500 BEST-EVER RECIPES
CHOCOLATE

A definitive collection of delectable recipes, from devilish chocolate
roulade to Mississippi mud pie, shown in over 500 photographs

Felicity Forster

southwater

This edition is published by Southwater
an imprint of Anness Publishing Ltd
Blaby Road, Wigston, Leicestershire LE18 4SE
info@anness.com

www.southwaterbooks.com; www.annesspublishing.com

If you like the images in this book and would like to investigate using
them for publishing, promotions or advertising, please visit our website
www.practicalpictures.com for more information.

Publisher: Joanna Lorenz
Senior Editor: Felicity Forster
Recipes: Christine France, Christine McFadden
and Elizabeth Wolf-Cohen
Photography: Karl Adamson, Edward Allwright,
David Armstrong, Steve Baxter, James Duncan,
Michelle Garrett, Amanda Heywood, Tim Hill and Don Last
Jacket Design: Nigel Partridge
Copy Editor: Jay Thundercliffe
Production Controller: Claire Rae

ETHICAL TRADING POLICY

At Anness Publishing we believe that business should be conducted
in an ethical and ecologically sustainable way, with respect for the
environment and a proper regard to the replacement of the natural
resources we employ. As a publisher, we use a lot of wood pulp to
make high-quality paper for printing, and that wood commonly comes
from spruce trees. We are therefore currently growing more than
750,000 trees in three Scottish forest plantations: Berrymoss
(130 hectares/320 acres), West Touxhill (125 hectares/305 acres) and
Deveron Forest (75 hectares/185 acres). The forests we manage
contain more than 3.5 times the number of trees employed each year
in making paper for the books we manufacture. Because of this
ongoing ecological investment programme, you, as our customer, can
have the pleasure and reassurance of knowing that a tree is being
cultivated on your behalf to naturally replace the materials used to
make the book you are holding. Our forestry programme is run in
accordance with the UK Woodland Assurance Scheme (UKWAS) and
will be certified by the internationally recognized Forest Stewardship
Council (FSC). The FSC is a non-government organization dedicated to
promoting responsible management of the world's forests. Certification
ensures forests are managed in an environmentally sustainable and
socially responsible way. For further information about this scheme,
go to www.annesspublishing.com/trees

A CIP catalogue record for this book is available
from the British Library.

PUBLISHER'S NOTE: Although the advice and information in this book
are believed to be accurate and true at the time of going to press,
neither the authors nor the publisher can accept any legal responsibility
or liability for any errors or omissions that may be made nor for any
inaccuracies nor for any harm or injury that comes about from
following instructions or advice in this book.

Notes

Bracketed terms are intended for American readers.
For all recipes, quantities are given in both metric and imperial measures and, where appropriate, in standard
cups and spoons. Follow one set of measures, but not a mixture, because they are not interchangeable.
Standard spoon and cup measures are level. 1 tsp = 5ml, 1 tbsp = 15ml, 1 cup = 250ml/8fl oz. Australian standard tablespoons
are 20ml. Australian readers should use 3 tsp in place of 1 tbsp for measuring small quantities.
American pints are 16fl oz/2 cups. American readers should use 20fl oz/2.5 cups in place of 1 pint when measuring liquids.
Electric oven temperatures in this book are for conventional ovens. When using a fan oven, the temperature will probably need to be
reduced by about 10–20°C/20–40°F. Since ovens vary, you should check with your manufacturer's instruction book for guidance.

The nutritional analysis given for each recipe is calculated per portion (i.e. serving or item), unless otherwise stated.
If the recipe gives a range, such as Serves 4–6, then the nutritional analysis will be for the smaller portion size, i.e. 6 servings.
Measurements for sodium do not include salt added to taste.
Medium (US large) eggs are used unless otherwise stated.

Main front cover image shows Chocolate Orange Marquise – for recipe, see page 61

Contents

Introduction   6

Cakes, Rolls and Loaves   8

Rich Cakes and Special Occasion Cakes   24

Hot Desserts   60

Cold Desserts   78

Ice Creams and Sorbets   102

Tarts, Pies and Cheesecakes   126

Little Cakes, Slices and Bars   144

Cookies   174

Candies and Truffles   206

Drinks   226

Basic Recipes and Techniques   236

Index   254

Introduction

One of the greatest treasures ever discovered was the bean from the tree *Theobroma cacao*, the original source of chocolate. Smooth in texture, intense in taste, subtly perfumed and elegant to behold, chocolate is a rich source of

sensory pleasure, adored by almost everyone. Divine it really is – the name *Theobroma* is a Greek word meaning "food of the gods". The ultimate decadent treat, it is hardly surprising that in the past chocolate has been credited with being an aphrodisiac. Chocolates are traditional lovers' gifts, and special events, such as Easter and Christmas, are celebrated with chocolate eggs or the traditional yuletide log.

Once the preserve of Aztec emperors, highly prized and coveted, chocolate was unknown in Europe until the middle of the 16th century, when it was introduced as a rare and wonderful beverage. It took almost 200 years before the sweetened chocolate bar made its appearance, and the rest, as they say, is history. Although chocolate is now accessible to all, familiarity has done nothing to dim its huge popularity. Consumption of all types of chocolate continues to rise. In recent years there has been an increased demand for the pure product with more than 50 per cent cocoa solids, and aficionados scout out new varieties of chocolate with all the enthusiasm and energy of the ardent wine buff or truffle fancier.

For the cook, the fascination with chocolate goes even deeper. It is a sensitive ingredient that needs careful handling, but which offers remarkable rewards. The velvety texture and rich flavour add a touch of luxury to numerous cakes, cookies, puddings and desserts, and it is equally good in hot or cold dishes.

As an added bonus, chocolate can be piped, shaped and moulded to make a variety of exciting decorations.

This book is for serious chocolate lovers. As you would expect, we've included classics like Black Forest Gateau and Double Chocolate Chip Muffins, but – and this is the mark of the true chocoholic – we've also investigated every conceivable way of introducing our favourite ingredient into familiar and much-loved dishes. There's a rich chocolate trifle, a rare chocolate pavlova (with cocoa giving the meringue a dusky appearance and delectable flavour), an unusual chocolate crème brûlée, a chocolate zabaglione and even a chocolate and cherry polenta cake.

Also in the luscious line-up are crunchy chocolate chip cookies, chocolate sponge cakes with fudgy centres, gloriously gooey puddings, voluptuous gateaux and sweet chocolate treats for gifts and after-dinner delights. In honour of those ancient Aztecs, there's a recipe for Mexican Hot Chocolate and even an iced chocolate and peppermint drink.

The book is helpfully divided into sections so that you can easily find the recipes you want – Cakes, Rolls and Loaves; Rich Cakes and Special Occasion Cakes; Hot Desserts; Cold Desserts; Ice Creams and Sorbets; Tarts, Pies and Cheesecakes; Little Cakes, Slices and Bars; Cookies; Candies and Truffles; and Drinks. All the classics are included, as well as many decadent recipes you may not have tried before.

To help you make the most of these incredibly tempting recipes, a section at the back of the book covers all the basic recipes for cakes, rolls, icings, frostings, sauces and fondues. There are standard recipes for Quick-mix Sponge Cakes, Sponge Rolls, Madeira Cakes, Glossy Chocolate Fudge Icing, Satin Chocolate Icing, Butter Icing, Royal Icing, French Chocolate Sauce, and many more. In addition, there are step-by-step instructions explaining basic chocolate techniques – melting chocolate over water, tempering chocolate, feathering, marbling and piping chocolate, making decorations such as chocolate curls, squiggles and leaves, and making chocolate bases such as cups, baskets and shortcrust pastry.

So go on, indulge yourself with every kind of chocolate recipe imaginable. But take it slow and easy – Death by Chocolate could be just around the corner.

Simple Chocolate Cake

This is an easy-to-make chocolate cake that is transformed into a terrific dessert when served with cream or a selection of mixed summer fruits.

Serves 6–8

115g/4oz plain (semisweet) chocolate, broken into squares
45ml/3 tbsp milk
150g/5oz/²⁄₃ cup unsalted (sweet) butter or margarine, softened, plus extra for greasing
150g/5oz/³⁄₄ cup light muscovado (brown) sugar
3 eggs

200g/7oz/1³⁄₄ cups self-raising (self-rising) flour
15ml/1 tbsp unsweetened cocoa powder
icing (confectioners') sugar and cocoa powder, for dusting

For the buttercream

75g/3oz/6 tbsp unsalted (sweet) butter or margarine, softened
175g/6oz/1¹⁄₂ cups icing (confectioners') sugar
15ml/1 tbsp unsweetened cocoa powder
2.5ml/¹⁄₂ tsp vanilla extract

1 Preheat the oven to 180°C/350°F/Gas 4. Grease two 18cm/7in round sandwich cake tins (layer pans) and line the base of each with baking parchment. Melt the chocolate with the milk in a heatproof bowl set over a pan of simmering water.

2 Cream the butter or margarine with the sugar in a mixing bowl until pale and fluffy. Add the eggs one at a time, beating well after each addition. Stir in the chocolate mixture.

3 Sift the flour and cocoa powder over the mixture and fold in with a metal spoon until evenly mixed. Turn into the prepared tins, level the surfaces and bake for 35–40 minutes or until well risen and firm. Turn out on to wire racks and leave to cool.

4 Make the buttercream. Beat the butter or margarine, icing sugar, cocoa powder and vanilla extract together in a bowl until the mixture is smooth.

5 Spread buttercream over one of the cakes, then top with the second layer. Dust with a mixture of icing sugar and cocoa just before serving.

One-stage Chocolate Sponge

Whipping marmalade into the cream gives this cake a tangy citrus flavour.

Serves 6–8

175g/6oz/³⁄₄ cup soft margarine, at room temperature
115g/4oz/generous ¹⁄₂ cup caster (superfine) sugar
50g/2oz/4 tbsp golden (light corn) syrup

175g/6oz/1¹⁄₂ cups self-raising (self-rising) flour, sifted
45ml/3 tbsp unsweetened cocoa powder, sifted
2.5ml/¹⁄₂ tsp salt
3 eggs, beaten
a little milk, as required
150ml/¹⁄₄ pint/²⁄₃ cup whipping cream
15–30ml/1–2 tbsp fine shred marmalade
icing (confectioners') sugar, for dusting

1 Preheat the oven to 180°C/350°F/Gas 4. Lightly grease or line two 18cm/7in shallow round cake tins (pans).

2 Place the margarine, sugar, syrup, flour, cocoa powder, salt and eggs in a large bowl, and cream together until well blended using a wooden spoon or electric whisk. If the mixture seems a little thick, stir in 15–30ml/1–2 tbsp milk, until you have a soft dropping consistency.

3 Spoon the mixture into the prepared tins and bake for about 30 minutes, changing shelves if necessary after 15 minutes, until the tops are just firm and the cakes are springy to the touch.

4 Leave the cakes to cool for 5 minutes, then remove from the tins and leave to cool completely on a wire rack.

5 Whip the cream and fold in the marmalade, then use to sandwich the two cakes together. Sprinkle the top with sifted icing sugar.

Cook's Tip
You could also use butter at room temperature cut into small pieces for this one-stage sponge mixture.

Cake Energy 567kcal/2377kJ; Protein 6.6g; Carbohydrate 71.4g, of which sugars 52.2g; Fat 30.4g, of which saturates 18.2g; Cholesterol 133mg; Calcium 141mg; Fibre 1.6g; Sodium 328mg.
Sponge Energy 3476kcal/14495kJ; Protein 47.3g; Carbohydrate 315.7g, of which sugars 177.1g; Fat 234g, of which saturates 78.4g; Cholesterol 732mg; Calcium 556mg; Fibre 10.9g; Sodium 2022mg.

Chocolate Frosted Layer Cake

The contrast between the frosting and the sponge creates a dramatic effect when the cake is cut.

Makes one 20cm/8in round cake
225g/8oz/1 cup butter or margarine, at room temperature
300g/11oz/scant 1½ cups caster (superfine) sugar
4 eggs, separated
10ml/2 tsp vanilla extract

385g/13½oz/3⅓ cups plain (all-purpose) flour
10ml/2 tsp baking powder
1.5ml/¼ tsp salt
250ml/8fl oz/1 cup milk

For the frosting
150g/5oz plain (semisweet) chocolate
120ml/4fl oz/½ cup sour cream
1.5ml/¼ tsp salt

1 Preheat the oven to 180°C/350°F/Gas 4. Line two 20cm/8in round cake tins (pans) with baking parchment and grease the paper. Dust the tins with flour. Tap to remove any excess.

2 Cream the butter or margarine until soft. Gradually add the sugar and beat until light and fluffy. Beat the egg yolks, then add to the butter mixture with the vanilla extract.

3 Sift the flour with the baking powder three times. Set aside. Beat the egg whites with the salt until they form stiff peaks.

4 Fold the dry ingredients into the butter mixture in three batches, alternating with the milk. Add a dollop of the egg white to the batter and fold in to lighten the mixture. Fold in the remainder until just blended.

5 Spoon into the cake tins and bake until the cakes pull away from the sides, about 30 minutes. Leave in the tins for 5 minutes, then turn out on to a wire rack to cool completely.

6 To make the frosting, melt the chocolate in the top of a double boiler or in a heatproof bowl over a pan of simmering water. When cool, stir in the sour cream and salt. Sandwich the layers with frosting, then spread on the top and side.

Mocha Chocolate Victoria Sponge

This light coffee- and cocoa-flavoured sponge is decorated with a rich buttercream topping.

Makes one 18cm/7in round cake
175g/6oz/¾ cup butter
175g/6oz/generous ¾ cup caster (superfine) sugar
3 eggs
175g/6oz/1½ cups self-raising (self-rising) flour, sifted
15ml/1 tbsp strong black coffee

15ml/1 tbsp unsweetened cocoa powder mixed with 15–30ml/ 1–2 tbsp boiling water

For the coffee buttercream
150g/5oz/10 tbsp butter
15ml/1 tbsp coffee extract or 10ml/2 tsp instant coffee powder dissolved in 15–30ml/ 1–2 tbsp warm milk
275g/10oz/2½ cups icing (confectioners') sugar

1 Preheat the oven to 180°C/350°F/Gas 4. Grease and base-line two 18cm/7in shallow round cake tins (pans). Cream the butter and sugar in a large bowl until light and fluffy. Add the eggs, one at a time, beating well after each addition. Fold in the flour.

2 Divide the mixture between two bowls. Fold the coffee into one and the cocoa mixture into the other.

3 Place alternate spoonfuls of each mixture side by side in the cake tins. Bake for 25–30 minutes. Turn out on to a wire rack to cool.

4 For the buttercream, beat the butter until soft. Gradually beat in the remaining ingredients until smooth.

5 Sandwich the cakes, bases together, with a third of the buttercream. Cover the top and side with the remainder.

> **Cook's Tip**
> When mixing eggs into creamed sugar and butter, whisk only briefly, and if the mixture begins to curdle add a spoonful of the flour before you add any more of the eggs.

Sponge Energy 4668kcal/19505kJ; Protein 42.2g; Carbohydrate 506.1g, of which sugars 371g; Fat 289.6g, of which saturates 176.4g; Cholesterol 1265mg; Calcium 612mg; Fibre 7.2g; Sodium 2355mg.
Cake Energy 5530kcal/23187kJ; Protein 83.4g; Carbohydrate 709.9g, of which sugars 415.2g; Fat 282.3g, of which saturates 167g; Cholesterol 1337mg; Calcium 1306mg; Fibre 15.7g; Sodium 1838mg.

Devil's Food Cake with Orange Frosting

The classic combination of chocolate and orange makes this dessert irresistible.

Serves 10

50g/2oz/½ cup unsweetened
  cocoa powder
175ml/6fl oz/¾ cup boiling water
175g/6oz/¾ cup butter, at
  room temperature
350g/12oz/1½ cups soft dark
  brown sugar
3 eggs, at room temperature
225g/8oz/2 cups plain
  (all-purpose) flour

25ml/1½ tsp bicarbonate of soda
  (baking soda)
1.5ml/¼ tsp baking powder
175ml/6fl oz/¾ cup sour cream
pared orange rind, shredded and
  blanched, to decorate

For the frosting

285g/10½oz/1½ cups sugar
2 egg whites
60ml/4 tbsp frozen orange
  juice concentrate
15ml/1 tbsp fresh lemon juice
grated rind of 1 orange

1 Preheat the oven to 180°C/350°F/Gas 4. Line two 23cm/9in cake tins (pans) with baking parchment and grease. In a bowl, mix the cocoa and the boiling water until smooth. Set aside.

2 With an electric whisk, cream the butter and sugar until light and fluffy. Add the eggs, one at a time, beating well.

3 When the cocoa mixture is lukewarm, stir into the butter mixture. Sift together the flour, bicarbonate of soda and baking powder twice. Fold into the cocoa mixture in three batches, alternately with the sour cream.

4 Pour into the tins. Bake for 30–35 minutes, until the cakes pull away from the sides. Stand for 15 minutes before turning out.

5 Make the frosting. Place all the ingredients in a bowl set over a pan of hot water. With an electric whisk, beat until the mixture holds soft peaks. Remove from the heat and continue beating until thick enough to spread. Sandwich the cake with frosting, then spread over the top and side. Decorate with orange rind.

Hazelnut and Chocolate Cake

A deliciously rich and nutty cake, perfect for those indulgent moments.

Serves 8–10

115g/4oz/½ cup unsalted (sweet)
  butter, softened, plus extra
  for greasing
150g/5oz plain (semisweet)
  chocolate, chopped into
  small pieces
115g/4oz/generous ½ cup caster
  (superfine) sugar
4 eggs, separated

115g/4oz/1 cup ground lightly
  toasted hazelnuts
50g/2oz/1 cup fresh breadcrumbs
grated rind of 1½ oranges
30ml/2 tbsp strained
  marmalade, warmed
60ml/4 tbsp chopped hazelnuts,
  to decorate

For the icing

150g/5oz plain (semisweet)
  chocolate, chopped into pieces
50g/2oz/¼ cup butter, diced

1 Preheat the oven to 180°C/350°F/Gas 4. Butter a 23cm/9in round cake tin (pan) and line the base of the tin with a sheet of baking parchment.

2 Melt the plain chocolate in the top of a double boiler or in a heatproof bowl over a pan of simmering water, stirring occasionally. Set aside when completely melted.

3 Beat the butter and sugar together, then gradually add the egg yolks, beating well. The mixture may curdle slightly. Beat in the melted chocolate, then the hazelnuts, breadcrumbs and orange rind. Whisk the egg whites until stiff, then fold into the chocolate mixture. Transfer to the cake tin. Bake for 40–45 minutes, until set.

4 Remove from the oven, cover with a damp dish towel for 5 minutes, then transfer to a wire rack until cold.

5 Make the icing. Place the chocolate and butter in the top of a double boiler or in a heatproof bowl over a pan of simmering water and stir until smooth. Leave until cool and thick.

6 Spread the cake with the marmalade, then the icing. Sprinkle over the nuts, then leave to set.

Devil's Food Cake Energy 537kcal/2262kJ; Protein 6.5g; Carbohydrate 86.2g, of which sugars 68.5g; Fat 20.9g, of which saturates 12.5g; Cholesterol 105mg; Calcium 101mg; Fibre 1.3g; Sodium 200mg.
Hazelnut Cake Energy 490kcal/2040kJ; Protein 7.2g; Carbohydrate 38.2g, of which sugars 33.8g; Fat 35.4g, of which saturates 15.1g; Cholesterol 113mg; Calcium 62mg; Fibre 2g; Sodium 172mg.

Chocolate Layer Cake

The surprise ingredient of this chocolate cake recipe – beetroot – makes a beautifully moist cake.

Makes one 23cm/9in cake
unsweetened cocoa powder, for dusting
225g/8oz can cooked whole beetroot, drained and juice reserved
115g/4oz/½ cup unsalted (sweet) butter, softened
550g/1lb 4oz/2¾ cups soft light brown sugar
3 eggs
15ml/1 tbsp vanilla extract
75g/3oz unsweetened chocolate, melted
275g/10oz/2½ cups plain (all-purpose) flour
10ml/2 tsp baking powder
2.5ml/½ tsp salt
120ml/4fl oz/½ cup buttermilk
chocolate curls, to decorate (optional)

For the frosting
475ml/16fl oz/2 cups double (heavy) cream
500g/1¼lb plain (semisweet) chocolate, chopped
15ml/1 tbsp vanilla extract

1 Preheat the oven to 180°C/350°F/Gas 4. Grease two 23cm/9in cake tins (pans) and dust with cocoa powder. Grate the beetroot and add it to its juice. Beat the butter, brown sugar, eggs and vanilla until pale and fluffy. Beat in the chocolate.

2 Sift together the flour, baking powder and salt. With the mixer on low speed and beginning and ending with flour mixture, alternately beat in flour and buttermilk. Add the beetroot and juice and beat for 1 minute. Transfer to the cake tins.

3 Bake for 30–35 minutes. Cool in the tins for 10 minutes, then unmould and transfer to a wire rack to cool.

4 To make the frosting, heat the cream in a pan until it just begins to boil, stirring occasionally to prevent scorching. Remove from the heat and stir in the chocolate, until melted and smooth. Stir in the vanilla extract. Strain into a bowl and chill, stirring every 10 minutes, for 1 hour.

5 Sandwich and cover the cake with the frosting, and top with chocolate curls, if you like. Allow to set for 20–30 minutes, then chill before serving.

Chocolate and Orange Angel Cake

This light-as-air sponge with its fluffy icing is the answer to a cake-lover's prayer.

Makes one 20cm/8in ring cake
25g/1oz/¼ cup plain (all-purpose) flour
15g/½oz/2 tbsp unsweetened cocoa powder
15g/½oz/2 tbsp cornflour (cornstarch)
a pinch of salt
5 egg whites
2.5ml/½ tsp cream of tartar
115g/4oz/generous ½ cup caster (superfine) sugar
blanched and shredded rind of 1 orange, to decorate

For the icing
200g/7oz/1 cup caster (superfine) sugar
1 egg white

1 Preheat the oven to 180°C/350°F/Gas 4. Sift the flour, cocoa powder, cornflour and salt together three times.

2 Beat the egg whites in a large bowl until foamy. Add the cream of tartar, then whisk until soft peaks form.

3 Add the caster sugar to the egg whites a spoonful at a time, whisking after each addition. Sift a third of the flour and cocoa mixture over the egg whites and gently fold in. Repeat twice more.

4 Spoon the mixture into a non-stick 20cm/8in ring mould and level the top. Bake for 35 minutes, or until springy when lightly pressed. Turn upside down on to a wire rack and leave to cool in the tin. Carefully ease out of the tin.

5 To make the icing, put the sugar in a pan with 75ml/5 tbsp cold water. Stir over a low heat until dissolved. Boil until the syrup reaches soft ball stage (119°C/238°F on a sugar thermometer). Remove from the heat.

6 Whisk the egg whites until stiff. Add the syrup in a thin stream, whisking all the time, until the mixture is very thick and fluffy.

7 Spread the icing over the top and sides of the cooled cake. Carefully sprinkle the orange rind over the top of the cake and serve.

Angel Cake Energy 1495kcal/6373kJ; Protein 24.1g; Carbohydrate 364.1g, of which sugars 329.6g; Fat 3.7g, of which saturates 2g; Cholesterol 0mg; Calcium 233mg; Fibre 2.6g; Sodium 535mg.
Layer Energy 9521kcal/39888kJ; Protein 94.2g; Carbohydrate 1196.3g, of which sugars 972.4g; Fat 518.1g, of which saturates 312.1g; Cholesterol 1472mg; Calcium 1419mg; Fibre 27.5g; Sodium 1382mg.

Best-ever Chocolate Sandwich

A three-layered cake is ideal for a birthday party.

Makes one 20cm/8in cake
115g/4oz/1 cup plain
  (all-purpose) flour
50g/2oz/½ cup unsweetened
  cocoa powder
5ml/1 tsp baking powder
6 eggs
225g/8oz/generous 1 cup caster
  (superfine) sugar
10ml/2 tsp vanilla extract

115g/4oz/½ cup unsalted (sweet)
  butter, melted

For the icing
225g/8oz plain (semisweet)
  chocolate, chopped
75g/3oz/6 tbsp unsalted
  (sweet) butter
3 eggs, separated
250ml/8fl oz/1 cup whipping cream
45ml/3 tbsp caster
  (superfine) sugar

1 Preheat the oven to 180°C/350°F/Gas 4. Line three 20cm/8in round shallow cake tins (pans) with baking parchment, grease the paper and dust with flour. Sift the flour, cocoa powder, baking powder and a pinch of salt together three times.

2 Place the eggs and sugar in the top of a double boiler. Beat until doubled in volume. Add the vanilla extract. Fold in the flour mixture in three batches, then the melted butter. Transfer the mixture into the tins. Bake until the cakes pull away from the tin sides, about 25 minutes. Transfer to a wire rack.

3 To make the icing, melt the chocolate in the top of a double boiler. Off the heat, stir in the butter and egg yolks. Return to the heat and stir until thick. Whip the cream until firm.

4 In another bowl, beat the egg whites until stiff peaks form. Add the sugar and beat until glossy. Fold the cream, then the egg whites, into the chocolate mixture. Chill the cake for 20 minutes, then sandwich together and cover with icing.

> **Variation**
> This chocolate sandwich cake can be made with coffee-flavoured butter icing instead of chocolate icing.

Chocolate Banana Cake

Fresh fruit is especially good for making a moist cake mixture. Here is a delicious sticky chocolate cake, moist enough to eat without the chocolate icing if you want to cut down on the calories.

Serves 8
225g/8oz/2 cups self-raising
  (self-rising) flour
45ml/3 tbsp reduced-fat
  unsweetened cocoa powder
115g/4oz/½ cup soft light
  brown sugar
30ml/2 tbsp malt extract

30ml/2 tbsp golden (light
  corn) syrup
2 eggs, beaten
60ml/4 tbsp skimmed milk
60ml/4 tbsp sunflower oil
2 large ripe bananas

For the icing
175g/6oz/1½ cups icing
  (confectioners') sugar, sifted
30ml/2 tbsp reduced-fat
  unsweetened cocoa
  powder, sifted
15–30ml/1–2 tbsp warm water

1 Preheat the oven to 160°C/325°F/Gas 3. Line and grease a deep 20cm/8in round cake tin (pan). Sift the flour into a mixing bowl with the cocoa powder. Stir in the sugar.

2 Make a well in the centre of the dry ingredients and add the malt extract, golden syrup, eggs, milk and oil. Mix well.

3 Mash the bananas thoroughly and stir them into the mixture until thoroughly combined.

4 Spoon the cake mixture into the prepared tin and bake for 1–1¼ hours, or until the centre of the cake springs back when lightly pressed.

5 Remove from the tin and turn on to a wire rack to cool.

6 To make the icing, put the icing sugar and cocoa in a mixing bowl and gradually add enough water to make a mixture thick enough to coat the back of a wooden spoon.

7 Pour over the top of the cake and ease to the edges, allowing the icing to dribble down the sides.

Sandwich Energy 5787kcal/24151kJ; Protein 95g; Carbohydrate 528g, of which sugars 432.6g; Fat 382.2g, of which saturates 220.4g; Cholesterol 2393mg; Calcium 879mg; Fibre 15.2g; Sodium 2352mg.
Banana Cake Energy 352kcal/1487kJ; Protein 6.5g; Carbohydrate 64.4g, of which sugars 41.9g; Fat 9.4g, of which saturates 2.3g; Cholesterol 48mg; Calcium 145mg; Fibre 2.3g; Sodium 233mg.

Chocolate Cake with Coffee Icing

This easy all-in-one recipe is a firm favourite, and can be quickly and easily dressed up to make a cake that looks extra special. The coffee icing perfectly complements the chocolate-flavoured cake.

Makes one 18cm/7in cake
175g/6oz/1 1/2 cups self-raising (self-rising) flour
25ml/1 1/2 tbsp unsweetened cocoa powder
pinch of salt
175g/6oz/3/4 cup butter, softened, or easy-spread margarine
175g/6oz/3/4 cup soft dark brown sugar
50g/2oz/1/2 cup ground almonds
3 large (US extra large) eggs, lightly beaten

For the coffee butter icing
175g/6oz/3/4 cup unsalted (sweet) butter, at warm room temperature
350g/12oz/3 cups sifted icing (confectioners') sugar
30ml/2 tbsp coffee extract
whole hazelnuts or pecan nuts, to decorate (optional)

1 Preheat the oven to 180°C/350°F/Gas 4 and butter two 18cm/7in round sandwich tins (layer pans).

2 Sift the flour, cocoa and salt into a mixing bowl. Cut in the butter or margarine and add the sugar, ground almonds and eggs.

3 Mix with a wooden spoon for 2–3 minutes, until thoroughly combined; the mixture should be smooth, with no traces of butter remaining.

4 Divide the mixture between the prepared tins and bake in the centre of the preheated oven for 25–30 minutes, or until springy to the touch. Turn out and cool on a wire rack. Meanwhile make the coffee butter icing: cream the butter well, then gradually beat in the sifted icing sugar and the coffee extract.

5 When the cakes are cold, sandwich them together with some of the icing and cover the top and sides with most of the remainder. Pipe the remaining icing around the top in rosettes, if you like, and decorate with whole hazelnuts or pecan nuts.

Chocolate and Cherry Polenta Cake

The combination of polenta and ground almonds add an unusual nutty texture to this tasty cake. It is delicious when served on its own, but it also tastes good served with a topping of thin cream or yogurt.

Serves 8–10
50g/2oz/1/3 cup quick-cook polenta
about 120ml/4fl oz/1/2 cup boiling water
oil, for greasing
200g/7oz plain (semisweet) chocolate, broken into small squares
5 eggs, separated
175g/6oz/3/4 cup caster (superfine) sugar
115g/4oz/1 cup ground almonds
50g/2oz/1/2 cup plain (all-purpose) flour
finely grated rind of 1 orange
115g/4oz/1/2 cup glacé (candied) cherries, halved
icing (confectioners') sugar, for dusting

1 Place the polenta in a heatproof bowl and pour over just enough of the boiling water to cover. Stir well, then cover the bowl and leave to stand for about 30 minutes, until the polenta has absorbed all the excess moisture.

2 Preheat the oven to 190°C/375°F/Gas 5. Grease a deep 22cm/8½in round cake tin (pan) and line the base of the tin with baking parchment. Melt the chocolate in the top of a double boiler or in a heatproof bowl set over a pan of simmering water, stirring occasionally until smooth.

3 Whisk the egg yolks with the sugar in a bowl until thick and pale. Beat in the chocolate, then fold in the polenta, ground almonds, flour and orange rind.

4 Whisk the egg whites in a clean bowl until stiff. Stir 15ml/ 1 tbsp of the whites into the chocolate mixture, then fold in the rest. Finally, fold in the cherries.

5 Scrape the mixture into the prepared tin and bake for 45–55 minutes or until well risen and firm to the touch. Turn the cake out on to a wire rack and leave to cool. Dust with icing sugar just before serving.

Chocolate Cake Energy 5899kcal/24,684kJ; Protein 56.2g; Carbohydrate 691.1g, of which sugars 556.9g; Fat 343.1g, of which saturates 193.7g; Cholesterol 1.43g; Calcium 1.06g; Fibre 2.2g; Sodium 3.28g.
Polenta Cake Energy 420kcal/1764kJ; Protein 9.6g; Carbohydrate 56.4g, of which sugars 45.5g; Fat 18.8g, of which saturates 5.8g; Cholesterol 120mg; Calcium 89mg; Fibre 2.2g; Sodium 53mg.

Chocolate and Prune Cake

Thanks to gram flour, this delicious cake is high in soluble fibre but it is also quite high in sugar from the prunes, so enjoy it as an occasional treat.

Makes one 20cm/8in cake
300g/11oz dark (bittersweet)
  chocolate, broken into pieces
150g/5oz/²⁄₃ cup low-fat spread

200g/7oz/generous 1 cup
  ready-to-eat pitted
  prunes, quartered
3 eggs, beaten
150g/5oz/1¼ cups gram flour,
  sifted with 10ml/2 tsp
  baking powder
120ml/4fl oz/½ cup soya milk

1 Preheat the oven to 180°C/350°F/Gas 4. Grease and base-line a deep 20cm/8in round cake tin (pan). Melt the chocolate in a heatproof bowl over a pan of hot water.

2 Mix the low-fat spread and prunes in a food processor. Process until light and fluffy, then scrape into a bowl.

3 Gradually fold in the melted chocolate and eggs, alternately with the flour mixture. Beat in the soya milk.

4 Spoon the mixture into the prepared cake tin, level the surface with a spoon, then bake for 20–30 minutes or until the cake is firm to the touch. A fine metal skewer inserted in the centre of the cake should come out clean. Leave to cool on a wire rack.

> **Variation**
> You can substitute ready-to-eat dried apricots in place of the prunes, if you wish.

> **Cook's Tip**
> Gram flour is made from chickpeas and is also known as besan. It is available is supermarkets or Asian food stores.

Walnut and Ricotta Cake with Chocolate Curls

Soft, tangy ricotta cheese is widely used in Italy for making desserts. Here, it is included along with walnuts and orange to flavour a whisked egg sponge.

Serves 10
115g/4oz/1 cup walnut pieces
150g/5oz/²⁄₃ cup butter, softened
150g/5oz/¾ cup caster
  (superfine) sugar

5 eggs, separated
finely grated rind of 1 orange
150g/5oz/²⁄₃ cup ricotta cheese
40g/1½oz/⅓ cup plain
  (all-purpose) flour

To finish
60ml/4 tbsp apricot jam
15ml/1 tbsp water
30ml/2 tbsp brandy
50g/2oz plain (semisweet)
  chocolate, coarsely grated

1 Preheat the oven to 190°C/375°F/Gas 5. Grease and line the base of a deep 23cm/9in round, loose-based cake tin (pan). Roughly chop the walnuts and toast them lightly.

2 Cream the butter and 115g/4oz/generous ½ cup of the sugar until light and fluffy. Add the egg yolks, orange rind, ricotta cheese, flour and walnuts and mix well.

3 Whisk the egg whites until stiff. Gradually whisk in the remaining sugar. Fold a quarter of the whisked whites into the ricotta mixture. Carefully fold in the rest. Turn the mixture into the prepared tin. Bake for about 30 minutes until risen and firm. Leave to cool in the tin.

4 Transfer the cake to a serving plate. Heat the apricot jam with the water in a small pan. Press through a sieve (strainer) into a bowl and stir in the brandy. Brush over the top and sides of the cake. Sprinkle the cake generously with the grated plain chocolate.

> **Variation**
> Use toasted and chopped almonds in place of the walnuts.

Prune Cake Energy 3173kcal/13,294kJ; Protein 65g; Carbohydrate 376.8g, of which sugars 259.8g; Fat 166.1g, of which saturates 72.6g; Cholesterol 598mg; Calcium 537mg; Fibre 23.6g; Sodium 1268mg.
Walnut Cake Energy 393kcal/1635kJ; Protein 7.9g; Carbohydrate 27.4g, of which sugars 24.2g; Fat 28.1g, of which saturates 12.4g; Cholesterol 138mg; Calcium 44mg; Fibre 0.7g; Sodium 131mg.

Custard Layer Cake with Chocolate Icing

A creamy custard makes the perfect filling for a layer cake.

Serves 8
225g/8oz/2 cups plain
  (all-purpose) flour
15ml/1 tbsp baking powder
pinch of salt
115g/4oz/½ cup butter, softened
225g/8oz/generous 1 cup caster
  (superfine) sugar
2 eggs
5ml/1 tsp vanilla extract
175ml/6fl oz/¾ cup milk

For the filling
3 egg yolks

115g/4oz/½ cup caster
  (superfine) sugar
25g/1oz/¼ cup plain
  (all-purpose) flour
250ml/8fl oz/1 cup hot milk
15g/½oz/1 tbsp butter
15ml/1 tbsp brandy

For the chocolate icing
25g/1oz plain (semisweet)
  chocolate
25g/1oz/2 tbsp butter
50g/2oz/½ cup icing
  (confectioners') sugar, plus
  extra for dusting
2.5ml/½ tsp vanilla extract
about 15ml/1 tbsp hot water

1 Preheat the oven to 190°C/375°F/Gas 5. Grease and base-line two deep round cake tins (pans). Sift the flour, baking powder and salt. Beat the butter and sugar until fluffy. Add the eggs one at a time, beating. Stir in the vanilla extract. Add the milk and dry ingredients alternately, and mix until blended. Divide the mixture between the tins and bake for 25 minutes.

2 For the filling, whisk the egg yolks in a heatproof bowl. Add the sugar and whisk until the mixture is thick. Beat in the flour, then add the hot milk, beating constantly. Place the bowl over a pan of boiling water and stir until thickened. Add the butter and brandy. Set aside until cold. When cool, place one cake on a plate and spread over the custard filling. Lay the other cake on top.

3 For the icing, melt the chocolate with the butter in a heatproof bowl over a pan of hot water. When smooth, remove from the heat and beat in the icing sugar and vanilla extract. Add enough hot water until able to spread the icing over the top of the cake. Dust with icing sugar.

Mississippi Mud Cake Ring

Dense, dark and utterly dreamy, this is definitely a special-occasion cake.

Serves 8–10
225g/8oz/2 cups plain
  (all-purpose) flour
pinch of salt
5ml/1 tsp baking powder
300ml/½ pint/1¼ cups strong
  black coffee

60ml/4 tbsp brandy
150g/5oz chocolate
225g/8oz/1 cup butter
450g/1lb/2 cups sugar
2 eggs, at room temperature
7.5ml/1½ tsp vanilla extract
unsweetened cocoa powder,
  for dusting
sweetened whipped cream,
  to serve

1 Preheat the oven to 140°C/275°F/ Gas 1. Grease a 3 litre/ 5 pint/12 cup bundt tin (see Cook's Tip, below). Dust it with cocoa powder. Sift the flour, salt and baking powder together.

2 Combine the coffee, brandy, chocolate and butter in the top of a double boiler. Heat until the chocolate and butter have melted and the mixture is smooth, stirring occasionally.

3 Pour the mixture into a large bowl. Using an electric mixer on low speed, gradually beat in the sugar until dissolved.

4 Raise the speed to medium and add the sifted dry ingredients. Mix well, then beat in the eggs and vanilla extract until thoroughly blended. Pour the batter into the tin and bake for 1¼–1½ hours or until a skewer, inserted in the cake, comes out clean.

5 Let the cake cool in the tin for 15 minutes, then turn it out on to a wire rack. Leave to cool completely, then transfer to a plate and dust lightly with cocoa powder. Serve with the sweetened whipped cream.

> **Cook's Tip**
> A bundt tin (pan) is a large fluted ring tin, also known as a kugelhopf tin. It is perfect for Mississippi Mud Cake, but you can use an angel cake tin instead.

Custard Cake Energy 529kcal/2224kJ; Protein 7.9g; Carbohydrate 79.8g, of which sugars 56g; Fat 21.6g, of which saturates 12.2g; Cholesterol 168mg; Calcium 154mg; Fibre 1.1g; Sodium 165mg.
Mississippi Ring Energy 526kcal/2208kJ; Protein 4.5g; Carbohydrate 74.2g, of which sugars 56.9g; Fat 24.1g, of which saturates 14.6g; Cholesterol 87mg; Calcium 70mg; Fibre 1.1g; Sodium 155mg.

Marbled Chocolate Ring Cake

Glaze this cake with runny glacé icing if you prefer.

Makes one 25cm/10in ring cake

115g/4oz plain
    (semisweet) chocolate
350g/12oz/3 cups plain
    (all-purpose) flour
5ml/1 tsp baking powder
450g/1lb/2 cups butter,
    at room temperature
725g/1lb 10oz/3¾ cups caster
    (superfine) sugar
15ml/1 tbsp vanilla extract
10 eggs, at room temperature
icing (confectioners') sugar,
    for dusting

1 Preheat the oven to 180°C/350°F/Gas 4. Line a 25 × 10cm/ 10 × 4in ring mould with baking parchment and grease the paper. Dust with flour. Melt the chocolate in the top of a double boiler or in a heatproof bowl over a pan of simmering water, stirring occasionally. Set aside.

2 Sift together the flour and baking powder. In another bowl, cream the butter, sugar and vanilla extract until light and fluffy. Add the eggs, two at a time, then gradually blend in the flour mixture.

3 Spoon half the mixture into the ring mould. Stir the melted chocolate into the remaining mixture, then spoon into the tin. With a metal spatula, swirl the mixtures to create a marbled effect.

4 Bake until a skewer inserted in the centre comes out clean, about 1¾ hours. Cover with foil halfway through baking. Leave to cool in the tin for 15 minutes, then unmould and transfer to a wire rack to cool completely. To serve, dust with icing sugar.

Cook's Tip
With marbling cake mixtures, less is definitely more. Three or four wide swirling movements are all you will need to create the effect. If you over-swirl the batter the definition of the marbling will become lost.

Marbled Chocolate and Peanut Cake

A deliciously rich treat for a special tea.

Makes 12–14 slices

115g/4oz unsweetened
    chocolate, chopped
225g/8oz/1 cup unsalted (sweet)
    butter, softened
225g/8oz/1 cup peanut butter
200g/7oz/1 cup caster
    (superfine) sugar
225g/8oz/1 cup soft light
    brown sugar
5 eggs
275g/10oz/2½ cups plain
    (all-purpose) flour
10ml/2 tsp baking powder
2.5ml/½ tsp salt
125ml/4fl oz/½ cup milk
50g/2oz/⅓ cup chocolate chips

For the chocolate-peanut butter glaze
25g/1oz/2 tbsp butter, diced
25g/1oz/2 tbsp smooth
    peanut butter
45ml/3 tbsp golden (light
    corn) syrup
5ml/1 tsp vanilla extract
175g/6oz plain (semisweet)
    chocolate, broken into pieces

1 Preheat the oven to 180°C/350°F/Gas 4. Grease and flour a 3-litre/5¼-pint/13¼-cup tube cake tin (pan) or ring mould. Melt the chocolate in a double boiler or in a heatproof bowl over a pan of simmering water.

2 Beat the butter, peanut butter and sugars until light and creamy. Add the eggs, one at a time, beating well after each addition. Sift together the flour, baking powder and salt. Add to the butter mixture alternately with the milk.

3 Pour half the batter into another bowl. Stir the melted chocolate into one half and stir the chocolate chips into the other half. Drop alternate large spoonfuls of the two batters into the tin or mould. Using a knife, pull through the batters to create a swirled marbled effect; do not let the knife touch the side or base of the tin. Bake for 50–60 minutes, or until the top springs back when touched. Cool in the tin on a wire rack for 10 minutes. Then unmould on to the wire rack.

4 Combine the glaze ingredients and 15ml/1 tbsp water in a small pan. Melt over a low heat, stirring. Cool slightly, then drizzle over the cake, allowing it to run down the sides.

Ring Cake Energy 8720kcal/36545kJ; Protein 107.5g; Carbohydrate 1105.3g, of which sugars 837.6g; Fat 462.1g, of which saturates 269.9g; Cholesterol 2869mg; Calcium 1278mg; Fibre 13.7g; Sodium 3488mg.
Peanut Cake Energy 450kcal/1876kJ; Protein 7.9g; Carbohydrate 34.4g, of which sugars 33.1g; Fat 32.3g, of which saturates 16g; Cholesterol 108mg; Calcium 46mg; Fibre 1.5g; Sodium 210mg.

Chocolate Orange Battenburg Cake

A tasty variation on the traditional pink-and-white Battenburg cake. Use good quality marzipan for the best flavour.

Serves 6–8

115g/4oz/½ cup soft margarine
115g/4oz/generous ½ cup caster
 (superfine) sugar
2 eggs, beaten
a few drops of vanilla extract
15g/½oz/1 tbsp ground almonds
115g/4oz/1 cup self-raising
 (self-rising) flour, sifted
grated rind and juice of ½ orange
15g/½oz/2 tbsp unsweetened
 cocoa powder, sifted
30–45ml/2–3 tbsp milk
1 jar chocolate and nut spread
225g/8oz white marzipan

1 Preheat the oven to 180°C/350°F/Gas 4. Grease and line an 18cm/7in square cake tin (pan) with baking parchment. Put a double piece of foil across the middle of the tin, to divide it into two equal oblongs.

2 Cream the margarine and sugar. Beat in the eggs, vanilla extract and almonds. Divide the mixture evenly into two halves.

3 Fold half of the flour into one half, with the orange rind and enough juice to give a soft dropping consistency. Fold the rest of the flour and the cocoa powder into the other half, with enough milk to give a soft dropping consistency. Fill the tin with the two mixes and level the top.

4 Bake for 15 minutes, reduce the heat to 160°C/325°F/Gas 3 and cook for 20–30 minutes, or until the top is just firm. Leave to cool in the tin for a few minutes. Turn out on to a board, cut each cake into two strips and trim evenly. Leave to cool.

5 Using the chocolate and nut spread, sandwich the portions of the cake together, alternating the pieces to achieve the Battenburg design.

6 Roll out the marzipan on a board lightly dusted with cornflour to a rectangle 18cm/7in wide and long enough to wrap around the cake. Wrap the marzipan around the cake, putting the join underneath. Press to seal.

Mocha Hazelnut Battenburg

Coffee and nuts give a tasty twist to the classic cake.

Serves 6–8

115g/4oz/½ cup butter, softened
115g/4oz/generous ½ cup caster
 (superfine) sugar
2 eggs
115g/4oz/1 cup self-raising
 (self-rising) flour, sifted
50g/2oz/⅔ cup ground hazelnuts
10ml/2 tsp coffee extract
15ml/1 tbsp unsweetened
 cocoa powder

To finish
7 tbsp strained apricot
 jam, warmed
225g/8oz yellow marzipan
50g/2oz/⅔ cup ground hazelnuts
sifted icing (confectioners') sugar,
 for rolling out and to decorate

1 Preheat the oven to 180°C/350°F/Gas 4. Grease an 18cm/7in square cake tin (pan), line with baking parchment.

2 Cream the butter and sugar in a bowl. Gradually beat in the eggs, then fold in the flour. Transfer half the mixture to another bowl. Stir the ground hazelnuts into one bowl and the coffee extract and cocoa powder into the other bowl.

3 Place a strip of foil down the centre of the tin to divide it into two equal oblong halves. Spoon the two mixtures into each half of the tin. Smooth the surface of both mixtures.

4 Bake for 30–35 minutes or until just firm. Leave the cakes to cool in the tin for 5 minutes, then turn out on to a wire rack, peel off the lining paper and leave to cool completely.

5 Cut each cake into half lengthways. Sandwich the cakes together with the apricot jam to achieve the alternating Battenburg design.

6 Knead the marzipan to soften, then add the ground hazelnuts and knead until blended. Roll out the marzipan on a board dusted with icing sugar into a rectangle that will wrap around the cake.

7 Brush the cake with apricot jam and wrap with marzipan, pressing to seal. Pinch the edges of the marzipan for an attractive finish. Score the top surface and sprinkle with ground hazelnuts.

Battenburg Energy 716kcal/2993kJ; Protein 11.5g; Carbohydrate 77.2g, of which sugars 65g; Fat 42.3g, of which saturates 6.9g; Cholesterol 49mg; Calcium 163mg; Fibre 2.9g; Sodium 204mg.
Hazelnut Battenberg Energy 457kcal/1914kJ; Protein 6.7g; Carbohydrate 54.1g, of which sugars 42.6g; Fat 25.3g, of which saturates 9g; Cholesterol 78mg; Calcium 77mg; Fibre 2g; Sodium 135mg.

Vanilla and Chocolate Marble Cake

White and dark chocolate, marbled together, make a cake that tastes as good as it looks. This cake is made in a bread machine, and you can mix it with fresh peach slices and add a sprinkling of orange or peach liqueur for an impressive dessert.

Makes one medium cake
125g/4¹/₂oz/generous ¹/₂ cup margarine or butter
125g/4¹/₂ oz/scant ³/₄ cup caster (superfine) sugar
2 eggs, lightly beaten
50g/2oz white chocolate, broken into pieces
50g/2oz plain (semisweet) chocolate, broken into pieces
2.5ml/¹/₂ tsp natural vanilla extract
200g/7oz/1³/₄ cups self-raising (self-rising) flour
icing (confectioners') sugar and unsweetened cocoa powder, for dusting

1 Remove the blade from the bread machine and line the base of the pan with baking parchment. Cream the margarine or butter and sugar together until light and fluffy. Slowly add the eggs, beating thoroughly. Place half the mixture in another bowl.

2 Place the white chocolate in a heatproof bowl over a pan of simmering water. Stir until the chocolate is melted. Melt the plain chocolate in a separate bowl, in the same way. Stir the white chocolate and the vanilla extract into one bowl of creamed mixture and the plain chocolate into the other. Divide the flour equally between the bowls and lightly fold it in.

3 Put alternate spoonfuls of the two mixtures into the prepared bread pan. Use a round-bladed knife to swirl the mixtures together three or four times to marble them.

4 Set the bread machine to the 'bake only' setting. Set the timer, if possible, for the recommended time. If not, set the timer and check the cake after the shortest recommended baking time. Bake the cake for 50–55 minutes, until well risen.

5 The cake should be just firm to the touch and a skewer inserted into the cake should come out clean. Remove the pan from the machine. Stand for 2–3 minutes, then turn out on to a wire rack. Dust with icing sugar and cocoa powder and serve.

Chocolate Cream Roll

The combination of fresh cream rolled inside a chocolate sponge will prove to be an irresistible treat.

Makes one 33cm/13in long roll
225g/8oz plain (semisweet) chocolate, chopped
45ml/3 tbsp water
30ml/2 tbsp rum, brandy or strong coffee
7 eggs, separated
175g/6oz/scant 1 cup caster (superfine) sugar
1.5ml/¹/₄ tsp salt
icing (confectioners') sugar, for dusting
350ml/12fl oz/1¹/₂ cups whipping cream

1 Preheat the oven to 180°C/350°F/Gas 4. Line and grease a 38 x 33cm/15 x 13in Swiss roll tin (jelly roll pan) with baking parchment. Combine the chocolate, water and rum or other flavouring in the top of a double boiler or in a heatproof bowl over a pan of simmering water. Heat until melted, stirring constantly. Set aside.

2 With an electric mixer, beat the egg yolks and sugar until thick. Stir in the melted chocolate. In another bowl, beat the egg whites and salt until they hold stiff peaks. Fold a large spoonful of egg whites into the yolk mixture to lighten it, then carefully fold in the rest of the egg whites.

3 Pour the mixture into the tin and smooth evenly with a metal spatula. Bake for 15 minutes. Remove from the oven, cover with baking parchment and a damp cloth. Leave to stand for 1–2 hours. With an electric mixer, whip the cream until stiff. Set aside.

4 Run a knife along the inside edge of the tin to loosen the cake, then invert the cake on to a sheet of baking parchment that has been dusted with icing sugar.

5 Whip the cream until it holds its shape. Peel off the lining paper from the cake. Spread with an even layer of whipped cream, then roll up the cake using the sugared paper. Chill for several hours until set. Before serving, dust with an even layer of icing sugar.

Marble Energy 6711kcal/28422kJ; Protein 44.2g; Carbohydrate 1392.7g, of which sugars 1239.8g; Fat 145.9g, of which saturates 86.2g; Cholesterol 650mg; Calcium 1107mg; Fibre 7.5g; Sodium 1029mg.
Roll Energy 3732kcal/15572kJ; Protein 62.9g; Carbohydrate 330g, of which sugars 327.9g; Fat 242.9g, of which saturates 137g; Cholesterol 1713mg; Calcium 567mg; Fibre 5.6g; Sodium 601mg.

Chocolate Rum Roulade

This delicious roll is filled with rum-flavoured cream and makes a good alternative to a traditional iced fruit cake at Christmas.

Makes one 28cm/11in roll
4 eggs, separated
150g/5oz/³⁄₄ cup caster
  (superfine) sugar
5ml/1 tsp vanilla extract

a pinch of cream of tartar
115g/4oz/1 cup plain
  (all-purpose) flour, sifted
250ml/8fl oz/1 cup
  whipping cream
300g/11oz plain (semisweet)
  chocolate, chopped
30ml/2 tbsp rum or Cognac
icing (confectioners') sugar,
  for dusting

1 Preheat the oven to 190°C/375°F/Gas 5. Grease, line and flour a 40 × 28cm/16 × 11in Swiss roll tin (jelly roll pan).

2 Whisk the egg yolks with all but 25g/1oz/2 tbsp of the sugar until pale and thick. Add the vanilla extract.

3 Whisk the egg whites with the cream of tartar until they form soft peaks. Add the reserved sugar and continue whisking until the mixture is stiff and glossy.

4 Fold half the flour into the yolk mixture. Add a quarter of the egg whites and fold in to lighten the mixture. Fold in the remaining flour, then the remaining egg whites.

5 Spread the mixture in the tin. Bake for 15 minutes. Turn on to paper sprinkled with caster sugar. Roll up and leave to cool.

6 Put the cream into a small pan and bring it to the boil. Put the chocolate in a bowl and add the cream. Stir until the chocolate has melted, then beat until it is fluffy and has thickened to a spreading consistency. Mix one-third of the chocolate cream with the rum or Cognac.

7 Unroll the cake and spread with the rum mixture. Re-roll and cut off about a quarter, at an angle. Arrange to form a branch. Spread the chocolate cream over the cake. You could also add Christmas decorations and dust with icing sugar.

Marbled Chocolate Swiss Roll

A sensational combination of chocolate sponge and rich walnut buttercream.

Serves 6–8
90g/3¹⁄₂oz/³⁄₄ cup plain
  (all-purpose) flour
15ml/1 tbsp unsweetened
  cocoa powder
25g/1oz plain (semisweet)
  chocolate, grated
25g/1oz white chocolate, grated
3 eggs

115g/4oz/generous ¹⁄₂ cup caster
  (superfine) sugar
30ml/2 tbsp boiling water

For the filling
75g/3oz/6 tbsp unsalted (sweet)
  butter or margarine, softened
175g/6oz/1¹⁄₂ cups icing
  (confectioners') sugar
15ml/1 tbsp unsweetened
  cocoa powder
2.5ml/¹⁄₂ tsp vanilla extract
45ml/3 tbsp chopped walnuts

1 Preheat the oven to 200°C/400°F/Gas 6. Grease a 30 × 20cm/12 × 8in Swiss roll tin (jelly roll pan) and line with baking parchment. Sift half the flour with the cocoa into bowl. Stir in the grated plain chocolate. Sift the remaining flour into another bowl; stir in the grated white chocolate.

2 Whisk the eggs and sugar in a heatproof bowl, set over a pan of hot water, until its shape holds when the whisk is lifted.

3 Remove from the heat and turn half the mixture into a separate bowl. Fold the white chocolate mixture into one half, then fold the plain chocolate mixture into the other. Stir 15ml/1 tbsp boiling water into each half to soften the mixtures.

4 Place alternate spoonfuls of mixture in the tin and swirl lightly together for a marbled effect. Bake for 12–15 minutes, or until firm. Turn out on to a sheet of baking parchment and cover with a damp, clean dish towel. Cool.

5 Make the filling. Beat the butter, icing sugar, cocoa and vanilla together in a bowl until smooth, then mix in the walnuts. Uncover the sponge, peel off the lining and spread the filling evenly over the surface. Roll up carefully from a long side, using the paper underneath as a guide, then place on a serving plate. For a special occasion you could decorate with chocolate curls.

Swiss Roll Energy 361kcal/1518kJ; Protein 5.6g; Carbohydrate 51.1g, of which sugars 42g; Fat 16.4g, of which saturates 7.4g; Cholesterol 92mg; Calcium 67mg; Fibre 1.1g; Sodium 125mg.
Roulade Energy 3826kcal/16020kJ; Protein 56.6g; Carbohydrate 443.4g, of which sugars 353g; Fat 208.4g, of which saturates 119.9g; Cholesterol 1042mg; Calcium 599mg; Fibre 11.1g; Sodium 373mg.

Chocolate Chip Walnut Loaf

A nutty, chocolate loaf that
will be the perfect treat to
accompany an afternoon
cup of coffee or tea.

Makes one loaf

115g/4oz/generous ½ cup caster
 (superfine) sugar
115g/4oz/1 cup plain
 (all-purpose) flour
5ml/1 tsp baking powder
60ml/4 tbsp cornflour (cornstarch)
115g/4oz/½ cup butter, softened

2 eggs, beaten
5ml/1 tsp vanilla extract
30ml/2 tbsp currants or raisins
25g/1oz/¼ cup walnuts,
 finely chopped
grated rind of ½ lemon
45ml/3 tbsp plain (semisweet)
 chocolate chips
icing (confectioners') sugar,
 for dusting

1 Preheat the oven to 180°C/350°F/Gas 4. Grease and line a
22 × 12cm/8½ × 4½in loaf tin (pan). Sprinkle 25ml/1½ tbsp
of the caster sugar into the tin and tilt to distribute the sugar in
an even layer over the bottom and sides. Shake out any excess
sugar from the tin.

2 Sift the flour, baking powder and cornflour into a mixing
bowl. Repeat this twice more. Set aside.

3 With an electric mixer, cream the butter until soft. Add the
remaining sugar and continue beating until light and fluffy. Add
the eggs, one at a time, beating after each addition.

4 Gently fold the dry ingredients into the butter mixture, in
three batches; do not overmix.

5 Fold in the vanilla extract, currants or raisins, walnuts, lemon
rind and chocolate chips until just blended.

6 Pour the mixture into the prepared tin and bake for
45–50 minutes. Leave to cool in the tin for 5 minutes before
transferring to a wire rack to cool completely. Place on
a serving plate and dust with an even layer of icing sugar
before serving. Alternatively, top with glacé icing and decorate
with walnut halves.

Bitter Marmalade Chocolate Loaf

Zesty marmalade provides
this cake with the delicious
combination of chocolate
and orange.

Serves 8

115g/4oz plain (semisweet)
 chocolate, chopped into pieces
3 eggs
200g/7oz/1 cup caster
 (superfine) sugar

175ml/6fl oz/¾ cup sour cream
200g/7oz/1¾ cups self-raising
 (self-rising) flour

For the filling and glaze
175g/6oz/⅔ cup bitter
 orange marmalade
115g/4oz plain (semisweet)
 chocolate, chopped into pieces
60ml/4 tbsp sour cream
shredded orange rind, to decorate

1 Preheat the oven to 180°C/350°F/Gas 4. Lightly grease a
900g/2lb loaf tin (pan), then line it with baking parchment. Melt
the chocolate in a double boiler or a heatproof bowl over a
pan of hot water, stirring occasionally, until smooth.

2 Combine the eggs and sugar in a mixing bowl. Using a hand-
held electric mixer, whisk the mixture until it is thick and
creamy, then stir in the sour cream and the melted chocolate.
Fold in the self-raising flour evenly, using a metal spoon and a
figure-of-eight action.

3 Scrape the mixture into the prepared tin and bake for about
1 hour or until well risen and firm to the touch. Cool for a few
minutes in the tin, then turn out on to a wire rack and leave
the loaf to cool completely.

4 Make the filling. Spoon two-thirds of the marmalade into a
small pan and melt over a gentle heat, stirring constantly. Melt
the chocolate and stir it into the marmalade. Add the sour
cream and mix until thoroughly combined.

5 Slice the cake across into three layers and sandwich the
layers back together with about half the marmalade filling.
Spread the rest of the filling mixture over the top of the cake
and set aside until set. Spoon the remaining marmalade over
the cake as a glaze. To finish, sprinkle the shredded orange rind
on top, to decorate.

Walnut Loaf Energy 3759kcal/15650kJ; Protein 60.1g; Carbohydrate 294g, of which sugars 149.5g; Fat 268.6g, of which saturates 76.5g; Cholesterol 626mg; Calcium 543mg; Fibre 12.5g; Sodium 913mg.
Marmalade Loaf Energy 475kcal/2004kJ; Protein 7.1g; Carbohydrate 80.1g, of which sugars 60.8g; Fat 16.3g, of which saturates 9.1g; Cholesterol 91mg; Calcium 101mg; Fibre 1.6g; Sodium 56mg.

Chocolate Bread

In Italy it is the custom to serve this chocolate dessert bread as a snack with mascarpone or Gorgonzola cheese and a glass of red wine. Although this combination may sound unusual, it is really delicious. Chocolate bread tastes good spread with butter at tea time, and is excellent toasted next day for breakfast and served with butter and jam.

Makes two loaves
450g/1lb/4 cups strong plain
   (all-purpose) flour
2.5ml/½ tsp salt
30ml/2 tbsp butter
30ml/2 tbsp caster
   (superfine) sugar
10ml/2 tsp easy-blend (rapid-rise)
   dried yeast
30ml/2 tbsp unsweetened
   cocoa powder
75g/3oz/½ cup plain (semisweet)
   chocolate chips
melted butter, for brushing

1 Sift the flour and salt into a bowl, cut in the butter with a knife, then stir in the sugar, yeast and cocoa powder.

2 Gradually add 300 ml/½ pint/1¼ cups of tepid water to the flour mixture, stirring with a spoon at first, then gathering the dough together with your hands.

3 Turn the dough out on to a floured surface and knead for about 10 minutes until smooth and elastic.

4 Cut the dough in half and knead half the chocolate chips into each piece of dough until they are evenly distributed.

5 Shape into rounds, place on lightly oiled baking sheets and cover with oiled clear film. Leave to rise in a warm place for 1–2 hours until the dough has doubled in bulk.

6 Preheat the oven to 220°C/425°F/Gas 7. Uncover the loaves and bake for 10 minutes, then reduce the oven temperature to 190°C/375°F/Gas 5 and bake for a further 15–20 minutes.

7 Place the loaves on a wire rack and brush liberally with butter. Cover with a dish towel and leave to cool.

Chocolate Chip Marzipan Loaf

The perfect sweet loaf for chocolate lovers who enjoy the rich, nutty taste of marzipan.

Makes one loaf
115g/4oz/½ cup unsalted
   (sweet) butter, softened
150g/5oz/¾ cup light muscovado
   (brown) sugar
2 eggs, beaten

45ml/3 tbsp unsweetened
   cocoa powder
150g/5oz/1¼ cups self-raising
   (self-rising) flour
130g/4½oz marzipan
60ml/4 tbsp plain (semisweet)
   chocolate chips

1 Preheat the oven to 180°C/350°F/Gas 4. Lightly grease a 900g/2lb loaf tin (pan) and line the base of it with a sheet of baking parchment.

2 Cream the butter and sugar together in a large mixing bowl, beating with a wooden spoon until the mixture becomes light and fluffy.

3 Add the eggs to the creamed mixture one at a time, beating well after each addition until well combined.

4 Sift the cocoa powder and flour over the mixture and fold in evenly with a metal spoon until blended.

5 Chop the marzipan into small pieces with a sharp knife. Transfer to a bowl and mix with the chocolate chips. Set aside about 60ml/4 tbsp and gently fold the rest of the mixture evenly into the cake batter.

6 Scrape the mixture into the prepared tin and level the top with a knife. Sprinkle the top with the reserved marzipan and chocolate chips.

7 Bake the loaf in the oven for 45–50 minutes or until the loaf is risen and firm. Leave to cool for a few minutes in the tin to firm up, then it turn out on to a wire rack to cool completely, before slicing and serving.

Bread Energy 1176kcal/4970kJ; Protein 26g; Carbohydrate 216.2g, of which sugars 42.6g; Fat 29g, of which saturates 16.5g; Cholesterol 34mg; Calcium 358mg; Fibre 9.8g; Sodium 244mg.
Loaf Energy 2919kcal/12240kJ; Protein 46.1g; Carbohydrate 368.6g, of which sugars 248.6g; Fat 150.7g, of which saturates 80.5g; Cholesterol 629mg; Calcium 513mg; Fibre 14.1g; Sodium 1305mg.

Three Chocolate Bread

If you like chocolate, you'll adore this bread. The recipe suggests three specific types of chocolate, but you can combine your own particular favourites.

Makes one medium loaf
250ml/8fl oz/1 cup water
1 egg
500g/1¼lb/4½ cups unbleached
 white bread flour

25g/1oz/2 tbsp caster
 (superfine) sugar
5ml/1 tsp salt
25g/1oz/2 tbsp butter
7.5ml/1½ tsp easy-blend
 (rapid-rise) dried yeast
50g/2oz plain (semisweet)
 chocolate with raisins
 and almonds
50g/2oz plain (semisweet)
 chocolate with ginger
75g/3oz Belgian milk chocolate

1 Pour the water into the bread machine pan and add the egg. If necessary for your machine, reverse the order in which you add the liquid and dry ingredients.

2 Sprinkle over the flour, ensuring that it covers the water. Add the sugar, salt and butter, placing them in separate corners of the bread pan.

3 Make a small indent in the centre of the flour. Add the easy-blend dried yeast into the indent.

4 Set the bread machine to the basic/normal setting, with raisin setting (if available), medium crust. Press Start. Coarsely chop all the chocolate (it is not necessary to keep them separate). Add the chocolate to the bread pan when the machine beeps, or after the first kneading (see Cook's Tip).

5 Remove the bread at the end of the baking cycle and turn out on to a wire rack to cool.

> **Cook's Tip**
> *Gradually add the chocolate to the bread machine pan, making sure that it is mixing into the dough evenly before adding any more to the pan.*

Pane al Cioccolato

This slightly sweet chocolate bread from Italy is often served with creamy mascarpone cheese as a dessert or snack. The dark chocolate pieces add texture to this light loaf.

Makes one loaf
350g/12oz/3 cups unbleached
 white bread flour
25ml/1½ tbsp unsweetened
 cocoa powder

2.5ml/½ tsp salt
25g/1oz/2 tbsp caster
 (superfine) sugar
15g/½ oz fresh yeast
250ml/8fl oz/1 cup
 lukewarm water
25g/1oz/2 tbsp butter, softened
75g/3oz plain (semisweet)
 continental chocolate,
 coarsely chopped
melted butter, for brushing

1 Lightly grease a 15cm/6in round deep cake tin (pan). Sift the flour, cocoa powder and salt together into a large bowl. Stir in the sugar. Make a well in the centre.

2 Cream the yeast with 60ml/1 tbsp of the water, then stir in the rest. Add to the centre of the flour mixture and gradually mix to a dough.

3 Knead in the softened butter, then knead on a floured surface until smooth and elastic. Place in a lightly oiled bowl, cover with lightly oiled clear film (plastic wrap) and leave to rise, in a warm place, for about 1 hour, or until doubled in bulk.

4 Turn out on to a lightly floured surface and knock back (punch down). Gently knead in the chocolate, then cover with lightly oiled clear film; leave to rest for 5 minutes.

5 Shape the dough into a round and place in the tin. Cover with lightly oiled clear film and leave to rise, in a warm place, for 45 minutes, or until doubled; the dough should reach the top of the tin.

6 Preheat the oven to 220°C/425°F/Gas 7. Bake for 10 minutes, then reduce to 190°C/375°F/Gas 5 and bake for a further 25–30 minutes. Brush with melted butter and cool on a wire rack.

Bread Energy 2890kcal/12205kJ; Protein 58g; Carbohydrate 521g, of which sugars 139g; Fat 78.1g, of which saturates 44.5g; Cholesterol 77mg; Calcium 916mg; Fibre 18.6g; Sodium 238mg.
Pane Energy 1939kcal/8188kJ; Protein 41.5g; Carbohydrate 348.7g, of which sugars 78.5g; Fat 51.5g, of which saturates 29.5g; Cholesterol 58mg; Calcium 565mg; Fibre 15.8g; Sodium 406mg.

Mocha Chocolate Panettone

Panettone is the traditional
Christmas bread from Milan.

Serves 8–10

*30ml/2 tbsp instant coffee
  granules or coffee powder
140ml/5fl oz/scant ⅔ cup milk
1 egg, plus 2 egg yolks
400g/14oz/3½ cups unbleached
  white bread flour
15ml/1 tbsp unsweetened
  cocoa powder*

*5ml/1 tsp ground cinnamon
2.5ml/½ tsp salt
75g/3oz/scant ½ cup caster
  (superfine) sugar
75g/3oz/6 tbsp butter, softened
7.5ml/1½ tsp easy-blend
  (rapid-rise) dried yeast
115g/4oz plain (semisweet)
  chocolate, chopped
45ml/3 tbsp pine nuts,
  lightly toasted
melted butter, for glazing*

1 Dissolve the coffee in 30ml/2tbsp hot water and pour into
the bread machine pan. Add the milk, egg and egg yolks. If
necessary for your machine, reverse the order in which you add
the liquid and dry ingredients. Add the flour, cinnamon and cocoa
powder, covering the liquid. Add the salt, sugar and butter in
separate corners. Make an indent in the flour and add the yeast.

2 Start the bread machine on the basic dough setting. Lightly
oil a 15cm/6in deep cake tin (pan). Using a double sheet of
baking parchment that is 7.5cm/3in wider than the depth of the
tin, line the container so the excess parchment forms a collar.

3 When the machine has finished, remove the dough and
knock it back (punch down). Knead in the chocolate and pine
nuts and shape into a ball. Cover with lightly oiled clear film
(plastic wrap) and leave it to rest for 5 minutes.

4 Shape into a plump round loaf. Place in the tin and cover
with oiled clear film. Leave to rise for 1 hour or until it is almost
at the top of the collar. Preheat the oven to 200°C/400°F/Gas 6.

5 Brush the top of the loaf with the melted butter and cut a
cross in the top. Bake for about 10 minutes, then reduce the
oven to 180°C/350°F/Gas 4 and bake for 30–35 minutes
more, or until golden all over. Leave in the tin for 5–10
minutes, then turn out on to a wire rack to cool.

Cappuccino Chocolate Panettone

This light Italian bread is
traditionally a tall loaf with
a dome on the top, formed
by the rich yeasted dough
as it rises. The chocolate
chips give a lovely texture.

Serves 8

*450g/1lb/4 cups strong plain
  (all-purpose) flour
2.5ml/½ tsp salt
75g/3oz/scant ½ cup caster
  (superfine) sugar*

*7g/¼oz sachet easy-blend
  (rapid-rise) dried yeast
115g/4oz/½ cup butter
100ml/3½fl oz/scant ½ cup
  very hot strong brewed
  espresso coffee
100ml/3½fl oz/scant ½ cup milk
4 egg yolks
115g/4oz/⅔ cup plain
  (semisweet) chocolate chips
beaten egg, to glaze*

1 Preheat the oven to 190°C/375°F/Gas 5. Lightly grease and
line a deep 14–15cm/5½–6in cake tin (pan) with baking
parchment. Sift the flour and salt into a large bowl. Stir in the
sugar and yeast.

2 Add the butter to the coffee and stir until melted. Stir in the
milk, then add to the dry ingredients with the egg yolks. Mix
together to make a dough.

3 Turn the dough out on to a lightly floured surface and knead
for 10 minutes, until smooth and elastic. Gently knead in the
chocolate chips.

4 Shape into a ball, place in the tin and cover with oiled clear
film (plastic wrap). Leave to rise in a warm place for 1 hour or
until the dough reaches the top of the tin. Lightly brush with
beaten egg and bake for 35 minutes.

5 Turn down the oven to 180°C/350°F/Gas 4 and cover the
panettone with foil if it has browned enough. Cook for a
further 10–15 minutes, or until done.

6 Allow the panettone to cool in the tin for 10 minutes, then
transfer to a wire rack. Remove the lining paper just before
slicing and serving.

Mocha Energy 336kcal/1412kJ; Protein 6.7g; Carbohydrate 47.3g, of which sugars 16.5g; Fat 14.7g, of which saturates 6.8g; Cholesterol 57mg; Calcium 90mg; Fibre 1.8g; Sodium 76mg.
Cappuccino Energy 445kcal/1871kJ; Protein 8g; Carbohydrate 63.3g, of which sugars 20.3g; Fat 19.5g, of which saturates 10.9g; Cholesterol 133mg; Calcium 118mg; Fibre 2.1g; Sodium 100mg.

Chocolate Date Cake

This is a stunning cake that tastes absolutely wonderful. Rich and gooey – it's a chocoholic's delight.

Serves 8
4 egg whites
115g/4oz/generous ½ cup caster (superfine) sugar
200g/7oz plain (semisweet) chocolate
175g/6oz/1 cup Medjool dates, stoned (pitted) and chopped
175g/6oz/1½ cups chopped walnuts or pecan nuts
5ml/1 tsp vanilla extract

For the frosting
200g/7oz/scant 1 cup fromage frais or ricotta cheese
200g/7oz/scant 1 cup mascarpone
a few drops of vanilla extract
icing (confectioners') sugar, to taste

1 Preheat the oven to 180°C/350°F/Gas 4. Grease and base-line a 20cm/8in springform tin (pan).

2 To make the frosting, mix together the fromage frais or ricotta and mascarpone, add a few drops of vanilla extract and icing sugar to taste, then set aside.

3 Whisk the egg whites until they form stiff peaks. Whisk in 30ml/2 tbsp of the caster sugar until the meringue is thick and glossy, then fold in the remainder.

4 Chop 175g/6oz of the chocolate. Carefully fold into the meringue with the dates, nuts and 5ml/1 tsp of the vanilla extract. Pour into the prepared tin, spread level and bake for about 45 minutes, or until risen around the edges.

5 Allow to cool in the tin for about 10 minutes, then unmould, peel off the lining paper and leave to cool completely. Swirl the frosting over the top of the cake.

6 Melt the remaining chocolate in a double boiler or in a heatproof bowl over a pan of simmering water. Spoon into a small paper piping (pastry) bag and drizzle the chocolate over the cake. Chill before serving.

Chocolate Ginger Crunch Cake

This delicious no-bake gingery cake is easy and quick to prepare.

Serves 6
150g/5oz plain (semisweet) chocolate, chopped into small pieces
50g/2oz/¼ cup unsalted (sweet) butter
115g/4oz ginger nut biscuits (gingersnaps)
4 pieces of preserved stem ginger
30ml/2 tbsp stem ginger syrup
45ml/3 tbsp desiccated (dry unsweetened shredded) coconut

To decorate
25g/1oz milk chocolate, chopped into small pieces
pieces of crystallized (candied) ginger

1 Grease a 15cm/6in flan ring and place it on a sheet of baking parchment. Melt the plain chocolate with the butter in a heatproof bowl over a pan of barely simmering water. Remove the bowl from the heat and set aside.

2 Crush the ginger nut biscuits into small pieces. Transfer them into a bowl.

3 Chop the stem ginger finely and mix with the crushed ginger nut biscuits.

4 Stir the biscuit mixture, ginger syrup and coconut into the melted chocolate and butter, mixing well until evenly combined.

5 Transfer the mixture into the prepared flan ring and press down firmly and evenly. Chill in the refrigerator until set.

6 Remove the flan ring and slide the cake on to a plate. Melt the milk chocolate, drizzle it over the top and decorate with the pieces of crystallized ginger.

> **Cook's Tip**
> When crushing biscuits, place them in a plastic bag and use a rolling pin to break up the biscuits to the required size.

Date Cake Energy 441kcal/1841kJ; Protein 10.2g; Carbohydrate 40.3g, of which sugars 39.9g; Fat 27.6g, of which saturates 9.1g; Cholesterol 14mg; Calcium 70mg; Fibre 1.8g; Sodium 45mg.
Ginger Cake Energy 340kcal/1420kJ; Protein 3.1g; Carbohydrate 33.9g, of which sugars 25.4g; Fat 22.3g, of which saturates 14.5g; Cholesterol 20mg; Calcium 46mg; Fibre 2g; Sodium 121mg.

Frosted Chocolate Fudge Cake

A sumptuously rich cake, perfect for chocolate lovers.

Serves 6–8
115g/4oz plain (semisweet) chocolate, chopped into small pieces
175g/6oz/¾ cup unsalted (sweet) butter or margarine, softened
200g/7oz/scant 1 cup light muscovado (brown) sugar
5ml/1 tsp vanilla extract
3 eggs, beaten
150ml/¼ pint/⅔ cup Greek (US strained plain) yogurt
150g/5oz/1¼ cups self-raising (self-rising) flour
icing (confectioners') sugar and chocolate curls, to decorate

For the frosting
115g/4oz dark (bittersweet) chocolate, chopped into small pieces
50g/2oz/¼ cup unsalted (sweet) butter
350g/12oz/3 cups icing (confectioners') sugar
90ml/6 tbsp Greek (US strained plain) yogurt

1 Preheat the oven to 190°C/375°F/Gas 5. Lightly grease two 20cm/8in round sandwich cake tins (pans) and line the base of each with baking parchment. Melt the chocolate.

2 In a mixing bowl, cream the butter or margarine with the sugar until light and fluffy. Beat in the vanilla extract, then gradually add the eggs, beating after each addition.

3 Stir in the melted plain chocolate and yogurt evenly. Fold in the flour with a metal spoon.

4 Divide the mixture between the tins. Bake for 25–30 minutes or until firm to the touch. Turn out and cool on a wire rack.

5 Make the frosting. Melt the chocolate and butter in a pan over a low heat. Remove from the heat and stir in the icing sugar and yogurt. Mix until smooth, then beat until the frosting thickens slightly. Use a third of the mixture to sandwich the cakes together.

6 Working quickly, spread the remainder over the top and sides. Sprinkle with icing sugar and decorate with the curls.

Rich Chocolate Leaf Cake

This delicious cake has a stunning topping that will impress dinner guests.

Serves 8
75g/3oz dark (bittersweet) chocolate, broken into squares
150ml/¼ pint/⅔ cup milk
175g/6oz/¾ cup unsalted (sweet) butter, softened
250g/9oz/generous 1 cup light muscovado (brown) sugar
3 eggs
250g/9oz/2¼ cups plain (all-purpose) flour
10ml/2 tsp baking powder
75ml/5 tbsp single (light) cream

For the filling and topping
60ml/4 tbsp raspberry conserve
1 quantity Chocolate Ganache
dark (bittersweet) and white chocolate leaves

1 Preheat oven to 190°C/375°F/Gas 5. Grease two 22cm/8½in round sandwich cake tins (pans) and line the bases with baking parchment.

2 Melt the chocolate with the milk in a small pan over a low heat, stirring until smooth. Remove the pan from the heat and allow to cool slightly.

3 Cream the butter with the light muscovado sugar in a mixing bowl until light and fluffy. Add the eggs, one at a time, beating well after each addition.

4 Sift the flour and baking powder over the mixture and fold in gently but thoroughly. Stir in the chocolate mixture and the cream, mixing until smooth. Divide between the prepared tins and level the tops.

5 Bake the cakes for 30–35 minutes or until they are well risen and firm to the touch. Cool in the tins for a few minutes, then turn out on to wire racks.

6 Sandwich the cake layers together with the raspberry conserve. Spread the chocolate ganache over the cake and swirl with a knife. Place the cake on a serving plate, then decorate with the dark and white chocolate leaves, overlapping the leaves to create an attractive finish.

Fudge Cake Energy 753kcal/3160kJ; Protein 8g; Carbohydrate 105.4g, of which sugars 90.9g; Fat 36.6g, of which saturates 21.7g; Cholesterol 133mg; Calcium 133mg; Fibre 1.3g; Sodium 224mg.
Leaf Cake Energy 476kcal/1986kJ; Protein 5.3g; Carbohydrate 49.4g, of which sugars 35.7g; Fat 29.9g, of which saturates 18.2g; Cholesterol 102mg; Calcium 84mg; Fibre 1g; Sodium 108mg.

Chocolate Cappuccino Cake

This cake can be left whole and rolled roulade-style, or baked in two 23cm/9in tins for a round cake.

Serves 8–10
175g/6oz plain (semisweet) chocolate, chopped
10ml/2 tsp instant espresso powder dissolved in 45ml/3 tbsp boiling water
6 eggs, separated
150g/5oz/³⁄₄ cup sugar
pinch of cream of tartar
chocolate coffee beans

For the cream filling
175ml/6fl oz/³⁄₄ cup whipping or double (heavy) cream

35g/1oz/2 tbsp sugar
225g/8oz mascarpone or cream cheese, softened
30ml/2 tbsp coffee-flavoured liqueur
25g/1oz plain (semisweet) chocolate, grated

For the buttercream
4 egg yolks, at room temperature
75ml/2¹⁄₂fl oz/¹⁄₃ cup golden (light corn) syrup
50g/2oz/¹⁄₃ cup sugar
225g/8oz/1 cup unsalted (sweet) butter, in pieces and softened
15ml/1 tbsp instant espresso powder dissolved in 5–10ml/ 1–2 tsp boiling water
15–30ml/1–2 tbsp coffee liqueur

1 Preheat the oven to 180°C/350°F/Gas 4. Grease and line a 40 × 20cm/16 × 8in baking sheet with baking parchment, leaving 5cm/2in over each end. Grease the paper. In a bowl over a pan of simmering water, melt the chocolate and coffee. Set aside. In a bowl with an electric mixer, beat the egg yolks and sugar until thick. Lower the speed and blend in the chocolate mixture.

2 In a bowl with an electric mixer beat the egg whites and cream of tartar until stiff peaks form. Fold into the chocolate mixture. Pour the batter into the tin, smoothing the top. Bake for 15 minutes or until just firm. Turn out on to a wire rack to cool and peel off the paper.

3 Prepare the filling. In a bowl with an electric mixer, whip the cream and sugar until soft peaks form. In another bowl, beat the mascarpone or cream cheese and liqueur until light and smooth. Stir in the grated chocolate and fold in the whipped cream. Cover and refrigerate until ready for use.

4 Prepare the buttercream. In a bowl with an electric mixer, beat the egg yolks until thick and pale-coloured. In a pan, cook the syrup and sugar until boiling, stirring constantly. With the mixer on medium-low speed, pour the hot syrup over the beaten yolks. Beat in the butter a few pieces at a time until smooth. Beat in the dissolved coffee and liqueur. Chill until ready to use.

5 Assemble the cake. Trim off any crisp edges of cake. Cut crossways into three equal strips. Place one cake strip on a cake plate and spread with half the coffee cream filling. Cover with a second strip and the remaining filling. Top with the last strip.

6 Spoon about one third of the coffee buttercream into a small piping (pastry) bag fitted with a small star tip. Spread the remaining buttercream on the top and sides of cake. Pipe lattice or scroll design on the top and around the edges and decorate with chocolate coffee beans. Refrigerate the cake if not serving immediately, but allow to stand at room temperature for 30 minutes before serving.

Mocha Sponge Cake

The Yemeni city of Mocha was once the coffee capital of the world, and still makes a coffee that tastes like chocolate. 'Mocha' may be the variety of coffee or a combination of coffee and chocolate, as in this recipe.

Serves 10
25ml/1¹⁄₂ tbsp strong-flavoured ground coffee
175ml/6fl oz/³⁄₄ cup milk
115g/4oz/¹⁄₂ cup soft light brown sugar
115g/4oz/¹⁄₂ cup butter

1 egg, lightly beaten
190g/6¹⁄₂oz/1²⁄₃ cups self-raising (self-rising) flour
5ml/1 tsp bicarbonate of soda (baking soda)
60ml/4 tbsp creamy liqueur, such as Baileys or Irish Velvet

For the chocolate icing
200g/7oz plain (semisweet) chocolate, broken into pieces
75g/3oz/6 tbsp unsalted (sweet) butter, cubed
120ml/4fl oz/¹⁄₂ cup double (heavy) cream

1 Preheat the oven to 180°C/350°F/Gas 4. Grease and line a 18cm/7in round fixed-base cake tin (pan) with baking parchment.

2 Put the coffee in a jug (pitcher). Heat the milk to near-boiling point and pour over. Leave for 4 minutes, then strain and cool.

3 Gently melt the sugar and butter until dissolved. Pour into a bowl and cool for 2 minutes, then stir in the egg.

4 Sift the flour over the mixture and fold in. Blend the bicarbonate of soda with the coffee-flavoured milk and gradually stir into the mixture.

5 Pour into the tin, smooth the top, and bake for 40 minutes, until well-risen and firm. Cool in the tin for 10 minutes. Spoon the liqueur over and leave until cold. Turn out on to a wire rack.

6 To make the icing, place the chocolate in a heatproof bowl over a pan of simmering water, stirring until melted. Remove from the heat and stir in the butter and cream until smooth. When cool, coat the top and sides of the cake, using a metal spatula. Leave until set.

Sponge Cake Energy 444kcal/1853kJ; Protein 4.2g; Carbohydrate 41.2g, of which sugars 27.3g; Fat 29.7g, of which saturates 17.6g; Cholesterol 78mg; Calcium 112mg; Fibre 1.1g; Sodium 206mg.
Cappuccino Cake Energy 545kcal/2270kJ; Protein 8.6g; Carbohydrate 39.6g, of which sugars 39.4g; Fat 39.9g, of which saturates 23.1g; Cholesterol 272mg; Calcium 60mg; Fibre 0.5g; Sodium 189mg.

White Chocolate Cappuccino Gateau

A sensational, rich gateau, guaranteed to impress.

Serves 8
4 eggs
115g/4oz/generous ½ cup caster (superfine) sugar
15ml/1 tbsp strong black coffee
2.5ml/½ tsp vanilla extract
115g/4oz/1 cup plain (all-purpose) flour
75g/3oz white chocolate, coarsely grated

For the filling
120ml/4fl oz/½ cup double (heavy) cream or whipping cream
15ml/1 tbsp coffee-flavoured liqueur

For the topping
15ml/1 tbsp coffee-flavoured liqueur
1 quantity White Chocolate Frosting
white chocolate curls
unsweetened cocoa powder or ground cinnamon, for dusting

1 Preheat the oven to 180°C/350°F/Gas 4. Grease two 18cm/7in round sandwich cake tins (layer cake pans) and line the base of each with baking parchment.

2 Combine the eggs, caster sugar, coffee and vanilla extract in a large heatproof bowl. Place over a pan of hot water and whisk until pale and thick.

3 Sift half the flour over the mixture; fold in gently and evenly. Fold in the remaining flour with the grated white chocolate, stirring until evenly blended.

4 Divide the mixture between the prepared tins and smooth the tops. Bake for 20–25 minutes, until firm and golden brown, then turn out on to wire racks and leave to cool completely.

5 Make the filling. Whip the cream with the coffee liqueur in a bowl until it holds its shape. Spread over one of the cakes, then place the second layer on top.

6 Stir the coffee liqueur into the frosting. Spread over the top and sides of the cake, swirling with a metal spatula. Top with curls of white chocolate and dust with cocoa powder or cinnamon. Transfer the cake to a serving plate and set aside until the frosting has set. Serve that day.

Mocha Brazil Layer Torte

A deliciously nutty cake, which contains layers of light meringue and chocolate sponge within.

Serves 8
3 egg whites
115g/4oz/generous ½ cup caster (superfine) sugar
15ml/1 tbsp coffee extract
75g/3oz/¾ cup brazil nuts, toasted and finely ground
20cm/8in chocolate-flavoured Quick-mix Sponge Cake

For the icing
175g/6oz/1 cup plain (semisweet) chocolate chips
30ml/2 tbsp coffee extract
30ml/2 tbsp water
600ml/1 pint/2½ cups double (heavy) cream, whipped

For the decoration
12 chocolate triangles
12 chocolate-coated coffee beans

1 Preheat the oven to 150°C/300°F/Gas 2. Draw two 20cm/8in circles on baking parchment and place on a baking sheet. Grease, base-line and flour a 20cm/8in round springform tin (pan).

2 Whisk the egg whites until stiff. Whisk in the sugar until glossy. Fold in the coffee extract and nuts. Using a 1cm/½in plain nozzle, pipe to cover circles drawn on the paper.

3 Bake the meringues for 2 hours, then remove from the oven and leave to cool. Increase the oven temperature to 180°C/350°F/Gas 4.

4 To make the icing, melt the chocolate chips, coffee extract and water in a bowl over a pan of simmering water. Remove from the heat and fold in the whipped cream.

5 Cut the cake into three equal layers. Trim the meringue discs to the same size. Assemble the cake with a layer of sponge, a thin layer of icing and a meringue disc. End with sponge. Reserve a little icing and use the rest to swirl over the top of the cake.

6 Using the reserved icing, and a piping (pastry) bag with a star nozzle, pipe 24 small rosettes on top of the cake. Top alternately with the coffee beans and the chocolate triangles.

Cappuccino Gateau Energy 337kcal/1418kJ; Protein 5.3g; Carbohydrate 50.5g, of which sugars 39.5g; Fat 13.6g, of which saturates 7.4g; Cholesterol 116mg; Calcium 61mg; Fibre 0.7g; Sodium 41mg.
Brazil Torte Energy 6236kcal/25900kJ; Protein 60.3g; Carbohydrate 395g, of which sugars 327.8g; Fat 501.5g, of which saturates 242g; Cholesterol 833mg; Calcium 770mg; Fibre 7.6g; Sodium 1624mg.

Walnut Coffee Gateau with Chocolate Frosting

This cake uses finely ground walnuts instead of flour.

Serves 8–10

150g/5oz/generous 1 cup walnuts
150g/5oz/¾ cup caster
  (superfine) sugar
5 eggs, separated
50g/2oz/scant 1 cup dry breadcrumbs
15ml/1 tbsp unsweetened
  cocoa powder

15ml/1 tbsp instant coffee
30ml/2 tbsp rum or lemon juice
1.5ml/¼ tsp salt
90ml/6 tbsp redcurrant jam
chopped walnuts, for decorating

For the frosting

225g/8oz plain
  (semisweet) chocolate
750ml/1¼ pint/3 cups
  whipping cream

1 To make the frosting, combine the chocolate and cream in the top of a double boiler until the chocolate melts. Cool, then cover and chill overnight, or until the mixture is firm.

2 Preheat the oven to 180°C/350°F/Gas 4. Line and grease a 23 × 5cm/9 × 2in cake tin (pan). Grind the nuts with 45ml/ 3 tbsp of the sugar in a food processor, blender or coffee grinder.

3 With an electric mixer, beat the egg yolks and remaining sugar until thick and pale. Fold in the walnuts. Stir in the breadcrumbs, cocoa, coffee and rum or lemon juice.

4 In another bowl, beat the egg whites and salt until they hold stiff peaks. Fold carefully into the walnut mixture. Pour the batter into the prepared tin and bake until the top of the cake springs back when touched, about 45 minutes. Leave in the tin for 5 minutes, then turn out and cool. Slice in half horizontally.

5 With an electric mixer, beat the frosting mixture on a low speed until it becomes lighter, about 30 seconds. Warm the redcurrant jam and brush some over the cut cake layer. Spread with some of the frosting, then sandwich with the remaining cake layer. Brush the top of the cake with some more jam, then cover the side and top with the remaining frosting. Make a starburst pattern with a knife and sprinkle the walnuts around the edge.

Chocolate Pecan Nut Torte

This torte uses finely ground nuts instead of flour. Toast and cool the nuts before grinding finely in a processor.

Makes one 20cm/8in round cake

200g/7oz plain (semisweet)
  chocolate, chopped
150g/5oz/10 tbsp unsalted
  (sweet) butter, diced
4 eggs
90g/3½oz/½ cup caster
  (superfine) sugar

10ml/2 tsp vanilla extract
115g/4oz/1 cup ground
  pecan nuts
10ml/2 tsp ground cinnamon
24 toasted pecan nut halves,
  to decorate (optional)

For the honey glaze

115g/4oz plain (semisweet)
  chocolate, chopped
60g/2oz/¼ cup unsalted (sweet)
  butter, cut into pieces
30ml/2 tbsp honey
a pinch of ground cinnamon

1 Preheat the oven to 180°C/350°F/Gas 4. Grease a 20cm/8in springform tin (pan), line with baking parchment, then grease the paper. Wrap the tin with foil.

2 Melt the chocolate and butter in a double boiler or in a heatproof bowl over a pan of simmering water, stirring until smooth. Set aside. Beat the eggs, sugar and vanilla extract until frothy. Stir in the melted chocolate and butter, ground nuts and cinnamon.

3 Pour into the tin. Place in a large roasting pan and pour boiling water into the roasting pan, to come 2cm/¾in up the side of the springform tin. Bake for 25–30 minutes, or until the edge of the cake is set, but the centre soft. Remove the foil and set on a wire rack.

4 To make the glaze, melt the chocolate, butter, honey and cinnamon as before, stirring until smooth. Remove from the heat. Dip the toasted pecan halves halfway into the glaze and place on baking parchment to set. Remove the cake from its tin and invert on to a wire rack. Remove the paper. Pour the glaze over the cake, tilting the rack to ensure it is evenly spread out. Use a metal spatula to smooth the sides. Arrange the pecan nut halves on top.

Walnut Gateau Energy 651kcal/2707kJ; Protein 9.5g; Carbohydrate 43.5g, of which sugars 38.5g; Fat 50.1g, of which saturates 24.9g; Cholesterol 175mg; Calcium 101mg; Fibre 1.8g; Sodium 149mg.
Torte Energy 4744kcal/19729kJ; Protein 53.2g; Carbohydrate 335.4g, of which sugars 330.8g; Fat 363.6g, of which saturates 175.2g; Cholesterol 1228mg; Calcium 380mg; Fibre 13.3g; Sodium 1582mg.

Luxurious Chocolate Cake

This attractive and delicious chocolate cake contains no flour and has a light mousse-like texture.

Makes one 20cm/8in round cake
225g/9oz squares plain (semisweet) chocolate
175g/6oz/¾ cup butter, softened
130g/4½oz/⅔ cup caster (superfine) sugar
225g/8oz/2 cups ground almonds
4 eggs, separated
115g/4oz squares white chocolate, melted, to decorate

1 Preheat the oven to 180°C/350°F/Gas 4. Grease and base-line a 20cm/8in springform cake tin (pan).

2 Melt the chocolate in a heatproof bowl over a pan of simmering water. Beat 115g/4oz/½ cup butter and all the sugar until light and fluffy in a large bowl. Add two-thirds of the plain chocolate, the almonds and egg yolks, and beat well.

3 Whisk the egg whites in another clean, dry bowl until stiff peaks form. Fold them into the chocolate mixture, then transfer to the tin and smooth the surface. Bake for 50–55 minutes, or until a skewer inserted into the centre comes out clean.

4 Cool in the tin for 5 minutes, then remove from the tin and transfer to a wire rack. Remove the lining paper and cool completely.

5 Place the remaining butter and remaining melted chocolate in a pan. Heat very gently, stirring constantly, until melted and smooth. Place a large sheet of baking parchment under the wire rack to catch any drips. Pour the chocolate topping over the cake, allowing the topping to coat the top and sides. Leave to set for at least 1 hour.

6 To decorate, fill a paper piping (pastry) bag with the melted white chocolate and snip the end. Drizzle the white chocolate around the edges. Use any remaining chocolate to pipe leaves on to baking parchment. Allow to set then place in the middle on top of the cake.

Torte Varazdin

This classic chocolate cake is a favourite worldwide, and appears in many guises.

Serves 8–12
225g/8oz/1 cup butter, at room temperature
225g/8oz/generous 1 cup caster (superfine) sugar
200g/7oz plain (semisweet) chocolate, melted
6 eggs, separated
130g/4½oz/generous 1 cup plain (all-purpose) flour, sifted
chocolate curls, to decorate

For the filling
250ml/8fl oz/1 cup double (heavy) cream, lightly whipped
450g/1lb/1¾ cups canned chestnut purée
115g/4oz/generous ½ cup caster (superfine) sugar

For the topping
150g/5oz/10 tbsp unsalted (sweet) butter
150g/5oz/1¼ cups icing (confectioners') sugar, sifted
115g/4oz plain (semisweet) chocolate, melted

1 Preheat the oven to 180°C/350°F/Gas 4. Grease and line the base and sides of a 20–23cm/8–9in round cake tin (pan). Cream the butter and sugar together in a bowl until pale and fluffy. Stir in the melted chocolate and egg yolks. Fold the flour carefully into the chocolate mixture.

2 In a grease-free bowl, whisk the egg whites until stiff. Add a spoonful of the egg white to the chocolate mixture to loosen it, then carefully fold in the remainder. Spoon the cake mixture into the prepared tin.

3 Bake the cake for 45–50 minutes, or until firm to the touch and a skewer inserted into the middle comes out clean. Cool on a wire rack. When cold, peel off the lining paper and slice the cake in half horizontally.

4 Meanwhile, gently mix the filling ingredients together in a bowl. Sandwich the two cake halves together firmly with the chestnut filling. In a mixing bowl, cream together the butter and sugar for the topping before stirring in the melted chocolate. Using a dampened knife, spread the chocolate topping over the sides and top of the cake. Chill for 60 minutes before serving if possible, decorated with chocolate curls.

Luxurious Energy 5823kcal/24249kJ; Protein 103.4g; Carbohydrate 426.5g, of which sugars 418.4g; Fat 424.1g, of which saturates 186.5g; Cholesterol 1148mg; Calcium 1436mg; Fibre 22.3g; Sodium 1641mg.
Varazdin Energy 731kcal/3055kJ; Protein 3.8g; Carbohydrate 82g, of which sugars 62.4g; Fat 45.4g, of which saturates 27.9g; Cholesterol 97mg; Calcium 79mg; Fibre 2.5g; Sodium 202mg.

French Chocolate Cake

This is typical of a French home-made cake – dense, dark and utterly delicious. Serve with cream or a fruit coulis.

Makes one 24cm/9½in round cake
150g/5oz/¾ cup caster (superfine) sugar
275g/10oz plain (semisweet) chocolate, chopped
175g/6oz/¾ cup unsalted (sweet) butter, cut into pieces
10ml/2 tsp vanilla extract
5 eggs, separated
40g/1½oz/⅓ cup plain (all-purpose) flour, sifted
a pinch of salt
icing (confectioners') sugar, for dusting

I Preheat the oven to 160°C/325°F/Gas 3. Butter a 24cm/9½in round springform tin (pan), sprinkle with sugar and tap out excess.

2 Set aside 45ml/3 tbsp of the caster sugar. Place the chopped chocolate, butter and remaining sugar in a heavy pan and cook gently over a low heat until melted, stirring occasionally.

3 Remove the pan from the heat, stir in the vanilla extract and leave to cool slightly.

4 Beat the egg yolks, one at a time, into the chocolate mixture, then stir in the flour.

5 Beat the egg whites with the salt until soft peaks form. Sprinkle over the reserved sugar and beat until stiff and glossy. Beat one-third of the whites into the chocolate mixture to lighten it, then fold in the rest.

6 Pour the mixture into the tin and tap it gently to release any air bubbles.

7 Bake the cake for 35–45 minutes, or until well risen and the top springs back when touched lightly. Transfer to a wire rack, remove the sides of the tin and leave the cake to cool. Remove the tin base, dust the cake with icing sugar and transfer to a serving plate.

French Chocolate Cake with Brandy

A deliciously dense dessert with an attractive topping.

Serves 10
250g/9oz dark (bittersweet) chocolate, chopped into pieces
225g/8oz/1 cup unsalted (sweet) butter, cut into small pieces
90g/3½oz/scant ½ cup sugar
30ml/2 tbsp brandy or orange-flavoured liqueur
5 eggs
15ml/1 tbsp plain (all-purpose) flour
icing (confectioners') sugar, for dusting
whipped or sour cream, to serve

I Preheat the oven to 180°C/350°F/Gas 4. Generously grease a 23 × 5cm/9 × 2in springform tin (pan). Line the base with baking parchment and grease. Wrap the bottom and sides of the tin in foil to prevent water from seeping into the cake.

2 In a pan, over a low heat, melt the chocolate, butter and sugar, stirring frequently until smooth. Remove from the heat, cool slightly and stir in the brandy or liqueur.

3 In a bowl, beat the eggs for 1 minute. Beat in the flour, then slowly blend in the chocolate mixture. Pour into the tin.

4 Place the springform tin in a large roasting pan. Add enough boiling water to come 2cm/¾in up the side of the springform tin. Bake for 25–30 minutes, until the edge of the cake is set but the centre is still soft. Remove the springform tin from the roasting pan and remove the foil. Cool on a wire rack. The cake will sink in the centre and become its classic slim shape as it cools. Don't worry if the surface cracks slightly.

5 Remove the side of the springform tin and turn the cake on to a wire rack. Lift off the tin base and then carefully peel back the paper, so the base of the cake is now the top. Leave the cake on the rack until it is quite cold.

6 Cut 6–8 strips of baking parchment 2.5cm/1in wide and place randomly over the cake. Dust the cake with icing sugar, then carefully remove the paper. Slide the cake on to a plate and serve with whipped or sour cream.

French Energy 3799kcal/15862kJ; Protein 50.6g; Carbohydrate 363.5g, of which sugars 330.6g; Fat 249.1g, of which saturates 145.2g; Cholesterol 1341mg; Calcium 400mg; Fibre 8.1g; Sodium 1437mg.
Brandy Energy 379kcal/1576kJ; Protein 4.7g; Carbohydrate 26.6g, of which sugars 25.2g; Fat 28.3g, of which saturates 16.7g; Cholesterol 145mg; Calcium 33mg; Fibre 0.7g; Sodium 173mg.

Chocolate and Almond Cake

This rich and sumptuous chocolate cake is filled with a sweet almond paste.

Serves 6
6 eggs, separated
115g/4oz/1 cup caster
  (superfine) sugar
150g/5oz/1¼ cups unsweetened
  cocoa powder
150g/5oz/1¼ cups
  ground almonds

For the almond paste
150g/5oz/1¼ cups caster
  (superfine) sugar
120ml/4fl oz/½ cup water
150g/5oz/1¼ cups
  ground almonds
15–30ml/1–2 tbsp lemon juice
½ vanilla pod (bean)

For the icing
115g/4oz dark (bittersweet)
  chocolate, chopped
25g/1oz/2 tbsp unsalted
  (sweet) butter, cubed
120ml/4fl oz/½ cup double
  (heavy) cream
50g/2oz/½ cup icing
  (confectioners') sugar, sifted

1 Preheat the oven to 200°C/400°F/Gas 6. Grease and line a 20cm/8in springform cake tin (pan). Beat the egg yolks in a large bowl, add the sugar and beat until the mixture is thick and creamy. Add the cocoa powder and almonds, and gently fold in.

2 Whisk the egg whites until stiff peaks form. Fold a spoonful of the whites into the yolk mixture, then mix in the remaining whites. Spoon into the tin and bake for 1 hour, or until a skewer inserted into the centre comes out clean. Cool in the tin.

3 Make the almond paste. Gently heat the sugar and water in a pan until the sugar has dissolved. Boil for 5 minutes, or until a thick syrup forms. Stir in the almonds and transfer to a bowl. Add the lemon juice and the seeds from the vanilla pod. Mix well.

4 Remove the cake from the tin and slice into two even layers. Sandwich the two halves together with the almond paste.

5 Make the icing. Melt the chocolate and butter in a heatproof bowl over a pan of simmering water. Remove from the heat and stir in the cream, then add the sugar and stir well. Cover the top of the cake with the chocolate icing. Leave to set.

Chocolate Gooey Cake

This is Sweden's favourite chocolate cake. For perfect results it is essential to undercook the cake so that it is really dense in the middle. It is made with ground almonds instead of flour so the cake is gluten-free and therefore the perfect tempting, self-indulgent treat for a coeliac dinner guest.

Serves 8
115g/4oz dark (bittersweet)
  chocolate with 75 per cent
  cocoa solids
5ml/1 tsp water
115g/4oz/½ cup unsalted
  (sweet) butter, plus extra
  to grease
2 eggs, separated
175g/6oz/1½ cups ground
  almonds
5ml/1 tsp vanilla sugar
whipped double (heavy) cream,
  to serve

1 Preheat the oven to 180°C/350°F/Gas 4. Grease a 20cm/8in shallow round cake tin (pan) with butter.

2 Break the dark chocolate into pieces and place in a pan. Add the water and heat gently, stirring constantly, until the chocolate has melted and the mixture is smooth. Remove from the heat and set aside.

3 Cut the butter into small pieces, add to the chocolate and stir until melted.

4 Add the egg yolks, ground almonds and vanilla sugar and stir together until the mixture is evenly blended. Transfer the mixture in a large bowl.

5 Whisk the egg whites until stiff, then carefully fold them into the chocolate mixture.

6 Spoon the mixture into the prepared tin and bake in the oven for 15–17 minutes, until just set. The mixture should still be soft in the centre.

7 Leave the cake to cool in the tin. When cold, serve with a spoonful of the whipped cream.

Almond Cake Energy 892kcal/3726kJ; Protein 23g; Carbohydrate 73.7g, of which sugars 69.3g; Fat 58.4g, of which saturates 19g; Cholesterol 228mg; Calcium 226mg; Fibre 7.2g; Sodium 349mg.
Gooey Cake Energy 311kcal/1288kJ; Protein 6.8g; Carbohydrate 10g, of which sugars 9.3g; Fat 27.4g, of which saturates 9.9g; Cholesterol 75mg; Calcium 66.2mg; Fibre 1.9g; Sodium 97mg.

Rich Tea-time Chocolate Cake

The first chocolate arrived in England in the 1500s, and the 17th century saw the opening of expensive chocolate houses, which were frequented by the rich and famous. Today, chocolate cake is a staple of every self-respecting tea table in England.

Serves 10–12
225g/8oz/2 cups plain
  (all-purpose) flour
5ml/1 tsp bicarbonate of soda
  (baking soda)
50g/2oz/1/2 cup unsweetened
  cocoa powder
125g/41/2oz/9 tbsp soft butter
250g/9oz/11/4 cups caster
  (superfine) sugar
3 eggs, beaten
250ml/8fl oz/1 cup buttermilk

For the chocolate buttercream
175g/6oz/11/2 cups icing
  (confectioners') sugar
115g/4oz/1/2 cup soft
  unsalted (sweet) butter
few drops of vanilla extract
50g/2oz dark (bittersweet)
  chocolate

1 Butter two 20cm/8in round sandwich tins (pans) and line the bases with baking parchment. Preheat the oven to 180°C/350°F/Gas 4. Sift the flour with the bicarbonate of soda and cocoa.

2 Beat the butter and sugar until light and fluffy. Gradually beat in the eggs. Add the flour and buttermilk, and mix well.

3 Spoon into the prepared tins. Place in the hot oven and cook for 30–35 minutes, until firm to the touch. Turn out of the tins, peel off the paper and leave on a wire rack to cool.

4 To make the chocolate buttercream, sift the icing sugar into a bowl. In a separate bowl, beat the butter until very soft and creamy.

5 Beat in half the sifted icing sugar until smooth and light. Gradually beat in the remaining sugar and the vanilla extract. Break the chocolate into squares. Melt in a bowl over a pan of hot water or in a microwave oven on low.

6 Mix the melted chocolate into the buttercream. Use half to sandwich the cakes together, and spread the rest on the top.

Tia Maria and Ginger Gateau

A feather-light coffee sponge cake with chocolate icing and a filling flavoured with liqueur and spiked with preserved stem ginger.

Serves 8
75g/3oz/3/4 cup plain
  (all-purpose) flour
30ml/2 tbsp instant
  coffee powder
3 eggs
115g/4oz/generous 1/2 cup caster
  (superfine) sugar

For the filling
175g/6oz/generous 3/4 cup
  soft cheese
15ml/1 tbsp clear honey
15ml/1 tbsp Tia Maria
50g/2oz/1/3 cup preserved stem
  ginger, chopped

For the icing
225g/8oz/2 cups icing
  (confectioners') sugar, sifted
10ml/2 tsp coffee extract
5ml/1 tsp cocoa
coffee beans (optional)

1 Preheat the oven to 190°C/375°F/Gas 5. Line and grease a 20cm/8in round cake tin (pan). Sift the flour and coffee powder together into a bowl.

2 Whisk the eggs and sugar in a bowl until thick and mousse-like, then fold in the flour mixture lightly. Turn the mixture into the prepared tin. Bake for 30–35 minutes, or until firm and golden. Leave to cool on a wire rack.

3 To make the filling, mix the soft cheese with the honey in a bowl. Beat until smooth, then stir in the Tia Maria and preserved stem ginger. Split the cake in half horizontally. Spread the bottom layer with the creamy Tia Maria filling and sandwich the other cake half on top.

4 To make the icing, mix the icing sugar and coffee extract in a bowl with enough water to make an icing which will coat the back of a wooden spoon. Pour three-quarters of the icing over the cake.

5 Stir the cocoa into the remaining icing and mix well, spoon it into a piping (pastry) bag fitted with a writing nozzle and drizzle the mocha icing over the coffee icing. Decorate with the coffee beans, if you like.

Tea-time Cake Energy 430kcal/1790kJ; Protein 7.8g; Carbohydrate 29.5g, of which sugars 28.8g; Fat 32.1g, of which saturates 13.6g; Cholesterol 96mg; Calcium 92mg; Fibre 1.9g; Sodium 125mg.
Tia Maria Energy 247kcal/1050kJ; Protein 4.9g; Carbohydrate 54.7g, of which sugars 47.4g; Fat 2.5g, of which saturates 1.5g; Cholesterol 12mg; Calcium 65mg; Fibre 0.5g; Sodium 120mg.

Chocolate Gateau Terrine

This rich chocolate terrine is a spectacular cake for a special-occasion meal.

Serves 10–12
115g/4oz/½ cup butter, softened
few drops of vanilla extract
115g/4oz/½ cup caster
  (superfine) sugar
2 size 3 eggs
115g/4oz/1 cup self-raising
  (self-rising) flour, sifted
50ml/2fl oz/¼ cup milk
25g/1oz/⅓ cup desiccated
  (dry unsweetened shredded)
  coconut, to decorate
fresh roses, to decorate

For the light chocolate filling
115g/4oz/½ cup butter, softened
2 tbsp icing (confectioners')
  sugar, sifted

75g/3oz plain (semisweet)
  chocolate, melted
225ml/8fl oz/1 cup double
  (heavy) cream, lightly whipped

For the dark chocolate filling
115g/4oz plain (semisweet)
  chocolate, chopped
115g/4oz/½ cup butter
2 size 3 eggs
2 tbsp caster (superfine) sugar
225ml/8fl oz/1 cup double
  (heavy) cream, lightly whipped
50g/2oz/½ cup unsweetened
  cocoa powder
1 tbsp dark rum (optional)
2 tbsp gelatine powder dissolved
  in 2 tbsp hot water

For the topping
225g/8oz white chocolate
115g/4oz/½ cup butter

1 Preheat the oven to 180°C/350°F/Gas 4. Grease a 900g/2lb loaf tin (pan), line the base and sides with greased baking parchment.

2 To make the cake, beat the butter, vanilla extract and sugar until light and fluffy. Add the eggs, one at a time, beating well. Fold the flour and the milk into the mixture. Transfer to the tin and bake in the centre of the oven for 25–30 minutes, or until a skewer inserted in the centre comes out clean. Leave in the tin for 5 minutes, then transfer to a wire rack to cool. Peel off the paper.

3 To make the light chocolate filling, beat the butter and icing sugar until creamy. Stir in the chocolate and cream until blended. Cover and chill until required. To make the dark chocolate filling, heat the chocolate and butter in a pan, stirring until melted. Set aside to cool. Place the eggs and sugar in a bowl and beat until thick and frothy. Fold in the dark chocolate mixture, cream, cocoa, rum and dissolved gelatine until evenly blended.

4 Line the cleaned tin with clear film (plastic wrap), allowing it to hang over the edges. Cut the cake into three layers. Spread two with the light chocolate filling, then place one of them, filling side up, in the tin. Cover with half the dark chocolate filling. Chill for 10 minutes. Place the second light chocolate-topped layer in the terrine, filling side up. Spread over the remaining dark chocolate filling. Chill for 10 minutes. Top with the remaining layer of cake and chill the terrine again for about 10 minutes.

5 To make the white chocolate topping, heat the chocolate and butter in a pan, stirring until melted. Allow to cool slightly.

6 Turn the terrine out on to a wire rack. Remove the clear film. Trim the edges, then pour over the white chocolate topping, spreading it over the sides. Sprinkle the coconut over the top and sides. When set transfer to a plate and decorate with the roses.

Black Forest Gateau

This is a perfect chocolate gateau for a special tea party, or for serving as a sumptuous dinner-party dessert for chocoholic guests.

Makes one 20cm/8in cake
5 eggs
175g/6oz/scant 1 cup caster
  (superfine) sugar
50g/2oz/½ cup plain
  (all-purpose) flour
50g/2oz/½ cup unsweetened
  cocoa powder
75g/3oz/6 tbsp butter, melted

For the filling
75–90ml/5–6 tbsp Kirsch
600ml/1 pint/2½ cups double
  (heavy) cream
425g/15oz can black
  cherries, drained, pitted
  and chopped

To decorate
chocolate curls
15–20 fresh cherries,
  preferably with stems
icing (confectioners') sugar

1 Preheat the oven to 180°C/350°F/Gas 4. Base-line and grease two deep 20cm/8in round cake tins (pans).

2 Beat together the eggs and sugar for 10 minutes, or until thick and pale. Sift over the flour and cocoa powder, and fold in gently. Trickle in the melted butter and fold in gently.

3 Transfer the mixture to the cake tins. Bake for 30 minutes, or until springy to the touch.

4 Leave in the tins for 5 minutes, then turn out on to a wire rack, peel off the lining paper and leave to cool. Cut each cake in half horizontally and sprinkle with the Kirsch.

5 Whip the cream until softly peaking. Combine two-thirds of the cream with the chopped cherries. Place a layer of cake on a serving plate and spread with one-third of the filling. Repeat twice, and top with a layer of cake. Use the reserved cream to cover the top and side of the gateau.

6 Decorate the side of the gateau with chocolate curls, and place more in the centre of the top of the cake. Arrange fresh cherries around the edge and finally dredge the top with icing sugar.

Terrine Energy 793kcal/3291kJ; Protein 7.2g; Carbohydrate 45.4g, of which sugars 37.4g; Fat 66.1g, of which saturates 40.8g; Cholesterol 198mg; Calcium 123mg; Fibre 1.5g; Sodium 329mg.
Forest Energy 5386kcal/22373kJ; Protein 58.3g; Carbohydrate 316.8g, of which sugars 272.9g; Fat 423.1g, of which saturates 253.7g; Cholesterol 1934mg; Calcium 742mg; Fibre 10.1g; Sodium 1458mg.

Berry Chocolate Savarin

This exquisite cake is soaked
in a wine and brandy syrup.

Serves 6–8
100ml/3½fl oz/scant ½ cup milk
4 eggs
225g/8oz/2 cups unbleached
  white bread flour
40g/1½oz/⅓ cup unsweetened
  cocoa powder
2.5ml/½ tsp salt
25g/1oz/¼ cup caster
  (superfine) sugar
90g/3½oz/7 tbsp butter, melted
5ml/1 tsp easy-blend (rapid-rise)
  dried yeast

For the syrup
115g/4oz/generous ½ cup sugar
75ml/2½fl oz/⅓ cup white wine
45ml/3 tbsp brandy

For the filling
150ml/¼ pint/⅔ cup double
  (heavy) cream, whipped, or
  crème fraîche

For the topping
225g/8oz/2 cups
  strawberries, halved
115g/4oz/1 cup raspberries
physalis and strawberry leaves

1 Pour the milk and eggs into the bread machine pan. If necessary
for your machine, reverse the order in which you add the liquid
and dry ingredients. Sprinkle the flour and cocoa powder over
the liquid in the pan, until covered. Place the salt, sugar and butter
in separate corners. Make an indent in the flour; add the yeast.

2 Start the machine on the dough setting (basic dough setting
if available). Oil a 1.5 litre/2½ pint/6¼ cup savarin or ring mould.
When the machine has finished mixing, leave on the dough setting
for 20 minutes, then stop it. Put the dough into the mould,
cover with oiled clear film (plastic wrap) and leave for 1 hour,
or until the dough is near the top of the mould. Meanwhile,
preheat the oven to 200°C/400°F/Gas 6. Bake for 25–30
minutes, or until golden and well risen. Cool on a wire rack.

3 Make the syrup. Place the sugar, wine and 75ml/2½fl oz/⅓ cup
water in a pan. Heat gently, stirring until the sugar dissolves. Bring
to the boil, then lower the heat and simmer for 2 minutes.
Remove from the heat and stir in the brandy. Spoon over the
savarin. Transfer to a serving plate and leave to cool. To serve, fill
the centre with the cream or crème fraîche and top with the
berries. Decorate with physalis and strawberry leaves.

Death by Chocolate

One of the richest
chocolate cakes ever.

Serves 16–20
225g/8oz dark (bittersweet)
  chocolate, broken into squares
115g/4oz/½ cup unsalted
  (sweet) butter
150ml/¼ pint/⅔ cup milk
225g/8oz/1 cup light muscovado
  (brown) sugar
10ml/2 tsp vanilla extract
2 eggs, separated
150ml/¼ pint/⅔ cup
  sour cream
225g/8oz/2 cups self-raising
  (self-rising) flour
5ml/1 tsp baking powder

For the filling
60ml/4 tbsp seedless
  raspberry jam
60ml/4 tbsp brandy
400g/14oz dark (bittersweet)
  chocolate, broken into squares
200g/7oz/scant 1 cup unsalted
  (sweet) butter

For the topping
250ml/8fl oz/1 cup double
  (heavy) cream
225g/8oz dark (bittersweet)
  chocolate, broken into squares
plain (semisweet) and white
  chocolate curls, to decorate
chocolate-dipped physalis or
  raspberries, to serve (optional)

1 Preheat the oven to 180°C/350°F/Gas 4. Grease and
base-line a deep 23cm/9in springform cake tin (pan). Place the
chocolate, butter and milk in a pan. Heat gently until smooth
Remove from the heat, beat in the sugar and vanilla, then cool.

2 Beat the egg yolks and cream in a bowl, then beat into the
chocolate mixture. Sift the flour and baking powder over the
surface and fold in. Whisk the egg whites in a grease-free bowl
until stiff; fold into the mixture.

3 Scrape into the prepared tin and bake for 45–55 minutes, or
until firm. Cool in the tin for 15 minutes, then turn out and cool.

4 Slice the cold cake across the middle to make three even
layers. In a small pan, warm the jam with 15ml/1 tbsp of
the brandy, then brush over two of the layers. Heat the
remaining brandy in a pan with the chocolate and butter,
stirring, until smooth. Cool until beginning to thicken.

5 Spread the bottom layer of the cake with half the chocolate
filling, taking care not to disturb the jam. Top with a second
layer, jam side up, and spread with the remaining filling. Top
with the final layer and press lightly. Leave to set.

6 Make the topping. Heat the cream and chocolate together
in a pan over a low heat, stirring frequently until the chocolate
has melted. Pour into a bowl, leave to cool, then whisk until
the mixture begins to hold its shape.

7 Spread the top and sides of the cake with the chocolate
topping. Decorate with chocolate curls and chocolate-dipped
physalis or raspberries, if you like.

> **Cook's Tip**
> For chocolate-coated physalis, melt the chocolate in a bowl,
> then dip in the fruit, holding them by their tops. Leave to set
> completely before using.

Savarin Energy 335kcal/1396kJ; Protein 4.9g; Carbohydrate 25.6g, of which sugars 21.7g; Fat 22.4g, of which saturates 13.1g; Cholesterol 146mg; Calcium 66mg; Fibre 0.8g; Sodium 116mg.
Death by Chocolate Energy 432kcal/1809kJ; Protein 4.7g; Carbohydrate 49.9g, of which sugars 38.4g; Fat 24.7g, of which saturates 14.9g; Cholesterol 57mg; Calcium 99mg; Fibre 1.4g; Sodium 120mg.

Mississippi Mud Cake with Filling

A rich dark chocolate cake, reminiscent of the black shores of the great Mississippi River.

Serves 8–10
150g/5oz unsweetened chocolate
225g/8oz/1 cup butter
300ml/¼ pint/1¼ cups strong
  coffee or espresso
pinch of salt
400g/14oz/2 cups sugar
60ml/4 tbsp bourbon or whisky
2 eggs, lightly beaten
10ml/2 tsp vanilla extract
275g/10oz/2½ cups plain
  (all-purpose) flour, sifted
130g/4½oz/1 cup sweetened
  desiccated (dry shredded) coconut

For the filling and topping
250ml/8fl oz/1 cup
  evaporated milk
115g/4oz/½ cup soft light
  brown sugar
115g/4oz/½ cup butter
75g/3oz plain (semisweet) chocolate
3 egg yolks, lightly beaten
5ml/1 tsp vanilla extract
225g/8oz/2 cups pecans, chopped
75g/3oz/1 cup small marshmallows
350ml/12fl oz/1½ cups whipping
  or double (heavy) cream
5ml/1 tsp vanilla extract
fresh coconut for ruffles,
  to decorate

1 Preheat the oven to 180°C/350°F/Gas 4. Grease two 23cm/9in cake tins (pans). Melt the chocolate, butter, coffee, salt and sugar in a pan. Stir in the bourbon or whisky. Cool in a bowl slightly. Beat in the eggs and vanilla, then beat in the flour and coconut. Pour into the tins. Bake for 25–30 minutes. Cool in the tins for 10 minutes, then transfer to a wire rack.

2 For the filling, cook the milk, sugar, butter, chocolate, egg yolks and vanilla in a pan for 8–10 minutes. Remove from heat and stir in the nuts and marshmallows. Chill until thick enough to spread. Slice both cakes in half. Spread each bottom layer with half the chocolate nut filling and cover with the top layers.

3 Whip the cream and the vanilla until firm peaks form. Spread a filled cake with half the whipped cream. Top with the second filled cake and spread with the remaining cream. To make the coconut ruffles, draw a swivel-bladed peeler along the curved edge of a coconut piece to make thin wide curls with a brown edge.

Multi-layer Chocolate Cake

For a change, try sandwiching the layers with softened vanilla ice cream. Freeze the cake before serving.

Makes one 20cm/8in cake
115g/4oz plain (semisweet)
  chocolate
175g/6oz/¾ cup butter
450g/1lb/2¼ cups caster
  (superfine) sugar
3 eggs
5ml/1 tsp vanilla extract

175g/6oz/1½ cups plain
  (all-purpose) flour
5ml/1 tsp baking powder
115g/4oz/1 cup chopped walnuts

For the filling and topping
350ml/12fl oz/1½ cups
  whipping cream
225g/8oz plain (semisweet)
  chocolate
15ml/1 tbsp vegetable oil

1 Preheat the oven to 180°C/350°F/Gas 4. Line two 20cm/8in shallow round cake tins (pans) with baking parchment and grease the paper.

2 Melt the chocolate and butter together in the top of a double boiler or in a heatproof bowl over a pan of simmering water. Transfer to a bowl and stir in the sugar. Add the eggs and vanilla and mix well. Sift over the flour and baking powder. Stir in the chopped walnuts.

3 Pour the mixture into the prepared cake tins. Bake until a skewer inserted into the centre comes out clean, about 30 minutes. Leave to stand for 10 minutes, then unmould on to a wire rack to cool completely.

4 To make the filling and topping, whip the cream until firm. Slice the cakes in half horizontally. Sandwich them together with the cream and cover the cake with the remainder. Chill.

5 To make the chocolate curls, melt the chocolate and oil as before. Stir to combine well. Spread on to a non-porous surface. Just before it sets, hold the blade of a knife at an angle to the chocolate and scrape across the surface to make curls. Use to decorate the cake and add tiny curls made with the tip of a rounded knife as well, if you like.

Multi Energy 7850kcal/32796kJ; Protein 79.4g; Carbohydrate 836.4g, of which sugars 699.2g Fat 488.8g, of which saturates 249.3g Cholesterol 1332mg; Calcium 1024mg; Fibre 17.9g; Sodium 1419mg.
Mississippi Energy 1108kcal/4624kJ; Protein 13g; Carbohydrate 102.8g, of which sugars 79.9g; Fat 73.1g, of which saturates 40.7g; Cholesterol 181mg; Calcium 227mg; Fibre 4.3g; Sodium 294mg.

Sachertorte

This glorious gateau was created in Vienna in 1832 by Franz Sacher, a royal chef.

Serves 10–12
225g/8oz dark (bittersweet) chocolate, broken into squares
150g/5oz/10 tbsp unsalted (sweet) butter, softened
115g/4oz/generous ½ cup caster (superfine) sugar
8 eggs, separated
115g/4oz/1 cup plain (all-purpose) flour
chocolate curls, to decorate

For the glaze
225g/8oz/¾ cup apricot jam
15ml/1 tbsp lemon juice

For the icing
225g/8oz plain dark (bittersweet) chocolate, broken into squares
200g/7oz/1 cup caster (superfine) sugar
15ml/1 tbsp golden (light corn) syrup
250ml/8fl oz/1 cup double (heavy) cream
5ml/1 tsp vanilla extract

1 Preheat the oven to 180°C/350°F/Gas 4. Grease a 23cm/9in round springform tin (pan). Line with baking parchment. Melt the chocolate in a heatproof bowl over a pan of hot water.

2 Cream the butter and sugar in a bowl until pale and fluffy. Add the egg yolks, one at a time, beating after each addition. Beat in the melted chocolate. Sift the flour over the mixture and fold in.

3 Whisk the egg whites until stiff, then stir a quarter into the chocolate mixture to lighten it. Fold in the remaining whites. Turn the mixture into the cake tin and smooth level. Bake for 50–55 minutes, or until firm. Turn out on to a wire rack to cool.

4 Heat the apricot jam with the lemon juice in a small pan until melted, then strain. Slice the cake horizontally into two even layers. Brush the cut surfaces and sides of each layer with the apricot glaze, then sandwich together. Place on a wire rack.

5 Mix the icing ingredients in a heavy pan. Heat gently, stirring until thick. Simmer for 3–4 minutes, without stirring, until the mixture registers 95°C/200°F on a sugar thermometer. Pour over the cake and spread evenly. Decorate with the curls and leave to set before serving.

Chocolate and Fresh Cherry Gateau

Make this sophisticated cake for a special occasion.

Makes one 20in/8in round cake
115g/4oz/½ cup butter
150g/5oz/¾ cup caster (superfine) sugar
3 eggs, lightly beaten
175g/6oz/1 cup plain (semisweet) chocolate chips, melted
60ml/4 tbsp Kirsch
150g/5oz/1¼ cups self-raising (self-rising) flour
5ml/1 tsp ground cinnamon
2.5ml/½ tsp ground cloves
350g/12oz fresh cherries, pitted and halved

45ml/3 tbsp morello cherry jam, warmed
5ml/1 tsp lemon juice

For the frosting
115g/4oz/⅔ cup plain (semisweet) chocolate chips
50g/2oz/¼ cup unsalted (sweet) butter
60ml/4 tbsp double (heavy) cream

To decorate
18 fresh cherries dipped in 75g/3oz/1½ cup white chocolate chips, melted, and a few rose leaves, washed and dried

1 Preheat the oven to 160°C/325°F/Gas 3. Grease, base-line and flour a 20cm/8in round springform tin (pan).

2 Cream the butter and 115g/4oz/½ cup of the sugar until pale. Beat in the eggs. Stir in the chocolate and half the Kirsch. Fold in the flour and spices. Transfer to the tin and bake for 55–60 minutes. Cool for 10 minutes, then transfer to a wire rack.

3 For the filling, bring the cherries, the remaining Kirsch and sugar to the boil, cover, and simmer for 10 minutes. Uncover for a further 10 minutes until syrupy. Leave to cool.

4 Halve the cake horizontally. Cut a 1cm/½in deep circle from the middle of the base, leaving a 1cm/½in edge. Crumble this cake into the filling mixture and fill the cut-away depression.

5 Strain the jam and lemon juice. Brush all over the cake. For the frosting, melt all the ingredients together and stir until combined. Cool, then pour over the cake. Decorate with chocolate-dipped cherries and rose leaves.

Sachertorte Energy 625kcal/2618kJ; Protein 7.6g; Carbohydrate 73.1g, of which sugars 65.5g; Fat 35.8g, of which saturates 20.8g; Cholesterol 184mg; Calcium 73mg; Fibre 1.2g; Sodium 143mg.
Cherry Energy 5172kcal/21630kJ; Protein 60.1g; Carbohydrate 587.6g, of which sugars 470.7g; Fat 287.9g, of which saturates 171.5g; Cholesterol 1022mg; Calcium 781mg; Fibre 16.6g; Sodium 1337mg.

Tia Maria and Walnut Gateau

Whipped cream and Tia Maria make a mouth-watering filling for this light chocolate and walnut cake.

Serves 6–8

150g/5oz/1¼ cups self-raising (self-rising) flour
25g/1oz/¼ cup unsweetened cocoa powder
7.5ml/1½ tsp baking powder
3 eggs, beaten
175g/6oz/¾ cup unsalted (sweet) butter, softened

175g/6oz/scant 1 cup caster (superfine) sugar
50g/2oz/½ cup chopped walnuts
walnut brittle, to decorate

For the filling and coating
600ml/1 pint/2½ cups double cream
45ml/3 tbsp Tia Maria
50g/2oz/⅔ cup desiccated (dry unsweetened shredded) coconut, toasted

1 Preheat the oven to 160°C/325°F/Gas 3. Grease and base-line two 18cm/7in sandwich tins. Sift the flour, cocoa powder and baking powder into a large bowl. Add the beaten eggs, butter, sugar and chopped walnuts and mix together thoroughly.

2 Divide the mixture between the cake tins, level the surface and bake for 35–40 minutes, until risen and browned. Turn out the cakes and leave to cool on a wire rack.

3 For the filling, add the Tia Maria to the cream and whisk until the mixture forms soft peaks.

4 Slice each cake horizontally in half to give four layers. Sandwich the layers together, spreading some of the flavoured cream between each layer.

5 Coat the sides of the cake with cream. Spread out the toasted coconut on a sheet of non-stick baking parchment. Then, holding the top and bottom of the cake, roll the side in the coconut until evenly coated. Put the cake on a serving plate, spread more of the cream on top and pipe the remainder around the outside rim. Decorate inside the rim with walnut brittle.

Rich Chocolate Nut Cake

Use walnuts or pecan nuts for the cake sides, if you prefer.

Makes one 23cm/9in round cake
225g/8oz/1 cup butter
225g/8oz plain (semisweet) chocolate
115g/4oz/1 cup unsweetened cocoa powder
350g/12oz/1¾ cups caster (superfine) sugar
6 eggs

100ml/3½fl oz/scant ½ cup brandy
225g/8oz/2 cups finely chopped hazelnuts

For the glaze
50g/2oz/¼ cup butter
150g/5oz cooking (unsweetened) chocolate
30ml/2 tbsp milk
5ml/1 tsp vanilla extract

1 Preheat the oven to 180°C/350°F/Gas 4. Line a 23 × 5cm/9 × 2in round tin (pan) with baking parchment and grease the paper.

2 Melt the butter and chocolate in the top of a double boiler. Leave to cool.

3 Sift the cocoa powder into a bowl. Add the sugar and eggs, stirring until combined. Add the chocolate mixture and brandy.

4 Fold in three-quarters of the hazelnuts, then pour the mixture into the prepared cake tin.

5 Set the tin in a roasting pan and pour 2.5cm/1in hot water into the outer pan. Bake until the cake is firm to the touch, about 45 minutes. Leave for 15 minutes, then unmould on to a wire rack. When cool, wrap in baking parchment and chill for at least 6 hours.

6 To make the glaze, melt the butter and chocolate with the milk and vanilla extract as before.

7 Place the cake on a wire rack over a plate. Drizzle the glaze over, letting it drip down the sides. Cover the cake sides with the remaining nuts. Transfer to a serving plate when set.

Tia Maria Energy 815kcal/3380kJ; Protein 7.4g; Carbohydrate 39.8g, of which sugars 25.1g; Fat 69.4g, of which saturates 41.1g; Cholesterol 221mg; Calcium 101mg; Fibre 2g; Sodium 209mg.
Nut Energy 7802kcal/32523kJ; Protein 113.7g; Carbohydrate 633.7g, of which sugars 612.6g; Fat 532.7g, of which saturates 241.2g; Cholesterol 1752mg; Calcium 1030mg; Fibre 37.9g; Sodium 3249mg.

Chocolate Fudge Gateau

A glorious dessert that is sure to delight everyone.

Serves 8–10
275g/10oz/2½ cups self-raising wholemeal (self-rising whole-wheat) flour
50g/2oz/½ cup unsweetened cocoa powder
45ml/3 tbsp baking powder
225g/8oz/generous 1 cup caster (superfine) sugar
few drops of vanilla extract
135ml/9 tbsp sunflower oil
350ml/12fl oz/1½ cups water
sifted unsweetened cocoa powder, for sprinkling
25g/1oz/¼ cup chopped nuts

For the chocolate fudge
50g/2oz/¼ cup soya margarine
45ml/3 tbsp water
250g/9oz/2¼ cups icing (confectioners') sugar
30ml/2 tbsp unsweetened cocoa powder
15–30ml/1–2 tbsp hot water

1 Preheat the oven to 160°C/325°F/Gas 3. Grease a deep 20cm/8in round cake tin (pan), line with baking parchment and grease the paper lightly with a little sunflower oil.

2 Sift the flour, cocoa and baking powder into a mixing bowl. Add the sugar and vanilla extract, then gradually beat in the oil. Gradually add the water, beating constantly to produce a thick batter. Pour into the prepared tin and level the surface.

3 Bake the cake for about 45 minutes or until a fine metal skewer inserted in the centre comes out clean. Leave in the tin for about 5 minutes, before turning out on to a wire rack. Peel off the lining and cool. Cut in half to make two equal layers.

4 Make the chocolate fudge. Place the margarine and water in a pan and heat gently until the margarine has melted. Remove from the heat and sift in the icing sugar and cocoa powder, beating until shiny, adding more hot water if needed. Pour into a bowl and cool until firm enough to spread and pipe.

5 Sandwich the cake layers together with two-thirds of the chocolate fudge. Pipe the remaining chocolate fudge over the cake. Sprinkle with cocoa powder and decorate with the nuts.

Chocolate Potato Cake

Mashed potato makes this cake moist and delicious.

Makes one 23cm/9in cake
200g/7oz/1 cup sugar
250g/9oz/1 cup and 2 tbsp butter
4 eggs, separated
275g/10oz dark (bittersweet) chocolate
75g/3oz/¾ cup ground almonds
165g/5½oz mashed potato
225g/8oz/2 cups self-raising (self-rising) flour
5ml/1 tsp cinnamon
45ml/3 tbsp milk
white and dark (bittersweet) chocolate shavings, to garnish
whipped cream, to serve

1 Preheat the oven to 180°C/350°F/Gas 4. Grease and line a 23cm/9in round cake tin (pan) with baking parchment.

2 In a bowl, cream together the sugar and 225g/8oz/1 cup of the butter until light and fluffy. Then beat the egg yolks into the creamed mixture one at a time until it is smooth and creamy.

3 Finely chop or grate 175g/6oz of the chocolate and stir it into the creamed mixture with the ground almonds. Pass the mashed potato through a sieve (strainer) or ricer and stir it into the creamed chocolate mixture. Sift together the flour and cinnamon and fold into the mixture with the milk.

4 Whisk the egg whites until they hold stiff but not dry peaks, and fold into the cake mixture.

5 Spoon into the tin and smooth the top, but make a slight hollow in the middle to keep the surface of the cake level while cooking. Bake in the oven for 1¼ hours, until a skewer inserted in the centre comes out clean. Allow the cake to cool slightly in the tin, then turn out and cool on a wire rack.

6 Break up the remaining chocolate into a heatproof bowl over a pan of hot water. Add the remaining butter in small pieces and stir until the mixture is smooth and glossy.

7 Peel off the lining paper and trim the top of the cake so it is level. Smooth over the chocolate icing. When set, decorate with the chocolate shavings and serve with whipped cream.

Chocolate Brandy Snap Gateau

This cake will be the talking point at any dinner party.

Serves 8

225g/8oz dark (bittersweet) chocolate, chopped
225g/8oz/1 cup unsalted (sweet) butter, softened
200g/7oz/generous 1 cup dark muscovado (molasses) sugar
6 eggs, separated
5ml/1 tsp vanilla extract
150g/5oz/1¼ cups ground hazelnuts
60ml/4 tbsp fresh white breadcrumbs

finely grated rind of 1 large orange
1 quantity Chocolate Ganache, for filling and frosting
icing (confectioners') sugar, for dusting

For the brandy snaps

50g/2oz/¼ cup unsalted (sweet) butter
50g/2oz/¼ cup caster (superfine) sugar
75g/3oz/⅓ cup golden (light corn) syrup
50g/2oz/½ cup plain (all-purpose) flour
5ml/1 tsp brandy

1 Preheat the oven to 180°C/350°F/Gas 4. Grease two 20cm/8in sandwich cake tins (layer pans) and line with baking parchment. Melt the chocolate and set aside to cool slightly. Cream the butter with the sugar in a bowl until pale and fluffy. Beat in the egg yolks and vanilla extract. Add the chocolate and mix well.

2 In a clean, grease-free bowl, whisk the egg whites to soft peaks, then fold them into the chocolate mixture with the ground hazelnuts, breadcrumbs and orange rind. Divide the mixture between the tins and smooth the tops. Bake for 25–30 minutes, or until well risen and firm. Turn out on to wire racks.

3 Make the brandy snaps. Line two baking sheets with baking parchment. Melt the butter, sugar and syrup together, stirring until smooth. Remove from the heat and stir in the flour and brandy. Place spoonfuls of the mixture on the sheets and bake for 8–10 minutes. Cool until just firm enough to lift on to a wire rack. Pinch the edges of each snap to create a frilled effect.

4 Sandwich the cakes with half the chocolate ganache and spread the remaining ganache on the top. Arrange the brandy snaps over the gateau and dust with icing sugar.

Caribbean Chocolate Ring with Rum Syrup

This delectable chocolate and rum cake brings you a taste of the Caribbean.

Serves 8–10

115g/4oz/½ cup unsalted (sweet) butter, plus extra for greasing
115g/4oz/scant ½ cup light muscovado (brown) sugar
2 eggs, beaten
2 ripe bananas, mashed
30ml/2 tbsp desiccated (dry unsweetened shredded) coconut
30ml/2 tbsp sour cream
115g/4oz/1 cup self-raising (self-rising) flour

45ml/3 tbsp unsweetened cocoa powder
2.5ml/½ tsp bicarbonate of soda (baking soda)

For the syrup

115g/4oz/generous ½ cup caster (superfine) sugar
60ml/4 tbsp water
30ml/2 tbsp dark rum
50g/2oz plain (semisweet) chocolate, chopped
mixture of tropical fruits and chocolate shapes or curls, to decorate

1 Preheat the oven to 180°C/350°F/Gas 4. Grease a 1.5 litre/2½ pint/6¼ cup ring tin (pan) with butter.

2 Cream the butter and sugar in a bowl until light and fluffy. Add the eggs gradually, beating well, then mix in the bananas, coconut and sour cream. Sift the flour, cocoa and bicarbonate of soda over the mixture and fold in thoroughly.

3 Transfer to the prepared tin and spread evenly. Bake for 45–50 minutes, until firm to the touch. Cool for 10 minutes in the tin, then turn out to finish cooling on a wire rack.

4 Make the syrup. Place the sugar in a small pan. Add the water and heat gently, stirring occasionally until dissolved. Bring to the boil and boil rapidly, without stirring, for 2 minutes. Remove from the heat.

5 Add the rum and chocolate to the syrup and stir until smooth, then spoon evenly over the top and sides of the cake. Decorate the ring with tropical fruits and chocolate shapes.

Brandy Snap Energy 870kcal/3622kJ; Protein 10.7g; Carbohydrate 70g, of which sugars 59g; Fat 62.7g, of which saturates 31.2g; Cholesterol 244mg; Calcium 102mg; Fibre 2.3g; Sodium 424mg.
Caribbean Ring Energy 315kcal/1319kJ; Protein 4g; Carbohydrate 40.5g, of which sugars 31g; Fat 15.6g, of which saturates 9.7g; Cholesterol 65mg; Calcium 72mg; Fibre 1.6g; Sodium 172mg.

Rich Chocolate Cake

This dark, fudgy cake is easy to make and is a chocolate lover's dream come true.

Serves 14–16
250g/9oz plain (semisweet) chocolate, chopped
225g/8oz/1 cup unsalted (sweet) butter, cut into pieces
5 eggs
100g/3½oz/½ cup caster (superfine) sugar, plus 15ml/ 1 tbsp and extra for sprinkling
15ml/1 tbsp unsweetened cocoa powder
10ml/2 tsp vanilla extract
unsweetened cocoa powder, for dusting
chocolate shavings, to decorate
icing (confectioners') sugar, for dusting

1 Preheat the oven to 170°C/325°F/Gas 3. Lightly butter a 23cm/9in springform tin (pan) and line the base with baking parchment. Butter the paper and sprinkle with a little sugar, then tip out the excess. The cake is baked in a *bain-marie*, so carefully wrap the base and sides of the tin with a double thickness of foil to prevent water leaking into the cake.

2 Melt the chocolate and butter in a pan over a low heat until smooth, stirring, then remove from the heat. Beat the eggs and 100g/3½oz/½ cup of the sugar with a mixer for 1 minute.

3 Mix together the cocoa and the remaining 15ml/1 tbsp sugar and beat into the egg mixture until well blended. Beat in the vanilla extract, then slowly beat in the melted chocolate until well blended. Pour the mixture into the prepared tin and tap gently to release any air bubbles.

4 Place the cake tin in a roasting pan and pour in boiling water to come 2cm/¾in up the sides of the wrapped tin. Bake for 45–50 minutes, until the edge of the cake is set and the centre still soft. Lift the tin out of the water and remove the foil. Place the cake on a wire rack, remove the sides of the tin and leave the cake to cool completely (the cake will sink in the centre).

5 Invert the cake on to the wire rack. Remove the base of the tin and the paper. Dust the cake with cocoa and arrange the shavings around the edge. Slide the cake on to a serving plate.

Chocolate Mousse Gateau

This special occasion dessert is a double batch of chocolate mousse, glazed with chocolate ganache and decorated with long, slim chocolate curls.

Serves 8–10
275g/10oz plain (semisweet) chocolate, chopped
115g/4oz/½ cup unsalted (sweet) butter, cut into pieces
8 eggs, separated
1.5ml/¼ tsp cream of tartar
45ml/3 tbsp brandy or rum (optional)
chocolate curls, to decorate

For the chocolate ganache
250ml/8fl oz/1 cup double (heavy) cream
225g/8oz plain (semisweet) chocolate, chopped
30ml/2 tbsp brandy or rum (optional)
25g/1oz/2 tbsp unsalted (sweet) butter, softened

1 Preheat the oven to 180°C/350°F/Gas 4. Grease two 20–23cm/8–9in springform tins (pans) and line the bases with buttered baking parchment.

2 In a pan, melt the chocolate and butter over a low heat until smooth, stirring frequently. Remove from the heat and whisk in the egg yolks until completely blended. Beat in the brandy or rum, if using, and pour into a bowl. Set aside.

3 In a clean, grease-free bowl, beat the egg whites slowly until frothy. Add the cream of tartar and continue beating until stiffer peaks form that just flop over a little at the top. Stir a large spoonful of whites into the chocolate mixture to lighten it, then fold in the remaining whites until they are just combined.

4 Divide about two-thirds of the mousse between the two prepared tins, smoothing the tops. Chill the remaining mousse. Bake for 30–35 minutes until puffed; the cakes will fall slightly. Cool in the tins for 15 minutes, then remove the sides and leave to cool completely. Invert the cakes on to a wire rack, remove the tin bases and peel off the paper. Wash the tins.

5 To assemble, place one layer, flat side down in one of the clean tins. Spread the remaining mousse over the surface, smoothing the top. Cover with the second cake layer, flat side up. Press down gently so the mousse is evenly distributed. Chill for 2–4 hours or overnight.

6 To make the ganache, bring the cream to the boil in a heavy pan over a medium heat. Remove the pan from the heat and add the chocolate all at once, stirring until melted and smooth. Stir in the brandy or rum, if using, and beat in the softened butter. Set the mixture aside for about 5 minutes to thicken slightly (ganache should be thick enough to coat the back of a spoon in a smooth layer).

7 Run a knife around the edge of the assembled cake to loosen it, then remove the sides of the tin. Invert the cake on to a wire rack, remove the base and place the rack over a baking tray. Pour the warm ganache over the cake all at once, tilting gently to help spread it evenly on all surfaces. Use a spatula to smooth the sides, decorate the top with chocolate curls, then leave to set.

Rich Chocolate Cake Energy 214kcal/888kJ; Protein 3g; Carbohydrate 11.1g, of which sugars 10.8g; Fat 17.9g, of which saturates 10.6g; Cholesterol 90mg; Calcium 18mg; Fibre 0.5g; Sodium 117mg.
Mousse Gateau Energy 542kcal/2252kJ; Protein 8g; Carbohydrate 32.3g, of which sugars 31.8g; Fat 43.4g, of which saturates 25.3g; Cholesterol 219mg; Calcium 54mg; Fibre 1.3g; Sodium 149mg.

Chocolate Almond Mousse Cake

A deliciously nutty cake with a light mousse filling

Serves 8

50g/2oz plain (semisweet) chocolate, broken into squares
200g/7oz marzipan, grated or chopped
200ml/7fl oz/scant 1 cup milk
115g/4oz/1 cup self-raising (self-rising) flour
2 eggs, separated
75g/3oz/1/2 cup light muscovado (brown) sugar

For the mousse filling

115g/4oz plain (semisweet) chocolate, chopped into small pieces
50g/2oz/1/4 cup unsalted (sweet) butter
2 eggs, separated
30ml/2 tbsp Amaretto Disaronno liqueur

For the topping

1 quantity Chocolate Ganache
toasted flaked (sliced) almonds

1 Preheat the oven to 190°C/375°F/Gas 5. Grease a deep 17cm/6½in square cake tin (pan) and line with baking parchment. Gently heat the chocolate, marzipan and milk in a pan, stirring until smooth.

2 Sift the flour into a bowl and add the chocolate mixture and egg yolks, beating until evenly mixed. Whisk the egg whites in a separate clean, grease-free bowl until they hold firm peaks. Whisk in the sugar. Stir a spoonful of the whites into the chocolate mixture to lighten it, then fold in the rest. Spoon the mixture into the tin. Bake for 45–50 minutes, until well risen and springy to the touch. Cool on a wire rack.

3 Make the mousse filling. Melt the chocolate with the butter in a pan over a low heat, then remove from the heat and beat in the egg yolks and Amaretto. Whisk the egg whites in a clean, grease-free bowl until stiff, then fold into the chocolate mixture.

4 Halve the cake across the middle to make two layers. Return one half to the clean cake tin and pour over the mousse. Top with the second cake and press down lightly. Chill until set.

5 Transfer the cake to a plate. Let the chocolate ganache soften slightly, then beat until spreadable and cover over the top and sides of the cake. Press the almonds on the sides. Serve chilled.

Coffee Chocolate Mousse Cake

Serve this dense, dark chocolate cake in small portions as it is very rich.

Serves 6

175g/6oz plain (semisweet) chocolate
30ml/2 tbsp strong brewed coffee
150g/5oz/10 tbsp butter, cubed
50g/2oz/1/4 cup caster (superfine) sugar
3 eggs

25g/1oz/1/4 cup ground almonds
about 25ml/1½ tbsp icing (confectioners') sugar, for dusting

For the mascarpone and coffee cream

250g/9oz/generous 1 cup mascarpone
30ml/2 tbsp icing (confectioners') sugar, sifted
30ml/2 tbsp strong brewed coffee

1 Preheat the oven to 200°C/400°F/Gas 6. Grease and line the base of a 15cm/6in square tin (pan) with baking parchment.

2 Put the chocolate and coffee in a small heavy pan and heat very gently until melted, stirring occasionally.

3 Add the butter and sugar to the pan and stir until dissolved. Whisk the eggs until frothy and gently stir into the chocolate mixture with the ground almonds until blended.

4 Pour into the prepared tin, then put in a large roasting pan and pour in enough hot water to come two-thirds up the cake tin. Bake for 50 minutes, or until the top feels springy. Leave to cool in the tin for 5 minutes, then turn the cake out on to a board and leave to cool.

5 Meanwhile, beat the mascarpone with the icing sugar and coffee. Dust the cake generously with icing sugar, then cut into slices. Serve on individual plates with the mascarpone and coffee cream alongside.

> **Cook's Tip**
> The top of this flourless cake, with its moist mousse-like texture, will crack slightly as it cooks.

Almond Cake Energy 420kcal/1766kJ; Protein 10g; Carbohydrate 55.4g, of which sugars 44.1g; Fat 18.7g, of which saturates 8.5g; Cholesterol 117mg; Calcium 99mg; Fibre 1.6g; Sodium 160mg.
Coffee Cake Energy 524kcal/2180kJ; Protein 9.5g; Carbohydrate 34.2g, of which sugars 33.8g; Fat 39.9g, of which saturates 22.7g; Cholesterol 168mg; Calcium 46mg; Fibre 1g; Sodium 190mg.

Classic Chocolate Roulade

This rich, squidgy chocolate roll should be made at least eight hours before serving to allow it to soften. Expect the roulade to crack a little when you roll it up. Sprinkle with a little grated chocolate, if you like, as a final decoration.

Serves 8
200g/7oz plain
(semisweet) chocolate
200g/7oz/1 cup caster (superfine)
sugar, plus extra caster or icing
(confectioners') sugar to dust
7 eggs, separated
300ml/½ pint/1¼ cups double
(heavy) cream

1 Preheat the oven to 180°C/350°F/Gas 4. Grease a 33 × 23cm/13 × 9in Swiss roll tin (jelly roll pan) and line the tin with baking parchment.

2 Break the chocolate into squares and melt in a heatproof bowl over a pan of barely simmering water. Remove from the heat and leave to cool for about 5 minutes.

3 In a large bowl, whisk the sugar and egg yolks until light and fluffy. Stir in the melted chocolate.

4 Whisk the egg whites until stiff, but not dry, and then gently fold into the chocolate mixture.

5 Pour the chocolate mixture into the prepared tin, spreading it level with a metal spatula. Bake for about 25 minutes, or until firm. Leave the cake in the tin and cover with a cooling rack, making sure that it does not touch the cake. Cover the rack with a damp dish towel, then wrap in clear film (plastic wrap). Leave in a cool place for 8 hours, preferably overnight.

6 Dust a sheet of baking parchment with caster or icing sugar and turn out the roulade on to it. Peel off the lining paper.

7 Whip the cream until soft peaks form and spread it evenly over the roulade. Roll up the cake from a short end.

8 Place the roulade, seam side down, on to a serving plate and dust generously with more caster or icing sugar before serving.

Chocolate Caramel Torte

This creamy rich cake, topped with shards of caramel, was created by Jozep Dobos in the former Yugoslavia in the 1880s.

Serves 10–12
6 eggs, separated
150g/5oz/1¼ cups icing
(confectioners') sugar, sifted
5ml/1 tsp vanilla sugar
130g/4½ oz/generous 1 cup
plain (all-purpose) flour, sifted

For the filling
75g/3oz plain (semisweet)
chocolate, broken into pieces
175g/6oz/¾ cup unsalted
(sweet) butter
130g/4½ oz/generous 1 cup
(confectioners') icing sugar
30ml/2 tbsp vanilla sugar
1 egg

For the caramel topping
150g/5oz/¾ cup sugar
30–45ml/2–3 tbsp water
10g/¼ oz/½ tbsp butter, melted

1 Preheat the oven to 220°C/425°F/Gas 7. Whisk the egg yolks and half the icing sugar together in a bowl until pale in colour, thick and creamy.

2 Whisk the egg whites in a grease-free bowl until stiff; whisk in half the remaining icing sugar until glossy, then fold in the vanilla sugar. Fold the egg whites into the egg yolk mixture, alternating carefully with spoonfuls of the flour.

3 Line four baking sheets with baking parchment. Draw a 23cm/9in circle on each piece of paper. Lightly grease the paper and dust with flour.

4 Spread the mixture evenly on the paper circles. Bake for 10 minutes, then leave to cool before layering and weighing them down with a board.

5 To make the filling, melt the chocolate in a small heatproof bowl set over a pan of gently simmering water. Stir until smooth. Cream the butter and icing sugar together well in a bowl. Beat in the melted chocolate, vanilla sugar and egg.

6 Sandwich the four sponge circles together with the chocolate cream filling, then spread the remainder of the cream over the top and around the sides of the cake.

7 To make the caramel topping, put the sugar and water in a heavy pan and dissolve slowly over a very gentle heat. Add the butter.

8 When the sugar has dissolved, increase the heat and cook until the mixture turns golden brown. Quickly pour the caramel on to a greased baking sheet. Leave to set and shatter into shards when cold.

9 Place the pieces of caramel on top of the cake, and cut it into slices to serve.

> **Cook's Tip**
> Vanilla sugar can be prepared at home by combining white sugar with vanilla bean pieces, letting it rest for a few weeks.

Roulade Energy 476kcal/1988kJ; Protein 7.4g; Carbohydrate 42.6g, of which sugars 42.4g; Fat 32g, of which saturates 18.1g; Cholesterol 219mg; Calcium 65mg; Fibre 0.6g; Sodium 73mg.
Torte Energy 368kcal/1543kJ; Protein 5.3g; Carbohydrate 49.9g, of which sugars 41.6g; Fat 17.8g, of which saturates 10g; Cholesterol 144mg; Calcium 56mg; Fibre 0.5g; Sodium 137mg.

Chocolate and Coffee Roulade

This version of the classic roll is flavoured with coffee and liqueur.

Serves 8
200g/7oz plain
  (semisweet) chocolate
200g/7oz/1 cup caster
  (superfine) sugar
7 eggs, separated

For the filling
300ml/½ pint/1¼ cups double
  (heavy) cream
30ml/2 tbsp cold brewed coffee
15ml/1 tbsp coffee liqueur, such as
  Tia Maria, Kahlúa or Toussaint
60ml/4 tbsp icing (confectioners')
  sugar, for dusting
little grated chocolate,
  for sprinkling

1 Preheat the oven to 180°C/350°F/Gas 4. Grease and line a 33 × 23cm/13 × 9in Swiss roll tin (jelly roll pan) with baking parchment. Break the chocolate into squares and melt in a heatproof bowl over a pan of barely simmering water. Remove from the heat and leave to cool for 5 minutes.

2 In a large bowl, whisk the sugar and egg yolks until light and fluffy. Stir in the melted chocolate.

3 Whisk the egg whites until stiff, but not dry, and then gently fold into the chocolate mixture.

4 Pour the chocolate mixture into the prepared tin, spreading it level with a metal spatula. Bake for about 25 minutes, or until firm. Leave the cake in the tin and cover with a cooling rack, making sure that it does not touch the cake. Cover the rack with a damp dish towel, then wrap in clear film (plastic wrap). Leave in a cool place for 8 hours, preferably overnight.

5 Dust a large sheet of baking parchment with icing sugar and turn out the roulade on to it. Peel off the lining.

6 Make the filling. Whip the double cream with the coffee and liqueur until soft peaks form and spread over the roulade. Carefully roll up the cake, using the paper to help.

7 Place the roulade, seam side down, on to a serving plate, dust with icing sugar and sprinkle with a little grated chocolate.

Chocolate Coconut Roulade

A delicious coconut version of the traditional chocolate roll. Use a vegetable peeler to create the coconut curls for the topping.

Serves 8
115g/4oz/generous ½ cup caster
  (superfine) sugar
5 eggs, separated
50g/2oz/½ cup unsweetened
  cocoa powder

For the filling
300ml/½ pint/1¼ cups double
  (heavy) cream
45ml/3 tbsp whisky or brandy
50g/2oz piece solid creamed
  coconut (US 100ml/6½ tsp
  coconut milk, reducing the
  liquid as necessary)
30ml/2 tbsp caster (superfine) sugar

For the topping
fresh coconut curls
dark (bittersweet) chocolate curls

1 Preheat the oven to 180°C/350°F/Gas 4. Grease and line a 33 × 23cm/13 × 9in Swiss roll tin (jelly roll pan). Dust a large sheet of baking parchment with 30ml/2 tbsp of the caster sugar.

2 Place the egg yolks in a heatproof bowl. Add the remaining caster sugar and whisk with a hand-held electric mixer until the mixture leaves a trail. Sift the cocoa over, then carefully fold in.

3 Whisk the egg whites in a clean, grease-free bowl until they form soft peaks. Fold about 15ml/1 tbsp of the whites into the chocolate mixture to lighten it, then fold in the rest evenly.

4 Scrape the mixture into the prepared tin and smooth the surface. Bake for 20–25 minutes or until well risen and springy. Turn the cooked roulade out on to the sugar-dusted baking parchment and carefully peel off the lining paper. Cover with a damp, clean dish towel and leave to cool completely.

5 Make the filling. Whisk the cream with the whisky until the mixture holds its shape. Stir in the creamed coconut and sugar.

6 Spread about three-quarters of the cream mixture on the sponge. Roll up carefully and transfer to a plate. Spoon the remaining cream mixture on top. Decorate with the coconut and chocolate curls.

Coffee Roulade Energy 511kcal/2134kJ; Protein 7.5g; Carbohydrate 51.1g, of which sugars 50.9g; Fat 32g, of which saturates 18.1g; Cholesterol 219mg; Calcium 69mg; Fibre 0.6g; Sodium 73mg.
Coconut Roulade Energy 414kcal/1724kJ; Protein 6.2g; Carbohydrate 30.5g, of which sugars 29.8g; Fat 29.3g, of which saturates 18g; Cholesterol 170mg; Calcium 60mg; Fibre 0.8g; Sodium 115mg.

Bûche de Noël

This is the traditional French Christmas cake. Meringue mushrooms provide festive decoration.

Serves 8
1 size 3 egg white
50g/2oz/¼ cup caster (superfine) sugar, plus extra for sprinkling
¾ quantity chocolate-flavoured Quick-mix Sponge Cake mixture

For the filling and icing
225g/8oz unsweetened chestnut purée
30ml/2 tbsp clear honey
30ml/2 tbsp brandy
300ml/½ pint/1¼ cups double (heavy) cream
150g/5oz/scant 1 cup plain (bittersweet) chocolate chips

To decorate
4 chocolate flakes, crumbled icing (confectioners') sugar and holly leaves

1 Preheat the oven to 110°C/225°F/ Gas ¼. Grease a baking tray, line with baking parchment and grease the paper. Grease a 33 × 23cm/13 × 9in Swiss roll tin (jelly roll pan), line with baking parchment and grease the paper.

2 To make the meringue mushrooms, whisk the egg white until stiff and gradually beat in the sugar a little at a time, until thick and glossy. Transfer to a piping (pastry) bag. Pipe eight tall 'stalks' and eight shorter 'caps' on to the baking tray. Bake for 2½–3 hours, until crisp and dried out. Remove from the oven and leave to cool. Increase the temperature to 200°C/400°F/Gas 6.

3 Make the whisked sponge cake mixture and transfer to the prepared Swiss roll tin. Bake for 10–12 minutes, until risen and springy to the touch. Lay a sheet of baking parchment on a lightly dampened dish towel and sprinkle liberally with caster sugar. Turn the cake over on to the paper and leave to cool completely with the tin in place.

4 To make the filling, blend the chestnut purée with the honey and brandy in a food processor until smooth, and gradually blend in half the cream until thick. Chill until required.

5 To make the icing, heat the chocolate and remaining cream in a pan over a low heat, until melted. Transfer to a bowl, cool and chill. Remove from the refrigerator and beat until thick.

6 Remove the Swiss roll tin and peel away the lining paper from the sponge. Spread with all but 30 ml/2 tbsp chestnut filling, leaving a border around the edges. Roll up from one narrow end, to form a roll. Transfer to a cake board. Coat the top and sides of the roll with the icing, leaving the ends plain. Swirl a pattern over the icing with a palette knife, to resemble tree bark. Sprinkle the flakes over the rest of the board.

7 Remove the meringue 'stalks' and 'caps' from the baking tray. Transfer the reserved chestnut filling to the piping bag, fitted with the star nozzle. Pipe a swirl on to the underside of each mushroom 'cap'. Press gently on to the 'stalks' to form the mushroom decorations. Place a small cluster of mushrooms on top of the chocolate log, arranging the rest around the board. Sprinkle over a little icing sugar and add a few festive holly leaves.

Two-chocolate Chestnut Roulade

A deservedly popular cake that contains dark and white chocolate and a delicious chestnut filling.

Serves 8
225g/8oz plain (semisweet) chocolate
50g/2oz white chocolate
4 eggs, separated
115g/4oz/generous ½ cup caster (superfine) sugar

For the chestnut filling
150ml/¼ pint/⅔ cup double (heavy) cream
225g/8oz can chestnut purée
50–65g/2–2½oz/ 4–5 tbsp icing (confectioners') sugar, plus extra for dusting
15–30ml/1–2 tbsp brandy

1 Preheat the oven to 180°C/350°F/Gas 4. Line and grease a 33 × 23cm/13 × 9in Swiss roll tin (jelly roll pan).

2 For the chocolate curls, melt 50g/2oz of the plain and all of the white chocolate in separate heatproof bowls set over pans of simmering water. When melted, spread on a non-porous surface and leave to set. Hold a long sharp knife at a 45-degree angle to the chocolate and push it along the chocolate, using a sawing motion. Put the curls on baking parchment.

3 Melt the remaining plain chocolate. Beat the egg yolks and caster sugar until thick and pale. Stir in the chocolate.

4 Whisk the egg whites until they form stiff peaks, then fold into the chocolate mixture. Turn into the prepared tin and bake for 15–20 minutes. Cool, covered with a just-damp dish towel, on a wire rack.

5 Sprinkle a sheet of baking parchment with caster sugar. Turn the roulade out on to it. Peel off the lining paper and trim the edges of the roulade. Cover with the dish towel.

6 To make the filling, whip the cream until softly peaking. Beat together the chestnut purée, icing sugar and brandy until smooth, then fold in the cream. Spread over the roulade and roll it up. Top with chocolate curls and dust with icing sugar.

Roulade Energy 3496kcal/14645kJ; Protein 48g; Carbohydrate 424.1g, of which sugars 355.5g; Fat 187.3g, of which saturates 104.4g; Cholesterol 980mg; Calcium 585mg; Fibre 14.9g; Sodium 416mg.
Bûche de Noël Energy 560kcal/2332kJ; Protein 5.5g; Carbohydrate 52.2g, of which sugars 35.1g; Fat 37g, of which saturates 18.4g; Cholesterol 95mg; Calcium 71mg; Fibre 2.3g; Sodium 173mg.

Chocolate and Chestnut Yule Log

This is another variation on the French *bûche de Noël*, a traditional Christmas treat.

Serves 8

3 large eggs, separated
large pinch of cream of tartar
115g/4oz/generous ½ cup caster
  (superfine) sugar
2–3 drops almond extract
25g/1oz/¼ cup plain
  (all-purpose) flour
30ml/2 tbsp unsweetened
  cocoa powder
pinch of salt
sifted cocoa powder and holly
  sprigs, to decorate

For the filling

5ml/1 tsp powdered gelatine
15ml/1 tbsp brandy
115g/4oz dark (bittersweet)
  chocolate, broken into squares
50g/2oz/¼ cup caster
  (superfine) sugar
250g/9oz canned chestnut purée
300ml/½ pint/1¼ cups double
  (heavy) cream

1 Preheat the oven to 180°C/350°F/Gas 4. Grease a 33 × 23cm/13 × 9in Swiss roll tin (jelly roll pan); line with baking parchment.

2 Whisk the egg whites until frothy. Add the cream of tartar and whisk until stiff. Add half the sugar and whisk until the mixture forms stiff peaks. In another bowl, whisk the egg yolks and the remaining sugar until thick. Add the almond extract. Sift in the flour, cocoa and salt. Fold in the whites until blended.

3 Spoon the mixture into the tin and level the top. Bake for 15–20 minutes. Turn the roll on to a sheet of baking parchment dusted with caster sugar, remove the lining paper, and roll up the cake with the parchment still inside. Cool on a wire rack.

4 Make the filling. Sprinkle the gelatine over the brandy; leave until spongy. Melt the chocolate in a heatproof bowl over a pan of hot water. Melt the sponged gelatine over hot water and add to the chocolate. Whisk in the sugar and chestnut purée. Remove from the heat and leave to cool. Whisk the cream until it holds soft peaks and fold into the chocolate mixture.

5 Unroll the cake, spread with half the filling and re-roll. Cover the cake with the rest of the chocolate cream. Chill until firm. Dust with sifted cocoa powder and decorate with holly sprigs.

Chocolate Christmas Log with Cranberry Sauce

This is the perfect cake for the festive table.

Serves 12–14

1 chocolate-flavoured Sponge Roll
1 quantity Chocolate Ganache
  or Chocolate Buttercream

For the cream filling

200g/7oz fine quality white
  chocolate, in small pieces
475ml/16fl oz/2 cups double
  (heavy) cream
30ml/2 tbsp brandy or
  chocolate-flavoured liqueur
  (optional)

For the cranberry sauce

450g/1lb fresh or frozen
  cranberries, rinsed
275g/10oz/1 cup seedless
  raspberry jam, melted
115g/4oz/½ cup sugar

1 Make the cranberry sauce. Process the cranberries in a food processor fitted with a metal blade until they become liquid. Press through a sieve (strainer) into a small bowl and discard the pulp. Stir in the melted raspberry preserve and the sugar to taste. If the sauce is too thick, add a little water to thin it out. Cover and place in the refrigerator.

2 Make the cream filling. In a small pan, heat the chocolate with 120ml/4fl oz/½ cup of the cream until melted, stirring. Strain into a bowl and cool to room temperature. In a separate bowl, beat the remaining cream with the brandy or liqueur until soft peaks form; fold into the chocolate mixture.

3 Unroll the sponge roll, spread with the cream filling mixture and roll up again from a long end. Cut off a quarter of the roll at an angle and arrange both the pieces on a cake board so they resemble a log.

4 If using chocolate ganache for the topping, allow it to soften to room temperature, then beat until it is soft and spreadable. Cover the log with ganache or buttercream and mark it with a fork to resemble bark. Dust lightly with icing sugar and top with a sprig of holly. Serve with the cranberry sauce.

Yule Log Energy 448kcal/1870kJ; Protein 5.4g; Carbohydrate 45.6g, of which sugars 33.4g; Fat 27.9g, of which saturates 16.2g; Cholesterol 124mg; Calcium 68mg; Fibre 2.2g; Sodium 76mg.
Christmas Log Energy 591kcal/2469kJ; Protein 5.4g; Carbohydrate 58.6g, of which sugars 51.6g; Fat 38.7g, of which saturates 23.2g; Cholesterol 117mg; Calcium 109mg; Fibre 2.1g; Sodium 74mg.

Chocolate-topped Coffee Gateau

This delicious coffee cake, topped with chocolate-dipped almonds and small beads of chocolate, can be made quite quickly. You could use a chocolate-flavoured sponge, or ring the changes by using a coffee-flavoured one.

Serves 8
475g/1lb 2oz/2¼ cups coffee-
  flavoured Butter Icing
2 x 20cm/8in round Quick-mix
  Sponge Cakes
75g/3oz plain (semisweet)
  chocolate
20 blanched almonds
4 chocolate-coated coffee beans

1 Reserve 60ml/4 tbsp of the butter icing for piping and use the rest to sandwich the sponge cakes together and cover the top and side of the cake. Smooth the top with a metal spatula and serrate the side with a scraper to give a ridged effect.

2 Melt the chocolate in a double boiler or in a heatproof bowl over a pan of simmering water. Remove the pan from the heat.

3 Dip half of each almond in the chocolate at a slight angle. Leave to dry on baking parchment. Leave the bowl of chocolate over the pan of hot water so it does not set.

4 Arrange the almonds on top of the cake to represent flowers. Place a chocolate-coated coffee bean for the flower centres. Spoon the remaining melted chocolate into a baking parchment piping (pastry) bag. Cut a small piece off the end in a straight line. Pipe the chocolate in wavy lines over the top of the cake and in small beads around the top edge.

5 Transfer the cake to a serving plate. Place the reserved butter icing in a fresh piping bag fitted with a fine writing nozzle. Pipe beads of icing all around the bottom of the cake, then top with small beads of chocolate.

> **Cook's Tip**
> The Quick-mix Sponge Cake recipe at the back of the book is suitable for this recipe.

Chocolate Mousse Strawberry Layer Cake

To ring the changes, try replacing the strawberries with raspberries or blackberries, and use a complementary liqueur. Chocolate and berries always go well together.

Serves 10
oil, for greasing
115g/4oz good-quality white
  chocolate, chopped
120ml/4fl oz/½ cup whipping or
  double (heavy) cream
120ml/4fl oz/½ cup milk
15ml/1 tbsp rum essence or
  vanilla extract
115g/4oz/½ cup unsalted (sweet)
  butter, softened
175g/6oz/¾ cup granulated
  (white) sugar

3 eggs
275g/10oz/2½ cups plain
  (all-purpose) flour, plus extra
  for dusting
5ml/1 tsp baking powder
pinch of salt
675g/1½lb fresh strawberries,
  sliced, plus extra for decoration
750ml/1¼ pints/3 cups
  whipping cream
30ml/2 tbsp rum or strawberry-
  flavoured liqueur

For the mousse
250g/9oz good-quality white
  chocolate, chopped
350ml/12fl oz/1½ cups whipping
  or double (heavy) cream
30ml/2 tbsp rum or strawberry-
  flavoured liqueur

1 Preheat the oven to 180°C/350°F/Gas 4. Grease and flour two 23cm/9in cake tins (pans). Line the base of the tins with baking parchment. Melt the chocolate and cream in a double boiler over a low heat, stirring until smooth. Stir in the milk and rum essence or vanilla extract; set aside to cool.

2 In a large bowl, beat the butter and sugar together with an electric whisk until light and creamy. Add the eggs one at a time, beating well after each addition.

3 In a small bowl, stir together the flour, baking powder and salt. Alternately add the flour and melted chocolate to the egg mixture, until just blended. Pour evenly into the tins.

4 Bake for 20–25 minutes, until a metal skewer inserted into the centre comes out clean. Cool in the tins on a wire rack for 10 minutes. Turn the cakes out on to the rack, peel off the lining and leave to cool completely.

5 Make the mousse. Melt the chocolate and cream in a medium pan over low heat, stirring frequently, until smooth. Stir in the rum or strawberry-flavoured liqueur and pour into a bowl. Chill until just set. Using a wire whisk, whip the mixture lightly until it has a 'mousse' consistency.

6 Using a large knife, carefully slice both cakes in half horizontally. Sandwich the four layers together with the mousse and strawberries.

7 To decorate the cake, whip the cream with the rum or liqueur to form firm peaks. Spread half the flavoured cream over the top and sides of the cake. Spoon the remaining cream into a piping (pastry) bag with a star nozzle and pipe scrolls on top. Decorate with fresh strawberries and serve.

Coffee Energy 5901kcal/24633kJ; Protein 58.9g; Carbohydrate 605.1g, of which sugars 491.7g; Fat 377.2g, of which saturates 150.2g; Cholesterol 990mg; Calcium 791mg; Fibre 13.8g; Sodium 2877mg
Layer Cake Energy 964kcal/4008kJ; Protein 10.9g; Carbohydrate 69g, of which sugars 48g; Fat 72.1g, of which saturates 44.1g; Cholesterol 210mg; Calcium 253mg; Fibre 1.6g; Sodium 174mg.

Chocolate-iced Anniversary Cake with Exotic Fruits

This attractive Madeira cake is special enough to celebrate any wedding anniversary. The unusual glossy chocolate icing looks delicious contrasted with the exotic fruits.

Serves 8
20cm/8in round Madeira Cake
475g/1lb 2oz/2¼ cups chocolate-flavoured Butter Icing

For the chocolate icing
175g/6oz plain (semisweet) chocolate
150ml/¼ pint/⅔ cup single (light) cream
2.5ml/½ tsp instant coffee powder

To decorate
chocolate buttons, quartered
selection of fresh fruits, such as kiwi fruit, nectarines, peaches, apricots and physalis, peeled and sliced as necessary

1 Carefully cut the Madeira cake horizontally into three layers. Sandwich each of the layers together using three-quarters of the butter icing. Place the cake on a wire rack over a baking sheet to catch any drips.

2 To make the satin chocolate icing, place all the ingredients in a small pan and melt over a very low heat, stirring constantly until smooth. Immediately pour the icing over the cake to coat completely. Use a metal spatula to ensure the icing is smooth all over. Leave to set.

3 Transfer the cake to a serving plate. Place the remaining butter icing in a piping (pastry) bag with the star nozzle attached. Pipe butter icing scrolls around the top edge of the cake. Decorate with chocolate button pieces and fruit.

4 Make seven ribbon decorations. For each one, make two small loops from ribbon and secure the ends with a twist of florist's wire.

5 Cut the wire to the length you want and use to position the decoration in the fruit. Remove before serving.

Chocolate Fruit Birthday Cake

The modelled marzipan fruits on this moist chocolate Madeira cake make a very eye-catching decoration. Piped stars and a shiny ribbon add the finishing touches to the edges.

Makes one 18cm/7in square cake
18cm/7in square deep chocolate-flavoured Madeira Cake
45ml/3 tbsp apricot jam, warmed and strained
450g/1lb marzipan

450g/1lb/2 cups Glossy Chocolate Fudge Icing
red, yellow, orange, green and purple food colouring
whole cloves
angelica strips

Materials/equipment
20cm/8in square silver cake board
medium gateau nozzle
nylon piping (pastry) bag
75cm/2½ft yellow ribbon, 1cm/½in wide

1 Level the cake top and invert. Brush over the top and sides of the cake with apricot jam.

2 Use two-thirds of the marzipan to cover the cake. Reserve the trimmings.

3 Place the cake on a wire rack over a tray and pour three-quarters of the chocolate fudge icing over the top, spreading it evenly over the top and sides with a metal spatula.

4 Leave for 10 minutes, then place on the cake board.

5 Using the reserved icing and a medium gateau nozzle, pipe large stars around the top edge and base of the cake. Leave to set.

6 Colour small quantities of the reserved marzipan for the fruits and use it to model bananas, peaches, pears, cherries and grapes. Use the angelica strips and cloves to make stalks for those fruits which require them.

7 Secure the ribbon around the sides of the cake. Decorate the top with the marzipan fruits.

Anniversary Energy 6708kcal/28073kJ; Protein 73g; Carbohydrate 800.4g, of which sugars 615g; Fat 379.1g, of which saturates 228.8g; Cholesterol 519mg; Calcium 767mg; Fibre 20.6g; Sodium 5031mg.
Birthday Energy 6127kcal/25877kJ; Protein 66.7g; Carbohydrate 1138g, of which sugars 984.6g; Fat 176.5g, of which saturates 72.3g; Cholesterol 39mg; Calcium 877mg; Fibre 14.9g; Sodium 2920mg.

Strawberry Chocolate Valentine Cake

This delicious cake is perfect to share with a loved one.

Serves 8

175g/6oz/1½ cups self-raising (self-rising) flour
10ml/2 tsp baking powder
75ml/5 tbsp unsweetened cocoa powder
115g/4oz/generous ½ cup caster (superfine) sugar
2 eggs, beaten
15ml/1 tbsp black treacle (molasses)
150ml/¼ pint/⅔ cup sunflower oil
150ml/¼ pint/⅔ cup milk

For the filling

45ml/3 tbsp strawberry jam
150ml/¼ pint/⅔ cup double (heavy) cream or whipping cream
115g/4oz strawberries, sliced

To decorate

1 quantity Chocolate Fondant
chocolate hearts
icing (confectioners') sugar, to dust

1 Preheat the oven to 160°C/325°F/Gas 3. Grease a deep 20cm/8in heart-shaped cake tin (pan) and line the base with baking parchment. Sift the self-raising flour, baking powder and cocoa powder into a large mixing bowl. Stir in the sugar, then make a well in the centre of the dry ingredients.

2 Add the eggs, treacle, oil and milk to the well. Mix with a spoon to incorporate the dry ingredients, then beat with a hand-held electric mixer until the mixture is smooth and creamy.

3 Spoon the mixture into the prepared cake tin and spread evenly. Bake for about 45 minutes, until well risen and firm to the touch. Cool in the tin for a few minutes, then turn out on to a wire rack to cool completely.

4 Using a sharp knife, slice the cake neatly into two layers. Place the bottom layer on a board or plate. Spread with the strawberry jam.

5 Whip the cream in a bowl. Stir in the strawberries, then spread over the jam. Top with the remaining cake layer.

6 Roll out the chocolate fondant and cover the cake. Decorate with chocolate hearts and dust with icing sugar.

White Chocolate Celebration Cake

A stunning cake, perfect for enjoying at the most special of occasions.

Serves 40–50

900g/2lb/8 cups plain (all-purpose) flour
2.5ml/½ tsp salt
20ml/4 tsp bicarbonate of soda (baking soda)
450g/1lb white chocolate, chopped
475ml/16fl oz/2 cups whipping cream
450g/1lb/2 cups unsalted (sweet) butter, softened
900g/2lb/4 cups caster (superfine) sugar
12 eggs
20ml/4 tsp lemon extract
grated rind of 2 lemons
335ml/11fl oz/1⅓ cups buttermilk
lemon curd, for filling
chocolate leaves, to decorate

For the lemon syrup

200g/7oz/scant 1 cup sugar
250ml/8fl oz/1 cup water
60ml/4 tbsp lemon juice

For the buttercream

675g/1½lb white chocolate, chopped
1kg/2¼lb cream cheese, softened
500g/1¼lb/2½ cups unsalted (sweet) butter, softened
60ml/4 tbsp lemon juice
5ml/1 tsp lemon extract

1 Divide all the ingredients into two equal batches and make a cake with each batch. Preheat the oven to 180°C/350°F/Gas 4. Grease a 30cm/12in round cake tin (pan). Line with baking parchment. Sift the flour, salt and bicarbonate of soda into a bowl and set aside. Melt the chocolate and cream in a pan over a medium heat, stirring until smooth. Set aside to cool.

2 Beat the butter and sugar until creamy. Beat in the eggs, then slowly beat in the melted chocolate, lemon extract and rind. Gradually add the flour mixture, alternately with the buttermilk, stirring until smooth. Pour into the tin and bake for 1 hour, or until a skewer inserted in the cake comes out clean. Cool in the tin for 10 minutes, then invert on to a wire rack and cool completely. Cover this cake while making another cake in the same way from the second batch of ingredients.

3 Make the lemon syrup. In a pan, combine the sugar and water. Bring to the boil, stirring until the sugar dissolves. Remove from the heat, stir in the lemon juice and cool completely.

4 Make the buttercream. Melt the chocolate. Cool slightly. Beat the cream cheese in a bowl until smooth. Beat in the cooled white chocolate, then the butter, lemon juice and extract. Chill.

5 Split each cake in half. Spoon syrup over each layer, let it soak in, then repeat. Spread the bottom half of each cake with lemon curd and replace the tops.

6 Spread a quarter of the buttercream over the top of one of the filled cakes. Place the second filled cake on top. Chill for 15 minutes, so that the buttercream sets a little. Place the cake on a serving plate. Set aside a quarter of the remaining buttercream for piping, then spread the rest evenly over the top and sides of the filled cake.

7 Spoon the reserved buttercream into a piping (pastry) bag fitted with a small star tip. Pipe a pattern around the rim of the cake. Decorate with chocolate leaves and fresh flowers.

Valentine Cake Energy 395kcal/1649kJ; Protein 6.5g; Carbohydrate 40.2g, of which sugars 22.5g; Fat 24.3g, of which saturates 8.1g; Cholesterol 68mg; Calcium 100mg; Fibre 2g; Sodium 126mg.
Celebration Cake Energy 550kcal/2295kJ; Protein 6.2g; Carbohydrate 50.7g, of which sugars 37g; Fat 37.3g, of which saturates 22.7g; Cholesterol 115mg; Calcium 141mg; Fibre 0.6g; Sodium 224mg.

Valentine's Box of Chocolates Cake

As well as being an excellent choice for Valentine's Day, this heart-shaped cake would also make a wonderful surprise for Mother's Day.

Makes one 20cm/8in heart-shaped cake
20cm/8in heart-shaped chocolate-flavoured Quick-mix Sponge Cake
275g/10oz marzipan
120ml/4fl oz apricot jam, warmed and strained
900g/2lb/6 cups Sugarpaste Icing
red food colouring
225g/8oz/about 16–20 hand-made chocolates

Materials/equipment
23cm/9in square piece of stiff card
23cm/9in square cake board
piece of string
small heart-shaped cutter
length of ribbon
small paper sweet (candy) cases

1 Place the cake on the card, draw around it and cut out the heart shape. It will be used to support the box lid. Cut through the cake horizontally just below the dome. Place the top section on the card and the base on the cake board.

2 Use the string to measure around the outside of the base. Roll the marzipan into a long sausage to the measured length. Place on the cake around the outside edge.

3 Brush both sections of the cake with apricot jam. Tint the sugarpaste icing red and cut off one-third. Cut off another 50g/2oz/8 tbsp portion from the larger piece. Set aside. Use the large piece to cover the base section of cake. Use your hand to smooth the sugarpaste around the curves.

4 Stand the lid on a raised surface. Use the reserved one-third of sugarpaste icing to cover the lid. Roll out the remaining piece of icing and stamp out small hearts with the cutter. Stick them around the edge of the lid with water. Tie the ribbon in a bow and secure on top of the lid with diluted sugarpaste.

5 Place the chocolates in the paper cases and arrange in the cake base. Position the lid slightly off-centre, to reveal the chocolates. Remove the ribbon before serving.

Double Heart Engagement Cake

For a celebratory engagement party, these sumptuous cakes make the perfect centrepiece.

Makes two 20cm/8in heart-shaped cakes
350g/12oz plain (semisweet) chocolate
2 x 20cm/8in heart-shaped chocolate-flavoured Quick-mix Sponge Cakes
675g/1½lb/3 cups coffee-flavoured Butter Icing
icing (confectioners') sugar, for dusting
fresh raspberries, to decorate

Materials/equipment
2 x 23cm/9in heart-shaped cake boards

1 Melt the chocolate in a double boiler or in a heatproof bowl over a pan of simmering water. Pour the chocolate on to a smooth, non-porous surface and spread it out with a metal spatula. Leave to cool until just set, but not hard.

2 To make the chocolate curls, hold a large knife at a 45-degree angle to the chocolate and push it along the chocolate in short sawing movements. Leave to set on a sheet of baking parchment.

3 Cut each cake in half horizontally. Use one-third of the butter icing to sandwich the cakes together. Use the remaining icing to coat the tops and sides of the cakes.

4 Place the cakes on the cake boards. Generously cover the tops and sides of the cakes with the chocolate curls, pressing them gently into the butter icing.

5 Sift a little icing sugar over the top of each cake and decorate with raspberries. Chill until ready to serve.

> **Variation**
> If you are making this cake when fresh raspberries are not available, try glacé-icing-coated physalis, crystallized fruits or tiny chocolate flowers instead.

Box Energy 9848kcal/41510kJ; Protein 103.8g; Carbohydrate 1647.4g, of which sugars 1428.4g; Fat 361.9g, of which saturates 40.6g; Cholesterol 14mg; Calcium 1389mg; Fibre 10.9g; Sodium 4466mg.
Engagement Energy 3459kcal/14461kJ; Protein 34.8g; Carbohydrate 383.6g, of which sugars 302.5g; Fat 209.1g, of which saturates 69.7g; Cholesterol 204mg; Calcium 394mg; Fibre 3.3g; Sodium 2157mg.

Jazzy Chocolate Gateau

Decorated with white and dark chocolate triangles, this is a fun celebration chocolate cake.

Serves 12–15

2 x quantity chocolate-flavoured
 Quick-mix Sponge Cake
 mixture
75g/3oz plain (semisweet)
 chocolate

75g/3oz white chocolate
175g/6oz Chocolate
 Fudge Frosting
115g/4oz/1 cup Chocolate
 Glacé Icing
5ml/1 tsp weak coffee
8 tbsp chocolate nut spread

1 Preheat the oven to 160°C/325°F/Gas 3. Grease two 20cm/8in cake tins (pans), line the bases with baking parchment and grease the paper. Divide the cake mixture evenly between the tins and smooth the surfaces.

2 Bake in the centre of the oven for about 20–30 minutes, or until firm to the touch. Turn out on to a wire rack, peel off the lining paper and leave to cool.

3 Melt the chocolates in two separate bowls over pans of simmering water, pour on to baking parchment and spread evenly. As they begin to set, place another sheet of baking parchment on each and turn the chocolate 'sandwiches' over. When set, peel off the parchment and turn the chocolate sheets over. Cut out haphazard triangular shapes of chocolate and set aside.

4 Sandwich the two cakes together using the fudge frosting. Place the cake on a stand or plate. Colour the glacé icing using the weak coffee and add enough water to form a spreading consistency. Spread the icing on top of the cake almost to the edges. Cover the side of the cake with chocolate nut spread.

5 Press the chocolate pieces around the side of the cake and, using a piping (pastry) bag fitted with a fine nozzle, decorate the top of the cake with 'jazzy' lines over the glacé icing.

Chocolate Redcurrant Torte

A sumptuously rich cake that will be the centrepiece of any table.

Serves 8–10

115g/4oz/1/2 cup unsalted
 (sweet) butter, softened
115g/4oz/1/2 cup dark
 muscovado (molasses) sugar
2 eggs
150ml/1/4 pint/2/3 cup sour cream
150g/5oz/11/4 cups self-raising
 (self-rising) flour
5ml/1 tsp baking powder

50g/2oz/1/2 cup unsweetened
 cocoa powder
75g/3oz/3/4 cup stemmed
 redcurrants, plus 115g/4oz/1 cup
 redcurrant sprigs, to decorate

For the icing

150g/5oz plain (semisweet)
 chocolate, chopped into
 small pieces
45ml/3 tbsp redcurrant jelly
30ml/2 tbsp dark rum
120ml/4fl oz/1/2 cup double
 (heavy) cream

1 Preheat the oven to 180°C/350°F/Gas 4. Grease a 1.2 litre/2 pint/5 cup ring tin (pan) and dust lightly with flour. Cream the butter with the sugar in a mixing bowl until pale and fluffy. Beat in the eggs and sour cream until thoroughly mixed.

2 Sift the flour, baking powder and cocoa over the mixture, then fold in evenly. Fold in the stemmed redcurrants. Spoon into the tin and level the surface. Bake for 40–50 minutes, or until well risen. Turn out on to a wire rack to cool completely.

3 Make the icing. Mix the chocolate, redcurrant jelly and rum in a heatproof bowl over a pan of simmering water. Stir until melted. Remove from the heat and cool to room temperature, then add the cream, stirring until the mixture is well blended.

4 Transfer the cake to a serving plate. Spoon the icing over, drizzling it down the sides. Decorate with redcurrant sprigs.

> **Cook's Tip**
> Use a decorative gugelhupf tin, if you have one. Add a little cocoa powder to the flour used for dusting the greased tin, as this will prevent the cake from being streaked with white.

Jazzy Gateau Energy 444kcal/1862kJ; Protein 6g; Carbohydrate 58g, of which sugars 43.5g; Fat 22.5g, of which saturates 2.6g; Cholesterol 2mg; Calcium 84mg; Fibre 0.2g; Sodium 304mg.
Redcurrant Torte Energy 347kcal/1444kJ; Protein 3.7g; Carbohydrate 26.5g, of which sugars 25.9g; Fat 25.2g, of which saturates 15.3g; Cholesterol 89mg; Calcium 50mg; Fibre 1.2g; Sodium 138mg.

Chocolate Leaf Wedding Cake

This moist chocolate Madeira cake is covered with marzipan and chocolate-flavoured sugarpaste. The decorations consist of pretty coral-coloured sugar flowers and assorted chocolate leaves.

Serves 130
30 x 25cm/12 x 10in oval, deep
  chocolate-flavoured Madeira Cake
25 x 20cm/10 x 8in oval, deep
  chocolate-flavoured Madeira Cake
120ml/4fl oz/½ cup apricot jam,
  warmed and strained
2.75kg/6lb marzipan
3.25kg/7lb/9 x quantity
  Sugarpaste Icing
450g/1lb/4 cups unsweetened
  cocoa powder
350g/12 oz/⅔ quantity
  Petal Paste
yellow and pink food colourings

175g/6oz/1 cup plain (semisweet)
  chocolate chips, melted
115g/4oz/¾ cup white chocolate
  chips, melted
115g/4oz/¾ cup milk chocolate
  chips, melted
115g/4oz/⅙ quantity Royal Icing

Materials/equipment
35 x 30cm/14 x 12in oval silver
  cake board
25 x 20cm/10 x 8in thin oval
  silver cake board
flower cutter
30 peach pearl stamens
plunger blossom cutter
flower tape and wire
greaseproof paper piping
  (pastry) bag
No 1 writing nozzle
peach ribbon, 2.5cm/1in and
  1cm/½in wide
coral ribbon, 5mm/¼in wide
light coral ribbon, 5mm/¼in wide

1 To level the cakes, cut a slice off the top of each. Invert the cakes on to their cake boards and brush with apricot jam. Cover each cake with marzipan and leave to dry for 12 hours.

2 Divide the sugarpaste icing into three pieces. Knead 115g/4oz/½ cup cocoa powder into each piece until the sugarpaste icing is evenly coloured, then knead all the pieces together.

3 Cover the larger cake using half the sugarpaste icing, so there is plenty of icing to manipulate, dusting the surface with plenty of cocoa powder and using cocoa powder on your hands to smooth the surface. Repeat to cover the smaller cake and the large cake board. Store the cakes in boxes in a warm, dry place for up to a week.

4 To make the sugar flowers, divide the petal paste into three pieces. Using the yellow and pink food colourings, tint one piece pale, one piece medium and one piece dark coral. Make five roses, starting with dark centres and working out to pale petals.

5 Make 25 cut-out flowers of varying shades of coral paste and add stamens. Make 40 plunger blossom flower sprays with the remaining stamens, wire and tape. Leave all the flowers to dry overnight and store in boxes in a warm, dry place.

6 Using a piece of petal paste, press 30 blossom sprays in position to make an arrangement for the top of the cake.

7 To make the chocolate leaves, collect a variety of different-shaped leaves (rose, bay, camellia, fruit) and coat 30 with plain chocolate, 15 with white chocolate and 15 with milk chocolate. Store in a cool place until required, then peel off the leaves and keep the chocolate leaves separate on kitchen paper.

8 The day before the wedding, place the royal icing in a baking parchment piping (pastry) bag fitted with a No 1 writing nozzle. Measure and fit the 2.5cm/1in wide peach ribbon around the larger cake board, securing it at the back with a pin. Fit the 1cm/½in wide peach ribbon around the base of the larger cake. Fix the coral ribbon over the top, and secure with a bead of royal icing.

9 Arrange the cut-out flowers, roses and assorted chocolate leaves around the base of the cake, securing with royal icing.

10 Measure and fit another length of the 1cm/½in wide peach ribbon around the base of the small cake with another coral ribbon over the top, securing with royal icing. Carefully place the cake in position on top of the larger cake so that the backs of the cakes are level.

11 Arrange the sprays of blossom, cut-out flowers and chocolate leaves at intervals around the base of the small cake on the edge of the larger cake. Secure all decorations with royal icing.

12 Carefully remove the top cake. Place the sugar flower arrangement on the top of the cake and arrange the chocolate leaves so they come over the edge. Secure each leaf with royal icing.

13 Using the remaining coral ribbon, the light coral ribbon and fine wire, make some ribbon loops with tails. Press these into the arrangement.

14 Re-box the cakes until the next day, then re-assemble just before the reception.

> **To make the cakes**
> For a 30 × 25cm/12 × 10in and a 25 × 20cm/10 × 8in oval cake, use quantities of cake mix suitable for a 30cm/12in and a 25cm/10in round cake. Bake the cakes one at a time and store for up to a week before icing.

Chocolate Leaf **Wedding Cake** Energy 377kcal/1592kJ; Protein 4.5g; Carbohydrate 68.6g, of which sugars 58g; Fat 11.3g, of which saturates 5.1g; Cholesterol 0mg; Calcium 51mg; Fibre 1.3g; Sodium 214mg.

Easter Egg Nest Cake

Celebrate Easter with this colourfully adorned lemon sponge cake. The marzipan nests with chocolate eggs are easy to make.

Makes one 20cm/8in ring cake
20cm/8in ring lemon-flavoured Quick-mix Sponge Cake

350g/12oz/1½ cups lemon-flavoured Butter Icing
225g/8oz marzipan
pink, green and purple food colouring
small foil-wrapped chocolate eggs

1 Cut the cake in half horizontally and sandwich together with one-third of the butter icing. Place on the 25cm/10in cake board.

2 Use the remaining icing to cover the cake. Smooth the top and swirl the side with a metal spatula.

3 For the marzipan braids, divide the marzipan into three and tint the pieces with the pink, green and purple food colouring.

4 Cut each portion in half. Using half of each colour, roll thin sausages long enough to go around the base of the cake. Pinch the ends together, then twist the strands into a rope. Pinch the other ends to seal.

5 Place the coloured marzipan rope on the cake board around the base of the cake.

6 To make the nests, take the remaining portions of coloured marzipan and divide each into five pieces. Roll each piece into a 16cm/6¼in rope.

7 Take a rope of each colour and pinch the ends together. Twist the strands to form a multicoloured rope and pinch the other ends to secure. Form into a circle. Repeat for five nests.

8 Space the nests evenly on the cake. Place small chocolate eggs in the nests.

Fudge-frosted Starry Roll

Whether it's for a birthday or another occasion, this delicious chocolate roll decorated with shooting stars is sure to please.

Makes one 23cm/9in long roll
23 x 33cm/9 x 13in Sponge Roll
175g/6oz/¾ cup chocolate-flavoured Butter Icing
50g/2oz white chocolate
50g/2oz plain (semisweet) chocolate

For the fudge frosting
75g/3oz plain (semisweet) chocolate, broken into pieces
350g/12oz/3 cups icing (confectioners') sugar, sifted
75g/3oz/6 tbsp butter or margarine
65ml/4½ tbsp milk or single (light) cream
7.5ml/1½ tsp vanilla extract

Materials/equipment
small star cutter
several baking parchment piping (pastry) bags
big star nozzle

1 Unroll the sponge roll and spread with the butter icing. Re-roll and set aside.

2 For the decorations, melt the white chocolate in a bowl set over a pan of simmering water and spread on to a non-porous surface. Leave to firm up slightly, then cut out stars with the star cutter. Leave to set on baking parchment. To make lace curls, melt the plain chocolate as before and then cool slightly. Cover a rolling pin with baking parchment. Pipe zigzags on the paper and leave on the rolling pin until cool.

3 To make the frosting, stir all the ingredients in a pan over a low heat until melted. Remove from the heat and beat the mixture frequently until cool and thick. Cover the cake with two-thirds of the frosting. Use a metal spatula to create a swirl pattern in the frosting.

4 With a big star nozzle, use the remaining frosting to pipe diagonal lines on to the cake.

5 Position the lace curls and stars. Transfer the cake to a serving plate and decorate with more stars.

Nest Energy 5187kcal/21670kJ; Protein 51.1g; Carbohydrate 571.9g, of which sugars 439.9g; Fat 315.1g, of which saturates 115.3g; Cholesterol 991mg; Calcium 643mg; Fibre 9.7g; Sodium 2916mg.
Roll Energy 5460kcal/23020kJ; Protein 60.6g; Carbohydrate 916.8g, of which sugars 837.4g; Fat 198g, of which saturates 70.5g; Cholesterol 150mg; Calcium 1066mg; Fibre 13.2g; Sodium 2139mg.

Chocolate Hallowe'en Pumpkin Cake

Celebrate Hallowe'en with
this autumn-coloured
chocolate sponge cake,
colourfully decorated with
sugarpaste pumpkins.

**Makes one 20cm/8in
round cake**
175g/6oz/1 cup Sugarpaste Icing
brown and orange food colouring
2 x 20cm/8in round chocolate-
flavoured Quick-mix Sponge
Cakes

675g/1½lb/3 cups orange-
flavoured Butter Icing
chocolate chips
angelica

Materials/equipment
wooden cocktail stick (toothpick)
fine paintbrush
23cm/9in round cake board
serrated scraper
thick writing nozzle
baking parchment piping
(pastry) bag

1 For the pumpkins, tint a very small piece of the sugarpaste
icing with the brown food colouring, and tint the rest of
the icing orange.

2 Shape some balls of the orange icing the size of walnuts
and some a bit smaller.

3 Make ridges on each pumpkin using a cocktail stick
(toothpick). Make stems from the brown icing and secure to
the pumpkins with water. Paint highlights on the pumpkins in
orange. Leave to dry on baking parchment.

4 Cut both cakes in half horizontally. Use one-quarter of the
butter icing to sandwich the cakes together.

5 Place the cake on the board. Use two-thirds of the
remaining icing to cover the cake. Texture the icing using
a serrated scraper.

6 Using a thick writing nozzle, pipe a twisted rope pattern
around the top and base edges of the cake with the remaining
butter icing. Decorate with chocolate chips.

7 Cut the angelica into diamond shapes and arrange on the
cake with the pumpkins.

Chocolate Box with Caramel Mousse

A moulded chocolate box
contains a sumptuous
mousse and fresh fruits.

Serves 8–10
275g/10oz plain (semisweet)
chocolate, chopped into pieces

For the caramel mousse
4 x 50g/2oz chocolate-coated
caramel bars, coarsely chopped
25ml/1½ tbsp milk
350ml/12fl oz/1½ cups
double (heavy) cream
1 egg white

For the caramel shards
115g/4oz/generous ½ cup sugar
60ml/4 tbsp water

For the topping
115g/4oz fine quality white
chocolate, chopped into pieces
350ml/12fl oz/1½ cups double
(heavy) cream
450g/1lb mixed berries or cut up
fruits such as raspberries,
strawberries, blackberries

1 Mould foil around the base of a 23cm/9in square baking
tin (pan), then line the inside with foil. Stir the chocolate in a
heatproof bowl over a pan of simmering water until melted.
Pour into the tin, coating the bottom and sides. Chill until firm.

2 Melt the caramel bars and milk in a heatproof bowl set over
a pan of simmering water. Set aside and cool. Whip the cream
until soft peaks form. Stir a spoonful into the caramel mixture
to lighten it, then fold in the rest. Beat the egg white until stiff.
Fold into the mousse mixture. Pour into the box. Chill until set.

3 Make the caramel shards. Dissolve the sugar in the water
over a low heat. Boil until it is a pale gold colour. Pour on to
an oiled baking sheet. Cool, then break into pieces.

4 For the topping, stir the chocolate and 120ml/4fl oz/½ cup of
the cream in a pan over a low heat until smooth. Set aside to
cool. In a bowl, beat the remaining cream until firm peaks form.
Stir a spoonful into the chocolate mixture, then fold in the rest.

5 Remove the box from the tin and peel off the foil. Spoon
the topping into a piping (pastry) bag with a star tip. Pipe shells
over the top. Decorate with the berries and the caramel shards.

Hallowe'en Energy 6909kcal/28947kJ; Protein 62.7g; Carbohydrate 874.6g, of which sugars 701g; Fat 375.6g, of which saturates 104.2g; Cholesterol 426mg; Calcium 875mg; Fibre 0g; Sodium 4679mg.
Chocolate Box Energy 639kcal/2659kJ; Protein 4.6g; Carbohydrate 46.2g, of which sugars 43.8g; Fat 49.8g, of which saturates 30.2g; Cholesterol 102mg; Calcium 93mg; Fibre 1.8g; Sodium 62mg.

Chocolate Christmas Cakes

These individual cakes make excellent presents.

Makes 4

275g/10oz/2½ cups self-raising (self-rising) flour
15g/1 tbsp baking powder
50g/2oz/¼ cup unsweetened cocoa powder
250g/9oz/1 cup 2 tbsp caster (superfine) sugar
150ml/¼ pint/⅔ cup sunflower oil
350ml/12 fl oz/1½ cups water

For the icing and decoration

4 x 15cm/6in square silver cake boards
90ml/6 tbsp Apricot Glaze
1 kg/2¼ lb marzipan
900g/2lb Chocolate Fondant
red, yellow and green food colourings
2m/2yd red ribbon
2m/2yd green ribbon

1 Preheat the oven to 160C°/325°F/Gas 3. Grease a 20cm/8in square cake tin (pan) and line it with baking parchment. Sift the flour, baking powder, cocoa powder and sugar into a bowl. Add the oil and water and mix together, beating until smooth and glossy. Pour into the prepared tin and bake in the oven for 1 hour, or until the cake springs back when pressed in the centre.

2 Cool the cake in the pan for 15 minutes, then turn out, remove the paper and invert on to a wire rack. When cold, cut into four equal pieces, place each on a separate cake board and brush with apricot glaze. Divide the marzipan into four equal pieces and roll out a piece large enough to cover one cake. Place over the cake, press neatly into shape and trim off the excess marzipan at the base of the board. Knead the trimmings together and repeat to cover the remaining three cakes.

3 Divide the fondant into four pieces and repeat the process, rolling out each piece thinly to cover each cake. Colour the remaining marzipan ⅓ red, ⅓ yellow and ⅓ green with the food colourings. Thinly roll out each piece and cut into ½ in strips.

4 Lay alternate strips together and cut out four shapes using biscuit (cookie) cutters. Arrange the shapes on top of each cake. Measure and fit the red and green ribbons around each cake and tie a bow. Pack into pretty boxes, tie with ribbons and label.

Chocolate Puppies in Love

Children will love making and eating these fun decorated chocolate cakes.

Serves 8–10

1 chocolate-flavoured Sponge Roll
115g/4oz yellow marzipan
60ml/4 tbsp Chocolate Buttercream
115g/4oz/1⅓ cups desiccated (dry unsweetened shredded) coconut
green, brown, pink and red food colourings
450g/1lb Sugarpaste Icing
60ml/4 tbsp apricot jam, warmed and strained

1 Cut the sponge roll in half to use as the puppies' bodies. Make the faces by cutting the marzipan in half, rolling it into a ball, then into a cone shape. Use buttercream to stick the faces on.

2 Add a few drops of green colouring and a few drops of water to the coconut. Stir until flecked with green and white. Sprinkle over a cake board, then place the puppies on the board.

3 Set aside about 25g/1oz of the sugarpaste and colour half the remainder brown and half pink. Set aside 50g/2oz of each. Roll out the larger portions into rectangles to wrap each puppy. Halve each portion widthways and trim the edges.

4 Roll out the reserved brown and white paste, then stamp out circles. Set aside the trimmings. Stick white circles on to a brown rectangle, and brown ones on to a pink rectangle.

5 Slash all four paste rectangles along the two short edges. Brush each half of cake with jam, then lay the brown paste without spots over one, and the pink paste without spots over the other. Put the brown spotty paste over the brown dog and the pink spotty paste over the pink dog.

6 Roll out half of the trimmings in your hands to make tails. Stick in place with jam. Make a fringe from brown icing for the brown puppy, and tie pink icing strands together with ribbon for the pink puppy. Stick them in place with a dab of water. Use the remaining pieces of sugarpaste to shape eyes, a nose and a mouth for each puppy. Stick them on to the faces.

Christmas Energy 3198kcal/13392kJ; Protein 26g; Carbohydrate 400.1g, of which sugars 345.8g; Fat 177.1g, of which saturates 80.8g; Cholesterol 270mg; Calcium 390mg; Fibre 9.7g; Sodium 940mg.
Puppies in Love Energy 376kcal/1582kJ; Protein 3.6g; Carbohydrate 60.7g, of which sugars 56.4g; Fat 14.8g, of which saturates 9.4g; Cholesterol 13mg; Calcium 57mg; Fibre 2g; Sodium 85mg.

Chocolate Porcupine Cake

Melt-in-the-mouth pieces of flaked chocolate give this porcupine its delicious spiky coating.

Serves 15–20
2 chocolate-flavoured Quick-mix
　Sponge Cakes, baked in a
　1.2 litre/2 pint/5 cup and
　a 600ml/1 pint/2½ cup
　pudding bowl
500g/1¼lb/2½ cups chocolate-
　flavoured Butter Icing

cream, black, green, brown and
　red food colouring
5–6 flaked chocolate bars
50g/2oz/⅓ cup white marzipan

Materials/equipment
35cm/14in long rectangular
　cake board
wooden cocktail stick (toothpick)
fine paintbrush

1 Use the smaller cake for the head and shape a pointed nose at one end. Reserve the trimmed wedges.

2 Place the cakes side-by-side on the cake board, inverted, and use the trimmings to fill in the sides and top where they meet. Secure with butter icing.

3 Cover the cake with the remaining butter icing and mark the nose with a cocktail stick (toothpick).

4 Make the spikes by breaking the flaked chocolate bars into thin strips and sticking them into the butter icing all over the body section of the porcupine.

5 Reserve a small portion of marzipan. Divide the remainder into three and tint cream, black and green. Tint a tiny portion of the reserved marzipan using the brown food colouring.

6 Shape cream ears and feet, black-and-white eyes, and black claws and nose. Arrange all the features on the cake and press them into the butter icing.

7 Make green apples and highlight in red with a fine paintbrush. Make the stalks from the brown marzipan and push them in to the apples.

Chocolate Apple Tree

Filled with chocolate buttercream, this novelty apple tree is an ideal decorated chocolate sponge cake to get the children excited at a party.

Serves 10–12
1 chocolate-flavoured Sponge Roll
½ quantity Chocolate
　Buttercream
225g/8oz/1 cup Simple
　Buttercream, tinted with pale
　green food colouring

1 chocolate-flavoured Quick-mix
　Sponge Cake, baked in a
　450g/1lb fluted round cake tin
225g/8oz marzipan
red and green food colouring
florist's tape and florist's wire,
　for the apples
green-coloured desiccated
　(dry unsweetened shredded)
　coconut (see Chocolate Puppies
　in Love, facing page, step 2)
tiny fresh flowers, to decorate
　(optional)

1 Stand the sponge roll upright on a cake board, trimming it, if necessary. Anchor it on the board with a dab of the buttercream. Spread with chocolate buttercream, swirling the icing. Using about three-quarters of the green buttercream, thickly cover the round sponge cake. Draw the icing into peaks and swirls. Position the cake on top of the trunk to make the top of the tree.

2 Colour about 25g/1oz of the marzipan green. Colour the remainder red, then roll it into cherry-size apples. Roll the green marzipan into tiny sausage shapes and shape the stalks and leaves. Use a cocktail stick to make tiny holes in the tops of the apples, then insert a stalk and leaf into each.

3 Twist the florist's tape around the florist's wire, then cut it into 7.5cm/3in lengths. Press the lengths of wire through most of the apples, bending the ends so the apples cannot fall off when hanging. Press the hanging apples into the tree, reserving the remaining apples to put at the bottom, around the trunk.

4 Fill a piping (pastry) bag with the remaining green buttercream. Pipe leaves all over the tree top. Sprinkle the green coconut around the base of the tree and pipe a few extra leaves. Add a few tiny fresh flowers for effect, if liked. Remove the wires from the cake before serving.

Box of Chocolates Cake

This sophisticated cake, made in the shape of a box filled with individually wrapped chocolates, is perfect for an adult's birthday and will delight all chocolate lovers.

30ml/2 tbsp apricot jam,
    warmed and strained
350g/12oz marzipan
350g/12oz/2¼ cups
    Sugarpaste Icing
red food colouring
wrapped chocolates

**Makes one 15cm/6in
square cake**
15cm/6in square Quick-mix
    Sponge Cake
50g/2oz/4 tbsp Butter Icing

1 Split the cake in half and sandwich together with butter icing. Cut a shallow square from the top of the cake, leaving a 1cm/¼in border around the edge.

2 Place on the cake board and brush with apricot jam. Cover with a layer of marzipan.

3 Roll out the sugarpaste icing and cut an 18cm/7in square. Ease it into the hollow dip and trim. Tint the remaining sugarpaste icing red and use to cover the sides.

4 Put the chocolates into paper cases and arrange in the box. Tie the ribbon around the sides with a big bow.

Cook's Tip

If you often make cakes using sugarpaste icing, it is worth investing in a smoother. This is a flat plastic tool with a handle, and it is useful for achieving a professional finish. Use the smoother to smooth the sugarpaste over the top of the cake, using your hand to finish rounded edges. Then push the smoother down the sides of the cake and press the edge along the base where the sugarpaste meets the board. This will give a neat edge for you to cut away with a knife.

Ice Cream Cones

Individual cakes make a change for a party. Decorate them with sprinkles and flaked chocolate bars and put a candle in the special person's cake.

350g/12oz/1½ cups Butter Icing
red, green and brown
    food colouring
coloured and chocolate vermicelli,
    wafers and flaked chocolate bars
sweets (candies)

Serves 9
115g/4oz/¾ cup marzipan
9 ice cream cones
9 sponge fairy cakes

Materials/equipment
3 x 12-egg egg boxes
foil

1 Make the stands for the cakes by turning the egg boxes upside down and pressing three balls of marzipan into evenly spaced holes in each box. Wrap the boxes in foil.

2 Pierce the foil above the marzipan balls and insert the cones, being careful to press them in gently so that you do not crush the bottom of the cones.

3 Gently push a fairy cake into each cone. If the bases of the cakes are too large, trim them down with a small, sharp knife. The cakes should be quite secure in the cones.

4 Divide the butter icing between three bowls and tint them pale red, green and brown.

5 Using a small metal spatula, spread each cake with some of the pink icing, making sure that the finish on the icing is a little textured so that it looks like ice cream. Use the other coloured icings in the same way until all the cones have been covered.

6 To insert a wafer or chocolate stick into an ice cream, use a small, sharp knife to make a hole through the icing and into the cake, then insert the wafer or stick.

7 Add the finishing touches to the cakes by sprinkling over some coloured and chocolate vermicelli. Arrange sweets around the cones.

Box Energy 4150kcal/17538kJ; Protein 46.5g; Carbohydrate 762.1g, of which sugars 641.6g; Fat 123g, of which saturates 46.5g; Cholesterol 388mg; Calcium 663mg; Fibre 6.7g; Sodium 2087mg.
Cones Energy 576kcal/2416kJ; Protein 5.6g; Carbohydrate 78.6g, of which sugars 56.8g; Fat 28.8g, of which saturates 10.5g; Cholesterol 86mg; Calcium 89mg; Fibre 1.1g; Sodium 326mg.

Strawberries in a Chocolate Basket

For a summer birthday party, what could be more enjoyable than a delicious chocolate basket full of sweet strawberries?

Makes one small rectangular cake

1 Quick-mix Sponge Cake baked in a 450g/1lb/3 cup loaf tin (pan)

45ml/3 tbsp apricot jam
675g/1½lb marzipan
350g/12oz/1½ cups chocolate-flavoured Butter Icing
red food colouring
50g/2oz/¼ cup caster (superfine) sugar

1 Level the top of the cake and make it perfectly flat. Score a 5mm/¼in border around the edge and scoop out the inside to make a shallow hollow.

2 Warm the jam and strain, then brush it over the sides and border edges of the cake.

3 Roll out 275g/10oz/scant 2 cups of the marzipan, cut into rectangles and use to cover the sides of the cake, overlapping the borders. Press the edges together lightly to seal.

4 Using the star nozzle and the butter icing, pipe vertical lines 2.5cm/1in apart all around the sides of the cake. Pipe short horizontal lines of butter icing alternately crossing over and then stopping at the vertical lines to give a basketweave effect.

5 Pipe a decorative line of icing around the top edge of the basket to finish.

6 Tint the remaining marzipan red and mould it into ten strawberry shapes. Roll in the caster sugar and press a plastic strawberry calyx into each top. Arrange in the 'basket'.

7 For the basket handle, fold the foil into a thin strip and wind the ribbon around it to cover. Bend up the ends and then bend into a curve. Push the ends into the sides of the cake. Decorate with bows made from the ribbon.

Chocolate Sailing Boat

This fun, ocean-themed cake is covered with flaked chocolate to represent the hull of the boat. For chocoholics, make the cake using chocolate sponge.

Makes one cake
20cm/8in square Quick-mix Sponge Cake
225g/8oz/1 cup Butter Icing
15ml/1 tbsp unsweetened cocoa powder

4 large flaked chocolate bars
blue and red powder tints
115g/4oz/¾ cup Royal Icing
blue food colouring

Materials/equipment
25cm/10in square cake board
rice paper
paintbrush
plastic drinking straw
wooden cocktail stick (toothpick)
2 small cake ornaments

1 Split the cake and fill with half of the butter icing. Cut 7cm/2¾in from one side of the cake. Shape the larger piece to resemble the hull of a boat. Place diagonally across the cake board. Mix the cocoa powder into the remaining butter icing and spread evenly over the top and sides of the boat.

2 Make the rudder and tiller from short lengths of flaked chocolate bars and place them at the stern of the boat. Split the rest of the flaked chocolate bars lengthways and press on to the sides of the boat, horizontally, to resemble planks of wood. Sprinkle the crumbs over the top.

3 Cut two rice paper rectangles, one 14 × 16cm/5¾ × 6½in and the other 15 × 7.5cm/6 × 3in. Cut the bigger one in a gentle curve to make the large sail and the smaller one into a triangle. Brush a circle of blue powder tint on to the large sail.

4 Wet the edges of the sails and stick on to the straw. Make a hole for the straw 7.5cm/3in from the bow of the boat and push into the cake.

5 Cut a rice paper flag and brush with red powder tint. Stick the flag on to a cocktail stick (toothpick) and insert into the top of the straw. Tint the royal icing blue and spread on the board in waves. Place the small ornaments on the boat.

Spider's Web Cake with Chocolate Icing

Make the marzipan spider several days before you need the cake, to give it time to dry.

Serves 8–10

20cm/8in Quick-mix Sponge Cake
225g/8oz/1 cup Butter Icing
45ml/3 tbsp apricot jam, warmed and strained
30ml/2 tbsp unsweetened cocoa powder
chocolate vermicelli
40g/1½oz marzipan

yellow, red, black and brown food colouring
225g/8oz/1½ cups icing (confectioners') sugar
15–30ml/1–2 tbsp water

Materials/equipment

25cm/10in round cake board
2 small baking parchment piping (pastry) bags
wooden cocktail stick (toothpick)
medium star nozzle
candles and holders

1 Split the cake and fill with half the butter icing. Brush the sides with apricot jam, add the cocoa to the remaining butter icing, then smooth a little over the sides of the cake. Roll the sides of the cake in chocolate vermicelli. Place on the board.

2 For the spider, tint the marzipan yellow. Roll half of it into two balls of equal size for the head and body. Tint a small piece of marzipan red and make a mouth, and three balls to stick on the spider's body. Tint a tiny piece of marzipan black for the eyes. Roll the rest of the yellow marzipan into eight legs and two smaller feelers. Stick together.

3 Gently heat the icing sugar and water over a pan of hot water. Use two-thirds of the glacé icing to cover the cake top. Tint the remaining glacé icing brown and use it to pipe concentric circles on to the cake. Divide the web into eighths by drawing lines across with a cocktail stick (toothpick). Leave to set.

4 Put the rest of the chocolate butter icing into a piping (pastry) bag fitted with a medium star nozzle and pipe a border around the web. Put candles around the border and the spider in the centre.

Chocolate Coin Treasure Chest

Allow yourself a few days before the party to make this cake. The lock and handles are made separately, then left to dry for 48 hours before sticking on to the cake.

Serves 8–10

1½ x quantity chocolate-flavoured Quick-mix Sponge Cake baked in a 20cm/8in square cake tin

115g/4oz/1⁄3 quantity Butter Icing
60ml/4 tbsp apricot jam, warmed and strained
350g/12oz marzipan
350g/12oz/1 quantity Sugarpaste Icing
brown, green and black food colourings
50g/2oz/1 cup desiccated (dry unsweetened shredded) coconut
115g/4oz/1⁄6 quantity Royal Icing
edible gold dusting powder
silver balls
chocolate coins

1 Split the cake and fill with butter icing. Cut the cake in half and sandwich the halves on top of each other. Place on a 30cm/12in cake board.

2 Cut the top to shape the rounded lid and brush with apricot jam. Cover with a layer of marzipan. Colour all but a small piece of the sugarpaste icing brown. On a work surface dusted with icing sugar, roll out the icing and use to cover the cake.

3 Mark the lid of the treasure chest with a sharp knife. Roll out the trimmings of the brown sugarpaste icing and stick on four 5 mm/¼ inch wide strips with water.

4 Put the coconut in a bowl and mix in a few drops of green colouring. Spread a little royal icing over the cake board and press the coconut into it to look like grass.

5 From the remaining sugarpaste icing, cut out the padlock and handles. Cut a keyhole shape from the padlock and shape the handles over a small box. Leave to dry. Stick the padlock and handles into place with royal icing. Paint them gold and stick silver balls on the handles and padlock with a little royal icing to look like nails. Arrange the chocolate money around the chest on the grass.

Web Energy 5660kcal/23728kJ; Protein 54.3g; Carbohydrate 768.6g, of which sugars 611.1g; Fat 284.2g, of which saturates 96.9g; Cholesterol 997mg; Calcium 744mg; Fibre 10.7g; Sodium 3214mg.
Chest Energy 615kcal/2581kJ; Protein 6.1g; Carbohydrate 87.3g, of which sugars 74.1g; Fat 29.2g, of which saturates 9.9g; Cholesterol 81mg; Calcium 83mg; Fibre 1.9g; Sodium 245mg.

Pirate's Hat with Chocolate Coin Treasure

If you prefer, buy ready-made black sugarpaste icing for the hat rather than tinting it yourself.

Serves 8–10
25cm/10in round chocolate-flavoured Quick-mix Sponge Cake
225g/8oz/1 cup Butter Icing

45ml/3 tbsp apricot jam, warmed and strained
450g/1lb marzipan
500g/1¼lb/3¾ cups Sugarpaste Icing
black and gold food colouring
chocolate money
'jewel' sweets (candies)

1 Split the cake and fill with butter icing. Cut in half and sandwich the halves together. Stand upright diagonally across the 30cm/12in cake board and cut shallow dips from each end to create the brim of the hat. Brush with apricot jam.

2 Cut a strip of marzipan to lay over the top of the cake. Then cover the whole of the cake with a layer of marzipan. Tint 450g/1lb/3 cups of the sugarpaste icing black. Use to cover the cake.

3 Roll out the remaining sugarpaste icing and cut some 1cm/½in strips. Stick the strips in place with a little water around the brim of the pirate's hat and mark with the prongs of a fork to make a braid.

4 Make a skull and crossbones template and mark on to the hat. Cut the shapes out of the white sugarpaste icing and stick in place on the cake with water. With a fine paintbrush, paint the braid strip gold and arrange the chocolate money and jewel sweets on the board.

> **Variation**
> To make a sandy board for your pirate's hat to rest on, simply cover the board with a thin layer of butter icing and sprinkle finely crushed biscuits (cookies) over.

Army Tank Cake

Create a camouflaged tank by combining green and brown sugarpaste icing and a chocolate log gun.

Makes one 25 x 15cm/ 10 x 6in cake
25cm/10in square chocolate-flavoured Quick-mix Sponge Cake
225g/8oz/1 cup Butter Icing
45ml/3 tbsp apricot jam, warmed and strained

450g/1lb marzipan
450g/1lb/3 cups Sugarpaste Icing
brown, green and black food colouring
1 flaked chocolate bar
liquorice strips
60ml/4 tbsp Royal Icing
round biscuits (cookies)
sweets (candies)

Materials/equipment
25 x 35cm/10 x 14in cake board

1 Split the sponge cake and fill with butter icing. Cut off a 10cm/4in strip from one side of the cake. Use the off-cut to make a 15 × 7.5cm/6 × 3in rectangle, and stick on the top.

2 Shape the sloping top and cut a 2.5cm/1in piece from both ends to form the tracks. Shape the rounded ends for the wheels and tracks. Place on the cake board and brush with apricot jam. Cover with a layer of marzipan.

3 Tint a quarter of the sugarpaste icing brown and the rest green. Roll out the green to a 25cm/10in square. Break small pieces of brown icing and place all over the green. Flatten and roll out together to give a camouflage effect. Turn the icing over and repeat.

4 Continue to roll out until the icing is 3mm/⅛in thick. Lay it over the cake and gently press to fit. Using your hand, smooth the sugarpaste around all the curves of the tank. Cut away the excess.

5 From the trimmings cut a piece into a 6cm/2½in disc and stick on the top with a little water. Cut a small hole in the front of the tank for the gun and carefully insert the flaked chocolate. Stick liquorice on for the tracks, using a little black royal icing. Stick on cookies for the wheels and sweets for the lights and portholes.

Chocolate Cinnamon Cake with Banana Sauce

This mouthwatering cake, bursting with lovely flavours, is brilliantly complemented by the tasty banana sauce.

Serves 6
25g/1oz plain (semisweet) chocolate, chopped into small pieces
115g/4oz/½ cup unsalted (sweet) butter, at room temperature
15ml/1 tbsp instant coffee powder
5 eggs, separated
225g/8oz/1 cup granulated (white) sugar

115g/4oz/1 cup plain (all-purpose) flour
10ml/2 tsp ground cinnamon

For the banana sauce
4 ripe bananas
45ml/3 tbsp soft light brown sugar
15ml/1 tbsp fresh lemon juice
175ml/6fl oz/¾ cup whipping cream
15ml/1 tbsp rum (optional)

1 Preheat the oven to 180°C/350°F/Gas 4. Grease a 20cm/8in round cake tin (pan).

2 Place the chocolate and butter in the top of a double boiler or in a heatproof bowl set over a pan of simmering water. Stir until the chocolate and butter have melted. Remove from the heat and stir in the coffee. Set aside.

3 Beat the egg yolks with the granulated sugar until thick and lemon-coloured. Add the chocolate mixture and mix until just blended.

4 Stir the flour and cinnamon together in a bowl. In another bowl, beat the egg whites until they hold stiff peaks.

5 Fold a spoonful of whites into the chocolate mixture to lighten it. Fold in the remaining whites in three batches, alternating with the sifted flour mixture.

6 Pour the mixture into the prepared tin. Bake for 40–50 minutes, or until a skewer inserted in the centre comes out clean. Remove from the oven and turn the cake out on to a wire rack. Preheat the grill (broiler).

7 Make the sauce. Slice the bananas into a shallow, flameproof dish. Stir in the brown sugar and lemon juice. Place under the grill for 8 minutes, stirring occasionally, until caramelized.

8 Mash the banana mixture until almost smooth. Tip into a bowl and stir in the cream and rum, if using. Slice the cake and serve with the sauce.

Hot Chocolate Cake

This warm chocolate cake is wonderfully wicked served as a dessert with a white chocolate sauce. The basic cake freezes well – thaw, then warm in the microwave before serving.

Makes 10–12 slices
200g/7oz/1¼ cups self-raising wholemeal (self-rising whole-wheat) flour
25g/1oz/¼ cup unsweetened cocoa powder
pinch of salt
175g/6oz/¾ cup soft margarine

175g/6oz/¾ cup soft light brown sugar
few drops vanilla extract
4 eggs
75g/3oz white chocolate, roughly chopped
chocolate leaves and curls, to decorate

For the chocolate sauce
75g/3oz white chocolate
150ml/¼ pint/⅔ cup single (light) cream
30–45ml/2–3 tbsp milk

1 Preheat the oven to 160°C/325°F/Gas 3. Sift the flour, cocoa and salt into a bowl, adding in the wholemeal flakes from the sieve (strainer).

2 Cream the margarine, sugar and vanilla extract together until light and fluffy, then gently beat in one egg.

3 Gradually stir in the remaining eggs, one at a time, alternately folding in some of the flour mixture, until the eggs and flour have been used up and the mixture is blended in.

4 Stir in the white chocolate and spoon into a 675–900g/1½–2lb loaf tin (pan) or an 18cm/7in greased cake tin (pan). Bake for 30–40 minutes, or until just firm to the touch and shrinking away from the sides of the tin.

5 Meanwhile, make the sauce. Heat the white chocolate and cream very gently in a pan until the chocolate is melted. Add the milk and stir until cool.

6 Serve the cake sliced, in a pool of sauce and decorated with chocolate leaves and curls.

> **Cook's Tip**
> Take care when folding the egg white and flour into the chocolate mixture – do not be tempted to stir, otherwise you will break down the air bubbles in the mixture and the cake will not rise well.

Chocolate Cake Energy 343kcal/1432kJ; Protein 5.4g; Carbohydrate 35.7g, of which sugars 23.1g; Fat 20.8g, of which saturates 7.1g; Cholesterol 71mg; Calcium 124mg; Fibre 0.8g; Sodium 221mg.
Cinnamon Cake Energy 642kcal/2691kJ; Protein 8.9g; Carbohydrate 80.9g, of which sugars 64.8g; Fat 33.8g, of which saturates 19.4g; Cholesterol 230mg; Calcium 100mg; Fibre 1.4g; Sodium 186mg.

Chocolate Orange Marquise

Rich Chocolate Brioche Bake

Here is a cake for people
who are passionate about
the combination of chocolate
and orange. The rich, dense
chocolate flavour is accentuated
by fresh orange to make it a
truly delectable treat.

Serves 6–8
200g/7oz/1 cup caster
　(superfine) sugar
60ml/4 tbsp freshly squeezed
　orange juice

350g/12oz dark (bittersweet)
　chocolate, broken into squares
225g/8oz/1 cup unsalted (sweet)
　butter, diced, plus extra
　for greasing
5 eggs
finely grated rind of 1 orange
45g/1¾oz/3 tbsp plain
　(all-purpose) flour
icing (confectioners') sugar and
　finely pared strips of orange
　rind, to decorate

1 Preheat the oven to 180°C/350°F/Gas 4. Grease a 23cm/9in shallow cake tin (pan) with a depth of 6cm/2½in. Line the base of the tin with baking parchment.

2 Place 90g/3½oz/½ cup of the sugar in a pan. Add the orange juice and stir over a low heat until dissolved.

3 Remove from the heat and stir in the chocolate until melted, then add the butter, piece by piece, until melted.

4 Whisk the eggs with the remaining sugar in a large bowl, until the mixture is pale and very thick. Add the orange rind, then lightly fold the chocolate mixture into the egg mixture. Sift the flour over the top and fold in.

5 Pour the mixture into the prepared tin. Place in a roasting pan, then pour hot water into the roasting pan to reach about halfway up the sides of the cake tin.

6 Bake for 1 hour, or until the cake is firm to the touch. Remove the tin from the roasting pan and cool for 20 minutes. Turn out the cake on to a baking sheet, place a serving plate upside down on top, then carefully turn the plate and baking sheet over together. Dust with a little icing sugar, decorate with strips of orange rind and serve slightly warm or chilled.

Rich Chocolate Brioche Bake

This dessert is amazingly
easy to make and doesn't
require many ingredients.
Richly flavoured and quite
delicious, it's the perfect
dish for entertaining, when
you are pushed for time.
Serve with a platter of
sliced tropical fruit as a foil
to the richness of the dish.

Serves 4
40g/1½oz/3 tbsp unsalted
　(sweet) butter, plus extra
　for greasing

200g/7oz plain (semisweet)
　chocolate, chopped into
　small pieces
60ml/4 tbsp bitter marmalade
4 individual brioches, cut into
　halves, or 1 large brioche
　loaf, cut into thick slices
3 eggs
300ml/½ pint/1¼ cups milk
300ml/½ pint/1¼ cups single
　(light) cream
30ml/2 tbsp demerara
　(raw) sugar
crème fraîche, to serve

1 Preheat the oven to 180°C/350°F/Gas 4. Using the extra butter, lightly grease a shallow ovenproof dish.

2 Place the plain chocolate with the marmalade and butter in a double boiler or in a heatproof bowl set over a pan of just simmering water, stirring the mixture occasionally, until melted and smooth.

3 Spread the melted chocolate mixture over the brioche slices, then carefully arrange them in the dish so that the slices overlap in neat rows.

4 Beat the eggs in a large bowl, then add the milk and cream and mix well. Transfer to a jug (pitcher) and pour evenly over the slices.

5 Sprinkle the mixture with the demerara sugar and place the dish in the oven. Bake for 40–50 minutes, or until the custard has set lightly and the brioche slices have turned a golden brown colour.

6 Serve immediately, topped with dollops of crème fraîche and a fruit platter, if you like.

Brioche Bake Energy 987kcal/4143kJ; Protein 25.9g; Carbohydrate 127.8g, of which sugars 59.1g; Fat 45g, of which saturates 25.4g; Cholesterol 213mg; Calcium 460mg; Fibre 4.4g; Sodium 1060mg.
Marquise Energy 553kcal/2309kJ; Protein 3.1g; Carbohydrate 59.1g, of which sugars 54.4g; Fat 35.5g, of which saturates 22g; Cholesterol 63mg; Calcium 41mg; Fibre 1.3g; Sodium 176mg.

Chocolate and Orange Soufflé

The base in this hot soufflé is an easy-to-make semolina mixture, rather than the thick white sauce that many soufflés call for.

Serves 4
butter, for greasing
600ml/1 pint/2½ cups milk
50g/2oz/generous ⅓ cup semolina
50g/2oz/scant ¼ cup soft light brown sugar
grated rind of 1 orange
90ml/6 tbsp fresh orange juice
3 eggs, separated
75g/3oz plain (semisweet) chocolate, grated
icing (confectioners') sugar, for sprinkling
single (light) cream, to serve

1 Preheat the oven to 200°C/400°F/Gas 6. Butter a shallow 1.75 litre/3 pint/7½ cup ovenproof dish.

2 Pour the milk into a heavy pan, sprinkle over the semolina and sugar, then heat, stirring the mixture constantly, until boiling and thickened.

3 Remove the pan from the heat, beat in the orange rind and juice, egg yolks and all but 15ml/1 tbsp of the grated plain chocolate.

4 Whisk the egg whites until stiff peaks form, then lightly fold one-third into the semolina mixture. Fold in another third, followed by the remaining egg whites. Spoon the mixture into the buttered dish and bake for about 30 minutes, until just set in the centre.

5 Sprinkle the soufflé with the reserved grated chocolate and the icing sugar, then serve immediately, with the cream handed around separately.

> **Variation**
> For a sophisticated touch, replace 30ml/2 tbsp of the orange juice with the same amount of orange-flavoured liqueur, such as Cointreau or Grand Marnier.

Hot Mocha Rum Soufflé

These delicious individual soufflés, flavoured with cocoa and coffee, are light enough to be the ideal dessert for serving after a substantial main course.

Serves 6
25g/1oz/2 tbsp unsalted (sweet) butter, melted
65g/2½oz/9 tbsp unsweetened cocoa powder
75g/3oz/scant ½ cup caster (superfine) sugar
60ml/4 tbsp made-up strong black coffee
30ml/2 tbsp dark rum
6 egg whites
icing (confectioners') sugar, for dusting

1 Preheat the oven to 190°C/375°F/Gas 5. Grease six 250ml/8fl oz/1 cup soufflé dishes with melted butter.

2 Mix 15ml/1 tbsp of the cocoa with 15ml/1 tbsp of the caster sugar in a bowl. Sprinkle the mixture into each of the dishes in turn, rotating them so that they are evenly coated.

3 Mix the remaining cocoa with the coffee and rum in a medium bowl.

4 Whisk the egg whites in a clean, grease-free bowl until they form firm peaks. Whisk in the remaining sugar. Stir a generous spoonful of the egg whites into the cocoa mixture to lighten it, then fold in the remaining whites.

5 Spoon the mixture into the prepared dishes, smoothing the tops. Place on a hot baking sheet, and bake in the oven for 12–15 minutes, or until well risen. Serve immediately, dusted with icing sugar.

> **Cook's Tip**
> You can use either a hand whisk or an electric version to beat the egg whites, but take care not to overbeat them if you are using electric beaters. The beaten whites should stand in soft peaks, with the tips gently flopping over. If they are overbeaten they will look dry.

Hot Mocha Rum Soufflé Energy 148kcal/619kJ; Protein 5g; Carbohydrate 14.3g, of which sugars 13.1g; Fat 5.8g, of which saturates 3.6g; Cholesterol 9mg; Calcium 23mg; Fibre 1.3g; Sodium 190mg.
Orange Soufflé Energy 321kcal/1353kJ; Protein 12.2g; Carbohydrate 43.7g, of which sugars 33.8g; Fat 12.2g, of which saturates 5.9g; Cholesterol 153mg; Calcium 219mg; Fibre 0.8g; Sodium 123mg.

Twice-baked Mocha Soufflé

The perfect way to end a meal, these mini mocha soufflés can be made up to 3 hours ahead, then reheated just before you serve them.

Serves 6

75g/3oz/6 tbsp unsalted (sweet) butter, softened
90g/3½oz bittersweet or plain (semisweet) chocolate, grated
30ml/2 tbsp ground coffee
400ml/14fl oz/1⅔ cup milk

40g/1½oz/⅓ cup plain (all-purpose) flour, sifted
15g/½oz/2 tbsp unsweetened cocoa powder, sifted
3 eggs, separated
50g/2oz/¼ cup caster (superfine) sugar
175ml/6fl oz/¾ cup creamy chocolate or coffee liqueur, such as Crème de Caçao or Tia Maria

1 Preheat the oven to 200°C/400°F/Gas 6. Lightly brush six 150ml/¼ pint/⅔ cup dariole moulds or mini pudding bowls with 25g/1oz/2 tbsp of the butter. Coat evenly with 50g/2oz of the grated chocolate.

2 Put the coffee in a bowl. Heat the milk until almost boiling and pour over the coffee. Leave for 5 minutes, then strain.

3 Melt the remaining butter in a pan. Stir in the flour and cocoa to make a roux. Cook for 1 minute, then add the coffee milk, stirring all the time to make a very thick sauce. Simmer for 2 minutes. Remove from the heat and stir in the egg yolks.

4 Cool for 5 minutes, then stir in the remaining chocolate. Whisk the egg whites until stiff, then whisk in the sugar. Fold half into the sauce to loosen, then fold in the remainder.

5 Spoon the mixture into the dariole moulds or bowls and place in a roasting pan. Pour in enough hot water to come two-thirds of the way up the sides of the tins.

6 Bake the soufflés for 15 minutes. Turn them out on to a baking tray and leave to cool completely. Before serving, spoon 15ml/1 tbsp of liqueur over each soufflé and reheat in the oven for 6–7 minutes. Serve with the remaining liqueur poured over.

French Chocolate Soufflé

These stylish French soufflés are actually extremely easy to make.

Serves 6

175g/6oz plain (semisweet) chocolate, chopped
150g/5oz/10 tbsp unsalted (sweet) butter, cut into small pieces
4 large (US extra large) eggs, separated
30ml/2 tbsp orange liqueur (optional)

1.5ml/¼ tsp cream of tartar
40g/1½oz/3 tbsp caster (superfine) sugar
icing (confectioners') sugar, for dusting
sprigs of redcurrants and white chocolate roses, to decorate

For the sauce

75g/3oz white chocolate, chopped
90ml/6 tbsp whipping cream
15–30ml/1–2 tbsp orange liqueur
grated rind of ½ orange

1 Generously butter six 150ml/¼ pint/⅔ cup ramekins, custard cups or small ovenproof dishes. Sprinkle each with a little sugar and tap out any excess. Place the dishes on a baking sheet.

2 Melt the chocolate and butter in a heavy pan over a very low heat, stirring until smooth. Remove from the heat and cool slightly, then beat in the egg yolks and orange liqueur, if using. Set aside, stirring occasionally.

3 Preheat the oven to 220°C/425°F/Gas 7. In a grease-free bowl, whisk the egg whites slowly until frothy. Add the cream of tartar, increase the speed and whisk to form soft peaks. Gradually whisk in the sugar until the whites are stiff and glossy. Stir a third of the whites into the cooled chocolate mixture, then fold this into the remaining whites. Spoon into the dishes.

4 Make the sauce. Put the white chocolate and cream in a small pan. Place over a low heat and cook, stirring constantly until smooth. Remove from the heat and stir in the liqueur and orange rind, then pour into a serving jug (pitcher); keep warm.

5 Bake the soufflés for 10–12 minutes until risen and set, but still slightly wobbly in the centre. Dust with icing sugar and decorate with redcurrants and chocolate roses. Serve with the sauce.

French Soufflé Energy 543kcal/2256kJ; Protein 7.1g; Carbohydrate 35g, of which sugars 34.7g; Fat 42.3g, of which saturates 25g; Cholesterol 198mg; Calcium 80mg; Fibre 0.7g; Sodium 218mg.
Mocha Soufflé Energy 395kcal/1650kJ; Protein 7.4g; Carbohydrate 33.6g, of which sugars 28.1g; Fat 23.5g, of which saturates 10.9g; Cholesterol 127mg; Calcium 124mg; Fibre 0.9g; Sodium 191mg.

Rich Chocolate and Coffee Pudding

This heavenly dessert boasts a rich sponge topping with a luscious sauce underneath.

Serves 6

90g/3½oz/¾ cup plain (all-purpose) flour
10ml/2 tsp baking powder
pinch of salt
50g/2oz/¼ cup butter or margarine
25g/1oz plain (semisweet) chocolate, chopped into small pieces
115g/4oz/generous ½ cup caster (superfine) sugar
75ml/2½fl oz/⅓ cup milk
1.5ml/¼ tsp vanilla extract
whipped cream, to serve

For the topping

30ml/2 tbsp instant coffee powder or granules
325ml/11fl oz/1⅓ cups hot water
90g/3½oz/½ cup soft dark brown sugar
65g/2½oz/5 tbsp caster (superfine) sugar
30ml/2 tbsp unsweetened cocoa powder

1 Preheat the oven to 180°C/350°F/Gas 4. Grease a 23cm/9in square non-stick baking tin (pan)

2 Sift the flour, baking powder and salt into a small mixing bowl. Set aside.

3 Melt the butter or margarine, chocolate and caster sugar in a heatproof bowl set over a pan of simmering water, stirring occasionally. Remove the bowl from the heat.

4 Add the flour mixture and stir well. Stir in the milk and vanilla extract. Mix well, then pour into the prepared tin.

5 Make the topping. Dissolve the coffee in the water in a bowl. Allow to cool. Mix the brown sugar, caster sugar and cocoa powder in a bowl. Sprinkle the mixture over the pudding mixture in the tin.

6 Pour the coffee evenly over the surface. Bake for 40 minutes, or until the pudding is risen and set on top. The coffee mixture will have formed a delicious creamy sauce underneath. Serve immediately with whipped cream.

Steamed Chocolate and Fruit Pudding with Chocolate Syrup

Some things always turn out well, just like these wonderful little puddings. Dark, fluffy chocolate sponge with tangy cranberries and apple is served with a honeyed chocolate syrup.

Serves 4

butter or oil, for greasing
115g/4oz/½ cup muscovado (molasses) sugar
1 eating apple, peeled and cored
75g/3oz/¾ cup cranberries, thawed if frozen
115g/4oz/½ cup soft margarine
2 eggs
75g/3oz/⅔ cup plain (all-purpose) flour
2.5ml/½ tsp baking powder
45ml/3 tbsp unsweetened cocoa powder

For the chocolate syrup

115g/4oz plain (semisweet) chocolate, broken into squares
30ml/2 tbsp clear honey
15ml/1 tbsp unsalted (sweet) butter
2.5ml/½ tsp vanilla extract

1 Prepare a steamer or half fill a pan with water and bring to the boil. Grease four individual heatproof bowls and sprinkle each one with a little of the muscovado sugar to coat all over.

2 Dice the apple into a bowl. Add the cranberries and mix well. Divide the mixture equally among the prepared bowls.

3 Put the remaining sugar in a mixing bowl. Add the margarine, eggs, flour, baking powder and cocoa. Beat well until smooth.

4 Spoon the mixture on to the fruit, and cover each bowl with a double thickness of foil. Steam for 45 minutes, topping up the water if necessary, until the puddings are well risen and firm.

5 Make the syrup. Mix together the chocolate, honey, butter and vanilla in a small pan. Heat gently, stirring, until smooth.

6 Run a knife around the edge of each pudding to loosen it, then turn out on to individual plates. Serve immediately, with the chocolate syrup poured over the top.

Rich Pudding Energy 325kcal/1371kJ; Protein 3g; Carbohydrate 60.6g, of which sugars 50.5g; Fat 9.5g, of which saturates 5.8g; Cholesterol 19mg; Calcium 66mg; Fibre 1.1g; Sodium 107mg.
Fruit Pudding Energy 672kcal/2811kJ; Protein 8.7g; Carbohydrate 73.1g, of which sugars 57.3g; Fat 40.4g, of which saturates 13.9g; Cholesterol 105mg; Calcium 84mg; Fibre 3.2g; Sodium 366mg.

Chocolate, Date and Walnut Pudding

This tempting pudding is not steamed in the traditional way, but baked in the oven. The result is still completely irresistible.

Serves 4

25g/1oz/¼ cup chopped walnuts
25g/1oz/2 tbsp chopped dates
2 eggs, separated
5ml/1 tsp vanilla extract
30ml/2 tbsp golden caster (superfine) sugar
45ml/3 tbsp plain wholemeal (all-purpose whole-wheat) flour
15ml/1 tbsp unsweetened cocoa powder
30ml/2 tbsp skimmed milk

1 Preheat the oven to 180°C/350°F/Gas 4. Grease a 1.2 litre/2 pint/5 cup ovenproof bowl and line with baking parchment. Spoon in the walnuts and dates.

2 Mix the egg yolks, vanilla extract and sugar in a heatproof bowl. Place over a pan of hot water and whisk the mixture until thick and pale, then remove the bowl from the heat.

3 Sift the flour and cocoa over the mixture and fold in with a metal spoon. Stir in the milk, to soften the mixture. Whisk the egg whites to soft peaks. then gradually fold them into the pudding mixture.

4 Spoon the mixture over the walnuts and dates in the bowl and bake for 40–45 minutes, or until well risen and firm to the touch. Run a knife around the pudding to loosen it from the bowl, and then turn it out on to a plate and serve immediately.

> **Cook's Tips**
> • Pudding fans will probably not be satisfied without custard to accompany this dessert. Why not serve a real custard, Crème Anglaise, made using cream, egg yolks, caster (superfine) sugar and a few drops of vanilla extract?
> • If you wish, the cocoa can be omitted and the sponge mix flavoured with grated orange rind instead.

Magic Chocolate Mud Cake

Guaranteed to be a big hit, this scrumptious dessert can be put together in no time at all.

Serves 4

50g/2oz/¼ cup butter, plus extra for greasing
90g/3½oz/¾ cup self-raising (self-rising) flour
5ml/1 tsp ground cinnamon
75ml/5 tbsp unsweetened cocoa powder
200g/7oz/1 cup light muscovado (brown) or demerara (raw) sugar
475ml/16fl oz/2 cups milk
crème fraîche, Greek (US strained plain) yogurt or vanilla ice cream, to serve

1 Preheat the oven to 180°C/350°F/Gas 4. Grease a 1.5 litre/2½ pint/6¼ cup ovenproof dish with butter. Place the dish on a baking sheet and set aside.

2 Sift the flour and ground cinnamon into a bowl. Sift in 15ml/1 tbsp of the cocoa and mix well.

3 Place the butter in a pan. Add 115g/4oz/½ cup of the sugar and 150ml/¼ pint/⅔ cup of the milk. Heat gently without boiling, stirring from time to time, until the butter has melted and all the sugar has completely dissolved. Remove the pan from the heat.

4 Stir in the flour mixture, mixing evenly. Pour the mixture into the prepared dish and level the surface.

5 Mix the remaining sugar and cocoa in a bowl, then sprinkle over the pudding mixture. Pour the remaining milk evenly over the pudding.

6 Bake for 45–50 minutes or until the sponge has risen to the top and is firm to the touch. Serve hot, with the crème fraîche, yogurt or ice cream.

> **Cook's Tip**
> A delicious sauce 'magically' appears beneath the sponge.

Date Pudding Energy 171kcal/716kJ; Protein 6.2g; Carbohydrate 19.5g, of which sugars 10.5g; Fat 8.2g, of which saturates 1.7g; Cholesterol 96mg; Calcium 55mg; Fibre 1.1g; Sodium 76mg.
Mud Cake Energy 480kcal/2025kJ; Protein 10g; Carbohydrate 77.6g, of which sugars 58.3g; Fat 16.7g, of which saturates 10.2g; Cholesterol 34mg; Calcium 227mg; Fibre 3g; Sodium 309mg.

Chocolate Chip and Banana Pudding

Hot and steamy, this superb light pudding tastes extra special when served with ready-made fresh chocolate sauce or custard.

Serves 4
200g/7oz/1¾ cups self-rising (self-rising) flour
75g/3oz/6 tbsp unsalted (sweet) butter or margarine

2 ripe bananas
75g/3oz/6 tbsp caster (superfine) sugar
60ml/4 tbsp milk
1 egg, beaten
60ml/4 tbsp plain (semisweet) chocolate chips or chopped chocolate
whipped cream and fresh chocolate sauce, to serve

1 Prepare a steamer or half fill a pan with water and bring to the boil. Grease a 1 litre/1¾ pint/4 cup ovenproof bowl.

2 Sift the flour into a bowl and rub in the butter or margarine until the mixture resembles breadcrumbs. Mash the bananas in a bowl. Stir them into the creamed mixture, with the sugar.

3 Whisk the milk with the egg in a bowl, then beat into the pudding mixture. Stir in the chocolate chips.

4 Spoon the mixture into the prepared bowl, cover closely with a double thickness of foil, and steam for 2 hours, topping up the water as required during cooking.

5 Run a knife around the top edge of the pudding to loosen it, then turn it out on to a warm serving dish. Serve hot, with chocolate sauce and a spoonful of whipped cream.

> **Cook's Tip**
> If you have a food processor, make a quick-mix version by processing all the ingredients, except the chocolate, until smooth. Then stir in the chocolate, spoon into the prepared bowl and finish as described in the recipe.

Chocolate Pudding with Rum Custard

With melting moments of chocolate in every mouthful, these little treats won't last long. The rum custard turns them into a more adult dessert; you could flavour the custard with vanilla or orange rind instead.

Serves 6
115g/4oz/½ cup butter, plus extra for greasing
115g/4oz/½ cup soft light brown sugar
2 eggs, beaten
drops of vanilla extract

45ml/3 tbsp unsweetened cocoa powder, sifted
115g/4oz/1 cup self-raising (self-rising) flour
75g/3oz plain (semisweet) chocolate, chopped
a little milk, warmed

For the rum custard
250ml/8fl oz/1 cup milk
15ml/1 tbsp caster (superfine) sugar
2 egg yolks
10ml/2 tsp cornflour (cornstarch)
30–45ml/2–3 tbsp rum (optional)

1 Lightly grease a 1.2 litre/2 pint/5 cup heatproof bowl or six individual dariole moulds. Cream the butter and sugar until pale and creamy. Gently blend in the eggs and the vanilla extract.

2 Sift together the cocoa powder and flour, and fold gently into the egg mixture with the chopped chocolate and sufficient milk to give a soft dropping consistency.

3 Spoon the mixture into the bowl or moulds, cover with buttered baking parchment and tie down.

4 Fill a pan with 2.5–5cm/1–2in water, place the puddings in the pan, cover with a lid and bring to the boil. Steam the large pudding for 1½–2 hours and the individual ones for 45–50 minutes, topping up with water if necessary. When firm, turn out on to warm plates.

5 Make the custard. Bring the milk and sugar to the boil. Whisk together the egg yolks and cornflour, then pour on the hot milk, whisking constantly. Return the mixture to the pan and stir while it comes back to the boil. Simmer gently as it thickens, stirring all the time. Remove from the heat and stir in the rum.

Banana Pudding Energy 528kcal/2220kJ; Protein 8.1g; Carbohydrate 79.3g, of which sugars 40.9g; Fat 22g, of which saturates 13g; Cholesterol 89mg; Calcium 222mg; Fibre 2.5g; Sodium 320mg.
Chocolate Pudding Energy 458kcal/1915kJ; Protein 8.3g; Carbohydrate 49g, of which sugars 31.5g; Fat 25.6g, of which saturates 14.5g; Cholesterol 186mg; Calcium 145mg; Fibre 1.8g; Sodium 302mg.

Chocolate Baked Alaska

Children will love the
surprise of this classic
dessert – hot meringue with
chocolate sponge and ice-
cold ice cream inside. Here's
a variation on the classic
version to try out.

Serves 3 to 4
3 large egg whites
150g/5oz/¾ cup caster
  (superfine) sugar

25g/1oz desiccated (dry
  unsweetened shredded)
  coconut
175–225g/6–8oz piece of
  ready-made chocolate cake
6 slices ripe, peeled pineapple
500ml/17fl oz/generous 2 cups
  vanilla ice cream, in a brick
a few cherries or figs,
  to decorate

1 Preheat the oven to 230°C/450°F/Gas 8. Whisk the egg
whites in a grease-free bowl until stiff, then whisk in the sugar
until the mixture is stiff and glossy. Fold in the coconut.

2 Slice the ready-made cake into two thick layers the same
rectangular shape as the ice cream. Cut the pineapple into
triangles or quarters, cutting it over the cake to catch any drips.

3 On a baking sheet, arrange the pineapple on top of one
layer of cake. Place the ice cream on top of the fruit and then
top with the second layer of cake.

4 Spread the meringue over the cake and ice cream, and bake
in the oven for 5–7 minutes, or until turning golden. Serve
immediately, topped with fruit.

> **Cook's Tip**
> Do not use soft-scoop ice cream for this dessert as it will
> soften too quickly.

> **Variation**
> For chocoholics, use chocolate ice cream in place of the vanilla.

Chocolate, Date and Almond Filo Coil

Experience the allure of
the Middle East with this
delectable dessert. Crisp filo
pastry conceals a chocolate
and rose water filling studded
with dates and almonds.

Serves 6
275g/10oz filo pastry, thawed
  if frozen
50g/2oz/¼ cup butter, melted
icing (confectioners') sugar,
  unsweetened cocoa powder and
  ground cinnamon, for dusting

For the filling
75g/3oz/6 tbsp butter
115g/4oz dark (bittersweet)
  chocolate, broken up into pieces
115g/4oz/1⅓ cup ground
  almonds
115g/4oz/⅔ cup chopped dates
75g/3oz/⅔ cup icing
  (confectioners') sugar
10ml/2 tsp rose water
2.5ml/½ tsp ground cinnamon

1 Preheat the oven to 180°C/350°F/Gas 4. Grease a 22cm/8½in
round cake tin (pan). To make the filling, melt the butter with
the chocolate in a heatproof bowl set over a pan of simmering
water, then remove from the heat and stir in the remaining
ingredients to make a thick paste. Leave to cool.

2 Lay one sheet of filo on a flat surface and brush with melted
butter. Lay a second sheet on top and brush with more butter.

3 Roll a handful of the chocolate and almond mixture into a
long sausage shape and place along one long edge of the layered
filo. Roll up the pastry tightly around the filling to make a roll.

4 Fit the filo roll in the cake tin, in such a way that it sits snugly
against the outer edge. Make more filo rolls in the same way,
adding them to the tin from the outside towards the centre,
until the coil fills the tin.

5 Brush the coil with the remaining melted butter. Bake for
30–35 minutes or until the pastry is golden. Transfer to a
serving plate. Serve the cake warm, dusted with icing sugar,
cocoa and cinnamon.

Alaska Energy 667kcal/2808kJ; Protein 10.8g; Carbohydrate 104.6g, of which sugars 93.9g; Fat 25.7g, of which saturates 9.8g; Cholesterol 33mg; Calcium 215mg; Fibre 2.3g; Sodium 317mg.
Filo Coil Energy 543kcal/2267kJ; Protein 8.2g; Carbohydrate 55.4g, of which sugars 32.4g; Fat 33.6g, of which saturates 15g; Cholesterol 46mg; Calcium 108mg; Fibre 3.2g; Sodium 133mg.

Chocolate Almond Meringue Pie

This dreamy dessert offers a velvety chocolate filling on a light orange pastry case, topped with fluffy meringue.

Serves 6
175g/6oz/1½ cups plain (all-purpose) flour
50g/2oz/⅓ cup ground rice
150g/5oz/10 tbsp unsalted (sweet) butter
finely grated rind of 1 orange
1 egg yolk
flaked almonds and melted chocolate, to decorate

For the filling
150g/5oz plain (semisweet) chocolate, broken into squares
50g/2oz/¼ cup unsalted (sweet) butter, softened
75g/3oz/6 tbsp caster (superfine) sugar
10ml/2 tsp cornflour (cornstarch)
4 egg yolks
75g/3oz/¾ cup ground almonds

For the meringue
3 egg whites
150g/5oz/¾ cup caster (superfine) sugar

1 Sift the flour and ground rice into a bowl. Rub in the butter to resemble breadcrumbs. Stir in the orange rind. Add the egg yolk; bring the dough together. Roll out and use to line a 23cm/9in round flan tin (pan). Chill for 30 minutes.

2 Preheat the oven to 190°C/375°F/Gas 5. Prick the pastry base all over with a fork, cover with baking parchment, weighed down with baking beans, and bake blind for 10 minutes. Remove the pastry case from the oven; take out the baking beans and paper.

3 Make the filling. Melt the chocolate in a heatproof bowl over hot water. Cream the butter with the sugar in a bowl, then beat in the cornflour and egg yolks. Fold in the almonds, then the chocolate. Spread in the pastry case. Bake for 10 minutes more.

4 Make the meringue. Whisk the egg whites until stiff, then gradually add half the sugar. Fold in the remaining sugar. Spoon the meringue over the chocolate filling, lifting it up with the back of the spoon to form peaks. Reduce the oven temperature to 180°C/350°F/Gas 4 and bake the pie for 15–20 minutes or until the topping is pale gold. Serve, sprinkled with almonds and drizzled with melted chocolate.

Chocolate Pecan Pie

A delicious version of an American favourite, this pie is great for any occasion.

Serves 6
200g/7oz/1¾ cups plain (all-purpose) flour
75ml/5 tbsp caster (superfine) sugar
90g/3½oz/7 tbsp unsalted (sweet) butter, softened
1 egg, beaten
finely grated rind of 1 orange

For the filling
200g/7oz/¾ cup golden (light corn) syrup
45ml/3 tbsp light muscovado (brown) sugar
150g/5oz plain (semisweet) chocolate, chopped into small pieces
50g/2oz/¼ cup butter
3 eggs, beaten
5ml/1 tsp vanilla extract
175g/6oz/1½ cups shelled pecan nuts

1 Sift the flour into a bowl and stir in the sugar. Work in the butter evenly with your fingertips until combined.

2 Beat the egg and orange rind in a bowl, then stir into the mixture to make a firm dough. Add a little water if the mixture is too dry, and knead briefly.

3 Roll out the pastry on a lightly floured surface and use to line a deep, 20cm/8in loose-based flan tin (pan). Chill for about 30 minutes.

4 Preheat the oven to 180°C/350°F/Gas 4. Make the filling. Melt the syrup, sugar, chocolate and butter together in a small pan over a low heat.

5 Remove the pan from the heat and beat in the eggs and vanilla extract. Sprinkle the pecan nuts into the pastry case and carefully pour over the chocolate mixture.

6 Place the tin on a baking sheet and bake the pie for 50–60 minutes or until the filling is set.

7 Leave the pie in the tin for 10 minutes, then remove the tin's sides and transfer to a plate. Serve the pie on its own, or with a little single (light) cream.

Meringue Pie Energy 792kcal/3312kJ; Protein 11.4g; Carbohydrate 87g, of which sugars 56g; Fat 46.4g, of which saturates 23.5g; Cholesterol 241mg; Calcium 128mg; Fibre 2.6g; Sodium 248mg.
Pecan Pie Energy 843kcal/3524kJ; Protein 11.6g; Carbohydrate 90.8g, of which sugars 64.8g; Fat 50.8g, of which saturates 19.1g; Cholesterol 178mg; Calcium 112mg; Fibre 3g; Sodium 282mg.

Chocolate Soufflé Crêpes

These tasty pancakes hide a light soufflé filling inside.

Makes 12 crêpes
75g/3oz/³⁄₄ cup plain
  (all-purpose) flour
15ml/1 tbsp unsweetened
  cocoa powder
5ml/1 tsp caster (superfine) sugar
5ml/1 tsp ground cinnamon
pinch of salt
2 eggs
175ml/6fl oz/³⁄₄ cup milk
5ml/1 tsp vanilla extract
50g/2oz/4 tbsp unsalted (sweet)
  butter, melted
raspberries, pineapple and mint
  sprigs, to decorate

For the pineapple syrup
¹⁄₂ medium pineapple, peeled,
  cored and finely chopped
120ml/4fl oz/¹⁄₂ cup water
30ml/2 tbsp natural maple syrup
5ml/1 tsp cornflour (cornstarch)
¹⁄₂ cinnamon stick
30ml/2 tbsp rum

For the soufflé filling
250g/9oz dark (bittersweet)
  chocolate, chopped into
  small pieces
75ml/3fl oz/¹⁄₃ cup double
  (heavy) cream
3 eggs, separated
25g/1oz/2 tbsp caster
  (superfine) sugar

1 Place the ingredients for the syrup in a pan and simmer until thick. Discard the cinnamon. Cool, then chill.

2 Make the crêpes. Sift the flour, cocoa, sugar, cinnamon and salt together. Beat the eggs, milk and vanilla and stir into the mixture. Stir in half the butter and set aside for 1 hour. Butter a 20cm/8in crêpe pan and, when hot, pour in 45ml/3 tbsp of batter and cook over a medium heat for 1–2 minutes, then flip.

3 Make the filling. In a pan, stir the chocolate and cream until melted. In a bowl, beat the yolks with half the sugar until light. Add to the chocolate mixture. In another bowl, whisk the egg whites until soft peaks form. Whisk in the remaining sugar until stiff. Fold a little into the chocolate mixture, then fold in the rest.

4 Preheat the oven to 200°C/400°F/Gas 6. Spread a little filling on a crêpe. Fold in half over the mixture, then halve again. Place on a buttered baking sheet. When all crêpes are made, brush with butter and bake for 15–20 minutes, or until the filling has souffléd. Decorate with the fruits and mint and serve with the syrup.

Chocolate Chip Banana Pancakes

These tasty little pancake morsels will go down well with both children and adults alike.

Makes 16
2 ripe bananas
2 eggs
200ml/7fl oz/scant 1 cup milk
150g/5oz/1¹⁄₄ cups self-raising
  (self-rising) flour, sifted
25g/1oz/¹⁄₄ cup ground almonds
15g/¹⁄₂oz/1 tbsp caster
  (superfine) sugar
pinch of salt

15ml/1 tbsp plain (semisweet)
  chocolate chips
butter, for frying
50g/2oz/¹⁄₂ cup toasted flaked
  (sliced) almonds

For the topping
150ml/¹⁄₄ pint/²⁄₃ cup double
  (heavy) cream
15g/¹⁄₂oz/1 tbsp icing
  (confectioners') sugar

1 Mash the bananas in a bowl. Beat in the eggs and half the milk. Mix in the flour, ground almonds, sugar and salt. Add the remaining milk and the chocolate chips.

2 Stir the mixture well until it makes a thick batter. Heat a knob (pat) of butter in a non-stick frying pan. Spoon the pancake mixture into the pan in heaps, allowing room for them to spread. When the pancakes are lightly browned underneath and bubbling on top, flip them over to cook the other side. Slide on to a plate and keep hot. Make more pancakes in the same way.

3 Make the topping. Pour the cream into a bowl. Add the icing sugar to sweeten it slightly, and whip to soft peaks. Spoon the cream on to the pancakes and decorate with flaked almonds. Serve immediately.

> **Variations**
> • You could add sliced banana, tossed in lemon juice, to the topping to enhance the banana flavour of the pancakes.
> • Use yogurt as a low-fat alternative to cream, if you prefer.

Soufflé Crêpes Energy 273kcal/1143kJ; Protein 5.2g; Carbohydrate 27.7g, of which sugars 22.7g; Fat 16g, of which saturates 9g; Cholesterol 100mg; Calcium 60mg; Fibre 1.3g; Sodium 79mg.
Banana Pancakes Energy 192kcal/798kJ; Protein 3.4g; Carbohydrate 13.7g, of which sugars 6.3g; Fat 14.1g, of which saturates 7.1g; Cholesterol 51mg; Calcium 70mg; Fibre 0.8g; Sodium 89mg.

Chocolate and Orange Scotch Pancakes

Fabulous mini pancakes in a rich orange liqueur sauce.

Serves 4
115g/4oz/1 cup self-raising
  (self-rising) flour
30ml/2 tbsp unsweetened
  cocoa powder
2 eggs
50g/2oz plain (semisweet)
  chocolate, broken into squares
200ml/7fl oz/scant 1 cup milk
finely grated rind of 1 orange

30ml/2 tbsp orange juice
butter or oil, for frying
60ml/4 tbsp chocolate curls,
  to decorate

For the sauce
2 large oranges
25g/1oz/2 tbsp unsalted
  (sweet) butter
40g/1½oz/3 tbsp light
  muscovado (brown) sugar
250ml/8fl oz/1 cup crème fraîche
30ml/2 tbsp orange liqueur

1 Sift the flour and cocoa into a bowl and make a well in the centre. Add the eggs and beat well, gradually incorporating the surrounding dry ingredients to make a smooth batter.

2 Mix the chocolate and milk in a heavy pan. Heat gently until the chocolate has melted, then beat into the batter until smooth and bubbly. Stir in the grated orange rind and juice.

3 Heat a large frying pan. Grease with butter or oil. Drop large spoonfuls of batter on to the hot surface. Cook over a medium heat. When the pancakes are lightly browned underneath and bubbling on top, flip them over to cook the other side. Slide on to a plate and keep hot, then make more in the same way.

4 Make the sauce. Grate the rind of 1 of the oranges into a bowl and set aside. Peel both oranges, taking care to remove all the pith, then slice the flesh fairly thinly. Heat the butter and sugar in a wide, shallow pan over a low heat, stirring until the sugar dissolves. Stir in the crème fraîche and heat gently.

5 Add the pancakes and orange slices to the sauce, heat gently for 1–2 minutes, then spoon on the liqueur. Sprinkle with the reserved orange rind and chocolate curls.

Chocolate Crêpes with Plums and Port

The crêpes, filling and sauce for this recipe can be made in advance and assembled at the last minute.

Serves 6
50g/2oz plain (semisweet)
  chocolate, broken into squares
200ml/7fl oz/scant 1 cup milk
120ml/4fl oz/½ cup single
  (light) cream
30ml/2 tbsp unsweetened
  cocoa powder
115g/4oz/1 cup plain
  (all-purpose) flour
2 eggs

For the filling
500g/1¼lb red or golden plums
50g/2oz/¼ cup caster
  (superfine) sugar
30ml/2 tbsp water
30ml/2 tbsp port
oil, for frying
175g/6oz/¾ cup crème fraîche

For the sauce
150g/5oz plain (semisweet)
  chocolate, broken into squares
175ml/6fl oz/¾ cup double
  (heavy) cream
30ml/2 tbsp port

1 Place the chocolate and milk in a heavy pan. Heat gently until the chocolate dissolves. Pour into a blender or food processor and add the cream, cocoa, flour and eggs. Process until smooth. Turn into a jug (pitcher) and chill for 30 minutes.

2 Meanwhile, make the filling. Halve and stone (pit) the plums. Place in a pan with the sugar and water. Bring to the boil, then lower the heat, cover and simmer for about 10 minutes, or until the plums are tender. Stir in the port and simmer for a further 30 seconds. Remove from the heat and keep warm.

3 Heat a crêpe pan, grease with oil, then pour in enough batter to cover the base, swirling to coat it evenly. Cook until the crêpe is set, then flip to cook the other side. Slide on to baking parchment, then cook about ten more crêpes in the same way.

4 Make the sauce. Put the chocolate and cream in a pan. Heat gently, stirring until smooth. Add the port and stir for 1 minute. Divide the plums between the crêpes, add a spoonful of crème fraîche to each and roll up. Serve with the sauce spooned over.

Scotch Pancakes Energy 752kcal/3131kJ; Protein 12.1g; Carbohydrate 58.1g, of which sugars 35.5g; Fat 53.2g, of which saturates 27g; Cholesterol 185mg; Calcium 282mg; Fibre 3.9g; Sodium 304mg.
Chocolate Crêpes Energy 867kcal/3604kJ; Protein 10.6g; Carbohydrate 57.4g, of which sugars 41.7g; Fat 67g, of which saturates 36.7g; Cholesterol 184mg; Calcium 175mg; Fibre 3.4g; Sodium 115mg.

Baked Ravioli with Chocolate and Ricotta Filling

These sweet ravioli have a wonderful chocolate and ricotta cheese filling.

Serves 4
175g/6oz/¾ cup ricotta cheese
50g/2oz/¼ cup caster (superfine) sugar
4ml/¾ tsp vanilla extract
small egg, beaten, plus 1 egg yolk
15ml/1 tbsp mixed glacé (candied) fruits
25g/1oz dark (bittersweet) chocolate, finely chopped

For the pastry
225g/8oz/2 cups plain (all-purpose) flour
65g/2½oz/5 tbsp caster (superfine) sugar
90g/3½oz/7 tbsp butter, diced
1 egg
5ml/1 tsp finely grated chocolate

1 Make the pastry. Place the flour and sugar in a food processor and gradually process in the butter. Keep the motor running while you add the egg and lemon rind to make a dough. Transfer the dough to a sheet of clear film (plastic wrap), cover with another sheet of film and flatten into a round. Chill.

2 Press the ricotta through a strainer into a bowl. Stir in the sugar, vanilla, egg yolk, glacé fruits and dark chocolate.

3 Bring the pastry back to room temperature. Divide in half and roll each between clear film to make rectangles measuring 15 × 56cm/6 × 22in. Preheat the oven to 180°C/350°F/Gas 4.

4 Arrange heaped tablespoonfuls of the filling in two rows along one of the pastry strips, leaving a 2.5cm/1in margin around each strip. Brush the pastry between the mounds of filling with beaten egg. Place the second strip of pastry on top and press down between each mound of filling to seal.

5 Use a 6cm/2½in plain pastry (cookie) cutter to cut around each mound of filling to make small ravioli. Gently pinch each ravioli with your fingertips to seal the edges. Place on a greased baking sheet and bake for 15 minutes, or until they turn golden brown. Serve warm, sprinkled with chocolate.

Luxury Dark Chocolate Ravioli

Serve this special treat with cream and grated chocolate.

Serves 4
175g/6oz/1½ cups plain (all-purpose) flour
25g/1oz/¼ cup unsweetened cocoa powder
salt
30ml/2 tbsp icing (confectioners') sugar
2 large eggs, beaten
15ml/1 tbsp olive oil

For the filling
175g/6oz white chocolate, chopped
350g/12oz/1½ cups cream cheese
1 egg, plus 1 beaten egg to seal

1 Make the pasta. Sift the flour with the cocoa, salt and icing sugar on to a work surface. Make a well in the centre and pour in the eggs and oil. Mix together with your fingers. Knead until smooth. Cover and rest for at least 30 minutes.

2 For the filling, melt the white chocolate in a heatproof bowl placed over a pan of simmering water. Cool slightly. Beat the cream cheese in a bowl, then beat in the chocolate and egg. Spoon into a piping (pastry) bag fitted with a plain nozzle.

3 Cut the dough in half and wrap one portion in clear film (plastic wrap). Roll the pasta out thinly to a rectangle on a lightly floured surface, or use a pasta machine. Cover with a clean damp dish towel and repeat with the remaining pasta.

4 Pipe small mounds (about 5ml/1 tsp) of filling in rows, spacing them at 4cm/1½in intervals across one piece of the dough. Brush the dough between the mounds with beaten egg.

5 Using a rolling pin, lift the remaining sheet of pasta over the dough with the filling. Press down firmly between the pockets of filling, pushing out any trapped air. Cut the filled chocolate pasta into rounds with a ravioli cutter or sharp knife. Transfer to a floured dish towel. Leave for 1 hour to dry out.

6 Bring a frying pan of water to the boil and add the ravioli a few at a time, stirring to prevent sticking. Simmer gently for 3–5 minutes, remove with a perforated spoon and serve.

Baked Ravioli Energy 628kcal/2636kJ; Protein 13.1g; Carbohydrate 81.4g, of which sugars 38.5g; Fat 30.1g, of which saturates 17.7g; Cholesterol 162mg; Calcium 119mg; Fibre 2.1g; Sodium 186mg.
Luxury Ravioli Energy 894kcal/3722kJ; Protein 16.2g; Carbohydrate 68.1g, of which sugars 34g; Fat 63.9g, of which saturates 36.5g; Cholesterol 226mg; Calcium 299mg; Fibre 2.1g; Sodium 424mg.

Fruit Kebabs with Chocolate and Marshmallow Fondue

Children love these barbecued kebab and fondue treats – and with supervision they will happily help you to make them too.

Serves 4
2 bananas
2 kiwi fruit
12 strawberries
15ml/1 tbsp melted butter

15ml/1 tbsp lemon juice
5ml/1 tsp ground cinnamon

For the fondue
225g/8oz plain (semisweet)
  chocolate
100ml/4fl oz/½ cup single
  (light) cream
8 marshmallows
2.5ml/½ tsp vanilla
  extract

1 Peel the bananas and cut each into six thick chunks. Peel the kiwi fruit thinly and quarter them. Thread the bananas, kiwi fruit and strawberries on to four wooden or bamboo skewers.

2 Mix together the butter, lemon juice and cinnamon and brush the mixture over the fruits.

3 Prepare the fondue. Place the plain chocolate, cream and marshmallows in a small pan and heat gently on the barbecue, without boiling, stirring constantly until the mixture has melted and is smooth.

4 Cook the kebabs on the barbecue for 2–3 minutes, turning once, or until golden. Stir the vanilla extract into the fondue and serve it with the kebabs.

> **Cook's Tips**
> • These kebabs taste great straight from the barbecue but if the weather is bad they can easily be cooked under a hot grill (broiler) indoors.
> • Soak wooden or bamboo skewers in water for 10 minutes before threading with the fruit to avoid them being burned while on the barbecue.

Chocolate Fruit Fondue

This particular version of a sweet fondue makes a fun dessert that also looks extremely attractive and is appealing to all ages. Guests will enjoy skewering their favourite tropical fruits on to long forks, then dipping them into swirls of decadent hot chocolate fondue.

Serves 6–8
16 fresh strawberries
4 rings fresh pineapple,
  cut into wedges
2 small nectarines, stoned (pitted)
  and cut into wedges
1 kiwi fruit, halved and
  thickly sliced

small bunch of black
  seedless grapes
2 bananas, chopped
1 small eating apple, cored
  and cut into wedges
lemon juice, for brushing

For the fondue
225g/8oz plain (semisweet)
  chocolate
15g/½oz/1 tbsp butter
150ml/¼ pint/⅔ cup single
  (light) cream
45ml/3 tbsp Irish
  cream liqueur
15ml/1 tbsp chopped
  pistachio nuts

1 Arrange the fruit on a serving platter and brush the banana and apple pieces with a little lemon juice. Cover and chill.

2 Place the chocolate, butter, cream and liqueur in a bowl over a pan of simmering water. Stir until smooth.

3 Pour into a warmed serving bowl and sprinkle with the pistachio nuts.

4 To eat, guests skewer the fruits on to forks, then dip them into the hot sauce.

> **Variation**
> Other delicious dippers for this fondue include: cubes of sponge cake; sweet biscuits (cookies) such as amaretti; miniature marshmallows; ready-to-eat dried fruit such as apricots; crêpes torn into pieces; and popcorn.

Fruit Kebabs Energy 442kcal/1853kJ; Protein 5.1g; Carbohydrate 57.5g, of which sugars 53.7g; Fat 22.9g, of which saturates 13.9g; Cholesterol 27mg; Calcium 59mg; Fibre 2.7g; Sodium 42mg.
Fruit Fondue Energy 305kcal/1282kJ; Protein 3.6g; Carbohydrate 39.7g, of which sugars 38.9g; Fat 15.2g, of which saturates 8.1g; Cholesterol 16mg; Calcium 51mg; Fibre 2.7g; Sodium 37mg.

Prune Beignets in Chocolate Sauce

Combining soft-textured prunes with a crisp batter coating works brilliantly. The rich chocolate sauce is the perfect finishing touch.

Serves 4

75g/3oz/⅔ cup plain (all-purpose) flour
45ml/3 tbsp ground almonds
45ml/3 tbsp oil or melted butter
1 egg white
60ml/4 tbsp water

oil, for deep frying
175g/6oz/1 cup ready-to-eat pitted prunes
45ml/3 tbsp vanilla sugar
15ml/1 tbsp unsweetened cocoa powder

For the sauce

200g/7oz milk chocolate, chopped into small pieces
120ml/4fl oz/½ cup crème fraîche
30ml/2 tbsp Armagnac or brandy

1 Make the sauce. Melt the chocolate in a bowl over a pan of hot water. Remove from the heat, stir in the crème fraîche until smooth, then add the Armagnac or brandy. Replace the bowl over the water, off the heat, so that the sauce stays warm.

2 Beat the flour, almonds, oil or butter and egg white in a bowl, then beat in enough of the water to make a thick batter.

3 Heat the oil for deep frying to 180°C/350°F or until a cube of dried bread browns in 30–45 seconds. Dip the prunes into the batter and fry a few at a time until the beignets rise to the surface and are golden brown. Remove each batch of beignets with a slotted spoon, drain on kitchen paper and keep hot.

4 Mix the vanilla sugar and cocoa in a bowl or stout paper bag, add the drained beignets and toss well to coat. Serve in individual bowls, with the chocolate sauce poured over the top.

Cook's Tip

Vanilla sugar is available from good food stores, but it's easy to make your own: simply store a vanilla pod in a jar of sugar for a few weeks until the sugar has taken on the vanilla flavour.

Pears in Chocolate Fudge Blankets

This dessert consists of warm poached pears coated in a rich chocolate fudge sauce – who could resist such a treat?

Serves 6

6 ripe eating pears
30ml/2 tbsp fresh lemon juice
75g/3oz/scant ½ cup caster (superfine) sugar
300ml/½ pint/1¼ cups water
1 cinnamon stick

For the sauce

200ml/7fl oz/scant 1 cup double (heavy) cream
150g/5oz/scant 1 cup light muscovado (brown) sugar
25g/1oz/2 tbsp unsalted (sweet) butter
60ml/4 tbsp golden (light corn) syrup
120ml/4fl oz/½ cup milk
200g/7oz plain (semisweet) chocolate, broken into squares

1 Peel the pears thinly, leaving the stalks on. Scoop out the cores from the base. Brush the cut surfaces with lemon juice to prevent browning.

2 Place the sugar and water in a large pan. Heat gently until the sugar dissolves. Add the pears and cinnamon stick with any remaining lemon juice, and, if necessary, a little more water, so that the pears are almost covered.

3 Bring to the boil, then lower the heat, cover the pan and simmer the pears gently for 15–20 minutes.

4 Meanwhile, make the sauce. Place the cream, sugar, butter, golden syrup and milk in a heavy pan. Heat gently until the sugar has dissolved and the butter and syrup have melted, then bring to the boil. Boil, stirring constantly, for about 5 minutes or until thick and smooth.

5 Remove the pan from the heat and stir in the chocolate, a few squares at a time, stirring until it has all melted.

6 Using a slotted spoon, transfer the poached pears to a dish. Keep hot. Boil the syrup rapidly to reduce to 45–60ml/3–4 tbsp. Remove the cinnamon stick and gently stir the syrup into the chocolate sauce. Serve the pears with the sauce spooned over.

Prune Beignets Energy 727kcal/3039kJ; Protein 11.3g; Carbohydrate 71.7g, of which sugars 56.5g; Fat 44.1g, of which saturates 24.2g; Cholesterol 69mg; Calcium 209mg; Fibre 4.8g; Sodium 176mg.
Pears in Blankets Energy 613kcal/2570kJ; Protein 3.6g; Carbohydrate 84.8g, of which sugars 84.5g; Fat 31.2g, of which saturates 19.1g; Cholesterol 58mg; Calcium 90mg; Fibre 4.1g; Sodium 77mg.

Bitter Chocolate Fondue with Rosemary and Vanilla Poached Pears

Vanilla-scented poached pears and scoops of ice cream are dipped into a rich chocolate fondue for this splendid dessert. The sprigs of rosemary add a herby flavour.

Serves 4–6
200g/7oz dark (bittersweet) chocolate, broken into pieces
75ml/2½fl oz/⅓ cup strong black coffee
75g/3oz/scant ⅓ cup soft light brown sugar

120ml/4fl oz/½ cup double (heavy) cream
small, firm scoops of vanilla ice cream, to serve

For the poached pears
juice of 1 lemon
90g/3½oz/½ cup vanilla caster (superfine) sugar
1–2 fresh rosemary sprigs
12–18 small pears, or 4–6 large pears

I To poach the pears, put the lemon juice, sugar, rosemary sprigs and 300ml/½ pint/1¼ cups water in a pan large enough to accommodate the pears all in one layer. Bring to the boil, stirring until the sugar dissolves in the water.

2 Peel the pears, and halve the large ones, if using, but leave the stalks intact. Add to the hot syrup and spoon over to cover.

3 Cook for 5–10 minutes, depending on size and ripeness, spooning the syrup over them and turning frequently, until they are just tender. Transfer to a serving plate, then remove the rosemary sprigs from the syrup. Stir about 15–30ml/1–2 tbsp of the rosemary leaves into the syrup and then leave to cool.

4 Put the chocolate in a heatproof bowl over a pan of barely simmering water. Add the coffee and sugar and heat, without stirring, until the chocolate is melted. Stir in the cream and heat gently. Transfer the fondue to a fondue pot and place on a burner set at a low heat at the table.

5 Serve the pears and syrup together with the vanilla ice cream to dip into the hot chocolate fondue.

Poached Pears with Chocolate

This is a classic combination of poached dessert pears served with a hot chocolate sauce. As a variation, try poaching the pears with white or red wine or a flavoured liqueur.

Serves 4
4 firm dessert pears, peeled
250g/9oz/1¼ cups caster (superfine) sugar
600ml/1 pint/2½ cups water

500ml/17fl oz/2¼ cups vanilla ice cream

For the chocolate sauce
250g/9oz good quality dark (bittersweet) chocolate (minimum 70 per cent cocoa solids)
40g/1½oz unsalted (sweet) butter
5ml/1 tsp vanilla extract
75ml/5 tbsp double (heavy) cream

I Cut the pears in half lengthways and remove the core. Place the sugar and water in a large pan and gently heat until the sugar has dissolved completely.

2 Add the pear halves to the pan, then simmer for 20 minutes, or until the pears are tender but not falling apart. Lift out of the sugar syrup with a slotted spoon and leave to cool.

3 To make the chocolate sauce, break the chocolate into small pieces and put into a pan. Add the butter and 30ml/2 tbsp water. Heat gently over a low heat, without stirring, until the chocolate has melted.

4 Add the vanilla extract and cream, and mix gently to combine. Place a scoop of ice cream into each of four glasses.

5 Add two cooled pear halves to each and pour over the hot chocolate sauce. Serve immediately.

> **Variation**
> Like apples, there are two types of pear: dessert varieties and those that need cooking. Ensure that you use firm ones, as they will hold their shape when poached, rather than turning to mush.

Poached Pears Energy 1014kcal/4255kJ; Protein 8.8g; Carbohydrate 145.1g, of which sugars 143.2g; Fat 46.7g, of which saturates 29.6g; Cholesterol 81mg; Calcium 206mg; Fibre 4.9g; Sodium 152mg.
Bitter Fondue Energy 464kcal/1949kJ; Protein 2.8g; Carbohydrate 71.9g, of which sugars 71.6g; Fat 20.3g, of which saturates 12.3g; Cholesterol 29mg; Calcium 59mg; Fibre 5.6g; Sodium 15mg.

Vanilla Poached Pears with Choc-dusted Cappuccino Sauce

Served with a bubbly espresso sauce and finished with a dusting of chocolate, these vanilla-scented pears make a light, elegant dessert.

Serves 6
1 vanilla pod
150g/5oz/³⁄₄ cup sugar
400ml/14fl oz/1²⁄₃ cups water
6 slightly under-ripe pears
juice of ¹⁄₂ lemon

For the cappuccino sauce
3 egg yolks
25g/1oz/2 tbsp caster
  (superfine) sugar
50ml/2fl oz/¹⁄₄ cup brewed
  espresso coffee
50ml/2fl oz/¹⁄₄ cup single
  (light) cream
10ml/2 tsp drinking chocolate
2.5ml/¹⁄₂ tsp ground cinnamon

1 Split the vanilla pod lengthways and scrape out the black seeds into a large pan. Add the split pod, sugar and water. Heat gently until the sugar has completely dissolved.

2 Meanwhile, peel and halve the pears, then rub with lemon juice. Scoop out the cores with a melon baller or teaspoon. Add the pears to the syrup and pour in extra water to cover.

3 Cut out a circle of baking parchment and cover the top of the pears. Bring to a light boil, cover the pan with a lid and simmer for 15 minutes, or until tender. Transfer the pears to a serving bowl. Bring the syrup to a rapid boil and cook for 15 minutes, or until reduced by half.

4 Strain the syrup over the pears and leave to cool. Cover with clear film (plastic wrap) and chill for several hours. Allow to come back to room temperature before serving.

5 Make the sauce. Whisk the egg yolks, sugar, coffee and cream in a heatproof bowl over a pan of simmering water until thick and frothy. Remove from the heat and whisk for 2–3 minutes.

6 Arrange the pears on plates and pour sauce over each. Mix the drinking chocolate and cinnamon and dust over the sauce.

Pear Tartlets with Chocolate Sauce

Pears go perfectly with puffy golden pastry, complemented by a rich, warm chocolate sauce.

Serves 6
3 firm pears, peeled
450ml/³⁄₄ pint/scant 2 cups water
strip of thinly pared orange rind
1 vanilla pod (bean)
1 bay leaf
50g/2oz/¹⁄₄ cup sugar
350g/12oz puff pastry

40g/1¹⁄₂oz/¹⁄₃ cup unsweetened
  cocoa powder
75ml/5 tbsp double
  (heavy) cream
15g/¹⁄₂oz/1 tbsp butter, softened
15ml/1 tbsp soft light
  brown sugar
25g/1oz/¹⁄₄ cup walnuts,
  chopped
1 egg, beaten
15g/¹⁄₂oz/1 tbsp caster
  (superfine) sugar

1 Cut the pears in half and scoop out just the cores. Put the water in a pan with the orange rind, vanilla pod, bay leaf and sugar. Bring to the boil, stirring well. Add the pears and water to cover. Cover and cook gently for 15 minutes, or until just tender. Remove the pears and set aside to cool. Reserve the syrup.

2 Meanwhile, roll out the pastry and cut out six pear shapes, slightly larger than the pear halves. Place the pastry shapes on greased baking sheets and chill for 30 minutes.

3 Remove the rind, vanilla pod and bay leaf from the syrup, then return the syrup to the heat and boil for 10 minutes. Blend the cocoa powder with 60ml/4 tbsp cold water in a separate pan.

4 Stir a large spoonful of the syrup into the cocoa paste, then whisk the paste into the syrup. Boil until reduced to about 150ml/¹⁄₄ pint/²⁄₃ cup. Remove the pan from the heat and add the cream to the syrup. Stir well.

5 Preheat the oven to 200°C/400°F/Gas 6. Mix together the butter, sugar and walnuts. and spoon a little of the mixture into each cavity. Brush the pastries with beaten egg. Put a pear half, filled side down, in the centre of each pastry and sprinkle with sugar. Bake for 12 minutes, or until the pastry has puffed up and is golden brown. Drizzle with the warm chocolate sauce.

Poached Pears Energy 228kcal/963kJ; Protein 2.4g; Carbohydrate 47g, of which sugars 47g; Fat 4.6g, of which saturates 1.9g; Cholesterol 105mg; Calcium 52mg; Fibre 3.3g; Sodium 17mg.
Pear Tartlets Energy 443kcal/1847kJ; Protein 6.7g; Carbohydrate 44.2g, of which sugars 22.5g; Fat 28.4g, of which saturates 6.8g; Cholesterol 54mg; Calcium 73mg; Fibre 2.6g; Sodium 277mg.

Chocolate Orange Fondue

This liqueur fondue goes with any fresh fruits.

Serves 4–6
225g/8oz plain (semisweet) chocolate, chopped into pieces
300ml/½ pint/1¼ cups double (heavy) cream

30ml/2 tbsp Grand Marnier
25g/1oz/2 tbsp butter, diced
cherries, strawberries, sliced bananas, mandarin segments and cubes of sponge cake, for dipping

1 Combine the chocolate, cream and Grand Marnier in a fondue pan or small pan. Heat until melted, stirring frequently. Stir the butter into the fondue until melted. Place the fondue pot or pan over a lighted spirit burner.

2 Arrange the fruit and cake on a plate. Guests spear the items of their choice on fondue forks and swirl them in the dip until coated. Anyone who loses his or her dipper pays a forfeit.

Hot Chocolate Zabaglione

This is a delicious twist on the classic Italian dessert.

Serves 6
6 egg yolks
150g/5oz/⅔ cup caster (superfine) sugar

45ml/3 tbsp unsweetened cocoa powder
200ml/7fl oz/scant 1 cup Marsala
unsweetened cocoa powder or icing (confectioners') sugar, for dusting

1 Whisk the egg yolks and sugar in a heatproof bowl over a pan of simmering until pale and all the sugar has dissolved.

2 Add the cocoa and Marsala, then place the bowl back over the simmering water. Whisk until the mixture is thick and foamy.

3 Pour the mixture into tall heatproof glasses, dust with cocoa powder or sugar and serve with chocolate cinnamon tuiles or amaretti biscuits.

Peachy Chocolate Bake

A sublime combination of peaches and chocolate, this lightweight baked dessert is guaranteed to be popular with everyone – and it has the added bonus of being easy to make. For smart presentation, drizzle cream or yogurt over each serving and sprinkle lightly with chocolate powder.

Serves 6
200g/7oz dark (bittersweet) chocolate, chopped into pieces
115g/4oz/½ cup unsalted (sweet) butter, plus extra for greasing
4 eggs, separated
115g/4oz/generous ½ cup caster (superfine) sugar
425g/15oz can peach slices, drained
whipped cream or Greek (US strained plain) yogurt, to serve

1 Preheat the oven to 160°C/325°F/Gas 3. Butter a wide ovenproof dish. Melt the chocolate with the butter in a heatproof bowl over barely simmering water, then remove from the heat.

2 Whisk the egg yolks with the sugar until thick and pale. In a clean, grease-free bowl, whisk the whites until stiff.

3 Beat the melted chocolate into the egg yolk mixture. Stir in a large spoonful of the egg whites, then gently fold in the remaining whites.

4 Fold the peach slices into the mixture, then turn into the prepared dish. Bake for 35–40 minutes or until risen and just firm. Serve hot with cream or yogurt.

Variations
• Pears also taste delicious with chocolate, and canned pears can be used very successfully in this recipe, instead of the canned peaches.
• During the summer months, try using very ripe fresh peaches or a mix of soft berries instead of the canned fruit.

Fondue Energy 470kcal/1949kJ; Protein 2.7g; Carbohydrate 24.7g, of which sugars 24.4g; Fat 40.8g, of which saturates 25.2g; Cholesterol 80mg; Calcium 38mg; Fibre 0.9g; Sodium 39mg.
Zabaglione Energy 235kcal/989kJ; Protein 4.5g; Carbohydrate 31g, of which sugars 30.1g; Fat 7.1g, of which saturates 2.5g; Cholesterol 202mg; Calcium 48mg; Fibre 0.9g; Sodium 83mg.
Peachy Bake Energy 465kcal/1942kJ; Protein 6.5g; Carbohydrate 48.2g, of which sugars 47.9g; Fat 28.8g, of which saturates 16.6g; Cholesterol 170mg; Calcium 47mg; Fibre 1.4g; Sodium 175mg.

Chocolate Amaretti Peaches

A delicious dish of peaches stuffed with chocolate. This is a simple dessert but nonetheless one that is simply bursting with Italian style and flavour.

Serves 4
115g/4oz amaretti, crushed
50g/2oz plain (semisweet)
  chocolate, chopped
finely grated rind of ½ orange
15ml/1 tbsp clear honey
1.5ml/¼ tsp ground cinnamon
1 egg white, lightly beaten
4 firm ripe peaches
150ml/¼ pint/⅔ cup
  white wine
15g/½oz/1 tbsp caster
  (superfine) sugar
whipped cream, to serve

1 Preheat the oven to 190°C/375°F/Gas 5. Mix together the crushed amaretti, chopped chocolate, orange rind, honey and cinnamon in a bowl. Add the beaten egg white and mix to bind the mixture.

2 Halve the peaches, remove the stones (pits) and fill the cavities with the chocolate mixture, mounding it up slightly.

3 Arrange the stuffed peaches in a lightly buttered, shallow ovenproof dish that will just hold the peaches comfortably in a single layer.

4 Mix the wine and sugar in a jug (pitcher). Pour the wine mixture around the peaches.

5 Bake the peaches for 30–40 minutes, or until they are tender when tested with a metal skewer and the filling has turned a golden colour.

6 Serve immediately with a little cooking juice spooned over. Accompany with cream.

> **Cook's Tip**
> To stone (pit) peaches, halve them and twist the two halves apart, then lever out the stone (pit) with the point of a knife.

Chocolate Risotto

If you've never tasted a sweet risotto, there's a treat in store. Chocolate risotto is delectable, and children of all ages love it.

Serves 4 to 6
175g/6oz/scant 1 cup risotto rice
600ml/1 pint/2½ cups milk
75g/3oz plain (semisweet)
  chocolate, broken into pieces
25g/1oz/2 tbsp butter
about 50g/2oz/¼ cup caster
  (superfine) sugar
pinch of ground cinnamon
60ml/4 tbsp double
  (heavy) cream
fresh raspberries and chocolate
  curls, to decorate
chocolate sauce, to serve

1 Put the rice in a heavy non-stick pan. Pour in the milk and bring to the boil over a low to medium heat. Reduce the heat to the lowest setting and simmer the rice very gently for about 20 minutes, stirring occasionally, until the rice is very soft.

2 Add the chocolate pieces, butter and sugar to the pan. Cook, stirring all the time over a very gentle heat for 1–2 minutes, until the chocolate has melted.

3 Remove the pan from the heat and add the ground cinnamon and the double cream to the pan. Mix thoroughly until well combined. Cover the pan and leave to stand for a few minutes.

4 Spoon the risotto into individual dishes or dessert plates, and decorate with fresh raspberries and chocolate curls. Serve with chocolate sauce.

> **Cook's Tips**
> • Ensure that you use the plump Italian risotto rice for this recipe, otherwise it will not work as well. Look out for varieties called arborio or carnaroli.
> • Stirring the rice frequently helps it to release the starch contained inside the grains, which gives this dish its delicious creamy texture.

Amaretti Peaches Energy 282kcal/1190kJ; Protein 4.1g; Carbohydrate 47g, of which sugars 34.4g; Fat 7.4g, of which saturates 3.8g; Cholesterol 1mg; Calcium 56mg; Fibre 2.4g; Sodium 117mg.
Risotto Energy 348kcal/1451kJ; Protein 6.3g; Carbohydrate 44.6g, of which sugars 21.2g; Fat 16.3g, of which saturates 10.1g; Cholesterol 37mg; Calcium 138mg; Fibre 0.3g; Sodium 72mg.

Double Chocolate Snowball

This is an ideal dish to make as a party dessert because it can be prepared ahead and decorated on the day.

Serves 12–14

350g/12oz plain (semisweet) chocolate, chopped
285g/10½oz/1½ cups caster (superfine) sugar
275g/10oz/1¼ cups unsalted (sweet) butter, diced

8 eggs
50ml/2fl oz/¼ cup orange-flavoured liqueur (optional)

For the chocolate cream
200g/7oz good-quality white chocolate, broken into pieces
475ml/16fl oz/2 cups double (heavy) or whipping cream
30ml/2 tbsp orange-flavoured liqueur (optional)

1 Preheat the oven to 180°C/350°F/Gas 4. Line a 1.75 litre/3 pint/7½ cup round ovenproof bowl with foil, smoothing the sides. In a bowl over a pan of simmering water, melt the plain chocolate. Add the sugar and stir until it dissolves. Strain into a medium bowl. Using an electric mixer at low speed, beat in the butter, then the eggs, one at a time. Stir in the liqueur, if using, and pour into the lined bowl. Tap to release large air bubbles.

2 Bake for 1¼–1½ hours until the surface is firm and slightly risen, but cracked. The centre will set on cooling. Transfer to a rack to cool. Cover with a plate, then cover completely with clear film (plastic wrap) and chill overnight. To unmould, remove the plate and film and invert the mould on to a plate; shake firmly to release. Peel off foil. Cover until ready to decorate.

3 Work the white chocolate in a food processor to form fine crumbs. In a small pan, heat 120ml/4fl oz/½ cup of the cream until just beginning to simmer. With the processor running, pour in the cream until the chocolate has melted. Strain into a bowl and cool to room temperature, stirring occasionally.

4 Beat the remaining cream until soft peaks form, add the liqueur, if using, and beat for 30 seconds or until the cream just holds its shape. Fold a spoonful of cream into the chocolate then fold in the remaining cream. Spoon into an icing (pastry) bag fitted with a star tip and pipe rosettes over the surface.

Chocolate Amaretto Marquise

This wickedly rich chocolate dessert is truly extravagant.

Serves 10–12
15ml/1 tbsp flavourless vegetable oil, such as groundnut (peanut) or sunflower
75g/3oz/7–8 amaretti, finely crushed
25g/1oz/¼ cup unblanched almonds, toasted and finely chopped
450g/1lb fine-quality plain or dark (bittersweet) chocolate, chopped into small pieces

75ml/5 tbsp Amaretto Disaronno liqueur
75ml/5 tbsp golden (light corn) syrup
475ml/16fl oz/2 cups double (heavy) cream
unsweetened cocoa powder, for dusting

For the Amaretto cream
350ml/12fl oz/1½ cups whipping cream or double (heavy) cream
30–45ml/2–3 tbsp Amaretto Disaronno liqueur

1 Lightly oil a 23cm/9in heart-shaped or springform cake tin (pan). Line the bottom with baking parchment, then oil the paper. In a small bowl, combine the crushed amaretti and the chopped almonds. Sprinkle evenly on to the base of the tin.

2 Place the chocolate, Amaretto liqueur and golden syrup in a medium pan over a very low heat. Stir frequently until the chocolate has melted and the mixture is smooth. Remove from the heat and allow it to cool for about 6–8 minutes, until the mixture feels just warm to the touch.

3 Whip the cream until it just begins to hold its shape. Stir a large spoonful into the chocolate mixture, to lighten it, then quickly add the remaining cream and gently fold in. Pour into the prepared tin, on top of the amaretti mixture. Level the surface. Cover the tin with clear film (plastic wrap) and chill overnight.

4 To unmould, run a slightly warmed, thin-bladed sharp knife around the edge of the dessert, then unmould. Carefully peel off the paper, replacing any crust that sticks to it, and dust with cocoa. In a bowl, whip the cream and Amaretto liqueur to soft peaks. Serve separately.

Snowball Energy 640kcal/2661kJ; Protein 6.7g; Carbohydrate 46.2g, of which sugars 46g; Fat 49g, of which saturates 29.3g; Cholesterol 199mg; Calcium 94mg; Fibre 0.6g; Sodium 185mg.
Marquise Energy 589kcal/2444kJ; Protein 3.9g; Carbohydrate 38.2g, of which sugars 35.1g; Fat 46.4g, of which saturates 27.5g; Cholesterol 87mg; Calcium 63mg; Fibre 1.2g; Sodium 57mg.

Chilled Chocolate Zucotto Sponge

An Italian-style dessert with a rich ricotta, fruit, chocolate and nut filling, zucotto is encased in a moist, chocolate and liqueur-flavoured sponge.

Serves 8

3 eggs
75g/3oz/6 tbsp caster (superfine) sugar
75g/3oz/²⁄₃ cup plain (all-purpose) flour
25g/1oz/¹⁄₄ cup unsweetened cocoa powder
90ml/6 tbsp Kirsch
250g/9oz/generous 1 cup ricotta cheese

50g/2oz/¹⁄₂ cup icing (confectioners') sugar
50g/2oz plain (semisweet) chocolate, finely chopped
50g/2oz/¹⁄₂ cup blanched almonds, chopped and toasted
75g/3oz/scant ¹⁄₂ cup natural glacé (candied) cherries, quartered
2 pieces preserved stem ginger, finely chopped
150ml/¹⁄₄ pint/²⁄₃ cup double (heavy) cream
unsweetened cocoa powder, for dusting

1 Preheat the oven to 180°C/350°F/Gas 4. Grease and line a 23cm/9in cake tin (pan). Whisk the eggs and sugar in a heatproof bowl over a pan of simmering water until the whisk leaves a trail. Remove the bowl from the heat and continue to whisk the mixture for 2 minutes.

2 Sift the flour and cocoa into the bowl and fold it in with a large metal spoon. Spoon the mixture into the prepared tin and bake for about 20 minutes until just firm. Leave to cool.

3 Cut the cake horizontally into three layers. Set aside 30ml/ 2 tbsp of the Kirsch. Drizzle the remaining Kirsch over the layers.

4 Beat the ricotta cheese in a bowl until softened, then beat in the icing sugar, chopped chocolate, toasted almonds, cherries, stem ginger and reserved Kirsch.

5 Pour the cream into a separate bowl and whip it lightly. Using a large metal spoon, fold the cream into the ricotta mixture. Chill. Cut a 20cm/8in circle from one sponge layer, using a plate as a guide, and set it aside.

6 Use the remaining sponge to make the case for the zucotto. Cut the cake to fit the bottom of a 2.8–3.4 litre/5–6 pint/ 12½–15 cup freezerproof mixing bowl lined with clear film (plastic wrap). Cut more sponge for the sides of the bowl, fitting the pieces together and taking them about one-third of the way up.

7 Spoon the ricotta filling into the bowl up to the height of the sponge, and level the surface.

8 Fit the reserved circle of sponge on top of the filling. Trim off the excess sponge around the edges. Cover the bowl and freeze overnight.

9 Transfer the zucotto to the refrigerator 45 minutes before serving, so that the filling softens slightly. Invert it on to a serving plate and peel away the clear film. Dust with cocoa powder and serve immediately in slices.

Fruity Chocolate Ricotta Creams

Ricotta is an Italian soft cheese with a smooth texture and a mild, slightly sweet flavour. Served here with candied fruit peel and delicious chocolate, it is quite irresistible.

Serves 4

350g/12oz/1½ cups ricotta cheese
30–45ml/2–3 tbsp Cointreau or other orange liqueur
10ml/2 tsp grated lemon rind

30ml/2 tbsp icing (confectioners') sugar
150ml/¹⁄₄ pint/²⁄₃ cup double (heavy) cream
150g/5oz/scant 1 cup candied peel, such as orange, lemon and grapefruit, finely chopped
50g/2oz plain (semisweet) chocolate, finely chopped
chocolate curls, to decorate
amaretti biscuits (cookies), to serve (optional)

1 Using the back of a wooden spoon, push the ricotta through a fine sieve (strainer) into a large bowl.

2 Add the liqueur, lemon rind and icing sugar to the ricotta and beat well until the mixture is light and smooth.

3 Whip the cream in a large bowl until it forms soft peaks.

4 Gently fold the cream into the ricotta mixture with the candied peel and chopped chocolate.

5 Spoon the mixture into four individual glass dishes and chill for about 1 hour. Decorate the ricotta creams with chocolate curls and serve with amaretti, if you like.

Cook's Tips

• For this uncooked, Italian-style dessert, you need to buy candied fruits in large pieces from a good delicatessen – tubs of chopped candied peel are too tough to eat raw, and should only be used in baking.
• The desserts can also be topped with a sprinkling of raspberries to add an extra fruitiness.

Zucotto Sponge Energy 391kcal/1631kJ; Protein 8.7g; Carbohydrate 33.8g, of which sugars 26.1g; Fat 22.7g, of which saturates 11.4g; Cholesterol 111mg; Calcium 66mg; Fibre 1.4g; Sodium 64mg.
Ricotta Creams Energy 546kcal/2276kJ; Protein 9.4g; Carbohydrate 43.1g, of which sugars 43g; Fat 36.7g, of which saturates 22.6g; Cholesterol 89mg; Calcium 75mg; Fibre 2.1g; Sodium 115mg.

Rice Pudding with Chocolate Sauce

Cook a rice pudding on top of the stove for a light creamy texture, which is particularly good served cold and topped with chocolate sauce and fruit.

5ml/1 tsp vanilla extract
2.5ml/½ tsp ground cinnamon
40g/1½oz sugar

To serve
strawberries, raspberries or
   blueberries
1 quantity Quick Chocolate Sauce
flaked toasted almonds

Serves 4
50g/2oz/⅓ cup pudding rice
600ml/1 pint/2½ cups milk

1 Put the rice, milk, vanilla extract, cinnamon and sugar into a medium-sized pan. Bring to the boil, stirring constantly, and then turn down the heat to a gentle simmer.

2 Cook the rice for about 30–40 minutes, stirring occasionally. You may need to add extra milk if the liquid in the pan reduces down too quickly.

3 Test the grains to make sure they are soft, then remove the pan from the heat and set aside to allow the rice to cool, stirring it occasionally. When the rice has gone cold, chill it in the refrigerator.

4 Just before serving, stir the rice and spoon into four sundae dishes. Top with fruits, chocolate sauce and almonds.

Variations
• Milk puddings are at last enjoying something of a comeback in popularity. Instead of simple pudding rice try using a Thai fragrant or jasmine rice for a delicious natural flavour. For a firmer texture, an Italian risotto rice, such as arborio, with its high starch content makes a good pudding, too.
• There's no need to use a lot of full-fat (whole) milk or cream either. A pudding made with semi-skimmed (low-fat) milk or even fat-free milk can be just as nice and is much more healthy for you.

Tiramisu in Chocolate Cups

Here is an Italian favourite served in an elegant new way, in chocolate cups.

15ml/1 tbsp unsweetened cocoa powder, plus extra for dusting
30ml/2 tbsp coffee liqueur
16 amaretti biscuits (cookies)

Serves 6
1 egg yolk
30ml/2 tbsp caster
   (superfine) sugar
2.5ml/½ tsp vanilla extract
250g/9oz/generous 1 cup
   mascarpone cheese
120ml/4fl oz/½ cup strong
   black coffee

For the chocolate cups
175g/6oz plain (semisweet)
   chocolate, chopped
25g/1oz/2 tbsp unsalted
   (sweet) butter

1 Make the chocolate cups. Cut out six 15cm/6in rounds of baking parchment. Melt the chocolate with the butter in a heatproof bowl over a pan of simmering water. Stir until smooth, then spread a spoonful of the chocolate mixture over each circle, to within 2cm/¾in of the edge.

2 Carefully lift each paper round and drape it over an upturned teacup or ramekin so that the edges curve into frills. Leave until completely set, then carefully peel away the paper.

3 Make the filling. Using a hand-held electric mixer, beat the egg yolk and sugar in a bowl until smooth, then stir in the vanilla extract. Soften the mascarpone if necessary, then stir it into the egg yolk mixture. Beat until smooth.

4 In a separate bowl, mix the coffee, cocoa and liqueur. Break up the amaretti roughly, then stir them into the mixture.

5 Place the chocolate cups on individual plates. Divide half the amaretti mixture among them, then spoon over half the mascarpone mixture.

6 Spoon over the remaining amaretti mixture (including any free liquid), top with the rest of the mascarpone mixture and dust lightly with cocoa. Chill for 30 minutes before serving.

Tiramisu Energy 351kcal/1469kJ; Protein 6.9g; Carbohydrate 34.5g, of which sugars 29.6g; Fat 20.4g, of which saturates 12.1g; Cholesterol 62mg; Calcium 33mg; Fibre 1.2g; Sodium 86mg.
Rice Pudding Energy 185kcal/782kJ; Protein 6.9g; Carbohydrate 34.8g, of which sugars 24.8g; Fat 2.7g, of which saturates 1.6g; Cholesterol 9mg; Calcium 204mg; Fibre 1.1g; Sodium 71mg.

Chocolate Vanilla Timbales

These elegantly turned-out timbales look particularly impressive if they are set in fluted moulds. It's worth investing in some.

Serves 6

350ml/12fl oz/1½ cups semi-skimmed (low-fat) milk
30ml/2 tbsp unsweetened cocoa powder, plus extra for dusting
2 eggs
10ml/2 tsp vanilla extract
45ml/3 tbsp caster (superfine) sugar
15ml/1 tbsp/1 sachet powdered gelatine
45ml/3 tbsp hot water
fresh mint sprigs, to decorate (optional)

For the sauce
115g/4oz/½ cup light Greek (US strained plain) yogurt
25ml/1½ tbsp vanilla extract

1 Place the milk and cocoa in a pan and stir until the milk is boiling. Separate the eggs and beat the egg yolks with the vanilla extract and sugar in a bowl, until the mixture is pale and smooth. Gradually pour in the chocolate milk, beating well.

2 Return the mixture to the pan and stir constantly over a gentle heat, without boiling, until it is slightly thickened and smooth in consistency.

3 Remove the pan from the heat. Pour the gelatine into the hot water and stir until it is completely dissolved, then quickly stir it into the milk mixture. Put this mixture aside and allow it to cool until almost setting.

4 Whisk the egg whites until they hold soft peaks. Fold the egg whites quickly into the milk mixture. Spoon the timbale mixture into six individual moulds. Chill them until set.

5 To serve, run a knife around the edge, dip the moulds quickly into hot water and turn out on to serving plates. For the sauce, stir together the yogurt and vanilla extract and spoon on to the plates next to the timbales. Lightly dust with cocoa and decorate with mint sprigs, if using.

Chocolate and Chestnut Pots

The chestnut purée adds substance and texture to these mousses. Crisp, delicate cookies, such as langues-de-chat, provide a good foil to the richness.

Serves 6

250g/9oz plain (semisweet) chocolate
60ml/4 tbsp Madeira
25g/1oz/2 tbsp butter, diced
2 eggs, separated
225g/8oz/scant 1 cup unsweetened chestnut purée
crème fraîche or whipped double (heavy) cream, to decorate

1 Make a few chocolate curls for decoration by rubbing a grater along the length of the bar of chocolate. Break the rest of the chocolate into squares and melt it in a pan with the Madeira over a gentle heat. Remove from the heat and add the butter, a few pieces at a time, stirring until melted and smooth.

2 Beat the egg yolks quickly into the mixture, then beat in the chestnut purée, mixing until smooth.

3 Whisk the egg whites in a clean, grease-free bowl until stiff. Stir about 15ml/1 tbsp of the whites into the chestnut mixture to lighten it, then fold in the rest smoothly and evenly.

4 Spoon the mixture into six small ramekin dishes and chill in the refrigerator until set.

5 Remove the pots from the refrigerator about 30 minutes before serving to allow the flavours to 'ripen'. Serve the pots topped with a generous spoonful of crème fraîche or whipped cream and decorated with chocolate curls.

> **Cook's Tips**
> • If Madeira is not available, use brandy or rum instead.
> • These chocolate pots can be frozen successfully for up to 2 months, making them ideal for a prepare-ahead dessert.

Vanilla Timbales Energy 89kcal/372kJ; Protein 6.2g; Carbohydrate 3.7g, of which sugars 3.1g; Fat 5.9g, of which saturates 2.8g; Cholesterol 67mg; Calcium 115mg; Fibre 0.6g; Sodium 110mg.
Chocolate Pots Energy 348kcal/1455kJ; Protein 5g; Carbohydrate 41.4g, of which sugars 29.9g; Fat 18g, of which saturates 9.9g; Cholesterol 75mg; Calcium 42mg; Fibre 2.6g; Sodium 56mg.

Mocha Velvet Cream Pots

These dainty pots of chocolate heaven are a fabulous way to round off a special meal.

Serves 8

15ml/1 tbsp instant
  coffee powder
475ml/16fl oz/2 cups milk
75g/3oz/6 tbsp caster
  (superfine) sugar

225g/8oz plain (semisweet)
  chocolate, chopped into
  small pieces
10ml/2 tsp vanilla extract
30ml/2 tbsp coffee-flavoured
  liqueur (optional)
7 egg yolks
whipped cream and crystallized
  mimosa balls, to decorate

1 Preheat the oven to 160°C/325°F/Gas 3. Place eight 120ml/4fl oz/½ cup custard cups or ramekins in a roasting pan. Set the pan aside.

2 Put the instant coffee in a saucepan. Stir in the milk, then add the sugar and place the pan over medium heat. Bring to the boil, stirring constantly, until both the coffee and the sugar have dissolved completely.

3 Remove the pan from the heat and add the chocolate. Stir until it has melted and the sauce is smooth. Stir in the vanilla extract and coffee liqueur, if using.

4 In a bowl, whisk the egg yolks to blend them lightly. Slowly whisk in the chocolate mixture until well mixed, then strain the mixture into a large jug (pitcher) and divide equally among the cups or ramekins. Pour enough boiling water into the roasting pan to come halfway up the sides of the cups or ramekins. Carefully place the roasting pan in the oven.

5 Bake for 30–35 minutes, until the custard is just set and a knife inserted into the custard comes out clean. Remove the cups or ramekins from the roasting pan and allow to cool. Place on a baking sheet, cover and chill completely.

6 Decorate the pots with whipped cream and crystallized mimosa balls, if you wish.

Petits Pots de Cappuccino

These very rich coffee custards, with a cream topping and a light dusting of drinking chocolate, look wonderful presented in fine china coffee cups.

Serves 6–8

75g/3oz/1 cup roasted
  coffee beans
300ml/½ pint/1¼ cups milk
300ml/½ pint/1¼ cups single
  (light) cream

1 whole egg
4 egg yolks
50g/2oz/4 tbsp caster
  (superfine) sugar
2.5ml/½ tsp vanilla extract

For the topping
120ml/4fl oz/½ cup
  whipping cream
45ml/3 tbsp iced water
10ml/2 tsp drinking chocolate

1 Preheat oven to 160°C/325°F/Gas 3. Put the coffee beans in a pan over a low heat for about 3 minutes, shaking the pan frequently. Pour the milk and cream over the beans. Heat until almost boiling; cover and leave to infuse (steep) for 30 minutes.

2 Whisk the egg, the egg yolks, sugar and vanilla together. Return the milk to boiling and pour through a sieve (strainer) on to the egg mixture. Discard the beans.

3 Pour the mixture into eight 75ml/5 tbsp coffee cups or six 120ml/4fl oz/½ cup ramekins. Cover each with a small piece of foil. Put in a roasting pan with hot water reaching about two-thirds of the way up the sides of the dishes. Bake for 30–35 minutes, or until lightly set. Let cool. Chill in the refrigerator for at least 2 hours.

4 Whisk the whipping cream and iced water until thick and frothy, and spoon on top of the custards. Dust with drinking chocolate before serving.

> **Cook's Tip**
> These petits pots may also be served warm, topped with a spoonful of clotted cream. Serve straight away, with the clotted cream just starting to melt.

Mocha Cream Pots Energy 261kcal/1095kJ; Protein 6g; Carbohydrate 30.5g, of which sugars 30.2g; Fat 13.7g, of which saturates 6.7g; Cholesterol 182mg; Calcium 106mg; Fibre 0.7g; Sodium 36mg.
Petits Pots Energy 226kcal/939kJ; Protein 5.6g; Carbohydrate 10.5g, of which sugars 10.5g; Fat 18.3g, of which saturates 10g; Cholesterol 197mg; Calcium 110mg; Fibre 0g; Sodium 49mg.

Belgian Chocolate Mousse

Every Belgian family has its favourite recipe for this culinary classic, usually involving some combination of melted chocolate with fresh eggs and cream, butter, coffee and liqueur. Whatever the recipe calls for, the essential ingredient is the chocolate, which must be of excellent quality. For professional results you can use callets (drop-like pieces of chocolate) made by the Belgian company Callebaut, or substitute other good-quality Belgian chocolate. The finished dish is magnificent.

Serves 4
150g/5oz Callebaut callets
  (semi-sweet bits) or other
  good-quality Belgian chocolate,
  cut into small pieces
200ml/7fl oz/scant 1 cup
  whipping or double
  (heavy) cream
75g/3oz/6 tbsp caster
  (superfine) sugar
2 eggs, separated, at
  room temperature
chocolate curls or sprinkles,
  roasted almond slivers, strips
  of candied orange peel,
  unsweetened cocoa powder
  or extra whipped cream,
  to decorate (optional)

1 Put the chocolate in a heatproof bowl over a small pan of simmering water. Melt the chocolate, stirring occasionally. When it is smooth, scrape it into a large bowl and leave to cool to room temperature.

2 In a clean bowl, whip the cream with 15ml/1 tbsp of the sugar until it stands in soft peaks. Set aside.

3 In a separate, grease-free, bowl, whisk the egg whites, gradually adding 50g/2oz/4 tbsp of the remaining sugar, until they are stiff and silky.

4 Whisk the egg yolks in a third bowl, gradually adding the last of the sugar, until foamy. Fold the yolks into the chocolate.

5 Using a spatula, fold in the whipped cream and then the egg whites, taking care not to deflate the mixture. Spoon or pipe into ramekins, dessert glasses or chocolate cups and leave to set for at least 4 hours. Serve plain or with any of the suggested decorations.

Heavenly Mud

This divine chocolate mousse, appropriately christened 'heavenly mud', is a dreamy combination of dark chocolate, eggs and cream. It is rich and full of flavour – the height of self-indulgence, and a classic sweet dessert dish in the Netherlands.

30ml/2 tbsp milk
4 eggs, separated
25ml/1½ tbsp soft light
  brown sugar
whipped double (heavy) cream
  and grated chocolate, to
  decorate

Serves 4
100g/3¾oz dark (bittersweet)
  chocolate, chopped

1 Put the chocolate and milk in a heatproof bowl and melt over a pan of barely simmering water, stirring constantly until smooth.

2 Beat the egg yolks with the sugar in another bowl. Stir the mixture into the melted chocolate mixture and warm briefly, stirring constantly, until slightly thickened.

3 Whisk the egg whites in a grease-free bowl until they are very stiff. Remove the chocolate mixture from the heat and fold it into the egg whites.

4 Divide the mixture among four individual dishes and chill in the refrigerator for at least 1 hour, until set. Decorate with whipped cream and grated chocolate.

> **Variation**
> To make another chocolate dessert called Mud from Gerritje, substitute icing (confectioners') sugar for the brown sugar and add some vanilla and ground cinnamon to the chopped chocolate. Stir 30ml/2 tbsp brandy into the chocolate mixture just before folding it into the egg whites.

Belgian Mousse Energy 550kcal/2290kJ; Protein 5.9g; Carbohydrate 44.3g, of which sugars 43.9g; Fat 40.1g, of which saturates 23.8g; Cholesterol 166mg; Calcium 61mg; Fibre 1g; Sodium 50mg.
Heavenly Mud Energy 226kcal/947kJ; Protein 7.8g; Carbohydrate 22g, of which sugars 21.8g; Fat 12.7g, of which saturates 5.8g; Cholesterol 192mg; Calcium 49mg; Fibre 0.6g; Sodium 75mg.

Bitter Chocolate Mousse

A classic and ever-popular dessert, these dishes of liqueur-flavoured chocolate mousse make a stylish and memorable finish to any dinner party.

Serves 8
225g/8oz plain (semisweet) chocolate, chopped into small pieces
60ml/4 tbsp water
30ml/2 tbsp orange-flavoured liqueur or brandy
25g/1oz/2 tbsp unsalted (sweet) butter, cut into small pieces
4 eggs, separated
90ml/6 tbsp whipping cream
1.5ml/¼ tsp cream of tartar
45ml/3 tbsp caster (superfine) sugar
crème fraîche and chocolate curls, to decorate

1 Melt the chocolate with the water in a heatproof bowl set over a pan of barely simmering water, stirring until completely smooth. Remove from the heat and whisk in the liqueur or brandy and butter.

2 With a hand-held electric mixer, beat the egg yolks for 2–3 minutes until thick and creamy, then slowly beat into the melted chocolate until well blended. Set aside.

3 Whip the cream until soft peaks form and stir a spoonful into the chocolate mixture to lighten it. Fold in the remaining cream.

4 In a grease-free bowl, beat the egg whites slowly until frothy. Add the cream of tartar, increase the speed and continue beating until they form soft peaks. Gradually sprinkle over the sugar and continue beating until the whites are stiff and glossy.

5 Using a rubber spatula or large metal spoon, stir a quarter of the egg whites into the chocolate mixture, then gently fold in the remaining whites, cutting down to the bottom, along the sides and up to the top in a semicircular motion until they are just combined. Gently spoon into eight individual dishes. Chill for at least 2 hours or until set.

6 Spoon a little crème fraîche over each mousse and decorate with the chocolate curls.

White Chocolate Mousse with Dark Sauce

In this delicious dessert, creamy, white chocolate mousse is set off by a dark rum and chocolate sauce.

Serves 6–8
200g/7oz white chocolate, broken into squares
2 eggs, separated
60ml/4 tbsp caster (superfine) sugar
300ml/½ pint/1¼ cups double (heavy) cream
15ml/1 tbsp/1 sachet powdered gelatine
150ml/¼ pint/⅔ cup Greek (US strained plain) yogurt
10ml/2 tsp vanilla extract

For the sauce
50g/2oz plain (semisweet) chocolate, broken into squares
30ml/2 tbsp dark rum
60ml/4 tbsp single (light) cream

1 Line a 1 litre/1¾ pint/4 cup loaf tin (pan) with baking parchment or clear film (plastic wrap). Melt the chocolate in a heatproof bowl over hot water, then remove from the heat.

2 Whisk the egg yolks and sugar in a bowl until pale and thick, then beat in the melted chocolate.

3 Heat the cream in a small pan until almost boiling, then remove from the heat. Sprinkle the powdered gelatine over, stirring gently until it is completely dissolved. Then pour on to the chocolate mixture, whisking vigorously to combine the gelatine until smooth.

4 Whisk the yogurt and vanilla extract into the mixture. In a clean, grease-free bowl, whisk the egg whites until stiff, then fold them into the mixture. Turn into the prepared loaf tin, level the surface and chill until set.

5 Make the sauce. Melt the chocolate with the rum and cream in a heatproof bowl over barely simmering water. Cool.

6 Remove the mousse from the tin with the aid of the lining. Serve sliced with the chocolate sauce poured around.

Bitter Mousse Energy 276kcal/1152kJ; Protein 4.8g; Carbohydrate 24.1g, of which sugars 23.9g; Fat 17.6g, of which saturates 9.9g; Cholesterol 115mg; Calcium 34mg; Fibre 0.7g; Sodium 61mg.
White Mousse Energy 433kcal/1796kJ; Protein 6g; Carbohydrate 25g, of which sugars 24.9g; Fat 34.4g, of which saturates 20.5g; Cholesterol 103mg; Calcium 133mg; Fibre 0.2g; Sodium 69mg.

Rich Chocolate Mousse with Glazed Kumquats

Perfumed kumquats, glazed in orange-flavoured liqueur, turn this mousse into a very special treat.

Serves 6

225g/8oz plain (semisweet) chocolate, broken into squares
4 eggs, separated
30ml/2 tbsp orange-flavoured liqueur

90ml/6 tbsp double (heavy) cream

For the glazed kumquats

275g/10oz/2¾ cups kumquats
115g/4oz/generous ½ cup sugar
150ml/¼ pint/⅔ cup water
15ml/1 tbsp orange-flavoured liqueur

1 To make the glazed kumquats, halve the fruit lengthways and place cut side up in a shallow serving dish.

2 Place the sugar in a small pan with the water. Heat gently, stirring constantly, until the sugar has dissolved, then bring to the boil and boil rapidly, without stirring, until a golden-brown caramel forms.

3 Remove the pan from the heat and very carefully stir in 60ml/4 tbsp boiling water. Stir in the orange-flavoured liqueur, then pour the caramel sauce over the kumquat slices and leave to cool. Once completely cold, cover and chill.

4 Line a shallow 20cm/8in round cake tin (pan) with clear film (plastic wrap). Melt the chocolate in a bowl over a pan of barely simmering water, then remove the bowl from the heat.

5 Beat the egg yolks and liqueur into the chocolate, then gently fold in the cream. In a separate mixing bowl, whisk the egg whites until stiff, then gently fold them into the chocolate mixture. Pour the mixture into the prepared tin and level the surface. Chill for several hours until set.

6 Turn the mousse out on to a plate and cut into slices. Serve with the glazed kumquats alongside.

Black and White Chocolate Mousse

Dark and dreamy or white and creamy – if you can't decide which mousse you prefer, have both.

Serves 8
For the white mousse
200g/7oz white chocolate, broken into squares
60ml/4 tbsp white rum
30ml/2 tbsp coconut cream
1 egg yolk
60ml/4 tbsp caster (superfine) sugar

250ml/8fl oz/1 cup double (heavy) cream
2 egg whites

For the black mousse
200g/7oz plain (semisweet) chocolate, broken into squares
30ml/2 tbsp unsalted (sweet) butter
60ml/4 tbsp dark rum
3 eggs, separated
chocolate curls, to decorate

1 Make the white chocolate mousse. Melt the chocolate with the rum and coconut cream in a heatproof bowl over barely simmering water. Remove from the heat.

2 Beat the egg yolk and sugar in a separate bowl, then whisk into the chocolate mixture. Whip the cream until it just begins to hold its shape, then carefully fold it into the chocolate mixture.

3 Whisk the egg whites in a clean, grease-free bowl until they form soft peaks, then fold quickly and evenly into the chocolate mixture. Chill until cold and set.

4 Make the dark chocolate mousse. Melt the chocolate with the butter and rum in a heatproof bowl over barely simmering water, stirring until smooth. Remove from the heat and beat in the egg yolks.

5 Whisk the egg whites to soft peaks, then fold them quickly and evenly into the chocolate mixture. Chill until cold and set.

6 Spoon the white and dark chocolate mixtures alternately into tall glasses or into one large glass serving bowl. Decorate with chocolate curls and serve.

Black and White Energy 569kcal/2366kJ; Protein 7.5g; Carbohydrate 39.1g, of which sugars 38.9g; Fat 39.9g, of which saturates 24.2g; Cholesterol 149mg; Calcium 111mg; Fibre 0.6g; Sodium 103mg.
Rich Mousse Energy 431kcal/1805kJ; Protein 6.9g; Carbohydrate 49.8g, of which sugars 49.5g; Fat 22.3g, of which saturates 12.4g; Cholesterol 150mg; Calcium 71mg; Fibre 1.7g; Sodium 56mg.

Liqueur-spiked Dark Chocolate Orange Mousse

Everything about this mousse is seductive and sophisticated. The smooth, creamy chocolate lingers on the tongue after being slowly sucked off the spoon. Only the best chocolates can create this divine effect, so save your most expensive, cocoa-solids-packed variety for this ultimate indulgence.

Serves 4
200g/7oz orange-flavoured dark
    (bittersweet) chocolate with
    more than 60 per cent
    cocoa solids
45ml/3 tbsp Grand Marnier or
    other orange-flavoured liqueur
25g/1oz/2 tbsp unsalted
    (sweet) butter
3 large (US extra large) eggs
salt
candied orange peel, to serve

1 Break the chocolate into pieces and put in a small bowl over a pan of barely simmering water. Pour in the liqueur and add the butter. Leave undisturbed for about 10 minutes until melted.

2 Separate the eggs and put the whites into a large mixing bowl with a tiny pinch of salt. Stir the chocolate mixture and remove from the heat. Quickly mix in the egg yolks.

3 Whisk the egg whites until stiff but not dry. Fold one large spoonful into the chocolate sauce to loosen the mixture, then carefully, but thoroughly, fold in the remaining egg whites.

4 Spoon the mixture into little pots or ramekins, cover and chill for at least 6 hours, or until set. Serve with thin strips of candied orange peel.

> **Cook's Tip**
> Grand Marnier is a liqueur made with cognac and orange extract. A common name for an orange liqueur is 'triple sec', and there are many brands, with Grand Marnier being one of the most famous. Also look out for Cointreau, which, along with Grand Marnier, has a high alcohol content of 40 per cent.

Chocolate and Orange Mousse

There's no hint of deprivation in this dairy-free dessert, made with dark chocolate flavoured with brandy. It makes a great treat when entertaining.

Serves 8
175g/6oz good-quality dark
    (bittersweet) chocolate, broken
    into squares
grated rind and juice of 1½ large
    oranges, plus extra pared rind
    for decoration
5ml/1 tsp powdered gelatine
4 size 2 eggs, separated
90ml/6 tbsp unsweetened
    soya cream
60ml/4 tbsp brandy
chopped pistachio nuts, to
    decorate

1 Melt the chocolate in a heatproof bowl over a pan of barely simmering water, stirring until smooth. Put 30ml/2 tbsp of the orange juice in a heatproof bowl and sprinkle the gelatine on top. When the gelatine is spongy, stand the bowl over a pan of hot water and stir until it has dissolved.

2 Let the chocolate cool slightly, then beat in the orange rind, egg yolks, soya cream and brandy, followed by the gelatine mixture and the remaining orange juice. Set aside.

3 Whisk the egg whites in a grease-free bowl until they form soft peaks. Gently fold the whites into the chocolate and orange mixture.

4 Spoon or pour the mixture into six sundae dishes or glasses, or into a single glass bowl. Cover and chill until the mousse sets. Decorate with the chopped pistachio nuts and extra pared orange rind before serving.

> **Cook's Tip**
> The percentage of cocoa solids in the chocolate influences not only the taste but also the texture of the mousse. The higher the percentage of the cocoa the firmer the mousse will become. Try to use a chocolate with a minimum of 70 per cent cocoa solids if you can.

Orange Energy 230kcals/966kJ; Fat, total 12.4g; saturated fat 4.6g;polyunsaturated fat 0.6g; monounsaturated fat 3.4g; Carbohydrate 17.3g; sugar, total 17g; Starch 0.2g; Fibre 0.55g; Sodium 113mg.
Liqueur Energy 382kcal/1593kJ; Protein 7.2g; Carbohydrate 31.8g, of which sugars 31.4g; Fat 23.3g, of which saturates 12.8g; Cholesterol 159mg; Calcium 39mg; Fibre 1.3g; Sodium 94mg.

Chocolate and Coffee Mousse

White Amaretto Mousse with Chocolate Sauce

These little desserts are extremely rich, and derive their flavour from Amaretto, an almond-flavoured liqueur, and amaretti, little almond-flavoured cookies.

Serves 8
115g/4oz amaretti, ratafia or macaroon biscuits (cookies)
60ml/4 tbsp Amaretto liqueur
350g/12oz white chocolate, broken into squares
15g/½oz powdered gelatine, soaked in 45ml/3 tbsp cold water
450ml/¾ pint/scant 2 cups double (heavy) cream

For the chocolate sauce
225g/8oz dark (bittersweet) chocolate, broken into squares
300ml/½ pint/1¼ cups single (light) cream
50g/2oz/4 tbsp caster (superfine) sugar

1 Lightly oil eight individual 120ml/4floz moulds and line the base of each with oiled baking parchment. Put the biscuits into a large bowl and crush finely with a rolling pin.

2 Melt the liqueur and white chocolate in a bowl over a pan of simmering water. Remove from the pan and leave to cool.

3 Melt the gelatine over hot water and stir into the chocolate mixture. Whisk the cream until it holds soft peaks. Fold in the chocolate mixture, with 60ml/4 tbsp of the crushed biscuits.

4 Put a teaspoonful of the crushed biscuits into the bottom of each mould and spoon in the chocolate mixture. Tap each mould to disperse any air bubbles. Level the tops and sprinkle the remaining biscuits on top. Press down and chill for 4 hours.

5 To make the chocolate sauce, put all the ingredients in a small pan and heat gently to melt the chocolate and dissolve the sugar. Simmer for 2–3 minutes. Leave to cool completely.

6 Slip a knife around the sides of each mould, and turn out on to individual plates. Remove the baking parchment and pour round a little dark chocolate sauce.

Chocolate and Coffee Mousse

A light chocolate mousse is always a popular way to end a meal. This Polish version is made with a good strong chocolate flavoured with coffee and rum, Polish spirit or vodka. You can omit all or any of these, depending on your preference.

Serves 4–6
250g/9oz good quality dark (bittersweet) chocolate (minimum 70 per cent cocoa solids)
60ml/4 tbsp cooled strong black coffee
8 eggs, separated
200g/7oz/1 cup caster (superfine) sugar
60ml/4 tbsp rum, or 95 per cent proof Polish spirit or vodka

1 Break the chocolate into small pieces and melt in a heatproof bowl over a pan of gently simmering water. Ensure the water in the pan does not touch the base of the bowl, or the chocolate may go hard.

2 Once the chocolate has completely melted, stir in the cold coffee. Leave to cool slightly.

3 Beat the egg yolks with half the sugar until it is pale, thick and creamy. Add the rum, Polish spirit or vodka and stir in the melted chocolate mixture.

4 Whisk the egg whites in a separate clean bowl until stiff peaks form.

5 Stir in the remaining sugar, then fold into the chocolate cream mixture. Spoon into chilled glasses or ramekins and chill for at least an hour before serving.

Variation
For a slightly less intense mousse, whip 300ml/½ pint/1¼ cups double (heavy) cream until soft peaks form, then fold into the mixture at the end of step 3.

Amaretto Mousse Energy 837kcal/3484kJ; Protein 7.9g; Carbohydrate 64.9g, of which sugars 58.4g; Fat 60.6g, of which saturates 37g; Cholesterol 99mg; Calcium 210mg; Fibre 0.9g; Sodium 121mg.
Coffee Mousse Energy 464kcal/1951kJ; Protein 10.6g; Carbohydrate 61.3g, of which sugars 60.9g; Fat 19.1g, of which saturates 9.1g; Cholesterol 256mg; Calcium 70mg; Fibre 1.1g; Sodium 98mg.

Chilled Chocolate and Espresso Mousse in Chocolate Cups

Heady, aromatic espresso coffee adds a distinctive flavour to this rich mousse.

Serves 4
225g/8oz plain (semisweet)
   chocolate
45ml/3 tbsp brewed espresso
25g/1oz/2 tbsp unsalted
   (sweet) butter

4 eggs, separated
sprigs of fresh mint, to
   decorate (optional)
mascarpone or clotted cream,
   to serve (optional)

For the chocolate cups
225g/8oz plain (semisweet)
   chocolate

1 For each chocolate cup, cut a double thickness, 15cm/6in square of foil. Mould it around a small orange, leaving the edges and corners loose to make a cup shape. Remove the orange and press the bottom of the foil case gently on a surface to make a flat base. Repeat to make four foil cups.

2 Break the plain chocolate into a heatproof bowl set over a pan of simmering water. Stir until the chocolate has melted and is smooth. Spoon the chocolate into the foil cups, spreading it up the sides with the back of a spoon to give a ragged edge. Chill for 30 minutes or until set hard. Gently peel away the foil, starting at the top edge.

3 To make the chocolate mousse, put the plain chocolate and brewed espresso into a bowl set over a pan of hot water and melt as before. When it is smooth and liquid, add the unsalted butter, a little at a time. Remove the pan from the heat, then stir in the egg yolks.

4 Whisk the egg whites in a bowl until stiff, but not dry, then fold them into the chocolate mixture. Pour into a bowl and refrigerate for at least 3 hours.

5 To serve, scoop the chilled mousse into the chocolate cups. Add a scoop of mascarpone or clotted cream and decorate with a sprig of fresh mint, if you wish.

Iced Coffee Mousse in a Chocolate Case

A dark chocolate bowl is filled with a light, iced coffee mousse.

Serves 8
1 sachet powdered gelatine
60ml/4 tbsp very strong
   brewed coffee
30ml/2 tbsp coffee liqueur, such
   as Tia Maria, Kahlúa or
   Toussaint

3 eggs, separated
75g/3oz/scant ½ cup caster
   (superfine) sugar
150ml/¼ pint/⅔ cup whipping
   cream, lightly whipped

For the chocolate case
225g/8oz plain (semisweet)
   chocolate squares, plus extra
   for decoration

1 Grease and line a deep 18cm/7in loose-based cake tin (pan) with baking parchment. Melt the chocolate in a bowl over a pan of simmering water. Using a pastry brush, brush a layer of chocolate over the base of the tin and about 7.5cm/3in up the sides, finishing with a ragged edge. Allow the chocolate to set before repeating. Put in the freezer to harden.

2 Sprinkle the gelatine over the coffee in a bowl and leave to soften for 5 minutes. Put the bowl over a pan of simmering water, stirring until dissolved. Remove from the heat and stir in the liqueur. Whisk the egg yolks and sugar in a bowl over the simmering water until thick enough to leave a trail. Remove from the pan and whisk until cool. Whisk the egg whites until stiff.

3 Pour the dissolved gelatine into the egg yolk mixture in a thin stream, stirring gently. Chill in the refrigerator for 20 minutes, or until just beginning to set, then fold in the cream, followed by the whisked egg whites.

4 Remove the chocolate case from the freezer and peel away the lining. Put it back in the tin, then pour in the mousse. Return to the freezer for at least 3 hours. Remove from the tin, place on a plate and allow to soften in the refrigerator for 40 minutes before serving. Decorate with grated chocolate. Use a knife dipped in hot water and wiped dry to cut into slices to serve.

Espresso Mousse Energy 694kcal/2901kJ; Protein 11.9g; Carbohydrate 71.5g, of which sugars 70.5g; Fat 42.2g, of which saturates 23.7g; Cholesterol 210mg; Calcium 67mg; Fibre 2.8g; Sodium 115mg.
Iced Coffee Mousse Energy 464kcal/1950kJ; Protein 10.6g; Carbohydrate 61.3g, of which sugars 60.9g; Fat 19.1g, of which saturates 9.1g; Cholesterol 256mg; Calcium 69mg; Fibre 1g; Sodium 98mg.

Luxury Mocha Mousse

As a variation, use an
orange-flavour liqueur,
brandy or even water
in place of the coffee.

Serves 6
225g/8oz fine quality dark
    (bittersweet) chocolate, chopped
50ml/2fl oz/¼ cup espresso or
    strong coffee
25g/1oz/2 tbsp butter, diced

30ml/2 tbsp brandy or rum
3 eggs, separated
pinch of salt
40g/1½oz/3 tbsp caster
    (superfine) sugar
120ml/4fl oz/½ cup
    whipping cream
30ml/2 tbsp coffee-flavour liqueur,
    such as Tia Maria or Kahlúa
chocolate coffee beans to
    decorate (optional)

1 In a medium pan over medium heat, melt the chocolate and coffee, stirring frequently until smooth. Remove from the heat and beat in the butter and brandy or rum.

2 In a bowl, beat the yolks lightly, then beat into the melted chocolate; the mixture will thicken. Set aside to cool. In a large bowl, beat the whites to 'break' them. Add a pinch of salt and beat until soft peaks form. Beat in the sugar, 15ml/1 tbsp at a time, beating well after each addition until the egg whites become glossy and stiff, but do not overbeat or they will become dry.

3 Beat 1 large spoonful of whites into the chocolate mixture to lighten it, then fold the chocolate into the remaining whites. Pour into a large glass serving bowl or six individual dishes and refrigerate for at least 3–4 hours before serving.

4 In a medium bowl, beat the cream and coffee-flavour liqueur until soft peaks form. Spoon into an icing (pastry) bag fitted with a medium star tip and pipe rosettes or shells on to the surface of the mousse. Garnish with a chocolate coffee bean.

Cook's Tip
It is essential to whip the egg whites while slowly adding the sugar; otherwise the whites will separate and become watery.

Coffee, Vanilla and Chocolate Stripe

This looks really special
layered in wine glasses and
decorated with cream.

Serves 6
285g/10½oz/1½ cups caster
    (superfine) sugar
90ml/6 tbsp cornflour
    (cornstarch)

900ml/1½ pints/3¾ cups milk
3 egg yolks
75g/3oz/6 tbsp unsalted (sweet)
    butter, at room temperature
20ml/generous 1 tbsp instant
    coffee powder
10ml/2 tsp vanilla extract
30ml/2 tbsp unsweetened
    cocoa powder

1 To make the coffee layer, place 90g/3½oz/½ cup of the sugar and 30ml/2 tbsp of the cornflour in a heavy pan. Gradually add one-third of the milk, whisking until well blended. Over a medium heat, whisk in one of the egg yolks and bring to the boil, whisking. Boil for 1 minute.

2 Remove the pan from the heat. Stir in 25g/1oz/2 tbsp of the butter and the instant coffee. Set aside the pan to cool slightly.

3 Divide the coffee mixture among six wine glasses. Smooth the tops before the mixture sets. Wipe any dribbles on the insides and outsides of the glasses with damp kitchen paper.

4 To make the vanilla layer, place half of the remaining sugar and cornflour in a heavy pan. Whisk in half the milk. Over a medium heat, whisk in another egg yolk and bring to the boil, whisking. Boil for 1 minute.

5 Remove the pan from the heat and stir in 25g/1oz/2 tbsp of the butter and the vanilla. Leave to cool slightly, then spoon into the glasses on top of the coffee layer. Smooth the tops.

6 To make the chocolate layer, place the remaining sugar and cornflour in a heavy pan. Gradually whisk in the remaining milk until blended. Over a medium heat, whisk in the last egg yolk and bring to the boil, whisking. Boil for 1 minute. Remove from the heat, stir in the remaining butter and the cocoa. Leave to cool slightly, then spoon on top of the vanilla layer. Chill to set.

Luxury Mousse Energy 389kcal/1621kJ; Protein 5.5g; Carbohydrate 32.5g, of which sugars 32.2g; Fat 25.5g, of which saturates 14.3g; Cholesterol 127mg; Calcium 43mg; Fibre 0.9g; Sodium 72mg.
Coffee Stripe Energy 448kcal/1891kJ; Protein 7.9g; Carbohydrate 71.1g, of which sugars 56.8g; Fat 16.8g, of which saturates 9.6g; Cholesterol 136mg; Calcium 228mg; Fibre 0.6g; Sodium 203mg.

Chocolate and Lemon Fromage Frais

What better excuse to add iron to your diet than by eating some good dark chocolate? Contrast the richness with the tanginess of fromage frais.

Serves 4

150g/5oz dark (bittersweet) chocolate

45ml/3 tbsp water
15ml/1 tbsp rum, brandy or whisky (optional)
grated rind of 1 lemon
200g/7oz low-fat fromage frais or low-fat cream cheese
sliced kumquats and sprigs of mint, to decorate

1 Break up the chocolate into a heatproof bowl. Add the water and melt very slowly over a pan of gently simmering water, stirring constantly until smooth. Alternatively, melt it in a microwave on full power for 2 minutes.

2 Stir well until smooth and allow the chocolate to cool for 10 minutes. Stir in the rum, brandy or whisky, if using, and the lemon rind and fromage frais or cream cheese.

3 Spoon into four elegant wine glasses and chill until set. Decorate with kumquats and sprigs of mint.

Cook's Tips
• Fromage frais (French for 'fresh cheese') can be hard to find in the US. Look for specialist stores and markets that stock European food or try to order some from online or mail-order retailers. If none is available, then low-fat cream cheese will also work in this recipe.
• Chocolate can be melted very successfully in the microwave. Place the pieces of chocolate in a plastic measuring jug (cup) or bowl. The chocolate may scorch if placed in a glass bowl. Microwave on high power for 1 minute, stir, and then heat again for up to 1 minute, checking halfway through to see if it is melted.

Fruits of the Forest with White Chocolate Creams

Colourful fruits macerated in a mixture of white coconut rum and sugar make a fantastic accompaniment to a delightfully creamy white chocolate mousse.

Serves 4

75g/3oz white cooking chocolate, in squares
150ml/1/4 pint/2/3 cup double (heavy) cream

30ml/2 tbsp crème fraîche
1 egg, separated
5ml/1 tsp powdered gelatine
30ml/2 tbsp cold water
a few drops of pure vanilla extract
115g/4oz/3/4 cup small strawberries, sliced
75g/3oz/1/2 cup raspberries
75g/3oz/3/4 cup blueberries
45ml/3 tbsp caster (superfine) sugar
75ml/5 tbsp white coconut rum
strawberry leaves, to decorate

1 Melt the chocolate in a heatproof bowl set over a pan of hot water. Heat the cream in a separate pan until almost boiling, then stir into the chocolate with the crème fraîche. Cool slightly, then beat in the egg yolk.

2 Sprinkle the gelatine over the water in another heatproof bowl and set aside for a few minutes to swell. Set the bowl in a pan of hot water until the gelatine has dissolved, then stir into the chocolate mixture and add the vanilla extract. Set aside.

3 Brush four dariole moulds or individual soufflé dishes with oil; line the base of each with baking parchment.

4 In a grease-free bowl, whisk the egg white to soft peaks, then fold into the chocolate mixture. Spoon the mixture into the moulds or dishes. Level the surface and chill for 2 hours until firm.

5 Meanwhile, place the fruits in a bowl. Add the sugar and coconut rum and stir to mix. Cover and chill until required.

6 Ease the chocolate cream away from the moulds or dishes and turn out on to plates. Spoon the fruits around the outside. Decorate with the strawberry leaves.

Fromage Frais Energy 220kcal/925kJ; Protein 5.7g; Carbohydrate 27.2g, of which sugars 26.9g; Fat 10.6g, of which saturates 6.4g; Cholesterol 3mg; Calcium 56mg; Fibre 1g; Sodium 19mg.
Fruits Energy 397kcal/1643kJ; Protein 4.5g; Carbohydrate 17g, of which sugars 16.2g; Fat 30.4g, of which saturates 18.4g; Cholesterol 107mg; Calcium 90mg; Fibre 1.2g; Sodium 50mg.

Chocolate Blancmange

An old-fashioned dessert that is worthy of a revival. Serve with pouring cream for a touch of luxury.

Serves 4

60ml/4 tbsp cornflour (cornstarch)
600ml/1 pint/2½ cups milk
45ml/3 tbsp sugar
50–115g/2–4oz plain (semisweet) chocolate, chopped
few drops of vanilla extract
white and plain (semisweet) chocolate curls, to decorate

1 Rinse a 750ml/1¼ pint/3 cup fluted mould with cold water and leave it upside down to drain. Blend the cornflour to a smooth paste with a little of the milk in a medium bowl.

2 Bring the remaining milk to the boil, preferably in a non-stick pan, then pour on to the blended paste, stirring constantly, until smooth in consistency.

3 Pour all the milk back into the pan and bring slowly back to the boil over a low heat, stirring constantly until the mixture boils and thickens.

4 Remove the pan from the heat, then add the sugar, chopped chocolate and vanilla extract and stir constantly until the sauce is smooth, all the sugar has dissolved and the chocolate pieces have melted completely.

5 Carefully pour the chocolate mixture into the mould, cover the top closely with dampened baking parchment (to prevent the formation of a skin) and leave in a cool place for several hours to set.

6 To unmould the blancmange, place a large serving plate upside down on top of the mould. Holding the plate and mould firmly together, turn them both over in one quick motion. Give both plate and mould a gentle but firm shake to loosen the blancmange, then carefully lift off the mould.

7 To serve, sprinkle the chocolate curls over the top.

Chocolate Mandarin Trifle

Rich chocolate custard is combined with mandarin oranges to make this delicious trifle that is too tempting to resist.

Serves 6–8

4 trifle sponges
14 amaretti
60ml/4 tbsp Amaretto Disaronno or sweet sherry
8 mandarin oranges

For the custard

200g/7oz plain (semisweet) chocolate, broken into squares
25g/1oz/2 tbsp cornflour (cornstarch) or custard powder
25g/1oz/2 tbsp caster (superfine) sugar
2 egg yolks
200ml/7fl oz/scant 1 cup milk
250g/9oz/generous 1 cup mascarpone

For the topping

250g/9oz/generous 1 cup mascarpone or fromage frais
chocolate shapes
mandarin slices

1 Break up the trifle sponges and place them in a large glass serving dish. Crumble the amaretti over and then sprinkle with Amaretto or sweet sherry.

2 Squeeze the juice from two of the mandarins and sprinkle into the dish. Segment the rest and put in the dish.

3 Make the custard. Melt the chocolate in a heatproof bowl over hot water. In a separate bowl, mix the cornflour or custard powder, sugar and egg yolks to a smooth paste.

4 Heat the milk in a small pan until almost boiling, then pour in a steady stream on to the egg yolk mixture, stirring constantly. Return to the pan and stir over a low heat until the custard has thickened slightly and is smooth.

5 Stir in the mascarpone until melted, then add the melted chocolate; mix well. Spread over the trifle, cool, then chill to set.

6 To finish, spread the mascarpone or fromage frais over the custard, then decorate with chocolate shapes and the remaining mandarin slices just before serving.

Blancmange Energy 230kcal/975kJ; Protein 5.9g; Carbohydrate 40.6g, of which sugars 26.6g; Fat 6.2g, of which saturates 3.7g; Cholesterol 10mg; Calcium 192mg; Fibre 0.3g; Sodium 74mg.
Mandarin Trifle Energy 569kcal/2394kJ; Protein 12.5g; Carbohydrate 80.3g, of which sugars 61.3g; Fat 23.1g, of which saturates 12.8g; Cholesterol 135mg; Calcium 162mg; Fibre 2.9g; Sodium 115mg.

Chocolate and Mandarin Truffle Slice

Chocoholics will love this rich dessert. The mandarins impart a delicious tang.

Serves 8

400g/14oz plain
  (semisweet) chocolate
4 egg yolks
3 mandarin oranges

200ml/7fl oz/scant 1 cup
  crème fraîche
30ml/2 tbsp raisins
chocolate curls, to decorate

For the sauce

30ml/2 tbsp Cointreau
120ml/4fl oz/½ cup
  crème fraîche

1 Grease a 450g/1lb loaf tin (pan) and line it with clear film (plastic wrap). Break the chocolate in to a large heatproof bowl. Place over a pan of hot water until melted. Remove the bowl of chocolate from the heat and whisk in the egg yolks.

2 Pare the rind from the mandarins, taking care to leave the pith behind. Cut the rind into slivers.

3 Stir the slivers of mandarin rind into the chocolate with the crème fraîche and raisins. Beat until smooth, then spoon the mixture into the prepared loaf tin and chill for 4 hours.

4 Cut the pith and any remaining rind from the mandarins, then slice thinly.

5 For the sauce, stir the Cointreau into the crème fraîche. Remove the truffle loaf from the tin, peel off the clear film and slice. Serve each slice on a dessert plate with some sauce and mandarin slices, and decorate.

> **Cook's Tip**
> Chocolate-tipped mandarin slices would also make a superb decoration. Use small segments; pat dry on kitchen paper, then half-dip them in melted chocolate. Leave on baking parchment until the chocolate has set.

Mango and Chocolate Crème Brûlée

Fresh mangoes, topped with a wickedly rich chocolate cream and a layer of crunchy caramel, make a fantastic dessert.

Serves 6

2 ripe mangoes, peeled, stoned
  (pitted) and chopped
300ml/½ pint/1¼ cups double
  (heavy) cream

300ml/½ pint/1¼ cups
  crème fraîche
1 vanilla pod (bean)
115g/4oz plain (semisweet)
  chocolate, chopped into
  small pieces
4 egg yolks
15ml/1 tbsp clear honey
90ml/6 tbsp demerara (raw)
  sugar, for the topping

1 Divide the mangoes among six flameproof dishes set on a baking sheet.

2 Mix the cream, crème fraîche and vanilla pod in a large heatproof bowl. Place the bowl over a pan of barely simmering water.

3 Heat the cream mixture for 10 minutes. Do not let the bowl touch the water or the cream may overheat. Remove the vanilla pod and stir in the chocolate, a few pieces at a time, until melted. When smooth, remove the bowl, but leave the pan of water over the heat.

4 Whisk the egg yolks and clear honey in a second heatproof bowl, then gradually pour in the chocolate cream, whisking constantly. Place over the pan of simmering water and stir constantly until the chocolate custard thickens enough to coat the back of a wooden spoon.

5 Remove from the heat and spoon the custard over the mangoes. Cool, then chill in the refrigerator until set.

6 Preheat the grill (broiler) to high. Sprinkle 15ml/1 tbsp demerara sugar evenly over each dessert and spray lightly with a little water. Grill (broil) briefly, as close to the heat as possible, until the sugar melts and caramelizes. Chill again before serving.

Chocolate Truffle Slice Energy 456kcal/1899kJ; Protein 5g; Carbohydrate 35.3g, of which sugars 34.7g; Fat 32.8g, of which saturates 20.1g; Cholesterol 152mg; Calcium 54mg; Fibre 1.3g; Sodium 19mg.
Mango Crème Brûlée Energy 670kcal/2782kJ; Protein 5.2g; Carbohydrate 38.9g, of which sugars 38.4g; Fat 56g, of which saturates 34.6g; Cholesterol 261mg; Calcium 90mg; Fibre 1.8g; Sodium 31mg.

White Chocolate Parfait

The ultimate cold dessert – white and dark chocolate in one mouthwatering slice.

Serves 10

225g/8oz white chocolate, chopped
600ml/1 pint/2½ cups
   whipping cream
120ml/4fl oz/½ cup milk
10 egg yolks
15ml/1 tbsp caster
   (superfine) sugar
25g/1oz/scant ½ cup
   desiccated (dry unsweetened
   shredded) coconut

120ml/4fl oz/½ cup canned
   sweetened coconut milk
150g/5oz/1¼ cups unsalted
   macadamia nuts

For the chocolate icing

225g/8oz plain (semisweet)
   chocolate
75g/3oz/6 tbsp butter
20ml/generous 1 tbsp golden
   (light corn) syrup
175ml/6fl oz/¾ cup
   whipping cream
curls of fresh coconut,
   to decorate

1 Line the base and sides of a 1.4 litre/2⅓ pint/6 cup terrine mould (25 × 10cm/10 × 4in) with clear film (plastic wrap).

2 Place the white chocolate and 120ml/4fl oz/½ cup of the cream in the top of a double boiler or in a heatproof bowl set over hot water. Stir until melted and smooth. Set aside.

3 Put 250ml/8fl oz/1 cup of the cream and the milk in a pan and bring to boiling point.

4 Meanwhile, whisk the egg yolks and caster sugar together in a large bowl, until thick and pale.

5 Add the hot cream mixture to the yolks, beating constantly. Pour back into the pan and cook over a low heat for 2–3 minutes, until thickened. Stir constantly and do not boil. Remove the pan from the heat. Add the melted chocolate, desiccated coconut and coconut milk, then stir well and leave to cool.

6 Whip the remaining cream until thick, then fold into the chocolate and coconut mixture.

7 Put 475ml/16fl oz/2 cups of the parfait mixture in the prepared mould and spread evenly. Cover and freeze for about 2 hours, until just firm. Cover the remaining mixture and chill.

8 Sprinkle the macadamia nuts evenly over the frozen parfait. Pour in the remaining parfait mixture. Cover the terrine and freeze for 6–8 hours or overnight, until the parfait is firm.

9 To make the icing, melt the chocolate with the butter and syrup in the top of a double boiler set over hot water. Stir occasionally. Heat the cream in a pan, until just simmering, then stir into the chocolate mixture. Remove from the heat; cool.

10 To turn out the parfait, wrap the terrine in a hot towel and invert on to a plate. Lift off the mould and clear film and place the parfait on a rack over a baking sheet. Pour the chocolate icing over the top and quickly smooth it down the sides with a palette knife. Leave to set slightly, then freeze for 3–4 hours. To serve, slice with a knife dipped in hot water and decorate with coconut curls.

Chocolate and Brandy Parfait

This parfait is traditionally made with a mixture of chocolate and coffee, but here it is blended with cocoa powder. Melted Belgian chocolate and a kick of brandy are the secret of its superb flavour.

Serves 6

45ml/3 tbsp unsweetened
   cocoa powder

60ml/4 tbsp boiling water
150g/5oz dark (bittersweet)
   chocolate, broken into squares
4 egg yolks
115g/4oz/generous ½ cup caster
   (superfine) sugar
120ml/4fl oz/½ cup water
300ml/½ pint/1¼ cups
   double (heavy) cream
60–75ml/4–5 tbsp brandy
drizzled white chocolate rings,
   to decorate

1 Mix the cocoa to a paste with the boiling water. Put the chocolate into a heatproof bowl. Bring a pan of water to the boil, remove from the heat and place the bowl on top until the chocolate melts, stirring constantly. In a separate bowl, whisk the yolks until frothy.

2 Heat the sugar and measured water gently in a small pan, stirring occasionally, until completely dissolved, then boil for 4–5 minutes, without stirring, until it registers 115°C/239°F on a sugar thermometer. You can also test the temperature by dropping a little syrup into cold water. The syrup should make a soft ball.

3 Quickly whisk the syrup into the yolks. Lift the bowl of melted chocolate off the pan and bring the water to a simmer. Place the bowl with the yolk mixture on top and whisk until very thick. Lift it off the pan and continue whisking until the mixture cools slightly.

4 Whisk in the cocoa mixture, then fold in the melted chocolate. Whip the cream lightly and fold it in, along with the brandy. Pour the mixture into six or eight freezerproof serving dishes, then freeze for 4 hours or until they are firm. Decorate with white chocolate rings, made by drizzling melted white chocolate on to baking parchment and leaving it to set before carefully peeling from the paper.

White Parfait Energy 792kcal/3280kJ; Protein 9.2g; Carbohydrate 34.8g, of which sugars 34.5g; Fat 69.4g, of which saturates 36g; Cholesterol 301mg; Calcium 165mg; Fibre 1.7g; Sodium 169mg.
Brandy Parfait Energy 537kcal/2235kJ; Protein 5.5g; Carbohydrate 37.6g, of which sugars 36.5g; Fat 39.1g, of which saturates 22.9g; Cholesterol 204mg; Calcium 68mg; Fibre 1.5g; Sodium 91mg.

Chocolate Loaf with Coffee Sauce

This rich chocolate dessert is popular in many French restaurants, where it is called *Marquise au Chocolat*.

Serves 6–8

175g/6oz plain (semisweet)
  chocolate, chopped
50g/2oz/¼ cup butter, softened
4 large (US extra large)
  eggs, separated
30ml/2 tbsp rum or
  brandy (optional)

pinch of cream of tartar
chocolate curls and chocolate
  coffee beans, to decorate

For the coffee sauce

600ml/1 pint/2½ cups milk
9 egg yolks
50g/2oz/¼ cup caster
  (superfine) sugar
5ml/1 tsp vanilla extract
15ml/1 tbsp instant coffee
  powder, dissolved in
  30ml/2 tbsp hot water

1 Line a 1.2 litre/2 pint/5 cup terrine or loaf tin (pan) with clear film (plastic wrap), smoothing it evenly.

2 Put the chocolate in a bowl over a pan of hot water and stir until melted. Remove the bowl from the pan and quickly beat in the butter, egg yolks, one at a time, and rum or brandy, if using.

3 In a clean grease-free bowl, using an electric mixer, beat the egg whites until frothy. Add the cream of tartar, increase the speed and mix until they form soft peaks, then stiffer peaks. Stir a third of the whites into the chocolate mixture, then fold in the remaining whites. Pour into the terrine or tin and smooth the top. Cover and freeze.

4 To make the coffee sauce, bring the milk to a simmer over a medium heat. Whisk the egg yolks and sugar until thick and creamy, then add the hot milk and return the mixture to the pan. Stir over a low heat until the sauce thickens and coats the back a spoon. Strain into a chilled bowl, stir in the vanilla extract and coffee and set aside to cool, stirring occasionally. Chill.

5 To serve, uncover the terrine or tin and dip the base into hot water for 10 seconds. Invert the dessert on to a board and peel off the clear film. Slice the loaf and serve with the coffee sauce. Decorate with the chocolate curls and coffee beans.

Pear and Hazelnut Meringue Torte

This stunning dessert with chocolate cream will raise gasps of admiration.

Serves 8–10

175g/6oz/generous ¾ cup
  granulated (white) sugar
1 vanilla pod (bean), split
475ml/16fl oz/2 cups water
4 ripe pears, peeled, halved
  and cored
30ml/2 tbsp hazelnut- or
  pear-flavoured liqueur
150g/5oz/1¼ cups
  hazelnuts, toasted
6 egg whites

pinch of salt
350g/12oz/3 cups icing
  (confectioners') sugar
5ml/1 tsp vanilla extract
50g/2oz plain (semisweet)
  chocolate, melted

For the chocolate cream

275g/10oz plain (semisweet)
  chocolate, chopped into
  small pieces
475ml/16fl oz/2 cups
  whipping cream
60ml/4 tbsp hazelnut-
  or pear-flavoured liqueur

1 In a pan large enough to hold the pears in a single layer, combine the sugar, vanilla pod and water. Over a high heat, bring to the boil, stirring, until the sugar dissolves. Lower the heat, add the pears to the syrup, cover and simmer gently for 12–15 minutes until tender. Remove the pan from the heat and allow the pears to cool in their poaching liquid. Carefully lift the pears out of the liquid and drain on kitchen paper. Transfer them to a plate, sprinkle with liqueur, cover and chill overnight.

2 Preheat the oven to 180°C/350°F/Gas 4. With a pencil, draw a 23cm/9in circle on each of two sheets of baking parchment. Turn the paper over on to two baking sheets (so that the pencil marks are underneath). Grind the toasted hazelnuts.

3 In a large bowl, beat the whites with a hand-held electric mixer until frothy. Add the salt and beat on high speed until soft peaks form. Reduce the mixer speed and gradually add the icing sugar, beating well after each addition until all the sugar has been added and the whites are stiff. Gently fold in the nuts and vanilla extract to the mixture and spoon the meringue on to the circles on the baking sheets, smoothing the tops and sides.

4 Bake for 1 hour until the tops are dry and firm. Turn off the oven and cool in the oven for 2–3 hours or overnight, until dry.

5 Make the chocolate cream. Melt the chocolate in a heatproof bowl set over a pan of simmering water and stir until melted and smooth. Cool to room temperature. Whip the cream in a bowl to soft peaks. Quickly fold the cream into the chocolate; fold in the liqueur. Spoon about one-third of the chocolate cream into a piping (pastry) bag fitted with a star tip. Set aside.

6 Thinly slice each pear in half lengthways. Place one meringue layer on a serving plate, spread with half the chocolate cream, and arrange half the pears on top. Pipe rosettes around the edge.

7 Top with the second meringue layer, spread with the remaining chocolate cream and arrange the remaining pear slices on top. Pipe a border of rosettes around the edge. Spoon the melted chocolate into a small paper cone and drizzle the chocolate over the pears. Chill for at least 1 hour before serving.

Loaf Energy 323kcal/1347kJ; Protein 10.1g; Carbohydrate 24g, of which sugars 23.8g; Fat 21.5g, of which saturates 10.3g; Cholesterol 341mg; Calcium 142mg; Fibre 0.6g; Sodium 117mg.
Meringue Torte Energy 706kcal/2960kJ; Protein 6.9g; Carbohydrate 86.1g, of which sugars 85.5g; Fat 37.4g, of which saturates 17.9g; Cholesterol 52mg; Calcium 97mg; Fibre 3.1g; Sodium 64mg.

Chocolate Pavlova with Passion Fruit Cream

This meringue dessert has a scrumptious chewy centre that is hard to resist.

Serves 6
4 egg whites
200g/7oz/1 cup caster (superfine) sugar
20ml/4 tsp cornflour (cornstarch)
45g/1¾oz/3 tbsp unsweetened cocoa powder
5ml/1 tsp vinegar
chocolate leaves, to decorate

For the filling
150g/5oz plain (semisweet) chocolate, chopped into small pieces
250ml/8fl oz/1 cup double (heavy) cream
150g/5oz/⅔ cup Greek (US strained plain) yogurt
2.5ml/½ tsp vanilla extract
4 passion fruit

1 Preheat the oven to 140°C/275°F/Gas 1. Cut a piece of baking parchment to fit a baking sheet. Draw on a 23cm/9in circle.

2 Whisk the egg whites in a clean, grease-free bowl until stiff. Gradually whisk in the sugar and continue to whisk until the mixture is stiff again. Whisk in the cornflour, cocoa and vinegar.

3 Place the baking parchment upside down on the baking sheet. Spread the mixture over the circle, making a slight dip in the centre. Bake for 1½–2 hours.

4 Make the filling. Melt the chocolate in a heatproof bowl over barely simmering water, then remove from the heat and cool slightly. In a separate bowl, whip the cream with the yogurt and vanilla extract until thick. Fold 60ml/4 tbsp into the chocolate, then set both mixtures aside.

5 Halve all the passion fruit and scoop out the pulp. Stir half into the plain cream mixture. Carefully transfer the meringue shell to a serving plate. Fill with the passion fruit cream, then spoon over the chocolate mixture and the remaining passion fruit pulp. Decorate with chocolate leaves. Serve immediately.

Meringue Gateau with Chocolate Mascarpone

A chocolatey meringue treat, ideal for a special occasion.

Serves about 10
4 egg whites
pinch of salt
175g/6oz/generous ¾ cup caster (superfine) sugar
5ml/1 tsp ground cinnamon
75g/3oz plain (semisweet) chocolate, grated

icing (confectioners') sugar and rose petals, to decorate

For the filling
115g/4oz plain (semisweet) chocolate, chopped into small pieces
5ml/1 tsp vanilla extract or rosewater
115g/4oz/½ cup mascarpone cheese

1 Preheat the oven to 150°C/300°F/Gas 2. Line two large baking sheets with baking parchment. Whisk the egg whites with the salt in a clean, grease-free bowl until they form stiff peaks.

2 Gradually whisk in half the sugar, then add the rest and whisk until stiff and glossy. Add the cinnamon and chocolate and mix.

3 Draw a 20cm/8in circle on the parchment on one of the sheets, replace it upside down and spread the circle evenly with about half the meringue. Spoon the remaining meringue in 28–30 small heaps on the sheets. Bake for 1½ hours, until crisp.

4 Make the filling. Melt the chocolate in a heatproof bowl over hot water. Cool slightly, then add the vanilla extract (or rosewater) and cheese. Cool the mixture until it holds its shape.

5 Spoon the chocolate mixture into a large piping (pastry) bag and sandwich the meringues together in pairs, reserving a small amount of filling for assembling the gateau.

6 Peel off the parchment from the large round of meringue, then pile the filled meringues on top, piling them in a pyramid. Keep them in position with a few dabs of the reserved filling. Dust the pyramid with icing sugar, sprinkle with the rose petals and serve immediately.

Pavlova Energy 541kcal/2260kJ; Protein 7.3g; Carbohydrate 56.4g, of which sugars 52.3g; Fat 33.6g, of which saturates 20.4g; Cholesterol 59mg; Calcium 96mg; Fibre 1.9g; Sodium 146mg.
Meringue Gateau Energy 701kcal/2941kJ; Protein 8.2g; Carbohydrate 94.2g, of which sugars 93.1g; Fat 35g, of which saturates 21g; Cholesterol 12mg; Calcium 49mg; Fibre 3g; Sodium 31mg.

Dark Chocolate and Coffee Mousse Cake

This double treat will prove irresistible – rich sponge filled with a delicious creamy coffee mousse.

Serves 8
4 eggs
115g/4oz/generous ½ cup caster (superfine) sugar
75g/3oz/⅔ cup plain (all-purpose) flour, sifted
25g/1oz/¼ cup unsweetened cocoa powder, sifted

60ml/4 tbsp coffee liqueur, such as Tia Maria, Kahlúa or Toussaint
icing (confectioners') sugar, to dust

For the coffee mousse
30ml/2 tbsp dark-roasted ground coffee beans
350ml/12fl oz/1½ cups double (heavy) cream
115g/4oz/generous ½ cup granulated (white) sugar
120ml/4fl oz/½ cup water
4 egg yolks

1 Preheat the oven to 180°C/350°F/Gas 4. Grease and line the bases of a 20cm/8in square and a 23cm/9in round cake tin (pan) with baking parchment. Whisk the eggs and sugar in a bowl over a pan of hot water until thick. Remove from the heat.

2 Fold in the flour and cocoa. Pour a third into the square tin and the remainder into the round tin. Bake the square sponge for 15 minutes and the round for 30 minutes. Cool on a wire rack, then halve the round cake horizontally. Place the bottom half back in the tin. Sprinkle with half the liqueur. Trim the edges of the square sponge and cut into four strips to line the sides of the tin.

3 Make the mousse. Heat 50ml/2fl oz/¼ cup of the cream and pour over the coffee in a bowl, stirring until dissolved. Heat the sugar and water until dissolved. Increase the heat and boil until the syrup reaches 107°C/225°F. Cool for 5 minutes, then pour on to the egg yolks, whisking until the mixture is very thick.

4 Add the coffee cream to the remaining cream and beat until soft peaks form. Fold into the egg mixture. Spoon into the sponge case and freeze for 20 minutes. Sprinkle the remaining liqueur over the second half and place on top of the mousse. Freeze for 4 hours. Remove from the tin and dust with icing sugar.

Cappuccino Chocolate Torte

The famous and much loved beverage of freshly brewed coffee, whipped cream, chocolate and cinnamon is transformed here into a sensational dessert.

Serves 6–8
75g/3oz/6 tbsp butter, melted
275g/10oz shortbread biscuits (cookies), crushed
1.5ml/¼ tsp ground cinnamon
25ml/1½ tbsp powdered gelatine

45ml/3 tbsp cold water
2 eggs, separated
115g/4oz/½ cup soft light brown sugar
115g/4oz plain (semisweet) chocolate, chopped
175ml/6fl oz/¾ cup brewed espresso
400ml/14fl oz/1⅔ cups whipping cream
whole coffee beans and ground cinnamon, to decorate

1 Mix the butter with the biscuits and cinnamon until thoroughly combined. Spoon into the base of a 20cm/8in loose-based tin (pan) and press down well. Chill in the refrigerator while making the filling.

2 Sprinkle the gelatine over the cold water. Leave to soften for 5 minutes, then place the bowl over a pan of hot water and stir to dissolve.

3 Whisk the egg yolks and sugar until thick. Put the chocolate in a bowl with the coffee and stir until melted. Add to the egg mixture, then cook gently in a pan for 1–2 minutes until thickened. Stir in the gelatine. Leave until just beginning to set, stirring occasionally.

4 Whip 150ml/¼ pint/⅔ cup of the cream until soft peaks form. Whisk the egg whites until stiff. Gently fold the cream into the coffee mixture, followed by the egg whites. Pour the mixture over the biscuit base and chill for 2 hours.

5 When ready to serve, remove the torte from the tin and transfer to a serving plate. Whip the remaining cream in a bowl until it has thickened slightly and place a dollop on top. Decorate the top with a little ground cinnamon and place a few whole coffee beans on each plate.

Mousse Cake Energy 465kcal/1940kJ; Protein 7g; Carbohydrate 40.1g, of which sugars 32.6g; Fat 31.1g, of which saturates 16.6g; Cholesterol 262mg; Calcium 82mg; Fibre 0.7g; Sodium 88mg.
Cappuccino Torte Energy 584kcal/2429kJ; Protein 5.5g; Carbohydrate 47.3g, of which sugars 30.8g; Fat 42.7g, of which saturates 26.6g; Cholesterol 146mg; Calcium 81mg; Fibre 1g; Sodium 181mg.

Raspberry Chocolate Mousse Gateau

A lavish quantity of raspberries gives this chocolatey-based gateau its vibrant colour and full flavour. Make it at the height of summer, when raspberries are plentiful.

Serves 8–10
2 eggs
50g/2oz/¼ cup caster
  (superfine) sugar
50g/2oz/½ cup plain
  (all-purpose) flour
30ml/2 tbsp unsweetened
  cocoa powder
600g/1lb 5oz/3½ cups
  raspberries
115g/4oz/1 cup icing
  (confectioners') sugar
60ml/4 tbsp whisky (optional)
300ml/½ pint/1¼ cups
  whipping cream
2 egg whites

1 Preheat the oven to 180°C/350°F/Gas 4. Grease and line a 23cm/9in springform cake tin (pan). Whisk the eggs and sugar in a heatproof bowl set over a pan of simmering water until it leaves a trail. Remove from the heat and whisk for 2 minutes.

2 Sift the flour and cocoa powder over the mixture and fold in. Spoon into the tin and spread to the edges. Bake for 12–15 minutes until just firm. Leave to cool, then remove the cake from the tin and place it on a wire rack. Wash and dry the tin.

3 Line the sides of the clean tin with baking parchment and lower the cake back in. Freeze until the filling is ready. Set aside 200g/7oz/generous 1 cup of the raspberries. Put the remainder in a bowl, stir in the icing sugar and process to a purée in a food processor or blender. Strain into a bowl, then stir in the whisky, if using.

4 Whip the cream to form soft peaks. Whisk the egg whites until stiff. Fold the cream, then the whites into the purée. Spread half the filling over the cake. Sprinkle with the reserved raspberries. Spread the remaining filling on top and level the surface. Cover and freeze the gateau overnight.

5 Transfer the gateau to the refrigerator at least 1 hour before serving. Remove it from the tin, place on a serving plate and serve in slices.

Rich Chocolate Mousse Gateau

Because this gateau is heavily laced with liqueur, you can easily get away with a bought sponge. The mousse is rich, so serve small portions.

Serves 12
400g/14oz chocolate-flavoured
  Quick-mix Sponge Cake
75ml/5 tbsp Cointreau or other
  orange-flavoured liqueur
finely grated rind and juice
  of 1 orange
300g/11oz plain (semisweet)
  chocolate, broken into pieces
25g/1oz/¼ cup unsweetened
  cocoa powder
45ml/3 tbsp golden (light
  corn) syrup
3 eggs
300ml/½ pint/1¼ cups
  whipping cream
150ml/¼ pint/⅔ cup double
  (heavy) cream, lightly whipped
unsweetened cocoa powder,
  for dusting

1 Cut the cake into 5mm/¼in thick slices. Set a third aside, and use the remainder to make a case for the mousse. Line the bottom of a 23cm/9in springform or loose-based cake tin (pan) with cake, trimming to fit neatly, then use more for the sides, making a case about 4cm/1½ in deep.

2 Mix 30ml/2 tbsp of the liqueur with the orange juice and drizzle over the sponge case. Put the chocolate in a heatproof bowl. Add the cocoa powder, syrup and remaining liqueur and place the bowl over a pan of simmering water. Leave until melted and smooth, then remove from the heat.

3 Whisk the eggs with the orange rind in a mixing bowl until they are thick and pale. Whip the whipping cream until it forms soft peaks. Fold the chocolate mixture into the whisked eggs, using a large metal spoon, then fold in the cream. Scrape the mixture into the sponge case and level the surface.

4 Cover with the reserved chocolate cake, trimming the pieces to fit. Cover and freeze overnight.

5 Transfer the gateau to the refrigerator 30 minutes before serving. Invert on to a plate, spread with the double cream and dust with cocoa powder.

Raspberry Gateau Energy 238kcal/996kJ; Protein 4.4g; Carbohydrate 25g, of which sugars 20.9g; Fat 14.1g, of which saturates 8.3g; Cholesterol 70mg; Calcium 58mg; Fibre 2g; Sodium 65mg.
Rich Mousse Gateau Energy 488kcal/2032kJ; Protein 6g; Carbohydrate 37.4g, of which sugars 29.6g; Fat 34.4g, of which saturates 15.3g; Cholesterol 92mg; Calcium 61mg; Fibre 1.2g; Sodium 175mg.

White Chocolate and Brownie Torte

An exceedingly rich dessert, this quick but impressive-looking dish is guaranteed to appeal to chocolate lovers. The great thing about this recipe is that it uses very few ingredients, making shopping a breeze.

Serves 10
300g/11oz white chocolate, broken into pieces
600ml/1 pint/2½ cups double (heavy) cream
250g/9oz rich chocolate brownies
unsweetened cocoa powder, for dusting

1 Dampen the sides of a 20cm/8in springform tin (pan) and line with a strip of baking parchment. Put the chocolate in a small pan. Add 150ml/¼ pint/⅔ cup of the cream and heat very gently until the chocolate has melted. Stir until smooth, then pour into a bowl and leave to cool.

2 Break the chocolate brownies into chunky pieces and sprinkle these on the bottom of the prepared tin. Pack them down lightly to make a fairly dense base.

3 Whip the remaining cream until it forms soft peaks, then fold in the white chocolate mixture.

4 Spoon into the tin to cover the layer of brownies, then tap the tin gently on the work surface to level the chocolate mixture. Cover the tin and freeze for a few hours or overnight.

5 Transfer the torte to the refrigerator about 45 minutes before serving, then remove the tin to serve. Decorate with a light dusting of cocoa powder before serving.

> **Cook's Tips**
> • If you are unable to find good quality brownies, use a moist chocolate sponge instead.
> • Serve with a fresh fruit salad as a foil to the richness. A mix of summer fruit topped with a purée made from lightly cooked raspberries is the perfect partner.

Chocolate and Brandied Fig Torte

A seriously rich torte for chocolate lovers. If you dislike figs, use dried prunes, dates or apricots instead.

Serves 8
250g/9oz/1½ cups dried figs
60ml/4 tbsp brandy
200g/7oz ginger nut biscuits (gingersnaps)

175g/6oz/¾ cup unsalted (sweet) butter, softened
150ml/¼ pint/⅔ cup milk
250g/9oz plain (semisweet) chocolate, broken into pieces
45ml/3 tbsp caster (superfine) sugar
unsweetened cocoa powder, for dusting
whipped cream, to serve

1 Chop the figs and put them into a bowl, pour over the brandy and leave for 2–3 hours until most of the brandy has been absorbed. Break the gingersnap biscuits into large chunks, put the pieces in a strong plastic bag and crush them with a rolling pin.

2 Melt half the butter and stir in the crumbs until combined. Pack on to the bottom and up the sides of a 20cm/8in loose-based flan tin (pan) that is about 3cm/1¼in deep Leave in the refrigerator to chill.

3 Pour the milk into a pan, add the chocolate pieces and heat gently until the chocolate has melted and the mixture is smooth, stirring frequently. Pour the chocolate mixture into a bowl and leave to cool.

4 In a separate bowl, beat the remaining butter with the caster sugar until the mixture is pale and creamy.

5 Add the chocolate mixture, whisking until it is well mixed. Fold in the figs, and any remaining brandy, and spoon the mixture into the chilled flan case. Level the surface, cover and freeze overnight.

6 Transfer the frozen torte to the refrigerator about 30 minutes before serving so that the filling softens slightly. Lightly dust the surface with cocoa powder and serve in slices, with dollops of lightly whipped cream.

Brownie Torte Energy 570kcal/2365kJ; Protein 5.2g; Carbohydrate 31.1g, of which sugars 25.7g; Fat 48.1g, of which saturates 25.6g; Cholesterol 82mg; Calcium 129mg; Fibre 0g; Sodium 154mg.
Fig Torte Energy 539kcal/2257kJ; Protein 5g; Carbohydrate 63.9g, of which sugars 54.2g; Fat 29.7g, of which saturates 17.7g; Cholesterol 50mg; Calcium 172mg; Fibre 4.1g; Sodium 241mg.

Iced Praline Chocolate Torte

This lovely torte will serve you well on any occasion.

Serves 8
115g/4oz/1 cup almonds
115g/4oz/generous ½ cup caster (superfine) sugar
115g/4oz/⅔ cup raisins
90ml/6 tbsp rum or brandy
115g/4oz dark (bittersweet) chocolate, broken into squares
30ml/2 tbsp milk
450ml/¾ pint/scant 2 cups double (heavy) cream
30ml/2 tbsp strong black coffee
16 sponge fingers

To finish
150ml/¼ pint/⅔ cup double (heavy) cream
50g/2oz/1½ cup flaked (sliced) almonds, toasted
15g/½oz dark (bittersweet) chocolate, melted

1 To make the praline, oil a baking sheet. Put the nuts into a heavy pan with the sugar and heat gently until the sugar melts and coats the nuts. Cook slowly until the nuts brown and the sugar caramelizes. Transfer the nuts quickly to the sheet; leave until cold. Break up and grind to a fine powder in a blender.

2 Soak the raisins in 45ml/3 tbsp of the rum or brandy for at least an hour to soften and absorb the rum. Melt the chocolate with the milk in a bowl over a pan of hot, but not boiling water. Remove and leave until cold. Lightly grease a 1.2 litre/2 pint/5 cup loaf tin (pan) and line it with baking parchment.

3 Whisk the cream in a bowl until it holds soft peaks. Whisk in the chocolate. Fold in the praline and the raisins, with any liquid.

4 Mix the coffee and remaining rum or brandy in a shallow dish. Dip in the sponge fingers and arrange half in a layer over the base of the prepared loaf tin. Cover with the chocolate mixture and add another layer of soaked sponge fingers. Leave in the freezer overnight.

5 To finish, whip the double cream. Dip the tin briefly in warm water and turn the torte out on to a serving plate. Cover with the whipped cream, sprinkle the top with toasted almonds and drizzle with melted chocolate. Freeze until needed.

Iced Paradise Chocolate Cake

Serve this rich and creamy delight chilled.

Makes one 23 x 13cm/9 x 5in cake
3 eggs
75g/3oz/scant ½ cup caster (superfine) sugar
65g/12½oz/9 tbsp plain (all-purpose) flour, sifted
15g/½oz/2 tbsp cornflour (cornstarch), sifted
90ml/6 tbsp dark rum
250g/9oz/1½ cups plain (semisweet) chocolate chips
30ml/2 tbsp golden (light corn) syrup
30ml/2 tbsp water
115g/4oz/generous 1 cup desiccated (dry unsweetened shredded) coconut, toasted
400ml/14fl oz/1⅔ cups double (heavy) cream, whipped
25g/1oz/2 tbsp unsalted (sweet) butter
30ml/2 tbsp single (light) cream
50g/2oz/⅓ cup white chocolate chips, melted
coconut curls, to decorate
unsweetened cocoa powder, to dust

1 Preheat the oven to 200°C/400°F/Gas 6. Grease and flour two baking sheets. Line a 23 × 13cm/9 × 5in loaf tin (pan) with clear film (plastic wrap).

2 Whisk the eggs and sugar together in a heatproof bowl. Place over a pan of simmering water and whisk until pale and thick. Whisk off the heat until cool. Fold in the flour and cornflour. Pipe 30 7.5cm/3in sponge fingers on to the baking sheets. Bake for 8–10 minutes. Cool slightly, then transfer to a wire rack.

3 Line the base and sides of the loaf tin with sponge fingers. Brush with rum. Melt 75g/3oz/½ cup chocolate chips, the syrup, water and 30ml/2 tbsp rum in a bowl over simmering water.

4 Stir the chocolate mixture and coconut into the cream. Pour into the tin and top with the remaining fingers. Brush with the remaining rum. Cover with clear film and freeze until firm.

5 Melt the remaining chocolate with the butter and single cream as before, then cool slightly. Turn the cake out on to a wire rack. Coat with the icing then chill. Drizzle with white chocolate zigzags and chill again. Sprinkle with coconut curls and dust with cocoa powder.

Praline Torte Energy 636kcal/2650kJ; Protein 7.7g; Carbohydrate 49.5g, of which sugars 43.5g; Fat 43.9g, of which saturates 22.3g; Cholesterol 134mg; Calcium 104mg; Fibre 1.9g; Sodium 47mg.
Paradise Energy 5502kcal/22864kJ; Protein 62.6g; Carbohydrate 349.1g, of which sugars 226.4g; Fat 416.4g, of which saturates 267.8g; Cholesterol 1204mg; Calcium 760mg; Fibre 26.4g; Sodium 653mg.

White Chocolate, Frosted Raspberry and Coffee Terrine

A white chocolate and raspberry layer and a contrasting smooth coffee layer make this attractive-looking terrine dessert doubly delicious.

Serves 6–8

30ml/2 tbsp ground coffee, e.g. mocha orange-flavoured
250ml/8fl oz/1 cup milk
4 eggs, separated
50g/2oz/¼ cup caster (superfine) sugar
30ml/2 tbsp cornflour (cornstarch)
150ml/¼ pint/⅔ cup double (heavy) cream
150g/5oz white chocolate, roughly chopped
115g/4oz/⅔ cup raspberries
shavings of white chocolate and cocoa powder, to decorate

1 Line a 1.5 litre/2½ pint/6¼ cup loaf tin (pan) with clear film (plastic wrap) and chill in the freezer. Put the coffee in a jug (pitcher). Heat 100ml/3½fl oz/scant ½ cup of the milk to near-boiling point and pour over the coffee. Leave to infuse (steep).

2 Blend the egg yolks, sugar and cornflour together in a pan and whisk in the remaining milk and the cream. Bring to the boil, stirring all the time, until thickened.

3 Divide the mixture between two bowls and add the white chocolate to one, stirring until melted. Strain the coffee into the other bowl and mix well. Leave until cool, stirring occasionally.

4 Whisk two of the egg whites until stiff. Fold into the coffee custard. Spoon into the tin. Freeze for 30 minutes. Whisk the remaining whites and fold into the chocolate mixture with the raspberries. Spoon into the tin and level. Freeze for 4 hours.

5 Turn the terrine out on to a flat serving plate and peel off the clear film. Cover with shavings and dust with cocoa powder.

> **Cook's Tip**
> Soften the terrine in the refrigerator for 20 minutes before slicing.

Classic Triple Chocolate Terrine

This variation on Neapolitan ice cream is made with smooth, dark, milk and white chocolate.

Serves 8–10

6 egg yolks
115g/4oz/generous ½ cup caster (superfine) sugar
5ml/1 tsp cornflour (cornstarch)
450ml/¾ pint/scant 2 cups semi-skimmed (low-fat) milk
115g/4oz dark (bittersweet) chocolate, broken into squares
115g/4oz milk chocolate, broken into squares
115g/4oz white chocolate, broken into squares
2.5ml/½ tsp natural vanilla extract
450ml/¾ pint/scant 2 cups whipping cream

1 Whisk the egg yolks, sugar and cornflour until thick. Pour the milk into a pan and bring to the boil. Pour it on to the yolk mixture, whisking constantly, then return the mixture to the pan and simmer, stirring, until the custard thickens and is smooth.

2 Divide the custard among three bowls. Add the chocolates: the dark to one, milk to another, and white and vanilla to the third. Stir with separate spoons until the chocolate has melted. Cool, then chill. Line a 25 × 7.5 × 7.5cm/10 × 3 × 3in terrine or large loaf tin (pan) with clear film (plastic wrap).

3 Stir a third of the cream into each bowl, then churn the milk chocolate custard mixture until thick. Return the remaining bowls of flavoured custard and cream mixture to the refrigerator. Spoon the milk chocolate ice cream into the terrine or tin, level the surface and freeze the ice cream until it is firm.

4 Churn the white chocolate ice cream in an ice cream maker until it is thick and smooth, then spoon it into the tin. Level the surface and freeze the ice cream until it is firm. Finally, churn the dark chocolate ice cream and spread it in the tin to form the top layer, making sure the surface is smooth and level.

5 Cover the terrine with clear film, then freeze it overnight. To serve, remove the clear film cover, then invert on to a plate. Peel off the clear film and serve in slices.

Raspberry Terrine Energy 285kcal/1189kJ; Protein 6.2g; Carbohydrate 23.4g, of which sugars 19.9g; Fat 19.2g, of which saturates 10.8g; Cholesterol 123mg; Calcium 119mg; Fibre 0.4g; Sodium 76mg.
Chocolate Terrine Energy 453kcal/1889kJ; Protein 6.6g; Carbohydrate 35.9g, of which sugars 35.8g; Fat 32.5g, of which saturates 18.9g; Cholesterol 174mg; Calcium 160mg; Fibre 0.4g; Sodium 60mg.

Mocha, Prune and Armagnac Terrine

A sophisticated iced chocolate dessert for entertaining in style.

Serves 6

115g/4oz/½ cup ready-to-eat
    pitted prunes, chopped
90ml/6 tbsp Armagnac
90g/3½oz/½ cup caster
    (superfine) sugar
150ml/¼ pint/⅔ cup water
45ml/3 tbsp coffee beans
150g/5oz plain (semisweet)
    chocolate, broken into pieces
300ml/½ pint/1¼ cups
    double (heavy) cream
unsweetened cocoa powder,
    for dusting

1 Put the prunes in a small bowl. Pour over 75ml/5 tbsp of the Armagnac and leave to soak for at least 3 hours or overnight in the refrigerator. Line the bases of six 100ml/3½fl oz/scant ½ cup ramekins with baking parchment.

2 Put the sugar and water in a heavy pan and heat gently until the sugar dissolves, stirring occasionally. Add the soaked prunes and any of the Armagnac that remains in the bowl; simmer the prunes gently in the syrup for 5 minutes.

3 Using a slotted spoon, lift the prunes out of the pan and set them aside. Add the coffee beans to the syrup and simmer gently for 5 minutes.

4 Lift out the coffee beans and put about a third of them in a bowl. Spoon over 120ml/4fl oz/½ cup of the syrup and stir in the remaining Armagnac.

5 Add the chocolate to the pan containing the remaining syrup and leave until melted. Whip the cream until it just holds its shape. Using a large metal spoon, fold the chocolate mixture and prunes into the cream until just combined. Spoon the mixture into the lined ramekins, cover and freeze for at least 3 hours.

6 To serve, loosen the edges of the ramekins with a knife, then dip in very hot water for 2 seconds and invert on to serving plates. Decorate with the syrup and a dusting of cocoa powder.

Iced Pear Terrine with Calvados and Chocolate Sauce

This terrine makes a refreshing and impressive end to a meal. Ensure the pears are ripe and juicy.

Serves 8

1.5kg/3–3½lb ripe Williams pears
juice of 1 lemon
115g/4oz/generous ½ cup caster
    (superfine) sugar
10 whole cloves
90ml/6 tbsp water
julienne strips of orange rind,
    to decorate

For the sauce
200g/7oz plain (semisweet)
    chocolate
60ml/4 tbsp hot strong
    black coffee
200ml/7fl oz/1 cup double
    (heavy) cream
30ml/2 tbsp Calvados or brandy

1 Peel, core and slice the pears. Place them in a pan with the lemon juice, sugar, cloves and water. Cover and simmer for 10 minutes. Remove the cloves. Allow the pears to cool.

2 Process the pears with their juice, in a food processor or blender, until smooth. Pour the purée into a freezerproof bowl, cover and freeze until firm.

3 Meanwhile, line a 900g/2lb loaf tin (pan) with clear film (plastic wrap). Allow the film to overhang the sides of the tin. Remove the frozen pear purée from the freezer and spoon it into a food processor or blender. Process until smooth. Pour into the prepared tin, cover and freeze until firm.

4 Make the sauce. Break the chocolate into a large heatproof bowl over a pan of simmering water, stirring until melted and smooth. Stir in the coffee and the cream and then the Calvados or brandy. Set the sauce aside.

5 About 20 minutes before serving, remove the tin from the freezer. Invert on to a plate, lift off the clear film and place the terrine in the refrigerator to soften slightly. Heat the sauce over hot water. Slice the terrine and spoon over some of the sauce. Decorate with julienne strips of orange rind.

Mocha Terrine Energy 495kcal/2060kJ; Protein 2.6g; Carbohydrate 38.9g, of which sugars 38.7g; Fat 33.9g, of which saturates 20.9g; Cholesterol 70mg; Calcium 47mg; Fibre 1.7g; Sodium 16mg.
Pear Terrine Energy 392kcal/1638kJ; Protein 2.3g; Carbohydrate 50.1g, of which sugars 49.9g; Fat 20.6g, of which saturates 12.6g; Cholesterol 36mg; Calcium 49mg; Fibre 4.8g; Sodium 14mg.

Chocolate and Vanilla Ice Cream

To make this popular classic, use good quality chocolate to give the best flavour.

Serves 6
750ml/1¼ pints/3 cups milk
10cm/4in piece of vanilla
   pod (bean)

4 egg yolks
150g/5oz/¾ cup granulated
   (white) sugar
225g/8oz dark (bittersweet)
   chocolate, melted

1 To make the custard, heat the milk with the vanilla pod in a small pan. Remove from the heat as soon as small bubbles start to form. Do not boil.

2 Beat the egg yolks with a wire whisk or electric beater. Gradually incorporate the sugar, and continue beating for about 5 minutes until the mixture is pale yellow. Strain the milk and slowly add it to the egg mixture, drop by drop.

3 Pour the mixture into a double boiler with the melted chocolate. Stir over moderate heat until the water in the pan is boiling, and the custard thickens enough to lightly coat the back of a spoon. Remove from the heat and allow to cool.

4 Pour the mixture into a freezer container and freeze until set, about 3 hours. Remove from the container and chop roughly into 7.5cm/3in pieces. Place in the bowl of a food processor and process until smooth. Return to the freezer container, and freeze again until firm. Repeat the freezing and chopping process two or three times, until a smooth consistency is reached, then freeze until required. Alternatively, you can use an ice cream maker and freeze the mixture following the manufacturer's instructions.

> **Cook's Tip**
> If you do not have a double boiler, cook the custard in a heatproof bowl set over a pan of water. Make sure that the custard does not boil, otherwise it will curdle.

Chocolate Flake Ice Cream

This enticing ice cream, speckled with chocolate, is difficult to resist. Serve with slices of tropical fruit, such as pineapple and mango, for a perfect balance.

Serves 6
300ml/½ pint/1¼ cups whipping
   cream, chilled

90ml/6 tbsp Greek (US strained
   plain) yogurt
75–90ml/5–6 tbsp caster
   (superfine) sugar
few drops of vanilla extract
150g/5oz/10 tbsp flaked or
   roughly grated chocolate
flaked chocolate pieces,
   to decorate

1 Have ready a 600–900ml/1–1½ pint/2½–3¾ cup freezer container, preferably with a lid.

2 Gently whip the cream in a large bowl until thickened slightly then fold in the yogurt, sugar, vanilla extract and chocolate. Stir gently to combine thoroughly, and then transfer to the freezer container.

3 Smooth the surface of the ice cream, then cover and freeze. Gently stir with a fork every 30 minutes for up to 4 hours until the ice cream is too hard to stir.

4 Alternatively, use an ice cream maker. Freeze the cream and chocolate mixture following the manufacturer's instructions.

5 Transfer to the refrigerator 15 minutes before serving to soften slightly. Serve in scoops, decorated with chocolate flakes.

> **Cook's Tips**
> • Transferring the ice cream from the freezer to the refrigerator for a short time before serving allows the full flavour of the dessert to develop and makes it easier to scoop it into neat balls for serving.
> • Use a metal scoop to serve the ice cream. Dipping the scoop briefly in warm water between servings helps to stop the ice cream sticking to the scoop.

Chocolate Energy 388kcal/1634kJ; Protein 8.2g; Carbohydrate 55.8g, of which sugars 55.5g; Fat 16.3g, of which saturates 8.7g; Cholesterol 144mg; Calcium 191mg; Fibre 0.9g; Sodium 64mg.
Flake Energy 385kcal/1600kJ; Protein 3.3g; Carbohydrate 30.6g, of which sugars 30.4g; Fat 28.7g, of which saturates 17.6g; Cholesterol 54mg; Calcium 66mg; Fibre 0.6g; Sodium 25mg.

White Chocolate Raspberry Ripple

A truly luscious treat that always impresses. Note that an ice cream maker is required for this recipe.

Serves 6
250ml/8fl oz/1 cup milk
475ml/16fl oz/2 cups
  whipping cream
7 egg yolks
30ml/2 tbsp sugar
225g/8oz good white chocolate,
  chopped into small pieces

5ml/1 tsp vanilla extract
mint sprigs, to decorate

For the sauce
275g/10oz raspberry preserve or
  275g/10oz frozen raspberries
  in light syrup
10ml/2 tsp golden (light
  corn) syrup
15ml/1 tbsp lemon juice
15ml/1 tbsp cornflour (cornstarch),
  if using frozen fruit in syrup,
  mixed with 15ml/1 tbsp water

1 For the sauce, put the preserve in a pan with the golden syrup, the lemon juice and the water but not the cornflour. If using frozen fruit, press the fruit and its syrup through a sieve (strainer) into a pan and add all the other sauce ingredients. Bring to the boil, stirring. Simmer for 2 minutes. Pour into a bowl, cool, then chill.

2 In a pan, combine the milk and 250ml/8fl oz/1 cup of the cream and bring to the boil. In a bowl, beat the yolks and sugar with a hand-held mixer for 2–3 minutes until thick and creamy. Gradually pour the hot milk mixture over the yolks and return to the pan. Cook over a medium heat, stirring constantly, until the custard coats the back of a wooden spoon.

3 Remove the pan from the heat and stir in the white chocolate until melted and smooth. Pour the remaining cream into a large bowl. Strain in the hot custard, mix well, then stir in the vanilla extract. Cool, then freeze in an ice cream maker.

4 When frozen but soft, transfer a third of the ice cream to a freezerproof bowl. Set aside half the sauce, spooning a third of the rest over the ice cream. Cover with another third of the ice cream and more sauce. Repeat. With a knife, lightly marble the mixture. Cover and freeze. Soften the ice cream for 15 minutes. Serve with the rest of the raspberry sauce, and the mint.

Chocolate Cookie Ice Cream

This wickedly indulgent ice cream is a favourite in the USA. To make the result even more luxurious, use freshly baked home-made cookies with large chunks of chocolate and nuts.

Serves 4–6
4 egg yolks
75g/3oz/scant ½ cup caster
  (superfine) sugar

5ml/1 tsp cornflour (cornstarch)
300ml/½ pint/1¼ cups
  semi-skimmed (low-fat) milk
5ml/1 tsp natural vanilla extract
300ml/½ pint/1¼ cups
  whipping cream
150g/5oz chunky chocolate and
  hazelnut cookies, crumbled into
  chunky pieces

1 Whisk the egg yolks, sugar and cornflour in a bowl until the mixture is thick and foamy. Pour the milk into a heavy pan, bring it just to the boil, then pour it on to the yolk mixture in the bowl, whisking constantly.

2 Return to the pan and cook over a gentle heat, stirring until the custard thickens and is smooth. Pour it back into the bowl and cover closely. Leave to cool, then chill.

3 Stir the vanilla into the custard. Stir in the whipping cream and churn in an ice cream maker until thick.

4 Scrape the ice cream into a freezerproof container. Fold in the cookie chunks and freeze for 2–3 hours until firm.

5 Remove the ice cream from the freezer about 15 minutes before serving to allow it to soften slightly.

> **Cook's Tip**
> • Experiment with different types of cookie to find the type that gives the best results.
> • Softening the ice cream before serving will not only help make the ice cream tastier, but will also ensure the pieces of cookie inside are the perfect texture.

Raspberry Ripple Energy 735kcal/3066kJ; Protein 10.3g; Carbohydrate 63.3g, of which sugars 61g; Fat 50.8g, of which saturates 29.2g; Cholesterol 321mg; Calcium 242mg; Fibre 1.2g; Sodium 110mg.
Cookie Energy 428kcal/1782kJ; Protein 6.2g; Carbohydrate 36.3g, of which sugars 27.1g; Fat 29.7g, of which saturates 16.4g; Cholesterol 189mg; Calcium 135mg; Fibre 0.5g; Sodium 129mg.

Ice Cream Sundae with Chocolate Sauce

This immensely popular sundae dessert consists of good quality vanilla ice cream with a decadent warm chocolate sauce.

Serves 4
350ml/12fl oz/1½ cups milk
250ml/8fl oz/1 cup double (heavy) cream
1 vanilla pod (bean)
4 egg yolks
90g/3½oz/½ cup caster (superfine) sugar

For the chocolate sauce
60ml/4 tbsp double (heavy) cream
150ml/¼ pint/⅔ cup milk
250g/9oz Callebaut callets (semisweet bits) or other good-quality chocolate, cut into small pieces
15ml/1 tbsp brandy, rum or liqueur such as Cointreau (optional)
sweetened whipped cream, chopped nuts, chocolate curls and ice cream wafers (optional), to serve

1 Pour 250ml/8fl oz/1 cup of the milk into a heavy pan. Add the cream. Slit the vanilla pod, scrape the seeds into the pan, then heat the mixture until nearly boiling. Remove from the heat and leave to stand for 10 minutes.

2 Beat the egg yolks and sugar in a bowl until thick and creamy. Still beating, add a third of the milk mixture in a steady stream. Add the remaining milk mixture and whisk for 2 minutes more.

3 Return to the pan and cook over medium-high heat, stirring, for 5 minutes, until the custard coats the back of a spoon. Remove the pan from the heat and stir in the remaining milk. When cooled, cover and chill. Scrape the chilled mixture into a freezer container and freeze until firm, whisking occasionally.

4 Make the chocolate sauce. Simmer the cream and milk in a pan. Remove from the heat and stir in the chocolate bits until dissolved. Stir in the brandy or liqueur, if using.

5 Pour about 20ml/4 tsp of the warm chocolate sauce into ice cream coupes or cups. Top with scoops of ice cream and more sauce. Pipe cream on top, add chopped nuts, curls and a wafer.

Chocolate Fudge and Banana Sundae

A banana and ice cream treat, highlighted with coffee.

Serves 4
4 scoops each vanilla and coffee ice cream
2 small ripe bananas
whipped cream
toasted flaked (sliced) almonds

For the sauce
50g/2oz/¼ cup soft light brown sugar
120ml/4fl oz/½ cup golden (light corn) syrup
45ml/3 tbsp strong black coffee
5ml/1 tsp ground cinnamon
150g/5oz plain (semisweet) chocolate, chopped into small pieces
75ml/2½fl oz/⅓ cup whipping cream
45ml/3 tbsp coffee-flavoured liqueur (optional)

1 Make the sauce. Place the sugar, syrup, coffee and cinnamon in a heavy pan. Bring to the boil, then boil for about 5 minutes, stirring the mixture constantly.

2 Turn off the heat and stir in the chocolate pieces. When the chocolate has melted and the mixture is smooth, stir in the cream and the coffee-flavoured liqueur, if using. Set the sauce aside to cool slightly.

3 Fill four glasses with a scoop each of vanilla and coffee ice cream.

4 Peel the bananas and slice them thinly. Sprinkle the sliced bananas over the ice cream. Pour the warm fudge sauce over the bananas, then top each sundae with a generous swirl of whipped cream. Sprinkle the sundaes with toasted almonds and serve immediately.

> **Cook's Tip**
> To make life easier you can make the chocolate sauce ahead of time and reheat it gently, until just warm, when you are ready to make the sundaes. Assemble the sundaes just before serving.

Ice Cream Energy 930kcal/3869kJ; Protein 11.2g; Carbohydrate 72.3g, of which sugars 71.7g; Fat 68.2g, of which saturates 40.2g; Cholesterol 324mg; Calcium 229mg; Fibre 1.6g; Sodium 80mg.
Fudge Energy 642kcal/2690kJ; Protein 5.5g; Carbohydrate 85.9g, of which sugars 84g; Fat 33.1g, of which saturates 20.5g; Cholesterol 64mg; Calcium 115mg; Fibre 1.4g; Sodium 132mg.

French-style Coupe Glacée with Chocolate Ice Cream

This dessert can be made with bought ice cream, but this extra rich chocolate ice cream is the main feature.

Serves 6–8

225g/8oz dark (bittersweet) chocolate, chopped
250ml/8fl oz/1 cup milk mixed with 250ml/8fl oz/1 cup single (light) cream
3 egg yolks
50g/1¾oz/¼ cup sugar
350ml/12fl oz/1½ cups double (heavy) cream
15ml/1 tbsp vanilla extract
chocolate triangles, to decorate

For the espresso cream

45g/3 tbsp instant espresso powder, dissolved in 45ml/ 3 tbsp boiling water, cooled
350ml/12fl oz/1½ cups double (heavy) cream
30ml/2 tbsp coffee-flavoured liqueur

For the sauce

300ml/10fl oz/1¼ cups double (heavy) cream
30g/2 tbsp instant espresso powder, dissolved in 45ml/ 3 tbsp boiling water
320g/11oz dark (bittersweet) chocolate, chopped
30ml/2 tbsp coffee-flavoured liqueur

1 Melt the chocolate in a pan over a low heat with 120ml/ 4fl oz/½ cup of the milk mixture. In another pan, boil the remaining milk mixture. Beat the egg yolks and sugar in a bowl until thick and creamy. Pour the milk mixture over the yolks, whisking, and return to the pan. Heat until it thickens, stirring. Pour over the melted chocolate, stirring until blended.

2 Pour the cream into a bowl, and strain in the custard with the vanilla. Blend, then cool. Refrigerate until cold. Transfer to an ice cream maker and freeze according to instructions.

3 Make the espresso cream. Stir the espresso powder into the cream and beat until soft peaks form. Add the liqueur and mix. Spoon into a piping (pastry) bag fitted with a star tip and chill.

4 Prepare the sauce. Boil the cream and espresso powder. Remove from the heat and stir in the chocolate and liqueur. Pipe a layer of espresso cream into six wine goblets. Add the ice cream. Spoon on the sauce and top with rosettes of espresso cream.

Black Forest Sundae

There's more than one way to enjoy the classic Black Forest Gateau. Here the traditional ingredients are layered in a sundae glass to make a superb cold sweet.

Serves 4

400g/14oz can stoned (pitted) black cherries in syrup
15ml/1 tbsp cornflour (cornstarch)

45ml/3 tbsp Kirsch
150ml/¼ pint/⅔ cup whipping cream
15ml/1 tbsp icing (confectioners') sugar
600ml/1 pint/2½ cups chocolate ice cream
115g/4oz chocolate-flavoured Sponge Cake
8 fresh cherries
vanilla ice cream, to serve

1 Strain the cherry syrup from the can into a pan. Spoon the cornflour into a small bowl and stir in 30ml/2 tbsp of the strained cherry syrup.

2 Bring the syrup in the pan to the boil. Stir in the cornflour and syrup mixture. Simmer briefly, stirring constantly, until the syrup thickens.

3 Add the drained canned cherries, stir in the Kirsch and spread on a metal tray to cool.

4 Whip the cream in a large bowl with the icing sugar until the mixture thickens.

5 Place a spoonful of the cherry mixture in the bottom of four sundae glasses. Continue with layers of ice cream, cake, cream and more cherry mixture until the glasses are full.

6 Finish with a piece of chocolate cake, two scoops of ice cream and more cream. Decorate with the fresh cherries.

> **Cook's Tip**
> Bottled black cherries often have a better flavour than canned ones, especially if the stones are left in. You needn't remove the stones – just remember to warn your guests.

Coupe Energy 1062kcal/4400kJ; Protein 8.6g; Carbohydrate 50.9g, of which sugars 50.3g; Fat 92.4g, of which saturates 56.4g; Cholesterol 262mg; Calcium 152mg; Fibre 1.8g; Sodium 55mg.
Black Forest Energy 727kcal/3031kJ; Protein 9.4g; Carbohydrate 68g, of which sugars 58.2g; Fat 45.4g, of which saturates 23.1g; Cholesterol 39mg; Calcium 213mg; Fibre 0.7g; Sodium 233mg.

Chocolate Bombes with Hot Sauce

These individual ice cream bombes, with a surprise vanilla and chocolate-chip centre, are served with a hot toffee cream sauce to make a truly indulgent hot-and-cold dessert.

Serves 6
1 litre/1¾ pints/4 cups soft-scoop chocolate ice cream

475ml/16fl oz/2 cups soft-scoop vanilla ice cream
50g/2oz/⅓ cup plain (semisweet) chocolate chips

For the sauce
115g/4oz toffees
75ml/5 tbsp double (heavy) cream

1 Divide the chocolate ice cream equally among six small cups. Push it roughly to the base and up the sides, leaving a small cup-shaped dip in the middle. Put them in the freezer and leave for 45 minutes. Take the cups out again and smooth the ice cream in each to make cup shapes with hollow centres. Return to the freezer.

2 Put the vanilla ice cream in a small bowl and break it up slightly with a spoon. Stir in the chocolate chips and use this mixture to fill the hollows in the cups of chocolate ice cream. Smooth the tops, then cover the cups with clear film (plastic wrap), return to the freezer and leave overnight.

3 Melt the toffees with the cream in a small pan over a very low heat, stirring constantly until smooth, warm and creamy.

4 Turn out the bombes on to individual plates and pour the toffee sauce over the top. Serve immediately.

> **Cook's Tips**
> • To make it easier to unmould the bombes, dip them briefly in hot water, then turn out immediately on to serving plates. If you wish, you can return the unmoulded bombes to the freezer for about 10 minutes to firm up.
> • Serve with crisp little biscuits (cookies) for a crunchy contrast.

Rocky Road Ice Cream

A gloriously rich chocolate ice cream with lots of texture.

Serves 6
115g/4oz plain (semisweet) chocolate, chopped into small pieces
150ml/¼ pint/⅔ cup milk
300ml/½ pint/1¼ cups double (heavy) cream

115g/4oz/2 cups marshmallows, chopped
115g/4oz/½ cup glacé (candied) cherries, chopped
50g/2oz/½ cup crumbled shortbread
30ml/2 tbsp chopped walnuts
chocolate sauce and wafers, to serve (optional)

1 Melt the chocolate in the milk in a pan over a gentle heat, stirring from time to time. Pour into a bowl and leave to cool.

2 Whip the cream in a separate bowl until it just holds its shape. Beat in the chocolate mixture, a little at a time, until the mixture is smooth and creamy.

3 Pour the chocolate mixture into a freezer container and transfer to the freezer. Freeze until ice crystals form around the edges, then whisk with a strong hand whisk or hand-held electric mixer until smooth. Alternatively, use an ice cream maker and churn the mixture until almost frozen, following the manufacturer's instructions.

4 Stir the marshmallows, glacé cherries, crumbled shortbread and nuts into the iced mixture, then return to the freezer container and freeze until firm.

5 Allow the ice cream to soften at room temperature for 15–20 minutes before serving in scoops. Add a wafer and chocolate sauce to each portion, if you wish.

> **Cook's Tip**
> Do not allow the ice cream mixture to freeze too hard before step 4, otherwise it will be difficult to stir in the remaining ingredients.

Layered Chocolate, Chestnut and Brandy Bombes

Using an ice cream maker takes all the effort out of making these triple-flavoured ice creams, which taste delicious and look stunning.

Serves 6

3 egg yolks
75g/3oz/scant ½ cup caster
  (superfine) sugar
5ml/1 tsp cornflour (cornstarch)
300ml/½ pint/1¼ cups milk
115g/4oz plain (semisweet)
  chocolate, chopped
150g/5oz/generous 1 cup
  sweetened chestnut purée
30ml/2 tbsp brandy or Cointreau
130g/4½oz/generous 1 cup
  mascarpone cheese
5ml/1 tsp vanilla extract
450ml/¾ pint/scant 2 cups
  double (heavy) cream
50g/2oz plain (semisweet)
  chocolate, to decorate

1 Whisk the egg yolks in a bowl with the sugar and cornflour. Boil the milk in a pan and pour over the egg mixture, whisking well. Return to the pan and cook over a gentle heat, stirring until thickened. Divide among three bowls. While hot, add the chocolate to one bowl, stirring until melted. Cool, then chill.

2 Beat the chestnut purée until soft, then beat it into the second bowl with the brandy or Cointreau. Beat the mascarpone and vanilla extract into the third bowl. Cool, then chill.

3 Add a third of the cream to each mixture. Turn the chestnut mixture into the ice cream maker and churn until it has a softly set consistency. Divide among six 150ml/¼ pint/⅔ cup metal moulds, level the surface and freeze.

4 Add the chocolate mixture to the ice cream maker and churn to the same consistency. Spoon into the moulds, level the top and freeze. Churn the remaining mixture to the same consistency. Spoon into moulds, level the surface and freeze for several hours or overnight.

5 To serve, melt the chocolate for the decoration in a bowl over a pan of simmering water. Transfer to a piping (pastry) bag and pipe lines on to plates. Soften the ice cream slightly, then serve.

Rainbow Ice Cream with Chocolate Candies

Speckled with roughly chopped sugar-coated chocolate sweets, this will soon be a family favourite with youngsters and adults alike, and it is especially good at children's parties.

Serves 6

4 egg yolks
75g/3oz/6 tbsp caster
  (superfine) sugar
5ml/1 tsp cornflour (cornstarch)
300ml/½ pint/1¼ cups
  semi-skimmed (low-fat) milk
300ml/½ pint/1¼ cups double
  (heavy) cream
5ml/1 tsp vanilla extract
115g/4oz sugar-coated
  chocolate sweets (candies)
whole sweets (candies),
  to decorate

1 Whisk the egg yolks, sugar and cornflour together in a bowl until thick and pale. Pour the milk into a heavy pan, bring it just to the boil, then gradually pour it on to the egg yolk mixture, whisking constantly.

2 Return the mixture to the pan and cook over a gentle heat, stirring constantly until the custard has thickened and is smooth.

3 Pour it back into the bowl, cover, leave to cool, then chill. Mix the cream and vanilla extract into the cooled custard, then pour into an ice cream maker. Churn until thick.

4 Roughly chop the sweets, stir them into the ice cream and churn for a minute or two until firm enough to scoop. Transfer to a plastic container and freeze until it is required.

5 Scoop into bowls or cones and decorate with the sweets.

> **Cook's Tip**
> The sugar coating on the sweets will dissolve slightly into the ice cream, but this just adds to the swirly coloured effect.

Bombes Energy 671kcal/2786kJ; Protein 7.9g; Carbohydrate 40.2g, of which sugars 31.1g; Fat 53.1g, of which saturates 31.7g; Cholesterol 217mg; Calcium 133mg; Fibre 1.5g; Sodium 48mg.
Rainbow Energy 438kcal/1823kJ; Protein 5.1g; Carbohydrate 30.4g, of which sugars 29.8g; Fat 33.8g, of which saturates 20g; Cholesterol 176mg; Calcium 132mg; Fibre 0g; Sodium 49mg.

Cranberry and White Chocolate Ice Cream

A traditional American combination – the creamy sweet white chocolate ice cream complements the slight sharpness of the ruby-red fruits for a richly contrasting marbled ice cream.

Serves 6
150g/5oz/1¼ cups frozen cranberries
125g/4½oz/scant ¾ cup caster (superfine) sugar
4 egg yolks
5ml/1 tsp cornflour (cornstarch)
300ml/½ pint/1¼ cups semi-skimmed (low-fat) milk
150g/5oz white chocolate
5ml/1 tsp vanilla extract
200ml/7fl oz/scant 1 cup double (heavy) cream
extra cranberries, to decorate

1 Put the cranberries into a pan with 60ml/4 tbsp water and cook uncovered for 5 minutes until softened. Drain off any fruit juices, mix in 60ml/4 tbsp of the sugar and leave to cool.

2 Whisk the egg yolks, remaining sugar and cornflour together in a bowl until thick and pale. Pour the milk into a heavy pan, bring it just to the boil, then gradually pour it on to the egg yolk mixture, whisking constantly.

3 Return the mixture to the pan and cook over a gentle heat, stirring constantly until the custard thickens and is smooth. Pour it back into the bowl.

4 Finely chop 50g/2oz of the chocolate and set aside. Break the remainder into pieces and stir into the hot custard until melted. Mix in the vanilla extract then cover, cool and chill.

5 Pour the cooled chocolate custard and cream into an ice cream maker and churn until thick. Gradually mix in the cooled cranberries and diced chocolate and churn for a few more minutes until firm enough to scoop. Transfer to a freezer container and freeze until required.

6 Scoop into tall glasses and decorate with a few cranberries.

Classic Dark Chocolate Ice Cream

Rich, dark and wonderfully luxurious, this ice cream can be served solo, with chocolate shavings or drizzled with warm chocolate sauce. If you are making it in advance, don't forget to soften the ice cream before serving so that the full intense flavour of the dark chocolate comes through.

Serves 4–6
4 egg yolks
75g/3oz/scant ½ cup caster (superfine) sugar
5ml/1 tsp cornflour (cornstarch)
300ml/½ pint/1¼ cups semi-skimmed (low-fat) milk
200g/7oz dark (bittersweet) chocolate
300ml/½ pint/1¼ cups whipping cream
shaved chocolate, to decorate

1 Whisk the egg yolks, sugar and cornflour in a bowl until thick and foamy. Pour the milk into a pan, bring just to the boil, then gradually whisk it into the yolk mixture.

2 Return the mixture to the pan and cook over a gentle heat, stirring constantly until the custard thickens and is smooth. Remove the pan from the heat.

3 Break the chocolate into small pieces and stir into the hot custard until it has melted. Leave to cool, then chill.

4 Whip the cream until it has thickened but still falls from a spoon. Fold into the custard, then pour into a freezer container. Freeze for 6 hours or until firm enough to scoop, beating once or twice with a fork or in a food processor as it thickens.

5 Alternatively, use an ice cream maker. Mix the chocolate custard with the whipped cream. Churn until the mixture is firm enough to scoop. Serve in scoops, decorated with chocolate shavings.

Cook's Tip
For the best flavour use a good-quality chocolate with at least 70 per cent cocoa solids, such as fine Belgian chocolate.

Cranberry Energy 296kcal/1245kJ; Protein 5.4g; Carbohydrate 41.8g, of which sugars 41g; Fat 13.1g, of which saturates 7g; Cholesterol 108mg; Calcium 153mg; Fibre 0.4g; Sodium 57mg.
Dark Chocolate Energy 349kcal/1461kJ; Protein 4.8g; Carbohydrate 36.8g, of which sugars 35.8g; Fat 21.4g, of which saturates 11.9g; Cholesterol 162mg; Calcium 78mg; Fibre 0.7g; Sodium 29mg.

Chocolate Double Mint Ice Cream

Full of body and flavour, this creamy, smooth ice cream combines the sophistication of dark chocolate with the satisfying coolness of fresh chopped mint.

Serves 4
4 egg yolks
75g/3oz/scant ¹/₂ cup caster
  (superfine) sugar
5ml/1 tsp cornflour (cornstarch)

300ml/¹/₂ pint/1¹/₄ cups
  semi-skimmed (low-fat) milk
200g/7oz dark (bittersweet)
  chocolate, broken into squares
40g/1¹/₂oz/¹/₄ cup peppermints
60ml/4 tbsp chopped
  fresh mint
300ml/¹/₂ pint/1¹/₄ cups
  whipping cream
sprigs of fresh mint dusted with
  icing (confectioners') sugar,
  to decorate

1 Put the egg yolks, sugar and cornflour in a bowl and whisk until thick and foamy. Pour the milk into a heavy pan, bring slowly to the boil, then gradually whisk the hot milk into the yolk mixture.

2 Scrape the mixture back into the pan and cook over a gentle heat, stirring constantly, until the custard thickens and is smooth. Scrape it back into the bowl, add the chocolate, a little at a time, and stir until melted and smooth. Cool, then chill.

3 Put the peppermints in a strong plastic bag and crush them with a rolling pin. Stir them into the custard with the chopped fresh mint.

4 Mix the custard and cream together and churn the mixture in an ice cream maker until firm enough to scoop.

5 Serve the ice cream in scoops and then decorate with mint sprigs dusted with sifted icing sugar.

> **Cook's Tip**
> If you freeze the ice cream in a tub, don't beat it in a food processor when breaking up the ice crystals, or the crunchy texture of the crushed peppermints will be lost.

Double White Chocolate Ice Cream

Crunchy chunks of white chocolate are a bonus in this delicious ice cream. Serve it scooped in waffle cones dipped in dark chocolate for a truly sensational treat.

Serves 8
4 egg yolks
75g/3oz/scant ¹/₂ cup caster
  (superfine) sugar

5ml/1 tsp cornflour (cornstarch)
300ml/¹/₂ pint/1¹/₄ cups
  semi-skimmed (low-fat) milk
250g/9oz white chocolate,
  chopped into pieces
10ml/2 tsp natural vanilla extract
300ml/¹/₂ pint/1¹/₄ cups
  whipping cream
8 chocolate-dipped cones,
  to serve

1 Whisk the egg yolks, sugar and cornflour in a bowl until the mixture is thick and foamy. Pour the milk into a heavy pan, bring it to the boil, then gradually pour the hot milk on to the yolk mixture, whisking constantly.

2 Return the custard mixture to the pan and cook over a gentle heat, stirring constantly, until the custard begins to thicken and is smooth. Pour the hot custard back into the same bowl.

3 Add 150g/5oz of the chopped white chocolate to the hot custard, along with the vanilla extract. Gently stir until the chocolate has completely melted, leave to cool to room temperature, then chill.

4 Stir the cream into the custard, then churn the mixture in an ice cream maker until thick. Add the remaining white chocolate and churn for 5–10 minutes until firm. Serve in cones dipped in dark chocolate.

> **Variation**
> If you prefer, scoop the ice cream into glass dishes and decorate with white chocolate curls or extra diced chocolate. Ice cream served this way won't go quite as far, so will only serve 4–6.

Double Mint Energy 757kcal/3159kJ; Protein 9.8g; Carbohydrate 68.3g, of which sugars 66.7g; Fat 51.4g, of which saturates 29.8g; Cholesterol 299mg; Calcium 186mg; Fibre 1.3g; Sodium 66mg.
White Chocolate Energy 395kcal/1646kJ; Protein 6g; Carbohydrate 31.4g, of which sugars 30.8g; Fat 28.2g, of which saturates 16.4g; Cholesterol 142mg; Calcium 168mg; Fibre 0g; Sodium 65mg.

Chunky Chocolate Ice Cream

This creamy milk chocolate ice cream, topped with delicious chunks of milk, dark and white chocolate will satisfy even the sweetest tooth and will be a hit with adults as well as children.

Serves 4–6
4 egg yolks
75g/3oz/scant ½ cup caster (superfine) sugar
5ml/1 tsp cornflour (cornstarch)
300ml/½ pint/1¼ cups semi-skimmed (low-fat) milk
200g/7oz milk chocolate
50g/2oz dark (bittersweet) chocolate, plus extra, to decorate
50g/2oz white chocolate
300ml/½ pint/1¼ cups whipping cream

1 Whisk the egg yolks, caster sugar and cornflour in a bowl until thick and foamy. Heat the milk in a pan and bring it to the boil, then pour it on to the egg mixture, whisking constantly.

2 Return the custard mixture to the pan and cook over a gentle heat, stirring constantly with a wooden spoon until the custard thickens and is smooth.

3 Pour the custard back into the bowl. Break 150g/5oz of the milk chocolate into squares, stir these into the hot custard, then cover closely. Leave to cool, then chill.

4 Chop the remaining milk, dark and white chocolate finely and set aside. Mix the chocolate custard and the whipping cream and churn in an ice cream maker for 25–30 minutes until thick.

5 Scoop the ice cream out of the machine and into a plastic tub. Fold in the pieces of chocolate and freeze for 2–3 hours until firm enough to scoop. To serve, scoop into glasses or bowls and decorate with more pieces of chopped chocolate.

> **Cook's Tip**
> For maximum flavour, use good quality chocolate or your favourite chocolate bar. Avoid dark, milk or white cake covering.

Chocolate and Hazelnut Brittle Ice Cream

For nut lovers and chocoholics everywhere, this luxurious ice cream is the ultimate indulgence. Rich, smooth dark chocolate is combined with crisp little chunks of sweet hazelnut brittle that provide a satisfying contrast. For a change, use other types of nuts, such as almonds, walnuts or pecan nuts.

Serves 4–6
4 egg yolks
175g/6oz/scant 1 cup sugar
5ml/1 tsp cornflour (cornstarch)
300ml/½ pint/1¼ cups semi-skimmed (low-fat) milk
150g/5oz dark (bittersweet) chocolate, broken into squares
115g/4oz/1 cup hazelnuts
60ml/4 tbsp water
300ml/½ pint/1¼ cups whipping cream

1 Whisk the egg yolks, sugar and cornflour in a bowl until thick and foamy. Pour the milk into a pan, bring it just to the boil, then gradually whisk it into the yolk mixture. Scrape back into the pan and cook over a gentle heat, stirring constantly, until the custard has thickened and is smooth.

2 Take the pan off the heat and stir in the chocolate, a few squares at a time. Cool, then chill. Lightly oil a baking sheet.

3 Meanwhile, put the hazelnuts, remaining sugar and water in a large frying pan. Gently heat without stirring until the sugar has dissolved. Increase the heat slightly and cook until the syrup has turned pale golden. Pour the mixture on to the oiled baking sheet and leave to stand until the hazelnut brittle hardens.

4 Pour the chocolate custard into the ice cream maker and add the cream. Churn for 25 minutes or until it is thick and firm enough to scoop.

5 Break the nut brittle into pieces. Reserve a few pieces for decoration and finely chop the rest. Scrape the ice cream into a tub and stir in the nut brittle. Freeze for 2–3 hours or until firm enough to scoop. Scoop on to plates and decorate with the reserved hazelnut brittle.

Hazelnut Brittle Energy 614kcal/2559kJ; Protein 8.3g; Carbohydrate 52g, of which sugars 50.6g; Fat 42.9g, of which saturates 19g; Cholesterol 158mg; Calcium 151mg; Fibre 1.9g; Sodium 43mg.
Chunky Energy 564kcal/2352kJ; Protein 7.9g; Carbohydrate 47.7g, of which sugars 47.5g; Fat 39.3g, of which saturates 23g; Cholesterol 197mg; Calcium 175mg; Fibre 0.8g; Sodium 64mg.

Chocolate Ripple Ice Cream

This creamy, dark chocolate ice cream, unevenly rippled with swirls of rich chocolate sauce, will stay deliciously soft even after freezing.

Serves 4–6
4 egg yolks
75g/3oz/scant ½ cup caster (superfine) sugar
5ml/1 tsp cornflour (cornstarch)

300ml/½ pint/1¼ cups semi-skimmed (low-fat) milk
250g/9oz dark (bittersweet) chocolate, broken into squares
25g/1oz/2 tbsp butter, diced
30ml/2 tbsp golden (light corn) syrup
90ml/6 tbsp single (light) cream or cream and milk mixed
300ml/½ pint/1¼ cups whipping cream

1 Put the egg yolks, sugar and cornflour in a bowl and whisk until thick and foamy. Pour the milk into a heavy pan, bring just to the boil, then gradually pour the milk on to the yolk mixture, whisking constantly.

2 Return the mixture to the pan and cook over a gentle heat, stirring constantly until the custard thickens and is smooth. Pour back into the bowl and stir in 150g/5oz of the chocolate until melted. Cover the custard closely, leave to cool, then chill.

3 Whip the cream in a bowl until it has thickened, but is still soft enough to fall from a spoon. Fold it into the custard. Pour the mixture into a freezer container and freeze for 5 hours until thick, beating twice with a fork or in a food processor during this time.

4 Alternatively, use an ice cream maker. Stir the whipped cream into the cooled custard and churn the mixture for 20–25 minutes until thick.

5 Put the remaining chocolate in a pan with the butter and golden syrup. Heat gently, stirring, until melted. Stir in the single cream or cream and milk mixture. Heat gently, stirring, until smooth, then leave to cool.

6 Add alternate spoonfuls of ice cream and sauce to a large freezer container. Freeze for 5–6 hours until firm.

Gingered Semi-freddo in Dark Chocolate Cases

This ice cream is made with a boiled sugar syrup rather than an egg custard.

Serves 6
4 egg yolks
115g/4oz/generous ½ cup caster (superfine) sugar
120ml/4fl oz/½ cup cold water

300ml/½ pints/1¼ cups double (heavy) cream
115g/4oz/⅔ cup drained stem ginger, finely chopped, plus extra slices, to decorate
45ml/3 tbsp whisky (optional)

For the chocolate cases
175g/6oz dark (bittersweet) chocolate, melted

1 Put the egg yolks in a large heatproof bowl and whisk until frothy. Bring a pan of water to the boil and simmer gently.

2 Mix the sugar and cold water in a pan and heat gently, stirring, until the sugar has dissolved. Increase the heat and boil for 4–5 minutes without stirring, until the syrup registers 115°C/239°F on a sugar thermometer. Pour the water away. You should be able to mould the syrup into a ball.

3 Put the bowl of egg yolks over the pan of simmering water and whisk in the sugar syrup. Continue whisking until the mixture is very thick. Remove from the heat and whisk until cool.

4 Whip the cream and lightly fold it into the yolk mixture, with the chopped ginger and whisky, if using. Pour into a plastic tub or similar freezerproof container and freeze for 1 hour.

5 To make cases, spread the melted chocolate over six squares of baking parchment in circles about 13cm/5in in diameter. Drape over upturned tumblers. Leave to cool and harden. Ease off the tumblers, then gently peel away the paper.

6 Stir the semi-freddo to bring any ginger that has sunk to the bottom of the tub to the top, then return to the freezer for 5–6 hours until firm. Scoop into the chocolate cases. Decorate with slices of ginger.

Chocolate Ripple Energy 594kcal/2474kJ; Protein 7.3g; Carbohydrate 48.3g, of which sugars 47.2g; Fat 42.6g, of which saturates 25.2g; Cholesterol 209mg; Calcium 140mg; Fibre 1.1g; Sodium 87mg.
Semi-freddo Energy 371kcal/1539kJ; Protein 3g; Carbohydrate 22.4g, of which sugars 22.3g; Fat 30.6g, of which saturates 17.8g; Cholesterol 203mg; Calcium 55mg; Fibre 0.5g; Sodium 23mg.

Chunky Chocolate-coffee Bean and Kahlúa Ice Cream

A wonderful combination of creamy dark coffee with a hint of coffee liqueur, peppered with crunchy chocolate-covered coffee beans. The beans used here have been coated with white, dark and milk chocolate, but all dark chocolate-covered beans would work just as well.

Serves 6

4 egg yolks
75g/3oz/scant ½ cup caster (superfine) sugar
5ml/1 tsp cornflour (cornstarch)
300ml/½ pint/1¼ cups semi-skimmed (low-fat) milk
30ml/2 tbsp instant coffee granules or powder
300ml/½ pint/1¼ cups double (heavy) cream
120ml/4fl oz/½ cup Kahlúa or other coffee liqueur
115g/4oz assorted chocolate-covered coffee beans
a little sifted unsweetened cocoa powder, to decorate

1 Whisk the egg yolks, sugar and cornflour in a bowl until the mixture is thick and pale. Heat the milk in a pan, then gradually whisk into the yolk mixture. Return the custard to the pan and cook over a gentle heat, stirring constantly so that it does not catch on the bottom and burn.

2 When the custard has thickened and is smooth, pour it back into the bowl and mix in the instant coffee granules or powder, stirring continuously until all of the coffee has completely dissolved. Cover the custard with clear film (plastic wrap) to prevent a skin from forming, leave to cool, then chill well before churning.

3 Stir the cream and Kahlúa into the coffee custard, then pour into an ice cream maker. Churn until thick. Roughly chop 75g/3oz of the chocolate-covered coffee beans, add to the ice cream and churn until firm enough to scoop. Transfer to a freezer container and freeze until required.

4 Scoop the ice cream into coffee cups and decorate with the remaining chocolate-covered coffee beans and a light dusting of cocoa powder.

Iced Tiramisu

This favourite Italian combination is not usually served as a frozen dessert, but in fact it does make a marvellous ice cream.

Serves 4

150g/5oz/¾ cup caster (superfine) sugar
150ml/¼ pint/⅔ cup water
250g/9oz/generous 1 cup mascarpone
200g/7oz/scant 1 cup virtually fat-free fromage frais or low-fat cream cheese
5ml/1 tsp vanilla extract
10ml/2 tsp instant coffee, dissolved in 30ml/2 tbsp boiling water
30ml/2 tbsp coffee liqueur or brandy
75g/3oz sponge fingers
unsweetened cocoa powder and chocolate curls, to decorate

1 Put 115g/4oz/generous ½ cup of the sugar into a small pan. Add the water and bring to the boil, stirring, until the sugar has dissolved. Leave the syrup to cool, then chill.

2 Put the mascarpone into a bowl. Beat with a spoon until it is soft, then stir in the fromage frais or cream cheese. Add the chilled syrup, a little at a time, then stir in the vanilla extract.

3 Spoon the mixture into a freezer container and freeze for 4 hours, beating twice with a fork, electric whisk or in a food processor to break up the ice crystals. Alternatively, use an ice cream maker and churn the mascarpone mixture until it is thick but too soft to scoop.

4 Meanwhile, put the coffee in a bowl, sweeten with the remaining sugar, then add the liqueur. Stir well, then cool. Crumble the sponge fingers and toss in the coffee mixture.

5 Spoon a third of the ice cream into a 900ml/1½ pint/3¾ cup freezer container, spoon over half the crumbled sponge, then top with half the remaining ice cream. Sprinkle over the rest of the crumbled sponge, then cover with the remaining ice cream.

6 Freeze for 2–3 hours until the ice cream is firm enough to scoop. Serve dusted with cocoa powder and decorated with chocolate curls.

Bean and Kahlúa Energy 504kcal/2094kJ; Protein 4.9g; Carbohydrate 32.2g, of which sugars 31.3g; Fat 38.2g, of which saturates 20.8g; Cholesterol 173mg; Calcium 112mg; Fibre 0.4g; Sodium 57mg.
Tiramisu Energy 362kcal/1526kJ; Protein 11.7g; Carbohydrate 54.5g, of which sugars 50.3g; Fat 10.5g, of which saturates 6.1g; Cholesterol 69mg; Calcium 78mg; Fibre 0.2g; Sodium 35mg.

Pistachio Ice Cream in Choc Cones

This continental favourite owes its enduring popularity to its delicate pale green colour and distinctive yet subtle flavour.

Serves 4–6

4 egg yolks
75g/3oz/scant ½ cup caster
    (superfine) sugar
5ml/1 tsp cornflour (cornstarch)
300ml/½ pint/1¼ cups
    semi-skimmed (low-fat) milk
115g/4oz/1 cup pistachios,
    plus a few extra, to decorate
300ml/½ pint/1¼ cups
    whipping cream
a little green food colouring
chocolate-dipped waffle cones,
    to serve

1 Place the egg yolks, sugar and cornflour in a bowl and whisk until the mixture is thick and foamy.

2 Pour the milk into a heavy pan, gently bring it to the boil, then gradually whisk it into the egg yolk mixture.

3 Return the mixture to the pan and cook it over a gentle heat, stirring constantly until the custard thickens and is smooth. Pour it back into the bowl, set aside to cool, then chill in the refrigerator until required.

4 Shell the pistachios and put them in a food processor or blender. Add 30ml/2 tbsp of the cream and grind the mixture to a coarse paste. Pour the rest of the cream into a small pan. Bring it to the boil, stir in the coarsely ground pistachios, then leave to cool.

5 Mix the chilled custard and pistachio cream together and tint the mixture delicately with a few drops of food colouring.

6 Churn the mixture in an ice cream maker until firm enough to scoop. Serve in chocolate-dipped cones, sprinkled with extra nuts.

> **Cook's Tip**
> Waffle cones can be decorated by dipping them in melted chocolate and sprinkling them with extra chopped pistachios.

Black Forest and Kirsch Ice Cream

All the flavours of boozy soaked dark cherries, cream and chocolate sponge combined in a light ice cream dessert.

Serves 6

425g/15oz can black cherries
90ml/6 tbsp Kirsch
4 egg yolks
75g/3oz/scant ½ cup caster
    (superfine) sugar
5ml/1 tsp cornflour (cornstarch)
300ml/½ pint/1¼ cups
    semi-skimmed (low-fat) milk
300ml/½ pint/1¼ cups double
    (heavy) cream
6 double chocolate muffins, each
    one weighing about 75g/3oz

To decorate
fresh cherries, on stalks
a little sifted unsweetened
    cocoa powder

1 Drain the cherries, discarding the juice, then put into a bowl and spoon over 30ml/2 tbsp of the Kirsch. Leave to soak for 2 hours or overnight.

2 Whisk the egg yolks, sugar and cornflour together in a bowl until thick and pale. Pour the milk into a heavy pan, bring it just to the boil, then gradually pour it on to the egg yolk mixture, whisking constantly.

3 Return the mixture to the pan and cook over a gentle heat, stirring constantly until the custard thickens and is smooth. Pour it back into the bowl, cover, leave to cool, then chill well.

4 Stir the cream into the custard, then pour into an ice cream maker. Churn until thick.

5 Gradually mix in the soaked cherries and any Kirsch juices and gently churn together.

6 Meanwhile, cut each muffin into two horizontal slices and drizzle with the remaining Kirsch.

7 To serve, sandwich the muffin slices back together with ice cream, arrange on serving plates and decorate with the fresh cherries and a light dusting of cocoa powder.

Pistachio Energy 422kcal/1749kJ; Protein 8.1g; Carbohydrate 19.1g, of which sugars 17.9g; Fat 35.3g, of which saturates 15.6g; Cholesterol 190mg; Calcium 133mg; Fibre 1.2g; Sodium 143mg.
Black Forest Energy 726kcal/3034kJ; Protein 9.1g; Carbohydrate 69.4g, of which sugars 50.7g; Fat 44.1g, of which saturates 26.1g; Cholesterol 224mg; Calcium 234mg; Fibre 1.6g; Sodium 234mg.

Iced Coffee Cups with Chocolate Dusting

Small, sturdy coffee cups make attractive containers for this richly flavoured ice cream topped with whipped cream and chocolate dusting.

Serves 6–8
150ml/¼ pint/⅔ cup water
75ml/5 tbsp ground
   espresso coffee

5ml/1 tsp cornflour (cornstarch)
4 egg yolks
65g/2½oz/5 tbsp light
   muscovado (brown) sugar
300ml/½ pint/1¼ cups
   whipping cream
30ml/2 tbsp Tia Maria or
   Kahlúa liqueur
lightly whipped cream and
   drinking chocolate powder,
   to decorate

1 Pour the water into a small pan and stir in the coffee powder. Bring to the boil, remove from the heat and leave to infuse (steep) for 15 minutes. Strain through a sieve (strainer) lined with a piece of muslin (cheesecloth) held over a bowl.

2 Spoon the cornflour into a small, heavy pan. Stir in a little of the hot coffee, then add the remaining coffee with the egg yolks and sugar. Cook over a gentle heat, stirring until thickened. Do not boil or the mixture may curdle. Scrape into a bowl, cover closely with baking parchment and leave to cool.

3 Whip the cream with the liqueur and cooled coffee mixture until it forms soft peaks. Spoon the mixture into the coffee cups, tapping them gently to level the surface. Freeze for at least 3 hours.

4 Transfer the coffee cups to the refrigerator about 30 minutes before serving to let the ice cream soften. Top with swirls of lightly whipped cream and dust with drinking chocolate powder.

> **Cook's Tip**
> The number of people this will serve depends on the size of the cups. If they are very small, this quantity will serve at least eight.

Minty Choc Madness Ice Cream

This creamy smooth peppermint ice cream is speckled with crushed peppermints and shards of chocolate-covered peppermint crisps, and looks particularly good served scooped in delicate glasses.

Serves 6
4 egg yolks
75g/3oz/scant ½ cup caster
   (superfine) sugar

5ml/1 tsp cornflour (cornstarch)
300ml/½ pint/1¼ cups
   semi-skimmed (low-fat) milk
250ml/8fl oz/1 cup
   crème fraîche
5ml/1 tsp peppermint extract
50g/2oz mint imperials or
   other hard mints
75g/3oz chocolate-covered
   peppermint crisps and
   chocolate curls, to decorate

1 Whisk the egg yolks, sugar and cornflour together in a bowl until thick and pale. Pour the milk into a pan, bring it just to the boil, then pour it on to the yolk mixture, whisking constantly. Return to the pan and cook over a gentle heat, stirring, until the custard thickens. Pour it back into the bowl, cover, cool, then chill.

2 Whisk the crème fraîche and peppermint extract into the chilled custard. Pour into an ice cream maker and churn until thick.

3 Put the mints into a plastic bag and roughly crush them with a rolling pin. Roughly chop the peppermint crisps with a knife. Stir both into the ice cream and churn until firm enough to scoop. Transfer to a freezer container and freeze.

4 Scoop the ice cream into glasses and sprinkle with extra pieces of peppermint crisps and chocolate curls.

> **Cook's Tip**
> To make delicate chocolate curls, hold a bar of dark, white or milk chocolate over a plate and pare curls away from the edge of the bar, using a swivel-blade vegetable peeler. Lift the pared curls carefully with a flat blade or a palette knife and arrange as desired.

Minty Choc Madness Energy 338kcal/1414kJ; Protein 4.2g; Carbohydrate 36.7g, of which sugars 35.8g; Fat 20.4g, of which saturates 12.6g; Cholesterol 151mg; Calcium 104mg; Fibre 0g; Sodium 38mg.
Iced Coffee Cups Energy 220kcal/911kJ; Protein 2.2g; Carbohydrate 10.9g, of which sugars 10.4g; Fat 18.4g, of which saturates 10.3g; Cholesterol 140mg; Calcium 39mg; Fibre 0g; Sodium 18mg.

Chocolate Ice Cream in Florentine Baskets

A similar mixture to that used when making florentines is perfect for shaping fluted baskets for holding scoops of ice cream. For convenience, make the baskets a couple of days in advance, but dip the edges in chocolate on the day you serve them.

Serves 8
115g/4oz/½ cup butter, plus extra for greasing
50g/2oz/¼ cup caster (superfine) sugar
90ml/6 tbsp golden (light corn) syrup
90g/3½oz/scant 1 cup plain (all-purpose) flour
50g/2oz/½ cup flaked (sliced) almonds
50g/2oz/¼ cup glacé (candied) cherries, finely chopped
25g/1oz/3 tbsp raisins, chopped
15ml/1 tbsp finely chopped preserved stem ginger
90g/3½oz plain (semisweet) chocolate, broken into pieces
about 750ml/1¼ pints/3 cups chocolate ice cream

1 Preheat oven to 190°C/375°F/Gas 5. Line two baking sheets with greased baking parchment. Melt the butter, sugar and syrup in a pan. Stir in the flour, almonds, cherries, raisins and ginger.

2 Place a shallow tablespoonful of the mixture at either end of a baking sheet and spread to a 13cm/5in round. Bake for 5 minutes until they look lacy and golden. Spread more circles on the second baking sheet ready to put in the oven. Have ready several metal dariole moulds for shaping the baskets.

3 Leave the biscuits (cookies) on the sheet for 2 minutes to firm up. Lay a biscuit over an upturned dariole mould. Shape the biscuit into flutes around the sides of the mould. Leave for 2 minutes until cool, then lift away. Process the remaining mixture until you have eight baskets.

4 Melt the chocolate in a heatproof bowl over a pan of gently simmering water. Carefully dip the edges of the baskets in the melted chocolate and place on individual dessert plates. Scoop the chocolate ice cream into the baskets to serve.

Ice Cream with Mexican Chocolate

This rich ice cream has a wonderfully complex flavour, thanks to the cinnamon and almonds in the chocolate.

Serves 4
2 large eggs
115g/4oz/generous ½ cup caster (superfine) sugar
2 bars Mexican chocolate, total weight about 115g/4oz
400ml/14fl oz/1⅔ cups double (heavy) cream
200ml/7fl oz/scant 1 cup full-fat (whole) milk
chocolate curls, to decorate

1 Put the eggs in a bowl and whisk them with an electric whisk until they are thick, pale and fluffy. Gradually whisk in the sugar.

2 Gently heat the chocolate in a heatproof bowl over a pan of simmering water, stirring until melted and smooth. Add it to the egg mixture and mix thoroughly.

3 Whisk in the cream to the chocolate mixture. Stir in the milk, a little at a time.

4 Cool the mixture, then chill. Pour the mixture into an ice cream maker and churn until thick.

5 Alternatively, freeze the mixture in a shallow plastic box in the fast-freeze section of the freezer for several hours, until ice crystals have begun to form around the edges. Process to break up the ice crystals, then freeze again. To serve, decorate with chocolate curls.

> **Cook's Tip**
> Mexican chocolate is richly flavoured with cinnamon, almonds and vanilla, and has a much grainier texture than other chocolates. It is available in Mexican food stores and some supermarkets. If you can't find it, then 25g/1oz plain (semisweet) chocolate, 2.5ml/½ tsp ground cinnamon and 1 drop of almond extract can be substituted for every 25g/1oz Mexican chocolate.

Baskets Energy 525kcal/2191kJ; Protein 6.8g; Carbohydrate 53.9g, of which sugars 45g; Fat 32.8g, of which saturates 18.2g; Cholesterol 31mg; Calcium 141mg; Fibre 1.2g; Sodium 180mg.
Mexican Chocolate Energy 966kcal/4016kJ; Protein 9.3g; Carbohydrate 69.7g, of which sugars 69.2g; Fat 74.2g, of which saturates 44.9g; Cholesterol 243mg; Calcium 156mg; Fibre 1.4g; Sodium 84mg.

Crumbled Chocolate Brownie Ice Cream

A double-chocolate dessert that combines chocolate ice cream with soft brownies.

Serves 6
1.2 litres/2 pints/5 cups good
   quality chocolate or chocolate
   chip ice cream

For the chocolate brownies
75g/3oz dark (bittersweet)
   chocolate, broken into pieces
115g/4oz/½ cup butter

4 eggs, beaten
10ml/2 tsp vanilla extract
400g/14oz/2 cups caster
   (superfine) sugar
115g/4oz/1 cup plain
   (all-purpose) flour
25g/1oz/¼ cup unsweetened
   cocoa powder
115g/4oz packet dark
   (bittersweet) chocolate chips
115g/4oz/1 cup chopped
   walnuts

1 Make the brownies. Preheat the oven to 190°C/375°F/Gas 5. Grease an 18 × 28cm/7 × 11in shallow baking tin (pan) and line the base with baking parchment. Melt the chocolate with the butter in a heatproof bowl over a pan of simmering water, stirring until smooth. Remove the bowl from the heat and stir in the beaten eggs, vanilla and sugar. Mix together well.

2 Sift the flour with the cocoa powder and beat into the chocolate mixture. Gently stir in the chocolate chips and walnuts. Pour the mixture into the pan and level the surface.

3 Bake for about 35 minutes. To test if the brownies are fully cooked, insert a metal skewer in the centre. The cake should be set but still moist. (Overcooking will make the brownies dry.) If you prefer a drier texture – which is better for the ice cream – cook for 10–15 minutes more. Leave the brownies to cool in the pan. When completely cold, cut into squares or bars.

4 To make the chocolate brownie ice cream, cut about 175g/6oz of the brownies into small cubes. Soften the ice cream and lightly stir in the chopped brownies. Spoon the mixture into a large freezerproof container, cover and freeze for at least 2 hours before serving.

White Chocolate and Brownie Ice Cream

This scrumptious recipe combines an irresistible contrast between the white chocolate ice cream and luscious chunks of chocolate brownie. Use good-quality, bought chocolate brownies, or even better still, make your own.

Serves 6
4 egg yolks
2.5ml/½tsp cornflour (cornstarch)
300ml/½ pint/1¼ cups full
   cream (whole) milk
200g/7oz white chocolate, chopped
200g/7oz chocolate brownies
300ml/½ pint/1¼ cups
   whipping cream

1 Put the egg yolks and cornflour in a bowl and whisk lightly to combine. Bring the milk to the boil in a heavy pan. Pour the milk over the whisked mixture, whisking constantly until the mixture is well combined.

2 Pour the custard back into the pan and cook over a very gentle heat, stirring continually until it slightly thickens and becomes smooth.

3 Pour into a bowl and add the chopped chocolate. Leave until the chocolate has melted, stirring frequently. Leave to cool.

4 Crumble the brownies into small pieces. Stir the cream into the chocolate custard and pour into the ice cream maker. Churn the mixture until it is thick.

5 Sprinkle the crumbled brownies over the ice cream mixture and churn until just mixed. Scoop into glasses or transfer to a freezerproof container and freeze the ice cream until ready to serve.

> **Variation**
> As an alternative, you could use chopped dark (bittersweet) chocolate in place of the white chocolate, and white chocolate brownies or 'blondies' in place of the dark chocolate brownies.

Brownie Energy 1255kcal/5248kJ; Protein 19.4g; Carbohydrate 139.4g, of which sugars 123.7g; Fat 72.8g, of which saturates 36.1g; Cholesterol 170mg; Calcium 319mg; Fibre 2.6g; Sodium 330mg.
White Chocolate Energy 570kcal/2365kJ; Protein 5.2g; Carbohydrate 31.1g, of which sugars 25.7g; Fat 48.1g, of which saturates 25.6g; Cholesterol 82mg; Calcium 129mg; Fibre 0g; Sodium 154mg.

Chocolate Ice Cream with Hot Cherry Sauce

Hot cherry sauce transforms chocolate ice cream into a delicious dessert for any occasion. Serve immediately to ensure that the sauce is still warm to the taste.

Serves 4
425g/15oz can stone (pitted) black cherries in juice
10ml/2 tsp cornflour (cornstarch)
finely grated rind of 1 lemon, plus 10ml/2 tsp juice
15ml/1 tbsp caster (superfine) sugar
2.5ml/½ tsp ground cinnamon
30ml/2 tbsp brandy or Kirsch (optional)
400ml/14fl oz/1⅔ cups dark (bittersweet) chocolate ice cream
400ml/14fl oz/1⅔ cups classic vanilla ice cream
drinking chocolate powder, for dusting

1 Drain the cherries, reserving the canned juice. Spoon the cornflour into a small pan and blend to a paste with a little of the reserved juice.

2 Stir in the remaining canned juice with the lemon rind and juice, sugar and cinnamon. Bring to the boil, stirring, until smooth and glossy. Add the cherries, with the brandy or kirsch, if using. Stir gently, then cook for 1 minute.

3 Scoop the chocolate and vanilla ice cream into shallow dishes. Spoon the sauce around, dust with drinking chocolate powder and serve.

Variation
The hot cherry sauce also makes a delicious filling for pancakes. For a speedy dessert, you can use heated, ready-made sweet pancakes – just spread a little sauce in the centre of each pancake and fold into a triangle shape or roll up. Then arrange in a serving dish and spoon the rest of the sauce over the top. Finish with spoonfuls of thick yogurt or whipped cream.

Chocolate and Coffee Bombe with Marsala

For the best results, use a good-quality ice cream for this delicious Italian dessert. The assembled bombe is very impressive.

Serves 6–8
15–18 sponge fingers
about 175ml/6fl oz/¾ cup sweet Marsala
75g/3oz amaretti
about 475ml/16fl oz/2 cups coffee ice cream, softened
about 475ml/16fl oz/2 cups vanilla ice cream, softened
50g/2oz dark (bittersweet) or plain (semisweet) chocolate, grated
chocolate curls and sifted cocoa powder or icing (confectioners') sugar, to decorate

1 Line a 1 litre/1¾ pint/4 cup freezer-proof bowl with a large piece of damp muslin (cheesecloth), letting it hang over the top edge. Trim the sponge fingers to fit the bowl, if necessary. Pour the Marsala into a shallow dish. Dip a sponge finger in the Marsala, turning it quickly so that it becomes saturated but does not disintegrate. Stand it against the side of the bowl, sugared side out. Repeat with the remaining sponge fingers to line the bowl fully. Fill in the base and any gaps around the side with any trimmings and sponge fingers cut to fit. Chill for 30 minutes.

2 Put the amaretti in a large bowl and crush them with a rolling pin. Add the coffee ice cream and any remaining Marsala, and beat until mixed. Spoon into the sponge-finger-lined bowl. Press the ice cream against the sponge to form an even layer with a hollow. Freeze for 2 hours.

3 Put the vanilla ice cream and grated chocolate in a bowl and beat together until evenly mixed. Spoon into the hollow in the centre of the mould. Smooth the top, then cover with the overhanging muslin. Place in the freezer overnight.

4 To serve, run a spatula between the muslin and the bowl, then unfold the top of the muslin. Place a chilled serving plate on top of the bombe, then invert so that the bombe is upside down on the plate. Carefully peel off the muslin. Decorate with the chocolate curls, then sift cocoa powder or icing sugar over.

Bombe Energy 391kcal/1631kJ; Protein 8.7g; Carbohydrate 33.8g, of which sugars 26.1g; Fat 22.7g, of which saturates 11.4g; Cholesterol 111mg; Calcium 66mg; Fibre 1.3g; Sodium 64mg.
Ice Cream with Cherry Energy 529kcal/2213kJ; Protein 8.4g; Carbohydrate 59.5g, of which sugars 57g; Fat 30.2g, of which saturates 18.1g; Cholesterol 0mg; Calcium 218mg; Fibre 0.7g; Sodium 130mg.

Coffee Ice Cream with Choc Beans

This bittersweet blend is a must for those who like their coffee strong and dark with just a hint of cream. When serving, decorate with the chocolate-covered coffee beans that are available from some larger supermarkets and high-class confectioners.

Serves 4–6

90ml/6 tbsp fine filter coffee

250ml/8fl oz/1 cup boiling water
4 egg yolks
75g/3oz/scant ½ cup caster (superfine) sugar
5ml/1 tsp cornflour (cornstarch)
300ml/½ pint/1¼ cups semi-skimmed milk
150ml/¼ pint/⅔ cup double (heavy) cream
chocolate-covered coffee beans, to decorate

1 Put the coffee in a cafetière (press pot) or jug (pitcher) and pour on the boiling water. Leave to cool, then strain and chill until required.

2 Whisk the egg yolks, caster sugar and cornflour in a bowl until the mixture is thick and foamy. Pour the milk into a heavy pan, bring to the boil, then gradually pour on to the yolk mixture, whisking constantly.

3 Return the mixture to the pan and cook over a gentle heat, stirring all the time, until the custard thickens and is smooth. Pour it back into the bowl and cover closely with clear film (plastic wrap). Cool, then chill.

4 By hand: Whip the cream until it has thickened but still falls from a spoon. Fold into the custard, add the coffee, then pour into a plastic tub or similar freezerproof container. Freeze for 6 hours until firm, beating once or twice with a fork, electric mixer or in a food processor to break up the crystals.

5 Ice cream maker: Mix the coffee and cream with the chilled custard, then churn the mixture until firm enough to scoop.

6 Scoop the ice cream into glass dishes, sprinkle with the chocolate-covered coffee beans and serve.

White Chocolate Brûlées with Blackberry Coulis

This ice cream is topped with caramel shards and fresh blackberries.

Serves 6
4 egg yolks
50g/2oz/¼ cup caster (superfine) sugar
5ml/1 tsp cornflour (cornstarch)
300ml/½ pint/1¼ cups semi-skimmed (low-fat) milk

150g/5oz white chocolate, broken into pieces
5ml/1 tsp vanilla extract
115g/4oz/generous 1 cup granulated (white) sugar
300ml/½ pint/1¼ cups double (heavy) cream
blackberries, for decoration

For the coulis
200g/7oz/scant 2 cups blackberries

1 Whisk the egg yolks, sugar and cornflour together until thick and pale. Pour the milk into a pan, bring it just to the boil, then pour it on to the egg yolk mixture, whisking constantly. Return to the pan and cook gently, stirring, until the custard thickens.

2 Take the pan off the heat and add the chocolate pieces and vanilla extract and stir until the chocolate has completely melted. Cover, leave to cool, then chill.

3 For the coulis, put the blackberries into a pan with 60ml/4 tbsp water, then cover and cook for 5 minutes until softened. Purée the berries in a liquidizer or food processor and strain, discarding the seeds. Stir in 30–45ml/2–3 tbsp extra water to make a sauce.

4 Put the granulated sugar in a small pan with 45ml/3 tbsp water and heat, without stirring, until the sugar has dissolved. Increase the heat and boil for 4–5 minutes until golden. Pour on to an oiled baking sheet. Leave to harden, then break into pieces.

5 Pour the cooled white chocolate custard and cream into an ice cream maker and churn until firm enough to scoop. Transfer to a freezer container and store in the freezer until required.

6 Scoop the ice cream into bowls and top with caramel pieces and whole blackberries. Serve with the coulis.

Coffee Ice Cream Energy 260kcal/1076kJ; Protein 2.6g; Carbohydrate 12.9g, of which sugars 10.2g; Fat 21.5g, of which saturates 12.5g; Cholesterol 53mg; Calcium 87mg; Fibre 0.1g; Sodium 39mg.
White Brûlées Energy 553kcal/2307kJ; Protein 6.4g; Carbohydrate 49g, of which sugars 48.2g; Fat 38.3g, of which saturates 22.6g; Cholesterol 172mg; Calcium 192mg; Fibre 1g; Sodium 67mg.

Miniature Choc Ices

For summer entertaining, these little chocolate-coated ice creams make a fun alternative to the more familiar after-dinner chocolates. You can be creative with toppings and adapt them to suit the occasion, from chopped nuts for adults to multicoloured sprinkles for children.

Makes about 25

750ml/1¼ pints/3 cups vanilla, chocolate or coffee ice cream
200g/7oz plain (semisweet) chocolate, broken into small pieces
25g/1oz milk chocolate, broken into small pieces
25g/1oz/¼ cup chopped hazelnuts, lightly toasted

1 Put a baking sheet in the freezer for 15 minutes. Use a melon baller to scoop balls of each of the different ice cream flavours on to the baking sheet. Freeze for 1 hour until firm.

2 Line a second baking sheet with baking parchment and place in the freezer for 15 minutes. Melt the plain and milk chocolates in separate heatproof bowls set over a pan of simmering water.

3 Transfer the ice cream scoops to the paper-lined sheet. Spoon a little plain chocolate over a scoop so that most of it is coated. Sprinkle with chopped nuts, before the chocolate sets.

4 Coat the remaining scoops with the dark chocolate. Sprinkle chopped nuts over half of the chocolate-covered scoops, working quickly so that the chocolate does not set.

5 Once the chocolate has set on the half that are not topped with nuts, drizzle each with milk chocolate, using a teaspoon. Freeze until ready to serve.

> **Cook's Tip**
> If the melted milk chocolate is very runny, leave it for a few minutes to thicken up slightly before spooning it over the ice cream scoops. The milk chocolate can be piped on the choc ices, using a bag fitted with a writing nozzle.

Chocolate Teardrops with Cherry Brandy Sauce

These stunning chocolate cases look impressive but are easy to make.

Serves 6

90g/3½oz plain (semisweet) chocolate, broken into pieces
115g/4oz amaretti
450ml/¾ pint/scant 2 cups double (heavy) cream
2.5ml/½ tsp almond extract
40g/1½oz/⅓ cup icing (confectioners') sugar
30ml/2 tbsp brandy or almond liqueur
75ml/5 tbsp full-fat (whole) milk
fresh cherries, to decorate

For the sauce

2.5ml/½ tsp cornflour (cornstarch)
75ml/5 tbsp water
225g/8oz pitted cherries, halved
45ml/3 tbsp caster (superfine) sugar
10ml/2 tsp lemon juice
45ml/3 tbsp brandy or almond liqueur

1 Cut out six 25 × 3cm/10 × 1¼in strips of Perspex (Plexiglas). Melt the chocolate in a heatproof bowl over a pan of hot water. Line a baking sheet with baking parchment.

2 Coat the underside of the Perspex strips in chocolate, apart from 1cm/½in at each end. Bring the ends together so the chocolate is on the inside. Secure the ends with paper clips, then set on the baking sheet. Chill until completely hardened.

3 Put the amaretti in a plastic bag and crush with a rolling pin. Put the cream in a bowl and beat in the almond extract, icing sugar and liqueur. Churn in an ice cream maker until thick. Spoon in the milk and crushed amaretti. Churn until mixed. Spoon carefully into the chocolate cases, making sure they're filled to the rim. Freeze for at least 2 hours or overnight.

4 Make the sauce. Put the cornflour in a pan and stir in a little of the water to make a paste. Stir in the remaining water with the cherries, sugar and lemon juice. Bring to the boil and stir until thick. Remove from the heat and cool. Stir in the liqueur.

5 Peel away the Perspex from the cases and put on a plate. Spoon sauce beside the cases and decorate with cherries.

Teardrops Energy 441kcal/1839kJ; Protein 3.3g; Carbohydrate 45g, of which sugars 36.1g; Fat 26.9g, of which saturates 16.3g; Cholesterol 53mg; Calcium 72mg; Fibre 1.1g; Sodium 78mg.
Choc Ices Energy 117kcal/488kJ; Protein 1.8g; Carbohydrate 10.7g, of which sugars 10.6g; Fat 7.7g, of which saturates 4.3g; Cholesterol 1mg; Calcium 36mg; Fibre 0.3g; Sodium 19mg.

Cappuccino Choc Cones

White and dark chocolate cones are filled with swirls of cappuccino cream and topped with a dusting of unsweetened cocoa powder.

Serves 6
115g/4oz each good quality plain (semisweet) and white cooking chocolate

For the cappuccino cream
30ml/2 tbsp ground espresso or other strong-flavoured coffee
30ml/2 tbsp near-boiling water
300ml/½ pint/1¼ cups double (heavy) cream
45ml/3 tbsp icing (confectioners') sugar, sifted
15ml/1 tbsp unsweetened cocoa powder, for dusting

1 Cut nine 13 × 10cm/5 × 4in rectangles from baking parchment, then cut each rectangle in half diagonally to make 18 triangles. Roll up each to make a cone and secure with tape.

2 Heat the plain chocolate in a heatproof bowl over a pan of gently simmering water, stirring, until melted. Using a small pastry brush, thickly brush the insides of half the paper cones with chocolate. Chill until set. Repeat with the white chocolate. Carefully peel away the paper and keep the cones in the refrigerator until needed.

3 To make the cappuccino cream, put the coffee in a small bowl. Pour the hot water over. Leave to infuse (steep) for 4 minutes, then strain into a bowl. Leave to cool. Add the cream and sugar and whisk until soft peaks form. Spoon into a piping (pastry) bag fitted with a medium star nozzle.

4 Pipe the cream into the chocolate cones. Put on a baking sheet and freeze for at least 2 hours or until solid. Arrange on individual plates, allowing three cones per person and dusting with cocoa powder before serving.

> **Cook's Tip**
> When melting the chocolate in bowls over pans of water, make sure that the water doesn't boil or touch the bottom of the bowl, otherwise the chocolate will overheat and stiffen.

Iced Chocolate Nut Gateau

A divine dessert of rich chocolate ice cream encased in brandy-soaked sponge.

Serves 6–8
75g/3oz/¾ cup shelled hazelnuts
about 32 sponge fingers
150ml/¼ pint/⅔ cup cold strong black coffee
30ml/2 tbsp brandy

475ml/16fl oz/2 cups double (heavy) cream
75g/3oz/⅔ cup icing (confectioners') sugar, sifted
150g/5oz plain (semisweet) chocolate, chopped into small pieces
icing (confectioners') sugar and unsweetened cocoa powder, for dusting

1 Preheat the oven to 200°C/400°F/Gas 6. Spread out the hazelnuts on a baking sheet and toast them in the oven for 5 minutes until golden. Turn the nuts on to a clean dish towel and rub off the skins while still warm. Cool, then chop finely.

2 Line a 1.2 litre/2 pint/5 cup loaf tin (pan) with clear film (plastic wrap) and cut the sponge fingers to fit the base and sides. Reserve the remaining fingers. Mix the coffee with the brandy in a shallow dish. Dip the sponge fingers briefly into the coffee mixture and return to the tin, sugar side down, to fit.

3 Whip the cream with the icing sugar until it holds soft peaks. Fold half the chopped chocolate into the cream with the hazelnuts. Use a gentle figure-of-eight action to distribute the chocolate and nuts evenly.

4 Melt the remaining chocolate in a bowl set over a pan of barely simmering water. Cool, then fold into the cream mixture. Spoon into the tin.

5 Moisten the remaining fingers in the coffee mixture – take care not to soak the fingers, otherwise they will go soft and collapse. Lay the moistened fingers over the filling. Wrap and freeze until firm.

6 To serve, remove from the freezer 30 minutes before serving to allow the ice cream to soften slightly. Turn out on to a serving plate and dust with icing sugar and cocoa powder.

Cones Energy 485kcal/2013kJ; Protein 3.8g; Carbohydrate 32.3g, of which sugars 31.9g; Fat 38.7g, of which saturates 23.8g; Cholesterol 70mg; Calcium 90mg; Fibre 0.8g; Sodium 58mg.
Nut Gateau Energy 573kcal/2380kJ; Protein 5.8g; Carbohydrate 36.8g, of which sugars 30.8g; Fat 44.9g, of which saturates 23.9g; Cholesterol 140mg; Calcium 73mg; Fibre 1.3g; Sodium 37mg.

Chocolate Mint Ice Cream Pie

This chocolate-flavoured cereal pie case is incredibly easy to make and offers a simple way to turn ready-made ice cream into a smart-looking dessert.

40g/1½oz/3 tbsp butter
or margarine
50g/2oz crisped rice cereal
1 litre/1¾ pints/4 cups
mint-chocolate-chip ice cream
chocolate curls, to decorate

Serves 8
75g/3oz plain (semisweet)
chocolate chips

1 Line a 23cm/9in pie tin (pan) with foil. Place a round of baking parchment over the foil in the bottom of the tin.

2 Put the chocolate chips and butter or margarine in a heatproof bowl that will fit over a pan of simmering water. Place the bowl over the pan and melt the chocolate and butter.

3 Remove the bowl from the heat and gently stir in the cereal, a little at a time.

4 Press the chocolate-cereal mixture evenly over the base and up the sides of the prepared tin, forming a 1cm/½in rim. Chill until completely hard.

5 Carefully remove the cereal case from the tin and peel off the foil and paper. Return the case to the pie tin.

6 Remove the ice cream from the freezer. Let it soften for 10 minutes and spread it evenly in the cereal case. Freeze until firm.

7 Sprinkle the ice cream with chocolate curls just before serving.

Variation
Use any flavour of ice cream that marries well with chocolate – coffee, orange or raspberry ripple would be a good choice. Try plain, milk or white chocolate for the base.

Chocolate Millefeuille Slice

This stunning dessert takes a little time to prepare but can be assembled days in advance, ready to impress dinner guests.

Serves 8
4 egg yolks
10ml/2 tsp cornflour (cornstarch)
300ml/½ pint/1¼ cups milk
175ml/6fl oz/¾ cup maple syrup
250ml/8fl oz/1 cup crème fraîche

115g/4oz/1 cup pecan
nuts, chopped

To finish
200g/7oz plain (semisweet)
chocolate, broken into pieces
300ml/½ pint/1¼ cups
double (heavy) cream
45ml/3 tbsp icing
(confectioners') sugar
30ml/2 tbsp brandy
lightly toasted pecan nuts

1 Whisk the egg yolks in a bowl with the cornflour and a little of the milk until smooth. Pour the remaining milk into a pan, bring to the boil, then pour over the yolk mixture, stirring. Return the mixture to the pan and stir in the maple syrup and crème fraîche. Heat gently, stirring until thick. Pour into a bowl, cover and cool.

2 Churn in an ice cream maker until thick, then add the pecan nuts. Scrape into a freezerproof container and freeze overnight.

3 Melt 150g/5oz of the chocolate in a bowl over a pan of hot water. On baking parchment draw four rectangles, each about 19 × 12cm/7½ × 4½in. Spoon the melted chocolate equally on to the rectangles, spreading to the edges. Leave to set. Make thin curls from the remaining chocolate using a potato peeler.

4 Whip the cream with the sugar and brandy until it forms soft peaks. Peel away the paper from a rectangle and place on a plate. Spread a third of the cream over the chocolate. Lay small scoops of ice cream over the cream. Cover with a second rectangle. Repeat the layering, finishing with chocolate.

5 Sprinkle with the toasted pecan nuts and chocolate curls. Freeze overnight until firm. Transfer the frozen dessert to the refrigerator 30 minutes before serving to soften it slightly. Serve in slices.

Mint Ice Cream Pie Energy 378kcal/1573kJ; Protein 6.1g; Carbohydrate 32g, of which sugars 27.2g; Fat 25.9g, of which saturates 15.5g; Cholesterol 11mg; Calcium 183mg; Fibre 0.2g; Sodium 108mg.
Millefeuille Energy 667kcal/2772kJ; Protein 6.7g; Carbohydrate 43.3g, of which sugars 42.6g; Fat 53.1g, of which saturates 27.2g; Cholesterol 191mg; Calcium 117mg; Fibre 1.3g; Sodium 99mg.

Chocolate, Rum and Raisin Roulade

This richly flavoured dessert can be assembled and frozen a week or two in advance.

Serves 6
For the roulade
115g/4oz plain (semisweet) chocolate, broken into pieces
4 eggs, separated
115g/4oz/generous ½ cup caster (superfine) sugar, plus extra for dusting

For the filling
75g/3oz/generous ½ cup raisins
60ml/4 tbsp dark rum
425g/15oz can custard
50g/2oz/¼ cup light muscovado (brown) sugar
200ml/7fl oz/scant 1 cup whipping cream
unsweetened cocoa powder and icing (confectioners') sugar, to decorate

1 Make the roulade. Preheat the oven to 180°C/350°F/Gas 4. Line a 33 × 23cm/13 × 9in Swiss roll tin (jelly roll pan) with baking parchment. Melt the chocolate in a heatproof bowl set over a pan of simmering water.

2 Whisk the egg yolks and sugar together until thick and pale. Fold in the melted chocolate. Whisk the egg whites until stiff and fold one quarter of the egg whites into the chocolate mixture to loosen it, then gently fold in the remainder.

3 Pour the mixture into the tin. Bake for about 20 minutes or until the cake has risen and is just firm. Leave to cool in the tin covered with a piece of baking parchment and a clean dish towel.

4 Meanwhile, warm the raisins in the rum in a small pan for a few minutes, then leave them to cool and soak for 2 hours.

5 Make the ice cream. Mix together the custard, sugar and cream and pour into an ice cream maker. Churn until it is thick, then add the raisins and churn until it is stiff enough to spread.

6 Turn the roulade out on to baking parchment dusted with caster sugar. Spread with the ice cream, then roll up from one of the short sides, using the paper to help. Cover and freeze. Dust with cocoa powder and icing sugar before slicing and serving.

White Chocolate Castles with Fresh Summer Berries

These romantic-looking chocolate cases serve a wide variety of uses. They can be frozen with iced mousses or filled with scoops of your favourite ice cream and succulent fresh blueberries.

Serves 6
225g/8oz white chocolate, broken into pieces
250ml/8fl oz/1 cup white chocolate ice cream
250ml/8fl oz/1 cup dark (bittersweet) chocolate ice cream
115g/4oz/1 cup blueberries
unsweetened cocoa powder, for dusting

1 Put the white chocolate in a heatproof bowl, set it over a pan of gently simmering water and leave until melted. Line a baking sheet with baking parchment. Cut out six 30 × 13cm/12 × 5in strips of baking parchment, then fold each in half lengthways.

2 Stand a 7.5cm/3in pastry (cookie) cutter on the baking sheet. Roll one strip of paper into a circle and fit inside the cutter with the folded edge on the base paper. Stick the edges together with tape.

3 Remove the cutter and make more paper collars in the same way, leaving the cutter in place around the final collar.

4 Spoon a little of the melted chocolate into the base of the collar supported by the cutter. Using a teaspoon, spread the chocolate over the base and up the sides of the collar, making the top edge uneven. Carefully lift away the cutter.

5 Make five more chocolate cases in the same way, using the cutter for extra support each time. Leave the cases in a cool place or in the refrigerator to set.

6 Carefully peel the baking parchment from the sides of the chocolate cases, then lift the cases off the base. Transfer to serving plates. Using a teaspoon, scoop the ice creams into the cases and decorate with the fruit. Dust with cocoa powder.

Roulade Energy 486kcal/2023kJ; Protein 10.2g; Carbohydrate 32.8g, of which sugars 32.4g; Fat 34.5g, of which saturates 19.9g; Cholesterol 190mg; Calcium 41mg; Fibre 1.3g; Sodium 143mg.
Castles Energy 351kcal/1463kJ; Protein 6g; Carbohydrate 34.3g, of which sugars 34.2g; Fat 22g, of which saturates 13.1g; Cholesterol 0mg; Calcium 182mg; Fibre 1.2g; Sodium 84mg.

Chocolate Ice Cream with Lime Sabayon

Sabayon sauce has a light, foamy texture that perfectly complements the rich, smooth flavour of ice cream. This tangy lime version is particularly delicious when spooned generously over chocolate ice cream.

Serves 4

2 egg yolks
65g/2½oz/5 tbsp caster (superfine) sugar
finely grated rind and juice of 2 limes
60ml/4 tbsp white wine or apple juice
45ml/3 tbsp single (light) cream
500ml/17fl oz/generous 2 cups chocolate chip or dark (bittersweet) chocolate ice cream
pared strips of lime rind, to decorate

1 Put the egg yolks and sugar in a heatproof bowl and beat until combined. Beat in the lime rind and juice, then the white wine or apple juice.

2 Whisk the mixture over a pan of gently simmering water until the sabayon is smooth and thick, and the mixture leaves a trail when the whisk is lifted from the bowl.

3 Lightly whisk in the cream. Remove the bowl from the pan and cover with a lid or plate.

4 Working quickly, scoop the ice cream into four glasses. Spoon the sabayon sauce over the ice cream, decorate with the strips of lime rind and serve immediately.

Variation
The tangy lime sauce marries just as well with vanilla ice cream. It is also very good served with individual servings of sliced tropical fruit – pineapple, papaya and kiwi would look pretty. Try the sabayon sauce as a topping for a selection of soft summer fruits, too.

Chocolate Sorbet

This is a delicious cooling treat for chocolate lovers. Serve with crisp little biscuits as a light way to end a meal.

Serves 6

150g/5oz dark (bittersweet) chocolate, chopped
115g/4oz plain (semisweet) chocolate, grated
225g/8oz/1 cup caster (superfine) sugar
475ml/16fl oz/2 cups water
chocolate curls, to decorate

1 Put all of the chocolate in a food processor, fitted with a metal blade, and process for approximately 20–30 seconds, or until finely chopped.

2 Place the sugar and water in a pan over medium heat. Bring to the boil, stirring until all of the sugar has completely dissolved. Boil for about 2 minutes, then remove the pan from the heat.

3 While the machine is running, carefully add the hot sugar-and-water syrup to the chocolate in the food processor. Keep the food processor running for 1–2 minutes until the chocolate is completely melted and the mixture is smooth. Scrape down the bowl once or twice to catch any mixture that is clinging to the sides.

4 Strain the chocolate mixture into a large measuring jug (cup) or bowl. Leave to cool completely, then chill, making sure that you stir the mixture occasionally.

5 Pour the chilled mixture into a freezer container and freeze until it is slushy.

6 Whisk the mixture until smooth, then freeze again until it is almost firm. Whisk it for a second time and return it to the freezer.

7 Allow to soften slightly before serving decorated with the chocolate curls.

Lime Sabayon Energy 395kcal/1648kJ; Protein 6.8g; Carbohydrate 38.3g, of which sugars 38.2g; Fat 23.8g, of which saturates 13.5g; Cholesterol 107mg; Calcium 157mg; Fibre 0g; Sodium 84mg.
Chocolate Sorbet Energy 301kcal/1266kJ; Protein 2.3g; Carbohydrate 48.1g, of which sugars 47.7g; Fat 12.4g, of which saturates 7.4g; Cholesterol 3mg; Calcium 25mg; Fibre 1.1g; Sodium 4mg.

Chocolate Sorbet with Red Fruits

Mouthwatering chocolate-flavoured sorbet tastes and looks stunning when served with a selection of luscious red berries.

Serves 6
475ml/16fl oz/2 cups water
45ml/3 tbsp clear honey
90g/3½oz/½ cup caster (superfine) sugar

75g/3oz/⅔ cup unsweetened cocoa powder
50g/2oz plain (semisweet) or dark (bittersweet) chocolate, chopped into small pieces
400g/14oz soft red fruits, such as raspberries, redcurrants or strawberries

1 Put the water in a pan with the honey, sugar and cocoa powder. Heat the mixture gently, stirring occasionally, until the sugar has completely dissolved.

2 Remove the pan from the heat, add the chocolate pieces and stir until melted. Leave until cool.

3 Pour the chocolate mixture into a freezer container and freeze until slushy. Whisk quickly until smooth, then return the mixture to the freezer again and freeze until almost firm. Whisk the iced mixture for a second time, cover the container and freeze until firm.

4 Alternatively, use an ice cream maker to freeze the mixture, following the manufacturer's instructions.

5 Remove the sorbet from the freezer 10–15 minutes before serving to soften slightly. Serve in scoops, in chilled dessert bowls, with the soft fruits.

> **Cook's Tip**
> Chocolate curls make an attractive decoration for a dessert and are very simple to create. Simply chill a bar of chocolate, then use a vegetable peeler to shave off curls along the length of the bar.

Choca Mocha Sherbet

This delicious dark chocolate sherbet is a cross between a water ice and light cream-free ice cream. It is an ideal way to end a meal for chocoholics who are trying to count calories but still feel the need to have an occasional taste of chocolate.

Serves 4–6
600ml/1 pint/2½ cups semi-skimmed (low-fat) milk
40g/1½oz/⅓ cup good quality unsweetened cocoa powder
115g/4oz/generous ½ cup caster (superfine) sugar
5ml/1 tsp instant coffee granules
chocolate-covered raisins, to decorate

1 Heat the milk in a pan. Meanwhile, put the cocoa powder in a bowl, add a little of the hot milk and mix to a paste.

2 Add the remaining milk to the cocoa mixture, stirring all the time, then pour the chocolate milk back into the pan. Bring to the boil, stirring continuously.

3 Take the pan off the heat and add the sugar and the coffee granules, stirring until the sugar and coffee have dissolved. Pour into a jug (pitcher), leave to cool, then chill well.

4 To make by hand, pour the mixture into a plastic tub or similar freezerproof container and freeze for 6 hours until firm, beating once or twice with a fork, electric mixer or in a food processor to break up the ice crystals. Allow to soften slightly before scooping into dishes. Sprinkle each portion with a few chocolate-covered raisins.

5 To make in an ice cream maker, churn the chilled mixture until very thick. Scoop into dishes. Sprinkle each portion with a few chocolate-covered raisins.

> **Cook's Tip**
> Use good-quality cocoa powder and don't overheat the milk mixture or the finished ice may taste bitter. If there are any lumps of cocoa in the milk, beat with a balloon whisk.

Sorbet Energy 179kcal/758kJ; Protein 3.8g; Carbohydrate 31.2g, of which sugars 29.7g; Fat 5.3g, of which saturates 3.1g; Cholesterol 1mg; Calcium 44mg; Fibre 3.4g; Sodium 123mg.
Choca Mocha Energy 142kcal/604kJ; Protein 4.7g; Carbohydrate 25.5g, of which sugars 24.7g; Fat 3.2g, of which saturates 1.9g; Cholesterol 6mg; Calcium 139mg; Fibre 0.8g; Sodium 108mg.

Coffee with Mocha Ice Cream

This coffee and mocha ice cream combination is a speciality of Belgium. You can enjoy it as an afternoon treat or serve it after dinner as the perfect way to finish off a good meal. The chocolatey topping – either a dusting of cocoa, shavings of chocolate or a chocolate-coated coffee bean – make an attractive and delicious decoration.

Serves I
*100ml/3 fl oz/scant ½ cup
double (heavy) cream
15ml/1 tbsp icing (confectioners')
sugar
45ml/3 tbsp freshly brewed
espresso coffee
10ml/2 tsp granulated
(white) sugar
2 scoops mocha ice cream
2.5ml/½ tsp unsweetened cocoa
powder, 5ml/1 tsp shaved
chocolate curls, or 3 chocolate
coffee beans, to decorate*

I Pour the cream into a bowl. Add the icing sugar and whip by hand or with an electric mixer until stiff.

2 Sweeten the espresso coffee by stirring in the granulated sugar.

3 Place the scoops of ice cream in a tall or wide heat-resistant glass.

4 Pour over the hot, sweet espresso and top with the whipped cream.

5 Decorate with a dusting of cocoa, a few shavings of chocolate or the chocolate coffee beans. Serve immediately.

> **Cook's Tip**
> *Chill the espresso before pouring it over the ice cream, if you prefer.*

Turkish Delight Sorbet with White Chocolate Drizzle

Anyone who likes Turkish delight will adore the taste and aroma of this intriguing dessert. Because of its sweetness, it is best served in small portions and is delicious with after-dinner coffee. Decorate with drizzled white chocolate and sugared almonds or slices of Turkish delight.

Serves 8
*250g/9oz rose water-flavoured
Turkish delight
25g/1oz/2 tbsp caster
(superfine) sugar
750ml/1¼ pints/3 cups water
30ml/2 tbsp lemon juice
50g/2oz white chocolate, broken
into pieces
roughly chopped sugared
almonds, to decorate*

I Cut the cubes of Turkish delight into small pieces. Put half of the pieces in a heavy pan with the sugar. Pour in half of the water. Heat gently until the Turkish delight has dissolved.

2 Cool, then stir in the lemon juice with the remaining water and Turkish delight. Chill well. Churn the mixture in an ice cream maker until it is firm enough to hold its shape.

3 While the sorbet is freezing, dampen eight very small plastic cups or glasses. Line them with clear film (plastic wrap).

4 Spoon the sorbet into the cups and tap them lightly on the surface to compact the mixture. Cover with the overlapping film and freeze for at least 3 hours or overnight.

5 Make a paper piping (pastry) bag. Put the chocolate in a heatproof bowl over a pan of gently simmering water, and stir until melted.

6 Meanwhile, remove the sorbets from the freezer, let them stand at room temperature for 5 minutes, then pull them out of the cups. Transfer to serving plates and peel away the film. Spoon the melted chocolate into the piping bag, snip off the tip and scribble a design on the sorbet and the plate. Sprinkle the sugared almonds over and serve.

Coffee with Mocha Energy 925kcal/3855kJ; Protein 6.2g; Carbohydrate 82.9g, of which sugars 81.6g; Fat 64g, of which saturates 40.7g; Cholesterol 166mg; Calcium 198mg; Fibre 0g; Sodium 97mg.
Turkish Delight Energy 280kcal/1188kJ; Protein 1.4g; Carbohydrate 63.8g, of which sugars 58g; Fat 3.9g, of which saturates 2.3g; Cholesterol 0mg; Calcium 44mg; Fibre 0g; Sodium 34mg.

Greek Chocolate Mousse Tartlets

Irresistible Greek-style
tartlets with a lightweight
chocolate and yogurt filling.

Makes 6 tarts
175g/6oz/1½ cups plain
   (all-purpose) flour
30ml/2 tbsp unsweetened
   cocoa powder
30ml/2 tbsp icing
   (confectioners') sugar
115g/4oz/½ cup butter
60ml/4 tbsp water

melted dark (bittersweet)
   chocolate, to decorate

For the filling
200g/7oz white chocolate
120ml/4fl oz/½ cup milk
10ml/2 tsp powdered gelatine
25g/1oz/2 tbsp caster
   (superfine) sugar
5ml/1 tsp vanilla extract
2 eggs, separated
250g/9oz/generous 1 cup Greek
   (US strained plain) yogurt

1 Preheat the oven to 190°C/375°F/Gas 5. Sift the flour, cocoa and icing sugar into a large bowl.

2 Place the butter in a pan with the water and heat gently until just melted. Cool, then stir into the flour to make a smooth dough. Chill until firm.

3 Roll out the pastry and line six deep 10cm/4in loose-based flan tins (pans). Prick the base of the pastry cases (pie shells), cover with baking parchment, weigh down with baking beans and bake blind for 10 minutes. Remove the beans and paper, return to the oven and bake for 15 minutes until firm. Leave to cool.

4 Make the filling. Melt the broken-up chocolate in a heatproof bowl over hot water. Pour the milk into a pan, sprinkle over the gelatine and heat gently, stirring, until the gelatine has dissolved. Remove from the heat and stir in the chocolate.

5 Whisk the sugar, vanilla and egg yolks in a large bowl, then beat in the chocolate mixture. Beat in the yogurt until mixed.

6 Whisk the egg whites in a clean, grease-free bowl until stiff, then carefully fold into the chocolate mixture. Spoon into the pastry cases and leave to set. Drizzle with melted chocolate to serve.

Chocolate Lemon Tartlets

These delicious individual
chocolate desserts have a
tasty lemony curd filling.

Makes 12 tartlets
1 quantity Chocolate
   Shortcrust Pastry
lemon twists and melted
   chocolate, to decorate

For the lemon custard sauce
grated rind and juice of 1 lemon
350ml/12fl oz/1½ cups milk
6 egg yolks
50g/2oz/½ cup caster
   (superfine) sugar

For the lemon curd filling
grated rind and juice of 2 lemons
175g/6oz/¾ cup unsalted
   (sweet) butter, diced
450g/1lb/2¼ cups granulated
   (white) sugar
3 eggs, lightly beaten

For the chocolate layer
175ml/6fl oz/¾ cup double
   (heavy) cream
175g/6oz dark (bittersweet) or
   plain (semisweet) chocolate,
   chopped into small pieces
25g/1oz/2 tbsp unsalted (sweet)
   butter, cut into pieces

1 Prepare the custard sauce. Boil the rind in a pan with the milk. Remove from the heat and leave for 5 minutes to infuse (steep). Strain the milk into a clean pan and reheat it gently. In a bowl beat the yolks and sugar with a hand-held electric mixer for 2–3 minutes, until pale and thick. Pour over about 250ml/8fl oz/1 cup of the flavoured hot milk, beating vigorously.

2 Return the yolk mixture to the milk in the pan and cook gently, stirring, until the mixture thickens. (Do not allow the sauce to boil or it will curdle.) Strain into a chilled bowl. Stir 30ml/2 tbsp lemon juice into the sauce. Cool, stirring occasionally, then chill until ready to use.

3 Prepare the lemon curd filling. Combine the lemon rind, juice, butter and sugar in the top of a double boiler. Set over simmering water and heat until the butter has melted and the sugar has completely dissolved. Reduce the heat to low. Stir the lightly beaten eggs into the mixture. Gently cook for 15 minutes, stirring constantly, until the mixture thickens. Strain into a bowl and cover with clear film (plastic wrap). Allow to cool, stirring occasionally, then chill to thicken, stirring occasionally.

4 Lightly butter twelve 7.5cm/3in tartlet tins (muffin pans). On a lightly floured surface, roll out the pastry to a thickness of 3mm/⅛in. Using a 10cm/4in fluted cutter, cut out 12 rounds and press each one into a tin. Prick the bases with a fork. Place the tins on a baking sheet and chill for 30 minutes.

5 Preheat the oven to 190°C/375°F/Gas 5. Cut out rounds of foil and line each pastry case (pie shell); fill with baking beans or rice. Bake blind for 5–8 minutes. Remove the foil and beans and bake for 5 minutes, until the cases are golden. Remove to a rack to cool.

6 Prepare the chocolate layer. Boil the cream in a pan. Remove from the heat and add the chocolate; stir until melted. Beat in the butter and cool slightly. Pour the filling into each tartlet to make a layer 5mm/¼in thick. Chill 10 minutes until set.

7 Fill the tartlets with lemon curd. Set aside. Spoon lemon custard sauce on to a plate and place a tartlet in the centre. Decorate with a lemon twist. Dot with melted chocolate.

Greek Tartlets Energy 555kcal/2320kJ; Protein 11.9g; Carbohydrate 55g, of which sugars 32.2g; Fat 34g, of which saturates 19.7g; Cholesterol 105mg; Calcium 242mg; Fibre 1.5g; Sodium 263mg.
Lemon Tartlets Energy 379kcal/1585kJ; Protein 6.1g; Carbohydrate 40.5g, of which sugars 27g; Fat 22.6g, of which saturates 12.9g; Cholesterol 163mg; Calcium 68mg; Fibre 0.7g; Sodium 127mg.

Fruit Tartlets with Chocolate Pastry

The cream and fresh fruit topping of these delightful tartlets contrast beautifully with the chocolate pastry.

Makes 8 tartlets
150g/5oz/10 tbsp cold butter, cut into pieces
65g/2½oz/5 tbsp dark brown sugar
45ml/3 tbsp unsweetened cocoa powder
175g/6oz/1½ cups plain (all-purpose) flour
1 egg white

For the filling
215g/7½oz/¾ cup redcurrant or grape jelly
15ml/1 tbsp fresh lemon juice
175ml/6fl oz/¾ cup whipping cream
675g/1½lb fresh fruit, such as strawberries, raspberries, kiwi fruit, peaches, grapes or blueberries, peeled and sliced as necessary

1 Make the pastry. Place the butter, brown sugar and cocoa in a medium pan over a low heat. When the butter has melted, remove from the heat and sift over the flour. Stir with a wooden spoon to combine, then add just enough egg white to bind the mixture. Gather into a ball, wrap in baking parchment and chill for at least 30 minutes.

2 Preheat the oven to 180°C/350°F/Gas 4. Grease eight 7.5cm/3in tartlet tins (muffin pans). Roll out the dough between two sheets of baking parchment and stamp out eight 10cm/4in rounds with a fluted cutter.

3 Line the tartlet tins with dough rounds. Prick the pastry bases with a fork. Chill for 15 minutes.

4 Bake for 20–25 minutes until firm. Leave to cool, then remove the tartlets from the tins.

5 Melt the jelly with the lemon juice in a pan over a low heat. Brush a thin layer over the base of the tartlets. Whip the cream in a bowl and spread a thin layer in the tartlet cases (shells). Arrange the fruit on top. Brush evenly with the fruit glaze and serve immediately.

Truffle Filo Tarts

These dainty filo pastry cups, decorated with twists of lemon, can be prepared a day ahead and then stored in an airtight container until they are needed.

Makes 24 tarts
3–6 sheets filo pastry (depending on size), thawed if frozen
45g/1½oz/3 tbsp unsalted (sweet) butter, melted
sugar, for sprinkling
lemon rind, to decorate

For the truffle mixture
250ml/8fl oz/1 cup double (heavy) cream
225g/8oz plain (semisweet) or dark (bittersweet) chocolate, chopped
50g/2oz/¼ cup unsalted (sweet) butter, diced
30ml/2 tbsp brandy

1 To make the truffle mixture, bring the double cream to the boil in a pan over medium heat. Remove from the heat and add the chocolate, stirring until melted. Beat in the butter and add the brandy. Strain into a bowl and chill for 1 hour.

2 Preheat the oven to 200°C/400°F/Gas 6. Grease a bun tray with 24 cups, each 4cm/1½in. Cut each filo sheet into 6cm/2½in squares. Cover with a damp dish towel. Keeping the other filo sheets covered, place one square on a work surface. Brush lightly with melted butter, turn over and brush the other side. Sprinkle with a pinch of sugar.

3 Butter another square and place it over the first at an angle. Sprinkle with sugar. Butter a third square and place over the first two, unevenly, so that the corners form an uneven edge. Press the layered square into the tray. Continue to fill the tray.

4 Bake the filo cups for 4–6 minutes, or until golden. Cool for 10 minutes on a wire rack in the tray. Remove from the tray and cool completely.

5 Stir the chocolate mixture, which should be just thick enough to pipe. Spoon the mixture into a piping (pastry) bag fitted with a medium star nozzle and pipe a swirl into each cup. Decorate with lemon rind.

Fruit Tartlets Energy 440kcal/1841kJ; Protein 5.4g; Carbohydrate 49.3g, of which sugars 32g; Fat 26g, of which saturates 16.1g; Cholesterol 63mg; Calcium 83mg; Fibre 3.5g; Sodium 192mg.
Filo Tarts Energy 149kcal/621kJ; Protein 1.2g; Carbohydrate 10.2g, of which sugars 6.1g; Fat 11.5g, of which saturates 7.1g; Cholesterol 23mg; Calcium 16mg; Fibre 0.4g; Sodium 27mg.

Tia Maria Truffle Tarts

The ideal dessert for a tea or coffee break, these mini coffee pastry cases are filled with a truffle centre and topped with fresh berries.

Serves 6
300ml/½ pint/1¼ cups double
  (heavy) cream
225g/8oz/generous ¾ cup seedless
  bramble or raspberry jam
150g/5oz plain (semisweet)
  chocolate, broken into squares
45ml/3 tbsp Tia Maria liqueur

450g/1lb mixed berries, such as
  raspberries, small strawberries
  or blackberries

For the pastry
225g/8oz/2 cups plain
  (all-purpose) flour
15ml/1 tbsp caster
  (superfine) sugar
150g/5oz/10 tbsp
  butter, cubed
1 egg yolk
30ml/2 tbsp very strong
  brewed coffee, chilled

1 Preheat the oven to 200°C/400°F/Gas 6. Put a baking sheet in the oven to heat. To make the pastry, sift the flour and sugar into a large bowl. Rub in the butter. Stir the egg yolk and coffee together, add to the bowl and mix to a stiff dough. Knead lightly on a floured surface for a few seconds until smooth. Wrap in clear film (plastic wrap) and chill for about 20 minutes.

2 Use the pastry to line six 10cm/4in fluted tartlet tins (pans). Prick the bases with a fork and line with baking parchment and baking beans. Put the tins on the hot baking sheet and bake for 10 minutes. Remove the paper and beans and bake for another 8–10 minutes longer, until cooked. Transfer to a wire rack and leave to cool completely.

3 Make the filling. Bring the cream and 175g/6oz/generous ½ cup of the jam to the boil, stirring continuously until dissolved.

4 Remove from the heat, add the chocolate and 30ml/2 tbsp of the liqueur. Stir until melted. Cool, then spoon into the pastry cases (pie shells) and smooth the tops. Chill for 40 minutes.

5 Heat the remaining jam and liqueur until smooth. Arrange the fruit on top of the tarts, then brush the jam glaze over it. Chill until ready to serve.

Dark Chocolate and Hazelnut Tart

The crisp, hazelnut-flavoured pastry tastes wonderful combined with a luxurious chocolate filling.

115g/4oz/1 cup toasted
  hazelnuts
10ml/2 tsp icing (confectioners')
  sugar, for dusting

Serves 10
300ml/½ pint/1¼ cups double
  (heavy) cream
150ml/¼ pint/⅔ cup creamy milk
150g/5oz dark (bittersweet)
  chocolate, chopped
4 eggs
50g/2oz/¼ cup caster
  (superfine) sugar
5ml/1 tsp vanilla extract
15ml/1 tbsp plain
  (all-purpose) flour

For the pastry
150g/5oz/1¼ cups plain
  (all-purpose) flour
pinch of salt
40g/1½oz/3 tbsp caster
  (superfine) sugar
50g/2oz/½ cup ground
  hazelnuts, toasted
90g/3½oz/scant ½ cup
  butter, diced
1 egg, lightly beaten

1 Make the pastry. Sift the flour, salt and sugar into a mixing bowl, then mix in the toasted hazelnuts. Rub or cut in the butter until the mixture resembles fine breadcrumbs.

2 Make a well in the centre, add the beaten egg and mix to a firm dough. Knead the dough on a lightly floured surface for a few seconds until smooth. Wrap in clear film (plastic wrap) and chill for 30 minutes.

3 Roll out the pastry on a floured surface and use to line a 23cm/9in loose-based heart-shaped flan tin (pan). Trim the edges. Cover and chill for a further 30 minutes.

4 Re-roll the pastry trimmings into a long strip, about 30cm/12in long. Cut this into six strips, each 5mm/¼in wide, and make two plaits (braids) with three pastry strips in each. Curve into a heart shape and press gently to join together at both ends. Carefully place the heart on a baking sheet lined with baking parchment, and chill.

5 Put a baking sheet in the oven and preheat to 200°C/400°F/Gas 6. Prick the base of the pastry case (pie shell) with a fork. Line with foil and baking beans and bake blind on the sheet for 10 minutes. Remove the foil and beans and bake for a further 5 minutes. Bake the pastry plait on the shelf below for 10 minutes, or until lightly browned.

6 Meanwhile, pour the cream and milk into a pan and bring to the boil. Add the chocolate and stir until melted. Whisk the eggs, caster sugar, vanilla and flour together in a bowl. Pour the hot chocolate cream over the egg mixture, whisking all the time. Stir the chopped hazelnuts into the mixture, stirring until well combined.

7 Pour the chocolate and hazelnut mixture into the pastry case and bake in the oven for 25 minutes, or until just set.

8 Allow the tart to cool completely, then remove from the tin and transfer on to a serving plate. Place the pastry rope on top of the tart, then lightly dust the surface with icing sugar.

Tia Maria Tarts Energy 844kcal/3519kJ; Protein 7.1g; Carbohydrate 79g, of which sugars 50.2g; Fat 55.9g, of which saturates 34.3g; Cholesterol 157mg; Calcium 112mg; Fibre 2.6g; Sodium 182mg.
Dark Tart Energy 544kcal/2261kJ; Protein 8.8g; Carbohydrate 35.6g, of which sugars 22.5g; Fat 41.8g, of which saturates 19.2g; Cholesterol 158mg; Calcium 105mg; Fibre 2g; Sodium 106mg.

Velvety Mocha Tart

A creamy smooth filling tops a dark light-textured base in this wondrous dessert decorated with cream and chocolate-coated coffee beans.

Serves 8
10ml/2 tsp instant
  espresso coffee
30ml/2 tbsp hot water
175g/6oz plain (semisweet)
  chocolate
25g/1oz bitter cooking
  chocolate

350ml/12fl oz/1½ cups
  whipping cream,
  slightly warmed
120ml/4fl oz/½ cup whipped
  cream, to decorate
chocolate-coated coffee beans,
  to decorate

For the base
150g/5oz/2½ cups crushed
  chocolate wafers
30ml/2 tbsp caster
  (superfine) sugar
65g/2½oz/5 tbsp butter,
  melted

1 To make the base, combine the crushed chocolate wafers with the sugar and butter in a bowl.

2 Press the mixture over the base and sides of a 23cm/9in pie dish. Chill.

3 Dissolve the coffee in the water. Set aside to cool.

4 Melt the plain and bitter chocolates in the top of a double boiler or in a heatproof bowl over a pan of simmering water.

5 Once the chocolate has melted, remove from the double boiler and set the base of the pan in cold water to cool.

6 Whip the cream until light and fluffy. Add the coffee and whip until the cream just holds its shape.

7 When the chocolate is at room temperature, fold it gently into the cream.

8 Pour into the wafer base and chill until firm. Decorate with piped whipped cream and chocolate-coated coffee beans just before serving.

Chocolate and Pine Nut Tart

Orange-flavoured pastry makes this a real winner.

Serves 8
200g/7oz/1¾ cups plain
  (all-purpose) flour
50g/2oz/¼ cup caster
  (superfine) sugar
pinch of salt
grated rind of ½ orange
115g/4oz/½ cup unsalted (sweet)
  butter, cut into small pieces
3 egg yolks, lightly beaten
15–30ml/1–2 tbsp chilled water

For the filling
2 eggs
45ml/3 tbsp caster
  (superfine) sugar
grated rind of 1 orange
15ml/1 tbsp orange liqueur
250ml/8fl oz/1 cup whipping cream
115g/4oz plain (semisweet)
  chocolate, cut into small pieces
75g/3oz/¾ cup pine nuts, toasted
thinly pared rind of 1 orange and
  50g/2oz/¼ cup granulated
  (white) sugar, to decorate

1 Process the flour, sugar, salt and orange rind in a food processor, add the butter and process again for 30 seconds. Add the yolks and pulse until the dough begins to stick together. If it seems dry, gradually add the water. Knead, then wrap and chill for 2–3 hours.

2 Grease a 23cm/9in loose-based flan tin (pan). Roll out the dough on a floured surface into a 28cm/11in round. Ease it into the tin and roll a rolling pin over the edge to trim. Prick the base. Chill for 1 hour. Preheat the oven to 200°C/400°F/Gas 6.

3 Line the pastry with foil, fill with baking beans and bake blind for 5 minutes. Remove the foil and beans and bake for 5 minutes more, then cool. Lower the temperature to 180°C/350°F/Gas 4.

4 Beat the eggs, sugar, orange rind and liqueur in a bowl. Stir in the cream. Sprinkle the chocolate and pine nuts over the base of the tart. Pour in the filling. Bake for 20–30 minutes, until golden.

5 Make the decoration. Cut the orange rind into strips. Dissolve the sugar in 120ml/4fl oz/½ cup water over a medium heat, add the rind and boil for 5 minutes. Remove from the heat and stir in 15ml/1 tbsp cold water. Brush the orange syrup over the tart and decorate with the caramelized strips. Serve warm.

Mocha Tart Energy 507kcal/2103kJ; Protein 3.6g; Carbohydrate 30.3g, of which sugars 27g; Fat 42.1g, of which saturates 26.2g; Cholesterol 83mg; Calcium 71mg; Fibre 0.8g; Sodium 83mg.
Pine Nut Tart Energy 543kcal/2261kJ; Protein 7.8g; Carbohydrate 42.7g, of which sugars 23.5g; Fat 38.6g, of which saturates 19.2g; Cholesterol 187mg; Calcium 84mg; Fibre 1.3g; Sodium 118mg.

Chocolate Truffle Tart

A dreamy chilled tart with a chocolate flavoured pastry case and a luscious filling, laced with brandy.

15–30ml/1–2 tbsp iced water
25g/1oz good-quality white or
  milk chocolate, melted
whipped cream for serving
  (optional)

Serves 12
115g/4oz/1 cup plain
  (all-purpose) flour
40g/1¼oz/⅓ cup unsweetened
  cocoa powder
50g/2oz/¼ cup caster
  (superfine) sugar
2.5ml/½ tsp salt
115g/4oz/½ cup unsalted (sweet)
  butter, cut into pieces
1 egg yolk

For the truffle filling
350ml/12fl oz/1½ cups double
  (heavy) cream
350g/12oz fine plain (semisweet)
  chocolate, chopped
50g/2oz/4 tbsp unsalted (sweet)
  butter, cut into small pieces
30ml/2 tbsp brandy or liqueur

1 Make the pastry. Sift the flour and cocoa into a bowl. In a food processor fitted with a metal blade, process the flour mixture with the sugar and salt. Add the butter and process for a further 15–20 seconds, or until the mixture resembles coarse breadcrumbs.

2 Lightly beat the yolk with the iced water in a bowl. Add to the flour mixture and pulse until the dough begins to stick together. Turn out the dough on to a sheet of clear film (plastic wrap). Use the film to help shape the dough into a flat disc. Wrap tightly. Chill for 1–2 hours, until firm.

3 Lightly grease a 23cm/9in flan tin (pan) with a removable base. Let the dough soften briefly, then roll it out between sheets of baking parchment or clear film to a 28cm/11in round, about 5mm/¼in thick. Peel off the top sheet and invert the dough into the flan tin. Remove the bottom sheet. Ease the dough into the tin. Prick all over with a fork. Chill in the refrigerator for 1 hour.

4 Preheat the oven to 180°C/350°F/Gas 4. Line the tart with foil or baking parchment; fill with baking beans. Bake blind for 5–7 minutes. Lift out the foil with the beans, return the pastry case (pie shell) to the oven and bake for a further 5–7 minutes, until the pastry is just set. Leave to cool completely in the tin on a rack.

5 Make the filling. In a medium pan, bring the cream to the boil over a medium heat. Remove the pan from the heat and stir in the chocolate until melted and smooth. Stir in the butter and brandy or liqueur. Strain into the prepared pastry case, tilting the tin slightly to level the surface. Do not touch the surface of the filling or it will spoil the glossy finish.

6 Spoon the melted chocolate into a paper piping (pastry) bag and cut off the tip. Drop rounds of chocolate over the surface of the tart and use a skewer or cocktail stick (toothpick) to draw a point gently through the chocolate to produce a marbled effect. Chill for 2–3 hours, until set.

7 Just before serving, allow the tart to soften slightly at room temperature, then serve with whipped cream, if you like.

Chocolate Lemon Tart

In this easy-to-make recipe, the chocolate-flavoured pastry is pressed into the tin rather than rolled out, helping to speed up the preparation. With a simple lemon filling, this is a great dessert for the busy cook.

2.5ml/½ tsp salt
115g/4oz/½ cup unsalted
  (sweet) butter or margarine,
  plus extra for greasing
15ml/1 tbsp water

For the filling
225g/8oz/1 cup caster
  (superfine) sugar
6 eggs
grated rind of 2 lemons
175ml/6fl oz/¾ cup freshly
  squeezed lemon juice
175ml/6fl oz/¾ cup
  double (heavy) or
  whipping cream
chocolate curls, to decorate

Serves 8–10
175g/6oz/1½ cups plain
  (all-purpose) flour
10ml/2 tsp unsweetened
  cocoa powder
25g/1oz/¼ cup icing
  (confectioners') sugar

1 Grease a 25cm/10in loose-based flan tin (pan). Sift the flour, cocoa, icing sugar and salt into a bowl. Set aside.

2 Melt the butter or margarine and water in a pan over a low heat. Add the flour mixture and stir until the flour has absorbed all the liquid and the dough is smooth.

3 Press the dough evenly over the base and side of the prepared tin. Chill the pastry case (pie shell).

4 Preheat the oven to 190°C/375°F/Gas 5, and place a baking sheet inside to heat up. Make the filling. Whisk the caster sugar and eggs in a bowl until the sugar has dissolved. Add the lemon rind and juice and mix well. Stir in the cream. Taste and add more lemon juice or sugar if needed, for a sweet taste with a touch of tartness.

5 Pour the filling into the pastry case and place the tin on the hot baking sheet. Bake for 20–25 minutes or until the filling is set. Cool the tart on a rack, then remove from the tin. Decorate with the chocolate curls and serve.

Lemon Tart Energy 379kcal/1585kJ; Protein 6.1g; Carbohydrate 40.5g, of which sugars 27g; Fat 22.6g, of which saturates 12.9g; Cholesterol 163mg; Calcium 68mg; Fibre 0.7g; Sodium 127mg.
Truffle Tart Energy 474kcal/1969kJ; Protein 3.7g; Carbohydrate 32.5g, of which sugars 24.6g; Fat 36.8g, of which saturates 22.6g; Cholesterol 88mg; Calcium 48mg; Fibre 1.4g; Sodium 117mg.

Chocolate Apricot Linzer Tart

This makes an excellent dinner party dessert.

Serves 10–12
50g/2oz/⅓ cup blanched
  almonds
115g/4oz/generous ½ cup caster
  (superfine) sugar
175g/6oz/1½ cups plain
  (all-purpose) flour
30ml/2 tbsp unsweetened
  cocoa powder
5ml/1 tsp ground cinnamon
2.5ml/½ tsp salt

5ml/1 tsp grated orange rind
225g/8oz/1 cup unsalted (sweet)
  butter, cut into small pieces
75g/3oz/½ cup chocolate chips
icing (confectioners') sugar,
  for dusting

For the apricot filling
350g/12oz/1½ cups dried apricots
120ml/4fl oz/½ cup orange juice
40g/1½oz/3 tbsp granulated
  (white) sugar
50g/2oz/2 tbsp apricot jam
2.5ml/½ tsp almond extract

1 For the filling, simmer the apricots, orange juice and 175ml/6fl oz/¾ cup water, stirring, until the liquid is absorbed. Stir in the remaining ingredients. Strain into a bowl, cool, cover and chill.

2 Grease a 28cm/11in loose-based flan tin (pan). Grind the almonds and half the sugar in a food processor. Sift in the flour, cocoa, cinnamon and salt, add the remaining sugar and process. Add the rind and butter. Process for 15–20 seconds until the mixture resembles breadcrumbs. Add 30ml/2 tbsp iced water and pulse, adding more water until the dough holds together.

3 Turn out and knead the dough on a lightly floured surface. Halve and press one piece on to the base and sides of the tin. Prick the base with a fork. Chill for 20 minutes. Roll out the rest of the dough between sheets of clear film (plastic wrap) to a 28cm/11in round, then slide on to a baking sheet and chill for 30 minutes.

4 Preheat the oven to 180°C/350°F/Gas 4. Spread the filling in the pastry case (pie shell) and sprinkle with chocolate chips. Cut the dough round into 1cm/½in strips. Leave to soften, then place the strips over the filling, 1cm/½in apart, to form a lattice. Press the ends on to the side of the tart and trim. Bake for 35–40 minutes, until golden. Cool on a rack and dust with icing sugar.

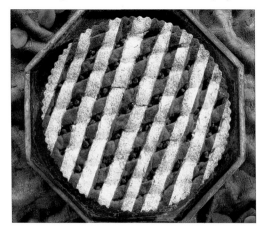

Chocolate Tiramisu Tart

This tart, based on the Italian dessert, has an utterly delicious creamy filling.

Serves 12–16
115g/4oz/½ cup butter
15ml/1 tbsp coffee liqueur
175g/6oz/1½ cups plain
  (all-purpose) flour
25g/1oz/¼ cup unsweetened
  cocoa powder, plus extra
  for dusting
25g/1oz/¼ cup icing
  (confectioners') sugar
pinch of salt
2.5ml/½ tsp vanilla extract

For the chocolate layer
350ml/12fl oz/1½ cups double
  (heavy) cream

15ml/1 tbsp golden (light
  corn) syrup
115g/4oz plain (semisweet)
  chocolate, chopped into pieces
25g/1oz/2 tbsp unsalted (sweet)
  butter, cut into small pieces
30ml/2 tbsp coffee liqueur

For the filling
250ml/8fl oz/1 cup
  whipping cream
350g/12oz/1½ cups mascarpone,
  at room temperature
45ml/3 tbsp icing
  (confectioners') sugar
45ml/3 tbsp cold espresso or
  strong black coffee
45ml/3 tbsp coffee liqueur
90g/3½oz plain (semisweet)
  chocolate, grated

1 Make the pastry. Grease a 23cm/9in springform tin (pan). Heat the butter and liqueur until melted. Sift the flour, cocoa, sugar and salt into a bowl. Remove the butter mixture from the heat, stir in the vanilla and stir into the flour mixture until soft dough forms. Knead until smooth. Press on to the base and up the sides of the tin. Prick the base for 40 minutes. Preheat the oven to 190°C/375°F/Gas 5. Bake for 8–10 minutes. Cool in the tin on a rack.

2 Mix the cream and syrup in a pan. Bring to a boil. Off the heat, stir in the chocolate until melted. Beat in the butter and liqueur and pour into the pastry case (pie shell). Cool and chill.

3 Make the filling. In one bowl, whip the cream until soft peaks form; in another, beat the cheese until soft, then beat in the sugar until smooth. Add the coffee, liqueur, cream and chocolate. Spoon into the pastry case, on top of the chocolate layer. Level the surface. Chill until ready to serve, dusted with cocoa powder.

Linzer Tart Energy 368kcal/1539kJ; Protein 4.4g; Carbohydrate 44.3g, of which sugars 32.8g; Fat 20.4g, of which saturates 11.4g; Cholesterol 40mg; Calcium 69mg; Fibre 3.1g; Sodium 147mg.
Tiramisu Tart Energy 399kcal/1657kJ; Protein 4.8g; Carbohydrate 24.4g, of which sugars 15.8g; Fat 30.9g, of which saturates 20.4g; Cholesterol 60mg; Calcium 49mg; Fibre 0.9g; Sodium 86mg.

White Chocolate and Mango Cream Tart

A rich, exotic tart designed to tantalize the taste buds.

Serves 8
175g/6oz/1½ cups plain
   (all-purpose) flour
75g/3oz/1 cup desiccated
   (dry unsweetened
   shredded) coconut
115g/4oz/½ cup butter, softened
30ml/2 tbsp caster
   (superfine) sugar
2 egg yolks
2.5ml/½ tsp almond extract
120ml/4fl oz/½ cup whipping
   cream, whipped to soft peaks

1 large mango, peeled and sliced
whipped cream and toasted
   almonds, to decorate

For the filling
150g/5oz good-quality white
   chocolate, chopped finely
120ml/4fl oz/½ cup whipping
   cream or double (heavy) cream
75ml/5 tbsp cornflour (cornstarch)
15ml/1 tbsp plain
   (all-purpose) flour
50g/2oz/¼ cup granulated
   (white) sugar
350ml/12fl oz/1½ cups milk
5 egg yolks

1 Beat the flour, coconut, butter, sugar, egg yolks and almond extract in a bowl to form a soft dough. Grease a 23cm/9in flan tin (pan) with a removable base and press the pastry into the tin to line. Prick the base with a fork. Chill for 30 minutes.

2 Preheat the oven to 180°C/350°F/Gas 4. Line the pastry case (pie shell) with baking parchment; fill with baking beans and bake blind for 10 minutes. Remove the paper and beans and bake for a further 5–7 minutes, until golden. Cool in the tin on a wire rack.

3 Make the filling. In a pan, melt the chocolate with the cream, stirring until smooth. Combine the cornflour, plain flour and sugar in another pan. Stir in the milk and cook, stirring until thick.

4 Beat the egg yolks in a bowl. Stir in some of the milk mixture. Return the yolk mixture to the rest of the sauce in the pan. Bring to a boil, stirring, until thick. Stir in the melted chocolate. Cool, then fold in the cream. Spoon half the custard into the case and arrange the mango on top. Cover with the rest of the custard. Remove from the tin and decorate with piped cream and nuts.

Rich Chocolate Tart with Blackberry Sauce

This magnificent chocolate tart is a gorgeous way to serve fresh summer berries.

Serves 10
115g/4oz/½ cup unsalted
   (sweet) butter, softened
90g/3½oz/½ cup caster
   (superfine) sugar
2.5ml/½ tsp salt
15ml/1 tbsp vanilla extract
50g/2oz/½ cup unsweetened
   cocoa powder
215g/7½oz/scant 2 cups plain
   (all-purpose) flour
450g/1lb fresh berries for topping

For the chocolate filling
475ml/16fl oz/2 cups double
   (heavy) cream
150g/5oz/½ cup seedless
   blackberry preserve
225g/8oz plain (semisweet)
   chocolate, chopped
25g/1oz/2 tbsp unsalted
   (sweet) butter

For the blackberry sauce
225g/8oz blackberries
15ml/1 tbsp lemon juice
25g/1oz/2 tbsp caster
   (superfine) sugar
30ml/2 tbsp blackberry liqueur

1 Make the pastry. Place the butter, sugar, salt and vanilla in a food processor and process until creamy. Add the cocoa and process for 1 minute. Add the flour all at once and process for 10–15 seconds, until just blended. Place a piece of clear film (plastic wrap) on a work surface. Turn out the dough on to the clear film. Use the clear film to help shape the dough into a flat disc and wrap tightly. Chill for 1 hour.

2 Lightly grease a 23cm/9in loose-based flan tin (pan). Roll out the dough between two sheets of clear film to a 28cm/11in round, about 5mm/¼in thick. Peel off the top sheet of clear film and invert the dough into the prepared tin. Ease the dough into the tin. Remove the clear film.

3 With floured fingers, press the dough on to the base and side of the tin, then roll a rolling pin over the edge of the tin to cut off any excess dough. Prick the base of the dough with a fork. Chill for 1 hour. Preheat the oven to 180°C/350°F/Gas 4. Line the pastry case (pie shell) with foil or baking paper and fill with baking beans. Bake for 10 minutes, then lift out the foil and beans and bake for 5 minutes more, until just set (the pastry may look underdone on the base, but will dry out). Place on a wire rack to cool completely.

4 Make the filling. Place the cream and blackberry preserve in a medium pan over medium heat and bring to the boil. Remove from the heat and add the chocolate, stirring until smooth. Stir in the butter and strain into the cooled tart, then level the surface. Leave the tart to cool completely.

5 Make the sauce. In a food processor, combine the blackberries, lemon juice and sugar and process until smooth. Strain into a small bowl and add the blackberry liqueur. If the sauce is too thick, thin with a little water.

6 To serve, remove the tart from the tin. Place on a serving plate and arrange the berries on top of the tart. With a pastry brush, coat the berries with a little of the blackberry sauce to glaze lightly. Serve the remaining sauce separately.

Mango Tart Energy 802kcal/3336kJ; Protein 12.3g; Carbohydrate 57.3g, of which sugars 30.3g; Fat 59.8g, of which saturates 41.9g; Cholesterol 217mg; Calcium 256mg; Fibre 3.1g; Sodium 195mg.
Rich Tart Energy 653kcal/2722kJ; Protein 6g; Carbohydrate 58.9g, of which sugars 41.8g; Fat 44.9g, of which saturates 27.7g; Cholesterol 96mg; Calcium 95mg; Fibre 3.5g; Sodium 152mg.

Chocolate Pear Tart

Serve slices of this tart drizzled with cream for a special treat.

Serves 8
115g/4oz plain (semisweet) chocolate, grated
3 large firm, ripe pears
1 egg
1 egg yolk
120ml/4fl oz/½ cup single (light) cream
2.5ml/½ tsp vanilla extract

40g/1½oz/3 tbsp caster (superfine) sugar

For the pastry
115g/4oz/1 cup plain (all-purpose) flour
pinch of salt
25g/1oz/2 tbsp caster (superfine) sugar
115g/4oz/½ cup cold unsalted (sweet) butter, cut into pieces
1 egg yolk
15ml/1 tbsp fresh lemon juice

1 Make the pastry. Sift the flour and salt into a bowl. Add the sugar and butter. Cut in with a pastry blender until the mixture resembles coarse crumbs. With a fork, stir in the egg yolk and lemon juice until the mixture forms a dough. Gather into a ball, wrap in baking parchment, and chill for at least 20 minutes.

2 Place a baking sheet in the oven and preheat to 200°C/400°F/Gas 6. On a lightly floured surface, roll out the dough to 3mm/⅛in thick and trim the edge. Use to line a 25cm/10in loose-based flan tin (pan).

3 Sprinkle the base of the pastry all over with the grated plain chocolate.

4 Peel, halve and core the pears. Cut in thin slices crossways, then fan them out slightly. Transfer the pear halves to the tart with a metal spatula and arrange on top of the chocolate in a pattern resembling the spokes of a wheel.

5 Whisk together the egg and egg yolk, cream and vanilla extract. Spoon over the pears, then sprinkle with sugar.

6 Bake for 10 minutes. Reduce the heat to 180°C/350°F/Gas 4 and continue to cook for about 20 minutes until the custard is set and the pears begin to caramelize. Serve warm.

Chocolate Nut Tart

This is a sophisticated tart – strictly for grown-ups.

Serves 6 – 8
225g/8oz Chocolate Shortcrust Pastry, thawed if frozen
200g/7oz/1¾ cups dry amaretti
90g/3½oz/generous ½ cup blanched almonds
50g/2oz/⅓ cup blanched hazelnuts

45ml/3 tbsp caster (superfine) sugar
200g/7oz plain (semisweet) cooking chocolate
45ml/3 tbsp milk
50g/2oz/¼ cup butter
45ml/3 tbsp amaretto liqueur or brandy
30ml/2 tbsp single (light) cream

1 Grease a shallow loose-based 25cm/10in flan tin (pan). Roll out the pastry on a lightly floured surface, and use it to line the tin. Trim the edge, prick the base with a fork and chill for 30 minutes.

2 Grind the amaretti in a blender or food processor. Tip into a mixing bowl.

3 Set eight whole almonds aside and place the rest in the food processor or blender with the hazelnuts and sugar. Grind to a medium texture. Add the nuts to the amaretti, and mix well to combine thoroughly.

4 Preheat the oven to 190°C/375°F/Gas 5. Slowly melt the chocolate with the milk and butter in the top of a double boiler or in a heatproof bowl over a pan of simmering water. Once the chocolate has melted, stir until smooth.

5 Pour the chocolate mixture into the dry ingredients and mix well. Add the liqueur or brandy and the cream.

6 Spread the filling evenly in the pastry case (pie shell). Bake for 35 minutes, or until the crust is golden brown and the filling has puffed up and is beginning to darken.

7 Allow to cool to room temperature. Split the reserved almonds in half and use to decorate the tart.

Pear Tart Energy 357kcal/1492kJ; Protein 4.5g; Carbohydrate 39.9g, of which sugars 28.8g; Fat 21.1g, of which saturates 12.3g; Cholesterol 114mg; Calcium 66mg; Fibre 2.9g; Sodium 107mg.
Nut Tart Energy 644kcal/2685kJ; Protein 9.6g; Carbohydrate 56.4g, of which sugars 32g; Fat 42.4g, of which saturates 13.4g; Cholesterol 21mg; Calcium 122mg; Fibre 3g; Sodium 241mg.

Black Rum and Chocolate Pie

A totally wicked rum and chocolate creation.

Serves 6–8
250g/9oz/2¼ cups plain (all-purpose) flour
150g/5oz/10 tbsp unsalted (sweet) butter
2 egg yolks
15–30ml/1–2 tbsp chilled water

For the filling
3 eggs, separated
20ml/4 tsp cornflour (cornstarch)

75g/3oz/6 tbsp golden caster (superfine) sugar
400ml/14fl oz/1⅔ cups milk
150g/5oz plain (semisweet) chocolate, chopped into small pieces
5ml/1 tsp vanilla extract
1 sachet powdered gelatine
45ml/3 tbsp water
30ml/2 tbsp dark rum
175ml/6fl oz/¾ cup whipping cream
chocolate curls, to decorate

1 Sift the flour into a bowl and rub in the butter until the mixture resembles coarse breadcrumbs. Stir in the egg yolks with just enough chilled water to bind the mixture to a soft dough. Roll out on a lightly floured surface and line a deep 23cm/9in flan tin (pan). Chill for about 30 minutes.

2 Preheat the oven to 190°C/375°F/Gas 5. Prick the pastry case (pie shell) all over with a fork, cover with baking parchment weighed down with baking beans and bake blind for 10 minutes. Remove the baking beans and the paper, return the pastry case to the oven and bake for 10 minutes, until golden. Cool in the tin.

3 Make the filling. Mix the egg yolks, cornflour and 25g/1oz/2 tbsp of the sugar in a bowl. Heat the milk in a pan until almost boiling, then beat into the egg mixture. Return to the clean pan and stir over a low heat until the custard has thickened and is smooth. Pour half the custard into a bowl.

4 Put the chocolate in a heatproof bowl. Place over a pan of barely simmering water until the chocolate has melted, stirring occasionally until smooth. Stir the melted chocolate into the custard in the bowl, with the vanilla extract.

5 Spread the chocolate filling in the pastry case and cover closely with dampened clear film (plastic wrap) to prevent a skin forming. Allow to cool, then chill until set.

6 Sprinkle the gelatine over the water in a bowl, leave until spongy, then place the bowl over a pan of simmering water until all the gelatine has dissolved. Stir into the remaining custard, then add the rum.

7 Whisk the egg whites in a clean, grease-free bowl until peaks form. Whisk in the remaining sugar, a little at a time, until stiff, then fold the egg whites quickly but evenly into the rum-flavoured custard.

8 Spoon the custard over the chocolate layer in the pastry shell. Level the mixture, making sure that none of the chocolate custard is visible. Chill the pie until the top layer has set, then remove the pie from the tin. Whip the cream, spread it over the top and sprinkle with chocolate curls, to decorate.

Chilled Chocolate and Date Tart

A delicious tart with a crisp gingery base.

Serves 6–8
115g/4oz/½ cup unsalted (sweet) butter, melted
225g/8oz ginger nut biscuits (gingersnaps), finely crushed

For the filling
50g/2oz/⅔ cup stale sponge cake crumbs

75ml/5 tbsp orange juice
115g/4oz/⅔ cup stoned (pitted) dates
25g/1oz/¼ cup finely chopped nuts
175g/6oz dark (bittersweet) chocolate
300ml/½ pint/1¼ cups whipping cream
grated chocolate and icing (confectioners') sugar, to decorate

1 Make the base. Mix the butter and biscuit crumbs in a bowl, then press the mixture on to the sides and base of an 18cm/7in loose-based flan tin (pan). Chill the crust while making the filling.

2 Make the filling. Put the sponge cake crumbs into a bowl. Pour over 60ml/4 tbsp of the orange juice, stir well with a wooden spoon and leave to soak. Put the dates in a pan and add the remaining orange juice. Warm the mixture over a low heat. Mash the warm dates thoroughly and stir in the cake crumbs, with the finely chopped nuts.

3 Mix the chocolate with 60ml/4 tbsp of the cream in a heatproof bowl. Place the bowl over a pan of barely simmering water and stir occasionally until melted. In a separate bowl, whip the rest of the cream to soft peaks, then fold in the melted chocolate.

4 Add the cooled date, crumb and nut mixture to the cream and chocolate and mix lightly but thoroughly. Pour into the crumb crust. Using a metal spatula, level the mixture. Chill until just set, then mark the tart into portions, using a sharp knife dipped in hot water. Chill until firm.

5 To decorate the tart, sprinkle the grated chocolate over the surface and dust with icing sugar. Serve in wedges, with single (light) cream, if desired. Fresh orange segments make an excellent accompaniment.

Date Tart Energy 575kcal/2394kJ; Protein 5.1g; Carbohydrate 51.3g, of which sugars 37.5g; Fat 40.2g, of which saturates 22.8g; Cholesterol 78mg; Calcium 87mg; Fibre 1.8g; Sodium 214mg.
Black Rum Pie Energy 545kcal/2276kJ; Protein 9.3g; Carbohydrate 51.3g, of which sugars 25.1g; Fat 34.2g, of which saturates 20g; Cholesterol 189mg; Calcium 148mg; Fibre 1.4g; Sodium 173mg.

Rich Chocolate Pie

A delicious rich and creamy pie generously decorated with chocolate curls.

Serves 8
75g/3oz plain (semisweet) chocolate
50g/2oz/¼ cup butter
  or margarine
45ml/3 tbsp golden (light corn) syrup
3 eggs, beaten
150g/5oz/¾ cup caster
  (superfine) sugar
5ml/1 tsp vanilla extract

115g/4oz milk chocolate
475ml/16fl oz/2 cups
  whipping cream

For the pastry
165g/5½oz/1⅓ cups plain
  (all-purpose) flour
2.5ml/½ tsp salt
115g/4oz/⅔ cup lard
  or white cooking fat
  (shortening), diced
30–45ml/2–3 tbsp iced water

1 Preheat the oven to 220°C/425°F/Gas 7. To make the pastry, sift the flour and salt into a bowl. Rub in the fat until the mixture resembles coarse breadcrumbs. Add water until the pastry forms a ball.

2 Roll out the pastry and use to line a 20–23cm/8–9in flan tin (pan). Flute the edge. Prick the base and sides of the pastry case (pie shell) with a fork. Bake for 10–15 minutes until lightly browned. Cool in the tin on a wire rack.

3 Reduce the oven temperature to 180°C/350°F/Gas 4. In the top of a double boiler or in a heatproof bowl over a pan of simmering water, melt the plain chocolate, the butter or margarine, and the golden syrup. Remove from the heat and stir in the eggs, sugar and vanilla extract. Pour the chocolate mixture into the pastry case. Bake until the filling is set, about 35–40 minutes. Cool in the tin on a wire rack.

4 For the decoration, use the heat of your hands to soften the milk chocolate slightly. Use a swivel-headed vegetable peeler to shave off short, wide curls. Chill until needed.

5 Before serving, lightly whip the cream until soft peaks form. Spread the cream over the surface of the chocolate filling. Decorate with the milk chocolate curls.

Black Bottom Pie

Chocolate and rum make a winning combination over a crunchy ginger base.

Serves 8
10ml/2 tsp powdered gelatine
45ml/3 tbsp cold water
2 eggs, separated
150g/5oz/¾ cup caster
  (superfine) sugar
15g/½oz/2 tbsp cornflour
  (cornstarch)

2.5ml/½ tsp salt
475ml/16fl oz/2 cups milk
50g/2oz plain (semisweet)
  chocolate, finely chopped
30ml/2 tbsp rum
1.5ml/¼ tsp cream of tartar
chocolate curls, to decorate

For the crust
175g/6oz/2 cups ginger nut
  biscuits (gingersnaps), crushed
65g/2½oz/5 tbsp butter, melted

1 Preheat the oven to 180°C/350°F/Gas 4. Mix together the crushed ginger nut biscuits and the melted butter. Press evenly over the base and side of a 23cm/9in pie plate. Bake in the oven for 6 minutes. Sprinkle the gelatine over the water and leave to soften.

2 Beat the egg yolks in a large bowl and set aside. In a pan, combine half the sugar, the cornflour and salt. Gradually stir in the milk. Boil for 1 minute, stirring constantly.

3 Whisk the hot milk mixture into the yolks, pour back into the pan and return to the boil, whisking. Cook for 1 minute, still whisking. Remove from the heat.

4 Pour 225g/8oz of the custard mixture into a bowl. Add the chopped chocolate and stir until melted. Stir in half the rum and pour into the pie crust. Whisk the softened gelatine into the plain custard until dissolved, then stir in the remaining rum. Set the pan in cold water to reach room temperature.

5 Beat the egg whites and cream of tartar until they form stiff peaks. Add the remaining sugar gradually, beating thoroughly after each addition. Fold the cooled custard into the egg whites, then spoon over the chocolate mixture in the pie crust. Chill the pie until it is set, about 2 hours. Decorate with chocolate curls and serve immediately.

Chocolate Pie Energy 712kcal/2962kJ; Protein 7.2g; Carbohydrate 55.8g, of which sugars 40g; Fat 52.7g, of which saturates 28.9g; Cholesterol 164mg; Calcium 121mg; Fibre 1g; Sodium 109mg.
Black Pie Energy 248kcal/1040kJ; Protein 5.2g; Carbohydrate 25.8g, of which sugars 14.6g; Fat 13.7g, of which saturates 7.6g; Cholesterol 69mg; Calcium 111mg; Fibre 0.5g; Sodium 166mg.

Italian Chocolate Ricotta Pie

Savour the full richness of Italy with this de luxe tart.

Serves 6

225g/8oz/2 cups plain
  (all-purpose) flour
30ml/2 tbsp unsweetened
  cocoa powder
50g/2oz/¼ cup caster
  (superfine) sugar
115g/4oz/½ cup unsalted
  (sweet) butter
60ml/4 tbsp dry sherry

For the filling

2 egg yolks
115g/4oz/generous ½ cup caster
  (superfine) sugar
500g/1¼lb/2½ cups
  ricotta cheese
finely grated rind of 1 lemon
90ml/6 tbsp dark (bittersweet)
  chocolate chips
75ml/5 tbsp mixed (candied)
  chopped peel
45ml/3 tbsp chopped
  angelica

1 Sift the flour and cocoa powder into a bowl. Stir in the sugar. Rub in the butter with your fingers. Work in the sherry to form a firm dough.

2 Preheat the oven to 200°C/400°F/Gas 6. Roll out three-quarters of the pastry on a lightly floured surface and line a 24cm/9½in loose-based flan tin (pan).

3 Make the filling. Beat the egg yolks and sugar in a bowl, then beat in the ricotta to mix thoroughly. Stir in the lemon rind, chocolate chips, mixed peel and angelica.

4 Scrape the ricotta mixture into the pastry case (pie shell) and level the surface. Roll out the remaining pastry and cut into strips. Arrange these in a lattice over the pie.

5 Bake for 15 minutes. Lower the oven temperature to 180°C/350°F/Gas 4 and cook for a further 30–35 minutes, until golden brown and firm. Cool the pie in the tin, then serve.

> **Cook's Tip**
> This dish is best served at room temperature, so if made in advance, chill it, then bring to room temperature before serving.

Crunchy-topped Coffee Meringue Pie

For a special treat, try this sweet pastry case filled with coffee custard and topped with meringue – crisp on the outside and soft and chewy underneath.

Serves 6

30ml/2 tbsp ground coffee
350ml/12fl oz/1½ cups
  milk
25g/1oz/¼ cup cornflour
  (cornstarch)
130g/4½oz/⅔ cup caster
  (superfine) sugar
4 egg yolks
15g/½oz/1 tbsp butter
chocolate curls, to decorate

For the pastry

175g/6oz/1½ cups plain
  (all-purpose) flour
15ml/1 tbsp icing
  (confectioners') sugar
75g/3oz/6 tbsp butter, diced
1 egg yolk
finely grated rind of ½ orange
15ml/1 tbsp orange juice

For the meringue

3 egg whites
1.5ml/¼ tsp cream of tartar
150g/5oz/¾ cup caster
  (superfine) sugar
15ml/1 tbsp demerara (raw) sugar
25g/1oz/¼ cup skinned hazelnuts

1 Preheat the oven to 200°C/400°F/Gas 6. Make the pastry. Sift the flour and icing sugar into a bowl. Rub or cut in the butter until the mixture resembles fine breadcrumbs. Add the egg yolk, orange rind and juice and mix to form a firm dough. Wrap in clear film (plastic wrap) and chill for 20 minutes.

2 Roll out the pastry and use to line a 23cm/9in loose-based flan tin (pan). Cover again with clear film and chill for 30 minutes more.

3 Prick the pastry all over with a fork, line with foil, fill with baking beans and bake for about 10 minutes. Remove the foil and beans and bake for a further 5 minutes. Lower the oven temperature to 160°C/325°F/Gas 3.

4 Put the coffee in a small bowl. Heat 250ml/8fl oz/1 cup of the milk until near-boiling and pour over the coffee. Leave to infuse (steep) for 4–5 minutes, then strain. Blend the cornflour and sugar with the remaining milk in a pan and whisk in the coffee-flavoured milk. Bring the mixture to the boil, stirring until thickened. Remove from the heat.

5 In a bowl, beat the egg yolks. Stir a little of the coffee mixture into the egg yolks, then add to the remaining coffee mixture in the pan with the butter. Cook the filling over a low heat for 4 minutes, until thick. Pour the coffee filling into the pastry case (pie shell).

6 Make the meringue. Whisk the egg whites and cream of tartar in a small bowl until stiff peaks form. Whisk in the caster sugar, a spoonful at a time.

7 Spoon the meringue over the filling and spread right up to the edge of the pastry, swirling into peaks. Sprinkle with demerara sugar and hazelnuts, leaving some whole and chopping others into pieces.

8 Bake for 30–35 minutes, or until the topping is golden brown and crisp. Cover the top with chocolate curls and serve either warm or cold.

Ricotta Pie Energy 701kcal/2938kJ; Protein 14.2g; Carbohydrate 83.4g, of which sugars 54.1g; Fat 35.6g, of which saturates 21.3g; Cholesterol 144mg; Calcium 115mg; Fibre 3g; Sodium 223mg.
Meringue Pie Energy 540kcal/2274kJ; Protein 9.5g; Carbohydrate 83.6g, of which sugars 57.4g; Fat 21g, of which saturates 10g; Cholesterol 203mg; Calcium 168mg; Fibre 1.2g; Sodium 160mg.

Boston Banoffee Pie

A great American creation, you simply press the biscuit pastry into the tin, rather than rolling it out. Add the toffee filling and sliced banana and chocolate topping and it'll prove irresistible.

Serves 6
115g/4oz/½ cup butter, diced
200g/7oz can skimmed, sweetened condensed milk
115g/4oz/½ cup soft light brown sugar
30ml/2 tbsp golden (light corn) syrup
2 small bananas, sliced
a little lemon juice
whipped cream, to decorate
5ml/1 tsp grated plain (semisweet) chocolate

For the pastry
150g/5oz/1¼ cups plain (all-purpose) flour
115g/4oz/½ cup butter, diced
50g/2oz/¼ cup caster (superfine) sugar

1 Make the pastry. Preheat the oven to 160°C/325°F/Gas 3. In a food processor, process the flour and diced butter until it forms crumbs. Stir in the caster sugar and mix to form a soft, pliable dough.

2 Press into the base and sides of a 20cm/8in loose-based flan tin (pan). Bake for 30 minutes.

3 Make the filling. Place the butter in a medium pan with the condensed milk, brown sugar and syrup. Heat gently, stirring constantly, until the butter has melted and the sugar has completely dissolved.

4 Bring the mixture to a gentle boil, then cook for 7–10 minutes, stirring constantly, until the mixture thickens and turns a light caramel colour.

5 Pour the hot caramel filling into the pastry case (pie shell) and leave until completely cold.

6 Sprinkle the banana slices with lemon juice and arrange in overlapping circles on top of the filling, leaving a gap in the centre. Pipe a generous swirl of whipped cream in the centre and sprinkle with the grated chocolate.

Double Chocolate Banoffee Pie

An extra chocolatey version of the classic American pie.

Serves 12–14
2 x 400ml/14fl oz cans sweetened condensed milk
150g/5oz dark (bittersweet) chocolate, broken in pieces
175ml/6fl oz/¾ cup whipping or double (heavy) cream
10ml/2 tsp corn or glucose syrup
40g/1½oz/3 tbsp unsalted (sweet) butter, cut into pieces
5ml/1 tsp vanilla extract

For the ginger crumb crust
250g/9oz/about 24–26 ginger nut biscuits (gingersnaps), crushed
75g/3oz/6 tbsp butter, melted

For the topping
150g/5oz fine quality white chocolate
450ml/16fl oz/2 cups double (heavy) cream
3 ripe bananas
white chocolate curls
unsweetened cocoa powder, for dusting

1 Puncture a small hole in each can. Place in a pan large enough to cover with water. Bring to a boil, then reduce the heat and simmer for 2 hours, partially covered. Remove cans and cool.

2 Prepare the crust. Preheat the oven to 180°C/350°F/Gas 4. Grease a 23cm/9in loose-bottomed flan tin (pan), 4cm/1½in deep. Mix the ginger crumbs with the butter and put on to the bottom and side of the tin. Bake for 5–7 minutes until set. Cool on rack.

3 In a pan, simmer the dark chocolate, cream and syrup until melted and smooth. Remove from the heat and beat in the butter and vanilla. Pour over the crust and chill until set, about 1 hour.

4 Empty the cans of milk into a bowl. Whisk until smooth. Spoon over the chocolate layer. In a food processor, process the white chocolate into crumbs. In a pan, heat 125ml/4fl oz/½ cup of the cream. With the machine running, pour in the cream and process until the chocolate has melted. Chill for 25–30 minutes. Whip the remaining cream until stiff. Beat in a spoonful of cream to the chocolate mixture, then fold in the remaining cream.

5 Slice the bananas and arrange over the toffee layer. Spread over the chocolate whipped cream. Decorate with white chocolate curls and a light dusting of cocoa powder.

Boston Banoffee Pie Energy 608kcal/2547kJ; Protein 6.4g; Carbohydrate 78.5g, of which sugars 58.9g; Fat 32g, of which saturates 20.1g; Cholesterol 82mg; Calcium 169mg; Fibre 1.1g; Sodium 299mg.
Double Pie Energy 682kcal/2845kJ; Protein 8.3g; Carbohydrate 64.7g, of which sugars 56.4g; Fat 45.1g, of which saturates 27.6g; Cholesterol 100mg; Calcium 246mg; Fibre 0.8g; Sodium 211mg.

Mississippi Pie

This American biscuit-based pie has a layer of chocolate mousse, topped with a coffee toffee layer and lots of freshly whipped cream.

Serves 8

For the base
275g/10oz digestive biscuits (graham crackers), crushed
150g/5oz/10 tbsp butter, melted

For the chocolate layer
10ml/2 tsp powdered gelatine
30ml/2 tbsp cold water
175g/6oz plain (semisweet) chocolate, broken into squares

2 eggs, separated
150ml/¼ pint/⅔ cup double (heavy) cream

For the coffee toffee layer
30ml/2 tbsp ground coffee
300ml/½ pint/1¼ cups double (heavy) cream
200g/7oz/1 cup caster (superfine) sugar
25g/1oz/4 tbsp cornflour (cornstarch)
2 eggs, beaten
15g/½oz/1 tbsp butter
150ml/¼ pint/⅔ cup whipping cream and chocolate curls, to decorate

1 Grease a 21cm/8½in loose-based tin (pan). Mix the biscuit crumbs and butter and press over the base and sides of the tin. Chill for 30 minutes.

2 Make the chocolate layer. Sprinkle the gelatine over the water. Leave for 5 minutes. Stir in a bowl over a pan of hot water until dissolved. Melt the chocolate in a bowl over hot water. Stir in the gelatine. Blend the egg yolks and cream and stir into the chocolate. Whisk the egg whites and fold into the mixture. Pour into the case and chill for 2 hours.

3 Make the coffee layer. Reserve 60ml/4 tbsp of cream. Heat the remaining cream to near-boiling and pour over the coffee. Leave for 4 minutes. Strain back into the pan. Add the sugar and dissolve. Mix the cornflour with the reserved cream and the eggs. Add to the coffee and cream mixture and simmer for 2–3 minutes. Stir in the butter. Cool for 30 minutes. Spoon over the chocolate layer. Chill for 2 hours.

4 Whip the cream until soft peaks form, and spread thickly over the pie. Decorate with chocolate curls and chill until serving.

Chocolate, Banana and Toffee Pie

As an alternative to the coffee topping, just decorate the pie with whipped cream and extra banana slices.

Serves 6
65g/2½oz/5 tbsp unsalted (sweet) butter, melted
250g/9oz milk chocolate digestive biscuits (graham crackers), crushed

For the filling
400g/14oz can sweetened condensed milk, unopened
150g/5oz plain (semisweet) chocolate, chopped
120ml/4fl oz/½ cup crème fraîche
15ml/1 tbsp golden (light corn) syrup

For the topping
2 bananas
250ml/8fl oz/1 cup crème fraîche
10ml/2 tsp strong black coffee
chocolate curls, to decorate

1 Mix the butter with the biscuit crumbs. Press on to the base and sides of a 23cm/9in loose-based flan tin (pan). Chill.

2 Make the filling. Place the unopened can of condensed milk in a deep pan of boiling water, making sure that it is completely covered. Lower the heat and simmer, covered, for 2 hours, topping up the water as necessary. The can must remain covered at all times.

3 Remove the pan from the heat and set aside, covered, until the can has cooled down completely in the water. Do not attempt to open the can until it is completely cold.

4 Gently melt the chocolate with the crème fraîche and golden syrup in a heatproof bowl over a pan of simmering water. Stir in the caramelized condensed milk and beat together until thoroughly combined. Pour the chocolate filling into the biscuit crust and spread it evenly.

5 Slice the bananas evenly and arrange them over the chocolate filling in an attractive pattern.

6 Stir the crème fraîche and coffee together in a bowl, then spoon the mixture over the bananas. Sprinkle the chocolate curls on top.

Toffee Pie Energy 900kcal/3758kJ; Protein 11.5g; Carbohydrate 90g, of which sugars 73.2g; Fat 57.4g, of which saturates 35.8g; Cholesterol 139mg; Calcium 275mg; Fibre 1.8g; Sodium 368mg.
Mississippi Energy 519kcal/2165kJ; Protein 8.5g; Carbohydrate 48.6g, of which sugars 20.6g; Fat 32.8g, of which saturates 19.3g; Cholesterol 178mg; Calcium 146mg; Fibre 1.2g; Sodium 164mg.

Mississippi Mud Pie

This is a pastry-based version of the Mississippi classic.

Serves 6–8
3 eggs, separated
20ml/4 tsp cornflour (cornstarch)
75g/3oz/6 tbsp sugar
400ml/14fl oz/1²/³ cups milk
150g/5oz plain (semisweet)
   chocolate, broken up
5ml/1 tsp vanilla extract
15ml/1 tbsp powdered gelatine

45ml/3 tbsp water
30ml/2 tbsp dark rum
175ml/6fl oz/³/₄ cup double
   (heavy) cream, whipped
a few chocolate curls, to decorate

For the pastry
250g/9oz/2¼ cups plain
   (all-purpose) flour
150g/5oz/10 tbsp butter, diced
2 egg yolks
15–30ml/1–2 tbsp chilled water

1 Make the pastry. Sift the flour into a bowl. Rub in the butter until the mixture resembles breadcrumbs. Stir in the yolks with enough chilled water to make a soft dough. Roll out and use to line a deep 23cm/9in flan tin (pan). Chill for 30 minutes. Preheat the oven to 190°C/375°F/Gas 5. Prick the pastry, line with foil and baking beans, and bake blind for 10 minutes. Remove the foil and beans, and return to the oven for 10 minutes until the pastry is crisp and golden. Cool.

2 Mix the yolks, cornflour and 30ml/2 tbsp of the sugar in a bowl. In a pan, bring the milk almost to a boil, then beat into the egg mixture. Return to the pan and stir over a low heat until thickened. Pour half into a bowl. Melt the chocolate in a heatproof bowl over a pan of hot water, then add to the custard in the bowl. Mix in the vanilla extract. Spread in the pastry case (pie shell), cover with baking parchment to prevent a skin forming, cool, then chill until set. Sprinkle the gelatine over the water in a small bowl, leave until spongy, then place over a pan of simmering water until the gelatine dissolves. Stir into the remaining custard, with the rum.

3 Whisk the egg whites until stiff peaks form, whisk in the rest of the sugar, then fold into the gelatine and custard mix before it sets. Spoon over the chocolate custard to cover. Chill until set, then remove from the tin. Spread whipped cream over the top, decorate with chocolate curls and serve immediately.

Chocolate-topped Candied Fruit Pie

Use good quality candied fruits for the best flavour. Try half digestive biscuits and half ginger nut biscuits (gingersnaps) for the crust, if you prefer.

Serves 10
15ml/1 tbsp rum
50g/2oz/¼ cup mixed glacé
   (candied) fruit, chopped
475ml/16fl oz/2 cups milk
20ml/4 tsp powdered gelatine
90g/3¹/₂oz/¹/₂ cup caster
   (superfine) sugar
2.5ml/¹/₂ tsp salt

3 eggs, separated
250ml/8fl oz/1 cup whipping
   cream, whipped
chocolate curls, to decorate

For the crust
175g/6oz/2 cups crushed
   digestive biscuits
   (graham crackers)
75g/3oz/6 tbsp butter, melted
15ml/1 tbsp caster
   (superfine) sugar

1 To make the crust mix the digestive biscuits, butter and sugar. Press evenly over the base and sides of a 23cm/9in pie plate. Chill.

2 Stir together the rum and glacé fruit. Set aside. Pour 120ml/4fl oz/¹/₂ cup of the milk into a small bowl. Sprinkle over the gelatine and leave for 5 minutes to soften.

3 In the top of a double boiler or in a heatproof bowl over a pan of simmering water, combine 50g/2oz/¹/₄ cup of the sugar, the remaining milk and the salt. Stir in the gelatine mixture. Cook, stirring, until the gelatine dissolves. Whisk in the egg yolks and cook, stirring, until thick enough to coat the back of the spoon. Pour the custard over the glacé fruit mixture, set in a bowl of iced water.

4 Beat the egg whites until they form soft peaks. Add the remaining sugar and beat until just blended. Fold a large dollop of the egg whites into the cooled gelatine mixture. Pour into the remaining egg whites and fold together. Fold in the cream.

5 Pour into the pie crust and chill until firm. Decorate with chocolate curls.

Mississippi Mud Pie Energy 571kcal/2385kJ; Protein 9.4g; Carbohydrate 53.5g, of which sugars 22.7g; Fat 36.2g, of which saturates 21.2g; Cholesterol 196mg; Calcium 160mg; Fibre 1.3g; Sodium 180mg.
Fruit Pie Energy 333kcal/1388kJ; Protein 5.2g; Carbohydrate 28.9g, of which sugars 19.3g; Fat 22.3g, of which saturates 12.8g; Cholesterol 109mg; Calcium 110mg; Fibre 0.6g; Sodium 213mg.

Chocolate Chiffon Pie

Decorate with chocolate
curls for a pretty finish.

Serves 8
175g/6oz plain (semisweet)
  chocolate squares, chopped
25g/1oz dark (bittersweet)
  chocolate, chopped
250ml/8fl oz/1 cup milk
15ml/1 tbsp powdered gelatine
130g/4½oz/⅔ cup sugar
2 eggs, separated

5ml/1 tsp vanilla extract
350ml/12fl oz/1½ cups
  whipping cream
pinch of salt
whipped cream, to decorate

For the base
75g/3oz/1½ cups digestive biscuit
  (graham cracker) crumbs
75g/3oz/6 tbsp butter, melted

1 Place a baking sheet in the oven and preheat to 180°C/
350°F/Gas 4. Make the crust. Mix the biscuit crumbs and butter
in a bowl. Press the crumbs evenly over the base and sides of a
23cm/9in pie tin (pan). Bake for 8 minutes. Allow to cool.

2 Grind both chocolates in a food processor or blender. Set aside.
Place the milk in the top of a double boiler or in a heatproof
bowl. Sprinkle over the gelatine. Let stand for 5 minutes to soften.

3 Set the top of the double boiler or heatproof bowl over hot
water. Add 50g/2oz/¼ cup of the sugar, the chocolate and egg
yolks. Stir until dissolved. Add the vanilla extract.

4 Place the top of the double boiler or the heatproof bowl
in a bowl of ice and stir until the mixture reaches room
temperature. Remove from the ice and set aside.

5 Whip the cream lightly. Set aside. With an electric whisk, beat
the egg whites and salt until they hold soft peaks. Add the
remaining sugar and beat only enough to blend. Fold a dollop
of egg whites into the chocolate mixture, then pour back into
the whites and gently fold in.

6 Fold in the cream and pour into the tin. Freeze for about
5 minutes until just set. If the centre sinks, fill with any remaining
mixture. Chill for 3–4 hours. Decorate with whipped cream.

Chocolate, Pear and Pecan Pie

A classic pie gets a tempting
new twist.

Serves 8–10
3 small pears, peeled
150ml/¼ pint/⅔ cup water
165g/5½oz/generous ¾ cup
  caster (superfine) sugar
pared rind of 1 lemon
50g/2oz plain (semisweet)
  chocolate, broken into pieces
50g/2oz/¼ cup butter, diced
225g/8oz/scant ¾ cup golden
  (light corn) syrup

3 eggs, beaten
5ml/1 tsp vanilla extract
150g/5oz/1¼ cups pecan
  nuts, chopped

For the pastry
175g/6oz/1½ cups plain
  (all-purpose) flour
115g/4oz/½ cup butter, diced
25g/1oz/2 tbsp caster
  (superfine) sugar
1 egg yolk, lightly beaten with
  10ml/2 tsp chilled water

1 Sift the flour into a bowl, rub in the butter and stir in the
sugar. Add the egg yolk and mix to a dough, adding more
water if necessary. Knead lightly, wrap and chill for 30 minutes.

2 Roll out the pastry and use to line a 23cm/9in flan tin (pan).
Chill for 20 minutes. Preheat the oven to 200°F/400°C/Gas 6.
Line the pastry case (pie shell) with foil, fill with baking beans
and bake for 10 minutes. Lift out the foil and beans and bake
for 5 minutes more. Set aside to cool.

3 Halve and core the pears. Bring the water, 50g/2oz/¼ cup
of the sugar and the lemon rind to the boil. Add the
pears, cover and simmer gently for 10 minutes. Remove
the pears from the pan.

4 Melt the chocolate over simmering water, beat in the butter
and set aside. Heat the remaining sugar and syrup until the
sugar has dissolved. Bring to the boil and simmer for 2 minutes.
Whisk the eggs into the chocolate mixture until combined,
then whisk in the syrup mixture. Stir in the vanilla and nuts.

5 Slice the pear halves lengthways without cutting all the way
through. Arrange them in the pastry case and pour in the nut
mixture. Bake for 25–30 minutes. Cool and serve sliced.

Chiffon Pie Energy 509kcal/2120kJ; Protein 5.5g; Carbohydrate 43.2g, of which sugars 37.8g; Fat 36.2g, of which saturates 21.7g; Cholesterol 121mg; Calcium 98mg; Fibre 0.8g; Sodium 158mg.
Pear and Pecan Pie Energy 499kcal/2090kJ; Protein 5.8g; Carbohydrate 59.9g, of which sugars 46.3g; Fat 28g, of which saturates 11g; Cholesterol 113mg; Calcium 68mg; Fibre 2.4g; Sodium 186mg.

Chocolate Cheesecake Tart

You can use all digestive
biscuits for the base of
this tart, if you prefer.

Serves 8

350g/12oz/1½ cups
  cream cheese
60ml/4 tbsp whipping cream
225g/8oz/generous 1 cup caster
  (superfine) sugar
50g/2oz/½ cup unsweetened
  cocoa powder
2.5ml/½ tsp ground cinnamon

3 eggs
whipped cream and chocolate
  curls, to decorate

For the base

75g/3oz/1 cup crushed digestive
  biscuits (graham crackers)
40g/1½oz/scant 1 cup
  crushed amaretti
75g/3oz/6 tbsp butter, melted

1 Preheat a baking sheet in the oven at 180°C/350°F/Gas 4.

2 To make the base, mix the crushed biscuits and melted
butter in a bowl.

3 Press the mixture over the base and sides of a 23cm/9in
pie dish. Bake for 8 minutes. Leave to cool, but keep the
oven on.

4 Beat the cream cheese and cream together until smooth.
Beat in the sugar, cocoa and cinnamon until blended.

5 Add the eggs, one at a time, beating just enough to blend.

6 Pour into the biscuit base and bake on the baking sheet for
25–30 minutes. The filling will sink down as it cools.

7 Decorate the top of the tart with whipped cream and
chocolate curls.

> **Cook's Tip**
> For short chocolate curls, run a vegetable peeler against the
> long side of a bar of chocolate. To make long curls, see p251.

American Chocolate Cheesecake

This popular variation of
the American classic is made
with a crunchy cinnamon
and chocolate base.

Serves 10–12

175g/6oz plain (semisweet)
  chocolate, chopped
115g/4oz dark (bittersweet)
  chocolate, chopped
1.2kg/2½lb/5 cups cream cheese,
  at room temperature

200g/7oz/1 cup caster
  (superfine) sugar
10ml/2 tsp vanilla extract
4 eggs, at room temperature
175ml/6fl oz/¾ cup
  sour cream

For the base

75g/3oz/1½ cups chocolate
  biscuit (cookie) crumbs
75g/3oz/6 tbsp butter, melted
2.5ml/½ tsp ground cinnamon

1 Preheat the oven to 180°C/350°F/Gas 4. Grease a 23cm/9in
springform cake tin (pan).

2 Make the base. Mix the chocolate biscuit crumbs with the
butter and cinnamon. Press evenly over the bottom of the tin.

3 Melt the plain and dark chocolate in the top of a double
boiler, or in a heatproof bowl set over a pan of simmering
water. Set aside.

4 With an electric whisk, beat the cream cheese until smooth,
then beat in the sugar and vanilla extract. Add the eggs, one at
a time, scraping the bowl with a spatula when necessary.

5 Add the sour cream to the cheese mixture, then stir in the
melted chocolate, mixing well.

6 Pour into the tin. Bake for 1 hour. Allow to cool, then remove
from the tin. Chill before serving.

> **Variation**
> For a chocolate-orange cheesecake, replace the vanilla extract
> with finely grated orange rind. Serve with sliced oranges coated
> in a light sugar syrup, flavoured with shredded orange rind.

Tart Energy 514kcal/2139kJ; Protein 6.1g; Carbohydrate 40.8g, of which sugars 32.7g; Fat 37.5g, of which saturates 22.3g; Cholesterol 145mg; Calcium 98mg; Fibre 1g; Sodium 350mg.
Cheesecake Energy 717kcal/2972kJ; Protein 5.2g; Carbohydrate 37.5g, of which sugars 34.9g; Fat 61.8g, of which saturates 38.4g; Cholesterol 118mg; Calcium 131mg; Fibre 0.7g; Sodium 362mg.

Marbled Chocolate Cheesecake

This attractive-looking dessert will be a big hit.

Serves 6

butter or margarine, for greasing
50g/2oz/½ cup unsweetened cocoa powder
75ml/5 tbsp hot water

900g/2lb/4 cups cream cheese, at room temperature
200g/7oz/1 cup caster (superfine) sugar
4 eggs
5ml/1 tsp vanilla extract
75g/3oz digestive biscuits (graham crackers), crushed

I Preheat the oven to 180°C/350°F/Gas 4. Line a deep 20cm/8in cake tin (pan) with baking parchment. Grease the paper.

2 Sift the cocoa powder into a bowl. Pour over the hot water and stir to dissolve.

3 In another bowl, beat the cheese until smooth, then beat in the sugar, followed by the eggs, one at a time. Do not overmix.

4 Divide the mixture evenly between two bowls. Stir the chocolate mixture into one bowl, then add the vanilla extract to the remaining mixture.

5 Pour a cup or ladleful of the plain mixture into the centre of the tin; it will spread out into an even layer. Slowly pour over a cupful of chocolate mixture in the centre. Continue to alternate the cake mixtures in this way until both are used up. Draw a metal skewer through the cake mixture for a marbled effect.

6 Place the tin in a roasting pan and pour in hot water to come 4cm/1½in up the sides of the cake tin. Bake the cheesecake for about 1½ hours, until the top is golden. (The cake will rise during baking but will sink later.) Cool in the tin on a wire rack.

7 Run a knife around the inside edge of the cheesecake. Invert a flat plate over the tin and turn out the cake. Sprinkle the crushed biscuits evenly over the cake, gently invert another plate on top, and turn over again. Cover and chill for 3 hours, preferably overnight, before serving.

Luxury White Chocolate Cheesecake

A luscious dessert for a special occasion.

Serves 16–20

150g/5oz (about 16–18) digestive biscuits (graham crackers)
50g/2oz/½ cup blanched hazelnuts, toasted
50g/2oz/¼ cup unsalted (sweet) butter, melted, plus extra for greasing
2.5ml/½ tsp ground cinnamon
white chocolate curls, to decorate
unsweetened cocoa powder, for dusting (optional)

For the filling
350g/12oz fine white chocolate, chopped into small pieces

120ml/4fl oz/½ cup whipping cream or double (heavy) cream
675g/1½lb/3 cups cream cheese, softened
50g/2oz/¼ cup granulated (white) sugar
4 eggs
30ml/2 tbsp hazelnut-flavoured liqueur or 15ml/1 tbsp vanilla extract

For the topping
450ml/¾ pint/scant 2 cups sour cream
50g/2oz/¼ cup granulated (white) sugar
15ml/1 tbsp hazelnut-flavoured liqueur or 5ml/1 tsp vanilla extract

I Preheat the oven to 180°C/350°F/Gas 4. Grease a deep 23cm/9in springform tin (pan).

2 Put the digestive biscuits and hazelnuts in a food processor and process to form fine crumbs. Pour in the butter and cinnamon. Process until the mixture is just blended. Using the back of a spoon, press on to the base and to within 1cm/½in of the top of the sides of the cake tin.

3 Bake the crumb crust for 5–7 minutes, or until it is just set. Cool the crust in the tin on a wire rack. Lower the oven temperature to 150°C/300°F/Gas 2 and place a baking sheet inside to heat up.

4 Make the filling. Melt the white chocolate and cream in a small pan over a low heat, until smooth, stirring frequently. Set aside to cool slightly.

5 Using an electric whisk, beat the cream cheese and sugar in a large bowl until smooth. Add the eggs one at a time, beating well. Slowly beat in the white chocolate mixture and liqueur or vanilla extract.

6 Pour the filling into the baked crust. Place the tin on the heated baking sheet. Bake for 45–55 minutes; be careful to ensure the top does not brown. Transfer to a wire rack while preparing the topping. Increase the oven temperature to 200°C/400°F/Gas 6.

7 Make the topping. In a small bowl whisk the sour cream, sugar and liqueur or vanilla extract until well combined. Pour over the cheesecake, spreading it evenly to the edges, and return to the oven. Bake for a further 5–7 minutes. Turn off the oven, but do not open the door for 1 hour.

8 Serve the cheesecake at room temperature, decorated with the white chocolate curls. Dust lightly with the cocoa powder, if you like.

Marbled Cheesecake Energy 923kcal/3828kJ; Protein 11.3g; Carbohydrate 44.4g, of which sugars 36.5g; Fat 79.3g, of which saturates 47.8g; Cholesterol 274mg; Calcium 206mg; Fibre 1.3g; Sodium 653mg.
Luxury Cheesecake Energy 421kcal/1746kJ; Protein 5.3g; Carbohydrate 22.3g, of which sugars 18.1g; Fat 34.6g, of which saturates 20g; Cholesterol 98mg; Calcium 124mg; Fibre 0.3g; Sodium 206mg.

Baked Chocolate and Raisin Cheesecake

This classic cheesecake will disappear in a flash.

Serves 8–10

75g/3oz/²⁄₃ cup plain
  (all-purpose) flour
45ml/3 tbsp unsweetened
  cocoa powder
75g/3oz/½ cup semolina
50g/2oz/¼ cup caster
  (superfine) sugar
115g/4oz/½ cup unsalted
  (sweet) butter, softened

For the filling
225g/8oz/1 cup cream cheese

120ml/4fl oz/½ cup natural
  (plain) yogurt
2 eggs, beaten
75g/3oz/6 tbsp caster
  (superfine) sugar
finely grated rind of 1 lemon
75g/3oz/½ cup raisins
45ml/3 tbsp plain (semisweet)
  chocolate chips

For the topping
75g/3oz plain (semisweet)
  chocolate, chopped into pieces
30ml/2 tbsp golden (light
  corn) syrup
40g/1½oz/3 tbsp butter

1 Preheat the oven to 150°C/300°F/Gas 2. Sift the flour and cocoa into a mixing bowl and stir in the semolina and sugar. Using your fingertips, work the butter into the flour mixture until it makes a firm dough.

2 Press the dough into the base of a 22cm/8½in springform tin (pan). Prick all over with a fork and bake in the oven for 15 minutes. Remove the tin but leave the oven on.

3 Make the filling. In a large bowl, beat the cream cheese with the yogurt, eggs and sugar until evenly mixed. Stir in the lemon rind, raisins and chocolate chips.

4 Smooth the cream cheese mixture over the chocolate base and bake for a further 35–45 minutes or until the filling is pale gold and just set. Cool in the tin on a wire rack.

5 Make the topping. Melt the chocolate, syrup and butter in a bowl over simmering water, then pour over the cheesecake. Leave until set. Remove the cheesecake from the tin and serve.

Raspberry and White Chocolate Cheesecake

An unbeatable combination: raspberries teamed with mascarpone and white chocolate on a crunchy ginger and pecan nut base.

Serves 8

50g/2oz/4 tbsp unsalted
  (sweet) butter
225g/8oz/2⅓ cups ginger nut
  biscuits (gingersnaps), crushed
50g/2oz/½ cup chopped pecan
  nuts or walnuts

For the filling
275g/10oz/1¼ cups
  mascarpone

175g/6oz/¾ cup fromage frais or
  soft white (farmer's) cheese
2 eggs, beaten
40g/1½oz/3 tbsp caster
  (superfine) sugar
250g/9oz white chocolate,
  broken into squares
225g/8oz/1⅓ cups fresh or
  frozen raspberries

For the topping
115g/4oz/½ cup mascarpone
  cheese
75g/3oz/⅓ cup fromage frais or
  soft white (farmer's) cheese
white chocolate curls and
  raspberries, to decorate

1 Preheat the oven to 150°C/300°F/Gas 2. Melt the butter in a pan, then stir in the crushed biscuits (cookies) and nuts. Press into the base of a 23cm/9in springform cake tin (pan).

2 Make the filling. Beat the mascarpone and fromage frais or white cheese in a bowl, then beat in the eggs and caster sugar until evenly mixed.

3 Melt the white chocolate gently in a heatproof bowl over a pan of simmering water. Stir the chocolate into the cheese mixture with the raspberries.

4 Turn into the prepared tin and spread evenly, then bake for about 1 hour or until just set. Switch off the oven, but do not remove the cheesecake. Leave it until cold and completely set.

5 Remove the cheesecake from the tin. Make the topping. Mix the mascarpone with the fromage frais and spread over the cheesecake. Decorate with chocolate curls and raspberries.

Raspberry Cheesecake Energy 551kcal/2305kJ; Protein 12.8g; Carbohydrate 53.9g, of which sugars 41.4g; Fat 33.1g, of which saturates 17g; Cholesterol 88mg; Calcium 170mg; Fibre 1.4g; Sodium 195mg.
Raisin Cheesecake Energy 441kcal/1841kJ; Protein 5.8g; Carbohydrate 41.4g, of which sugars 29.3g; Fat 29.3g, of which saturates 17.7g; Cholesterol 93mg; Calcium 86mg; Fibre 1.4g; Sodium 243mg.

Chocolate Fairy Cakes

Make these delightful butter-iced chocolate fairy cakes to serve for a children's party.

Makes 24
115g/4oz good quality plain (semisweet) chocolate, cut into small pieces
15ml/1 tbsp water
300g/10oz/2½ cups plain (all-purpose) flour
5ml/1 tsp baking powder
2.5ml/½ tsp bicarbonate of soda (baking soda)
a pinch of salt
300g/11oz/generous 1½ cups caster (superfine) sugar
175g/6oz/¾ cup butter or margarine, at room temperature
150ml/¼ pint/⅔ cup milk
5ml/1 tsp vanilla extract
3 eggs
1 quantity Butter Icing, flavoured to taste

1 Preheat the oven to 180°C/350°F/Gas 4. Grease and flour 24 deep bun cups, about 6.5cm/2¾in in diameter, or use paper cases in the tins (pans).

2 Put the chocolate and water in a bowl set over a pan of almost-simmering water. Heat until melted and smooth, stirring. Remove from the heat and leave to cool.

3 Sift the flour, baking powder, bicarbonate of soda, salt and sugar into a large bowl. Add the chocolate mixture, butter or margarine, milk and vanilla extract.

4 With an electric mixer on medium-low speed, beat until smoothly blended. Increase the speed to high and beat for 2 minutes. Add the eggs and beat for 2 more minutes.

5 Divide the mixture evenly among the prepared bun tins and bake for 20–25 minutes, or until a skewer inserted into the centre of a cake comes out clean.

6 Cool in the tins for 10 minutes, then turn out to cool completely on a wire rack.

7 Ice the top of each cake with butter icing, swirling it into a peak in the centre.

Chocolate Mint-filled Cupcakes

For extra mint flavour, chop eight thin cream-filled after-dinner mints and fold into the cake batter.

Makes 12
225g/8oz/2 cups plain (all-purpose) flour
5ml/1 tsp bicarbonate of soda (baking soda)
a pinch of salt
50g/2oz/½ cup unsweetened cocoa powder
150g/5oz/10 tbsp unsalted (sweet) butter, softened
300g/11oz/generous 1½ cups caster (superfine) sugar
3 eggs
5ml/1 tsp peppermint extract
250ml/8fl oz/1 cup milk

For the filling
300ml/½ pint/1¼ cups double (heavy) or whipping cream
5ml/1 tsp peppermint extract

For the glaze
175g/6oz plain (semisweet) chocolate
115g/4oz/½ cup unsalted (sweet) butter
5ml/1 tsp peppermint extract

1 Preheat the oven to 180°C/350°F/Gas 4. Line a 12-cup bun tray with paper cases. Sift together the dry ingredients.

2 In another bowl, beat the butter and sugar until light and creamy. Add the eggs, one at a time, beating well after each addition; beat in the peppermint. On low speed, beat in the flour mixture alternately with the milk, until just blended. Spoon into the paper cases.

3 Bake for 12–15 minutes. Transfer to a wire rack to cool. When cool, remove the paper cases.

4 To make the filling, whip the cream and peppermint extract until stiff. Spoon into a piping (pastry) bag fitted with a small plain nozzle. Pipe 15ml/1 tbsp of the mixture into each cake through the base.

5 To make the glaze, melt the chocolate and butter in a heatproof bowl over a pan of simmering water, stirring until smooth. Remove from the heat and stir in the peppermint extract. Cool, then spread on top of each cake.

Fairy Cakes Energy 228kcal/957kJ; Protein 2.5g; Carbohydrate 30.6g, of which sugars 21g; Fat 11.5g, of which saturates 3.3g; Cholesterol 33mg; Calcium 40mg; Fibre 0.5g; Sodium 95mg.
Cupcakes Energy 535kcal/2234kJ; Protein 6.3g; Carbohydrate 52g, of which sugars 37.1g; Fat 35.1g, of which saturates 21.4g; Cholesterol 123mg; Calcium 100mg; Fibre 1.4g; Sodium 209mg.

Chocolate Chip Muffins

These classic cakes are studded inside with plain chocolate chips.

Makes 10

115g/4oz/¹/₂ cup butter or
   margarine, softened
75g/3oz/scant ¹/₂ cup granulated
   (white) sugar

30ml/2 tbsp soft dark
   brown sugar
2 eggs
175g/6oz/1¹/₂ cups plain
   (all-purpose) flour,
5ml/1 tsp baking powder
120ml/4fl oz/¹/₂ cup milk
175g/6oz/1 cup plain (semisweet)
   chocolate chips

1 Preheat the oven to 190°C/375°F/Gas 5. Grease a ten-cup muffin tin (pan), or use paper cases in the tin.

2 In a bowl, beat the butter or margarine with the white and brown sugars until light and creamy.

3 Add the eggs, one at a time. Beat the mixture well after each egg is added.

4 Sift together the flour and baking powder and then add into the mixture, alternating with the milk. Stir until the mixture is well combined.

5 Divide half the mixture among the muffin cups or cases, filling each one halfway to the top.

6 Sprinkle the chocolate chips on top, then cover with the remaining mixture.

7 Bake for 25 minutes until a skewer inserted in a muffin comes out clean but slightly sticky.

8 Leave the cakes in the tin for 5 minutes, then transfer to a rack to cool.

Variation
You can use milk, dark (bittersweet) or white chocolate chips.

Chunky Chocolate and Banana Muffins

Luxurious but not overly sweet, these muffins are simple and quick to make. Serve warm while the chocolate is still gooey.

Makes 12

90ml/6 tbsp semi-skimmed
   (low-fat) milk
2 eggs
150g/5oz/10 tbsp unsalted
   (sweet) butter, melted

225g/8oz/2 cups unbleached
   plain (all-purpose) flour
pinch of salt
5ml/1 tsp baking powder
150g/5oz/³/₄ cup golden caster
   (superfine) sugar
150g/5oz plain (semisweet)
   chocolate, cut into
   large chunks
2 small bananas

1 Place 12 large paper cases in a deep muffin tin (pan). Preheat the oven to 200°C/400°F/Gas 6.

2 Place the semi-skimmed milk, eggs and melted butter in a medium bowl and whisk until well combined.

3 Sift together the flour, salt and baking powder into a separate large bowl.

4 Add the sugar and chocolate to the flour mixture and then stir until well combined. Slowly stir in the milk mixture, but do not beat it.

5 Peel the bananas. Using a potato masher or fork, mash the bananas in a bowl. Fold into the batter mixture.

6 Spoon the mixture into the paper cases. Bake for 20 minutes until golden. Cool on a wire rack.

Cook's Tip
Bananas are rich in potassium, which is vital for muscle and nerve function. They are also a good source of energy.

Chip Muffins Energy 296kcal/1238kJ; Protein 4.3g; Carbohydrate 36.4g, of which sugars 22.9g; Fat 15.8g, of which saturates 3.4g; Cholesterol 40mg; Calcium 56mg; Fibre 1g; Sodium 113mg.
Chunky Muffins Energy 240kcal/1003kJ; Protein 3.7g; Carbohydrate 26.3g, of which sugars 11.6g; Fat 14.1g, of which saturates 8.4g; Cholesterol 59mg; Calcium 47mg; Fibre 1g; Sodium 92mg.

Double Chocolate Chip Muffins

Chunks of white and plain chocolate will ensure that these delectable muffins go down a treat with chocoholics everywere.

Makes 16
400g/14oz/3½ cups plain (all-purpose) flour
15ml/1 tbsp baking powder
30ml/2 tbsp unsweetened cocoa powder
115g/4oz/⅔ cup dark muscovado (molasses) sugar

2 eggs
150ml/¼ pint/⅔ cup sour cream
150ml/¼ pint/⅔ cup milk
60ml/4 tbsp sunflower oil
175g/6oz white chocolate, chopped into small pieces
175g/6oz plain (semisweet) chocolate, chopped into small pieces
unsweetened cocoa powder, for dusting

1 Preheat the oven to 180°C/350°F/Gas 4. Place 16 paper muffin cases in muffin tins (pans) or deep patty tins.

2 Sift the flour, baking powder and cocoa into a bowl and stir in the sugar. Make a well in the centre.

3 In a separate bowl, mix the eggs with the sour cream, milk and oil, beating until well combined. Stir into the well in the dry ingredients. Beat thoroughly, gradually incorporating all the surrounding flour mixture to make a thick and creamy batter.

4 Stir the white chocolate and plain chocolate pieces into the batter mixture.

5 Spoon the chocolate mixture into the muffin cases, filling them almost to the top. Bake for 25–30 minutes, until well risen and firm to the touch. Cool the muffins on a wire rack, then dust them lightly with cocoa powder before serving.

Variation
These muffins are just as delicious with a different mix of chocolates. Try using milk and dark (bittersweet) chocolate.

Chocolate Walnut Muffins

These delicious cakes benefit from the addition of chunky walnut pieces.

Makes 12
175g/6oz/¾ cup unsalted (sweet) butter
150g/5oz plain (semisweet) chocolate, chopped into small pieces
200g/7oz/1 cup caster (superfine) sugar

50g/2oz/¼ cup soft dark brown sugar
4 eggs
5ml/1 tsp vanilla extract
1.5ml/¼ tsp almond extract
110g/3¾oz/scant 1 cup plain (all-purpose) flour
15ml/1 tbsp unsweetened cocoa powder
115g/4oz/1 cup walnuts, chopped

1 Preheat the oven to 180°C/350°F/Gas 4. Grease a 12-cup muffin tin (pan), or use paper cases supported in a bun tin.

2 Mix the butter with the chocolate in the top of a double boiler or in a heatproof bowl set over a pan of simmering water. Stir well until the chocolate is melted and smooth. Transfer to a large mixing bowl.

3 Stir both the sugars into the chocolate mixture. Mix in the eggs, one at a time, then add the vanilla and almond extracts.

4 Sift the flour and cocoa powder over the mixture, fold in, then stir in the walnuts.

5 Fill the muffin cups or cases almost to the top and bake for 30–35 minutes, until a skewer inserted in a muffin comes out clean but slightly sticky.

6 Leave the muffins to stand in the tin for 5 minutes before cooling completely on a wire rack.

Variation
You can replace the chopped walnuts with the same amount of chopped pecan nuts, if you prefer.

Walnut Muffins Energy 374kcal/1563kJ; Protein 4.9g; Carbohydrate 37.1g, of which sugars 32.2g; Fat 24g, of which saturates 10.8g; Cholesterol 95mg; Calcium 46mg; Fibre 0.8g; Sodium 115mg.
Double Muffins Energy 281kcal/1183kJ; Protein 4.7g; Carbohydrate 41.3g, of which sugars 21.9g; Fat 11.9g, of which saturates 5.7g; Cholesterol 7mg; Calcium 94mg; Fibre 1.3g; Sodium 40mg.

Chocolate Blueberry Muffins

Paper cases not only make for easier washing up, but keep the muffins fresher.

Makes 12
115g/4oz/½ cup butter
90g/3½oz unsweetened chocolate, chopped
200g/7oz/1 cup sugar
1 egg, lightly beaten
250ml/8fl oz/1 cup buttermilk
10ml/2 tsp vanilla extract
285g/10oz/2½ cups plain (all-purpose) flour
5ml/1 tsp bicarbonate of soda (baking soda)
175g/6oz/1½ cups fresh or frozen blueberries, thawed
25g/1oz dark (bittersweet) chocolate, melted

1 Preheat the oven to 190°C/375°F/Gas 5. Grease a 12-cup muffin tin (pan), or use paper cases supported in a bun tin.

2 Mix the butter with the unsweetened chocolate in the top of a double boiler or in a heatproof bowl set over a pan of simmering water. Stir well until the chocolate is melted and smooth. Transfer to a large mixing bowl.

3 Stir in the sugar, egg, buttermilk and vanilla extract to the chocolate mixture, mixing until well combined.

4 Gently fold in the flour and bicarbonate of soda until just blended. (Do not overblend; the mixture may be lumpy with some unblended flour.) Fold in the blueberries.

5 Spoon batter into the cups or cases, filling to the top. Bake for 25–30 minutes until a skewer inserted in the centre comes out with just a few crumbs attached. Remove muffins in their paper cases to a wire rack immediately (if left in the tin they will go soggy). Drizzle with the melted chocolate and serve warm or cool.

> **Cook's Tip**
> When melting the chocolate in a bowl over a pan of water, make sure that the water doesn't boil or touch the bottom of the bowl, otherwise the chocolate will overheat and stiffen.

Autumn Passionettes

Perfect for a tea party or packed lunch, this passion cake mixture can also be made as one big cake to serve for a celebration or as a dessert.

Makes 24
150g/5oz/10 tbsp butter, melted
200g/7oz/scant 1 cup soft light brown sugar
115g/4oz/1 cup carrots, peeled and finely grated
50g/2oz/1 cup dessert apples, peeled and finely grated
pinch of salt
5–10ml/1–2 tsp mixed spice (apple pie spice)
2 eggs
200g/7oz/1¾ cups self-raising (self-rising) flour, sifted
10ml/2 tsp baking powder, sifted
115g/4oz/1 cup shelled walnuts, finely chopped

For the topping
175g/6oz/¾ cup full-fat soft cheese
60–75ml/4–5 tbsp single (light) cream
50g/2oz/½ cup icing (confectioners') sugar, sifted
25g/1oz/¼ cup shelled walnuts, halved
10ml/2 tsp unsweetened cocoa powder, sifted

1 Preheat the oven to 180°C/350°F/Gas 4. Arrange 24 fairy cake paper cases in bun tins (pans). Mix the butter, sugar, carrots, apples, salt, mixed spice and eggs in a mixing bowl. Fold in the flour, baking powder and walnuts until evenly blended.

2 Half fill the cases with the mixture. Bake for 20–25 minutes, or until a skewer comes out clean. Leave in the tins for about 5 minutes, before transferring to a wire rack to cool completely.

3 Make the topping. Beat the cheese in a bowl with the cream and sugar until smooth. Put a spoonful on each cake, then top with the walnuts. Dust with the cocoa powder.

> **Variation**
> To make one cake, grease a 20cm/8in fluted cake tin and line with greased baking parchment. Fill with the mixture and bake for 1¼ hours. Leave for 5 minutes then turn out on to a wire rack and peel off the paper. Decorate as with the small cakes.

Blueberry Muffins Energy 279kcal/1172kJ; Protein 4.1g; Carbohydrate 43.5g, of which sugars 25.4g; Fat 11g, of which saturates 6.6g; Cholesterol 38mg; Calcium 73mg; Fibre 1.2g; Sodium 75mg.
Passionettes Energy 194kcal/808kJ; Protein 3.1g; Carbohydrate 18.3g, of which sugars 11.8g; Fat 12.6g, of which saturates 5.5g; Cholesterol 37mg; Calcium 38mg; Fibre 0.7g; Sodium 75mg.

Chocolate Cinnamon Doughnuts

Delicious, light doughnuts have a hidden nugget of chocolate inside.

Makes 16

500g/1¼lb/5 cups strong plain (all-purpose) flour
30ml/2 tbsp unsweetened cocoa powder
2.5ml/½ tsp salt
1 sachet easy-blend (rapid-rise) dried yeast
300ml/½ pint/1¼ cups milk

40g/1½oz/3 tbsp butter, melted
1 egg, beaten
115g/4oz plain (semisweet) chocolate, broken into 16 pieces
sunflower oil, for deep frying

For the coating

45ml/3 tbsp caster (superfine) sugar
15ml/1 tbsp unsweetened cocoa powder
5ml/1 tsp ground cinnamon

1 Sift the flour, cocoa and salt into a large bowl. Stir in the yeast. Warm the milk in a pan, then add to a well in the centre of the flour mixture along with the melted butter and egg. Stir, incorporating the dry ingredients, to make a soft dough.

2 Knead the dough on a lightly floured surface for about 5 minutes, until smooth and elastic. Return to the clean bowl, cover with clear film (plastic wrap) or a clean dry dish towel and leave in a warm place until the dough has doubled in bulk.

3 Knead the dough lightly again, then divide into 16 pieces. Shape each into a round, press a piece of plain chocolate into the centre, then fold the dough over to enclose the filling, pressing firmly to make sure the edges are sealed. Re-shape the doughnuts when sealed, if necessary.

4 Heat the oil for frying to 180°C/350°F, or until a cube of dried bread browns in 30–45 seconds. Deep fry the doughnuts in batches. As each doughnut rises and turns golden brown, turn it over carefully to cook the other side. Drain the cooked doughnuts well on kitchen paper.

5 Mix the sugar, cocoa and cinnamon in a shallow bowl. Toss the doughnuts in the mixture to coat them evenly. Pile on a plate and serve warm.

Chocolate Orange Sponge Drops

Light and crispy, with a zesty marmalade filling, these sponge drops are truly delightful.

Makes 14–15

2 eggs
50g/2oz/¼ cup caster (superfine) sugar

2.5ml/½ tsp grated orange rind
50g/2oz/½ cup plain (all-purpose) flour
60ml/4 tbsp fine-shred orange marmalade
40g/1½oz plain (semisweet) chocolate

1 Preheat the oven to 200°C/400°F/Gas 6. Line three baking sheets with baking parchment.

2 Put the eggs and sugar in a heatproof bowl over a pan of simmering water. Whisk until the mixture becomes thick and pale. Remove from the heat and whisk until cool.

3 Whisk the orange rind into the egg mixture. Sift the flour over and fold it in gently until well combined.

4 Place 28–30 dessertspoonfuls of the mixture on to the prepared baking sheets. Bake for 8 minutes, or until golden.

5 Remove from the oven and leave to cool slightly on the baking sheets, then carefully transfer the cakes to a wire rack to cool completely.

6 Spread a cake with about 5ml/1 tsp of marmalade and sandwich another one on top. Repeat this process until all the cakes have been sandwiched together.

7 Melt the plain chocolate in a heatproof bowl over a pan of simmering water, stirring until smooth. Drizzle over the cakes.

Cook's Tip
If you have only thick-cut marmalade with large chunks inside, then simply push the marmalade through a sieve (strainer) to filter out the large pieces of orange.

Doughnuts Energy 235kcal/989kJ; Protein 5.1g; Carbohydrate 33.2g, of which sugars 9g; Fat 10.1g, of which saturates 2.7g; Cholesterol 14mg; Calcium 76mg; Fibre 1.5g; Sodium 48mg.
Sponge Drops Energy 58kcal/247kJ; Protein 1.3g; Carbohydrate 10.5g, of which sugars 8g; Fat 1.5g, of which saturates 0.7g; Cholesterol 26mg; Calcium 12mg; Fibre 0.2g; Sodium 12mg.

Chocolate Eclairs

This tempting recipe is a delicious version of a popular French dessert.

Makes 12
300ml/½ pint/1¼ cups double (heavy) cream
10ml/2 tsp icing (confectioners') sugar, sifted
1.5ml/¼ tsp vanilla extract
115g/4oz plain (semisweet) chocolate
30ml/2 tbsp water
25g/1oz/2 tbsp butter

For the pastry
65g/2½oz/9 tbsp plain (all-purpose) flour
pinch of salt
50g/2oz/¼ cup butter, diced
150ml/¼ pint/⅔ cup water
2 eggs, lightly beaten

1 Preheat the oven to 200°C/400°F/Gas 6. Grease a large baking sheet and line with baking parchment. Make the pastry. Sift the flour and salt on to a sheet of parchment. Heat the butter and water in a pan until the butter melts. Increase the heat to a rolling boil. Remove from the heat and pour in the flour all at once. Return to a low heat, then beat with a wooden spoon until the mixture forms a ball. Set the pan aside and cool for 2–3 minutes.

2 Gradually beat in the beaten eggs until you have a smooth paste thick enough to hold its shape. Spoon the pastry into a piping (pastry) bag with a 2.5cm/1in plain nozzle. Pipe 10cm/4in lengths on to the prepared baking sheet. Bake for 25–30 minutes, until the pastries are well risen and golden brown. Remove from the oven and make a slit along the side of each to release steam. Lower the heat to 180°C/350°F/Gas 4 and bake for 5 minutes. Cool on a wire rack.

3 Make the filling. Whip the cream with the icing sugar and vanilla extract until it just holds its shape. Spoon into a piping bag fitted with a 1cm/½in plain nozzle and use to fill the éclairs.

4 Place the chocolate and water in a small heatproof bowl set over a pan of hot water. Melt, stirring until smooth. Remove from the heat and gradually stir in the butter. Dip the top of each éclair in the melted chocolate, place on a wire rack and leave in a cool place to set. Ideally, serve within 2 hours of making.

Fruity Chocolate Cookie-cakes

The combination of light spongy cookie, fruity preserve and dark chocolate makes irresistible eating for children of all ages. These cookie-cakes are ideal as a tea-time treat or for a kid's party. As cookies go, they are a little time-consuming to make, but that's all part of the fun.

Makes 18
90g/3½oz/½ cup caster (superfine) sugar
2 eggs
50g/2oz/½ cup plain (all-purpose) flour
75g/3oz/6 tbsp apricot-orange marmalade or apricot jam
125g/4¼oz plain (semisweet) chocolate

1 Preheat the oven to 190°C/375°F/Gas 5. Grease 18 patty tins (muffin pans), preferably non-stick. (If you don't have that many patty tins, you'll need to bake the cookies in batches.)

2 Stand a mixing bowl in very hot water for a couple of minutes to heat through, keeping the inside of the bowl dry. Place the sugar and eggs in the bowl and whisk with a hand-held electric mixer until light and frothy and the beaters leave a ribbon trail when lifted. Sift the flour over the mixture and stir in gently using a large metal spoon.

3 Divide the mixture among the patty tins. Bake for 10 minutes until just firm and pale golden around the edges. Using a metal spatula, lift from the tins and transfer to a wire rack to cool.

4 Press the marmalade or jam through a sieve (strainer) to remove any rind or fruit pieces. Spoon a little of the smooth jam on to the centre of each cookie.

5 Break the chocolate into pieces and place in a heatproof bowl set over a pan of gently simmering water. Heat, stirring frequently, until melted and smooth.

6 Spoon a little chocolate on to the top of each cookie and spread gently to the edges. Once the chocolate has just started to set, very gently press it with the back of a fork to give a textured surface. Leave to set for at least 1 hour.

Fruity Cookie-cakes Energy 84kcal/353kJ; Protein 1.3g; Carbohydrate 14.7g, of which sugars 12.5g; Fat 2.6g, of which saturates 1.3g; Cholesterol 22mg; Calcium 12mg; Fibre 0.3g; Sodium 11mg.
Chocolate Eclairs Energy 253kcal/1050kJ; Protein 2.5g; Carbohydrate 11.6g, of which sugars 7.4g; Fat 22.2g, of which saturates 13.5g; Cholesterol 80mg; Calcium 29mg; Fibre 0.4g; Sodium 56mg.

Chocolate Puffs

These delicious cream-filled choux pastry puffs are an exquisite treat.

Serves 6
65g/2½oz/9 tbsp plain
(all-purpose) flour
150ml/¼ pint/⅔ cup water
50g/2oz/¼ cup butter
2 eggs, beaten

For the filling and icing
150ml/¼ pint/⅔ cup double
(heavy) cream
225g/8oz/1½ cups icing
(confectioners') sugar
15ml/1 tbsp unsweetened
cocoa powder
30–60ml/2–4 tbsp water

1 Preheat the oven to 220°C/425°F/Gas 7. Sift the flour into a bowl. Put the water in a pan over a medium heat, add the butter and heat gently until it melts. Increase the heat and bring to the boil, then remove from the heat. Add all the flour at once and beat quickly until the mixture sticks together and becomes thick and glossy, leaving the side of the pan clean. Leave the mixture to cool slightly.

2 Add the eggs, a little at a time, to the mixture and beat by hand with a wooden spoon or with an electric whisk, until the mixture (choux pastry) is thick and glossy and drops reluctantly from a spoon. (You may not need to use all of the egg.) Spoon the choux pastry into a piping (pastry) bag fitted with a 2cm/¾in nozzle. Dampen two baking sheets with cold water.

3 Pipe walnut-size spoonfuls of the choux pastry on to the dampened baking sheets. Leave some space for them to rise. Cook for 25–30 minutes, until they are golden brown and well risen. Use a metal spatula to lift the puffs on to a wire rack, and make a small hole in each one with the handle of a wooden spoon to allow the steam to escape. Leave to cool.

4 Make the filling and icing. Whip the cream until thick. Put it into a piping bag fitted with a plain or star nozzle. Push the nozzle into the hole in each puff and squirt a little cream inside. Put the icing sugar and cocoa in a small bowl and stir together. Add enough water to make a thick glossy icing. Spread a little icing on each puff and serve when set.

Chocolate Cream Puffs

These light pastry puffs are filled with chocolate cream.

Makes 12 large puffs
115g/4oz/1 cup plain
(all-purpose) flour
30ml/2 tbsp unsweetened
cocoa powder
250ml/8fl oz/1 cup water
2.5ml/½ tsp salt
15ml/1 tbsp sugar
115g/4oz/½ cup unsalted
(sweet) butter, diced
4 eggs

For the pastry cream
450ml/¾ pint/scant 2 cups milk
6 egg yolks

115g/4oz/generous ½ cup sugar
50g/2oz/½ cup plain
(all-purpose) flour
150g/5oz plain (semisweet)
chocolate, chopped into pieces
120ml/4fl oz/½ cup
whipping cream

For the chocolate glaze
225g/8oz dark (bittersweet) or
plain (semisweet) chocolate
300ml/½ pint/1¼ cups
whipping cream
50g/2oz/¼ cup unsalted
(sweet) butter, diced
15ml/1 tbsp golden (light
corn) syrup
5ml/1 tsp vanilla extract

1 Preheat the oven to 220°C/425°F/Gas 7. Lightly grease two large baking sheets. Sift the flour and cocoa powder. In a pan, bring to the boil the water, salt, sugar and butter. Remove from the heat and add the flour and cocoa mixture in one go, stirring vigorously until smooth and it leaves the sides of the pan clean.

2 Return the pan to the heat to cook the choux pastry for 1 minute, beating constantly. Remove from the heat. With a hand-held electric mixer, beat in four of the eggs, one at a time, beating well after each addition, until well blended. The mixture should be thick and shiny. Spoon the mixture into a large piping (pastry) bag fitted with a plain nozzle. Pipe 12 mounds about 7.5cm/3in across at least 5cm/2in apart on the baking sheet.

3 Bake for 35–40 minutes until puffed and firm, then remove. With a knife, slice off and reserve the top third of each puff, then return the opened puffs to the oven for 5–10 minutes to dry out. Transfer to a wire rack to cool.

4 Prepare the pastry cream. Bring the milk to the boil in a small pan. In a bowl, heat the yolks and sugar until pale and thick. Stir in the flour. Slowly pour about 250ml/8fl oz/1 cup of the hot milk into the yolks, stirring constantly. Return the yolk mixture to the remaining milk in the pan and cook, stirring, until the sauce boils for a minute. Remove from the heat and stir in the chocolate until smooth.

5 Strain into a bowl and cover closely with clear film (plastic wrap). Cool to room temperature. In a bowl, whip the cream until stiff. Fold into the pastry cream.

6 Using a large piping bag, fill each puff bottom with pastry cream, then cover each puff with its top. Arrange the cream puffs on a large serving plate in a single layer, or as a pile.

7 Make the glaze. Break the chocolate and heat with the cream, butter, syrup and vanilla extract in a pan over a low heat until melted, stirring frequently. Cool for 30 minutes until thickened. Pour glaze over each of the cream puffs to serve.

Chocolate Puffs Energy 403kcal/1687kJ; Protein 4.2g; Carbohydrate 48.4g, of which sugars 39.8g; Fat 22.8g, of which saturates 13.6g; Cholesterol 115mg; Calcium 62mg; Fibre 0.6g; Sodium 106mg.
Cream Puffs Energy 527kcal/2196kJ; Protein 8.8g; Carbohydrate 44.7g, of which sugars 33.6g; Fat 36.1g, of which saturates 20.8g; Cholesterol 224mg; Calcium 121mg; Fibre 1.5g; Sodium 164mg.

Coffee Profiteroles with White Chocolate Sauce

Irresistible coffee-flavoured choux puffs, with a liqueur-laced white chocolate sauce.

Makes 24
65g/2½oz/9 tbsp plain
  (all-purpose) flour
pinch of salt
50g/2oz/¼ cup butter, diced
150ml/¼ pint/⅔ cup freshly
  brewed coffee
2 eggs, lightly beaten

250ml/8fl oz/1 cup double
  (heavy) cream, whipped

For the sauce
50g/2oz/¼ cup sugar
120ml/4fl oz/½ cup water
150g/5oz white chocolate,
  broken into pieces
25g/1oz/2 tbsp unsalted
  (sweet) butter
45ml/3 tbsp double (heavy) cream
30ml/2 tbsp coffee liqueur

1 Preheat the oven to 220°C/425°F/Gas 7. Sift the flour and salt on to a piece of baking parchment.

2 Place the butter in a pan with the coffee. Bring to a rolling boil, then remove from the heat and pour in the sifted flour in one go. Beat hard until the mixture leaves the side of the pan, forming a ball of thick paste. Leave to cool for 5 minutes.

3 Gradually add the eggs, beating well after each addition, until the mixture forms a stiff dropping consistency. Spoon into a piping (pastry) bag fitted with a 1cm/½in plain nozzle. Pipe 24 small buns on a dampened baking sheet, leaving plenty of room between them. Bake for 20 minutes, until risen. Remove the buns from the oven and pierce the side of each one with a sharp knife to let out the steam.

4 Make the sauce. Put the sugar and water in a heavy pan, and heat gently until the sugar has completely dissolved. Bring to the boil and simmer for 3 minutes. Remove the pan from the heat, and add the white chocolate and butter, stirring constantly until smooth. Stir in the double cream and liqueur.

5 Spoon the whipped cream into a piping bag and fill the buns through the slits. Serve with the chocolate sauce poured over.

Chocolate Profiteroles

These mouthwatering treats are served in cafés throughout France. Sometimes the profiteroles are filled with whipped cream instead of ice cream.

Makes 12
275g/10oz plain
  (semisweet) chocolate
120ml/4fl oz/½ cup warm water
750ml/1¼ pints/3 cups vanilla
  ice cream

For the profiteroles
100g/3¾oz/scant 1 cup plain
  (all-purpose) flour
1.5ml/¼ tsp salt
pinch of freshly grated nutmeg
75g/3oz/6 tbsp unsalted (sweet)
  butter, cut into 6 pieces,
  plus extra for greasing
175ml/6fl oz/¾ cup water
3 eggs

1 Preheat the oven to 200°C/400°F/Gas 6 and lightly butter a baking sheet.

2 Make the profiteroles. Sift together the flour, salt and nutmeg. In a medium pan, bring the butter and the water to the boil. Remove from the heat and add the dry ingredients all at once. Beat with a wooden spoon for about 1 minute until blended and the mixture starts to pull away from the sides of the pan, then set the pan over a low heat and cook the mixture for about 2 minutes, beating constantly. Remove from the heat.

3 Beat one egg in a small bowl and set aside. Add the remaining eggs, one at a time, to the flour mixture, beating well. Add the beaten egg gradually until the dough is smooth and shiny; it should fall slowly when dropped from a spoon.

4 Using a tablespoon, drop the dough on to the baking sheet in 12 mounds. Bake for 25–30 minutes until the pastry is well risen and browned. Turn off the oven and leave the puffs to cool with the oven door open.

5 Melt the chocolate and warm water in a bowl over a pan of hot water. Split the profiteroles in half and put a small scoop of ice cream in each. Pour the sauce over the top and serve.

Chocolate Profiteroles Energy 647kcal/2707kJ; Protein 11.7g; Carbohydrate 68.2g, of which sugars 52.4g; Fat 36.9g, of which saturates 22.7g; Cholesterol 155mg; Calcium 182mg; Fibre 1.7g; Sodium 189mg.
Coffee Profiteroles Energy 577kcal/2393kJ; Protein 6g; Carbohydrate 34.3g, of which sugars 26g; Fat 46.4g, of which saturates 28.1g; Cholesterol 157mg; Calcium 123mg; Fibre 0.3g; Sodium 139mg.

Brioches au Chocolat

Serve for breakfast as a luxurious start to the day.

Makes 12
250g/9oz/2¼ cups strong
  white flour
pinch of salt
30ml/2 tbsp caster
  (superfine) sugar

1 sachet easy-blend (rapid-rise)
  dried yeast
3 eggs, beaten, plus extra beaten
  egg, for glazing
45ml/3 tbsp hand-hot milk
115g/4oz/½ cup unsalted
  (sweet) butter, diced
175g/6oz plain (semisweet)
  chocolate, broken into squares

1 Sift the flour and salt into a mixing bowl and stir in the sugar and yeast. Make a well in the centre and add the eggs and milk. Beat well, gradually incorporating the dry ingredients to make a fairly soft dough. Turn the dough on to a lightly floured surface and knead well for about 5 minutes, until smooth and elastic, adding a little more flour if necessary.

2 Add the butter to the dough, a few pieces at a time, kneading until each addition is absorbed before adding the next. When all the butter has been incorporated and small bubbles appear in the dough, wrap it in clear film (plastic wrap) and chill for at least 1 hour. If you intend serving the brioches for breakfast, the dough can be left overnight.

3 Grease 12 individual brioche tins (pan) set on a baking sheet or a 12-hole brioche or patty tin (muffin pan). Divide the dough into 12 pieces and shape into smooth rounds. Place a chocolate square in the centre of each. Bring up the sides of the dough and press the edges together to seal.

4 Place the brioches, join side down, in the prepared tins. Cover and leave them in a warm place for about 30 minutes or until doubled in size. Preheat the oven to 200°C/400°F/Gas 6.

5 Brush the brioches with beaten egg. Bake for 12–15 minutes, until well risen and golden brown. Place on wire racks and leave to cool slightly. They should be served warm and can be made in advance and reheated if necessary. Do not serve straight from the oven, as the chocolate will be very hot.

Sicilian Brioches with Hot Chocolate Fudge Sauce

For sheer indulgence, this dessert is unbeatable. Warm brioches filled with ice cream and topped with a glorious hot fudge sauce will make anyone's day.

Serves 2
2 individual brioches
2 large scoops of best vanilla
  or coffee ice cream

For the hot fudge sauce
50g/2oz best dark (bittersweet)
  chocolate with 70 per cent
  cocoa solids
15g/½oz/1 tbsp butter
75ml/5 tbsp boiling water
30ml/2 tbsp golden (light
  corn) syrup
150g/5oz/¾ cup soft light brown
  sugar, sifted
5ml/1 tsp vanilla extract

1 Preheat the oven to 200°C/400°F/Gas 6. Meanwhile, make the hot fudge sauce. Break up the chocolate into small pieces and place in a heatproof bowl set over a pan of barely simmering water. Leave, without stirring, for about 10 minutes until the chocolate has completely melted, then add the butter and stir to combine.

2 Add the boiling water to the melted chocolate and butter, stir well to blend, then stir in the syrup, sugar and vanilla extract. Pour and scrape the chocolate mixture into a pan and bring to the boil, then turn down the heat and allow to barely bubble for 5 minutes.

3 Meanwhile, put the brioches on a baking sheet and warm them in the oven for approximately 5 minutes – or until they are slightly crisp on the outside but are still soft, fluffy and warm on the inside.

4 Remove the pan of chocolate sauce from the heat. Immediately split the brioches open and gently pull out a little of the insides. Generously fill each brioche base with ice cream and gently press down on the tops.

5 Put the filled brioches into individual bowls or on to dessert plates, and pour over the hot fudge sauce. Serve immediately.

Brioches Energy 236kcal/988kJ; Protein 4.3g; Carbohydrate 27g, of which sugars 11g; Fat 13.1g, of which saturates 7.6g; Cholesterol 69mg; Calcium 48mg; Fibre 1g; Sodium 79mg.
Sicilian Brioches Energy 913kcal/3853kJ; Protein 13.8g; Carbohydrate 163.3g, of which sugars 121.5g; Fat 27.2g, of which saturates 15.4g; Cholesterol 18mg; Calcium 257mg; Fibre 3g; Sodium 674mg.

Pain au Chocolat

Buttery, flaky yet crisp pastry conceals a delectable chocolate filling.

Makes 9

250g/9oz/2¼ cups unbleached
    white bread flour
30ml/2 tbsp skimmed milk
    powder (non-fat dry milk)
15ml/1 tbsp caster
    (superfine) sugar
2.5ml/½ tsp salt

7.5ml/1½ tsp easy-blend
    (rapid-rise) dried yeast
150g/5oz/10 tbsp butter, softened
125ml/4½fl oz/generous ½ cup
    hand-hot water
225g/8oz plain (semisweet)
    chocolate, broken into pieces

For the glaze
1 egg yolk
15ml/1 tbsp milk

1 Mix the flour, milk powder, sugar and salt in a bowl. Stir in the yeast and make a well in the middle. Melt 25g/1oz/2 tbsp of the butter and pour it into the well in the middle of the mixture. Pour in the water and then mix to form a firm dough.

2 Turn the dough out on to a lightly floured surface and knead it for about 10 minutes, until smooth and elastic. When pressed on the surface it should spring back rather than retain the dent.

3 Dust the bowl with flour and return the dough to it. Cover with clear film (plastic wrap) and leave in a warm place until doubled in size. Meanwhile, shape the remaining softened butter into an oblong block, about 2cm/¾in thick.

4 Grease two baking sheets. When the dough has doubled, turn it out on to a floured surface. Knock back (punch down) and shape into a ball. Cut a cross halfway through the top. Roll out around the cross, leaving a risen centre. Place the butter in the centre. Fold the dough over the butter. Seal the edges.

5 Roll to a rectangle 2cm/¾in thick, twice as long as wide. Fold the bottom third up and the top down; seal the edges with a rolling pin. Wrap in lightly oiled clear film. Chill for 20 minutes. Do the same again twice more, giving a quarter turn and chilling each time. Chill again for 30 minutes.

6 Roll out the dough to a rectangle measuring 52 × 30cm/ 21 × 12in. Using a knife, cut into three strips lengthways and widthways to make nine 18 × 10cm/7 × 4in rectangles. Divide the chocolate among the three dough rectangles, placing the pieces lengthways at one short end.

7 Mix together the egg yolk and milk for the glaze. Brush the mixture over the edges of the dough. Roll up each piece of dough to completely enclose the chocolate, then press the edges together to seal.

8 Place the pastries seam side down on the prepared baking sheets. Cover with oiled clear film and leave to rise in a warm place for about 30 minutes or until doubled in size.

9 Meanwhile, preheat the oven to 200°C/400°F/Gas 6. Brush the pastries with the remaining glaze and bake for 15 minutes, or until golden. Turn out on to a wire rack to cool just slightly and serve warm.

Ice Cream Croissants with Chocolate Sauce

A deliciously easy-to-make croissant sandwich with a tempting filling of vanilla custard, ice cream and chocolate sauce melting inside the warmed bread.

Makes 4

75g/3oz plain (semisweet)
    chocolate, broken into pieces
15g/½oz/1 tbsp unsalted
    (sweet) butter

30ml/2 tbsp golden (light
    corn) syrup
4 croissants
90ml/6 tbsp good quality
    ready-made vanilla custard
4 large scoops of vanilla
    ice cream
icing (confectioners') sugar,
    for dusting

1 Preheat the oven to 180°C/350°F/Gas 4. Put the chocolate in a small, heavy pan. Add the butter and syrup and heat very gently until smooth, stirring the mixture frequently.

2 Split each of the croissants in half horizontally and place the base halves on a baking sheet. Spoon over the ready-made custard so that it covers the croissant bases, cover with the lids and bake in the oven for approximately 5 minutes, or until warmed through.

3 Remove the lids and place a scoop of ice cream in each croissant. Spoon half the chocolate sauce over the ice cream and press the lids down gently. Put the croissants in the oven for 1 minute more.

4 Dust the filled croissants with icing sugar, spoon over the remaining chocolate sauce and serve immediately.

> **Variation**
> Add a dash of brandy to the chocolate sauce for a treat for adults. Experiment with different ice creams – try using some coffee-flavoured ice cream instead of vanilla.

Pain au Chocolat Energy 345kcal/1441kJ; Protein 4g; Carbohydrate 39.3g, of which sugars 17.9g; Fat 20.1g, of which saturates 12.4g; Cholesterol 35mg; Calcium 51mg; Fibre 1.5g; Sodium 206mg.
Ice Cream Croissants Energy 498kcal/2086kJ; Protein 8.7g; Carbohydrate 59.4g, of which sugars 35g; Fat 29.5g, of which saturates 14.6g; Cholesterol 55mg; Calcium 134mg; Fibre 1.5g; Sodium 341mg.

Puffy Chocolate Pears

These pear-shaped pastries
will go down a treat with
children – who will also love
to help make them.

Makes 4
225g/8oz puff pastry, thawed
  if frozen

2 pears, peeled
2 squares plain (semisweet)
  chocolate, roughly chopped
15ml/1 tbsp lemon juice
1 egg, beaten
15ml/1 tbsp caster
  (superfine) sugar

1 Roll out the pastry into a 25cm/10in square on a lightly
floured surface. Trim the edges, then cut it into four equal
smaller squares. Cover the pastry with clear film (plastic wrap)
and set aside.

2 Remove the core from each pear half and pack the gap
with the chopped chocolate. Place a pear half, cut side down,
on each piece of pastry and brush them with the lemon juice,
to prevent them from going brown.

3 Preheat the oven to 190°C/375°F/Gas 5. Cut the pastry
into a pear shape, by following the lines of the fruit, leaving a
2.5cm/1in border. Use the trimmings to make leaves and brush
the pastry border with the beaten egg.

4 Arrange the pastry and pears on a baking sheet. Make deep
cuts in the pears, taking care not to cut right through the fruit,
and sprinkle them with the sugar. Cook for 20–25 minutes, until
lightly browned. Serve hot or cold.

Variation
*Try using apples instead of pears for this recipe, if preferred.
Cut the puff pastry into 10cm/4in rounds. Slice 2 peeled and
cored eating apples. Toss with a little lemon juice to avoid the
fruit discolouring, drain and arrange on the pastry. Dot with
25g/1oz/2 tbsp butter and chopped milk chocolate. Bake as
for Puffy Chocolate Pears. While still hot, brush the apple slices
with warmed redcurrant jam.*

Choux Pastries with Two Custards

These sweetly scented
Italian pastry treats have
two contrasting custards –
chocolate and vanilla.

Makes about 48
200ml/7fl oz/scant 1 cup water
115g/4oz/½ cup butter
2cm/1in piece vanilla pod (bean)
pinch of salt
150g/5oz/1¼ cups plain
  (all-purpose) flour
5 eggs

For the custard fillings
50g/2oz cooking chocolate
300ml/½ pint/1¼ cups milk
4 egg yolks
65g/2½ oz/scant ⅓ cup sugar
40g/1½oz/⅓ cup plain
  (all-purpose) flour
5ml/1 tsp pure vanilla extract
300ml/½ pint/1¼ cups
  whipping cream
unsweetened cocoa powder and
  icing (confectioners') sugar,
  to garnish

1 Preheat the oven to 190°C/375°F/Gas 5. Heat the water
with the butter, vanilla and salt. When melted, beat in the flour.
Cook over low heat, stirring, for 10 minutes. Remove from the
heat. Mix in the eggs one at a time. Remove the vanilla pod.

2 Butter a flat baking tray. Using a piping (pastry) bag fitted
with a round nozzle, pipe walnut-size balls on to the tray. Bake
for 20–25 minutes, or until golden brown. Cool before filling.

3 Prepare the custard fillings. Melt the chocolate in the top half
of a double boiler, or in a bowl set over a pan of simmering
water. Heat the milk in a small pan, taking care not to let it boil.

4 Whisk the egg yolks. Add the sugar, and beat until pale. Beat
in the flour. Slowly pour in the hot milk, stirring until combined.
Pour into a pan, and bring to a boil. Simmer for 5–6 minutes,
stirring constantly. Remove from the heat and divide the custard
between two bowls. Add the chocolate to one, and stir the
vanilla extract into the other. Allow to cool completely.

5 Whip the cream. Fold half into each custard. Fill two pastry
bags fitted with round nozzles with each custard. Fill half the
pastries with chocolate custard, and the rest with vanilla custard,
through a little hole in the side. Dust the chocolate pastries
with cocoa powder, and the rest with sugar. Serve immediately.

Puffy Pears Energy 464kcal/1944kJ; Protein 6.9g; Carbohydrate 56.1g, of which sugars 35.6g; Fat 25.8g, of which saturates 6.7g; Cholesterol 50mg; Calcium 62mg; Fibre 2.6g; Sodium 197mg.
Choux Pastries Energy 79kcal/331kJ; Protein 1.8g; Carbohydrate 7.3g, of which sugars 3.3g; Fat 5g, of which saturates 3g; Cholesterol 44mg; Calcium 24mg; Fibre 0.2g; Sodium 32mg.

Chocolate Brownies

Traditional American brownies are usually rich in butter. This version uses sunflower oil in place of butter. It still tastes rich and gooey, but is best eaten on the day it is made.	150g/5oz plain (semisweet) chocolate, chopped
	2 eggs
	115g/4oz/1 cup self-raising (self-rising) flour
	115g/4oz/generous ½ cup caster (superfine) sugar
	5ml/1 tsp vanilla extract
Makes 20	75g/3oz/¾ cup halved
120ml/4fl oz/½ cup sunflower oil	pecan nuts

1 Preheat the oven to 200°C/400°F/Gas 6. Use a little of the oil to grease a 23cm/9in square shallow cake tin (pan) and then line it with lightly oiled baking parchment.

2 Melt the chocolate with the remaining oil in a heatproof bowl set over a pan of barely simmering water, stirring constantly until smooth.

3 Beat the eggs lightly and add them to the melted chocolate, stirring vigorously. Beat in the flour, caster sugar and vanilla extract and pour the mixture into the prepared tin. Arrange the pecan nut halves over the top.

4 Bake for 10–15 minutes. If you like chewy brownies, take them out of the oven at this point. However, if you prefer a more cake-like finish, leave the brownies to bake for a further 5 minutes. Cut into squares and leave to cool before removing them from the tin.

> **Cook's Tip**
> Ingredients can be melted easily in a microwave oven. To soften chocolate, butter, sugar or syrup, microwave on High power for a few seconds, until soft. Remember that chocolate and butter may not look melted, so check them carefully by stirring before returning them to the microwave for a few seconds more.

American Chocolate Fudge Brownies

This is the classic American recipe. The delicious chocolate frosting makes the brownies taste decadently rich.	2.5ml/½ tsp vanilla extract
	115g/4oz/1 cup chopped pecan nuts
	50g/2oz/½ cup self-raising (self-rising) flour
Makes 12	**For the frosting**
175g/6oz/¾ cup butter	115g/4oz plain
40g/1½oz/⅓ cup unsweetened cocoa powder	(semisweet) chocolate
	25g/1oz/2 tbsp butter
2 eggs, lightly beaten	15ml/1 tbsp sour cream
175g/6oz/¾ cup soft light brown sugar	

1 Preheat the oven to 180°C/350°F/Gas 4. Grease a 20cm/8in square shallow cake tin (pan) and line with baking parchment. Melt the butter in a pan and stir in the unsweetened cocoa powder. Set aside to cool.

2 Beat together the eggs, sugar and vanilla extract in a bowl, then stir in the cooled cocoa mixture with the nuts. Sift over the flour and fold into the mixture with a metal spoon.

3 Pour the mixture into the cake tin and bake in the oven for 30–35 minutes, or until risen. Remove from the oven (it will still be soft and wet, but firms while cooling). Cool in the tin.

4 To make the frosting, melt the chocolate and butter together in a pan and remove from the heat. Beat in the sour cream until smooth and glossy. Leave to cool slightly, and then spread over the top of the brownies. When set, cut into 12 pieces.

> **Cook's Tip**
> Brownies are firm family favourites and, once you find a recipe you like, you will want to make them regularly. For brownie enthusiasts you can now buy a special pan with a slide-out base, which makes removing the cooked brownies so much easier.

Chocolate Brownies Energy 152kcal/635kJ; Protein 1.9g; Carbohydrate 15.5g, of which sugars 11g; Fat 9.6g, of which saturates 2.2g; Cholesterol 19mg; Calcium 19mg; Fibre 0.5g; Sodium 8mg.
American Brownies Energy 335kcal/1396kJ; Protein 3.6g; Carbohydrate 25.6g, of which sugars 21.9g; Fat 25.1g, of which saturates 11.7g; Cholesterol 69mg; Calcium 45mg; Fibre 1.2g; Sodium 161mg.

LITTLE CAKES, SLICES AND BARS

Chocolate Chip Brownies

A double dose of chocolate is incorporated into these melt-in-the-mouth brownies.

Makes 24

115g/4oz plain
 (semisweet) chocolate
115g/4oz/½ cup butter

3 eggs
200g/7oz/1 cup caster
 (superfine) sugar
2.5ml/½ tsp vanilla extract
a pinch of salt
150g/5oz/1¼ cups plain
 (all-purpose) flour
175g/6oz/1 cup chocolate chips

1 Preheat the oven to 180°C/350°F/Gas 4. Line a 33 × 23cm/13 × 9in baking tin (pan) with baking parchment and grease the paper.

2 Melt the chocolate and butter together in the top of a double boiler, or in a heatproof bowl set over a pan of gently simmering water.

3 Beat together the eggs, sugar, vanilla extract and salt. Stir in the chocolate mixture. Sift over the flour and fold in. Add the chocolate chips.

4 Pour the mixture into the baking tin and spread evenly. Bake until just set, about 30 minutes. The brownies should be slightly moist inside. Leave to cool in the tin.

5 To turn out, run a knife all around the edge and invert on to a baking sheet. Remove the paper. Place another sheet on top and invert again. Cut into bars for serving.

Variations

Rich chocolate: Use the best quality chocolate (consisting of at least 70 per cent cocoa solids) cut into chunks to give the brownies a fantastic flavour.
Chunky choc and nut: Use 75g/3oz coarsely chopped white chocolate and 75g/3oz/¾ cup chopped walnuts.
Almond: Use almond extract, add 75g/3oz/¾ cup chopped almonds and reduce the chocolate chips to 75g/3oz/½ cup.

Raisin Chocolate Brownies

Cover these divine fruity brownies with a light chocolate frosting for a truly decadent treat.

Makes 16

115g/4oz/½ cup butter
 or margarine
50g/2oz/½ cup unsweetened
 cocoa powder
2 eggs

225g/8oz/generous 1 cup caster
 (superfine) sugar
5ml/1 tsp vanilla extract
40g/1½oz/⅓ cup plain
 (all-purpose) flour
75g/3oz/¾ cup finely
 chopped walnuts
75g/3oz/generous ½ cup
 raisins

1 Preheat the oven to 180°C/350°F/Gas 4. Line the base and sides of a 20cm/8in square baking tin (pan) with baking parchment and grease the paper.

2 Gently melt the butter or margarine in a small pan. Remove from the heat and stir in the cocoa powder.

3 With an electric mixer, beat the eggs, caster sugar and vanilla extract together until light. Add the cocoa and butter mixture and stir to blend.

4 Sift the flour over the cocoa mixture and gently fold in. Do not overmix.

5 Add the walnuts and raisins, and scrape the mixture into the prepared baking tin.

6 Bake in the centre of the oven for 30 minutes. Leave in the tin to cool before cutting into 5cm/2in squares and removing from the tin. The brownies should be soft and moist.

Cook's Tip

Adding dried fruit makes brownies a little more substantial and adds to their delicious flavour. Try to find Californian or Spanish raisins for the best flavour and texture.

Chip Brownies Energy 161kcal/674kJ; Protein 2g; Carbohydrate 21.3g, of which sugars 16.4g; Fat 8.1g, of which saturates 4.7g; Cholesterol 35mg; Calcium 22mg; Fibre 0.5g; Sodium 39mg.
Raisin Brownies Energy 181kcal/759kJ; Protein 2.5g; Carbohydrate 20.4g, of which sugars 18.1g; Fat 10.5g, of which saturates 4.6g; Cholesterol 39mg; Calcium 26mg; Fibre 0.7g; Sodium 86mg.

Maple and Pecan Nut Brownies

This recipe provides a delicious adaptation of the classic American chocolate brownie, using maple syrup and pecan nuts.

Makes 12
115g/4oz/¹/₂ cup butter, melted
75g/3oz/scant ¹/₂ cup soft light brown sugar
90ml/6 tbsp maple syrup
2 eggs

115g/4oz/1 cup self-raising (self-rising) flour
75g/3oz/³/₄ cup pecan nuts, chopped

For the topping
115g/4oz/²/₃ cup plain (semisweet) chocolate chips
50g/2oz/¹/₄ cup unsalted (sweet) butter
12 pecan nut halves, to decorate

1 Preheat the oven to 180°C/350°F/Gas 4. Line and grease a 25 × 18cm/10 × 7in cake tin (pan).

2 Beat together the melted butter, sugar, 60ml/4 tbsp of the maple syrup, the eggs and flour for 1 minute, or until smooth.

3 Stir in the nuts and transfer to the cake tin. Smooth the surface and bake for 30 minutes, or until risen and firm to the touch. Cool in the tin for 10 minutes, then transfer to a wire rack to cool completely.

4 Melt the chocolate chips, butter and remaining syrup over a low heat. Cool slightly, then spread over the cake. Press in the pecan nut halves, leave to set for about 5 minutes, then cut into squares or bars.

Cook's Tips
• Maple syrup is a sweet sugar syrup made from the sap of the sugar maple tree. It has a distinctive flavour which is delightful in a variety of sweet recipes as well as when added to ice creams and waffles.
• Buy a good quality maple syrup as blends are often disappointing.
• Store opened maple syrup in the refrigerator, as its delicate flavour will deteriorate once the bottle is opened.

Banana Chocolate Brownies

Nuts traditionally give brownies their chewy texture. Here oat bran is used instead, creating a wonderful alternative.

Makes 9
75ml/5 tbsp unsweetened cocoa powder
15ml/1 tbsp caster (superfine) sugar
75ml/5 tbsp milk

3 large bananas, mashed
215g/7¹/₂oz/scant 1 cup soft light brown sugar
5ml/1 tsp vanilla extract
5 egg whites
75g/3oz/²/₃ cup self-raising (self-rising) flour
75g/3oz/²/₃ cup oat bran
icing (confectioners') sugar, for dusting

1 Preheat the oven to 180°C/350°F/Gas 4. Line a 20cm/8in square cake tin (pan) with baking parchment.

2 Blend the cocoa powder and caster sugar with the milk. Add the bananas, soft brown sugar and vanilla extract. Lightly beat the egg whites with a fork. Add the chocolate mixture and continue to beat well. Sift the flour over the mixture and fold in with the oat bran. Pour into the prepared tin.

3 Cook in the oven for 40 minutes, or until firm. Cool in the tin for 10 minutes, then turn out on to a wire rack. Cut into slices or squares and lightly dust with icing sugar before serving.

Cook's Tips
Win a few brownie points by getting to know what makes them great.
• They should be moist and chewy with a sugary crust on the outside but squidgy on the inside.
• True versions contain a high proportion of sugar and fat and most contain nuts. Lighter versions often contain white chocolate and are often referred to as blondies.
• Brownies make superb individual cakes but the cooked slab can also be left whole and then served as a larger cake for dessert, decorated with cream and fruit.

Maple Brownies Energy 285kcal/1189kJ; Protein 3.1g; Carbohydrate 26.2g, of which sugars 18.9g; Fat 19.4g, of which saturates 9.4g; Cholesterol 62mg; Calcium 52mg; Fibre 0.8g; Sodium 151mg.
Banana Brownies Energy 223kcal/947kJ; Protein 5.7g; Carbohydrate 46.4g, of which sugars 32.4g; Fat 2.9g, of which saturates 1.2g; Cholesterol 0mg; Calcium 70mg; Fibre 2.2g; Sodium 151mg.

Fudge-glazed Chocolate Brownies

These pecan nut-topped brownies are irresistible, so you may find that you have to hide them from your friends!

Makes 16
250g/9oz dark (bittersweet)
  chocolate, chopped
25g/1oz unsweetened
  chocolate, chopped
115g/4oz/1/2 cup unsalted
  (sweet) butter, cut
  into pieces
90g/31/2oz/scant 1/2 cup soft
  light brown sugar
50g/2oz/1/4 cup caster
  (superfine) sugar
2 eggs

15ml/1 tbsp vanilla extract
65g/21/2oz/9 tbsp plain
  (all-purpose) flour
115g/4oz/1 cup pecan nuts or
  walnuts, toasted and chopped
150g/5oz white chocolate,
  chopped
pecan nut halves, to decorate
  (optional)

For the glaze
175g/6oz dark (bittersweet)
  chocolate, chopped
50g/2oz/1/4 cup unsalted (sweet)
  butter, cut into pieces
30ml/2 tbsp golden (light
  corn) syrup
10ml/2 tsp vanilla extract
5ml/1 tsp instant coffee

1 Preheat the oven to 180°C/350°F/Gas 4. Line a 20cm/8in square baking tin (pan) with foil, then grease the foil.

2 Melt the dark chocolates and butter in a pan over a low heat. Off the heat, add the sugars and stir for 2 minutes. Beat in the eggs and vanilla extract, and then blend in the flour.

3 Stir in the pecan nuts or walnuts and the chopped white chocolate.

4 Pour into the tin. Bake for 20–25 minutes. Cool in the tin for 30 minutes then lift, using the foil, on to a wire rack to cool for 2 hours.

5 To make the glaze, melt the chocolate in a pan with the butter, golden syrup, vanilla extract and instant coffee. Stir until smooth. Chill the glaze for 1 hour, then spread over the brownies. Top with pecan nut halves, if you like. Chill until set, then cut into bars.

Nutty Chocolate Squares

These delicious squares are incredibly rich, so cut them smaller if you wish.

Makes 16
2 eggs
10ml/2 tsp vanilla extract
1.5ml/1/4 tsp salt
175g/6oz/11/2 cups pecan nuts,
  coarsely chopped

50g/2oz/1/2 cup plain
  (all-purpose) flour
50g/2oz/1/4 cup caster
  (superfine) sugar
120ml/4fl oz/1/2 cup golden
  (light corn) syrup
75g/3oz plain (semisweet)
  chocolate, finely chopped
40g/11/2oz/3 tbsp butter
16 pecan nut halves, to decorate

1 Preheat the oven to 160°C/325°F/Gas 3. Line the base and sides of a 20cm/8in square baking tin (pan) with baking parchment and lightly grease the paper.

2 Whisk together the eggs, vanilla extract and salt. In another bowl, mix together the chopped pecan nuts and flour. Set both aside until needed.

3 In a pan, bring the sugar and golden syrup to the boil. Watch it carefully and remove from the heat as soon as it comes to the boil. Stir in the chocolate and butter, and blend thoroughly with a wooden spoon. Mix in the beaten egg mixture, then fold in the pecan nut mixture.

4 Pour the mixture into the baking tin and bake until set, about 35 minutes. Cool in the tin for 10 minutes before unmoulding.

5 Cut into 5cm/2in squares and press pecan nut halves into the tops while warm. Cool on a wire rack.

> **Variation**
> Toasted hazelnuts also taste great in this recipe in place of the pecan nuts. Simply brown the hazelnuts under a hot grill (broiler), turning them every so often. When toasted all over, leave to cool, then rub them in a clean dish towel until the skins are removed.

Brownies Energy 382kcal/1595kJ; Protein 4.1g; Carbohydrate 37.6g, of which sugars 34.1g; Fat 25g, of which saturates 12.4g; Cholesterol 47mg; Calcium 55mg; Fibre 1.2g; Sodium 89mg.
Nutty Squares Energy 172kcal/719kJ; Protein 2.4g; Carbohydrate 15.2g, of which sugars 12.7g; Fat 11.8g, of which saturates 2.9g; Cholesterol 29mg; Calcium 19mg; Fibre 0.7g; Sodium 45mg.

Marbled Chocolate Brownies

These fancy chocolate brownies have an impressive flavour as well a pretty, marbled appearance.

Makes 24

225g/8oz plain (semisweet) chocolate
75g/3oz/6 tbsp butter
4 eggs
300g/11oz/1½ cups caster (superfine) sugar
150g/5oz/1¼ cups plain (all-purpose) flour
2.5ml/½ tsp salt
5ml/1 tsp baking powder
10ml/2 tsp vanilla extract
115g/4oz/1 cup chopped walnuts

For the plain mixture

50g/2oz/¼ cup butter, at room temperature
175g/6oz/¾ cup cream cheese
90g/3½oz/1½ cups caster (superfine) sugar
2 eggs
25g/1oz/¼ cup plain (all-purpose) flour
5ml/1 tsp vanilla extract

1 Preheat the oven to 180°C/350°F/Gas 4. Line a 33 × 23cm/ 13 × 9in baking tin (pan) with baking parchment and grease.

2 Melt the chocolate and butter in a small pan over a very low heat, stirring. Set aside to cool. Meanwhile, beat the eggs until light and fluffy. Gradually beat in the sugar. Sift over the flour, salt and baking powder, and fold to combine.

3 Stir in the cooled chocolate mixture. Add the vanilla extract and chopped walnuts. Measure and set aside 475ml/16fl oz/ 2 cups of the chocolate mixture.

4 For the plain mixture, cream the butter and cream cheese with an electric mixer. Add the sugar and continue beating until blended. Beat in the eggs, flour and vanilla extract.

5 Spread the unmeasured chocolate mixture in the tin. Pour over the plain mixture. Drop spoonfuls of the reserved chocolate mixture on top.

6 With a metal spatula, swirl the mixtures to marble them. Do not blend completely. Bake until just set, 35–40 minutes. Turn out when cool and cut into squares for serving.

Butterscotch and White Chocolate Brownies

These gorgeous treats are made with brown sugar, white chocolate chips and walnuts. Who could possibly have the will power to resist? You might want to make two batches at a time.

Makes 12

450g/1lb white chocolate chips
75g/3oz/6 tbsp unsalted (sweet) butter
3 eggs
175g/6oz/¾ cup light muscovado (brown) sugar
175g/6oz/1½ cups self-raising (self-rising) flour
175g/6oz/1½ cups walnuts, chopped
5ml/1 tsp vanilla extract

1 Preheat the oven to 190°C/375°F/Gas 5. Line the base of a 28 × 18cm/11 × 7in shallow tin (pan) with baking parchment. Lightly grease the sides.

2 Melt 90g/3½oz of the chocolate chips with the butter in a heatproof bowl set over a pan of simmering water, stirring until smooth. Leave to cool slightly.

3 Put the eggs and light muscovado sugar into a large bowl and whisk well, then whisk in the melted chocolate mixture.

4 Sift the flour into the bowl and gently fold in along with the chopped walnuts, vanilla extract and the remaining chocolate chips. Mix until all the ingredients are combined, but be careful not to overmix.

5 Spread the mixture out in the prepared tin, pushing it to the edges, and bake for about 30 minutes.

6 When the mixture is risen and golden brown, remove from the oven. The centre of the brownie should still be quite firm to the touch but will be slightly soft. As it cools down it will become firmer.

7 Leave to cool slightly in the tin, then cut into 12 bars, or more if you prefer, when the brownie is completely cool.

Butterscotch Energy 469kcal/1961kJ; Protein 8.1g; Carbohydrate 48.7g, of which sugars 37.7g; Fat 28.3g, of which saturates 11.4g; Cholesterol 61mg; Calcium 182mg; Fibre 1g; Sodium 151mg.
Marbled Brownies Energy 259kcal/1083kJ; Protein 3.8g; Carbohydrate 28.8g, of which sugars 23.1g; Fat 15.1g, of which saturates 7.1g; Cholesterol 66mg; Calcium 42mg; Fibre 0.6g; Sodium 73mg.

Nutty Marshmallow and Chocolate Squares

Unashamedly sweet, with chocolate, marshmallows, cherries, nuts and coconut, this recipe is a favourite with children of all ages, and sweet-toothed adults too.

Makes 9

200g/7oz digestive biscuits
   (graham crackers)
90g/3¹/₂oz plain
   (semisweet) chocolate
200g/7oz mini coloured
   marshmallows
150g/5oz/1¹/₄ cups
   chopped walnuts
90g/3¹/₂oz/scant ¹/₂ cup glacé
   (candied) cherries, halved
50g/2oz/²/₃ cup sweetened
   desiccated (dry shredded)
   coconut
350g/12oz milk chocolate

1 Put the digestive biscuits in a plastic bag and, using a rolling pin, crush them until they are fairly small. Place them in a bowl.

2 Melt the plain chocolate in the microwave or in a heatproof bowl set over a pan of hot water. Pour the melted plain chocolate over the broken biscuits and stir well. Spread the mixture in the base of a 20cm/8in square shallow cake tin (pan).

3 Put the marshmallows, walnuts, cherries and coconut in a large bowl. Melt the milk chocolate in the microwave or in a heatproof bowl set over a pan of hot water.

4 Pour the melted milk chocolate over the marshmallow and nut mixture and toss together until almost everything is coated.

5 Spread the mixture over the chocolate base, but leave in chunky lumps – do not spread flat. Chill until set, then cut into squares or bars.

> **Variation**
> A variety of nuts can be used in this recipe instead of the walnuts – the choice is yours.

Very Low-fat Chocolate Brownies

If you ever need proof that you can still enjoy sweet treats even when you are on a low-fat diet, here it is. These brownies are not only tasty, but also very quick and easy to make.

Makes 16

90g/3¹/₂oz/³/₄ cup plain
   (all-purpose) flour
2.5ml/¹/₂ tsp baking powder
45ml/3 tbsp unsweetened
   cocoa powder
200g/7oz/1 cup caster
   (superfine) sugar
100ml/3¹/₂fl oz/scant ¹/₂ cup
   natural (plain) low-fat yogurt
2 eggs, beaten
5ml/1 tsp vanilla extract
25ml/1¹/₂ tbsp vegetable oil

1 Preheat the oven to 180°C/350°F/Gas 4. Line a 20cm/8in square cake tin (pan) with baking parchment.

2 Sift the flour, baking powder and cocoa powder into a large mixing bowl.

3 Stir in the caster sugar to the flour mixture, then beat in the natural yogurt, eggs, vanilla extract and vegetable oil until thoroughly combined.

4 Spoon the mixture into the prepared tin, filling it to the edges. Bake for about 25 minutes.

5 Remove the tin from the oven when the cake is just firm to the touch. Leave in the tin until cooled completely.

6 Using a sharp knife, cut into 16 squares, then remove from the tin using a metal spatula.

> **Variation**
> Try adding some dried fruits to the brownies. They will keep the fat content down while adding a delicious succulent flavour to the brownie. Mix in 75g/3oz/generous ¹/₂ cup of raisins, sultanas (golden raisins) or a similar quantity of finely chopped prunes or dates, in step 3.

Nutty Squares Energy 603kcal/2523kJ; Protein 8.6g; Carbohydrate 69.7g, of which sugars 53.2g; Fat 34.1g, of which saturates 14.7g; Cholesterol 19mg; Calcium 133mg; Fibre 2.5g; Sodium 179mg.
Low-fat Brownies Energy 101kcal/426kJ; Protein 4.6g; Carbohydrate 16.6g, of which sugars 10.8g; Fat 2.2g, of which saturates 1.2g; Cholesterol 0mg; Calcium 31mg; Fibre 2.8g; Sodium 167mg.

Oat, Date and Chocolate Brownies

These brownies are marvellous as a break-time treat. The secret of chewy, moist brownies is not to overcook them.

Makes 16
150g/5oz plain (semisweet) chocolate
50g/2oz/¼ cup butter
75g/3oz/scant 1 cup rolled oats
25g/1oz/3 tbsp wheatgerm
25g/1oz/⅓ cup milk powder
2.5ml/½ tsp baking powder
2.5ml/½ tsp salt
50g/2oz/½ cup chopped walnuts
50g/2oz/⅓ cup finely chopped dates
50g/2oz/¼ cup muscovado (molasses) sugar
5ml/1 tsp vanilla extract
2 eggs, beaten

1 Break the chocolate into a heatproof bowl and add the butter. Place over a pan of simmering water and stir until completely melted.

2 Cool the chocolate, stirring occasionally. Preheat the oven to 180°C/350°F/Gas 4. Grease and line a 20cm/8in square cake tin (pan).

3 Combine the oats, wheatgerm, milk powder and baking powder together in a bowl. Add the salt, walnuts, chopped dates and sugar, and mix well. Beat in the melted chocolate, vanilla and beaten eggs.

4 Pour the mixture into the cake tin, level the surface and bake in the oven for 20–25 minutes, or until firm around the edges yet still soft in the centre.

5 Cool the brownies in the tin, then chill in the refrigerator. When they are more solid, turn them out of the tin and cut into 16 squares.

Cook's Tip
When melting chocolate always make sure that the water in the pan does not touch the bowl, or it might bubble up the side of the bowl and splash into the chocolate, changing its texture.

Chunky White Chocolate and Coffee Brownies

Brownies – unlike cakes – should have a gooey texture, so take care not to overcook them. When ready, the mixture should still be slightly soft under the crust, but it will become firm as it cools.

Makes 12
25ml/1½ tbsp ground coffee
45ml/3 tbsp near-boiling water
300g/11oz plain (semisweet) chocolate, broken into pieces
225g/8oz/1 cup butter
225g/8oz/1 cup caster (superfine) sugar
3 eggs
75g/3oz/⅔ cup self-raising (self-rising) flour, sifted
225g/8oz white chocolate, chopped

1 Preheat the oven to 190°C/375°F/Gas 5. Grease and line the base of a 18 × 28cm/7 × 11in square cake tin (pan) with baking parchment.

2 Put the ground coffee in a bowl and pour the hot water over. Leave to infuse (steep) for 4 minutes, then strain through a sieve (strainer).

3 Put the plain chocolate and butter in a heatproof bowl over a pan of simmering water and stir occasionally until melted. Remove from the heat and cool for 5 minutes.

4 Mix the sugar and eggs together. Stir in the chocolate and butter mixture and the coffee. Stir in the sifted flour.

5 Fold in the white chocolate pieces and mix until just combined. Pour the mixture into the prepared tin, ensuring it is spread to the edges.

6 Bake for 45–50 minutes, or until just firm to the touch and the top is crusty. Leave to cool in the tin.

7 When the cake is completely cold, cut into 12 squares and remove from the tin.

Oat Brownies Energy 138kcal/577kJ; Protein 2.8g; Carbohydrate 13.3g, of which sugars 9.3g; Fat 8.6g, of which saturates 3.6g; Cholesterol 31mg; Calcium 32mg; Fibre 1g; Sodium 36mg.
Chunky Energy 480kcal/2005kJ; Protein 5.1g; Carbohydrate 51.4g, of which sugars 46.4g; Fat 29.7g, of which saturates 17.8g; Cholesterol 89mg; Calcium 88mg; Fibre 0.8g; Sodium 155mg.

Chocolate Cheesecake Brownies

A very dense chocolate brownie mixture is swirled with creamy cheesecake mixture to give a marbled effect. Cut into tiny squares for little mouthfuls of absolute heaven.

Makes 16

For the cheesecake mixture
1 egg
225g/8oz/1 cup full-fat
  cream cheese
50g/2oz/¼ cup caster
  (superfine) sugar
5ml/1 tsp vanilla extract

For the brownie mixture
115g/4oz dark (bittersweet)
  chocolate (minimum 70 per
  cent cocoa solids)
115g/4oz/½ cup unsalted
  (sweet) butter
150g/5oz/⅔ cup light muscovado
  (brown) sugar
2 eggs, beaten
50g/2oz/½ cup plain
  (all-purpose) flour

1 Preheat the oven to 160°C/325°F/Gas 3. Line the base and sides of a 20cm/8in cake tin (pan) with baking parchment.

2 To make the cheesecake mixture, beat the egg in a mixing bowl, then add the cream cheese, caster sugar and vanilla extract. Beat together until smooth and creamy.

3 To make the brownie mixture, melt the chocolate and butter together in the microwave or in a heatproof bowl set over a pan of gently simmering water. When the mixture is melted, remove from the heat, stir well, then add the sugar. Gradually pour in the beaten eggs, a little at a time, and beat well until thoroughly combined. Gently stir in the flour.

4 Spread two-thirds of the brownie mixture over the base of the prepared tin. Spread the cheesecake mixture on top, then spoon on the remaining brownie mixture in heaps. Using a metal skewer, swirl the two mixtures together to achieve a marbled effect.

5 Bake for 30–35 minutes, or until just set in the centre. Leave to cool in the tin, then cut into squares.

White Chocolate Brownies

These irresistible brownies are packed full of creamy white chocolate and juicy dried fruit. They are best served cut into very small portions as they are incredibly rich.

Makes 18
75g/3oz/6 tbsp unsalted
  (sweet) butter, diced
400g/14oz white
  chocolate, chopped

3 eggs
90g/3½oz/½ cup golden caster
  (superfine) sugar
10ml/2 tsp vanilla extract
90g/3½oz/¾ cup sultanas
  (golden raisins)
coarsely grated rind of 1 lemon,
  plus 15ml/1 tbsp juice
200g/7oz/1¾ cups plain
  (all-purpose) flour

1 Preheat the oven to 190°C/375°F/ Gas 5. Grease and line a 28 × 20cm/ 11 × 8in shallow rectangular baking tin (pan) with baking parchment.

2 Put the butter and 300g/11oz of the white chocolate in a heatproof bowl and melt over a pan of gently simmering water, stirring frequently until smooth.

3 Remove from the heat and beat in the eggs and sugar, then add the vanilla extract, sultanas, lemon rind and juice, and stir well to combine all the ingredients.

4 Sift in the flour and fold in until well combined. Mix in the remaining chocolate.

5 Tip the mixture into the prepared tin, ensuring it is spread into the corners. Bake for about 20 minutes.

6 Remove from the oven when slightly risen and the surface is only just turning golden. The centre should still be slightly soft as the brownie mixture will firm up a little as it cools down. Leave to cool completely in the tin.

7 Cut the brownies into about 18 small squares and remove from the tin.

Cheesecake Brownies Energy 228kcal/952kJ; Protein 2.6g; Carbohydrate 20.1g, of which sugars 17.7g; Fat 15.9g, of which saturates 9.5g; Cholesterol 72mg; Calcium 35mg; Fibre 0.3g; Sodium 103mg.
White Chocolate Brownies Energy 235kcal/984kJ; Protein 4.3g; Carbohydrate 30.3g, of which sugars 21.8g; Fat 11.6g, of which saturates 6.6g; Cholesterol 47mg; Calcium 88mg; Fibre 0.4g; Sodium 65mg.

Chocolate Dominoes

A recipe for children to eat rather than make, these fun bars are ideal for birthday parties, when you can match the spots on the dominoes to the children's ages.

Makes 16
175g/6oz/³/4 cup soft margarine
175g/6oz/generous ³/4 cup caster
 (superfine) sugar
150g/5oz/1¹/4 cups self-raising
 (self-rising) flour
25g/1oz/¹/4 cup unsweetened
 cocoa powder, sifted
3 eggs

For the topping
175g/6oz/³/4 cup butter
25g/1oz/¹/4 cup unsweetened
 cocoa powder
300g/11oz/2²/3 cups icing
 (confectioners') sugar
a few liquorice strips and
 115g/4oz packet candy-coated
 chocolate drops, to decorate

1 Preheat the oven to 180°C/350°F/Gas 4. Lightly brush an 18 × 28cm/7 × 11in rectangular baking tin (pan) with a little oil and line the base with baking parchment.

2 Put all the cake ingredients into a large mixing bowl and beat until smooth and creamy. Spoon the mixture evenly into the prepared cake tin, filling it to the edges and levelling the surface with a metal spatula.

3 Bake for 30 minutes, or until the cake springs back when pressed with the fingertips.

4 Cool in the tin for 5 minutes, then loosen the edges with a knife and transfer to a wire rack. Peel off the lining paper and leave the cake to cool completely. When cold, turn it out on to a chopping board.

5 To make the topping, place the butter in a bowl. Sift together the cocoa powder and the icing sugar into the bowl and beat until smooth. Spread the topping evenly over the cake with a metal spatula.

6 Cut the cake into 16 bars. Place a strip of liquorice across the middle of each bar, then decorate with candy-coated chocolate drops to make the domino spots.

Cranberry and Chocolate Squares

The flavour of the cranberries in these cake squares will add a pleasing tartness that perfectly complements the rich chocolate taste.

Makes 12
150g/5oz/1¹/4 cups self-raising
 (self-rising) flour, plus extra
 for dusting
115g/4oz/¹/2 cup unsalted
 (sweet) butter
60ml/4 tbsp unsweetened
 cocoa powder
225g/8oz/1 cup light muscovado
 (brown) sugar
2 eggs, beaten
115g/4oz/1 cup fresh or thawed
 frozen cranberries
75ml/5 tbsp coarsely grated plain
 (semisweet) chocolate,
 for sprinkling

For the topping
150ml/¹/4 pint/²/3 cup sour cream
75g/3oz/ scant ¹/2 cup caster
 (superfine) sugar
30ml/2 tbsp self-raising
 (self-rising) flour
50g/2oz/¹/4 cup soft margarine
1 egg, beaten
2.5ml/¹/2 tsp vanilla extract

1 Preheat the oven to 180°C/350°F/Gas 4. Lightly grease a 27 × 18cm/10¹/2 × 7in rectangular cake tin (pan) and dust lightly with flour.

2 Combine the butter, cocoa powder and sugar in a pan and stir over a low heat until melted and smooth.

3 Remove the melted mixture from the heat and stir in the flour and eggs, beating until thoroughly mixed.

4 Add in the cranberries, mixing until thoroughly combined. Spread the mixture in the prepared tin, ensuring it is filled to the corners.

5 Make the topping by mixing all the ingredients in a large bowl. Beat until smooth, then spread over the base.

6 Sprinkle with the grated chocolate and bake for 40–45 minutes, or until risen and firm. Cool in the tin for 10 minutes, then cut neatly into 12 squares. Remove from the tin and cool completely on a wire rack.

Dominoes Energy 335kcal/1400kJ; Protein 2.9g; Carbohydrate 38.8g, of which sugars 31.3g; Fat 19.8g, of which saturates 6.4g; Cholesterol 59mg; Calcium 41mg; Fibre 0.7g; Sodium 199mg.
Cranberry Squares Energy 343kcal/1439kJ; Protein 4.8g; Carbohydrate 42.9g, of which sugars 30.8g; Fat 18.2g, of which saturates 8.7g; Cholesterol 76mg; Calcium 63mg; Fibre 1.4g; Sodium 164mg.

White Chocolate Slices

If you wish, toasted and skinned hazelnuts can be substituted for the macadamia nuts in the topping for these white chocolate slices.

Serves 12
150g/5oz/1 1/4 cups plain
(all-purpose) flour
2.5ml/1/2 tsp baking powder
a pinch of salt
175g/6oz fine quality white
chocolate, chopped
90g/3 1/2oz/1/2 cup caster
(superfine) sugar

115g/4oz/1/2 cup unsalted
(sweet) butter, cut into pieces
2 eggs, lightly beaten
5ml/1 tsp vanilla extract
175g/6oz/1 cup plain (semisweet)
chocolate chips

For the topping
200g/7oz milk chocolate,
chopped
215g/7 1/2oz/1 1/3 cups unsalted
macadamia nuts, chopped

1 Preheat the oven to 180°C/350°F/Gas 4. Grease a 23cm/9in springform tin (pan). Sift together the flour, baking powder and salt, and set aside.

2 In a medium pan over a medium heat, melt the white chocolate, sugar and butter until smooth, stirring frequently. Cool slightly, then beat in the eggs and vanilla. Stir in the chocolate chips. Spread evenly in the prepared tin, smoothing the top.

3 Bake for 20–25 minutes, or until a cocktail stick (toothpick) inserted 5cm/2in from the side of the tin comes out clean. Remove from the oven to a heatproof surface, sprinkle chopped milk chocolate over the surface (avoid touching the side of tin) and return to the oven for 1 minute.

4 Remove from the oven and, using the back of a spoon, gently spread out the softened chocolate. Sprinkle with the macadamia nuts and gently press into the chocolate. Cool on a wire rack for 30 minutes, and then chill for 1 hour.

5 Run a sharp knife around the side of the tin to loosen, then unclip and remove. Cut the brownies into thin wedges to serve.

Almond-scented Chocolate Cherry Wedges

These cookies are a chocoholic's dream, and use the very best quality chocolate. Erratically shaped, they are packed with crunchy cookies, juicy raisins and munchy nuts.

Makes about 15
50g/2oz ratafia biscuits (almond
macaroons) or small amaretti
90g/3 1/2oz shortcake
biscuits (cookies)

150g/5oz/1 cup jumbo raisins
50g/2oz/1/4 cup undyed glacé
(candied) cherries, quartered
450g/1lb dark (bittersweet)
chocolate (minimum
70 per cent cocoa solids)
90g/3 1/2oz/7 tbsp unsalted
(sweet) butter, diced
30ml/2 tbsp amaretto
liqueur (optional)
25g/1oz/1/4 cup toasted flaked
(sliced) almonds

1 Line a baking sheet with baking parchment. Put the ratafia biscuits or amaretti in a large bowl. Leave half whole and break the remainder into coarse pieces. Break each of the shortcake biscuits into three or four jagged pieces and add to the bowl. Add the raisins and cherries and toss lightly together.

2 Melt the chocolate and butter with the liqueur, if using, in a heatproof bowl over a pan of hot water. When melted, remove from the heat and stir until combined. Set aside to cool slightly.

3 Pour the chocolate over the biscuit mixture and stir together until combined. Spread out over the prepared baking sheet. Sprinkle over the almonds and push them in at angles so they stick well to the chocolate-coated biscuits.

4 When the mixture is cold and set, cut or break into crazy shapes, such as long thin triangles or short stumpy squares.

Cook's Tip
If you cannot find undyed glacé cherries in the supermarket, look for them in your local delicatessen instead.

White Slices Energy 526kcal/2190kJ; Protein 6.3g; Carbohydrate 43.8g, of which sugars 34g; Fat 37.4g, of which saturates 16.1g; Cholesterol 64mg; Calcium 82mg; Fibre 2.1g; Sodium 154mg.
Cherry Wedges Energy 288kcal/1206kJ; Protein 2.7g; Carbohydrate 34.6g, of which sugars 29.7g; Fat 16.4g, of which saturates 9.5g; Cholesterol 20mg; Calcium 31mg; Fibre 1.3g; Sodium 75mg.

Bitter Chocolate and Pistachio Wedges

These are rich and grainy in texture, with a delicious bitter chocolate flavour. They go well with vanilla ice cream and are good with bananas and custard.

Makes 16
200g/7oz/scant 1 cup unsalted
  (sweet) butter, at room
  temperature, diced
90g/3½oz/½ cup golden caster
  (superfine) sugar
250g/9oz/2¼ cups plain
  (all-purpose) flour
50g/2oz/½ cup unsweetened
  cocoa powder
25g/1oz/¼ cup shelled pistachio
  nuts, finely chopped
unsweetened cocoa powder,
  for dusting

1 Preheat the oven to 180°C/350°F/Gas 4 and line a 23cm/9in round sandwich tin (layer pan) with baking parchment.

2 Beat the butter and sugar until light and creamy. Sift the flour and cocoa powder, then add the flour mixture to the butter and work in with your hands until the mixture is smooth. Knead until soft and pliable, then press into the prepared tin.

3 Using the back of a tablespoon, spread the mixture evenly in the tin. Sprinkle the pistachio nuts over the top and press in gently. Prick with a fork, then mark into 16 segments using a round-bladed knife.

4 Bake for 15–20 minutes. Do not allow to brown at all or the wedges will taste bitter.

5 Remove the tin from the oven and dust the wedges with cocoa powder. Cut through the marked sections with a round-bladed knife and leave to cool completely before removing from the tin and serving.

> **Variation**
> Try using almonds or hazelnuts instead of pistachio nuts.

Rocky Road Wedges

This is a gluten-free recipe for chocolate and marshmallow treats. These crumbly chocolate wedges contain home-made popcorn in place of broken cookies, which are the main ingredient in no-bake cookies. This recipe uses an orange-flavoured bar, but any chocolate can be used.

Makes 8
15ml/1 tbsp vegetable oil
25g/1oz/2½ tbsp popping corn
150g/5oz orange-flavoured plain
  (semisweet) chocolate
25g/1oz/2 tbsp unsalted
  (sweet) butter, diced
75g/3oz soft vanilla fudge, diced
icing (confectioners') sugar,
  for dusting

1 Heat the oil in a heavy pan. Add the popping corn, cover with a lid and heat, shaking the pan once or twice, until the popping noises die down. (It is important not to lift the lid until the popping stops.)

2 Remove the pan from the heat and leave for about 30 seconds before removing the lid. Be careful, as there may be quite a lot of steam trapped inside. Transfer the popcorn to a bowl and leave to cool for about 5 minutes.

3 Meanwhile, line the base of an 18cm/7in sandwich tin (pan) with baking parchment.

4 Once cooled, tip the corn into a plastic bag and tap with a rolling pin to break up into small pieces.

5 Break the chocolate into a heatproof bowl. Add the butter and rest the bowl over a pan of gently simmering water. Stir frequently until melted. Remove the bowl from the heat and leave to cool for 2 minutes.

6 Stir the popcorn and fudge into the chocolate until well coated, then turn the mixture into the tin and press down firmly in an even layer. Leave to set for about 30 minutes.

7 Turn the cookie out on to a board and cut into eight wedges. Serve lightly dusted with sugar.

Pistachio Wedges Energy 188kcal/783kJ; Protein 2.4g; Carbohydrate 18.6g, of which sugars 6.3g; Fat 12g, of which saturates 7.1g; Cholesterol 27mg; Calcium 33mg; Fibre 1g; Sodium 115mg.
Rocky Road Energy 191kcal/798kJ; Protein 1.5g; Carbohydrate 21g, of which sugars 19.3g; Fat 11.8g, of which saturates 5.9g; Cholesterol 11mg; Calcium 19mg; Fibre 0.5g; Sodium 33mg.

Chocolate and Coconut Slices

These are easier to slice if
they are chilled overnight.

Makes 24
175g/6oz digestive biscuits
  (graham crackers)
50g/2oz/¼ cup caster
  (superfine) sugar
a pinch of salt

115g/4oz/½ cup butter or
  margarine, melted
75g/3oz/1 cup desiccated (dry
  unsweetened shredded) coconut
250g/9oz plain (semisweet)
  chocolate chips
250ml/8fl oz/1 cup sweetened
  condensed milk
115g/4oz/1 cup chopped walnuts

1 Preheat the oven to 180°C/350°F/Gas 4. Put the digestive
biscuits in a plastic bag and, using a rolling pin, crush them until
they are fairly small.

2 In a bowl, combine the crushed digestive biscuits, sugar, salt
and butter or margarine. Mix the ingredients until thoroughly
combined. Press the mixture evenly over the base of an
ungreased 33 × 23cm/13 × 9in baking tin (pan).

3 Sprinkle the desiccated coconut over the cookie base, then
sprinkle over the chocolate chips.

4 Pour the condensed milk evenly over the chocolate chips,
spreading to the edges of the tin with a metal spatula. Sprinkle
the chopped walnuts on top.

5 Bake in the oven for 30 minutes, until just firm to the touch
and golden brown.

6 Leave in the tin to cool slightly before turning out on to a
board. Leave to cool completely before cutting into 24 slices.

> **Variations**
> • Try substituting 75g/3oz ginger nut biscuits (gingersnaps) for
> half the digestive biscuits.
> • Other nuts can be used in place of the walnuts, such as
> pecans, hazelnuts or almonds.

White Chocolate Macadamia Slices

Nutty, fruity and chocolatey
slices – what more could
anybody want?

Makes 16
150g/5oz/1¼ cups macadamia
  nuts, blanched almonds
  or hazelnuts
400g/14oz white chocolate,
  broken into squares

115g/4oz/½ cup ready-to-eat
  dried apricots
75g/3oz/6 tbsp unsalted
  (sweet) butter
5ml/1 tsp vanilla extract
3 eggs
150g/5oz/generous ½ cup light
  muscovado (brown) sugar
115g/4oz/1 cup self-raising
  (self-rising) flour

1 Preheat the oven to 190°C/375°F/Gas 5. Lightly grease two
20cm/8in round sandwich cake tins (layer pans) and line the
base of each with baking parchment.

2 Roughly chop the nuts and half the white chocolate, making
sure that the pieces are more or less the same size, then use
scissors to cut the apricots to similar size pieces. Set aside.

3 In a heatproof bowl over a pan of barely simmering water,
add the remaining white chocolate with the butter, stirring until
melted and smooth. Remove from the heat and stir in the
vanilla extract.

4 Whisk the eggs and sugar together in a mixing bowl until
thick and pale. Pour in the melted chocolate mixture, whisking
constantly until well combined.

5 Sift the flour over the mixture and fold it in evenly, ensuring
that all the ingredients are well mixed.

6 Add the nuts, chopped white chocolate and chopped dried
apricots to the mixture, stirring to combine.

7 Spoon the mixture into the tins, filling the corners. Level the
tops of the mixtures with a metal spatula. Bake for 30–35
minutes, or until the top is firm to the touch, crusty and golden
brown. Leave to cool in the tins before cutting each cake into
eight slices.

Coconut Slices Energy 217kcal/907kJ; Protein 2.8g; Carbohydrate 20g, of which sugars 15.8g; Fat 14.6g, of which saturates 7.5g; Cholesterol 18mg; Calcium 48mg; Fibre 1g; Sodium 89mg.
Macadamia Slices Energy 317kcal/1326kJ; Protein 4.8g; Carbohydrate 31.6g, of which sugars 26g; Fat 20g, of which saturates 8.4g; Cholesterol 46mg; Calcium 95mg; Fibre 0.9g; Sodium 97mg.

Chocolate Salami

This after-dinner sweetmeat resembles a salami in shape, hence its curious name – although, of course, the flavour is somewhat different. It is very rich and will serve a lot of people. Slice it very thinly and serve with espresso coffee and amaretto liqueur.

Makes 10–12
24 Petit Beurre cookies, broken into pieces

350g/12oz dark (bittersweet) or plain (semisweet) chocolate, broken into squares
225g/8oz/1 cup unsalted (sweet) butter, softened
60ml/4 tbsp amaretto liqueur
2 egg yolks
50g/2oz/¹⁄₂ cup flaked (sliced) almonds, lightly toasted and thinly shredded lengthways
25g/1oz/¹⁄₄ cup ground almonds

1 Place the cookies in a food processor and process until crushed into coarse crumbs. Place the chocolate in a large heatproof bowl over a pan of barely simmering water, add a small knob (pat) of the butter and all the liqueur, and heat, stirring, until the chocolate melts. Remove from the heat.

2 Leave the chocolate to cool for a minute, then stir in the egg yolks, followed by the remaining butter, a little at a time. Add in most of the crushed cookies, reserving a handful, and mix well. Stir in the almonds. Leave the mixture to cool for about 1 hour.

3 Process the remaining crushed cookies in the food processor until finely ground. Transfer to a bowl and mix with the ground almonds. Cover and set aside until you are ready to serve.

4 Turn the chocolate and cookie mixture on to a sheet of lightly oiled baking parchment, then shape into a 35cm/14in long sausage with a metal spatula, tapering the ends slightly so the roll resembles a salami. Wrap securely in the paper and freeze the roll for at least 4 hours, until solid.

5 Spread the finely ground cookies and almonds out on baking parchment and roll the 'salami' in them until coated. Leave to stand on a board for about 1 hour before serving in slices.

Marbled Caramel Chocolate Slice

This classic recipe is made even more special here with a decorative marbled topping swirled into the chocolate.

Makes about 24
250g/9oz/2¹⁄₄ cups plain (all-purpose) flour
75g/3oz/scant ¹⁄₂ cup caster (superfine) sugar
175g/6oz/³⁄₄ cup unsalted (sweet) butter, softened

For the filling
90g/3¹⁄₂oz/7 tbsp unsalted (sweet) butter, diced
90g/3¹⁄₂oz/scant ¹⁄₂ cup light muscovado (brown) sugar
2 x 400g/14oz cans evaporated milk

For the topping
90g/3¹⁄₂oz plain (semisweet) chocolate
90g/3¹⁄₂oz milk chocolate
50g/2oz white chocolate

1 Preheat the oven to 180°C/350°F/Gas 4. Lightly grease a 33 × 23cm/13 × 9in Swiss roll tin (jelly roll pan) and line with baking parchment. Put the flour and sugar in a bowl and rub in the butter until the mixture resembles breadcrumbs, then form into a soft dough.

2 Press the dough over the base of the tin. Prick all over with a fork and bake for about 20 minutes, or until firm to the touch and very light brown. Set aside and leave in the tin to cool.

3 Make the filling. Put the butter, muscovado sugar and milk in a pan and heat gently, stirring, until the sugar has dissolved. Simmer the mixture very gently, stirring constantly, for about 5–10 minutes, or until it has thickened and has turned a caramel colour. Remove from the heat.

4 Pour the filling mixture over the pastry base, spread evenly, then leave until cold.

5 Make the topping. Melt each type of chocolate separately in a microwave or in a heatproof bowl set over hot water. Spoon lines of plain and milk chocolate over the set caramel filling.

6 Add small spoonfuls of white chocolate. Use a skewer to form a marbled effect on the topping. Leave to cool until set.

Marbled Slice Energy 305kcal/1279kJ; Protein 4.5g; Carbohydrate 39.8g, of which sugars 31.8g; Fat 15.3g, of which saturates 9.5g; Cholesterol 36mg; Calcium 125mg; Fibre 0.5g; Sodium 117mg.
Salami Energy 453kcal/1885kJ; Protein 4.5g; Carbohydrate 36.6g, of which sugars 26.9g; Fat 32.3g, of which saturates 16.8g; Cholesterol 96mg; Calcium 47mg; Fibre 1.4g; Sodium 173mg.

Rich Chocolate Cookie Slice

These rich, dark chocolate refrigerator cookies are perfect when served with strong coffee, either as a mid-morning treat or even in place of dessert. They are always very popular, so don't expect them to last for long.

Makes about 10
275g/10oz fruit and nut plain (semisweet) chocolate
130g/4¹⁄₂oz/¹⁄₂ cup unsalted (sweet) butter, diced
90g/3¹⁄₂oz digestive biscuits (graham crackers)
90g/3¹⁄₂oz white chocolate

1 Grease and line the base and sides of a 450g/1lb loaf tin (pan) with baking parchment.

2 Break the fruit and nut chocolate into even pieces and place them in a heatproof bowl along with the butter.

3 Set the bowl over a pan of simmering water and stir gently until melted. Remove the bowl from the heat and leave to cool for 20 minutes.

4 Break the digestive biscuits into small pieces with your fingers. Finely chop the white chocolate.

5 Stir the broken biscuits and white chocolate into the cooled, melted fruit and nut chocolate until combined.

6 Turn the mixture into the prepared tin and pack down gently. Chill for 2 hours, or until set.

7 To serve, turn out the mixture and remove the lining paper. Cut into slices with a sharp knife.

> **Variation**
> *You can use this simple basic recipe to create all kinds of variations. Try different kinds of chocolate, such as ginger, hazelnut, honey and almond, peanut or mocha. You can also experiment with different kinds of biscuits or cookies.*

Chocolate Nut Slice

Children of all ages will love this combination of broken cookies, chocolate and nuts. Although the unsliced bar looks small, it's very rich so is best sliced very thinly. If you have any other plain cookies in the cupboard, you can use them instead of the rich tea, with equally good results.

Makes 10
225g/8oz milk chocolate
40g/1¹⁄₂oz/3 tbsp unsalted (sweet) butter, diced
75g/3oz rich tea biscuits (cookies)
50g/2oz/¹⁄₂ cup flaked (sliced) almonds
75g/3oz plain (semisweet) or white chocolate, roughly chopped
icing (confectioners') sugar, for dusting

1 Break the milk chocolate into pieces and place in a heatproof bowl with the butter. Rest the bowl over a pan of simmering water and stir frequently until melted.

2 Meanwhile, dampen a 450g/1lb loaf tin (pan) and line the base and sides with clear film (plastic wrap). Don't worry about smoothing out the creases in the film.

3 When the chocolate has melted, remove it from the heat and leave for 5 minutes until slightly cooled.

4 Break the biscuits into small pieces, then stir into the melted chocolate with the almonds. Add the chopped chocolate to the bowl and fold in quickly and lightly.

5 Turn the mixture into the tin and pack down with a fork. Tap the base of the tin gently on the work surface. Chill for 2 hours until set.

6 To serve, turn the chocolate loaf on to a board and peel away the clear film. Dust lightly with icing sugar and slice thinly.

> **Variation**
> *Use whatever biscuits or cookies you have available. To add a ginger taste, use ginger nut biscuits (gingersnaps).*

Cookie Slice Energy 326kcal/1361kJ; Protein 2.7g; Carbohydrate 29g, of which sugars 23.8g; Fat 23g, of which saturates 13.9g; Cholesterol 33mg; Calcium 44mg; Fibre 0.9g; Sodium 144mg.
Nut Slice Energy 248kcal/1034kJ; Protein 3.7g; Carbohydrate 23.5g, of which sugars 19.4g; Fat 16.1g, of which saturates 8.2g; Cholesterol 16mg; Calcium 74mg; Fibre 0.9g; Sodium 75mg.

Double Chocolate Slices

These delicious gluten-free cookies have a smooth chocolate base, topped with a mint-flavoured cream and drizzles of melted chocolate. Perfect for a tea-time treat – or at any time of day.

Makes 12
200g/7oz/1¾ cups
  gluten-free flour
25g/1oz/¼ cup unsweetened
  cocoa powder

150g/5oz/10 tbsp unsalted (sweet)
  butter, cut into small pieces
75g/3oz/⅔ cup icing
  (confectioners') sugar

For the topping
75g/3oz white chocolate
  mint crisps
50g/2oz/¼ cup unsalted (sweet)
  butter, softened
90g/3½oz/scant 1 cup icing
  (confectioners') sugar
50g/2oz milk chocolate

1 Preheat the oven to 180°C/350°F/Gas 4. Grease an 18cm/7in square shallow baking tin (pan) and line with a strip of baking parchment that comes up over two opposite sides. This will make it easier to remove the cookie base from the tin after baking.

2 Put the flour and cocoa powder into a food processor and add the pieces of butter. Process briefly until the mixture resembles fine breadcrumbs. Add the icing sugar and mix briefly again to form a smooth soft dough.

3 Turn the flour mixture into the prepared tin and gently press out to the edges with your fingers to make an even layer. Bake for 25 minutes, then remove from the oven and leave the base to cool completely in the tin.

4 To make the topping, put the chocolate mint crisps in a plastic bag and tap firmly with a rolling pin until crushed. Beat the butter and sugar together until creamy, then beat in the crushed chocolate mint crisps. Spread the mixture over the cookie base.

5 Melt the milk chocolate in a small heatproof bowl set over a pan of hot water. Lift the cookie base out of the tin; remove the paper. Using a teaspoon, drizzle the melted chocolate over the topping. Leave to set, then cut into squares.

Chilled Chocolate and Date Slice

This richly flavoured chocolate and date dessert is wonderful served in wedges, accompanied by fresh orange segments.

Serves 6–8
115g/4oz/½ cup unsalted
  (sweet) butter, melted
225g/8oz ginger nut biscuits
  (gingersnaps) finely crushed
50g/2oz/⅔ cup stale sponge
  cake crumbs
75ml/5 tbsp orange juice

115g/4oz/⅔ cup stoned
  (pitted) dates
25g/1oz/¼ cup finely
  chopped nuts
175g/6oz dark (bittersweet)
  chocolate
300ml/½ pint/1¼ cups
  whipping cream
grated chocolate and icing
  (confectioners') sugar,
  to decorate
single (light) cream, to serve
  (optional)

1 Mix the butter and ginger biscuit crumbs in a bowl, then press the mixture on to the sides and base of an 18cm/7in loose-based flan tin (pan). Chill while making the filling.

2 Put the cake crumbs in a bowl. Pour over 60ml/4 tbsp of the orange juice, stir well with a wooden spoon and leave to soak. Put the dates in a pan and add the remaining orange juice. Warm the mixture over a low heat. Mash the warm dates thoroughly and stir in the cake crumbs, with the chopped nuts.

3 Mix the chocolate with 60ml/4 tbsp of the cream in a heatproof bowl. Place the bowl over a pan of barely simmering water and stir occasionally until melted. In a separate bowl, whip the rest of the cream to soft peaks, then fold in the melted chocolate.

4 Add the cooled date, crumb and nut mixture to the cream and chocolate and mix lightly but thoroughly. Pour into the tin. Using a spatula, level the mixture. Chill until just set, then mark the tart into portions, using a sharp knife dipped in hot water. Return the tart to the refrigerator and chill until firm.

5 To decorate, sprinkle the grated chocolate over the surface and dust with icing sugar. Serve with cream, if you wish.

Double Slices Energy 299kcal/1248kJ; Protein 2.3g; Carbohydrate 34.4g, of which sugars 20.8g; Fat 17.3g, of which saturates 10.8g; Cholesterol 37mg; Calcium 28mg; Fibre 0.8g; Sodium 126mg.
Date Slice Energy 575kcal/2394kJ; Protein 5.1g; Carbohydrate 51.3g, of which sugars 37.5g; Fat 40.2g, of which saturates 22.8g; Cholesterol 78mg; Calcium 87mg; Fibre 1.8g; Sodium 214mg.

Chocolate-topped Date Crunch

A tasty mixture of dried fruit, syrup and chocolate is guaranteed to be a success with the younger members of the family – and they will need to keep an eye on the adults, too.

Makes 24

225g/8oz digestive biscuits (graham crackers)

75g/3oz/⅓ cup butter
30ml/2 tbsp golden (light corn) syrup
75g/3oz/½ cup finely chopped pitted dried dates
75g/3oz/⅔ cup sultanas (golden raisins)
150g/5oz milk or plain (semisweet) chocolate, chopped into small pieces

1 Line an 18cm/7in square shallow cake tin (pan) with foil. Put the biscuits in a plastic bag, keep the opening sealed and crush coarsely with a rolling pin.

2 Gently heat the butter and syrup together in a small pan until the butter has melted.

3 Stir the crushed biscuits, dates and sultanas into the butter and syrup mixture and mix well with a wooden spoon until evenly combined.

4 Spoon into the prepared tin, spreading it out evenly, press flat with the back of the spoon and chill for 1 hour.

5 Melt the chocolate in a heatproof bowl set over a pan of simmering water, stirring until smooth. Remove from the heat and spoon over the cookie mixture, spreading evenly with a metal spatula. Chill until set.

6 Lift the foil out of the cake tin and peel away. Cut the crunch into 24 pieces to serve.

Variation
You could drizzle 75g/3oz each melted white and dark (bittersweet) chocolate over the topping.

Fudge-nut Chocolate Bars

Although your kids will be desperate to tuck into these fudgy treats, it's well worth chilling them for a few hours before slicing so that they can be easily cut into neat pieces.

Makes 16

150g/5oz/10 tbsp unsalted (sweet) butter, chilled and diced
250g/9oz/2¼ cups plain (all-purpose) flour

75g/3oz/scant ½ cup caster (superfine) sugar

For the topping
150g/5oz milk chocolate, broken into pieces
40g/1½oz/3 tbsp unsalted (sweet) butter
400g/14oz can sweetened condensed milk
50g/2oz/½ cup chopped nuts

1 Preheat the oven to 160°C/325°F/Gas 3. Lightly grease a 28 × 18cm/11 × 7in shallow baking tin (pan).

2 Put the butter and flour in a food processor and process until the mixture resembles fine breadcrumbs.

3 Add the sugar to the flour mixture and process again until the mixture starts to cling together.

4 Tip the mixture into the baking tin and spread out with the back of a wooden spoon to fill the base in an even layer.

5 Bake for 35–40 minutes, or until the surface of the cookie base is very lightly coloured.

6 To make the topping, put the chocolate in a heavy pan with the butter and the condensed milk. Heat gently, stirring occasionally, until the chocolate and butter have melted, then increase the heat and cook, stirring, for 3–5 minutes until the mixture starts to thicken.

7 Add the chopped nuts to the pan and pour the mixture over the cookie base, spreading it in an even layer with a metal spatula. Leave to cool, then chill for at least 2 hours until firm. Serve cut into bars.

Date Crunch Energy 120kcal/503kJ; Protein 1.3g; Carbohydrate 15.3g, of which sugars 10.1g; Fat 6.4g, of which saturates 3.6g; Cholesterol 12mg; Calcium 27mg; Fibre 0.4g; Sodium 85mg.
Fudge Bars Energy 315kcal/1317kJ; Protein 4.9g; Carbohydrate 36.6g, of which sugars 24.7g; Fat 17.5g, of which saturates 9.7g; Cholesterol 37mg; Calcium 123mg; Fibre 0.7g; Sodium 116mg.

Chocolate and Toffee Bars

The irresistible combination of chocolate, toffee and nuts will ensure that these bars go down a treat at any time of day or night. It is possible to use white chocolate instead of plain, if you prefer.

Makes 32
350g/12oz/2 cups soft light
   brown sugar
450g/1lb/2 cups butter or
   margarine, softened
2 egg yolks
7.5ml/1½ tsp vanilla extract
450g/1lb/4 cups plain
   (all-purpose) or wholemeal
   (whole-wheat) flour
2.5ml/½ tsp salt
175g/6oz plain (semisweet)
   chocolate, broken into squares
115g/4oz/1 cup walnuts or pecan
   nuts, chopped

1 Preheat the oven to 180°C/350°F/Gas 4. Lightly grease a 33 × 23 × 5cm/13 × 9 × 2in baking tin (pan)

2 Beat the sugar and butter or margarine in a large mixing bowl until light and fluffy. Beat in the egg yolks and vanilla extract, then stir in the flour and salt to make a soft dough.

3 Spread the dough evenly into the prepared tin. Level the surface. Bake for 25–30 minutes, until lightly browned. The texture will be soft.

4 Remove the bake from the oven and immediately place the broken chocolate on top. Set aside until the chocolate is soft, then spread it out with a metal spatula. Sprinkle with the chopped nuts.

5 While the bake is still warm, cut it into 5 × 4cm/2 × 1½in bars. Remove from the tin and leave to cool completely on a wire rack.

> **Cook's Tip**
> If you find that the chocolate isn't softening enough to be easily spread over the base, then put the tin back in the oven for a minute or two to melt the chocolate a little.

Chocolate Raspberry Macaroon Bars

Any seedless preserve, such as strawberry or apricot, can be substituted for the raspberry in this fruity macaroon recipe.

Makes 16–18
115g/4oz/½ cup unsalted
   (sweet) butter, softened
50g/2oz/½ cup icing
   (confectioners') sugar
25g/1oz/¼ cup unsweetened
   cocoa powder
a pinch of salt
5ml/1 tsp almond extract
115g/4oz/1 cup plain
   (all-purpose) flour

For the topping
150g/5oz/½ cup seedless
   raspberry preserve
15ml/1 tbsp raspberry
   flavour liqueur
175g/6oz/1 cup milk
   chocolate chips
175g/6oz/1½ cups finely
   ground almonds
4 egg whites
a pinch of salt
200g/7oz/1 cup caster
   (superfine) sugar
2.5ml/½ tsp almond extract
50g/2oz/½ cup flaked
   (sliced) almonds

1 Preheat the oven to 160°C/325°F/Gas 3. Line a 23 × 33cm/ 9 × 13in baking tin (pan) with foil and then grease the foil. Beat together the butter, sugar, cocoa and salt until blended. Beat in the almond extract and flour to make a crumbly dough.

2 Turn the dough into the tin and smooth the surface. Prick all over with a fork. Bake for 20 minutes, or until just set. Remove the tin from the oven and increase the temperature to 190°C/375°F/Gas 5.

3 To make the topping, combine the raspberry preserve and liqueur. Spread over the cooked crust, then sprinkle with the chocolate chips.

4 In a food processor fitted with a metal blade, process the almonds, egg whites, salt, caster sugar and almond extract. Pour this mixture over the jam layer, spreading evenly. Sprinkle with almonds.

5 Bake for 20–25 minutes, or until the top is golden and puffed. Cool in the tin for 20 minutes. Carefully remove from the tin and cool completely. Peel off the foil and cut into bars.

Toffee Bars Energy 252kcal/1053kJ; Protein 2.4g; Carbohydrate 26g, of which sugars 15.2g; Fat 16.1g, of which saturates 8.6g; Cholesterol 43mg; Calcium 35mg; Fibre 0.7g; Sodium 87mg.
Macaroon Bars Energy 266kcal/1115kJ; Protein 4.5g; Carbohydrate 32.1g, of which sugars 26.6g; Fat 14.1g, of which saturates 5.7g; Cholesterol 16mg; Calcium 66mg; Fibre 1.2g; Sodium 79mg.

Chunky Chocolate Bars

Chocolate is combined here with dried fruit and nuts to create these heavenly bars.

Makes 12

350g/12oz plain (semisweet) chocolate, chopped into small pieces
115g/4oz/½ cup unsalted (sweet) butter
400g/14oz can condensed milk

225g/8oz digestive biscuits (graham crackers), broken
50g/2oz/⅓ cup raisins
115g/4oz ready-to-eat dried peaches, roughly chopped
50g/2oz/½ cup hazelnuts or pecan nuts, roughly chopped

1 Line a 28 × 18cm/11 × 7in cake tin (pan) with clear film (plastic wrap).

2 Melt the chocolate and butter together in a large heatproof bowl or double boiler set over a pan of simmering water. Stir until well melted and smooth.

3 Pour the condensed milk into the chocolate and butter mixture. Beat with a wooden spoon until creamy.

4 Add the broken biscuits, raisins, chopped peaches and hazelnuts or pecans. Mix well until all the ingredients are coated in the rich chocolate sauce.

5 Tip the mixture into the prepared tin, making sure it is pressed well into the corners. Leave the top craggy. Cool, then chill until set.

6 Lift the cake out of the tin using the clear film and then peel off the film. Cut into 12 bars and serve immediately.

Variations
You can make these chunky bars with a variety of fruits. Try making with dried apricots instead of the peaches, or use glacé (candied) cherries, prunes, or dates if you prefer. Preserved stem ginger, in place of the fruit, would make a tasty gingery bar.

Chocolate Walnut Bars

These delicious double-decker bars should be stored in the refrigerator in an airtight container.

Makes 24

50g/2oz/⅓ cup walnuts
55g/2¼oz/generous ¼ cup caster (superfine) sugar
100g/3¾oz/scant 1 cup plain (all-purpose) flour, sifted
90g/3½oz/7 tbsp cold unsalted (sweet) butter, cut into pieces

For the topping
25g/1oz/2 tbsp unsalted (sweet) butter
90ml/6 tbsp water
25g/1oz/¼ cup unsweetened cocoa powder
90g/3½oz/½ cup caster (superfine) sugar
5ml/1 tsp vanilla extract
1.5ml/¼ tsp salt
2 eggs
icing (confectioners') sugar, for dusting

1 Preheat the oven to 180°C/350°F/Gas 4. Grease the base and sides of a 20cm/8in square baking tin (pan).

2 Grind the walnuts with a few tablespoons of the caster sugar in a food processor or blender. In a bowl, combine the ground walnuts, remaining sugar and the flour.

3 Rub in the butter using your fingertips or a biscuit (cookie) cutter until the mixture resembles coarse breadcrumbs. Alternatively, use a food processor.

4 Pat the walnut mixture evenly into the base of the baking tin. Bake for 25 minutes.

5 To make the topping, gently melt the butter with the water in a pan. Whisk in the cocoa powder and sugar. Remove from the heat, stir in the vanilla extract and salt until well combined, then cool for 5 minutes.

6 Whisk in the eggs until blended. Pour the topping over the baked crust.

7 Return to the oven and bake until set, about 20 minutes. Set the tin on a wire rack to cool, then cut into bars and dust with icing sugar before serving.

Chunky Bars Energy 462kcal/1935kJ; Protein 6.3g; Carbohydrate 53.7g, of which sugars 43g; Fat 26.2g, of which saturates 13.9g; Cholesterol 42mg; Calcium 135mg; Fibre 1.9g; Sodium 220mg.
Walnut Bars Energy 97kcal/407kJ; Protein 1.5g; Carbohydrate 9.8g, of which sugars 6.5g; Fat 6.1g, of which saturates 2.9g; Cholesterol 26mg; Calcium 16mg; Fibre 0.3g; Sodium 45mg.

Chocolate Butterscotch Bars

The blend of chocolate and butterscotch makes these bars exquisitely chewy.

Makes 24

225g/8oz/2 cups plain (all-purpose) flour
2.5ml/½ tsp baking powder
150g/5oz plain (semisweet) chocolate, chopped
115g/4oz/½ cup unsalted (sweet) butter, diced
50g/2oz/⅓ cup light muscovado (brown) sugar
30ml/2 tbsp ground almonds

For the topping

175g/6oz/¾ cup unsalted (sweet) butter, diced
115g/4oz/½ cup caster (superfine) sugar
30ml/2 tbsp golden (light corn) syrup
175ml/6fl oz/¾ cup condensed milk
150g/5oz/1¼ cups whole toasted hazelnuts
225g/8oz plain (semisweet) chocolate, chopped into small pieces

1 Preheat the oven to 160°C/325°F/Gas 3. Grease a shallow 30 × 20 cm/12 × 8 in tin (pan). Sift the flour and baking powder into a large bowl. Melt the chocolate in a bowl over a pan of simmering water.

2 Rub the butter into the flour until the mixture resembles coarse breadcrumbs, then stir in the sugar. Work in the melted chocolate and ground almonds to make a light biscuit dough.

3 Spread the dough roughly in the tin, then use a rubber spatula to press it down evenly into the sides and the corners. Prick the surface with a fork and bake for 25–30 minutes until firm. Leave to cool in the tin.

4 Make the topping. Heat the butter, sugar, golden syrup and condensed milk in a pan, stirring until the butter and sugar have melted. Simmer until golden, then stir in the hazelnuts.

5 Pour over the cooked base. Leave to set.

6 Melt the chocolate for the topping in a heatproof bowl over barely simmering water. Spread evenly over the butterscotch layer, then leave to set again before cutting into bars to serve.

Rocky Road Chocolate Bars

If you have eaten versions of rocky road in various coffee bars and, although delicious, have always thought "I could improve on that" – well, you can, and this recipe is a dream to make with children. They will love smashing up the biscuits, and can do most of the rest, apart from melting the chocolate and lining the pan. Adults will also enjoy the contrast of melting chocolate chips, crunchy biscuits and soft marshmallows all blended together – it's not just kid's stuff.

Makes 16

225g/8oz/1 cup salted butter
115g/4oz dark (bittersweet) chocolate, roughly broken up
30ml/2 tbsp caster (superfine) sugar
30ml/2 tbsp golden (light corn) syrup
30ml/2 tbsp good quality unsweetened cocoa powder
350g/12oz mixed digestive biscuits (graham crackers) and ginger nut biscuits (gingersnaps)
50g/2oz mini marshmallows
75g/3oz mixed white and milk chocolate chips
icing (confectioners') sugar, for dusting (optional)

1 Line a 20cm/8in square cake pan, measuring about 2.5cm/1in deep, with baking parchment.

2 Put the butter in a pan with the chocolate, sugar, syrup and cocoa powder. Place over a gentle heat until completely melted.

3 Put the biscuits into a large plastic bag and smash with a rolling pin until broken up into rough chunks.

4 Stir the biscuits into the chocolate mixture, followed by the marshmallows and chocolate chips. Mix together well until everything is well coated in chocolate.

5 Spoon the mixture into the pan, but don't press down too much – it should look like a rocky road. Chill for at least 1 hour, or until firm.

6 Remove the cake from the pan and cut into 16 bars. If you like, dust the bars with icing sugar before serving.

Butterscotch Bars Energy 305kcal/1273kJ; Protein 3.5g; Carbohydrate 30g, of which sugars 22.5g; Fat 19.8g, of which saturates 9.7g; Cholesterol 29mg; Calcium 57mg; Fibre 1.2g; Sodium 89mg.
Rocky Road Energy 296kcal/1237kJ; Protein 2.7g; Carbohydrate 28.6g, of which sugars 15.7g; Fat 19.9g, of which saturates 11.6g; Cholesterol 40mg; Calcium 39mg; Fibre 0.9g; Sodium 245mg.

Chocolate Chip and Walnut Cookies

A perennial favourite with all the family, these cookies contain walnuts as well as chocolate chips.

Makes 24

115g/4oz/½ cup butter or margarine, at room temperature
45g/1¾oz/scant ¼ cup caster (superfine) sugar
100g/3¾oz/scant ½ cup soft dark brown sugar
1 egg
2.5ml/½ tsp vanilla extract
175g/6oz/1½ cups plain (all-purpose) flour
2.5ml/½ tsp bicarbonate of soda (baking soda)
1.5ml/¼ tsp salt
175g/6oz/1 cup chocolate chips
50g/2oz/⅓ cup walnuts, chopped

1 Preheat the oven to 180°C/350°F/Gas 4. Lightly grease two large baking sheets. With an electric mixer, cream the butter or margarine and both the sugars together until light and fluffy.

2 In another bowl, mix the egg and the vanilla extract, then gradually beat into the butter mixture. Sift over the flour, bicarbonate of soda and salt and stir. Add the chocolate chips and walnuts, and mix to combine well.

3 Place heaped teaspoonfuls of the dough 5cm/2in apart on the baking sheets. Bake in the oven until lightly coloured, about 10–15 minutes. Transfer to a wire rack to cool.

Variations
All chocolate: Substitute 15ml/1tbsp unsweetened cocoa powder for the same quantity of flour, and omit the vanilla.
Mocha: Use coffee extract instead of vanilla extract.
Macadamia nut or hazelnut: Instead of the walnuts, add whole or coarsely chopped macadamia nuts or hazelnuts.
Dried fruit: Instead of the walnuts and chocolate chips, add chopped dried fruit, such as rains, sultanas (golden raisins), glacé (candied) cherries, or tropical fruit.
Banana: Substitute a ripe, mashed banana and 50g/2oz/¼ cup chopped banana chips for the walnuts and chocolate chips.

Gluten-free Chocolate Chip Cookies

This gluten-free version of these perennially popular cookies is bound to be a big hit with all the family because of their lovely, light texture.

Makes 16

75g/3oz/6 tbsp soft margarine
50g/2oz/¼ cup soft light brown sugar
50g/2oz/¼ cup caster (superfine) sugar
1 egg, beaten
few drops of vanilla extract
75g/3oz/¾ cup rice flour
75g/3oz/¾ cup gluten-free cornmeal
5ml/1 tsp gluten-free baking powder
pinch of salt
115g/4oz/⅔ cup plain (semisweet) chocolate chips, or a mixture of milk and white chocolate chips

1 Preheat the oven to 190°C/375°F/Gas 5. Lightly grease two baking sheets.

2 Place the margarine and sugars in a bowl and cream together until light and fluffy.

3 Beat in the egg and vanilla extract. Fold in the rice flour, cornmeal, baking powder and salt, then fold in the chocolate chips.

4 Place spoonfuls of the mixture on the prepared baking sheets, leaving space for spreading between each one. Bake for about 10–15 minutes, until the cookies are firm and lightly browned.

5 Remove the cookies from the oven and leave on the baking sheets for a few minutes to cool slightly, then carefully transfer to a wire rack using a metal spatula and leave them to cool completely before serving.

Cook's Tip
Once the cookies are cold, they can be stored in an airtight container for up to a week. Alternatively, pack them into plastic bags and freeze.

Walnut Cookies Energy 139kcal/582kJ; Protein 1.7g; Carbohydrate 16.7g, of which sugars 11.1g; Fat 7.7g, of which saturates 3.9g; Cholesterol 19mg; Calcium 20mg; Fibre 0.5g; Sodium 33mg.
Gluten-free Energy 135kcal/565kJ; Protein 1.6g; Carbohydrate 18.3g, of which sugars 11.1g; Fat 6.4g, of which saturates 3.7g; Cholesterol 22mg; Calcium 10mg; Fibre 0.4g; Sodium 34mg.

Chocolate Chip and Hazelnut Cookies

This version of the classic cookie combines chopped hazelnuts with plain chocolate chips.

Makes 36
115g/4oz/1 cup plain
   (all-purpose) flour
5ml/1 tsp baking powder
5ml/1 tsp salt
75g/3oz/6 tbsp butter
   or margarine
115g/4oz/1 cup caster
   (superfine) sugar
50g/2oz/¼ cup soft light
   brown sugar
1 egg
5ml/1 tsp vanilla extract
115g/4oz/⅔ cup plain
   (semisweet) chocolate chips
50g/2oz/½ cup hazelnuts,
   chopped

1 Preheat the oven to 180°C/350°F/Gas 4. Grease 2–3 baking sheets. Sift the flour, baking powder and salt into a small bowl. Set the bowl aside.

2 With a hand-held electric mixer, cream the butter or margarine and caster and brown sugars together. Beat in the egg and vanilla extract. Add the flour mixture and beat well on low speed.

3 Stir in the chocolate chips and half of the hazelnuts. Drop teaspoonfuls of the mixture on to the prepared baking sheets, to form 2cm/¾in mounds. Space the cookies about 5cm/2in apart to allow room for spreading.

4 Flatten each cookie lightly with a wet fork. Sprinkle the remaining hazelnuts on top of the cookies and press lightly into the surface.

5 Bake for 10–12 minutes, until golden brown. Transfer the cookies to a wire rack and allow to cool.

> **Variation**
> *Try using whatever nuts you have available, such as pecans, macadamia nuts or walnuts.*

Candied Peel Crumble Cookies

Crumbly, melt-in-the-mouth cookies, these incorporate candied peel, walnuts and white chocolate chips and are coated with a zingy lemon glaze.

Makes about 24
175g/6oz/¾ cup unsalted
   (sweet) butter, at room
   temperature, diced
90g/3½oz/½ cup caster
   (superfine) sugar
1 egg, beaten
finely grated rind of 1 lemon
200g/7oz/1¾ cups self-raising
   (self-rising) flour
90g/3½oz/generous ½ cup
   candied peel, chopped
75g/3oz/¾ cup chopped
   walnuts
50g/2oz/⅓ cup white
   chocolate chips

For the glaze
50g/2oz/½ cup icing
   (confectioners') sugar, sifted
15ml/1 tbsp lemon juice
thin strips of candied peel, to
   decorate (optional)

1 Preheat the oven to 180°C/350°F/Gas 4. Grease two baking sheets or line them with baking parchment.

2 Put the butter and sugar in a large mixing bowl and cream together until pale and fluffy.

3 Add the egg and beat thoroughly. Add the lemon rind and flour and stir together gently.

4 Finally, fold the candied peel, walnuts and chocolate chips into the mixture.

5 Place tablespoonfuls of mixture, spaced slightly apart, on the baking sheets to allow for spreading.

6 Bake for 12–15 minutes, until the cookies are firm but still pale in colour. Transfer the cookies to a wire rack using a metal spatula to cool.

7 For the glaze, put the icing sugar in a bowl and stir in the lemon juice. Spoon glaze over each cookie.

8 Decorate with thin slices of candied peel, if using.

Crumble Cookies Energy 150kcal/626kJ; Protein 1.8g; Carbohydrate 16.2g, of which sugars 9.8g; Fat 9.2g, of which saturates 4.4g; Cholesterol 23mg; Calcium 31mg; Fibre 0.5g; Sodium 61mg.
Hazelnut Cookies Energy 64kcal/271kJ; Protein 0.8g; Carbohydrate 9.9g, of which sugars 5g; Fat 2.7g, of which saturates 1.2g; Cholesterol 4mg; Calcium 14mg; Fibre 0.3g; Sodium 68mg.

Chocolate Chip Oat Cookies

Oat cookies are given a delicious lift by the inclusion of chocolate chips. Try caramel chips for a change, if you like.

Makes 60

115g/4oz/1 cup plain
　(all-purpose) flour
2.5ml/½ tsp bicarbonate of
　soda (baking soda)
1.5ml/¼ tsp baking powder
1.5ml/¼ tsp salt
115g/4oz/½ cup butter or
　margarine, at room temperature
115g/4oz/generous ½ cup
　caster (superfine) sugar
90g/3½oz/scant ½ cup soft
　light brown sugar
1 egg
2.5ml/½ tsp vanilla extract
75g/3oz/scant 1 cup rolled oats
175g/6oz/1 cup plain
　(semisweet) chocolate chips

1 Preheat the oven to 180°C/350°F/Gas 4. Grease three or four baking sheets. Sift the flour, bicarbonate of soda, baking powder and salt into a mixing bowl. Set aside.

2 With an electric mixer, cream the butter or margarine and the sugars together. Add the egg and vanilla, and beat until light and fluffy.

3 Add the flour mixture to the egg and vanilla, and beat on low speed until thoroughly blended. Stir in the rolled oats and plain chocolate chips, mixing well with a wooden spoon. The dough should be crumbly.

4 Drop heaped teaspoonfuls on to the baking sheets, about 2.5cm/1in apart. Bake until just firm around the edges but still soft in the centres, about 15 minutes. With a metal spatula, transfer the cookies to a wire rack to cool.

> **Variation**
> For an elegant look suitable to accompany a chilled dessert, melt plain (semisweet) chocolate over a pan of hot, but not boiling water, stirring until smooth. Dip each baked cookie into the chocolate to cover one half of the cookie. Leave to set before serving.

Chewy Chocolate Cookies

The texture of these dark and delicious cookies is sublime – soft on the inside with a crisper, crunchier outside – matched only by their subtle mocha flavour.

Makes 18

4 egg whites
300g/11oz/2¾ cups icing
　(confectioners') sugar
115g/4oz/1 cup unsweetened
　cocoa powder
30ml/2 tbsp plain
　(all-purpose) flour
5ml/1 tsp instant
　coffee powder
15ml/1 tbsp water
115g/4oz/1 cup walnuts,
　finely chopped

1 Preheat the oven to 180°C/350°F/Gas 4.

2 Line two or three baking sheets with baking parchment and grease the paper well.

3 Place the egg whites in a large bowl. Using an electric mixer, whisk the egg whites until frothy.

4 Sift the sugar, cocoa powder, flour and coffee into the egg whites. Add the water and continue beating on low speed to blend, then on high for a few minutes until the mixture thickens. Fold in the walnuts.

5 Place spoonfuls of the mixture 2.5cm/1in apart on the baking sheets to allow for spreading.

6 Bake in batches for 12–15 minutes, until firm and cracked on top but soft inside. Transfer to a wire rack to cool.

> **Cook's Tip**
> Electric mixers take out some of the hard work from preparing this recipe. Hand-held electric whisks are widely available and will be a wise investment if you make lots of recipes that call for whisking ingredients. Don't worry if you don't have one as a balloon whisk will work fine – it just needs a bit more effort.

Oat Cookies Energy 207kcal/864kJ; Protein 3.2g; Carbohydrate 22.1g, of which sugars 12g; Fat 12.4g, of which saturates 5g; Cholesterol 32mg; Calcium 30mg; Fibre 1.1g; Sodium 46mg.
Chewy Cookies Energy 138kcal/580kJ; Protein 3g; Carbohydrate 19.7g, of which sugars 17.6g; Fat 5.8g, of which saturates 1.2g; Cholesterol 0mg; Calcium 26mg; Fibre 1.1g; Sodium 76mg.

Chunky Chocolate Drops

Do not allow these cookies to cool completely on the baking sheet or they will break when you lift them.

Makes 18
175g/6oz plain
   (semisweet) chocolate
115g/4oz/½ cup unsalted
   (sweet) butter
2 eggs
90g/3½oz/½ cup caster
   (superfine) sugar
50g/2oz/¼ cup soft light
   brown sugar
40g/1½oz/⅓ cup plain
   (all-purpose) flour

25g/1oz/¼ cup unsweetened
   cocoa powder
5ml/1 tsp baking powder
10ml/2 tsp vanilla extract
pinch of salt
115g/4oz/1 cup pecan
   nuts, toasted and
   coarsely chopped
175g/6oz/1 cup
   plain (semisweet)
   chocolate chips
115g/4oz fine quality white
   chocolate, chopped into
   5mm/¼in pieces
115g/4oz fine quality milk
   chocolate, chopped into
   5mm/¼in pieces

1 Preheat the oven to 160°C/325°F/Gas 3. Grease two large baking sheets.

2 In a medium pan over a low heat, melt the plain chocolate and butter until smooth, stirring frequently. Remove from the heat to cool slightly.

3 Beat the eggs with the sugars until pale and creamy. Gradually beat in the melted chocolate mixture. Beat in the flour, cocoa, baking powder, vanilla extract and salt, until just blended. Add in the nuts, chocolate chips and the white chocolate pieces.

4 Drop 4–6 heaped tablespoonfuls of the mixture on to each baking sheet 10cm/4in apart and flatten each to a round about 7.5cm/3in. Bake for 8–10 minutes, or until the tops are shiny and cracked and the edges look crisp.

5 Cool the cookies on the baking sheets for about 2 minutes, or until they are just set, then remove them to a wire rack to cool completely.

Nutty Chocolate Chip Cookies

These crunchy cookies are easy enough for children to make and are sure to disappear as soon as they are baked. Cook with the children to create their future comfort food.

Makes about 20
115g/4oz/½ cup butter, plus
   extra for greasing
115g/4oz/½ cup soft
   dark brown sugar
2 eggs, lightly beaten

45–60ml/3–4 tbsp milk
5ml/1 tsp vanilla extract
150g/5oz/1¼ cups plain
   (all-purpose) flour
5ml/1 tsp baking powder
pinch of salt
115g/4oz/generous 1 cup
   rolled oats
175g/6oz/1 cup plain (semisweet)
   chocolate chips
115g/4oz/1 cup pecan
   nuts, chopped

1 Cream the butter and sugar together in a large bowl until pale and fluffy. Add the beaten eggs, milk and vanilla extract, and beat thoroughly.

2 Sift in the flour, baking powder and salt, and stir in until well mixed. Fold in the rolled oats, chocolate chips and chopped pecan nuts.

3 Chill the mixture for at least 1 hour. Preheat the oven to 180°C/350°F/Gas 4. Grease two large baking trays.

4 Using two teaspoons, place mounds well apart on the trays and flatten with a spoon or fork.

5 Bake for 10–12 minutes, until the edges are just beginning to colour, then carefully transfer the cookies on to wire racks to cool completely.

Cook's Tip
Don't flatten these cookies too much on the baking sheets. They cook better when they are left chunky – and they look more appealing as well.

Chocolate Drops Energy 264kcal/1101kJ; Protein 3.4g; Carbohydrate 21.1g, of which sugars 20.7g; Fat 19.1g, of which saturates 9.1g; Cholesterol 37mg; Calcium 48mg; Fibre 0.9g; Sodium 73mg.
Nutty Cookies Energy 208kcal/871kJ; Protein 3.3g; Carbohydrate 22.1g, of which sugars 12g; Fat 12.5g, of which saturates 5g; Cholesterol 36mg; Calcium 30mg; Fibre 1.1g; Sodium 47mg.

Giant Triple Chocolate Cookies

Here is the ultimate cookie for serious chocoholics. Packed with chocolate and macadamia nuts, each cookie is a super-stress buster. You will have to be patient when they come out of the oven, as they are too soft to move until completely cold: that's stress enough to deserve at least two!

Makes 12 large cookies
90g/3½oz milk chocolate
90g/3½oz white chocolate
300g/11oz dark (bittersweet) chocolate (minimum 70 per cent cocoa solids)
90g/3½oz/7 tbsp unsalted (sweet) butter, at room temperature, diced
5ml/1 tsp vanilla extract
150g/5oz/¾ cup light muscovado (brown) sugar
150g/5oz/1¼ cups self-raising (self-rising) flour
100g/3½oz/scant 1 cup macadamia nut halves

1 Preheat the oven to 180°C/350°F/Gas 4. Line two baking sheets with baking parchment.

2 Coarsely chop the milk and white chocolate and put them in a bowl. Chop 200g/7oz of the dark chocolate into very large chunks, at least 2cm/¾in in size. Set aside.

3 Break up the remaining dark chocolate and place in a heatproof bowl set over a pan of barely simmering water. Stir until melted and smooth.

4 Remove from the heat and stir in the butter, then the vanilla extract and muscovado sugar.

5 Add the flour and mix gently. Add half the dark chocolate chunks, all the milk and white chocolate and the nuts and fold together.

6 Spoon 12 mounds on to the baking sheets. Press the remaining dark chocolate chunks into the top of each cookie. Bake for about 12 minutes, until just beginning to colour. Cool on the baking sheets.

Ladies' Kisses

These old-fashioned chocolate-sandwich cookies from the Piedmont region of Italy are sweet, light and a rare treat, just like their name. They certainly merit bone china cups.

Makes 20
150g/5oz/10 tbsp butter, softened
115g/4oz/generous ½ cup caster (superfine) sugar
1 egg yolk
2.5ml/½ tsp almond extract
115g/4oz/1 cup ground almonds
175g/6oz/1½ cups plain (all-purpose) flour
50g/2oz plain (semisweet) chocolate

1 Cream the butter and sugar with an electric mixer until light and fluffy, then beat in the egg yolk, almond extract, ground almonds and flour until evenly mixed. Chill for about 2 hours until firm.

2 Preheat the oven to 160°C/325°F/Gas 3. Line several baking sheets with baking parchment.

3 Break off small pieces of dough and roll into balls with your hands, making 40 altogether.

4 Place the balls on the baking sheets, spacing them out as they will spread in the oven.

5 Bake for 20 minutes, or until golden. Remove the baking sheets from the oven, lift off the parchment with the cookies still on it, then place on wire racks. Leave to cool. Repeat with the remaining mixture.

6 Lift the cooled cookies off the paper. Melt the chocolate in a bowl over a pan of hot water. Use to sandwich the cookies in pairs, then leave to cool and set before serving.

> **Cook's Tip**
> These cookies look extra dainty served in frilly petits fours cases.

Giant Cookies Energy 413kcal/1727kJ; Protein 3.9g; Carbohydrate 48.4g, of which sugars 38.6g; Fat 24g, of which saturates 11.6g; Cholesterol 18mg; Calcium 69mg; Fibre 1.8g; Sodium 117mg.
Ladies' Kisses Energy 159kcal/665kJ; Protein 2.4g; Carbohydrate 14.8g, of which sugars 8g; Fat 10.5g, of which saturates 4.7g; Cholesterol 26mg; Calcium 32mg; Fibre 0.8g; Sodium 47mg.

Cappuccino Chocolate Swirls

A melt-in-the-mouth, mocha-flavoured cookie drizzled with white and dark chocolate is just the thing to have with that mid-morning café latte, as well as for afternoon tea with friends.

Makes 18

10ml/2 tsp instant
  coffee powder
10ml/2 tsp boiling water
150g/5oz/1¼ cups plain
  (all-purpose) flour

115g/4oz/½ cup cornflour
  (cornstarch)
15ml/1 tbsp unsweetened
  cocoa powder
225g/8oz/1 cup unsalted
  (sweet) butter, at room
  temperature, diced
50g/2oz/¼ cup golden caster
  (superfine) sugar

For the decoration

50g/2oz white chocolate
25g/1oz dark (bittersweet)
  chocolate

1 Preheat the oven to 190°C/375°F/Gas 5. Line two baking sheets with baking parchment. Put the coffee powder in a cup, add the boiling water and stir until dissolved. Set aside to cool. Sift together the flour, cornflour and cocoa powder.

2 Put the butter and sugar in a bowl and beat until creamy. Add the coffee and the sifted flour and mix well. Spoon into a piping (pastry) bag fitted with a plain nozzle.

3 Pipe 18 spirals, slightly apart, on to the baking sheets. Bake for 10–15 minutes, or until firm but not browned. Leave on the baking sheets for 1 minute, then transfer to a wire rack to cool.

4 Melt the white and dark chocolate separately in heatproof bowls set over a pan of hot water.

5 Place the cooled cookies close together on kitchen paper. Using a teaspoon, take some white chocolate and flick over the cookies to create small lines of drizzle.

6 When all the white chocolate has been used, repeat the process with the dark chocolate, flicking it over the cookies so the dark chocolate is at an angle to the white chocolate. Leave to set and then remove the cookies from the paper.

Chocolate Crackle-tops

These dainty treats are always popular and are best eaten on the day they are baked, as they dry slightly on storage.

Makes 38

200g/7oz plain (semisweet)
  chocolate, chopped
90g/3½oz/7 tbsp unsalted
  (sweet) butter
115g/4oz/generous ½ cup
  caster (superfine) sugar
3 eggs

5ml/1 tsp vanilla extract
215g/7½oz/scant 2 cups
  plain (all-purpose) flour
25g/1oz/¼ cup unsweetened
  cocoa powder
2.5ml/½ tsp baking powder
a pinch of salt
175g/6oz/1½ cups icing
  (confectioners') sugar,
  for coating

1 Heat the chocolate and butter over a low heat until smooth, stirring frequently. Remove from the heat. Stir in the sugar, and continue stirring until dissolved. Add the eggs, one at a time, beating well after each addition; stir in the vanilla.

2 In a separate bowl, sift together the flour, cocoa, baking powder and salt. Gradually stir into the chocolate mixture until just blended. Cover and chill for at least 1 hour.

3 Preheat the oven to 160°C/325°F/Gas 3. Grease two or three large baking sheets. Place the icing sugar in a small, deep bowl. Using a teaspoon, scoop the dough into small balls and roll in your hands into 4cm/1½in balls.

4 Drop the balls, one at a time, into the icing sugar and roll until heavily coated. Remove each ball with a slotted spoon and tap against the bowl to remove any excess sugar. Place on the baking sheets 4cm/1½in apart.

5 Bake the cookies for 10–15 minutes, or until the tops feel slightly firm when touched with your fingertip.

6 Remove the baking sheets to a wire rack for 2–3 minutes, then remove the cookies to the wire rack to cool.

Cappuccino Swirls Energy 179kcal/746kJ; Protein 1.3g; Carbohydrate 18.1g, of which sugars 5.7g; Fat 11.8g, of which saturates 7.3g; Cholesterol 27mg; Calcium 19mg; Fibre 0.5g; Sodium 88mg.
Crackle-tops Energy 102kcal/428kJ; Protein 1.5g; Carbohydrate 15.8g, of which sugars 11.4g; Fat 4.1g, of which saturates 2.3g; Cholesterol 20mg; Calcium 17mg; Fibre 0.4g; Sodium 27mg.

Chocolate Amaretti

Although it is always said that chocolate does not go with wine, enjoy these delightful cookies Italian-style with a glass of chilled champagne.

Makes 24

150g/5oz/scant 1 cup blanched, toasted whole almonds

115g/4oz/generous ½ cup caster (superfine) sugar
15ml/1 tbsp unsweetened cocoa powder
30ml/2 tbsp icing (confectioners') sugar
2 egg whites
a pinch of cream of tartar
5ml/1 tsp almond extract
flaked (sliced) almonds, to decorate

1 Preheat the oven to 160°C/325°F/Gas 3. Line a large baking sheet with baking parchment or foil. In a food processor fitted with a metal blade, process the toasted almonds with half the sugar until they are finely ground but not oily. Transfer to a large bowl and sift in the cocoa and icing sugar; stir to blend evenly. Set aside.

2 Beat the egg whites and cream of tartar until stiff peaks form. Sprinkle in the remaining sugar 15ml/1 tbsp at a time, beating well after each addition, and continue beating until the whites are glossy and stiff. Beat in the almond extract.

3 Sprinkle over the almond mixture and gently fold into the egg whites until just blended. Spoon the mixture into a large piping (pastry) bag fitted with a plain 1cm/½in nozzle. Pipe 4cm/1½in rounds, 2.5cm/1in apart, on the baking sheet. Press a flaked almond into the centre of each.

4 Bake the cookies for 12–15 minutes, or until they appear crisp. Remove the baking sheet to a wire rack to cool for 10 minutes. With a metal spatula, remove the cookies to the wire rack to cool completely.

> **Variation**
> As an alternative decoration, lightly press a few coffee sugar crystals on top of each cookie before baking.

Chocolate Kisses

These delicious light and dark chocolate cookies are ideal as a special treat.

Makes 24

75g/3oz plain (semisweet) chocolate, chopped into small pieces
75g/3oz white chocolate, chopped into small pieces

115g/4oz/½ cup butter, softened
115g/4oz/½ cup caster (superfine) sugar
2 eggs
225g/8oz/2 cups plain (all-purpose) flour
icing (confectioners') sugar, to decorate

1 Melt the plain and white chocolates in separate heatproof bowls over pans of simmering water, stirring until smooth. Set both aside to cool.

2 Beat the butter and caster sugar together until pale and fluffy. Beat in the eggs, one at a time, then sift in the flour and mix well until combined.

3 Halve the creamed mixture and divide it between the two bowls of chocolate. Mix each chocolate in thoroughly so that each forms a dough.

4 Knead the doughs until smooth, wrap them separately in clear film (plastic wrap) and chill for 1 hour. Preheat the oven to 190°C/375°F/Gas 5.

5 Shape slightly rounded teaspoonfuls of both doughs roughly into balls. Roll the balls between your palms to neaten them. Arrange the balls on greased baking sheets.

6 Bake for 10–12 minutes. Dust liberally with sifted icing sugar and cool on a wire rack.

> **Cook's Tip**
> If you are serving these cookies at Christmas, decorate a plateful with some holly for a truly festive experience.

Amaretti Energy 65kcal/270kJ; Protein 1.8g; Carbohydrate 5.8g, of which sugars 5.5g; Fat 4g, of which saturates 0.4g; Cholesterol 0mg; Calcium 20mg; Fibre 0.6g; Sodium 12mg.
Chocolate Kisses Energy 125kcal/524kJ; Protein 1.9g; Carbohydrate 16.1g, of which sugars 9g; Fat 6.4g, of which saturates 3.7g; Cholesterol 26mg; Calcium 28mg; Fibre 0.4g; Sodium 39mg.

Chocolate Thumbprint Cookies

Chunky, chocolatey and gooey all at the same time, these gorgeous cookies are filled with a spoonful of chocolate spread after baking to really add to their indulgent feel.

Makes 16
115g/4oz/¹/₂ cup unsalted
  (sweet) butter, at room
  temperature, diced
115g/4oz/¹/₂ cup light muscovado
  (brown) sugar
I egg

75g/3oz/²/₃ cup plain
  (all-purpose) flour
25g/1oz/¹/₄ cup unsweetened
  cocoa powder
2.5ml/¹/₂ tsp bicarbonate of soda
  (baking soda)
115g/4oz/generous I cup
  rolled oats
75–90ml/5–6 tbsp chocolate
  spread

I Preheat the oven to 180°C/350°F/Gas 4. Grease a large baking sheet.

2 In a bowl, beat together the butter and sugar until pale and creamy.

3 Add the egg, flour, cocoa powder, bicarbonate of soda and rolled oats to the bowl and mix well.

4 Using your hands, roll spoonfuls of the mixture into balls. Place the balls on the baking sheet, spacing them well apart to allow room for spreading. Flatten slightly.

5 Dip a thumb in flour and press into the centre of each cookie to make an indent for the topping.

6 Bake the cookies for 10 minutes until they are firm and just beginning to go crisp on the edges. Leave for 2 minutes to cool slightly on the baking sheets, then transfer to a wire rack to cool completely.

7 Spoon a little of the chocolate spread into the centre of each cookie.

Chocolate Marzipan Cookies

These light cookies are perfect for anyone who loves the taste of marzipan with their chocolate.

Makes about 36
200g/7oz/scant I cup unsalted
  (sweet) butter, softened
200g/7oz/scant I cup light
  muscovado (brown) sugar

I egg, beaten
300g/11oz/2³/₄ cups plain
  (all-purpose) flour
60ml/4 tbsp unsweetened
  cocoa powder
200g/7oz white almond paste
115g/4oz white chocolate,
  chopped into small pieces

I Preheat oven to 190°C/375°F/Gas 5. Lightly grease two large baking sheets. Using a hand-held electric mixer, cream the butter with the sugar in a mixing bowl until pale and fluffy. Add the egg and beat well.

2 Sift the flour and cocoa over the mixture. Stir in with a wooden spoon until all the flour mixture has been smoothly incorporated, then use clean hands to press the mixture together to make a fairly soft dough.

3 Using a rolling pin and keeping your touch light, roll out about half the dough on a lightly floured surface to a thickness of about 5mm/¹/₄in. Using a 5cm/2in plain or fluted cookie cutter, cut out 36 rounds, re-rolling the dough as required. Wrap the remaining dough in clear film (plastic wrap) and set it aside.

4 Cut the almond paste into 36 equal pieces. Roll into balls, flatten slightly and place one on each round of dough. Roll out the remaining dough, cut out more rounds, then place on top of the almond paste. Press the dough edges to seal.

5 Bake for 10–12 minutes, or until the cookies have risen well and are beginning to crack on the surface. Cool on the baking sheet for about 2–3 minutes, then finish cooling on a wire rack.

6 Melt the white chocolate, then either drizzle it over the cookies to decorate, or spoon into a paper piping (pastry) bag and quickly pipe a design on to the cookies.

Marzipan Cookies Energy 137kcal/576kJ; Protein 1.9g; Carbohydrate 18.1g, of which sugars 11.6g; Fat 6.9g, of which saturates 3.8g; Cholesterol 17mg; Calcium 31mg; Fibre 0.6g; Sodium 57mg.
Thumbprint Cookies Energy 163kcal/682kJ; Protein 2.3g; Carbohydrate 19.3g, of which sugars 10.3g; Fat 9g, of which saturates 4.1g; Cholesterol 27mg; Calcium 19mg; Fibre 0.8g; Sodium 66mg.

Chocolate Treacle Snaps

These elegantly thin, treacle-flavoured snap cookies have a delicate hint of spice and a decorative lick of chocolate on top. They are particularly good with a steaming cup of hot coffee.

Makes about 35
90g/3¹/₂oz/7 tbsp unsalted (sweet) butter, diced
175ml/6fl oz/³/₄ cup golden (light corn) syrup
50ml/2fl oz/¹/₄ cup black treacle (molasses)
250g/9oz/2¹/₄ cups plain (all-purpose) flour
150g/5oz/³/₄ cup golden caster (superfine) sugar
5ml/1 tsp bicarbonate of soda (baking soda)
1.5ml/¹/₄ tsp mixed (apple pie) spice
100g/3³/₄oz milk chocolate
100g/3³/₄oz white chocolate

1 Preheat the oven to 180°C/350°F/Gas 4. Line two or three baking sheets with baking parchment.

2 Put the butter, syrup and treacle in a small pan. Heat gently, stirring constantly, until the butter has melted. Remove from the heat and set aside until required.

3 Sift the flour into a large mixing bowl. Add the sugar, bicarbonate of soda and mixed spice, and mix well using a wooden spoon. Slowly pour in the butter and treacle mixture and stir to combine well.

4 Place large teaspoonfuls of the mixture well apart on the prepared baking sheets. Bake the cookies for 10–12 minutes, until just beginning to brown around the edges.

5 Leave them to cool for a few minutes on the baking sheets. When firm enough to handle, transfer the cookies to a wire rack to cool completely.

6 Melt the milk chocolate and white chocolate separately in the microwave or in heatproof bowls set over pans of simmering water. Swirl a little of each into the centre of each cookie and leave to set.

Mini Chocolate Marylands

These tasty little cookies are perfect for any age group. They're easy to make and even young children can get involved with helping to press the chocolate chips into the unbaked dough.

Makes 40–45
125g/4¹/₂oz/generous ¹/₂ cup unsalted (sweet) butter, at room temperature, diced
90g/3¹/₂oz/¹/₂ cup caster (superfine) sugar
1 egg
1 egg yolk
5ml/1 tsp vanilla extract
175g/6oz/1¹/₂ cups self-raising (self-rising) flour
130ml/4¹/₂fl oz/generous ¹/₂ cup milk
90g/3¹/₂oz/generous ¹/₂ cup chocolate chips

1 Preheat the oven to 180°C/350°F/Gas 4. Lightly grease two baking sheets.

2 In a large mixing bowl, beat together the butter and sugar until pale and creamy. Add the egg, egg yolk, vanilla extract, flour, milk and half the chocolate chips and stir well until thoroughly combined.

3 Using two teaspoons, place small mounds of the mixture on the baking sheets, spacing them slightly apart to allow room for spreading during baking.

4 Press the remaining chocolate chips on to the mounds of cookie dough and press down gently.

5 Bake for 10–15 minutes until pale golden. Leave the cookies on the baking sheet for 2 minutes to firm up, then transfer to a wire rack to cool completely.

> **Cook's Tip**
> This recipe makes quite a large quantity. If you like, you can freeze half of the cookies for another time. Simply thaw, then return to the oven for a few minutes to re-crisp before serving.

Treacle Snaps Energy 109kcal/459kJ; Protein 1.2g; Carbohydrate 18.2g, of which sugars 12.8g; Fat 4g, of which saturates 2.4g; Cholesterol 6mg; Calcium 35mg; Fibre 0.2g; Sodium 38mg.
Mini Marylands Energy 54kcal/227kJ; Protein 0.7g; Carbohydrate 6.4g, of which sugars 3.5g; Fat 3g, of which saturates 1.8g; Cholesterol 10mg; Calcium 19mg; Fibre 0.2g; Sodium 33mg.

Mini Chocolate Macaroons

These little macaroons can be served as petits fours or with coffee. To make plain macaroons, replace the unsweetened cocoa powder with cornflour.

Makes 30
50g/2oz/½ cup ground almonds
50g/2oz/¼ cup caster (superfine) sugar
15ml/1 tbsp unsweetened cocoa powder
1.5–2.5ml/¼–½ tsp almond extract
1 egg white
15 flaked (sliced) almonds
4 glacé (candied) cherries, quartered
icing (confectioners') sugar or unsweetened cocoa powder, to dust

1 Preheat the oven to 160°C/325°F/Gas 3. Line two baking sheets with baking parchment.

2 Place the almonds, sugar, cocoa powder and almond extract into a bowl and mix together well using a wooden spoon.

3 In a separate bowl, whisk the egg white until frothy. Stir in enough egg white to the almond mixture to form a soft piping consistency.

4 Place the mixture into a nylon or baking parchment piping (pastry) bag fitted with a 1cm/½in plain piping nozzle.

5 Pipe about 15 rounds of mixture on to each baking sheet well spaced apart. Press a flaked almond on to half the macaroons and quartered glacé cherries on to the remainder.

6 Bake in the oven for 10–15 minutes, until firm to the touch. Cool completely on the paper and dust liberally with the sugar or unsweetened cocoa powder before removing from the baking parchment.

> **Cook's Tip**
> These cookies make a perfect present. Simply pack them into a pretty gift box or container.

Late Night Cookies

Take a pile of these to bed with you and all that will be left next morning will be the crumbs in the duvet. These are dangerous cookies. Crisp yet crumbly and packed with chocolate chips, they are a must with tall glasses of ice-cold milk or stacked with an obscene amount of ice cream.

Makes about 12 large or 20 small cookies
75g/3oz/6 tbsp butter, softened
75g/3oz/scant ½ cup golden caster (superfine) sugar
75g/3oz soft light brown sugar, sifted
1 large (US extra large) egg, beaten
2.5ml/½ tsp vanilla extract
150g/5oz/1¼ cups self-raising (self-rising) flour
25g/1oz/¼ cup unsweetened cocoa powder
1.5ml/¼ tsp salt
115g/4oz chopped chocolate or plain (semisweet) chocolate chips, ice cream or milk, to serve

1 Preheat the oven to 180°C/350°F/Gas 4. Butter two heavy non-stick baking sheets.

2 Cream the butter and sugars together until pale and fluffy. Beat in the egg and vanilla extract.

3 Sift the flour with the cocoa and salt. Gently fold into the egg mixture with the chopped chocolate or chocolate chips.

4 Place four heaped tablespoonfuls of the mixture spaced well apart on each baking sheet. Press down and spread out with the back of a wet spoon.

5 Bake the cookies in the oven for 12 minutes. Cool on the baking sheet for 1 minute, then remove to a cooling rack.

6 Repeat with the remaining mixture. Store the cookies in an airtight container when completely cold. Serve with ice cream sandwiched between, or enjoy on their own with a glass of ice-cold milk.

Late Night Cookies Energy 170kcal/711kJ; Protein 2.8g; Carbohydrate 21g, of which sugars 11.5g; Fat 8.9g, of which saturates 5.2g; Cholesterol 34mg; Calcium 72mg; Fibre 0.7g; Sodium 117mg.
Mini Macaroons Energy 102kcal/426kJ; Protein 2.8g; Carbohydrate 7.8g, of which sugars 7.5g; Fat 6.9g, of which saturates 0.6g; Cholesterol 13mg; Calcium 33mg; Fibre 0.9g; Sodium 5mg.

Crunchy Chocolate Chip Jumbles

For crunchier cookies, add 50g/2oz/½ cup chopped walnuts with the cereal.

Makes 36
115g/4oz/½ cup butter or
   margarine, at room temperature
225g/8oz/generous 1 cup caster
   (superfine) sugar

1 egg
5ml/1 tsp vanilla extract
150g/5oz/1¼ cups plain
   (all-purpose) flour, sifted
2.5ml/½ tsp bicarbonate of soda
   (baking soda)
1.5ml/¼ tsp salt
50g/2oz/2¼ cups rice cereal
175g/6oz/1 cup chocolate chips

1 Preheat the oven to 180°C/350°F/Gas 4. Grease two baking sheets. Cream the butter or margarine and sugar until fluffy. Add the egg and vanilla extract. Add the flour, bicarbonate of soda and the salt, and fold in.

2 Add the cereal and chocolate chips and mix thoroughly. Drop spoonfuls 5cm/2in apart on to baking sheets and bake for 10–12 minutes. Transfer to a wire rack to cool.

Chocolate Macaroons

Serve these delicious macaroons with coffee.

Makes 24
50g/2oz plain (semisweet)
   chocolate, melted
175g/6oz/1 cup blanched almonds

225g/8oz/generous 1 cup caster
   (superfine) sugar
3 egg whites
2.5ml/½ tsp vanilla extract
1.5ml/¼ tsp almond extract
icing (confectioners') sugar,
   for dusting

1 Preheat the oven to 160°C/325°F/Gas 3. Line two baking sheets with baking parchment. Grind the almonds in a food processor. Blend in the sugar, egg whites, vanilla and almond extracts.

2 Stir in the melted chocolate. Shape into walnut-size balls. Place on the sheets and flatten slightly. Brush with a little water and dust with icing sugar. Bake until just firm, 10–12 minutes. With a metal spatula, transfer to a wire rack to cool.

Chunky Double Chocolate Cookies

Delicious, chunky cookies with a moist gooey centre and an extra hit of chocolate.

Makes 18–20
115g/4oz/½ cup unsalted
   (sweet) butter, softened
115g/4oz/½ cup light
   muscovado (brown) sugar
1 egg

5ml/1 tsp vanilla extract
150g/5oz/1¼ cups self-raising
   (self-rising) flour
75g/3oz/¾ cup rolled oats
115g/4oz plain (semisweet)
   chocolate, roughly chopped
115g/4oz white chocolate,
   roughly chopped

1 Preheat the oven to 190°C/375°F/Gas 5. Lightly grease two baking sheets.

2 Cream the butter with the sugar in a bowl until pale and fluffy. Add the egg and vanilla extract and beat well.

3 Sift the flour over the mixture and fold in lightly with a metal spoon, then add the oats and chopped plain and white chocolate and stir until evenly mixed.

4 Place small spoonfuls of the mixture in 18–20 rocky heaps on the baking sheets, leaving space for spreading.

5 Bake for 12–15 minutes, or until the cookies are beginning to turn pale golden.

6 Cool for 2–3 minutes on the baking sheets, then lift on to wire racks. The cookies will be soft when freshly baked but will harden on cooling.

> **Variation**
> Instead of the porridge oats, use 75g/3oz/¾ cup ground almonds. Omit the chopped chocolate and use 175g/6oz/ 1 cup chocolate chips instead. Top each heap of cake mixture with half a glacé (candied) cherry before baking.

Crunchy Jumbles Energy 95kcal/398kJ; Protein 0.9g; Carbohydrate 14.2g, of which sugars 9.8g; Fat 4.2g, of which saturates 2.5g; Cholesterol 12mg; Calcium 18mg; Fibre 0.3g; Sodium 31mg.
Chocolate Macaroons Energy 94kcal/393kJ; Protein 2.1g; Carbohydrate 11.6g, of which sugars 11.4g; Fat 4.7g, of which saturates 0.7g; Cholesterol 0mg; Calcium 23mg; Fibre 0.6g; Sodium 9mg.
Chunky Cookies Energy 169kcal/710kJ; Protein 2.3g; Carbohydrate 21.6g, of which sugars 13.1g; Fat 8.8g, of which saturates 5.1g; Cholesterol 22mg; Calcium 36mg; Fibre 0.6g; Sodium 47mg.

Mocha Viennese Swirls

These crumbly, buttery cookies will go down a treat.

Makes about 20

115g/4oz plain (semisweet)
  chocolate, chopped into
  small pieces
200g/7oz/scant 1 cup unsalted
  (sweet) butter, softened
90ml/6 tbsp icing
  (confectioners') sugar
30ml/2 tbsp strong black coffee
200g/7oz/1¾ cups plain
  (all-purpose) flour
50g/2oz/½ cup cornflour
  (cornstarch)

To decorate

about 20 blanched almonds
150g/5oz plain (semisweet)
  chocolate, chopped into
  small pieces

1 Preheat the oven to 190°C/375°F/Gas 5. Melt the chocolate in a heatproof bowl over barely simmering water, stirring constantly until smooth.

2 Cream together the butter and the icing sugar in a bowl until smooth and pale. Beat in the melted chocolate, then the strong black coffee.

3 Sift the plain flour and cornflour over the mixture. Fold in lightly and evenly to make a soft cookie dough.

4 Lightly grease two large baking sheets. Spoon the dough into a piping (pastry) bag fitted with a large star nozzle. Pipe about 20 swirls on the baking sheets, allowing room for spreading. Keep the nozzle close to the sheet so that the swirls are flat.

5 Press an almond into the centre of each cookie. Bake for about 15 minutes, or until the cookies are firm and just starting to brown.

6 Leave the cookies to cool for about 10 minutes on the baking sheets, then lift carefully on to a wire rack using a metal spatula to cool completely.

7 When cool, melt the chocolate and dip the base of each swirl to coat. Place on a sheet of baking parchment and leave to set completely.

Chocolate Walnut Delights

Simple and delicious, this method of making cookies ensures they are all of a uniform size.

Makes 50

25g/1oz plain (semisweet)
  chocolate
25g/1oz dark (bittersweet)
  cooking chocolate
225g/8oz/2 cups plain
  (all-purpose) flour
2.5ml/½ tsp salt
225g/8oz/1 cup unsalted
  (sweet) butter, at
  room temperature
225g/8oz/generous 1 cup caster
  (superfine) sugar
2 eggs
5ml/1 tsp vanilla extract
115g/4oz/1 cup finely
  chopped walnuts

1 Melt the chocolate in the top of a double boiler, or in a heatproof bowl set over a pan of gently simmering water. Set aside. In a bowl, sift together the flour and salt. Set aside.

2 Cream the butter until soft. Add the sugar and continue beating until the mixture is light and fluffy. Mix the eggs and vanilla extract, then gradually stir into the butter mixture. Stir in the chocolate, then the flour. Finally, stir in the nuts.

3 Divide the mixture into four equal parts, and roll each into a 5cm/2in diameter log. Wrap tightly in foil and chill or freeze until firm.

4 Preheat the oven to 190°C/375°F/Gas 5. Grease two baking sheets. Cut the logs into 5mm/¼in slices. Place the circles on the baking sheets and bake until lightly coloured, about 10 minutes. Using a metal spatula, transfer to a wire rack to cool.

Variation
Try other nuts in this recipe, such as almonds, or use 50g/2oz/scant ½ cup chopped ready-to-eat dried apricots, peaches or dates and halve the amount of nuts used. Almonds and apricots make a particularly pleasing combination, or try dates and pecan nuts.

Viennese Swirls Energy 210kcal/877kJ; Protein 2.2g; Carbohydrate 21.3g, of which sugars 11.2g; Fat 13.5g, of which saturates 7.6g; Cholesterol 22mg; Calcium 28mg; Fibre 0.8g; Sodium 64mg.
Delights Energy 90kcal/377kJ; Protein 1.1g; Carbohydrate 8.9g, of which sugars 5.5g; Fat 5.8g, of which saturates 2.7g; Cholesterol 17mg; Calcium 13mg; Fibre 0.2g; Sodium 31mg.

Chocolate Caramel Nuggets

Inside each of these buttery cookies lies a soft-centred chocolate-coated piece of caramel. The cookies are at their most delicious served an hour or so after baking, so you might want to shape them in advance, then put the baking sheet of uncooked nuggets in the refrigerator until you are ready to bake them.

Makes 14
150g/5oz/1¼ cups self-raising (self-rising) flour
90g/3½oz/7 tbsp unsalted (sweet) butter, chilled and diced
50g/2oz/¼ cup golden caster (superfine) sugar
1 egg yolk
5ml/1 tsp vanilla extract
14 soft-centred chocolate caramels
icing (confectioners') sugar and unsweetened cocoa powder, for dusting

1 Put the flour and diced butter in a food processor and process until the mixture resembles fairly fine breadcrumbs.

2 Add the sugar, egg yolk and vanilla extract to the food processor and process to a smooth dough. Wrap the dough in clear film (plastic wrap) and chill for 30 minutes.

3 Preheat the oven to 200°C/400°F/Gas 6. Grease a large baking sheet.

4 Roll out the dough thinly on a lightly floured surface and cut out 28 rounds using a 5cm/2in cookie cutter.

5 Place one chocolate caramel on a cookie round, then lay a second round on top. Pinch the edges of the dough together so that the chocolate caramel is completely enclosed, then place on the baking sheet.

6 Make the remaining cookies in the same way. Bake for about 10 minutes until pale golden.

7 Transfer to a wire rack and leave to cool. Serve lightly dusted with icing sugar and cocoa powder.

Chocolate-dipped Hazelnut Crescents

These elegant cookies are perfect for a special occasion, or give them as a gift to a chocolate-lover.

Makes about 35
275g/10oz/2 cups plain (all-purpose) flour
pinch of salt
225g/8oz/1 cup unsalted butter, softened
75g/3oz/scant ½ cup caster (superfine) sugar
15ml/1 tbsp hazelnut-flavoured liqueur or water
5ml/1 tsp vanilla extract
75g/3oz plain (semisweet) chocolate, chopped into small pieces
50g/2oz/½ cup hazelnuts, toasted and finely chopped
icing (confectioners') sugar, for dusting
350g/12oz plain (semisweet) chocolate, melted, for dipping

1 Preheat the oven to 160°C/325°F/Gas 3. Grease two large baking sheets.

2 Sift the flour and salt into a bowl. In a separate bowl, beat the butter until creamy. Add the sugar and beat until pale and fluffy, then beat in the hazelnut liqueur or water and the vanilla extract. Gently stir in the flour mixture, then the chocolate and hazelnuts until combined.

3 With floured hands, shape the dough into 5 × 1cm/2 × ½in crescent shapes. Place on the baking sheets, 5cm/2in apart.

4 Bake for 20–25 minutes, until the edges are set and the biscuits slightly golden.

5 Remove the cookies from the oven and cool on the baking sheets for 10 minutes, then transfer the cookies to wire racks to cool completely.

6 Have the melted chocolate ready in a small bowl. Dust the cookies lightly with icing sugar.

7 Using a pair of kitchen tongs or your fingers, dip half of each crescent into the melted chocolate. Place the crescents on a non-stick baking sheet until the chocolate has set.

Caramel Nuggets Energy 149kcal/625kJ; Protein 1.8g; Carbohydrate 18.7g, of which sugars 9.5g; Fat 8g, of which saturates 4.6g; Cholesterol 30mg; Calcium 34mg; Fibre 0.3g; Sodium 58mg.
Hazelnut Crescents Energy 102kcal/427kJ; Protein 1.9g; Carbohydrate 13.8g, of which sugars 7.6g; Fat 4.7g, of which saturates 2g; Cholesterol 2mg; Calcium 38mg; Fibre 0.5g; Sodium 9mg.

Chocolate Pretzels

Pretzels come in many different flavours – here is a delicious chocolate version that is guaranteed to please the tastebuds.

Makes 28
150g/5oz/1¼ cups plain
  (all-purpose) flour
1.5ml/¼ tsp salt

20g/¾oz/3 tbsp unsweetened
  cocoa powder
115g/4oz/½ cup butter,
  at room temperature
130g/4½oz/scant ¾ cup caster
  (superfine) sugar
1 egg
1 egg white, lightly beaten,
  for glazing
sugar crystals, for sprinkling

1 Sift together the flour, salt and cocoa powder. Set aside. Cream the butter until light. Add the sugar and continue beating until light and fluffy. Beat in the egg.

2 Add the dry ingredients and stir to blend thoroughly. Gather the dough into a ball, wrap it in clear film (plastic wrap) and chill for 1 hour.

3 Roll the dough into 28 small balls. Chill the balls until needed. Preheat the oven to 190°C/375°F/Gas 5. Lightly grease two baking sheets.

4 Roll each ball into a rope about 25cm/10in long. With each rope, form a loop with the two ends facing you. Twist the ends and fold them back on to the circle, pressing them in to make a pretzel shape. Place on the prepared baking sheets.

5 Brush each of the pretzels with the egg white. Sprinkle sugar crystals over the tops and bake in the oven until firm, about 10–12 minutes. Using a metal spatula, transfer to a wire rack to cool.

Variation
Try making coffee-flavoured pretzels. Simply replace 10ml/ 1 tsp of the unsweetened cocoa powder with some instant coffee powder.

Tiramisu Biscuits

These sophisticated biscuits taste like the famed Italian dessert, with its flavours of coffee, chocolate and rum. A perfect luxurious accompaniment to ices, fools or other light dishes.

Makes 14
50g/2oz/¼ cup butter, at room
  temperature, diced
90g/3½oz/½ cup caster
  (superfine) sugar
1 egg, beaten
50g/2oz/½ cup plain
  (all-purpose) flour

For the filling
150g/5oz/⅔ cup mascarpone
15ml/1 tbsp dark rum
2.5ml/½ tsp instant
  coffee powder
15ml/1 tbsp light muscovado
  (brown) sugar

For the topping
75g/3oz white chocolate
15ml/1 tbsp milk
30ml/2 tbsp crushed
  chocolate flake

1 Make the filling. Put the mascarpone in a bowl. Mix together the rum and coffee powder until the coffee has dissolved. Add to the cheese, with the sugar, and mix together well. Cover with clear film (plastic wrap) and chill until required.

2 Preheat the oven to 200°C/400°F/Gas 6. Line two or three baking sheets with baking parchment. Make the biscuits (cookies). Cream together the butter and sugar in a bowl until light and fluffy. Add the egg and mix well. Stir in the flour and mix thoroughly.

3 Put the mixture into a piping (pastry) bag fitted with a 1.5cm/½in plain nozzle and pipe 28 small blobs on to the baking sheets, spaced slightly apart. Cook for 6–8 minutes, until firm in the centre and just beginning to brown on the edges. Remove from the oven and set aside to cool.

4 To assemble, spread a little of the filling on to half the biscuits and place the other halves on top. Put the chocolate and milk in a heatproof bowl and melt over a pan of hot water. When melted, stir vigorously until spreadable. Spread the chocolate evenly over the biscuits, then top with crushed chocolate flake.

Chocolate Pretzels Energy 72kcal/303kJ; Protein 1g; Carbohydrate 9.1g, of which sugars 5g; Fat 3.8g, of which saturates 2.3g; Cholesterol 16mg; Calcium 13mg; Fibre 0.3g; Sodium 37mg.
Tiramisu Biscuits Energy 178kcal/742kJ; Protein 2.4g; Carbohydrate 15.5g, of which sugars 12.8g; Fat 7.2g, of which saturates 4.3g; Cholesterol 26mg; Calcium 28mg; Fibre 0.2g; Sodium 34mg.

Chocolate Florentines

These big, flat, crunchy cookies are just like traditional florentines but use tiny seeds instead of nuts. Rolling the edges in milk or white chocolate makes them feel like a real treat.

Makes 12
50g/2oz/¼ cup unsalted (sweet) butter
50g/2oz/¼ cup caster (superfine) sugar
15ml/1 tbsp milk
25g/1oz/scant ¼ cup pumpkin seeds
40g/1½oz/generous ¼ cup sunflower seeds
50g/2oz/scant ½ cup raisins
25g/1oz/2 tbsp multi-coloured glacé (candied) cherries, chopped
30ml/2 tbsp plain (all-purpose) flour
125g/4¼oz milk or white chocolate

1 Preheat the oven to 180°C/350°F/Gas 4. Line two baking sheets with baking parchment and grease the paper well.

2 In a pan, melt the butter with the sugar, stirring, until the sugar has dissolved, then cook until bubbling. Remove the pan from the heat and stir in the milk, pumpkin and sunflower seeds, raisins, glacé cherries and flour. Mix well.

3 Spoon six teaspoonfuls of the mixture on to each baking sheet, spacing them well apart. Bake for 8–10 minutes until the cookies are turning dark golden. Using a metal spatula, push back the edges of the cookies to neaten. Leave on the baking sheets for about 5 minutes to firm up, then transfer to a wire rack to cool.

4 Break up the chocolate and put in a heatproof bowl set over a pan of gently simmering water. Heat, stirring frequently, until melted. Roll the edges of the cookies in the chocolate and leave to set on a clean sheet of baking parchment for about 1 hour.

> **Variation**
> *If you prefer, use plain (semisweet) or dark (bittersweet) chocolate to decorate the cookies.*

Oat Florentines

These irresistible 'bakes' make the best of familiar flapjacks and old-fashioned, chocolate-coated florentine biscuits. They take just minutes to microwave.

Makes 16
75g/3oz/6 tbsp butter
45ml/3 tbsp/¼ cup golden (light corn) syrup
115g/4oz/1¼ cups rolled oats
25g/1oz/2 tbsp soft light brown sugar
25g/1oz/2 tbsp chopped mixed (candied) peel
25g/1oz/2 tbsp glacé (candied) cherries, coarsely chopped
25g/1oz/¼ cup hazelnuts, coarsely chopped
115g/4oz plain (semisweet) chocolate

1 Lightly grease a 20cm/8in square microwaveproof shallow dish and line the base with a sheet of rice paper.

2 Place the butter and golden syrup in a microwaveproof bowl and microwave on high for 1½ minutes to melt. Stir well. Add the oats, sugar, peel, cherries and hazelnuts, mixing well to blend.

3 Spoon the mixture into the dish and level the surface with the back of a spoon. Microwave the mixture on medium high for 6 minutes, giving the dish a half turn about every 2 minutes. Allow to cool in the dish slightly, then cut into 16 fingers and place on a wire rack to cool completely.

4 Break the chocolate into pieces and place in a microwaveproof bowl. Microwave on high for 2–3 minutes, stirring twice, until melted and smooth. Spread over the tops of the florentines and mark in a zig-zag pattern with the prongs of a fork. Leave to set.

> **Cook's Tip**
> *Rice paper is used for cooking in traditional recipes as well as in microwave methods. It helps to prevent mixtures, such as this sweet oat base, from sticking by cooking on to them. When cooked, the rice paper can just be eaten along with the biscuits or other bakes.*

Chocolate Florentines Energy 157kcal/656kJ; Protein 2.2g; Carbohydrate 17.5g, of which sugars 14.8g; Fat 9.1g, of which saturates 4.3g; Cholesterol 11mg; Calcium 40mg; Fibre 0.6g; Sodium 38mg.
Oat Florentines Energy 133kcal/555kJ; Protein 1.5g; Carbohydrate 15.7g, of which sugars 10.4g; Fat 7.5g, of which saturates 3.7g; Cholesterol 10mg; Calcium 14mg; Fibre 0.9g; Sodium 44mg.

Ginger Florentines

These colourful, chewy cookies are delicious served with vanilla or other flavoured ice cream.

Makes 30
50g/2oz/¼ cup butter
115g/4oz/generous ½ cup caster (superfine) sugar
50g/2oz/¼ cup mixed glacé (candied) cherries, chopped
25g/1oz/generous 1 tbsp candied orange peel, chopped
50g/2oz/½ cup flaked (sliced) almonds
50g/2oz/½ cup chopped walnuts
25g/1oz/1 tbsp glacé (candied) ginger, chopped
30ml/2 tbsp plain (all-purpose) flour
2.5ml/½ tsp ground ginger

To finish
50g/2oz plain (semisweet) chocolate, melted
50g/2oz white chocolate, melted

1 Preheat the oven to 180°C/350°F/Gas 4. Beat the butter and sugar together until light and fluffy.

2 Add the glacé cherries, candied orange peel, flaked almonds, chopped walnuts and glacé ginger to the mixture, and blend thoroughly. Sift the plain flour and ground ginger into the mixture and stir well to combine.

3 Line some baking sheets with baking parchment. Put four small spoonfuls of the mixture on to each sheet, spacing them well apart to allow for spreading. Flatten the cookies and bake for 5 minutes.

4 Remove the cookies from the oven and flatten with a wet fork, shaping them into neat rounds.

5 Return to the oven for about 3–4 minutes, until they are golden brown. Work in batches if necessary.

6 Let them cool on the baking sheets for 2 minutes to firm up, and then transfer them to a wire rack. When they are cold and firm, spread plain chocolate on the undersides of half the cookies and white chocolate on the rest. Allow the chocolate to set before serving.

Mini Florentines with Grand Marnier

Orange liqueur adds a touch of luxury to these ever-popular biscuits.

Makes 8
50g/2oz/¼ cup soft light brown sugar
15ml/1 tbsp clear honey
15ml/1 tbsp Grand Marnier
50g/2oz/¼ cup unsalted (sweet) butter
40g/1½oz/⅓ cup plain (all-purpose) flour
25g/1oz/¼ cup hazelnuts and almonds, chopped
50g/2oz/¼ cup glacé (candied) cherries, chopped
115g/4oz plain (semisweet) chocolate, broken into squares

1 Preheat the oven to 180°C/350°F/Gas 4 and line three or four baking sheets with baking parchment.

2 Put the sugar, honey, Grand Marnier and unsalted butter in a small pan and melt over a low heat, stirring occasionally.

3 Remove the pan from the heat and tip in the flour, chopped hazelnuts, almonds and glacé cherries. Stir the mixture until it is well combined.

4 Spoon small heaps of the mixture on to the baking sheets, spacing them slightly apart to allow for spreading while they are baking.

5 Bake for 10 minutes until golden brown. Leave the florentines on the baking sheets until the edges begin to harden a little, then transfer to a wire rack to cool.

6 Melt the chocolate in a double boiler or in a heatproof bowl set over a pan of barely simmering water, stirring constantly until smooth. While still warm, spread a little over one side of each florentine. As the chocolate begins to set, drag a fork through to make wavy lines. Leave to set completely, then turn the florentines over and drizzle thin chocolate lines over the tops of the biscuits.

Ginger Florentines Energy 71kcal/298kJ; Protein 0.9g; Carbohydrate 8.6g, of which sugars 7.8g; Fat 3.9g, of which saturates 1.3g; Cholesterol 2mg; Calcium 16mg; Fibre 0.3g; Sodium 11mg.
Mini Energy 214kcal/897kJ; Protein 2.7g; Carbohydrate 22.57g, of which sugars 18.9g; Fat 12.87g, of which saturates 5.35g; Cholesterol 12mg; Calcium 34mg; Fibre 1.08g; Sodium 37mg.

Midnight Chocolate Chip Cookies

These cookies are so called because you can make them up before you go to bed and leave them to bake slowly in the switched-off oven. Hey presto – there they are in the morning, lightly crunchy on the outside and deliciously soft in the middle. A wonderfully indulgent way to start the day.

Makes 9
1 egg white
90g/3½oz/½ cup caster (superfine) sugar
50g/2oz/½ cup ground almonds
90g/3½oz/generous ½ cup milk chocolate chips
90g/3½oz/scant ½ cup glacé (candied) cherries, chopped
50g/2oz/⅔ cup sweetened, shredded coconut

1 Preheat the oven to 220°C/425°F/Gas 7. Line a baking sheet with baking parchment.

2 Put the egg white in a large, clean, grease-free bowl and whisk until stiff peaks form.

3 Add the caster sugar to the whisked egg white, a spoonful at a time, whisking well between each addition until the sugar is fully incorporated. The mixture should be completely smooth and glossy in appearance. Use an electric mixer for speed.

4 Fold in the almonds, chocolate chips, cherries and coconut, mixing until well combined.

5 Place nine spoonfuls of the mixture on the baking sheet, spacing them slightly apart.

6 Place in the oven, close the door then turn the oven off. Leave overnight and don't open the door. Serve the cookies for breakfast.

Cook's Tip
Instead of leaving the cookies in the oven overnight you can put them in for about 6 hours during the day.

Sticky Chocolate, Maple and Walnut Swirls

These delicious syrupy cakes are a great tea-time treat.

Makes one 23cm/9in round cake
450g/1lb/4 cups strong white flour
2.5ml/½ tsp ground cinnamon
50g/2oz/¼ cup unsalted (sweet) butter, cut into small pieces
50g/2oz/¼ cup caster (superfine) sugar
1 sachet easy-blend (rapid-rise) dried yeast

1 egg yolk
120ml/4fl oz/½ cup water
60ml/4 tbsp milk
45ml/3 tbsp maple syrup, to finish

For the filling
40g/1½oz/3 tbsp unsalted (sweet) butter, melted
50g/2oz/¼ cup light muscovado (brown) sugar
175g/6oz/1 cup plain (semisweet) chocolate chips
75g/3oz/¾ cup chopped walnuts

1 Grease a deep 23cm/9in springform cake tin (pan). Sift the flour and cinnamon into a bowl, then rub in the butter until the mixture resembles coarse breadcrumbs.

2 Stir in the sugar and yeast. In a jug (pitcher) or bowl, beat the egg yolk with the water and milk, then stir into the dry ingredients to make a soft dough.

3 Knead the dough on a lightly floured surface until smooth, then roll out to a rectangle measuring 40 × 30cm/16 × 12in.

4 For the filling, brush the dough with the melted butter and sprinkle with the sugar, chocolate chips and nuts.

5 Roll up the dough from one long side like a Swiss roll, then cut into 12 even slices. Pack close together in the prepared tin, cut sides up. Cover and leave in a warm place for 1½ hours, or until the dough is well risen and springy. Meanwhile, preheat the oven to 220°C/425°F/Gas 7.

6 Bake for 30–35 minutes, until golden brown. Remove from the tin and cool on a wire rack. Brush with maple syrup while still warm. Pull swirls apart to serve.

Midnight Cookies Energy 185kcal/777kJ; Protein 2.7g; Carbohydrate 23.5g, of which sugars 23.4g; Fat 9.6g, of which saturates 5g; Cholesterol 2mg; Calcium 48mg; Fibre 1.3g; Sodium 21mg.
Sticky Swirls Energy 341kcal/1433kJ; Protein 5.7g; Carbohydrate 47.6g, of which sugars 18.8g; Fat 15.6g, of which saturates 7g; Cholesterol 34mg; Calcium 77mg; Fibre 1.7g; Sodium 51mg.

Nut Bar Chocolate Cookies

If you love chocolate, condensed milk, nuts and crumb crust then these are the cookies for you. It's fortunate that they are incredibly easy to make because they are even easier to eat, and are sure to become firm favourites with all the family. Children enjoy helping to make them.

Makes 16–18
250g/9oz digestive biscuits (graham crackers)
115g/4oz/½ cup butter, melted
150g/5oz/scant 1 cup milk chocolate chips
200g/7oz mixed whole nuts, such as pecan nuts, hazelnuts, brazil nuts, walnuts and almonds
200ml/7fl oz/scant 1 cup sweetened condensed milk

1 Preheat the oven to 180°C/350°F/Gas 4. Crush the biscuits in a plastic bag, remembering to close the open end, with a rolling pin until broken into fine crumbs.

2 Melt the butter in a pan over a low heat. Put the biscuit crumbs in a large bowl and stir in the melted butter. Mix well.

3 Press the mixture evenly into the base of a 10 × 36cm/ 4 × 14in cake tin (pan).

4 Sprinkle the chocolate chips over the biscuit base. Arrange the nuts on top and pour the condensed milk over the top, spreading it evenly.

5 Bake in the oven for about 20–25 minutes, or until bubbling and golden.

6 Leave to cool slightly in the tin. Loosen from the sides, then cool completely and slice into thin bars.

> **Cook's Tip**
> *If you prefer, you can use a shallow 20cm/8in cake tin (pan) instead for this recipe. When the cookies are done, cut them into squares rather than thin bars.*

Chocolate and Prune Cookies

When freshly baked, these cookies have a deliciously gooey centre. As they cool down the mixture hardens slightly to form a firmer, fudge-like consistency. Try these with a glass of brandy.

Makes 18
150g/5oz/10 tbsp butter, at room temperature, diced
150g/5oz/¾ cup caster (superfine) sugar
1 egg yolk
250g/9oz/2¼ cups self-raising (self-rising) flour
25g/1oz/¼ cup unsweetened cocoa powder
about 90g/3½oz plain (semisweet) chocolate, coarsely chopped

For the topping
50g/2oz plain (semisweet) chocolate
9 ready-to-eat prunes, halved

1 Preheat the oven to 190°C/375°F/Gas 5. Line two baking sheets with baking parchment. Cream the butter and sugar together until light and creamy. Beat in the egg yolk. Sift over the flour and cocoa powder and stir in to make a firm yet soft dough.

2 Roll out about a third of the dough on baking parchment. Using a 5cm/2in round biscuit (cookie) cutter, stamp out 18 rounds and place them on the baking sheets.

3 Sprinkle the chopped chocolate in the centre of each cookie. Roll out the remaining dough in the same way as before and, using a 7.5cm/3in round biscuit (cookie) cutter, stamp out 18 'lids'. Lay the lids over the cookie bases and press the edges together to seal. Don't worry if the lids crack slightly.

4 Bake for about 10 minutes, until the cookies have spread a little and are just firm to a light touch. Leave them on the baking sheets for about 5 minutes to firm up slightly, then, using a metal spatula, transfer to a wire rack to cool completely.

5 For the topping, melt the chocolate in a heatproof bowl set over a pan of hot water. Dip the cut side of the prunes in the chocolate then place one on top of each cookie. Spoon any remaining chocolate over the prunes.

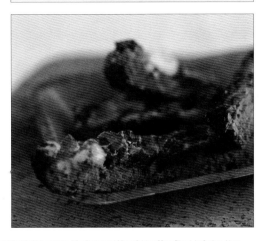

Prune Cookies Energy 197kcal/825kJ; Protein 2.3g; Carbohydrate 26.4g, of which sugars 15.5g; Fat 9.8g, of which saturates 5.9g; Cholesterol 29mg; Calcium 33mg; Fibre 1.1g; Sodium 66mg.
Nut Bar Cookies Energy 259kcal/1078kJ; Protein 3.4g; Carbohydrate 20g, of which sugars 12.2g; Fat 18.9g, of which saturates 7.1g; Cholesterol 25mg; Calcium 67mg; Fibre 0.9g; Sodium 143mg.

Shape and Bake Chocolate Cookies

The mixture for these simple Maryland-style cookies can be made and stored in the refrigerator. It's so easy to cook some each day – and there's nothing like a warm, freshly baked cookie.

Makes about 12 giant or 20 standard size cookies
115g/4oz/1/2 cup unsalted (sweet) butter, at room temperature, diced
115g/4oz/generous 1/2 cup granulated (white) sugar
115g/4oz/1/2 cup light muscovado (brown) sugar
1 large (US extra large) egg
5ml/1 tsp vanilla extract
200g/7oz/1¾ cups self-raising (self-rising) flour
150g/5oz/scant 1 cup chocolate chips
50g/2oz/1/2 cup chopped toasted hazelnuts or walnuts
50g/2oz/scant 1/2 cup raisins

1 Preheat the oven to 180°C/350°F/Gas 4. Line two baking sheets with baking parchment. Put the butter and sugars in a large bowl and beat together until light and fluffy. Add the egg and vanilla extract and beat again until well combined.

2 Add the flour, chocolate chips, chopped toasted hazelnuts or walnuts and raisins, and mix together until the ingredients have just blended. The dough should have a slightly crumbly consistency.

3 Depending on whether you want giant or standard size cookies, place tablespoonfuls or teaspoonfuls of the mixture on the prepared baking sheets. Bake for 15 minutes until golden.

4 Leave the cookies on the baking sheets for 5 minutes, then use a metal spatula to transfer to a wire rack to cool.

Cook's Tip
If you don't want to bake the mixture all at once, simply spoon into a plastic container, cover with clear film (plastic wrap) and replace the lid. Keep in the refrigerator for up to 1 week. When required, remove the dough from the refrigerator 15 minutes before baking the cookies, and shape and bake as before.

Chocolate Crispy Cookies

These little chocolate-coated cornflake cakes are always a hit with kids. They couldn't be easier to make – and are great for young aspiring cooks who want to get involved in the kitchen. The only problem is giving the mixture time to set before they've been gobbled up by hungry helpers.

Makes 10
90g/3½oz milk chocolate
15ml/1 tbsp golden (light corn) syrup
90g/3½oz/4½ cups cornflakes
icing (confectioners') sugar, for dusting

1 Line a large baking sheet with baking parchment.

2 Break the chocolate into a heatproof bowl and add the syrup. Rest the bowl over a pan of gently simmering water and leave until melted, stirring frequently. Ensure that the water doesn't touch the bowl.

3 Put the cornflakes in a plastic bag and, using a rolling pin, lightly crush them, breaking them all up into fairly small pieces but not too fine.

4 Remove the bowl from the heat and tip in the cornflakes. Mix well until the cornflakes are thoroughly coated in the chocolate mixture.

5 Place a 6cm/2½in round biscuit (cookie) cutter on the paper and put a spoonful of the chocolate mixture in the centre. Pack the mixture down firmly with the back of the spoon to make a thick cookie.

6 Gently ease away the cutter, using the spoon to help keep the mixture in place. Continue making cookies in this way until all the mixture has been used up. Chill for 1 hour.

7 Put a little icing sugar in a small bowl. Lift each cookie from the paper and carefully roll the edges in the icing sugar, until coated, to finish.

Shape and Bake Energy 187kcal/786kJ; Protein 2.1g; Carbohydrate 26.5g, of which sugars 18.7g; Fat 8.8g, of which saturates 4.5g; Cholesterol 22mg; Calcium 30mg; Fibre 0.7g; Sodium 41mg.
Crispy Cookies Energy 84kcal/355kJ; Protein 1.4g; Carbohydrate 14.2g, of which sugars 7.2g; Fat 2.8g, of which saturates 1.7g; Cholesterol 2mg; Calcium 21mg; Fibre 0.2g; Sodium 112mg.

Chocolate Fruit and Nut Cookies

These simple, chunky gingerbread cookies make a delicious gift, especially when presented in a decorative box. The combination of walnuts, almonds and cherries is very effective, but you can use any other mixture of glacé or candied fruits and nuts.

Makes 20

50g/2oz/¼ cup caster
   (superfine) sugar
75ml/5 tbsp water
225g/8oz plain (semisweet)
   chocolate, chopped
40g/1½oz/scant ½ cup
   walnut halves

75g/3oz/⅓ cup glacé (candied)
   cherries, chopped into
   small wedges
115g/4oz/1 cup whole
   blanched almonds

For the Lebkuchen

115g/4oz/½ cup unsalted
   (sweet) butter
115g/4oz/½ cup light
   muscovado (brown) sugar
1 egg, beaten
115g/4oz/⅓ cup black
   treacle (molasses)
400g/14oz/3½ cups self-raising
   (self-rising) flour
5ml/1 tsp ground ginger
2.5ml/½ tsp ground cloves
1.5ml/¼ tsp chilli powder

1 To make the cookies, cream together the butter and sugar until pale and fluffy. Beat in the egg and black treacle. Sift in the flour, ginger, cloves and chilli powder. Gradually mix the ingredients to make a stiff paste. Turn on to a floured surface and knead until smooth. Wrap and chill for 30 minutes.

2 Shape the dough into a roll, 20cm/8in long. Chill for 30 minutes. Preheat the oven to 180°C/350°F/Gas 4. Grease two baking sheets. Cut the roll into 20 slices and place on the sheets. Bake for 10 minutes. Leave to cool for 5 minutes, then transfer to a wire rack.

3 Put the sugar and water in a pan. Heat gently until the sugar has dissolved. Boil without stirring for 1 minute, until slightly syrupy. Leave off the heat for 3 minutes to cool, and then stir in the chocolate until it has melted and made a smooth sauce.

4 Spoon the chocolate mixture over the cookies. Gently press a walnut half into the centre. Arrange pieces of glacé cherry and almonds alternately around the nuts. Leave to set.

Ice Cream Sandwich Cookies

These are great when you get those midnight munchies – either keep the chocolate cookies in an airtight container and sandwich together each time with the softened ice cream of your choice, or make the sandwiches complete with ice cream and coating and freeze until required.

Makes 12

115g/4oz/½ cup unsalted
   (sweet) butter, at room
   temperature, diced
115g/4oz/generous ½ cup
   caster (superfine) sugar
1 egg, beaten
200g/7oz/1¾ cups plain
   (all-purpose) flour
25g/1oz/¼ cup unsweetened
   cocoa powder, sifted
ice cream, to fill
toasted nuts, biscuit (cookie)
   crumbs, chocolate flakes
   or demerara (raw) sugar,
   to coat

1 Preheat the oven to 180°C/350°F/Gas 4. Cream the butter and sugar together until light and fluffy, then beat in the egg. Stir in the flour and cocoa powder to make a firm dough.

2 Roll the dough out to a thickness of 5mm/¼in on baking parchment. Using a 7.5cm/3in plain round biscuit (cookie) cutter, stamp out 24 rounds and place on the prepared baking sheets. Alternatively, cut into squares or rectangles, ensuring they are an equal size.

3 Bake the cookies for about 15 minutes until firm. Set aside on the baking sheets to cool.

4 To make the ice cream cookies, spread two good spoonfuls of softened ice cream on a cookie and press a second on top. Squeeze down gently so that the ice cream reaches the edges of the cookies.

5 Put your chosen coating on a plate and roll the cookies in it to coat the sides. Either eat straight away or wrap individually in foil and freeze. The cookies may be kept for up to 2 weeks in the freezer.

Fruit and Nut Energy 278kcal/1166kJ; Protein 4.4g; Carbohydrate 38.2g, of which sugars 22.6g; Fat 13g, of which saturates 5.4g; Cholesterol 22mg; Calcium 88mg; Fibre 1.4g; Sodium 52mg.
Sandwich Energy 184kcal/771kJ; Protein 3.3g; Carbohydrate 20.1g, of which sugars 13.5g; Fat 10.7g, of which saturates 4.7g; Cholesterol 18mg; Calcium 36mg; Fibre 0.8g; Sodium 73mg.

Triple Chocolate Sandwiches

Chocolate shortbread
is a brilliant base for
sandwiching or coating
in lashings of melted
chocolate. Kids of any age
can enjoy making them
as they don't need to
be perfectly uniform.

150g/5oz/1¼ cups plain
(all-purpose) flour
30ml/2 tbsp unsweetened
cocoa powder
50g/2oz/¼ cup caster
(superfine) sugar
75g/3oz white chocolate
25g/1oz/2 tbsp unsalted
(sweet) butter
115g/4oz milk chocolate

Makes 15
125g/4¼oz/generous ½ cup
unsalted (sweet) butter, chilled
and diced

1 Put the butter, flour and cocoa in a food processor. Process until the mixture resembles breadcrumbs. Add the sugar and process again until the mixture forms a dough. Knead lightly then wrap in clear film (plastic wrap) and chill for 30 minutes.

2 Preheat the oven to 200°C/400°F/ Gas 6. Grease a large baking sheet. Roll out the chilled dough on a floured surface to a 33 × 16cm/13 × 6¼in rectangle. Lift on to the baking sheet and trim the edges. Cut the dough in half lengthways, then cut across at 2cm/¾in intervals to make 30 small bars.

3 Prick each bar with a fork and bake for 12–15 minutes until just beginning to darken around the edges. Remove from the oven and cut between the bars again while the cookies are still warm. Leave for 2 minutes, then transfer to a wire rack to cool.

4 Make the filling. Break the white chocolate into a heatproof bowl. Add half the butter and set the bowl over a pan of hot water and stir until melted. Spread the filling evenly on to one of the bars. Place another bar on top and press to sandwich the cookies. Continue with the remaining cookies and filling.

5 Make the topping. Break the milk chocolate into a heatproof bowl. Add the remaining butter and set over a pan of hot water. Drizzle the chocolate over the cookies, then leave to set.

Dark Chocolate Fingers

With their understated
elegance and distinctly
grown-up flavour, these
deliciously decadent
chocolate fingers add
a touch of luxury to
compotes and other
fruity desserts.

30ml/2 tbsp unsweetened
cocoa powder
50g/2oz/¼ cup unsalted
(sweet) butter, softened
50g/2oz/¼ cup caster
(superfine) sugar
20ml/4 tsp golden
(light corn) syrup
150g/5oz dark
(bittersweet) chocolate
chocolate flake, broken up,
for sprinkling

Makes about 26
115g/4oz/1 cup plain
(all-purpose) flour
2.5ml/½ tsp baking powder

1 Preheat the oven to 160°C/325°F/Gas 3. Line two baking sheets with baking parchment. Put the flour, baking powder, cocoa powder, butter, sugar and syrup in a large mixing bowl.

2 Work the ingredients together with your hands to combine and form into a dough.

3 Roll the dough out between sheets of baking parchment to an 18 × 24cm/7 × 9½in rectangle. Remove the top sheet. Cut in half lengthways, then into bars 2cm/¾in wide. Transfer to the baking sheets.

4 Bake for about 15 minutes, taking care not to allow the bars to brown or they will taste bitter. Transfer to a wire rack to cool.

5 Melt the chocolate in a heatproof bowl set over a pan of hot water. Half-dip the bars into the chocolate, then carefully place on a sheet of baking parchment. Sprinkle with chocolate flake, then leave to set.

Variation
For an extra touch of sophistication, add a dash of orange-flavoured liqueur to the chocolate.

Dark Fingers Energy 72kcal/303kJ; Protein 0.9g; Carbohydrate 9.9g, of which sugars 6.3g; Fat 3.5g, of which saturates 2.1g; Cholesterol 4mg; Calcium 11mg; Fibre 0.4g; Sodium 25mg.
Sandwiches Energy 189kcal/790kJ; Protein 2.4g; Carbohydrate 18.8g, of which sugars 11g; Fat 12.1g, of which saturates 7.5g; Cholesterol 22mg; Calcium 50mg; Fibre 0.6g; Sodium 88mg.

Nut Wafers with Chocolate Drizzle

Delicate wafers filled with
a sweet, peanut-flavoured
buttercream and drizzled
with chocolate make a fun,
no-bake recipe that kids of
any age can help with. Just
remember to chill the wafer
sandwiches after they have
been assembled, otherwise
they will be almost
impossible to cut.

Makes 12

65g/2½oz/4 tbsp unsalted
  (sweet) butter, at room
  temperature, diced
65g/2½oz/9 tbsp icing
  (confectioners') sugar
115g/4oz/½ cup crunchy
  peanut butter
12 fan-shaped wafers
50g/2oz plain
  (semisweet) chocolate

1 Put the butter and sugar in a bowl and beat with a hand-held electric whisk until very light and creamy. Beat in the peanut butter, until well combined.

2 Using a small metal spatula, spread a thick layer of the mixture on to a wafer and spread to the edges. Place another wafer on top of the peanut buttercream and press it down very gently. Spread the top wafer with more buttercream, then place another wafer on top and press down gently.

3 Use the remaining buttercream and wafers to assemble three more fans in the same way. Spread any remaining buttercream around the sides of the fans. Chill for at least 30 minutes until firm.

4 Using a serrated knife, carefully slice each fan into three equal wedges and arrange in a single layer on a small tray.

5 Break the chocolate into pieces and put in a heatproof bowl placed over a pan of gently simmering water. Stir frequently until melted.

6 Remove the bowl from the heat and leave to stand for a few minutes to cool slightly.

7 Drizzle lines of chocolate over the wafers, then leave to set in a cool place for at least 1 hour.

Chocolate Whirls

These cookies are so easy
that you don't even have
to make any dough. They're
made with ready-made
puff pastry rolled up with
a chocolate filling. They're
not too sweet and are
similar to Danish pastries,
so you could even make
them as a special treat
for breakfast.

Makes about 20

75g/3oz/scant ½ cup golden
  caster (superfine) sugar
40g/1½oz/⅓ cup unsweetened
  cocoa powder
2 eggs
500g/1¼lb puff pastry
25g/1oz/2 tbsp butter, softened
75g/3oz/generous ½ cup sultanas
  (golden raisins)
90g/3½oz milk chocolate

1 Preheat the oven to 220°C/425°F/Gas 7. Lightly grease two baking sheets.

2 Put the sugar, cocoa powder and eggs in a large bowl and mix to a paste.

3 Roll out the pastry on a lightly floured surface to make a 30cm/12in square. Trim off any rough edges using a sharp knife.

4 Dot the pastry all over with the softened butter, then spread evenly with the chocolate paste and sprinkle the sultanas over the top.

5 Roll the pastry into a sausage-shape, then cut the roll into 1cm/½in slices. Place the slices on the baking sheets, spacing them apart.

6 Bake the cookies for 10 minutes, until risen and pale golden. Transfer to a wire rack and leave to cool.

7 Break the milk chocolate into small pieces and put in a heatproof bowl set over a pan of gently simmering water. Heat, stirring frequently, until melted and smooth.

8 Spoon or pipe lines of melted chocolate over the tops of the cookies, taking care not to completely hide the swirls of chocolate filling.

Nut Wafers Energy 184kcal/769kJ; Protein 3.7g; Carbohydrate 19.4g, of which sugars 9.1g; Fat 10.7g, of which saturates 4.8g; Cholesterol 12mg; Calcium 30mg; Fibre 0.6g; Sodium 79mg.
Whirls Energy 165kcal/689kJ; Protein 2.9g; Carbohydrate 18.6g, of which sugars 9.4g; Fat 9.5g, of which saturates 1.9g; Cholesterol 23mg; Calcium 34mg; Fibre 0.4g; Sodium 117mg.

Gingerbread Family

You can have great fun with these cookies by creating characters with different features. By using an assortment of different gingerbread cutters you can make a gingerbread family of all shapes and sizes. If you want to make decorating the cookies simpler, use just one colour of chocolate rather than three. Coloured writer icing and candy are also good for decorating.

Makes about 12

350g/12oz/3 cups plain (all-purpose) flour

5ml/1 tsp bicarbonate of soda (baking soda)
5ml/1 tsp ground ginger
115g/4oz/½ cup unsalted (sweet) butter, chilled and diced
175g/6oz/¾ cup light muscovado (brown) sugar
1 egg
30ml/2 tbsp black treacle (molasses) or golden (light corn) syrup
50g/2oz each plain (semisweet), milk and white chocolate, to decorate

1 Preheat the oven to 180°C/350°F/Gas 4. Lightly grease two large baking sheets.

2 Put the flour, bicarbonate of soda, ginger and butter into the food processor. Process until the mixture resembles fine breadcrumbs. Add the sugar, egg and treacle or syrup to the processor and process the mixture until it forms into a ball. Turn out on to a floured surface, and knead until smooth.

3 Roll out the dough on a lightly floured surface. Cut out figures using people-shaped cutters, then transfer to the baking sheets. Re-roll any trimmings and cut out more figures. Bake for 15 minutes until slightly risen and starting to colour around the edges. Leave for 5 minutes, then transfer to a wire rack to cool.

4 To decorate the cookies, break each type of chocolate into a separate bowl. One at a time, set a bowl over a pan of simmering water and heat, stirring until melted. Spoon into paper piping (pastry) bags, snip off the merest tip, then pipe faces and clothes on to the cookies. Leave to set.

Iced Chocolate Ginger Cookies

If your children enjoy cooking with you, mixing and rolling the dough and cutting out all sorts of different shapes, this is the ideal recipe to let them practise on.

Makes 16

115g/4oz/½ cup soft light brown sugar

115g/4oz/½ cup soft margarine
pinch of salt
a few drops of vanilla extract
175g/6oz/1¼ cups wholemeal (whole-wheat) flour
15ml/1 tbsp unsweetened cocoa powder, sifted
10ml/2 tsp ground ginger
glacé icing and glacé (candied) cherries, to decorate

1 Preheat the oven to 190°C/375°F/Gas 5. Lightly grease one or two large baking sheets.

2 Cream together the sugar, margarine, salt and vanilla extract until very soft and light.

3 Work in the flour, cocoa powder and ginger, mixing until well combined. Add a little water, if necessary, in order to bind the mixture together.

4 Turn the mixture out on to a lighty floured surface and knead until smooth.

5 Roll out the dough to about 5mm/¼in thick. Stamp out shapes using floured biscuit (cookie) cutters and place on the baking sheet.

6 Bake the cookies for about 10–15 minutes, until just firm to a light touch.

7 Leave to cool on the baking sheets until completely firm, then transfer to a wire rack to cool completely.

8 To decorate the cookies, spread glacé icing over the tops, spreading it evenly to the edges. Gently press pieces of glacé cherries into the icing. You can use other decorations, such as mixed (candied) peel, if you prefer.

Gingerbread Energy 305kcal/1281kJ; Protein 4.1g; Carbohydrate 47.6g, of which sugars 25.2g; Fat 12.2g, of which saturates 7.3g; Cholesterol 37mg; Calcium 71mg; Fibre 1.2g; Sodium 71mg.
Ginger Cookies Energy 119kcal/497kJ; Protein 1.6g; Carbohydrate 14.7g, of which sugars 7.8g; Fat 6.4g, of which saturates 3.9g; Cholesterol 15mg; Calcium 11mg; Fibre 1.1g; Sodium 53mg.

Double Gingerbread Cookies

Packed in little bags, these festive two-tone cookies would make a lovely Christmas gift. They are easy to make, but will have everyone wondering how you did it.

Makes 25
For the golden gingerbread
175g/6oz/1½ cups plain (all-purpose) flour
1.5ml/¼ tsp bicarbonate of soda (baking soda)
pinch of salt
5ml/1 tsp ground cinnamon
65g/2½oz/5 tbsp unsalted (sweet) butter, cut into pieces
75g/3oz/scant ½ cup caster (superfine) sugar

30ml/2 tbsp maple syrup
1 egg yolk, beaten

For the chocolate gingerbread
175g/6oz/1½ cups plain (all-purpose) flour
pinch of salt
10ml/2 tsp mixed (apple pie) spice
2.5ml/½ tsp bicarbonate of soda (baking soda)
25g/1oz/¼ cup unsweetened cocoa powder
75g/3oz/6 tbsp unsalted (sweet) butter, chopped
75g/3oz/6 tbsp light muscovado (brown) sugar
1 egg, beaten

1 To make the golden gingerbread mixture, sift together the flour, bicarbonate of soda, salt and cinnamon into a large bowl. Rub the butter into the flour mixture until it resembles fine breadcrumbs. Add the sugar, syrup and egg yolk and mix to a firm dough. Knead lightly. Wrap in clear film (plastic wrap) and chill in the refrigerator for 30 minutes before shaping.

2 To make the chocolate gingerbread mixture, sift together the flour, salt, spice, bicarbonate of soda and cocoa powder. Knead the butter into the flour in a large bowl. Add the sugar and egg and mix to a firm dough. Knead lightly. Wrap in clear film and chill for 30 minutes.

3 Roll out half of the chocolate dough on a floured surface to a 28 × 4cm/11 × 1½in rectangle, 1cm/½in thick. Repeat with half of the golden gingerbread dough. Using a knife, cut both lengths into seven long, thin strips. Lay the strips together, side by side, alternating the chocolate and golden dough.

4 Roll out the remaining golden gingerbread dough with your hands to a long sausage, 2cm/¾in wide and the length of the strips. Lay the sausage of dough down the centre of the striped dough. Carefully bring the striped dough up around the sausage and press it in position, to enclose the sausage completely.

5 Roll out the remaining chocolate dough to a 28 × 13cm/ 11 × 5in rectangle. Bring the chocolate dough up around the striped dough, to enclose it. Press gently into place. Wrap and chill for 30 minutes.

6 Preheat the oven to 180°C/350°F/Gas 4. Grease a large baking sheet. Cut the gingerbread roll into thin slices and place them, slightly apart, on the prepared baking sheet.

7 Bake for about 12–15 minutes, until just beginning to colour around the edges. Leave on the baking sheet for 3 minutes, then transfer to a wire rack to cool completely.

Gingerbread Teddies

These endearing teddies, dressed in striped pyjamas, would make a perfect gift for friends. Children love to help make them, but might need a hand with the chocolate decorating.

Makes 6
75g/3oz white chocolate, melted
175g/6oz white Sugarpaste Icing
blue food colouring
25g/1oz plain (semisweet) or milk chocolate, melted

For the gingerbread
175g/6oz/1½ cups plain (all-purpose) flour
1.5ml/¼ tsp bicarbonate of soda (baking soda)
pinch of salt
5ml/1 tsp ground ginger
5ml/1 tsp ground cinnamon
65g/2½oz/5 tbsp unsalted (sweet) butter, diced
75g/3oz/scant ½ cup caster (superfine) sugar
30ml/2 tbsp maple or golden (light corn) syrup
1 egg yolk, beaten

1 To make the gingerbread, sift together the flour, bicarbonate of soda, salt, ginger and cinnamon into a bowl. Add the butter and rub it into the flour until it resembles breadcrumbs. Stir in the sugar, syrup and egg yolk and mix to a firm dough. Knead on a floured surface. Wrap and chill in the refrigerator for 30 minutes.

2 Preheat the oven to 180°C/350°F/Gas 4. Grease two large baking sheets. Roll out the dough on a floured surface, then stamp out teddies, using a 13cm/5in shaped cutter. Transfer the teddies to the baking sheets and bake for 10–15 minutes. Leave on the sheets for 3 minutes, then transfer to a wire rack to cool.

3 Spoon half the melted white chocolate into a piping (pastry) bag. Make a template for the clothes: draw an outline of the cutter on to paper, finishing at the neck, halfway down the arms and around the legs. Roll out the sugarpaste. Use the template to cut out the clothes, and secure with the chocolate. Use the trimmings to add ears, eyes and snouts. Dilute the blue colouring with water and use to paint the striped pyjamas.

4 Use the remaining white chocolate to pipe a decorative outline around the pyjamas and use the plain or milk chocolate to pipe the teddies' faces.

Cookies Energy 125kcal/526kJ; Protein 1.9g; Carbohydrate 18.2g, of which sugars 7.5g; Fat 5.4g, of which saturates 3.2g; Cholesterol 28mg; Calcium 27mg; Fibre 0.6g; Sodium 51mg.
Teddies Energy 375kcal/1576kJ; Protein 4.6g; Carbohydrate 58.4g, of which sugars 36.1g; Fat 15.2g, of which saturates 9g; Cholesterol 57mg; Calcium 94mg; Fibre 1g; Sodium 97mg.

Chocolate-dipped Cinnamon and Orange Tuiles

These lightweight tuiles
dipped in Belgian chocolate
will make a divine
accompaniment to fruit
or creamy desserts.

Makes 12–15
2 egg whites
90g/3½oz/½ cup caster
(superfine) sugar
7.5ml/1½ tsp ground cinnamon
finely grated rind of 1 orange

50g/2oz/½ cup plain
(all-purpose) flour
75g/3oz/6 tbsp butter, melted
15ml/1 tbsp recently boiled water

For the dipping chocolate
75g/3oz Belgian plain
(semisweet) chocolate
45ml/3 tbsp milk
75–90ml/5–6 tbsp double
(heavy) or whipping cream

1 Preheat the oven to 200°C/400°F/Gas 6. Line three large baking trays with baking parchment.

2 Whisk the egg whites until softly peaking, then whisk in the sugar until smooth and glossy. Add the cinnamon and orange rind, sift over the flour and fold in with the melted butter. When well blended, add water to thin the mixture.

3 Place 4–5 teaspoons of the mixture on each tray, well apart. Flatten out and bake, one tray at a time, for 7 minutes, until just turning golden. Cool for a few seconds, then remove from the tray with a metal spatula and immediately roll around the handle of a wooden spoon. Place on a rack to cool.

4 Melt the chocolate in the milk until smooth; stir in the cream. Dip one or both ends of the tuiles in the chocolate, then cool.

Cook's Tip
If you haven't made these before, cook only one or two at a time until you get the hang of it. If they harden too quickly to allow you time to roll them, return the baking sheet to the oven for a few seconds, then try rolling them again.

Chocolate Cinnamon Tuiles

These French treats
are named after their
resemblance to continental
roofing tiles. You may need
a bit of practice to get the
shaping process right as they
need to be formed before
the tuiles harden, but they
are so delicious they are
well worth the effort.

Makes 12
1 egg white
50g/2oz/¼ cup caster
(superfine) sugar
30ml/2 tbsp plain
(all-purpose) flour
40g/1½oz/3 tbsp butter, melted
15ml/1 tbsp unsweetened
cocoa powder
2.5ml/½ tsp ground cinnamon

1 Preheat the oven to 200°C/400°F/Gas 6. Lightly grease two large baking sheets. Whisk the egg white in a clean, grease-free bowl until it forms soft peaks. Gradually whisk in the sugar to make a smooth, glossy mixture.

2 Sift the flour over the meringue mixture and fold in evenly; try not to deflate the mixture. Stir in the butter. Transfer about 45ml/3 tbsp of the mixture to a small bowl and set it aside.

3 In a separate bowl, mix together the cocoa and cinnamon. Stir into the larger quantity of mixture until well combined.

4 Leaving room around each for spreading, drop spoonfuls of the chocolate-flavoured mixture on to the prepared baking sheets, then spread each gently with a metal spatula to make a neat round.

5 Using a small spoon, drizzle the reserved plain mixture over the rounds, swirling it lightly to give a marbled effect.

6 Bake in the oven for 4–6 minutes, until the tuiles are just set and beginning to colour.

7 Using a metal spatula, and working quickly, lift each tuile and drape it over a rolling pin, to give a curved shape. They will harden into this shape. Allow the tuiles to set completely, then remove them from the pin and finish cooling on a wire rack. Serve on the same day.

Chocolate-dipped Tuiles Energy 125kcal/523kJ; Protein 1.2g; Carbohydrate 12.3g, of which sugars 9.7g; Fat 8.3g, of which saturates 5.2g; Cholesterol 18mg; Calcium 17mg; Fibre 0.2g; Sodium 42mg.
Cinnamon Tuiles Energy 55kcal/229kJ; Protein 0.8g; Carbohydrate 6.5g, of which sugars 4.4g; Fat 3g, of which saturates 1.9g; Cholesterol 7mg; Calcium 8mg; Fibre 0.2g; Sodium 38mg.

Chocolate Wands

You need to work quickly making these cookies – it might take a few attempts to get the technique right. Bake only two at a time; any more and they will become brittle before you have time to shape them into wands.

Makes 10–12
3 egg whites
90g/3½oz/ ½ cup caster
  (superfine) sugar

25g/1oz/2 tbsp unsalted
  (sweet) butter, melted
30ml/2 tbsp plain
  (all-purpose) flour
15ml/1 tbsp unsweetened
  cocoa powder
30ml/2 tbsp single (light) cream
90g/3½oz milk chocolate
  and multi-coloured sprinkles,
  to decorate

I Preheat the oven to 180°C/350°F/Gas 4. Line two large baking sheets with baking parchment and grease the paper well. In a bowl, briefly beat together the egg whites and sugar until the whites are broken up. Add the melted butter, flour, cocoa powder and cream to the egg whites and beat until smooth.

2 Place two teaspoonfuls of the mixture to one side of a baking sheet and spread the mixture into an oval shape, about 15cm/6in long. Spoon more mixture on to the other side of the baking sheet and shape in the same way.

3 Bake for 7–8 minutes, until the edges begin to darken. Prepare two more cookies on the second baking sheet so you can put them in the oven while shaping the first batch.

4 Leave the cookies on the paper for 30 seconds, then lift one off and wrap it around the handle of a wooden spoon. Once it hardens, ease it off the spoon and shape the second cookie. Continue baking and shaping the cookies.

5 Break the chocolate into pieces and place in a heatproof bowl set over a pan of hot water, stirring until melted. Dip the ends of the cookies in the chocolate, until thickly coated. Sprinkle the chocolate-coated ends with coloured sprinkles and place on baking parchment. Leave for 1 hour until set.

Chocolate Alphabetinis

These funny little letters are great for kids – and might even be a good way to encourage them to practise their spelling. They are lots of fun to make and even better to eat afterwards.

Makes about 30
2 egg whites
15ml/1 tbsp cornflour
  (cornstarch)
50g/2oz/½ cup plain
  (all-purpose) flour
150g/5oz/¾ cup caster
  (superfine) sugar
10ml/2 tsp vanilla extract
90g/3½oz milk chocolate

I Preheat the oven to 180°C/350°F/Gas 4. Line two large baking sheets with baking parchment.

2 In a clean glass bowl, whisk the egg whites until peaking. Sift the cornflour and plain flour over the egg whites and add the sugar and vanilla extract. Fold in using a large metal spoon.

3 Spoon half the mixture into a plastic bag and gently squeeze it into a corner of the bag. Snip off the tip of the corner so that the cookie mixture can be squeezed out in a thin line, 1cm/½in wide.

4 Very carefully, pipe letters on to one of the lined baking sheets, making each letter about 6cm/2½in tall. Spoon the remaining cookie mixture into the bag and pipe more letters on to the second lined baking sheet.

5 Bake the cookies for 12 minutes, or until crisp and golden. Carefully transfer to a wire rack to cool.

6 Break the chocolate into pieces and put in a heatproof bowl set over a pan of simmering water. Heat, stirring frequently, until melted and smooth.

7 Spoon the melted chocolate into a small paper piping (pastry) bag, or use a smaller plastic bag, and snip off the merest tip.

8 Pipe the chocolate in lines over the cookies to highlight the shape of each letter. Leave to set for at least 1 hour.

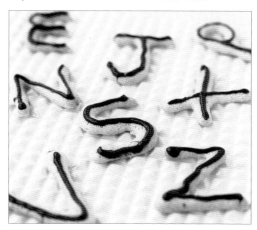

Chocolate Wands Energy 103kcal/432kJ; Protein 1.6g; Carbohydrate 14.3g, of which sugars 12.2g; Fat 4.8g, of which saturates 2.9g; Cholesterol 8mg; Calcium 28mg; Fibre 0.3g; Sodium 41mg.
Alphabetinis Energy 42kcal/178kJ; Protein 0.5g; Carbohydrate 8.5g, of which sugars 6.9g; Fat 0.9g, of which saturates 0.6g; Cholesterol 1mg; Calcium 10mg; Fibre 0g; Sodium 8mg.

Simnel Cookies with Chocolate Eggs

Enjoy these mini variations on the sweet, marzipan-covered simnel cake that is traditionally eaten at Easter and, originally, Mothering Sunday in Britain. Children will enjoy decorating them.

Makes about 18
175g/6oz/³/4 cup unsalted (sweet) butter, at room temperature, diced
115g/4oz/generous ¹/2 cup caster (superfine) sugar
finely grated rind of 1 lemon
2 egg yolks
225g/8oz/2 cups plain (all-purpose) flour
50g/2oz/¹/4 cup currants

For the topping
400g/14oz/1³/4 cup marzipan
200g/7oz/1³/4 cups icing (confectioners') sugar, sifted
2–3 shades of food colouring
mini sugar-coated chocolate Easter eggs

1 Preheat the oven to 180°C/350°F/Gas 4. Put the butter, sugar and lemon rind in a bowl and beat until light and fluffy. Beat in the egg yolks, then stir in the flour and currants and mix to a firm dough. If it is a little soft, chill until firm.

2 Roll the dough out on a sheet of baking parchment to just under 5mm/¹/4in thickness. Using a 9cm/3¹/2in fluted cutter, stamp out rounds and place on two non-stick baking sheets.

3 To make the topping, roll out the marzipan to just under 5mm/¹/4in thickness and use a 6cm/2¹/2in plain or fluted cutter to stamp out the same number of rounds as there are cookies. Place a marzipan round on top of each cookie and press down very gently to fix the marzipan to the cookie dough. Bake the cookies for about 12 minutes, or until just golden. Remove from the oven and leave to cool on the baking sheets.

4 Put the icing sugar in a bowl and add enough water to mix to a spreadable consistency. Divide the icing among two or three bowls and add different food colouring to each one.

5 Divide the cooled cookies into three batches and spread each batch with icing of a different colour. Gently press a few sugar-coated eggs on top of each cookie and leave to set.

Chocolate Box Cookies

These prettily decorated, bitesize cookies look as though they've come straight out of a box of chocolates.

Makes about 50
175g/6oz/1¹/2 cups self-raising (self-rising) flour
25g/1oz/¹/4 cup unsweetened cocoa powder
5ml/1 tsp mixed (apple pie) spice
50g/2oz/¹/4 cup unsalted (sweet) butter, softened and diced
115g/4oz/generous ¹/2 cup caster (superfine) sugar
1 egg
1 egg yolk

For the decoration
150g/5oz milk chocolate, melted
150g/5oz white chocolate, melted
100g/3³/4oz plain (semisweet) chocolate, melted
whole almonds or walnuts
unsweetened cocoa powder, for dusting

1 Preheat the oven to 180°C/350°F/ Gas 4. Grease two baking sheets. Put the flour, cocoa powder, spice and butter into a food processor. Process until the ingredients are thoroughly blended. Add the sugar, egg and egg yolk and mix to a smooth dough.

2 Turn the dough out on to a floured surface and knead gently. Cut in half and roll out each piece to form two long logs, each 33cm/13in long. Cut each log into 1cm/¹/2in slices. Place on the baking sheet, spacing apart, and chill for 30 minutes. Bake for 10 minutes, until slightly risen. Transfer to a wire rack to cool.

3 To decorate, divide the cookies into six batches. Dip one batch into the milk chocolate to coat completely. Place on a sheet of baking parchment. Half-dip the next batch in milk chocolate. Continue with the next two batches and the white chocolate. Coat one batch, then half-coat the second. Continue with the plain chocolate, coating one batch and half-dipping the other. Press a whole nut on to the plain chocolate cookies.

4 Put the leftover white chocolate in a small plastic bag and squeeze it into one corner. Snip off the tip, then drizzle lines of chocolate over the milk chocolate-coated cookies. Dust the white chocolate-coated cookies with a little cocoa powder. Store all the cookies in a cool place until ready to serve.

Simnel Cookies Energy 285kcal/1197kJ; Protein 2.9g; Carbohydrate 45g, of which sugars 35.4g; Fat 11.6g, of which saturates 5.5g; Cholesterol 43mg; Calcium 48mg; Fibre 0.9g; Sodium 66mg.
Box Cookies Energy 74kcal/312kJ; Protein 1.2g; Carbohydrate 9.9g, of which sugars 7.2g; Fat 3.6g, of which saturates 2.1g; Cholesterol 11mg; Calcium 23mg; Fibre 0.2g; Sodium 19mg.

Decorated Chocolate Lebkuchen

Wrapped in paper or beautifully boxed, these decorated Lebkuchen cookies make a lovely present.

Makes 20

For the Lebkuchen
115g/4oz/½ cup unsalted (sweet) butter, softened
50g/2oz/¼ cup soft light brown sugar
1 egg, beaten
350g/12oz/1 cup black treacle (molasses)

350g/12oz/3 cups self-raising (self-rising) flour
5ml/1 tsp ground ginger
2.5ml/½ tsp ground cloves
pinch of chilli powder

For the decoration
115g/4oz plain (semisweet) chocolate, melted
115g/4oz milk chocolate, melted
115g/4oz white chocolate, melted
chocolate vermicelli (sprinkles)
unsweetened cocoa powder or icing (confectioners') sugar

1 For the Lebkuchen, cream together the butter and sugar until pale and fluffy. Beat in the egg and black treacle. Sift the flour, ginger, cloves and chilli powder and then beat into the egg and treacle mixture to make a stiff paste. Turn out on to a floured surface and knead lightly. Wrap and chill for about 30 minutes.

2 Grease two baking sheets. Roll out just over half the mixture to 1cm/½in thickness. Cut out heart shapes using a 4cm/1½in heart-shaped cutter and arrange on the baking sheets. Gather the trimmings with the remaining dough and cut into 20 pieces. Roll into balls and place on the baking sheets. Flatten each one slightly and then chill the sheets for 30 minutes.

3 Preheat the oven to 180°C/350°F/Gas 4. Bake the Lebkuchen for about 8–10 minutes. Cool on a wire rack. Spoon a little of each of the melted chocolates into three piping (pastry) bags.

4 Spoon a little of the plain chocolate over a third of the cookies. Drizzle lines of white chocolate over a few of the plain chocolate cookies and sprinkle the remainder with the vermicelli. Coat the remaining cookies with the milk and white chocolate and decorate some with chocolate from the piping bags. Sprinkle the remaining chocolate-coated cookies with vermicelli, or dust with the cocoa powder or sugar. Leave to set.

Sweet Hearts

These cookies are for Valentine's Day or an anniversary, but you could use different-shaped cutters in the same way to make cookies for other occasions.

Makes 12–14
50g/2oz/¼ cup unsalted (sweet) butter, softened

75g/3oz/scant ½ cup caster (superfine) sugar
1 egg yolk
150g/5oz/1¼ cups plain (all-purpose) flour
25g/1oz dark (bittersweet) chocolate, melted and cooled
25–50g/1–2oz dark (bittersweet) chocolate, to decorate

1 Preheat the oven to 180°C/350°F/Gas 4. Line two baking sheets with baking parchment. Put the butter, sugar and egg yolk in a mixing bowl and beat well. Stir in the flour and then knead until smooth.

2 Divide the dough in half, then knead the melted chocolate into one half until it is evenly coloured. Roll out the chocolate dough between two sheets of baking parchment, to a thickness of about 3mm/⅛in. Roll out the plain dough in the same way.

3 Cut out hearts from both doughs using a 7.5cm/3in biscuit (cookie) cutter. Place the hearts on the baking sheets. Using a smaller heart-shaped cutter, stamp out the centres from all the hearts. Place a light-coloured heart in the centre of a larger chocolate heart and vice versa.

4 Bake the cookies for about 10 minutes, or until just beginning to turn brown. Remove from the oven and leave to cool.

5 To decorate, melt the chocolate in a microwave or in a heatproof bowl set over a pan of hot water. Put into a disposable piping (pastry) bag. Leave the chocolate to cool slightly.

6 Snip the end off the piping bag and carefully pipe dots directly onto the outer part of the large chocolate hearts (with the plain centres). Then pipe zigzags on the pale part of the large plain hearts (with the chocolate centres). Put the cookies aside in a cool place and leave until they are set.

Lebkuchen Energy 233kcal/982kJ; Protein 2.94g; Carbohydrate 34.4g, of which sugars 24.7g; Fat 10.3g, of which saturates 6.2g; Cholesterol 23mg; Calcium 147mg; Fibre 0.6g; Sodium 82mg.
Sweet Hearts Energy 107kcal/449kJ; Protein 1.4g; Carbohydrate 16.2g, of which sugars 8g; Fat 4.5g, of which saturates 2.6g; Cholesterol 22mg; Calcium 21mg; Fibre 0.4g; Sodium 23mg.

Spicy Hearts and Stars

These soft, sweet cookies have a wonderfully chewy texture and a deliciously warm, fragrant flavour. Serve them with coffee at the end of a festive meal, or make them as a gift to give for a special occasion.

Makes about 25

115g/4oz/½ cup unsalted (sweet) butter, softened
115g/4oz/½ cup light muscovado (brown) sugar

1 egg
50g/2oz/1½ tbsp golden (light corn) syrup
50g/2oz/1½ tbsp black treacle (molasses)
400g/14oz/3½ cups self-raising (self-rising) flour
10ml/2 tsp ground ginger

For the toppings

200g/7oz plain (semisweet) or milk chocolate
150g/5oz/1¼ cups icing (confectioners') sugar, sifted

1 Beat together the butter and sugar until pale and creamy. Beat in the egg, syrup and treacle together, until well combined. Sift in the flour and ginger and mix to form a firm dough. Chill for 20 minutes.

2 Meanwhile, preheat the oven to 180°C/350°F/Gas 4 and line two large baking sheets with a layer of baking parchment.

3 Roll out the dough on a lightly floured surface to just under 1cm/½in thick and use shaped cutters to stamp out heart and star shapes. Place, spaced slightly apart, on the prepared baking sheets and bake for about 10 minutes, or until risen. Cool on a wire rack.

4 To make the toppings, melt the chocolate in a microwave or in a heatproof bowl set over a pan of barely simmering water, stirring constantly until smooth. Use the melted chocolate to completely coat the heart-shaped cookies, laying them on a wire rack to set.

5 Put the icing sugar into a bowl and mix with enough warm water to make a coating consistency, then use this to glaze the star-shaped cookies. Place next to the heart-shaped cookies and leave to set.

Tree Cookies

These vibrant cookies look really effective with their chocolate 'trunks' and brightly coloured 'fruits'. Kids will love helping to decorate them. Arrange the finished cookies in a line on the tea table (preferably on a multi-coloured cloth if you have one).

Makes 10

50g/2oz/¼ cup unsalted (sweet) butter, at room temperature, diced
115g/4oz/½ cup light muscovado (brown) sugar

1 egg
150g/5oz/1¼ cups self-raising (self-rising) flour
2.5ml/½ tsp bicarbonate of soda (baking soda)
finely grated rind of 1 lemon

For the decoration

50g/2oz/½ cup icing (confectioners') sugar
10ml/2 tsp lemon juice
10 milk chocolate fingers
brightly coloured sweets (candies)

1 Preheat the oven to 180°C/350°F/Gas 4. Lightly grease two baking sheets.

2 In a large bowl, beat together the butter and sugar until smooth and creamy. Beat in the egg. Add the flour, bicarbonate of soda and lemon rind and mix until smooth.

3 Place five large spoonfuls of the mixture on to each baking sheet, spacing them well apart. Bake for 15 minutes, until the cookies have risen. Leave on the baking sheet for 5 minutes to firm up, then transfer to a wire rack to cool.

4 To decorate the cookies, mix together the icing sugar and lemon juice to make a thick spreadable paste. Use a little of the paste to secure one end of a chocolate finger to each of the cookies as a tree trunk.

5 Attach the coloured sweets in the same way, securing each sweet to the cookie with a little more of the icing paste. Leave the cookies to set for at least 1 hour. (Handle the decorated cookies with care.)

Hearts and Stars Energy 185kcal/781kJ; Protein 2.3g; Carbohydrate 31.5g, of which sugars 19.3g; Fat 6.5g, of which saturates 3.8g; Cholesterol 18mg; Calcium 44mg; Fibre 0.7g; Sodium 41mg.
Tree Cookies Energy 162kcal/681kJ; Protein 1.3g; Carbohydrate 24g, of which sugars 21.6g; Fat 7.2g, of which saturates 2.8g; Cholesterol 30mg; Calcium 24mg; Fibre 0.2g; Sodium 54mg.

Dolly Cookies with Chocolate Centres

These pretty chocolate-filled cookies look like they belong at a doll's tea party and are great fun for kids to join in making and decorating. The cookies are made by simply chilling a roll of dough, then slicing off pieces on to a baking sheet, so you don't even need to use cookie cutters. Baking doesn't get much easier than this.

Makes 14
115g/4oz/½ cup unsalted (sweet) butter, softened and diced
50g/2oz/¼ cup caster (superfine) sugar
pink food colouring
5ml/1 tsp vanilla extract
175g/6oz/1½ cups plain (all-purpose) flour
90g/3½oz white chocolate
75g/3oz multi-coloured sweets (candies)

1 Put the butter and sugar in a bowl with a dash of pink food colouring and the vanilla extract. Beat together until smooth and creamy.

2 Add the flour to the butter and sugar mixture and stir well until thoroughly combined. Turn the dough out on to a lightly floured surface and knead until smooth.

3 Using your hands, roll the dough into a thick sausage shape, about 12cm/4½in long and 5cm/2in in diameter. Wrap the dough in clear film (plastic wrap) and chill for at least 30 minutes.

4 Preheat the oven to 180°C/350°F/Gas 4. Grease two large baking sheets.

5 Cut the dough into 5mm/¼in slices and space them slightly apart on the baking sheets. Bake for 15–18 minutes, until the cookies begin to colour. Transfer to a wire rack to cool.

6 Break the chocolate into pieces and put in a heatproof bowl set over a pan of simmering water. Heat, stirring frequently, until the chocolate is melted and smooth. Using a sharp knife, cut the sweets in half.

7 Using a small metal spatula, swirl a little chocolate on to each cookie and decorate with a ring of sweets. Leave to set.

Giant Birthday Cookie

This enormous cookie is decorated with a mix of chocolate peanuts and shiny balls. To personalize the cookie, write the recipient's name in icing.

Makes one 28cm/11in cookie
175g/6oz/¾ cup unsalted (sweet) butter, at room temperature, diced
125g/4¼oz/generous ½ cup light muscovado (brown) sugar
1 egg yolk
175g/6oz/1½ cups plain (all-purpose) flour
5ml/1 tsp bicarbonate of soda (baking soda)
finely grated rind of 1 orange or lemon
75g/3oz/scant 1 cup rolled oats

For the decoration
125g/4¼oz/generous ½ cup cream cheese
225g/8oz/2 cups icing (confectioners') sugar
5–10ml/1–2 tsp lemon juice
birthday candles
white and milk chocolate-coated raisins or peanuts
unsweetened cocoa powder, for dusting
gold or silver balls, for sprinkling

1 Preheat the oven to 190°C/375°F/Gas 5. Grease a 28cm/11in metal flan tin (pan) and place on a large baking sheet. Put the diced butter and the sugar in a large bowl and beat together until pale and creamy.

2 Add the egg yolk to the butter and sugar mixture and stir well to mix. Add the flour, bicarbonate of soda, grated orange or lemon rind and rolled oats and stir until combined.

3 Turn the mixture into the tin and flatten with a wet wooden spoon. Bake for 15–20 minutes, until risen and golden. Leave to cool in the tin. Carefully slide the cookie from the tin on to a large, flat serving plate or board.

4 To decorate, beat the cream cheese in a bowl, then add the icing sugar and 5ml/1 tsp of the lemon juice. Beat until smooth and peaking. Spoon the mixture into a piping (pastry) bag and pipe swirls around the edge. Press the candles into the topping. Sprinkle with chocolate raisins or peanuts and dust with cocoa powder. Finish by sprinkling with gold or silver balls.

Dolly Cookies Energy 169kcal/709kJ; Protein 1.8g; Carbohydrate 21.9g, of which sugars 12.4g; Fat 8.9g, of which saturates 5.5g; Cholesterol 18mg; Calcium 39mg; Fibre 0.4g; Sodium 59mg.
Giant Energy 4188kcal/17559kJ; Protein 35.3g; Carbohydrate 557.4g, of which sugars 369.4g; Fat 217.5g, of which saturates 130.2g; Cholesterol 694mg; Calcium 649mg; Fibre 10.5g; Sodium 1496mg.

Chocolate Cookies on Sticks

Let your imagination run riot when decorating these fun chocolate cookies. Use plenty of brightly coloured sweets or create a real chocolate feast by using only chocolate decorations. Whichever you choose, these cookies are very sweet, so they should be kept as a real treat for special occasions.

Makes 12

125g/4¼oz milk chocolate
75g/3oz white chocolate
50g/2oz chocolate-coated digestive (sweetmeal) cookies, crumbled into chunks
a selection of small coloured sweets (candies), chocolate chips or chocolate-coated raisins
12 wooden ice lolly (popsicle) sticks

I Break the milk and white chocolate into pieces and put in separate heatproof bowls. Place each bowl in turn over a pan of gently simmering water and heat, stirring frequently, until melted and smooth.

2 Meanwhile, draw six 7cm/2¾in rounds on baking parchment and six 9 × 7cm/3½ × 2¾in rectangles. Invert the paper on to a large tray.

3 Spoon the milk chocolate into the outlines on the paper, reserving one or two spoonfuls of chocolate. Using the back of a spoon, carefully spread the chocolate to the edges to make neat shapes.

4 Press the end of a wooden ice lolly stick into each of the shapes, and spoon over a little more melted milk chocolate to cover the stick. Sprinkle the chocolate shapes with the crumbled cookies.

5 Pipe or drizzle the cookies with the melted white chocolate, then sprinkle the cookies with the coloured sweets, chocolate chips or chocolate-coated raisins, pressing them gently to make sure they stick.

6 Chill the cookies for about 1 hour until set, then carefully peel away the paper.

Striped White Chocolate Canes

These cookies can be made in different flavours and colours and look wonderful tied in bundles or packed into decorative jars or boxes. Eat them with ice cream or light desserts.

Makes 25

25g/1oz white chocolate, melted

red and green food colouring dusts
2 egg whites
90g/3½oz/½ cup caster (superfine) sugar
50g/2oz/½ cup plain (all-purpose) flour
50g/2oz/¼ cup unsalted (sweet) butter, melted

I Preheat the oven to 190°C/375°F/Gas 5. Line two baking sheets with baking parchment. Divide the melted chocolate in half, add a little food colouring dust to each half and put each colour in a separate baking parchment piping (pastry) bags.

2 Place the egg whites in a bowl and whisk until stiff. Add the sugar, whisking well. Add the flour and butter and whisk.

3 Drop four separate teaspoonfuls of the mixture on to the prepared baking sheets and spread into thin rounds. Pipe lines or zigzags of green and red chocolate over each round.

4 Bake one sheet at a time for 3 minutes, until pale golden. Loosen the rounds and return to the oven for a few seconds to soften. Taking one cookie out of the oven at a time, turn it over and roll it around a lightly oiled spoon handle. Leave to set. Repeat with the remaining cookies. Put the second sheet of cookies in the oven to bake. Repeat the process.

5 When the cookies are set, slip them off the spoon handles on to a wire rack. Repeat with the remaining mixture and the red and green coloured chocolate until all the mixture has been used, baking only one sheet of cookies at a time. If the cookies are too hard to shape, simply return them to the oven for a few seconds to soften.

6 When the cookies are cold, tie them together with coloured ribbon and pack into boxes, glass jars or tins as gifts.

Cookies on Sticks Energy 107kcal/448kJ; Protein 1.5g; Carbohydrate 12.3g, of which sugars 10.9g; Fat 6.1g, of which saturates 3.5g; Cholesterol 2mg; Calcium 43mg; Fibre 0.2g; Sodium 30mg.
Striped Canes Energy 42kcal/177kJ; Protein 0.5g; Carbohydrate 5.9g, of which sugars 4.4g; Fat 2g, of which saturates 1.2g; Cholesterol 4mg; Calcium 8mg; Fibre 0.1g; Sodium 18mg.

Jelly Bean Chocolate-topped Cones

Chocolate-dipped cookie cones filled with jelly beans make great treats for kids of all ages. The filled cones look very pretty arranged in glasses or other small containers to keep them upright. This way they can double as a tasty treat and a delightful table decoration.

Makes 10
3 egg whites
90g/3½oz/½ cup caster (superfine) sugar
25g/1oz/2 tbsp unsalted (sweet) butter, melted
40g/1½oz/⅓ cup plain (all-purpose) flour
30ml/2 tbsp single (light) cream
90g/3½oz plain (semisweet) chocolate jelly beans or other small sweets (candies)

1 Preheat the oven to 190°C/375°F/Gas 5. Line two baking sheets with baking parchment and lightly grease.

2 Put the egg whites and sugar in a bowl and whisk lightly with a fork until the whites are broken up. Add the melted butter, flour and cream and stir to make a smooth batter.

3 Using a 15ml/1 tbsp measure, place a rounded tablespoon of the mixture on one side of a baking sheet. Spread to a 9cm/3½in round. Spoon more mixture on to the other side of the baking sheet and spread out to make another round.

4 Bake for about 8–10 minutes, until the edges are deep golden. Meanwhile, spoon two more rounds of cookie mixture on to the second baking sheet.

5 Remove the first batch of cookies from the oven and replace with the second batch. Peel away the paper from the baked cookies and roll them into cone shapes. Leave to set. Continue in this way until you have made 10 cones.

6 Break the chocolate into a heatproof bowl set over a pan of simmering water and stir until melted. Dip the wide ends of the cookies in the chocolate and prop them inside narrow glasses to set, then fill with jelly beans or sweets.

Chocolate Flake Cookies

You don't need a special cutter to make these party cookies. They're shaped using an ordinary round cutter to which you add a V-shaped cone when cutting them out – quite simple once you've made one or two. Children will find these fun cookies irresistible.

Makes 15
150g/5oz/1¼ cups self-raising (self-rising) flour
90g/3½oz/7 tbsp unsalted (sweet) butter, diced
50g/2oz/¼ cup light muscovado (brown) sugar
1 egg yolk
5ml/1 tsp vanilla extract

For the decoration
75g/3oz/6 tbsp unsalted (sweet) butter, softened
5ml/1 tsp vanilla extract
115g/4oz/1 cup icing (confectioners') sugar
2 chocolate flakes

1 Put the flour and butter in a food processor and process until it resembles breadcrumbs. Add the sugar, egg yolk and vanilla, blending to a smooth dough. Wrap and chill for 30 minutes.

2 Preheat the oven to 200°C/400°F/Gas 6. Grease a large baking sheet. Roll the dough out thinly on a floured surface. Lay a 5cm/2in round cutter on the dough. Using a ruler, mark a point 5cm/2in away from the edge of the cutter, then cut two lines from either side of the cutter to the point, to make cornet shapes. Cut around the rest of the cutter and transfer the shape to the baking sheet. Make the rest in the same way.

3 Make shallow cuts 5mm/¼in apart across the cone area of each cookie, then make more cuts diagonally across the first to create a 'wafer' effect. Bake for 8–10 minutes, until pale golden. Leave for 2 minutes, then transfer to a wire rack to cool.

4 For the buttercream, beat together the butter, vanilla and icing sugar. Add 5ml/1 tsp hot water, beating until light and airy. Place in a piping (pastry) bag fitted with a large plain nozzle. Pipe swirls on to the cookies to resemble swirls of ice cream.

5 Cut the flakes into 5cm/2in lengths and then lengthways into four small lengths. Push a piece into each cookie.

Flake Cookies Energy 182kcal/762kJ; Protein 1.5g; Carbohydrate 21.4g, of which sugars 13.8g; Fat 10.6g, of which saturates 6.5g; Cholesterol 38mg; Calcium 31mg; Fibre 0.3g; Sodium 71mg.
Jelly Bean Cones Energy 160kcal/670kJ; Protein 1.9g; Carbohydrate 18.3g, of which sugars 15.2g; Fat 9.3g, of which saturates 5.8g; Cholesterol 18mg; Calcium 18mg; Fibre 0.4g; Sodium 66mg.

Easy Chocolate Hazelnut Fudge

An easy way to make a batch of delicious nutty fudge.

Makes 16 squares
150ml/¼ pint/⅔ cup evaporated milk

350g/12oz/1½ cups sugar
large pinch of salt
50g/2oz/½ cup hazelnuts, halved
350g/12oz/2 cups plain
   (semisweet) chocolate chips

1 Generously grease a 20cm/8in square cake tin (pan).

2 Place the evaporated milk, sugar and salt in a heavy pan. Bring to the boil over a medium heat, stirring constantly until smooth. Lower the heat and simmer gently, stirring, for about 5 minutes.

3 Remove the pan from the heat and add the hazelnuts and chocolate chips. Stir gently with a metal spoon until the chocolate has completely melted.

4 Quickly pour the fudge mixture into the prepared tin and spread evenly, ensuring that it is spread right into the corners. Leave to cool and set.

5 When the chocolate hazelnut fudge has set, cut it into 2.5cm/1in squares. Store in an airtight container, separating the layers of fudge with sheets of baking parchment to stop them sticking together.

Variation
For two-tone fudge, make the Easy Chocolate Hazelnut Fudge and spread it in a 23cm/9in square cake tin, to make a slightly thinner layer than for the main recipe. While it is cooling, make a batch of plain fudge, substituting white chocolate chips for the plain chocolate chips and leaving out the hazelnuts. Let the plain fudge cool slightly before pouring it carefully over the darker chocolate layer. Use a metal spatula to evenly spread the plain layer to the corners, then leave to set as detailed in the recipe above. Cut into squares.

Creamy Fudge

A good selection of fudge always makes a welcome change from more traditional sweets and chocolate confections.

Makes 900g/2lb
50g/2oz/¼ cup unsalted
   (sweet) butter, plus extra
   for greasing
450g/1lb/2 cups sugar
300ml/½ pint/1¼ cups double
   (heavy) cream
150ml/¼ pint/⅔ cup milk

45ml/3 tbsp water (or use
   orange, apricot or cherry
   brandy, or strong coffee)

For the flavourings
225g/8oz/1⅓ cups plain
   (semisweet) or milk
   chocolate chips
115g/4oz/1 cup chopped
   almonds, hazelnuts, walnuts
   or brazil nuts
115g/4oz/½ cup chopped glacé
   (candied) cherries, dates or
   ready-to-eat dried apricots

1 Butter a 20cm/8in shallow square tin (pan). Place the sugar, cream, butter, milk and water or other flavouring into a pan. Heat very gently, stirring occasionally, until all the sugar has dissolved.

2 Bring the mixture to a boil, and boil steadily, stirring only occasionally to prevent the mixture from burning over the base of the pan. Boil until the fudge forms a soft ball if a spoonful is dropped in iced water; 110°C/225°F for a soft fudge.

3 If you are making chocolate-flavoured fudge, add the chocolate at this stage. Remove the pan from the heat and beat thoroughly until the mixture thickens and becomes opaque. Just before this consistency has been reached, add chopped nuts for a nutty fudge, or glacé cherries or dried fruit for a fruity fudge.

4 Pour the fudge into the prepared pan, taking care as the mixture is exceedingly hot. Leave the mixture until cool and almost set. Using a sharp knife, mark the fudge into small squares and leave in the tin until quite firm.

5 Turn the fudge out on to a board and invert. Using a long-bladed knife, cut into neat squares. You can dust some with icing (confectioners') sugar and drizzle others with melted chocolate, if desired.

Creamy Energy 5886kcal/24635kJ; Protein 40.4g; Carbohydrate 708.8g, of which sugars 704.5g; Fat 340.8g, of which saturates 171g; Cholesterol 540mg; Calcium 874mg; Fibre 14.1g; Sodium 512mg.
Hazelnut Fudge Energy 231kcal/975kJ; Protein 2.4g; Carbohydrate 38.3g, of which sugars 38g; Fat 8.7g, of which saturates 4.2g; Cholesterol 3mg; Calcium 48mg; Fibre 0.8g; Sodium 14mg.

Chocolate Fudge Triangles

A fun way to prepare fudge, with a plain chocolate layer sandwiched between layers of white chocolate fudge.

Makes about 48 triangles
600g/1lb 6oz fine quality white chocolate, chopped into small pieces
375g/13oz can sweetened condensed milk
15ml/1 tbsp vanilla extract
7.5ml/1½ tsp lemon juice
pinch of salt
175g/6oz/1½ cups hazelnuts or pecan nuts, chopped (optional)
175g/6oz plain (semisweet) chocolate, chopped into small pieces
40g/1½ oz/3 tbsp unsalted (sweet) butter, cut into pieces
50g/2oz dark (bittersweet) chocolate, for drizzling

1 Line a 20cm/8in square baking tin (pan) with foil. Brush the foil lightly with oil.

2 In a pan over low heat, melt the white chocolate and condensed milk until smooth, stirring frequently. Remove from the heat and stir in the vanilla extract, lemon juice and salt. Stir in the nuts, if using. Spread half the mixture in the tin. Chill for 15 minutes.

3 In a pan over a low heat, melt the plain chocolate and butter until smooth, stirring frequently. Remove from the heat, cool slightly, then pour over the chilled white layer and chill for 15 minutes until set.

4 Gently reheat the remaining white chocolate mixture and pour over the set chocolate layer. Smooth the top, then chill for 2–4 hours, until set.

5 Using the foil as a guide, remove the fudge from the pan and turn it on to a cutting board. Carefully lift off the foil and use a sharp knife to cut the fudge into 24 squares. Cut each square into a triangle.

6 Melt the dark chocolate in a heatproof bowl over a pan of barely simmering water. Leave to cool slightly, then drizzle over the triangles.

Rich Chocolate Pistachio Fudge

This melt-in-the-mouth chocolate fudge is extremely rich – so you should try to eat it sparingly.

Makes 36
250g/9oz/1¼ cup sugar
375g/13oz can sweetened condensed milk
50g/2oz/¼ cup unsalted (sweet) butter
5ml/1 tsp vanilla extract
115g/4oz plain (semisweet) chocolate, grated
75g/3oz/½ cup pistachio nuts, almonds or hazelnuts

1 Lightly grease a 19cm/7½in square cake tin (pan) and line with baking parchment.

2 Mix the sugar, condensed milk and butter in a heavy pan. Heat gently, stirring occasionally, until the sugar has dissolved completely and the mixture is smooth.

3 Bring the mixture to the boil, stirring occasionally, and boil until it registers 116°C/240°F on a sugar thermometer, or until a small amount of the mixture dropped into a cup of iced water forms a soft ball.

4 Remove the pan from the heat and beat in the vanilla extract, chocolate and nuts. Beat vigorously until the mixture is smooth and creamy.

5 Pour the mixture into the prepared cake tin and spread evenly. Leave until just set, then mark into squares.

6 Leave the fudge to set completely before cutting into squares and removing from the tin. Store in an airtight container in a cool place.

> **Variation**
> Try making this fudge with different varieties of nut. Almonds, hazelnuts and brazil nuts will all work as well as the pistachios. Simply substitute the same quantity in the recipe.

Pistachio Fudge Energy 112kcal/472kJ; Protein 1.5g; Carbohydrate 18.2g, of which sugars 18.1g; Fat 4.2g, of which saturates 2.1g; Cholesterol 7mg; Calcium 39mg; Fibre 0.2g; Sodium 35mg.
Fudge Triangles Energy 120kcal/503kJ; Protein 1.5g; Carbohydrate 15.3g, of which sugars 15.1g; Fat 6.3g, of which saturates 3.8g; Cholesterol 6mg; Calcium 28mg; Fibre 0.4g; Sodium 17mg.

Chocolate Almond Torrone

Torrone is a type of Italian nougat believed to be of Roman origin. This delicious version is an ideal way to finish a dinner party.

Makes about 20 slices
115g/4oz plain (semisweet)
  chocolate, chopped into pieces
50g/2oz/¼ cup unsalted
  (sweet) butter
1 egg white
115g/4oz/generous ½ cup caster
  (superfine) sugar
75g/3oz/¾ cup chopped
  toasted almonds
50g/2oz/½ cup ground almonds
75ml/5 tbsp chopped mixed
  (candied) peel

For the coating
175g/6oz white chocolate,
  chopped into small pieces
25g/1oz/2 tbsp unsalted
  (sweet) butter
115g/4oz/1 cup flaked (sliced)
  almonds, toasted

1 Melt the chocolate with the butter in a heatproof bowl over a pan of barely simmering water until smooth.

2 In a clean, grease-free bowl, whisk the egg white with the sugar until stiff. Gradually beat in the melted chocolate mixture, then stir in the toasted almonds, ground almonds and peel.

3 Transfer the mixture on to a sheet of baking parchment and shape into a thick roll.

4 As the mixture cools, use the paper to press the roll firmly into a triangular shape. When you are satisfied with the shape, twist the paper over the triangular roll and chill until it is completely set.

5 Make the coating. Melt the white chocolate with the butter in a heatproof bowl over a pan of simmering water. Unwrap the chocolate roll and with a clean knife spread the white chocolate quickly over the surface. Press the flaked almonds in a thin even coating over the chocolate, working quickly before the chocolate sets.

6 Chill the coated chocolate roll again until firm, then cut the torrone into fairly thin slices to serve.

Chocolate Nut Clusters

The classic combination of chocolate and nuts are here made into tasty morsels, perfect for a mouthful of chocolate heaven.

Makes about 30
550ml/18fl oz/2½ cups double
  (heavy) cream
25g/1oz/2 tbsp unsalted (sweet)
  butter, cut into small pieces
350ml/12fl oz/1½ cups golden
  (light corn) syrup
200g/7oz/1 cup sugar
75g/3oz/scant ½ cup soft light
  brown sugar
pinch of salt
15ml/1 tbsp vanilla extract
350g/12oz/3 cups combination of
  hazelnuts, pecans, walnuts, brazil
  nuts and unsalted peanuts
400g/14oz plain (semisweet)
  chocolate, chopped into pieces
15g/½oz/1 tbsp white vegetable
  fat (shortening)

1 Lightly brush two baking sheets with vegetable oil. In a pan over a low heat, cook the cream, butter, golden syrup, sugars and salt, stirring until the sugars dissolve and the butter melts.

2 Bring to the boil and continue cooking, stirring, for about 1 hour, until the caramel reaches 119°C/238°F on a sugar thermometer, or until a small amount of caramel dropped into a cup of iced water forms a hard ball. Plunge the bottom of the pan into cold water to stop the cooking process. Cool slightly, then stir in the vanilla extract.

3 Stir the nuts into the caramel until well coated. Using an oiled tablespoon, drop spoonfuls of nut mixture on to the prepared sheets, about 2.5cm/1in apart. If the mixture hardens, return to the heat to soften. Chill the clusters for 30 minutes until firm and cold, or leave in a cool place until hardened.

4 Using a metal spatula, transfer the clusters to a wire rack placed over a baking sheet to catch drips. In a pan, over a low heat, melt the chocolate with the white vegetable fat, stirring until the mixture is smooth. Set aside to cool slightly.

5 Spoon chocolate over each cluster, being sure to cover completely. Place on the wire rack. Allow to set for 2 hours until hardened. Store in an airtight container.

Almond Torrone Energy 186kcal/775kJ; Protein 3.7g; Carbohydrate 11.8g, of which sugars 11.4g; Fat 14.1g, of which saturates 5.1g; Cholesterol 8mg; Calcium 60mg; Fibre 1.2g; Sodium 48mg.
Nut Clusters Energy 311kcal/1298kJ; Protein 2.7g; Carbohydrate 28.3g, of which sugars 27.9g; Fat 21.6g, of which saturates 9.2g; Cholesterol 27mg; Calcium 36mg; Fibre 1.1g; Sodium 46mg.

Chocolate-coated Nut Brittle

This chocolatey version of the classic nut praline will prove to be an instant, and very short-lived, success.

Makes 20–24 pieces
115g/4oz/1 cup mixed pecan nuts and whole almonds
115g/4oz/generous ½ cup caster (superfine) sugar
60ml/4 tbsp water
200g/7oz plain (semisweet) chocolate, chopped into small pieces

1 Lightly grease a baking sheet with butter or oil.

2 Mix the nuts, sugar and water in a heavy pan. Place the pan over a gentle heat, stirring frequently until all the sugar has completely dissolved.

3 Bring the mixture to the boil, then lower the heat to moderate. Cook until the mixture turns a rich golden brown and registers 155°C/310°F on a sugar thermometer. If you do not have a sugar thermometer, test the syrup by adding a few drops to a cup of iced water. The mixture should solidify to a very brittle mass.

4 Quickly remove the pan from the heat and tip the mixture on to the prepared baking sheet, spreading it around evenly with a metal spatula. Leave until completely cold and hard.

5 Break the nut brittle into bitesize pieces. Melt the chocolate in a heatproof bowl set over a pan of barely simmering water. Stir frequently until the chocolate is melted and smooth.

6 While the chocolate is still warm, dip in the nut brittle pieces to half-coat them. Leave on a sheet of baking parchment to set.

> **Cook's Tip**
> If the nut brittle proves too hard to break by hand, then cover with a clean dish towel and hit gently with a rolling pin or, if you have one, a toffee hammer.

Chocolate Christmas Cups

These fabulous little confections would be perfect to serve during the Christmas festivities. You will need about 70–80 foil or paper sweet cases to make and serve them.

Makes about 35 cups
275g/10oz plain (semisweet) chocolate, broken into pieces
175g/6oz cooked, cold Christmas pudding
75ml/2½fl oz/⅓ cup brandy or whisky
chocolate leaves and a few crystallized cranberries, to decorate

1 Place the chocolate in a double boiler or in a bowl over a pan of hot water. Heat gently until the chocolate is melted, stirring until the chocolate is smooth.

2 Using a pastry brush, brush or coat the base and sides of about 35 paper or foil sweet (candy) cases. Allow to set, then repeat, reheating the melted chocolate if necessary, and apply a second coat. Leave to cool and set completely, for 4–5 hours or overnight. Reserve the remaining chocolate.

3 Crumble the Christmas pudding in a small bowl, sprinkle with the brandy or whisky and allow to stand for 30–40 minutes, until the spirit is absorbed.

4 Spoon a little of the pudding mixture into each cup, smoothing the top. Reheat the remaining chocolate and spoon over the top of each cup to cover the surface of each cup to the edge. Leave to set.

5 When the cups are completely set, peel off the cases and place in clean foil cases. Decorate with chocolate leaves and crystallized cranberries.

> **Cook's Tip**
> To crystallize cranberries for decoration, beat an egg white until frothy. Dip each berry in egg white, then in sugar. Leave to dry.

Nut Brittle Energy 94kcal/395kJ; Protein 0.9g; Carbohydrate 10.6g, of which sugars 10.4g; Fat 5.7g, of which saturates 1.7g; Cholesterol 1mg; Calcium 8mg; Fibre 0.4g; Sodium 1mg.
Christmas Cups Energy 59kcal/249kJ; Protein 0.6g; Carbohydrate 7.5g, of which sugars 6.6g; Fat 2.7g, of which saturates 1.3g; Cholesterol 0mg; Calcium 7mg; Fibre 0.3g; Sodium 10mg.

Chocolate Citrus Candies

Home-candied peel makes a superb sweetmeat, especially when dipped in melted chocolate. You can also use bought candied peel for this recipe, but make sure it is the very best quality. If you buy the peel in one piece, it can then be simply sliced and dipped.

Makes about 100g/4oz petits fours
1 orange or 2 lemons
25g/1oz/2 tbsp sugar
about 50g/2oz good quality plain (semisweet) chocolate

1 Using a vegetable knife or peeler, cut the rind from the orange or lemons. Take care not to cut off too much of the pith. Slice into matchsticks.

2 Blanch the chopped peel in boiling water for 4–5 minutes, until beginning to soften, then refresh under cold water and drain thoroughly.

3 In a small pan, heat the sugar and 30ml/2 tbsp water gently together until the sugar has completely dissolved. Add the strips of fruit peel and simmer gently for about 8–10 minutes, or until the water has evaporated and the matchsticks of peel have turned transparent.

4 Lift out the peel with a slotted spoon and spread out on a sheet of baking parchment to cool. When cold, the peel can be stored in an airtight container in the refrigerator for up to 2 days before using, if required.

5 To coat, melt the chocolate carefully in a double boiler or in a heatproof bowl over a pan of hot water. Spear each piece of peel on to a cocktail stick (toothpick) and dip one end into the melted chocolate.

6 To set the chocolate on the candies, stick the cocktail sticks into a large potato. When the chocolate is completely dry, remove the sticks and then arrange the citrus candies attractively on a dish to serve as petits fours.

Marzipan Chocolate Logs

These rich confections are made from orange-flavoured marzipan rolled into logs then covered in a variety of tasty toppings. They will help to liven up any festive table, or serve at any other special occasion feast.

Makes about 12
225g/8oz marzipan, at room temperature
115g/4oz/⅔ cup candied orange peel, chopped
30ml/2 tbsp orange-flavoured liqueur
15ml/1 tbsp soft light brown sugar
edible gold powder
75g/3oz plain (semisweet) chocolate
gold-coated sweets (candies)

1 Knead the marzipan well on a lightly floured surface, then mix in the chopped peel and liqueur. Set aside for about 1 hour, to dry out.

2 Break off small pieces of the mixture and roll them into log shapes in the palms of your hands.

3 Separate the marzipan logs into two equal batches. Dip half of the logs in the brown sugar and brush them lightly with the edible gold powder using a clean, dry pastry brush or a small paintbrush, if available.

4 Melt the chocolate in a double boiler or heatproof bowl over a pan of barely simmering water. Stir the chocolate until it is completely melted and smooth.

5 Dip the remaining logs in the melted chocolate. Place on baking parchment and press a gold-coated sweet in the centre of each. When set, arrange all the logs on a plate.

Cook's Tip
There are a variety of orange-flavoured liqueurs on the market. Look out for Cointreau or Grand Marnier. The mandarin-flavoured Mandarine Napoleon will also work here.

Marzipan Logs Energy 138kcal/584kJ; Protein 1.3g; Carbohydrate 24.4g, of which sugars 24.4g; Fat 4.2g, of which saturates 1.2g; Cholesterol 0mg; Calcium 28mg; Fibre 1g; Sodium 31mg.
Citrus Candies Energy 438kcal/1845kJ; Protein 4.4g; Carbohydrate 74g, of which sugars 72.6g; Fat 15.8g, of which saturates 8.9g; Cholesterol 15mg; Calcium 208mg; Fibre 3.6g; Sodium 270mg.

Double Chocolate-dipped Fruit

These sweets have a multi-coloured chocolate layer covering various fruits.

Makes 24 coated pieces

*fruits – about 24 pieces
(strawberries, cherries, orange
segments, large seedless
grapes, physalis, kumquats,
pitted prunes, pitted dates,
ready-to-eat dried apricots,
dried peaches or dried pears)*

*115g/4oz white chocolate,
chopped into small pieces*
*115g/4oz dark (bittersweet) or
plain (semisweet) chocolate,
chopped into small pieces*

1 Clean and prepare fruits; wipe strawberries with a soft cloth or brush gently with a pastry brush. Wash firm-skinned fruits such as cherries and grapes and dry well. Peel and leave whole or cut up any other fruits being used.

2 Melt the white chocolate. Remove from the heat and cool to tepid (about 29°C/84°F), stirring frequently. Line a baking sheet with baking parchment.

3 Holding each fruit by the stem or end and at an angle, dip about two-thirds of the fruit into the chocolate. Allow the excess to drip off and place on the baking sheet. Chill the fruits for about 20 minutes until the chocolate has completely set.

4 Melt the dark or plain chocolate, stirring frequently until smooth. Remove the chocolate from the heat and cool to just below body temperature, about 30°C/86°F.

5 Take each white chocolate-coated fruit in turn from the baking sheet and, holding by the stem or end and at the opposite angle, dip the bottom third of each piece into the darker chocolate, creating a chevron effect. Set on the baking sheet. Chill for 15 minutes or until set.

6 Allow the fruit to stand at room temperature for about 15 minutes before serving.

Swedish Rose Chocolates

These rich chocolate balls are simple to make and completely delicious. They are a popular Swedish Christmas treat, where they might be offered as a gift or served on Christmas Eve. Here, they are served with crystallized rose petals.

Makes 12
*150g/5oz plain
(semisweet) chocolate*
30ml/2 tbsp ground almonds

*30ml/2 tbsp caster
(superfine) sugar*
2 egg yolks
10ml/2 tsp strong brewed coffee
15ml/1 tbsp dark rum
15ml/1 tbsp rose water
*40g/1½oz/¼ cup chocolate
vermicelli (sprinkles)*
*crystallized rose petals,
for decoration*

1 Grate the chocolate finely or grind in batches in a coffee or spice mill. Place in a bowl and add the ground almonds, caster sugar, egg yolks, coffee and rum.

2 Roll the mixture into balls by rolling small teaspoonfuls between your fingers. Chill well.

3 Dip each of the chocolate balls into the rose water, then roll in the chocolate vermicelli until completely coated.

4 Wrap the chocolate balls individually in cellophane tied with natural raffia before packing them in decorative boxes, or pile them high on a serving plate, sprinkled with crystallized rose petals.

> **Cook's Tip**
> *For crystallized rose petals, coat clean and dry petals with a thin and even layer of beaten egg white and, working quickly, sprinkle with sifted icing (confectioners') sugar. Allow the petals to dry for 30 minutes on a wire rack. The petals will keep for up to a week, stored in an airtight container between layers of paper towels.*

Chocolate-dipped Fruit Energy 54kcal/227kJ; Protein 0.8g; Carbohydrate 6.8g, of which sugars 6.8g; Fat 2.8g, of which saturates 1.7g; Cholesterol 0mg; Calcium 17mg; Fibre 0.3g; Sodium 7mg.
Rose Chocolates Energy 114kcal/476kJ; Protein 1.9g; Carbohydrate 13.3g, of which sugars 10.5g; Fat 5.8g, of which saturates 2.5g; Cholesterol 34mg; Calcium 16mg; Fibre 0.5g; Sodium 3mg.

Chocolate Apricots

You can use almost any
dried fruit for this
sophisticated sweetmeat.
In this recipe, the sweet
but sharp flavour of
apricots contrasts
beautifully with the
velvet-smooth chocolate.

Makes 24–36
*50g/2oz plain (semisweet)
chocolate
12 large ready-to-eat
dried apricots*

1 Take a length of foil or baking parchment and use it to line
a baking sheet. Set the baking sheet aside.

2 Break the chocolate into a double pan or a heatproof bowl
set over a pan of barely simmering water. Heat until melted,
stirring occasionally.

3 Cut each dried apricot into 2–3 strips. Dip the long cut
side of each strip into the melted chocolate and immediately
place it on the prepared baking sheet. Repeat the process
until all the apricots are covered.

4 Chill the chocolate apricots in the freezer for about
30 minutes, until set.

5 Use a metal spatula to slide the apricots off the foil or
baking paper, or press them from underneath. Store the
apricots in a cool place, in an airtight container.

Cook's Tips
• *To melt this quantity of chocolate in the microwave, put it on
a plate and cook on high for about 1 minute. If the chocolate
in the bowl starts to set before you have finished dipping all of
the apricots, put the bowl back over the heat for a minute or
two, or microwave again briefly.*
• *These chocolate treats will make an excellent gift for a loved
one. Simply pack the apricots into a pretty gift box, protecting
them with some coloured tissue paper.*

Stuffed Chocolate Prunes

Chocolate-covered prunes,
soaked in liqueur, hide a
delicious melt-in-the-mouth
coffee filling.

Makes approximately 30
*225g/8oz/1 cup unpitted prunes
50ml/2fl oz/¼ cup Armagnac
30ml/2 tbsp ground coffee*

*150ml/¼ pint/⅔ cup double
(heavy) cream
350g/12oz plain (semisweet)
chocolate, broken into squares
10g/¼oz/½ tbsp vegetable fat
30ml/2 tbsp unsweetened
cocoa powder, sifted,
for dusting*

1 Put the unpitted prunes in a bowl and pour the Armagnac
over. Stir, then cover with clear film (plastic wrap) and set aside
for 2 hours, or until the prunes have absorbed the liquid.

2 Make a slit along each prune to remove the pit, making a
hollow for the filling, but leaving the fruit intact.

3 Put the coffee and cream in a pan and heat almost to boiling
point. Cover, infuse (steep) for 4 minutes, then heat again until
almost boiling. Put 115g/4oz of the chocolate into a bowl and
pour over the coffee cream through a sieve (strainer).

4 Stir until the chocolate has melted and the mixture is smooth.
Leave to cool, until it has the consistency of softened butter.

5 Fill a piping (pastry) bag with a small plain nozzle with the
chocolate mixture. Pipe into the cavities of the prunes. Chill in
the refrigerator for 20 minutes.

6 Melt the remaining chocolate in a bowl over a pan of hot
water. Using a fork, dip the prunes one at a time into the
chocolate to give them a generous coating. Place on a sheet
of baking parchment until they have hardened. Dust each
with a little cocoa powder.

Cook's Tip
Dates can be used instead of prunes, if preferred.

Chocolate Apricots Energy 207kcal/872kJ; Protein 3.3g; Carbohydrate 34.2g, of which sugars 33.9g; Fat 7.3g, of which saturates 4.2g; Cholesterol 2mg; Calcium 45mg; Fibre 3.8g; Sodium 9mg.
Stuffed Prunes Energy 100kcal/419kJ; Protein 0.9g; Carbohydrate 10.1g, of which sugars 9.9g; Fat 6.3g, of which saturates 3.8g; Cholesterol 8mg; Calcium 10mg; Fibre 0.8g; Sodium 7mg.

Peppermint Chocolate Sticks

These minty treats are perfect with an after-dinner cup of coffee.

Makes about 80

115g/4oz/generous ½ cup sugar
150ml/¼ pint/⅔ cup water
2.5ml/½ tsp peppermint extract
200g/7oz plain (semisweet) chocolate, chopped into small pieces
60ml/4 tbsp toasted desiccated (dry unsweetened shredded) coconut

1 Lightly oil a large baking sheet. Place the sugar and water in a pan and heat gently, stirring until the sugar has dissolved.

2 Bring to the boil and boil rapidly without stirring until the syrup registers 138°C/280°F on a sugar thermometer. Remove the pan from the heat and stir in the peppermint extract.

3 Pour the mixture on to the greased baking sheet and leave until set.

4 Break up the peppermint mixture into a small bowl and use the end of a rolling pin to crush it into small pieces.

5 Melt the chocolate. Remove from the heat and stir in the mint pieces and desiccated coconut.

6 Lay a 30 × 25cm/12 × 10in sheet of baking parchment on a flat surface. Spread the chocolate mixture over the paper, leaving a narrow border all around, to make a rectangle measuring about 25 × 20cm/10 × 8in. Leave to set. When firm, use a sharp knife to cut into thin sticks, each about 6cm/2½in long.

> **Variations**
> • Make orange chocolate sticks by replacing the peppermint extract with the same amount of an orange-flavoured liqueur.
> • You can replace the coconut with the same quantity of ginger nut biscuits (gingersnaps) for crunchy gingery sticks.

Cognac and Ginger Creams

Ginger is arguably the perfect partner to rich and creamy plain chocolate. Add in some cognac and these confections become utterly irresistible.

Makes 18–20

300g/11oz plain (semisweet) chocolate, chopped into pieces
45ml/3 tbsp double (heavy) cream
30ml/2 tbsp cognac
4 pieces of stem ginger, finely chopped, plus 15ml/1 tbsp syrup from the jar
crystallized ginger, to decorate

1 Polish the insides of 18–20 chocolate moulds carefully with cotton wool.

2 Melt about two-thirds of the chocolate in a heatproof bowl over a pan of barely simmering water, then spoon a little into each mould. Reserve a little of the melted chocolate for sealing the creams.

3 Using a small brush, sweep the chocolate up the sides of the moulds to coat them evenly, then invert them on to a sheet of baking parchment. Set aside in a cool place until the chocolate has completely set.

4 Melt the remaining chopped chocolate over simmering water, then stir in the cream, cognac, stem ginger and ginger syrup, mixing well.

5 Spoon the mixture into the chocolate-lined moulds. If the reserved chocolate has solidified, melt, then spoon a little into each mould to seal.

6 Leave the chocolates in a cool place (not the refrigerator) until set. To remove them from the moulds, gently press them out on to a cool surface, such as a marble slab.

7 Decorate each cream with small pieces of crystallized ginger. Keep the chocolates cool if you are not planning on serving them immediately.

Cognac Creams Energy 92kcal/383kJ; Protein 0.8g; Carbohydrate 10.2g, of which sugars 10g; Fat 5.4g, of which saturates 3.3g; Cholesterol 4mg; Calcium 6mg; Fibre 0.4g; Sodium 3mg.
Peppermint Sticks Energy 23kcal/96kJ; Protein 0.2g; Carbohydrate 3.1g, of which sugars 3.1g; Fat 1.2g, of which saturates 0.8g; Cholesterol 0mg; Calcium 2mg; Fibre 0.2g; Sodium 0mg.

Chocolate and Coffee Mint Thins

These coffee-flavoured chocolate squares contain pieces of crisp minty caramel and are ideal for serving with after-dinner coffee.

Makes 16
75g/3oz/scant ½ cup sugar
75ml/5 tbsp water
3 drops oil of peppermint
15ml/1 tbsp strong-flavoured ground coffee
75ml/5 tbsp near-boiling double (heavy) cream
225g/8oz plain (semisweet) chocolate
10g/¼oz/½ tbsp unsalted (sweet) butter

1 Line an 18cm/7in square tin (pan) with baking parchment. Gently heat the sugar and water in a heavy pan until dissolved. Add the peppermint, and boil until a light caramel colour.

2 Pour the caramel on to an oiled baking sheet and leave to harden, then crush into small pieces.

3 Put the coffee in a small bowl and pour the hot cream over. Leave to infuse (steep) for about 4 minutes, then strain through a fine sieve (strainer).

4 Melt the chocolate and unsalted butter in a bowl over barely simmering water. Remove from the heat and beat in the hot coffee cream. Stir in the mint caramel.

5 Pour the mixture into the prepared tin and smooth the surface level. Leave in a cool place to set for at least 4 hours, preferably overnight.

6 Carefully turn out the chocolate on to a board and peel off the lining paper. Cut the chocolate into squares with a sharp knife and store in an airtight container until needed.

> **Cook's Tip**
> Don't put the chocolate in the refrigerator to set, or it may lose its glossy appearance and become too brittle to cut easily into neat squares.

Chocolate and Cherry Colettes

Tasty maraschino cherries are hidden inside these double-chocolate treats. A perfect gift for adults.

Makes 18–20
115g/4oz plain (semisweet) chocolate, chopped into pieces
75g/3oz white or milk chocolate, chopped into small pieces
25g/1oz/2 tbsp unsalted (sweet) butter, melted
15ml/1 tbsp Kirsch or brandy
60ml/4 tbsp double (heavy) cream
18–20 maraschino cherries or liqueur-soaked cherries
milk chocolate curls, to decorate

1 Melt the dark chocolate in a heatproof bowl over a pan of simmering water, then remove it from the heat. Spoon into 18–20 foil sweet cases, spread evenly up the sides with a small brush, then leave the cases in a cool place until the chocolate has completely set.

2 Melt the white or milk chocolate in a pan with the butter over a gentle heat. Remove from the heat and stir in the Kirsch or brandy, then the cream. Cool until the mixture is thick enough to hold its shape.

3 Carefully peel away the paper from the chocolate cases. Place one cherry in each chocolate case.

4 Spoon the white or milk chocolate cream mixture into a piping (pastry) bag fitted with a small star nozzle and pipe over the cherries until the cases are full.

5 Top each colette with a generous swirl of the chocolate, and decorate each one with milk chocolate curls. Leave to set before serving.

> **Cook's Tip**
> To make the chocolate curls for the decoration, put a bar of chocolate in the fridge until well chilled and then run a vegetable peeler down the long edge of the bar.

Chocolate Mint Thins Energy 118kcal/494kJ; Protein 0.8g; Carbohydrate 13.9g, of which sugars 13.8g; Fat 7g, of which saturates 4.3g; Cholesterol 9mg; Calcium 10mg; Fibre 0.4g; Sodium 6mg.
Cherry Colettes Energy 163kcal/675kJ; Protein 0.7g; Carbohydrate 6.9g, of which sugars 6.8g; Fat 14.7g, of which saturates 9.2g; Cholesterol 31mg; Calcium 17mg; Fibre 0.2g; Sodium 82mg.

Chocolate Fondant Hearts

If you're looking for a gift for your Valentine, look no further.

Makes 50
60ml/4 tbsp liquid glucose
50g/2oz plain (semisweet) chocolate, plus extra for decorating

50g/2oz white chocolate, plus extra for decorating
1 egg white
450g/1lb/4 cups icing (confectioners') sugar, sifted, plus extra for dusting

1 Divide the glucose between two heatproof bowls. Place each bowl over a pan of barely simmering water and heat gently. Break the two types of chocolate into pieces. Add the plain chocolate to one bowl and the white chocolate to the other and continue to heat until melted.

2 Remove both bowls of chocolate from the heat and set them aside to cool. Whisk the egg white until stiff, then add one-third to each bowl, reserving the remaining third.

3 Divide the icing sugar equally between the bowls and stir in thoroughly to mix. Turn the mixtures out of the bowls and knead each piece separately, with your hands, until smooth and pliable.

4 Lightly dust a work surface with icing sugar and roll out each piece of fondant to a 3mm/⅛in thickness.

5 Brush the surface of the dark chocolate fondant with the remaining egg white and place the white chocolate fondant on top. Roll the surface of the fondants with a rolling pin to press the pieces together.

6 Using a heart-shaped cutter, stamp out about 50 hearts from the fondant. Melt the extra plain and white chocolate and pipe or drizzle over the top of each chocolate heart.

7 Leave to set completely before packing in an airtight container, or put them in a decorative gift box.

Fruit Fondant Chocolates

These chocolates are simple to make using pre-formed plastic moulds, yet look very professional. Fruit fondant is available from sugarcraft stores and comes in a variety of flavours including coffee and nut. Try a mixture of flavours using a small quantity of each, or use just a single flavour.

Makes 24
225g/8oz plain (semisweet), milk or white chocolate
115g/4oz/1 cup real fruit liquid fondant
15–20ml/3–4tsp cooled boiled water
15ml/1 tbsp melted plain (semisweet), milk or white chocolate, to decorate

1 Melt the chocolate in a bowl over a pan of hot water. Use a piece of cotton wool to polish the insides of plastic chocolate moulds, ensuring that they are clean. Fill up the shapes in one plastic tray to the top with the chocolate, leave for a few seconds, then invert the tray over the bowl of melted chocolate allowing the excess chocolate to fall back into the bowl. Sit the tray on the work surface and draw a metal spatula across the top to remove the excess chocolate and to neaten the edges. Chill until set. Repeat to fill the remaining trays.

2 Sift the fruit fondant mixture into a bowl. Gradually stir in enough water to give it the consistency of thick cream. Place the fondant in a baking parchment piping (pastry) bag, fold down the top and snip off the end. Fill each chocolate case almost to the top by piping in the fondant. Leave for about 30 minutes, or until a skin has formed on the surface of the fondant.

3 Spoon the remaining melted chocolate over the fondant to fill each mould level with the top. Chill until the chocolate has set hard. Invert the tray and press out the chocolates one by one. Place the melted chocolate of a contrasting colour into a baking parchment piping bag, fold down the top, snip off the point and pipe lines across the top of each chocolate. Allow to set, then pack into pretty boxes and tie with ribbon.

Fruit Chocolates Energy 88kcal/368kJ; Protein 0.7g; Carbohydrate 13.1g, of which sugars 10.8g; Fat 4g, of which saturates 2.4g; Cholesterol 1mg; Calcium 5mg; Fibre 0.4g; Sodium 8mg.
Fondant Hearts Energy 50kcal/212kJ; Protein 0.2g; Carbohydrate 11.6g, of which sugars 11.1g; Fat 0.6g, of which saturates 0.4g; Cholesterol 0mg; Calcium 8mg; Fibre 0g; Sodium 5mg.

Chocolate Birds' Nests

These delightful crispy chocolate nests make a perfect Easter tea-time treat and are a real favourite with kids. They're so quick and easy to make and young children can have great fun shaping the chocolate mixture inside the paper cases and tucking the pastel-coloured chocolate eggs inside.

Makes 12
200g/7oz milk chocolate
25g/1oz/2 tbsp unsalted (sweet) butter, diced
90g/3½oz shredded wheat cereal
36 small pastel-coloured, sugar-coated chocolate eggs

1 Line the sections of a tartlet tin (muffin pan) with 12 decorative paper cake cases.

2 Break the milk chocolate into pieces and put in a heatproof bowl with the butter. Rest the bowl over a pan of gently simmering water and stir frequently until melted. Remove the bowl from the heat and leave to cool for a few minutes.

3 Using your fingers, crumble the Shredded Wheat into the melted chocolate. Stir well until the cereal is completely coated in chocolate.

4 Divide the mixture among the paper cases, pressing it down gently with the back of a spoon, and make a slight indentation in the centre. Tuck three eggs into each nest and leave to set for about 2 hours.

Cook's Tip
Bags of sugar-coated chocolate eggs are widely available in supermarkets and food stores around Easter time. However, if you have trouble finding them out of season, try visiting an old-fashioned sweet (candy) store. Often these stores have large jars of this type of chocolate sweet, which they sell all year round, and you can choose how many to buy.

Fruit-and-nut White Chocolate Clusters

This is a no-bake recipe that children will like, although if they are making it themselves, supervision for melting the chocolate is recommended.

Makes 24
225g/8oz white chocolate
50g/2oz/⅓ cup sunflower seeds
50g/2oz/½ cup flaked (sliced) almonds
50g/2oz/¼ cup sesame seeds
50g/2oz/⅓ cup seedless raisins
5ml/1 tsp ground cinnamon

1 Break the white chocolate into small pieces. Put the chocolate in a microwave-proof container and cook in a microwave on medium for 2–3 minutes, following the manufacturer's instructions.

2 Alternatively, melt the chocolate by putting it into a heatproof bowl set over a pan of barely simmering water on a low heat. Do not allow the water to touch the base of the bowl, or the chocolate may become too hot and stiffen.

3 Stir the melted chocolate constantly until it takes on a smooth and glossy appearance.

4 Mix the remaining ingredients together until thoroughly combined. Pour on the melted chocolate and stir well until all the ingredients are evenly covered in chocolate.

5 Using a teaspoon, spoon the mixture into paper cases supported in a bun tin (pan) if necessary. When all the cases are full, leave in a cool place to set, but do not put the clusters in the refrigerator.

Cook's Tip
As with any recipe that contains nuts, always check that the people who will be eating the cookies do not have nut allergies. You could always substitute other dried fruit, such as dates or apricots, for the nuts.

Birds' Nests Energy 214kcal/896kJ; Protein 3.4g; Carbohydrate 24.4g, of which sugars 19g; Fat 12.1g, of which saturates 7.2g; Cholesterol 12mg; Calcium 77mg; Fibre 1g; Sodium 42mg.
Fruit-and-nut Clusters Energy 93kcal/386kJ; Protein 2g; Carbohydrate 7.5g, of which sugars 7g; Fat 6.3g, of which saturates 2.1g; Cholesterol 0mg; Calcium 48mg; Fibre 0.5g; Sodium 12mg.

White Chocolate Snowballs

These little spherical cookies are particularly popular during the Christmas season. They're simple to make, yet utterly delicious and bursting with creamy, buttery flavours. If you like, make them in advance of a special tea as they will keep well in the refrigerator for a few days.

Makes 16
200g/7oz white chocolate
25g/1oz/2 tbsp butter, diced
90g/3½oz/generous 1 cup
   desiccated (dry unsweetened
   shredded) coconut
90g/3½oz syrup sponge or
   Madeira cake
icing (confectioners') sugar,
   for dusting

1 Break the chocolate into pieces and put in a heatproof bowl with the butter. Rest the bowl over a pan of gently simmering water and stir frequently until melted. Remove the bowl from the heat and set aside for a few minutes.

2 Meanwhile, put 50g/2oz/⅔ cup of the coconut on a plate and set aside.

3 Crumble the sponge or Madeira cake and add to the melted chocolate with the remaining coconut. Mix well to form a chunky paste.

4 Take spoonfuls of the mixture and roll into balls, about 2.5cm/1in in diameter, and immediately roll them in the reserved coconut. Place the balls on baking parchment and leave to set.

5 Before serving, dust the snowballs liberally with plenty of icing sugar.

Cook's Tip
Be prepared to shape the mixture into balls as soon as you've mixed in the desiccated coconut and the cake. The mixture will set extremely quickly and you won't be able to shape it once it has hardened.

Florentine Bites

Extremely sweet and rich, these little mouthfuls – based on a classic Italian biscuit (cookie) – are really delicious when served with after-dinner coffee and liqueurs. Nicely wrapped, they would also make a very special gift for anyone – your dinner party host, for example.

50g/2oz/2½ cups cornflakes
50g/2oz/scant ½ cup sultanas
   (golden raisins)
115g/4oz/1 cup toasted flaked
   (sliced) almonds
115g/4oz/½ cup glacé
   (candied) cherries, halved
50g/2oz/⅓ cup mixed
   (candied) peel
200ml/7fl oz/scant 1 cup
   sweetened condensed milk

Makes 36
200g/7oz good quality plain
   (semisweet) chocolate
   (minimum 70 per cent
   cocoa solids)

1 Preheat the oven to 180°C/350°F/Gas 4. Line the base of a shallow 20cm/8in cake tin (pan) with baking parchment. Lightly grease the sides.

2 Melt the chocolate in a heatproof bowl over a pan of barely simmering water on a low heat. Stir and spread the melted chocolate over the base of the tin. Chill in the refrigerator until set.

3 Meanwhile, put the cornflakes, sultanas, almonds, cherries and mixed peel in a large bowl.

4 Pour the condensed milk over the cornflake mixture and toss the mix gently, using a fork.

5 Spread the mixture evenly over the chocolate base and bake for 12–15 minutes, or until golden brown.

6 Put the cooked florentine mixture aside in the tin until completely cooled, then chill for 20 minutes.

7 Cut into approximately 36 tiny squares and serve.

Snowballs Energy 133kcal/554kJ; Protein 1.6g; Carbohydrate 10.9g, of which sugars 9.7g; Fat 9.5g, of which saturates 6.6g; Cholesterol 3mg; Calcium 38mg; Fibre 0.8g; Sodium 46mg.
Florentine Bites Energy 87kcal/364kJ; Protein 1.6g; Carbohydrate 12g, of which sugars 10.7g; Fat 3.9g, of which saturates 1.4g; Cholesterol 2mg; Calcium 30mg; Fibre 0.5g; Sodium 28mg.

Mini Chocolate Meringues

These mini meringues are perfect for a child's birthday party and could be tinted pink or green. Any spares are delicious crunched into your next batch of vanilla ice cream.

50g/2oz chocolate mint sticks, chopped
unsweetened cocoa powder, sifted (optional)

For the filling
150ml/¼ pint/⅔ cup double or whipping cream
5–10ml/1–2 tsp crème de menthe, or mint extract

Makes about 50
2 egg whites
115g/4oz/generous ½ cup caster (superfine) sugar

1 Preheat the oven to 110°C/225°F/Gas ¼. Line two or three large baking sheets with baking parchment.

2 Whisk the egg whites until stiff, then gradually whisk in the sugar until the mixture becomes thick and glossy.

3 Carefully fold in the chopped mint sticks to the mixture until well combined.

4 Place heaped teaspoons of the mixture on the prepared baking sheets.

5 Bake for 1 hour, or until crisp. Remove from the oven and allow to cool, then dust with cocoa powder, if using.

6 Lightly whip the cream, stir in the crème de menthe, and sandwich the meringues together just before serving.

> **Cook's Tips**
> • You can store these meringues in airtight tins or jars; they will keep for several days.
> • Crème de menthe is an alcoholic mint-flavoured liqueur, available in green or clear varieties. Use the mint extract if you plan on making these meringues for children.

Mini Praline Pavlovas

Melt-in-the-mouth meringue topped with rich, velvety chocolate and nutty praline.

Makes 14
2 large (US extra large) egg whites
large pinch of ground cinnamon
90g/3½oz/½ cup caster (superfine) sugar
50g/2oz/½ cup pecan nuts, finely chopped

For the filling
50g/2oz/¼ cup unsalted (sweet) butter, diced
100g/3¾oz/scant 1 cup icing (confectioners') sugar, sifted
50g/2oz plain (semisweet) chocolate, broken into pieces

For the praline
50g/2oz/¼ cup caster (superfine) sugar
15g/½oz/1 tbsp finely chopped toasted almonds

1 Preheat the oven to 140°C/275°F/Gas 1. Line two baking sheets with baking parchment. Whisk the egg whites until stiff. Stir the cinnamon into the sugar. Add a spoonful of sugar to the egg whites and whisk well. Continue whisking in the sugar, a spoonful at a time, until thick and glossy. Stir in the pecan nuts, until well combined.

2 Place 14 spoonfuls of meringue on the prepared baking sheets, well spaced. Using the back of a wet teaspoon, make a small hollow in the top of each meringue. Bake in the oven for 45–60 minutes until dry and just beginning to colour. Cool.

3 Make the filling. Beat together the butter and icing sugar until light and creamy. Place the chocolate in a heatproof bowl. Set over a pan of barely simmering water and stir occasionally until melted. Cool the chocolate slightly, then add to the butter mixture and stir well. Divide the filling among the meringues.

4 Make the praline. Put the sugar in a small non-stick frying pan. Heat gently until the sugar melts to form a clear liquid. When the mixture begins to turn brown, stir in the nuts. When the mixture is a golden brown, remove from the heat and pour immediately on to a lightly oiled or non-stick baking sheet. Leave to cool completely and then break into small pieces. Sprinkle over the meringues and serve.

Mini Pavlovas Energy 148kcal/621kJ; Protein 1.3g; Carbohydrate 21.2g, of which sugars 21.1g; Fat 7g, of which saturates 2.7g; Cholesterol 8mg; Calcium 16mg; Fibre 0.3g; Sodium 32mg.
Mint Meringues Energy 30kcal/123kJ; Protein 0.2g; Carbohydrate 3.1g, of which sugars 3.1g; Fat 1.9g, of which saturates 1.2g; Cholesterol 4mg; Calcium 3mg; Fibre 0g; Sodium 3mg.

Meringues with Chestnut Cream

This dessert is a great way to end a dinner party or other special-occasion meal.

Serves 6
2 egg whites
pinch of cream of tartar
90g/3½oz/½ cup caster
(superfine) sugar
2.5ml/½ tsp vanilla extract
chocolate shavings, to decorate

For the chestnut cream
65g/2½oz/generous ¼ cup caster
(superfine) sugar

120ml/4fl oz/½ cup water
450g/1lb can unsweetened
chestnut purée
5ml/1 tsp vanilla extract
350ml/12fl oz/1½ cups double
(heavy) cream

For the chocolate sauce
225g/8oz plain (semisweet)
chocolate, chopped
175ml/6fl oz/¾ cup whipping
cream
30ml/2 tbsp rum or brandy
(optional)

1 Preheat the oven to 140°C/275°F/Gas 1. Line a baking sheet with baking parchment. Use a saucer to outline six 9cm/3½in circles and turn the paper over. Whisk the egg whites until frothy. Add the cream of tartar, and beat until soft peaks form. Gradually add the sugar, beating until the whites are stiff. Beat in the vanilla.

2 Spoon the whites into a piping (pastry) bag fitted with a medium plain or star nozzle and pipe six spirals following the outlines on the paper. Bake for about 1 hour, until the meringues feel firm. Transfer to a wire rack to cool completely.

3 Make the chestnut cream. Boil the sugar and water in a pan until dissolved. Boil for 5 minutes. Put the chestnut purée in a food processor and process until smooth. Add the sugar syrup until the purée is soft, but holds its shape. Add the vanilla. Whisk the cream until soft peaks form, then stir a spoonful into the mixture. Spoon the chestnut cream into a piping bag and pipe swirls on to the meringues. Pipe the cream on top.

4 Make the chocolate sauce. Heat the chocolate and cream in a pan. Remove from the heat and stir in the rum or brandy. Set aside to cool. To serve, place each meringue on a plate and sprinkle with chocolate shavings. Serve the sauce separately.

Chocolate Meringues with Mixed Fruit Compote

A glamorous dessert that is very hard to beat.

Serves 6
105ml/7 tbsp unsweetened
red grape juice
105ml/7 tbsp unsweetened
apple juice
30ml/2 tbsp clear honey
450g/1lb/4 cups mixed fresh
summer berries, such as
blackcurrants, redcurrants,
raspberries and blackberries

For the meringues
3 egg whites
150g/5oz/¾ cup caster
(superfine) sugar
75g/3oz good-quality plain
(semisweet) chocolate,
finely grated
175g/6oz/¾ cup crème fraîche

1 Preheat the oven to 110°C/225°F/Gas ¼. Grease and line two large baking sheets with baking parchment.

2 Make the meringues. Whisk the egg whites in a large mixing bowl until stiff. Gradually whisk in half the sugar, then fold in the remaining sugar, using a metal spoon. Gently fold in the grated plain chocolate. Carefully spoon the meringue mixture into a large piping (pastry) bag fitted with a large star nozzle. Pipe small round whirls of the mixture on to the prepared baking sheets. Bake the meringues for 2½–3 hours until they are firm and crisp. Remove from the oven. Carefully peel the meringues off the paper, then transfer them to a wire rack to cool.

3 Meanwhile, make the compote. Heat the fruit juices and honey in a pan until the mixture is almost boiling. Place the mixed berries in a large bowl and pour over the hot fruit juice and honey mixture. Stir gently to mix, then set aside and leave to cool. Once cool, cover the bowl with clear film (plastic wrap) and chill until required.

4 To serve, sandwich the cold meringues together with crème fraîche. Spoon the mixed fruit compote on to individual plates, top with the meringues and serve immediately.

Meringues with Cream Energy 825kcal/3439kJ; Protein 6g; Carbohydrate 80g, of which sugars 57.5g; Fat 55.6g, of which saturates 33.5g; Cholesterol 113mg; Calcium 107mg; Fibre 4g; Sodium 53mg.
Meringues with Fruit Energy 343kcal/1442kJ; Protein 4g; Carbohydrate 50.2g, of which sugars 50g; Fat 15.4g, of which saturates 10.1g; Cholesterol 34mg; Calcium 61mg; Fibre 2.2g; Sodium 44mg.

Chocolate Cherry Brandy Truffles

Gloriously rich chocolate truffles are given a really wicked twist in this recipe simply by the addition of a small quantity of cherry brandy – the perfect indulgent way to end a special dinner party. Instead of adding cherry brandy, try experimenting with some other of your favourite alcoholic spirits or liqueurs.

Makes 18
50g/2oz/½ cup plain
  (all-purpose) flour
25g/1oz/¼ cup unsweetened
  cocoa powder
2.5ml/½ tsp baking powder
90g/3½oz/½ cup caster
  (superfine) sugar
25g/1oz/2 tbsp butter, diced
1 egg, beaten
5ml/1 tsp cherry brandy
50g/2oz/½ cup icing
  (confectioners') sugar

1 Preheat the oven to 200°C/400°F/Gas 6. Line two baking sheets with baking parchment.

2 Sift the flour, cocoa and baking powder into a bowl and stir in the sugar.

3 Rub the butter into the flour mixture with your fingertips until the mixture resembles coarse breadcrumbs.

4 Mix together the beaten egg and cherry brandy and stir thoroughly into the flour mixture. Cover with clear film (plastic wrap) and chill for approximately 30 minutes.

5 Put the icing sugar in a bowl. Shape walnut-size pieces of dough roughly into a ball and drop into the icing sugar. Toss until thickly coated, then place on the baking sheets.

6 Bake for about 10 minutes, or until just set. Transfer to a wire rack to cool completely.

Variation
If you are making these for children try using fresh orange juice instead of cherry brandy.

Mixed Chocolate Truffles

Give these delectable truffles as a gift and you will have a friend for life.

Makes 20 large or 30 medium truffles
250ml/8fl oz/1 cup double
  (heavy) cream
275g/10oz fine quality dark
  (bittersweet) or plain
  (semisweet) chocolate,
  chopped into small pieces

40g/1½oz/3 tbsp unsalted
  (sweet) butter, cut into
  small pieces
unsweetened cocoa powder,
  for dusting (optional)
finely chopped pistachio nuts,
  to decorate (optional)
400g/14oz dark (bittersweet)
  chocolate, to decorate
  (optional)

1 Pour the cream into a pan. Bring to the boil over a medium heat. Remove from the heat and add the chocolate. Stir gently until melted. Stir in the butter. Strain into a bowl and cool to room temperature. Cover with clear film (plastic wrap) and chill for 4 hours or overnight.

2 Line a baking sheet with baking parchment. Using a small ice cream scoop, melon baller or tablespoon, form the mixture into 20 large or 30 medium balls and place on the baking sheet.

3 If dusting with cocoa powder, sift a thick layer of cocoa on to a plate. Roll the truffles in the cocoa, rounding them between the palms of your hands. Do not worry if the truffles are not perfectly round as an irregular shape looks more authentic. Alternatively, roll the truffles in very finely chopped pistachios. Chill on the paper-lined baking sheet until firm. Keep in the refrigerator for up to 10 days or freeze for up to 2 months.

4 If coating with chocolate, do not roll the truffles in cocoa, but freeze them for 1 hour. For perfect results, temper the chocolate. Alternatively, simply melt it in a heatproof bowl over a pan of barely simmering water. Using a fork, dip the truffles, one at a time, into the melted chocolate, tapping the fork on the edge of the bowl to shake off excess. Place on a baking sheet, lined with baking parchment. If the chocolate begins to thicken, reheat it gently until smooth. Chill the truffles until set.

Cherry Brandy Truffles Energy 60kcal/251kJ; Protein 0.9g; Carbohydrate 10.5g, of which sugars 8.2g; Fat 1.8g, of which saturates 1g; Cholesterol 14mg; Calcium 12mg; Fibre 0.3g; Sodium 26mg.
Mixed Truffles Energy 169kcal/705kJ; Protein 1.3g; Carbohydrate 14.4g, of which sugars 14.2g; Fat 11.9g, of which saturates 7.3g; Cholesterol 16mg; Calcium 12mg; Fibre 0.6g; Sodium 11mg.

Classic Belgian Chocolate Truffles

When made with the best dark Belgian chocolate, these sweet truffles are the ultimate heavenly indulgence.

Makes 30
250g/9oz Belgian dark (bittersweet) chocolate, such as Callebaut, finely chopped
150g/5oz/10 tbsp unsalted (sweet) butter, diced and softened
100ml/3½fl oz/scant ½ cup double (heavy) cream
15–30ml/1–2 tbsp brandy or liqueur of own choice
15ml/1 tbsp vanilla extract (optional)
100g/3¾oz sifted unsweetened cocoa powder, icing (confectioners') or caster (superfine) sugar, chopped nuts or grated coconut, for coating

1 Melt the chocolate in a heatproof bowl over just boiled water, stirring until smooth. Stir in the butter until melted. Pour the cream into a pan and bring it to simmering point. Remove from the heat and leave to stand for 2 minutes.

2 Pour the cream into the chocolate, stirring until blended. Stir in the brandy or liqueur, with the vanilla extract, if using. Cover and refrigerate for at least 4 hours, stirring frequently, until the mixture is stiff but still malleable.

3 Transfer the chocolate mixture to a glass tray or shallow dish and spread it out so that it is about 3cm/1¼in deep. Cover and put in the refrigerator for 5 hours or overnight.

4 Line a baking sheet with baking parchment. Scoop up the teaspoonfuls of chocolate mixture and transfer to the baking sheet. Continue until all the chocolate has been shaped. Put the mixture back in the refrigerator for 30 minutes.

5 Working quickly, roll each piece of chocolate into a ball. Place slightly apart on parchment-lined baking sheets. Cover lightly with clear film (plastic wrap) and chill again for 1 hour.

6 To coat the truffles, roll them in separate bowls of cocoa powder, icing sugar, caster sugar, chopped nuts or grated coconut until coated. Cover and chill for 10 minutes to firm up again. Store in an airtight container for up to a week.

Chocolate Truffle Medley

These are popular with almost everybody; simply use different combinations of chocolate and flavourings to make your favourites.

Makes 60
115g/4oz plain (semisweet) chocolate
115g/4oz milk chocolate
175g/6oz white chocolate
175ml/6fl oz/¾ cup double (heavy) cream

For the flavouring
30ml/2 tbsp dark rum
30ml/2 tbsp Tia Maria
30ml/2 tbsp apricot brandy

For the coating
45g/3 tbsp coarsely grated plain (semisweet) chocolate
45g/3 tbsp coarsely grated milk chocolate
45g/3 tbsp coarsely grated white chocolate

1 Melt each type of chocolate in a separate bowl. Place the cream in a small pan and heat gently until hot but not boiling. Allow to cool. Stir one-third of the cream into each of the bowls and blend evenly.

2 Add the rum to the plain chocolate and whisk until the mixture becomes lighter in colour. Whisk the Tia Maria into the milk chocolate, and lastly whisk the apricot brandy into the white chocolate.

3 Allow the three mixtures to thicken, giving them an occasional stir, until they are thick enough to divide into equal spoonfuls. Line three baking sheets with baking parchment. Place about 20 teaspoons of each flavoured chocolate mixture, well spaced apart, on to the three baking sheets and chill until firm enough to roll into small balls.

4 Place each of the grated chocolates into separate dishes. Shape the plain chocolate truffles into neat balls and roll in grated plain chocolate to coat evenly.

5 Repeat with the milk chocolate truffles and grated milk chocolate, and the white chocolate truffles and grated white chocolate. Chill the truffles until firm, then arrange neatly in boxes, bags or tins and tie with festive ribbon.

Chocolate Truffle Medley Energy 65kcal/269kJ; Protein 0.7g; Carbohydrate 5.4g, of which sugars 5.4g; Fat 4.3g, of which saturates 2.6g; Cholesterol 5mg; Calcium 18mg; Fibre 0.1g; Sodium 7mg.
Belgian Chocolate Truffles Energy 108kcal/447kJ; Protein 1.1g; Carbohydrate 5.8g, of which sugars 5.3g; Fat 9g, of which saturates 5.5g; Cholesterol 16mg; Calcium 10mg; Fibre 0.6g; Sodium 63mg.

Coffee Chocolate Truffles

Because these classic chocolates contain fresh cream, they should be stored in the refrigerator and eaten within a few days.

Makes 24
350g/12oz plain (semisweet) chocolate

75ml/5 tbsp double (heavy) cream
30ml/2 tbsp coffee liqueur, such as Tia Maria, Kahlúa or Toussaint
115g/4oz good quality white dessert chocolate
115g/4oz good quality milk dessert chocolate

1 Melt 225g/8oz of the plain chocolate in a bowl over a pan of barely simmering water. Stir in the cream and liqueur, then chill the mixture in the refrigerator for 4 hours, until firm.

2 Divide the mixture into 24 equal pieces and quickly roll each into a ball. Chill for one more hour, or until they are firm again.

3 Melt the remaining plain, white and milk chocolate in separate small bowls. Using two forks, carefully dip eight of the truffles, one at a time, into the melted milk chocolate.

4 Repeat with the white and plain chocolate. Place the truffles on a board, covered with baking parchment or foil. Leave to set before removing and placing in a serving bowl or individual paper cases.

Variations
Ginger: Stir in 40g/1½oz/¼ cup finely chopped crystallized ginger.
Candied fruit: Stir in 50g/2oz/⅓ cup finely chopped candied fruit, such as pineapple and orange.
Pistachio: Stir in 25g/1oz/¼ cup, chopped skinned pistachio nuts.
Hazelnut: Roll each ball of chilled truffle mixture around a whole skinned hazelnut.
Raisin: Soak 40g/1½oz/generous ¼ cup raisins overnight in 15ml/1 tbsp coffee liqueur, such as Tia Maria or Kahlúa and stir into the truffle mixture.

Malt Whisky Truffles

Whisky aficionados will adore these heavenly alcoholic-flavoured chocolate truffles.

Makes 25–30
200g/7oz plain (semisweet) chocolate, chopped into small pieces

150ml/¼ pint/⅔ cup double (heavy) cream
45ml/3 tbsp malt whisky
115g/4oz/1 cup icing (confectioners') sugar
unsweetened cocoa powder, for coating

1 Melt the chocolate in a heatproof bowl or a double boiler set over a pan of simmering water, stir until smooth, then allow to cool slightly.

2 Using a wire whisk, whip the cream with the whisky in a bowl until thick enough to hold its shape.

3 Stir in the melted chocolate and icing sugar, mixing evenly until well combined. Leave the mixture until it is firm enough to handle. Chill it for about 30 minutes in the refrigerator if necessary.

4 Dust your hands with a little cocoa powder to stop the mixture from sticking to them. Shape the mixture into bitesize balls by rolling a small portion of the mixture between your hands.

5 Coat each ball in cocoa powder and pack them into pretty cases or gift boxes. Store in an airtight container in the refrigerator for up to 3–4 days if necessary.

Variation
Try this recipe with your favourite brand of whisky, whether Scottish or Irish, but try to use malt whisky for its superior taste. American bourbon such as Jack Daniel's or Jim Beam will work just as well as Scotch in this recipe. Simply replace the malt whisky with the same quantity of bourbon.

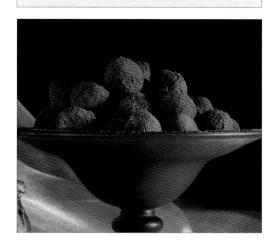

Bourbon Balls

This rich American delicacy laces biscuit and pecan nut truffles with an enticing dash of bourbon.

Makes about 25
175g/6oz Nice biscuits (cookies)
115g/4oz/1 cup pecan
  nuts, chopped

30ml/2 tbsp unsweetened
  cocoa powder
75g/3oz/²⁄₃ cup icing
  (confectioners') sugar, sifted
30ml/2 tbsp clear honey
120ml/4fl oz/½ cup bourbon

1 Put the biscuits in a plastic bag, sealing the open end, and crush them finely, using a rolling pin.

2 Transfer the crumbs into a bowl and add the chopped nuts, cocoa powder and half of the icing sugar. Stir until the mixture is well combined.

3 Add the honey and bourbon to the biscuit mixture. Stir until the mixture forms a stiff paste, adding a touch more bourbon if necessary.

4 Coat your hands in a little cocoa powder and shape the mixture into small balls. Place the balls on a plate and chill in the refrigerator until firm.

5 Roll the balls in the remaining icing sugar, then chill in the refrigerator for 15 minutes and roll again in the sugar.

6 Store in an airtight container until ready to serve, or pack in a decorative gift box.

Variations
• Nice biscuits are a plain coconut-flavoured biscuit, which have been made in the UK for over 100 years. If you can't find them, use any variety of plain coconut-flavoured biscuit or cookie.
• Brandy snaps can also be used and cognac or brandy in place of bourbon.

Gingered Truffles

Wonderfully creamy, these rich chocolate truffles are flecked with ginger, coated in dark chocolate and piped with melted white chocolate: a truly impressive gift.

Makes about 30
150ml/¼ pint/²⁄₃ cup double
  (heavy) cream

400g/14oz plain (semisweet)
  chocolate, broken into squares
25g/1oz butter
25g/1oz/2 tbsp brandy
30ml/2 tbsp glacé (candied)
  ginger, finely chopped
15ml/1 tbsp unsweetened
  cocoa powder
50g/2oz white chocolate, broken
  into squares

1 Place the cream in a heavy pan and bring to the boil. Remove from the heat and add 150g/5oz of the plain chocolate and the butter. Leave to stand for 5 minutes, stirring, until the chocolate and butter have melted. Return the pan to the heat for a few seconds if the chocolate and butter don't melt completely. Stir in the brandy, then, using an electric whisk, beat for 4–5 minutes, until the mixture is thick. Add 15ml/1 tbsp of the glacé ginger and stir well. Cover and chill for 2–3 hours until firm.

2 For the decoration, dip a teaspoon of the mixture in the cocoa powder and roll it into a ball, using your hands. Set aside and continue until all the mixture is used up. Freeze the truffles for 30 minutes until hard.

3 Place the remaining dark chocolate in a bowl set over a pan of simmering water. Heat until melted, stirring occasionally. Holding a truffle on a fork, spoon the melted chocolate over it until completely coated.

4 Carefully transfer to a baking sheet lined with baking parchment. Sprinkle the remaining glacé ginger over the truffles and leave to cool and harden. Melt the white chocolate and spoon into a baking parchment piping (pastry) bag. Pipe squiggly lines over the truffles and leave in the refrigerator to harden. Pack the truffles into petit four cases and arrange in boxes. Cover with a lid or some clear film (plastic wrap) and tie with a decorative ribbon.

Gingered Truffles Energy 111kcal/463kJ; Protein 0.97g; Carbohydrate 9.58g, of which sugars 9.41g; Fat 7.7g, of which saturates 4.7g; Cholesterol 9mg; Calcium 12mg; Fibre 0.4g; Sodium 14mg.
Bourbon Balls Energy 93kcal/389kJ; Protein 1.1g; Carbohydrate 8.8g, of which sugars 6g; Fat 5g, of which saturates 1.2g; Cholesterol 2.6mg; Calcium 12mg; Fibre 0.46g; Sodium 37mg.

Mocha Truffles with Café Noir

The combination of coffee liqueur and chocolate is irresistible. Give these as a gift and you'll have a friend for life.

Makes about 25

175g/6oz plain (semisweet) chocolate
50g/2oz/¼ cup unsalted (sweet) butter
10ml/2 tsp instant coffee granules
30ml/2 tbsp double (heavy) cream
225g/8oz/4 cups Madeira cake crumbs
50g/2oz/½ cup ground almonds
30ml/2 tbsp coffee-flavoured liqueur
unsweetened cocoa powder, chocolate vermicelli (sprinkles) or ground almonds, to coat

1 Break the chocolate into a heatproof bowl with the butter and instant coffee. Set the bowl over a pan of barely simmering water and heat gently until the chocolate and butter have melted and the coffee has dissolved.

2 Remove from the heat and stir in the cream, cake crumbs, ground almonds and coffee-flavoured liqueur.

3 Chill the mixture in the refrigerator until it has firmed up and is more easily handled.

4 Shape into small balls, roll in the cocoa powder, chocolate vermicelli or ground almonds, and place in foil petit four cases. Pack the truffles in gift boxes or arrange them on a decorative plate ready for serving.

> **Cook's Tip**
> There are a number of coffee-flavoured liqueurs that are widely available. The Jamaican liqueur Tia Maria is a little drier and lighter than Kahlúa, which has been made in Mexico for over 50 years. Kahlúa is more complex, with chocolate and vanilla flavours as well as coffee. Toussaint, from Haiti, is drier still and is the ideal choice for anybody who finds Tia Maria and Kahlúa a little too sweet.

Rose Petal Truffles

These glamorous chocolates are fun to make as a Valentine gift or for an engagement.

Makes about 25

500g/1¼lb plain (semisweet) chocolate
300ml/½ pint/1¼ cups double (heavy) cream
15ml/1 tbsp rose water
2 drops rose essential oil
250g/9oz plain (semisweet) chocolate, for coating
crystallized rose petals, for decoration

1 Break the chocolate into a heatproof bowl or into the top of a double boiler. Add the cream and set over a pan of barely simmering water. Heat gently, stirring constantly, until the chocolate has melted and the mixture is smooth.

2 Mix in the rose water and the essential oil, then pour into a baking tin (pan) lined with baking parchment and set aside to allow the mixture to cool.

3 When almost firm, take teaspoonfuls of the chocolate and shape into balls, using your hands. Coat your hands in a little cocoa powder if you find the mixture is sticking to them. Chill the truffles until they are hard.

4 Melt the chocolate for the coating in a heatproof bowl over a pan of simmering water. Skewer a truffle and dip it into the melted chocolate.

5 Decorate with a crystallized rose petal before the chocolate has set, then leave on a sheet of baking parchment until the truffles have set completely.

6 Sprinkle the truffles with crystallized rose petals before packing in a box.

> **Cook's Tip**
> Look out for crystallized rose petals in specialist food stores and large supermarkets.

Mocha Truffles Energy 108kcal/450kJ; Protein 1.36g; Carbohydrate 10.2g, of which sugars 8.2g; Fat 6.9g, of which saturates 3.5g; Cholesterol 6mg; Calcium 13mg; Fibre 0.43g; Sodium 47.5mg.
Rose Petal Truffles Energy 212kcal/886kJ; Protein 1.7g; Carbohydrate 19.2g, of which sugars 19g; Fat 14.8g, of which saturates 9g; Cholesterol 18mg; Calcium 16mg; Fibre 0.75g; Sodium 4.5mg

Truffle Christmas Puddings

Truffle Christmas puddings are great fun both to make and receive.

Makes 20
15ml/1 tbsp unsweetened cocoa powder
15ml/1 tbsp icing (confectioners') sugar
225g/8oz/1 cup white chocolate, melted
50g/2oz/¼ cup white marzipan

green and red food colouring
yellow food colouring dust

For the truffle mixture
175ml/6fl oz/¾ cup double (heavy) cream
275g/10oz plain (semisweet) chocolate, chopped
25g/1oz/2 tbsp unsalted (sweet) butter, cut into pieces
30–45ml/2–3 tbsp brandy (optional)

1 Prepare the truffle mixture. In a pan over a medium heat, bring the cream to a boil. Remove from the heat and add the chocolate, stirring until melted. Beat in the butter and add the brandy if using. Strain into a bowl, cover and chill overnight.

2 Line a large baking sheet with baking parchment. Using two teaspoons, form the truffle mixture into 20 balls and place in lines on the paper. Chill if the mixture becomes soft.

3 Sift the cocoa and icing sugar together and coat the truffles. Spread ⅔ of the white chocolate over a new sheet of baking parchment. Using a small daisy cutter, stamp out 20 rounds. Put a truffle on the centre of each daisy, securing with a little of the reserved melted chocolate.

4 Colour ⅔ of the marzipan green and the rest red, using the food colourings. Roll out the green marzipan thinly and stamp out 40 leaves with a tiny holly leaf cutter. Mark the veins with a sharp knife. Mould lots of tiny red marzipan beads.

5 Colour the remaining white chocolate with yellow food colouring and place in a baking parchment piping bag. Fold down the top of the bag, cut off the tip and and pipe the chocolate over the top of each truffle to resemble custard. Arrange the holly leaves and berries on the top of the puddings. Leave until completely set.

Chocolate Mint Truffle Filo Parcels

These exquisite little mint truffle parcels are utterly irresistible: there will be no leftovers. The use of fresh mint in the recipe gives a wonderfully fresh flavour.

Makes 18 parcels
15ml/1 tbsp very finely chopped fresh mint
75g/3oz/¾ cup ground almonds
50g/2oz plain (semisweet) chocolate, grated

115g/4oz/½ cup crème fraîche or fromage frais
2 dessert apples, peeled and grated
9 large sheets filo pastry
75g/3oz/6 tbsp butter, melted
15ml/1 tbsp icing (confectioners') sugar, to dust
15ml/1 tbsp unsweetened cocoa powder, to dust

1 Mix the chopped fresh mint, almonds, grated chocolate, crème fraîche or fromage frais and grated apple in a large mixing bowl. Set aside.

2 Cut the filo pastry sheets into 7.5cm/3in squares and cover with a damp cloth to prevent the sheets from drying out while you prepare the parcels.

3 Brush a square of filo with melted butter, lay on a second sheet, brush again and place a spoonful of filling in the middle of the top sheet. Bring in all four corners and twist to form a purse shape. Repeat to make 18 parcels.

4 Place the filo parcels on a griddle or baking sheet, well brushed with melted butter. Cook on a medium-hot barbecue for about 10 minutes, until the filo pastry is crisp.

5 Leave to cool, then dust lightly with sifted icing sugar and then with sifted cocoa powder.

> **Cook's Tip**
> If you can't find crème fraîche or fromage frais, then low-fat cream cheese would work equally well in this recipe.

Truffle Puddings Energy 169kcal/705kJ; Protein 1.3g; Carbohydrate 14.4g, of which sugars 14.2g; Fat 11.9g, of which saturates 7.3g; Cholesterol 16mg; Calcium 12mg; Fibre 0.6g; Sodium 11mg.
Filo Parcels Energy 140kcal/584kJ; Protein 2.3g; Carbohydrate 12.7g, of which sugars 4.1g; Fat 9.2g, of which saturates 4.6g; Cholesterol 16mg; Calcium 32mg; Fibre 0.9g; Sodium 28mg.

Frothy Hot Chocolate

Good hot chocolate should be made with the finest chocolate available. The vanilla pod will impart a delicious flavour to the milk. This is true comfort in a mug, the perfect way to unwind from a busy day after work or after a walk on a cold winter's day.

Serves 4
1 litre/1³⁄₄ pints/4 cups milk
1 vanilla pod (bean)
50–115g/2–4oz good quality dark (bittersweet) chocolate, minimum 60 per cent cocoa solids, grated

1 Pour the milk into a small pan and gently heat.

2 Split the vanilla pod lengthways using a sharp knife to reveal the seeds.

3 Add the pod to the milk and leave for a couple of minutes to let the milk take on the flavour of the vanilla.

4 Add the grated chocolate.

5 Heat the chocolate milk gently, stirring until all the chocolate has melted and the mixture is smooth, then whisk until the mixture boils.

6 Remove the vanilla pod from the pan and divide the drink among four mugs or heatproof glasses.

7 Serve the hot chocolate immediately.

> **Cook's Tips**
> • *Large mugs are essential for this drink. They will provide plenty of room to accommodate the lip-smackingly good froth as well as the dark, rich chocolate underneath.*
> • *The amount of chocolate to use depends on personal taste – start with a smaller amount if you are unsure of the flavour and taste at the beginning of step 4, adding more if necessary.*

Real Hot Chocolate

There are few better ways to enjoy the heavenly pleasures of chocolate than with a warming mug of proper hot chocolate. If you want a more chocolatey flavour, then simply increase the amount of chocolate. It's all a matter of taste.

Serves 2
115g/4oz plain (semisweet) chocolate with more than 60 per cent cocoa solids
400ml/14fl oz/1²⁄₃ cups milk

1 Break up the chocolate and put it in a heatproof bowl or double boiler set over a pan of barely simmering water.

2 Leave the chocolate in the bowl for 10 minutes until it has completely melted and is smooth.

3 Add the milk to a small pan and, over a medium heat, bring it just to a boil.

4 Stir a little of the hot milk into the melted chocolate.

5 Whisk in the remaining milk – a hand-held blender is good for this – until frothy.

6 Pour the hot chocolate into mugs and drink while hot.

> **Cook's Tips**
> • *This is the essence of real hot chocolate. The powdered version that comes in a packet doesn't even compare. Try to make it with the best chocolate you can afford – you'll really notice the difference if you use a cheaper version. This is how the Spanish and Mexicans have been making hot chocolate for centuries, and it's pure heaven.*
> • *For an utterly indulgent treat, enjoy your hot chocolate with your favourite chocolate treat, be it a cookie, truffle, cake or other delight. The perfect way to wind down from a busy day and give yourself a treat at supper time.*

Real Chocolate Energy 386kcal/1619kJ; Protein 9.7g; Carbohydrate 45.9g, of which sugars 45.4g; Fat 19.5g, of which saturates 11.8g; Cholesterol 15mg; Calcium 259mg; Fibre 1.5g; Sodium 90mg.
Frothy Chocolate Energy 179kcal/755kJ; Protein 9.1g; Carbohydrate 19.7g, of which sugars 19.6g; Fat 7.8g, of which saturates 4.8g; Cholesterol 16mg; Calcium 304mg; Fibre 0.3g; Sodium 108mg.

Mexican Hot Chocolate

The Mexicans have been drinking hot chocolate and other chocolate drinks for many hundreds of years. With drinks that taste this good it is easy to see why. Enjoy this drink at any time of day, or night.

Serves 4
1 litre/1¾ pints/4 cups milk
1 cinnamon stick
2 whole cloves
115g/4oz plain (semisweet)
   chocolate, chopped into
   small pieces
2–3 drops of almond extract

1 Put the milk into a small pan over a gentle heat.

2 Add the cinnamon stick and whole cloves to the pan and heat until the milk is almost boiling.

3 Stir in the plain chocolate over a medium heat until melted and smooth.

4 Strain the mixture into a blender, discarding the whole spices.

5 Add the almond extract and whizz on high speed for about 30 seconds until frothy. Alternatively, whisk the mixture in a bowl with a hand-held electric mixer or wire whisk.

6 Pour into warmed heatproof glasses and serve immediately.

> **Cook's Tips**
> • This drink is a liquid simulation of Mexican chocolate, which is flavored with cinnamon, almonds and vanilla, and has a much grainier texture than other chocolates. It is available in Mexican food stores and some supermarkets. If you can find some, why not try grating a little over the top of your drink for a full Mexican experience.
> • Few cultures have a longer history of cultivating and consuming chocolate than the Mexicans. The word itself comes from the Aztecs, who lived in Mexico over 500 years ago. They made a drink from cocoa beans called 'xocolatl', meaning 'bitter water'. No wonder this version of hot chocolate is one of the best.

Champurrada

This popular version of atole is made with Mexican chocolate. A special wooden whisk called a molinollo is traditionally used when making this frothy drink.

Serves 6
115g/4oz Mexican chocolate,
   about 2 discs
1.2 litres/2 pints/5 cups water
   or milk, or a mixture
200g/7oz white masa harina
30ml/2 tbsp soft dark brown sugar

1 Put the chocolate in a mortar and grind with a pestle until it becomes a fine powder. Alternatively, grind the chocolate in a food processor.

2 Put the liquid in a heavy pan and gradually stir in all the masa harina until a smooth paste is formed. Use a traditional wooden molinollo, if you have one, or use a wire whisk to create a frothier drink.

3 Place the pan over a moderate heat and bring the mixture to the boil, stirring all the time until the frothy drink thickens.

4 Stir in the ground chocolate, then add the sugar, stirring until the sugar has completely dissolved.

5 Pour into warmed glasses or mugs and serve immediately.

> **Cook's Tips**
> • Atole is a very thick beverage that's popular in Mexico and some parts of the American Southwest. It's a combination of masa harina (a heavy type of white flour made from maize), water or milk, crushed fruit and sugar or honey. Latin markets sell instant atole, which can be mixed with milk or water. Atole can be served hot or at room temperature.
> • This version of champurrada is also very popular in Mexico. In the morning in Mexican cities you will see people crowd around street-corner tamale carts as non-alcoholic champurrada is served in styrofoam cups or in plastic bags with straws as part of an on-the-go breakfast.

Mexican Chocolate Energy 220kcal/924kJ; Protein 8.1g; Carbohydrate 25.3g, of which sugars 25.1g; Fat 10.4g, of which saturates 6.4g; Cholesterol 13mg; Calcium 248mg; Fibre 0.6g; Sodium 88mg.
Champurrada Energy 250kcal/1048kJ; Protein 6g; Carbohydrate 41.6g, of which sugars 18.8g; Fat 6.8g, of which saturates 3.5g; Cholesterol 5mg; Calcium 89mg; Fibre 1.1g; Sodium 30mg.

White Hot Chocolate

This rich beverage is a delicious variation on the traditional dark chocolate drink. Flavoured with coffee and orange liqueur, it is the perfect way to round off a dinner party with friends or any other special-occasion meal.

Serves 4
1.75 litres/3 pints/7½ cups milk
175g/6oz white chocolate,
    chopped into small pieces
10ml/2 tsp coffee powder
10ml/2 tsp orange-flavoured
    liqueur (optional)
whipped cream and ground
    cinnamon, to serve

1 Pour the milk into a large heavy pan and heat until it is almost boiling.

2 As soon as bubbles form around the edge of the pan remove the milk from the heat.

3 Add the white chocolate pieces, coffee powder and the orange-flavoured liqueur, if using.

4 Stir the mixture until all the chocolate has melted and the mixture is smooth.

5 Pour the hot chocolate into four mugs.

6 Top each with a swirl or spoonful of whipped cream and a sprinkling of ground cinnamon. Serve immediately.

> **Variations**
> A variety of different flavoured liqueurs can be substituted in this recipe for the orange-flavoured liqueur.
> **Crème de cacao:** Use this chocolate liqueur to make the drink extra chocolatey. Only use the clear version, however, rather than the dark brown variety.
> **Crème de banane:** Give your drink a banana flavour with this liqueur.
> **Maraschino:** Try this bittersweet cherry-flavoured liqueur to give the drink a hint of maraschino cherries.

Iced Mint and Chocolate Cooler

This delicious chocolate drink is suprisingly invigorating thanks to the inclusion of peppermint extract and fresh mint leaves. For an even bigger minty kick, replace the chocolate ice cream for some mint chocolate chip ice cream.

Serves 4
60ml/4 tbsp drinking chocolate
400ml/14fl oz/1⅔ cups
    chilled milk
150ml/¼ pint/⅔ cup natural
    (plain) yogurt
2.5ml/½ tsp peppermint extract
4 scoops of chocolate ice cream,
    (or mint chocolate chip
    ice cream, if you prefer)
mint leaves and chocolate
    shapes, to decorate

1 Place the drinking chocolate in a small pan and stir in about 120ml/4fl oz/½ cup of the milk. Heat gently, stirring, until almost boiling, then remove the pan from the heat.

2 Pour the hot chocolate milk into a heatproof bowl or large jug (pitcher) and whisk in the remaining milk. Add the natural yogurt and peppermint extract and whisk again.

3 Pour the mixture into four tall glasses, filling them no more than three-quarters full. Top each drink with a scoop of chocolate ice cream. Decorate with mint leaves and chocolate shapes. Serve immediately.

> **Variations**
> Use this recipe as a base for other delicious milk drinks.
> **Chocolate vanilla cooler:** Make the drink as in the main recipe, but use single (light) cream instead of the natural yogurt and 5ml/1 tsp natural vanilla extract instead of the peppermint extract.
> **Mocha cooler:** Make the drink as in the main recipe, but dissolve the chocolate in 120ml/4fl oz/½ cup strong black coffee, and reduce the amount of milk to 300ml/½ pint/1¼ cups. Use single (light) cream instead of natural yogurt and omit the peppermint extract and mint leaves.

White Chocolate Energy 433kcal/1821kJ; Protein 18.4g; Carbohydrate 46.1g, of which sugars 46.1g; Fat 21g, of which saturates 12.7g; Cholesterol 26mg; Calcium 643mg; Fibre 0g; Sodium 236mg.
Mint Cooler Energy 231kcal/968kJ; Protein 8.1g; Carbohydrate 27.9g, of which sugars 27.5g; Fat 10.5g, of which saturates 6.3g; Cholesterol 6mg; Calcium 247mg; Fibre 0g; Sodium 138mg.

Warm Chocolate Float

Hot chocolate milkshake, scoops of chocolate ice cream and vanilla ice cream are combined here to make a meltingly delicious drink which will prove a big success with children and adults alike.

250ml/8fl oz/1 cup milk
15ml/1 tbsp caster sugar
4 large scoops vanilla
  ice cream
4 large scoops dark chocolate
  ice cream
a little lightly whipped cream
grated chocolate or chocolate
  curls, to decorate

Serves 2
115g/4oz plain chocolate, broken
  into pieces

1 Put the chocolate in a saucepan and add the milk and sugar.

2 Heat gently, stirring with a wooden spoon until the chocolate has melted and the mixture is smooth.

3 Place two scoops of each type of ice cream alternately in two heatproof tumblers.

4 Pour the chocolate milk over and around the ice cream. Top with lightly whipped cream and grated chocolate or big chocolate curls.

Variation

For a simpler – and decadently rich – version of a chocolate smoothie, try making the recipe with just two ingredients. Break 150g/5oz good quality chocolate into pieces and place in a heatproof bowl set over a pan of simmering water, making sure that the bowl does not rest in the water. Add 60ml/4 tbsp full cream (whole) milk and leave until the chocolate melts, stirring occasionally with a wooden spoon. Remove the bowl from the heat, pour another 290ml/10fl oz/1 cup milk over the chocolate and stir to combine. Pour the mixture into a blender or food processor and blend until frothy. Pour into glasses, add ice and chocolate curls or shavings, to serve.

Irish Chocolate Velvet

Few things are more deliciously indulgent than this velvety chocolate drink, heavily spiked with Irish whiskey. It is the perfect way to enjoy the end of a splendid feast.

115g/4oz milk chocolate,
  chopped into small pieces
30ml/2 tbsp unsweetened
  cocoa powder
60ml/4 tbsp Irish whiskey
whipped cream, for topping
chocolate curls, to decorate

Serves 4
250ml/8fl oz/1 cup double
  (heavy) cream
400ml/14fl oz/1²⁄₃ cups milk

1 Using a hand-held electric mixer, whip half the cream in a bowl until it is thick enough to hold its shape.

2 Place the milk and chocolate in a pan and heat gently, stirring, until the chocolate has melted and the mixture is smooth and glossy.

3 Whisk in the cocoa, then bring to the boil. Remove from the heat and stir in the remaining cream and the Irish whiskey.

4 Pour quickly into four warmed heatproof mugs or glasses.

5 Top each serving with a generous spoonful of the whipped cream, then the chocolate curls.

6 Serve with peppermint sticks for extra indulgence.

Cook's Tips

• *If you don't have any Irish whiskey, then this recipe will work equally well with your favourite brand of Scotch whisky. Even American bourbon makes a successful substitute.*
• *To make quick chocolate curls, chill a bar of your preferred chocolate in the refrigerator until hard. Run a vegetable peeler down the long side of the bar to peel off curls.*

Irish Velvet Energy 390kcal/1623kJ; Protein 7.5g; Carbohydrate 22.4g, of which sugars 21.6g; Fat 28.3g, of which saturates 17.3g; Cholesterol 54mg; Calcium 208mg; Fibre 1.1g; Sodium 145mg.
Warm Float Energy 918kcal/3834kJ; Protein 16.9g; Carbohydrate 92.2g, of which sugars 91.5g; Fat 56g, of which saturates 33.7g; Cholesterol 11mg; Calcium 423mg; Fibre 1.5g; Sodium 208mg.

Honey and Banana Smoothie with Hot Chocolate Sauce

This is a delicious blend of honey and banana, served with a hot chocolate sauce.

Serves 2 generously

450g/1lb/2 cups mashed
    ripe banana
200ml/7fl oz/scant 1 cup natural
    (plain) yogurt
30ml/2 tbsp mild honey
350ml/12fl oz/1½ cups orange
    juice ice cubes, crushed

For the hot chocolate sauce

175g/6oz plain (semisweet)
    chocolate with more than
    60 per cent cocoa solids
60ml/4 tbsp water
15ml/1 tbsp golden
    (light corn) syrup
15g/½oz/1 tbsp butter

1 First make the hot chocolate sauce. Break up the chocolate and put the pieces into a heatproof bowl placed over a pan of barely simmering water.

2 Leave undisturbed for 10 minutes until the chocolate has completely melted, then add the water, syrup and butter and stir until smooth. Keep warm over the hot water while you make the smoothie.

3 Place all the smoothie ingredients in a blender or food processor and blend until smooth. Pour into big, tall glasses, then pour in some chocolate sauce from a height and serve.

> **Cook's Tips**
> • *Pouring the chocolate sauce from a height cools the thin stream of sauce slightly on the way down, so that it thickens on contact with the cold smoothie. The sauce swirls around the glass to give a marbled effect, which is very attractive.*
> • *The secret to a successful smoothie is to always serve them ice-cold. Whizzing them up with a handful of ice is the perfect way to ensure this. Keep an ice tray of frozen orange juice at the ready. It's a great way to add extra flavour.*

Grasshopper Coffee

This hot drink is named for the crème de menthe flavour suggestive of a green grasshopper colour.

Serves 2

dark and white chocolate
    'after-dinner' style
    chocolate mints

50ml/2fl oz/¼ cup green
    crème de menthe
50ml/2fl oz/¼ cup coffee
    liqueur, such as Tia Maria
    or Kahlúa
350ml/12fl oz /1½ cups
    hot strong coffee
50ml/2fl oz/¼ cup
    whipping cream

1 Cut the dark and white chocolate mints diagonally in half.

2 Divide the two liqueurs equally between two tall, strong latte glasses. Combine well.

3 Fill each glass with the hot coffee and top them with whipped cream.

4 Decorate with the chocolate mint triangles, dividing the white and dark chocolate evenly between the drinks.

> **Cook's Tip**
> *It is important to use strong coffee to prevent the drink from tasting watery or being too diluted by the liqueurs, though it should be weaker than espresso, which might be overpowering.*

> **Variation**
> *Another great use for crème de menthe is in a chocolatey alcoholic milkshake. You'll need a few scoops of mint chocolate chip ice cream, 120ml/4fl oz/½ cup milk, 30ml/2 tbsp crème de menthe, a sprig of fresh mint and 1 miniature or broken cream-filled chocolate sandwich cookie. In a food processor or blender, combine the ice cream, milk and crème de menthe. Whirl until smooth and pour into a chilled tall glass. Garnish with the broken cookie and a mint sprig.*

Smoothie Energy 901kcal/3790kJ; Protein 13.2g; Carbohydrate 148.1g, of which sugars 142.2g; Fat 32.5g, of which saturates 19.4g; Cholesterol 23mg; Calcium 253mg; Fibre 4.9g; Sodium 176mg.
Grasshopper Coffee Energy 210kcal/868kJ; Protein 0.5g; Carbohydrate 6.4g, of which sugars 6.4g; Fat 14g, of which saturates 6.3g; Cholesterol 26mg; Calcium 19mg; Fibre 0g; Sodium 29mg.

Vanilla and Chocolate Caffè Latte

This luxurious vanilla and chocolate version of the classic coffee drink can be served at any time of the day topped with whipped cream, with cinnamon sticks to stir and flavour the drink. Caffè latte is a popular breakfast drink in Italy and France, and is now widely available elsewhere.

Serves 2
750ml/1¼ pints/3 cups milk
250ml/8fl oz/1 cup espresso or
    very strong coffee
45ml/3 tbsp vanilla sugar,
    plus extra to taste
115g/4oz dark (bittersweet)
    chocolate, grated
2 cinnamon sticks (optional)

1 Pour the milk into a small pan and bring to the boil, then remove from the heat.

2 Mix the espresso or very strong coffee with 475ml/16fl oz/ 2 cups of the boiled milk in a large heatproof jug (pitcher). Sweeten with vanilla sugar to taste.

3 Return the remaining boiled milk in the pan to the heat and add the 45ml/3 tbsp vanilla sugar. Stir constantly until dissolved. Bring to the boil, then reduce the heat.

4 Add the dark chocolate and continue to heat, stirring constantly until all the chocolate has melted and the mixture is smooth and glossy.

5 Pour the chocolate milk into the jug of coffee and whisk thoroughly. Serve in tall mugs or glasses. Top each serving with a swirl of whipped cream, and add cinnamon sticks, if you like, for stirring the drink.

> **Cook's Tip**
> Vanilla sugar is available from good food stores and large supermarkets, but it's easy to make your own: simply store a vanilla pod (bean) in a jar of sugar for a few weeks until the sugar has taken on the vanilla flavour.

New York Egg Cream

No eggs, no cream, just the best chocolate soda you will ever sip. This legendary drink is evocative of Old New York. No one knows why it is called egg cream but some say it was a witty way of describing richness at a time when no one could afford to put both expensive eggs and cream together in a drink.

Serves 1
45–60ml/3–4 tbsp good quality
    chocolate syrup
120ml/4fl oz/½ cup chilled milk
175ml/6fl oz/¾ cup chilled
    carbonated water
unsweetened cocoa powder,
    to sprinkle

1 Carefully pour the chocolate syrup into the bottom of a tall glass.

2 Pour the chilled milk on to the chocolate syrup.

3 Pour the carbonated water into the glass, sip up any foam that rises to the top of the glass and continue to add the remaining water.

4 Dust with the cocoa powder and serve.

5 Stir the egg cream well before drinking.

> **Cook's Tips**
> • An authentic egg cream is made with an old-fashioned seltzer dispenser that you press and spritz.
> • Chocolate syrup is available in supermarkets and food stores. It is a ready-to-use syrup, usually a combination of unsweetened cocoa powder, sugar or golden (light corn) syrup and various other flavourings. It is usually quite sweet and is most often used to flavour milk or as a dessert sauce. It cannot be substituted for melted chocolate in recipes. New Yorkers invariably use the chocolate syrup made by Fox's of Brooklyn called U-bet in their egg creams.

Caffè Latte Energy 543kcal/2290kJ; Protein 14.9g; Carbohydrate 76.5g, of which sugars 76g; Fat 22.1g, of which saturates 13.4g; Cholesterol 24mg; Calcium 451mg; Fibre 1.5g; Sodium 156mg.
Egg Cream Energy 302kcal/1266kJ; Protein 6.9g; Carbohydrate 32.9g, of which sugars 32.5g; Fat 16.9g, of which saturates 5.8g; Cholesterol 8mg; Calcium 202mg; Fibre 0.4g; Sodium 74mg.

Barbara

This cocktail recipe is variation on the classic White Russian (vodka, coffee liqueur and cream), but with a chocolatey flavour replacing the original coffee.

Makes 1 cocktail
1 measure/1½ tbsp vodka
1 measure/1½ tbsp white
  crème de cacao
½ measure/2 tsp double
  (heavy) cream
white chocolate, to decorate

Shake all the ingredients well with ice, and strain into a chilled cocktail glass. Grate white chocolate over the surface.

Cook's Tips
• Endlessly useful in the cocktail repertoire, the world of chocolate-flavoured liqueurs begins with simple crème de cacao, which comes in two versions, brown or dark (which may also contain some vanilla flavouring) and white (which tends to be considerably sweeter). If the designation "Chouao" appears on the label, then the cocoa beans used have come from that particular district of the Venezuelan capital, Caracas.
• For all cocktail recipes, 1 measure should be taken as the standard cocktail measure, that is 25ml/1fl oz.

Whiteout

A highly indulgent chocolate cream cocktail preparation which blends gin with sweet white crème de cacao. It tastes delicious and far more innocuous than it actually is.

Makes 1 cocktail
1½ measures/2 tbsp gin
1 measure/1½ tbsp white
  crème de cacao
1 measure/1½ tbsp double
  (heavy) cream
white chocolate, to decorate

Shake all the ingredients very well with ice to amalgamate the cream fully, and then strain into a chilled cocktail glass. Grate a small piece of white chocolate over the surface.

Arago

This delightful creamy chocolate and banana-flavoured creation is quite irresistible.

Makes 1 cocktail
1½ measures/2 tbsp cognac

1 measure/1½ tbsp crème
  de banane
1 measure/1½ tbsp double
  (heavy) cream
grated dark (bittersweet)
  chocolate, to decorate

Shake all the ingredients well with ice, and strain into a chilled cocktail glass. Sprinkle the surface of the drink with grated dark chocolate.

Pompeii

Here is a spin on the formula for an Alexander cocktail (gin, crème de cacao and cream), but with the chocolate component given a sweeter, nutty edge.

Makes 1 cocktail
1 measure/1½ tbsp cognac
¾ measure/3 tsp crème de cacao
½ measure/2 tsp amaretto
1 measure/1½ tbsp double
  (heavy) cream
flaked almonds, to decorate

Shake all the ingredients well with ice and strain into a chilled cocktail glass. Sprinkle the surface with flaked almonds.

Cook's Tips
• Use crème de cacao to boost the richness of your most chocolatey desserts, or add it to a cup of hot, strong coffee on a cold day for a quick chocolate fix.
• When using hot chocolate in a cocktail, it is always preferable to use good quality unsweetened cocoa powder with a good, high proportion of real cacao solids in it. The alternative – drinking chocolate – is mostly sugar and has a much less concentrated flavour.

Barbara Energy 201kcal/833kJ; Protein 0.2g; Carbohydrate 5.9g, of which sugars 5.9g; Fat 10.9g, of which saturates 4.3g; Cholesterol 18mg; Calcium 11mg; Fibre 0g; Sodium 25mg.
Whiteout Energy 305kcal/1262kJ; Protein 0.4g; Carbohydrate 6.1g, of which sugars 6.1g; Fat 17.3g, of which saturates 8.3g; Cholesterol 34mg; Calcium 17mg; Fibre 0g; Sodium 28mg.
Araga Energy 261kcal/1078kJ; Protein 0.4g; Carbohydrate 6.1g, of which sugars 6.1g; Fat 17.3g, of which saturates 8.3g; Cholesterol 34mg; Calcium 17mg; Fibre 0g; Sodium 28mg.
Pompeii Energy 271kcal/1121kJ; Protein 0.4g; Carbohydrate 8.6g, of which sugars 8.6g; Fat 16.2g, of which saturates 8.3g; Cholesterol 34mg; Calcium 16mg; Fibre 0g; Sodium 23mg.

Coffee and Chocolate Flip

Use only the freshest egg in this recipe, as it isn't cooked. The result is a smoothly frothy, intensely rich drink with a strong, beguiling coffee flavour. The chocolate element is in the garnish.

Makes I cocktail
I egg
5ml/1tsp sugar
I measure/1½ tbsp cognac
I measure/1½ tbsp Kahlúa
5ml/1tsp dark-roast instant coffee granules
3 measures/4½ tbsp double (heavy) cream
unsweetened cocoa powder, to decorate

I Separate the egg and lightly beat the white until frothy. In a separate bowl, beat the egg yolk with the sugar.

2 In a small pan, combine the brandy, Kahlúa, coffee and cream and warm over a very low heat. Allow the mixture to cool, then whisk it into the egg yolk.

3 Add the egg white to the egg and cream, and pour the mixture back and forth until it is smooth. Pour into a tall glass over crushed ice and sprinkle the top with cocoa powder.

Alhambra Royale

Perfect for relaxing with in front of a warm fire.

Makes I cocktail
250ml/8fl oz/1 cup hot chocolate
I small piece orange rind
1½ measures/2 tbsp cognac
15ml/1 tbsp whipped cream
unsweetened cocoa powder, to decorate

Drop the orange rind into the hot chocolate. Heat the cognac in a metal ladle over a gas flame or over boiling water, and set it alight. Pour it, flaming, into the chocolate. Stir it in, and spoon a blob of whipped cream on to the surface of the drink. Sprinkle with cocoa powder.

Hollywood Nuts

Almond, chocolate and hazelnut are among the flavours in this cocktail.

Makes I cocktail
I measure/1½ tbsp white rum
½ measure/2 tsp amaretto
½ measure/2 tsp brown crème de cacao
½ measure/2 tsp Frangelico
I measure/1½ tbsp sparkling lemonade

Shake all but the last ingredient with ice and strain into a rocks glass half-filled with cracked ice. Add the lemonade and stir. Garnish with a slice of lemon.

Mistress

This is a long, creamy chocolate cocktail.

Makes I cocktail
1½ measures/2 tbsp gin
I measure/1½ tbsp white crème de cacao
2 measures/3 tbsp pineapple juice
I measure/1½ tbsp passion fruit juice
I measure/1½ tbsp whipping cream
¼ measure/1 tsp Campari

Shake all but the last ingredient with ice and strain into a highball glass, half-filled with ice. Drizzle the Campari on top.

Blue Lady

This is a sweet, creamy cocktail that combines the flavours of two popular liqueurs, creating a most striking hue.

Makes I cocktail
1½ measures/2 tbsp blue curaçao
½ measure/2 tsp white crème de cacao
½ measure/2 tsp double (heavy) cream

Shake all the ingredients thoroughly with ice and strain into a chilled cocktail glass. Do not garnish.

Flip Energy 602kcal/2489kJ; Protein 7.5g; Carbohydrate 12.2g, of which sugars 12.2g; Fat 49.7g, of which saturates 26.6g; Cholesterol 293mg; Calcium 72mg; Fibre 0g; Sodium 109mg.
Alhambra Energy 361kcal/1512kJ; Protein 9.5g; Carbohydrate 27.9g, of which sugars 27.4g; Fat 15.1g, of which saturates 9.5g; Cholesterol 40mg; Calcium 300mg; Fibre 0g; Sodium 151mg.
Hollywood Nuts Energy 170kcal/706kJ; Protein 0g; Carbohydrate 7.2g, of which sugars 7.2g; Fat 3.9g, of which saturates 0g; Cholesterol 0mg; Calcium 6mg; Fibre 0g; Sodium 24mg.
Mistress Energy 300kcal/1249kJ; Protein 0.7g; Carbohydrate 14.3g, of which sugars 14.3g; Fat 14g, of which saturates 6.3g; Cholesterol 26mg; Calcium 25mg; Fibre 0g; Sodium 35mg.
Blue Lady Energy 201kcal/836kJ; Protein 0.2g; Carbohydrate 15.4g, of which sugars 15.4g; Fat 8.7g, of which saturates 4.2g; Cholesterol 17mg; Calcium 10mg; Fibre 0g; Sodium 18mg.

Piranha

This is one of those
deceptive chocolate-
flavoured cocktails that
tastes relatively harmless,
but in fact packs quite
a punch, much like the
predatory fish after
which it is named.

Makes 1 cocktail
1½ measures/2 tbsp vodka
1 measure/1½ tbsp brown
   crème de cacao
1 measure/1½ tbsp ice-cold cola

Pour the alcohol into a rocks glass or short tumbler
containing plenty of cracked ice and stir vigorously before
adding the cola.

Brandy Alexander

One of the best chocolate-
flavoured cocktails of them
all, Brandy Alexander can be
served at the end of a grand
dinner with coffee, or as the
first drink of the evening at
a cocktail party, since the
cream in it helps to line
the stomach.

Makes 1 cocktail
1 measure/1½ tbsp cognac
1 measure/1½ tbsp brown
   crème de cacao
1 measure/1½ tbsp double
   (heavy) cream
grated dark (bittersweet)
   chocolate or nutmeg,
   to decorate

Shake the ingredients thoroughly with ice and strain into
a tall cocktail glass. Scatter ground nutmeg, or grate a little
whole nutmeg, on top. Alternatively, sprinkle with coarsely
grated dark chocolate.

> **Cook's Tip**
> *Creamy cocktails should generally be made with double
> (heavy) cream, as the single (light) version tends to be
> too runny.*

Hammer Horror

Use the best vanilla ice
cream you can find for
this smooth cocktail, and
preferably one that is made
with whole egg and real
vanilla, for extra richness.

Makes 1 cocktail
1 measure/1½ tbsp vodka
1 measure/1½ tbsp Kahlúa
60ml/4 tbsp vanilla ice cream
grated dark chocolate,
   to decorate

Add all the ingredients to a liquidizer with cracked ice, blend for
a few seconds and then strain into a cocktail glass. Sprinkle the
surface of the drink with grated dark chocolate.

Alexander the Great

This cocktail is another
variation on the chocolate/
coffee/cream combination.
Related to the classic
Brandy Alexander, this drink
is reputed to have been
invented by the late
Hollywood singing star
Nelson Eddy.

Makes 1 cocktail
1½ measure/2 tbsp vodka
½ measure/2 tsp Kahlúa
½ measure/2 tsp brown
   crème de cacao
½ measure/2 tsp double
   (heavy) cream

Shake all the ingredients well with plenty of ice, and strain into
a cocktail glass. Add a couple of chocolate-coated coffee beans
to the drink.

> **Cook's Tips**
> • *The liqueur components in Alexander the Great are Kahlúa
> and the brown version of chocolate liqueur. If your guests do
> not have such a sweet tooth, substitute Tia Maria and white
> crème de cacao.*
> • *Chocolate-coated coffee beans are quite fashionable to serve
> on chocolate cocktails. They are naturally quite crunchy, but
> have the extra caffeine kick of the chocolate coating.*

Piranha Energy 174kcal/725kJ; Protein 0g; Carbohydrate 8.3g, of which sugars 8.3g; Fat 3.9g, of which saturates 0g; Cholesterol 0mg; Calcium 6mg; Fibre 0g; Sodium 24mg.
Brandy Alexander Energy 288kcal/1190kJ; Protein 0.6g; Carbohydrate 6.3g, of which sugars 6.3g; Fat 22.7g, of which saturates 11.7g; Cholesterol 48mg; Calcium 22mg; Fibre 0g; Sodium 30mg.
Hammer Horror Energy 243kcal/1012kJ; Protein 2.2g; Carbohydrate 17.6g, of which sugars 16.9g; Fat 9g, of which saturates 3.7g; Cholesterol 15mg; Calcium 65mg; Fibre 0g; Sodium 58mg.
Alexander the Great Energy 227kcal/938kJ; Protein 0.2g; Carbohydrate 5.9g, of which sugars 5.9g; Fat 10.6g, of which saturates 4.2g; Cholesterol 17mg; Calcium 11mg; Fibre 0g; Sodium 25mg.

Coffee Cognac Cooler

Topped with decorative chocolate curls, this drink is unabashedly decadent, and not for those who are counting calories. The recipe serves two, so you can both feel guilty together.

Makes 2 cocktails
*250ml/8fl oz cold strong
    dark-roast coffee
80ml/3fl oz cognac
50ml/2fl oz coffee liqueur
50ml/2fl oz double (heavy) cream
10ml/2 tsp sugar
2 scoops coffee ice cream
chocolate curls or shavings,
    to decorate*

1 Shake or blend all the ingredients except the ice cream together with plenty of crushed ice. Pour into tall cocktail glasses and gently add a scoop of ice cream to each.

2 Garnish with chocolate curls or shavings, and serve with a long-handled spoon. For more of a chocolate hit, pour a little melted chocolate on to a baking tray, allow it to cool and then chisel it carefully away in long curls with the point of a knife.

Savoy Hotel

It's a short step from London's Savoy Theatre to the American Bar in the hotel itself, where this delightful chocolate and brandy flavoured cocktail was created. It's a pousse-café or layered drink that requires a steady hand.

Makes 1 cocktail
*1 measure/1½ tbsp brown
    crème de cacao
1 measure/1½ tbsp Bénédictine
1 measure/1½ tbsp cognac*

Carefully pour each of the ingredients, in this order, over the back of a spoon into a liqueur glass or sherry schooner to create a multi-layered drink. Serve immediately, while the effect is intact.

Coffee-chocolate Soda

This is a fun, refreshing drink that tastes as good as it looks. The combination of chocolate ice cream and coffee-flavoured fizz makes for an unusually textured but thoroughly exciting cocktail. This recipe makes enough to serve two.

Makes 2 cocktails
*250ml/8fl oz strong cold coffee
60ml/4 tbsp double (heavy)
    cream, or 30ml/2 tbsp
    evaporated milk (optional)
250ml/8fl oz cold soda water
2 scoops chocolate ice cream
chocolate-covered coffee
    beans, roughly chopped,
    to garnish*

Pour the coffee into tall cocktail glasses. Add the cream or evaporated milk, if using. Add the soda water and stir. Gently place a scoop of ice cream into the mixture. Garnish with some of the roughly chopped chocolate-covered coffee beans. Serve with a long spoon or a straw.

> **Variation**
> *Try chocolate mint ice cream and sprinkle with good quality grated chocolate.*

Captain Kidd

Brandy and dark rum make a heady, but very successful mix in a powerful cocktail, and this one is further enhanced by the addition of strong chocolate flavour. There are no non-alcoholic ingredients, you'll notice, so watch out.

Makes 1 cocktail
*1½ measures/2 tbsp cognac
1 measure/1½ tbsp dark rum
1 measure/1½ tbsp brown
    crème de cacao*

Shake well with ice, and strain into a chilled champagne saucer. Garnish with a physalis or a half-slice of orange.

Coffee Cognac Energy 298kcal/1237kJ; Protein 0.5g; Carbohydrate 13.9g, of which sugars 13.9g; Fat 13.5g, of which saturates 8.4g; Cholesterol 34mg; Calcium 16mg; Fibre 0g; Sodium 9mg.
Savoy Hotel Energy 192kcal/798kJ; Protein 0g; Carbohydrate 5.7g, of which sugars 5.7g; Fat 3.9g, of which saturates 0g; Cholesterol 0mg; Calcium 5mg; Fibre 0g; Sodium 22mg.
Soda Energy 255kcal/1057kJ; Protein 2.7g; Carbohydrate 12.4g, of which sugars 11.8g; Fat 21.3g, of which saturates 13.7g; Cholesterol 56mg; Calcium 75mg; Fibre 0g; Sodium 43mg.
Captain Kidd Energy 220kcal/912kJ; Protein 0g; Carbohydrate 5.7g, of which sugars 5.7g; Fat 3.9g, of which saturates 0g; Cholesterol 0mg; Calcium 5mg; Fibre 0g; Sodium 22mg.

Quick-mix Sponge Cake

Choose chocolate flavouring for this light and versatile sponge cake, or omit the cocoa powder and leave it plain, if you prefer.

Makes one 20cm/8in round or ring cake
115g/4oz/1 cup self-raising (self-rising) flour
5ml/1 tsp baking powder
115g/4oz/½ cup soft margarine

115g/4oz/generous ½ cup caster (superfine) sugar
2 eggs*

For a chocolate flavouring
15ml/1 tbsp unsweetened cocoa powder blended with 15ml/1 tbsp boiling water

1 Preheat the oven to 160°C/325°F/Gas 3. Grease a 20cm/8in round or ring cake tin (pan), line the base with baking parchment and grease the paper.

2 Sift the flour and baking powder into a mixing bowl. Add the margarine, sugar and eggs, and blend with the cocoa powder and boiling water, if using.

3 Beat with a wooden spoon for 2–3 minutes. The mixture should be pale in colour and slightly glossy.

4 Spoon the mixture into the cake tin and smooth the surface. Bake in the centre of the oven for 30–40 minutes, or until a skewer inserted into the centre of the cake comes out clean. Turn out on to a wire rack, remove the lining paper and leave to cool completely.

Cook's Tips
• This sponge cake is ideal for a celebration cake that will be simply iced, but do not use it for a cake that needs to be cut into an intricate shape. Madeira cake is best for that purpose.
• Always leave any cake to cool completely before decorating it. It is best to leave it overnight in a sealed, airtight container to settle if possible.

Sponge Roll

You can use cocoa powder to flavour this basic Swiss roll. Vary the flavour of the cake by adding a little grated orange, lime or lemon rind to the mixture, if you like.

Serves 6–8
4 eggs, separated
115g/4oz/generous ½ cup caster (superfine) sugar, plus extra for sprinkling

115g/4oz/1 cup plain (all-purpose) flour
5ml/1 tsp baking powder

For a chocolate flavouring
Replace 25ml/1½ tbsp of the flour with 25ml/1½ tbsp unsweetened cocoa powder

1 Preheat the oven to 180°C/350°F/Gas 4. Base-line and grease a 33 × 23cm/13 × 9in Swiss roll tin (jelly roll pan).

2 Whisk the egg whites until stiff peaks form and then beat in 30ml/2 tbsp of the caster sugar.

3 Beat the egg yolks with the remaining caster sugar and 15ml/1 tbsp water for about 2 minutes, or until the mixture is pale and leaves a thick ribbon trail.

4 Sift together the flour and baking powder into another bowl. Carefully fold the beaten egg yolks into the egg whites, then fold in the flour mixture.

5 Pour the mixture into the prepared tin and gently smooth the surface with a plastic spatula. Bake in the centre of the oven for 12–15 minutes, or until the cake starts to come away from the edges of the tin.

6 Turn the cake out on to a piece of baking parchment lightly sprinkled with caster sugar. Peel off the lining paper and cut off any crisp edges. Spread with jam, if you like, and roll up, using the baking parchment to help you.

7 Leave to cool on a wire rack, then dust the finished roll with icing sugar.

Quick-mix Cake Energy 1504kcal/6260kJ; Protein 28.2g; Carbohydrate 107.8g, of which sugars 3.2g; Fat 110g, of which saturates 5.3g; Cholesterol 381mg; Calcium 270mg; Fibre 6g; Sodium 1207mg.
Sponge Roll Energy 142kcal/603kJ; Protein 4.6g; Carbohydrate 26.2g, of which sugars 15.2g; Fat 3g, of which saturates 0.8g; Cholesterol 95mg; Calcium 42mg; Fibre 0.5g; Sodium 36mg.

Madeira Cake

This sponge cake is excellent to use as a basic sponge for celebration cakes to be decorated with chocolate icing or frosting. You can flavour the base with cocoa if required.

Serves 6–8

225g/8oz/2 cups plain (all-purpose) flour
5ml/1 tsp baking powder

225g/8oz/1 cup butter or margarine, at room temperature
225g/8oz/generous 1 cup caster (superfine) sugar
grated rind of 1 lemon
5ml/1 tsp vanilla extract
4 eggs

For a chocolate flavouring

Replace 25ml/1½ tbsp of the flour with 25ml/1½ tbsp unsweetened cocoa powder

1 Preheat the oven to 160°C/325°F/Gas 3. Base-line and grease a 20cm/8in cake tin (pan). Sift the plain flour and baking powder into a bowl.

2 Cream the butter or margarine, adding the caster sugar about 30ml/2 tbsp at a time, until light and fluffy. Stir in the lemon rind and vanilla extract.

3 Add the eggs one at a time, beating for 1 minute after each addition. Add the flour mixture and stir until just combined. Pour the cake mixture into the prepared tin and tap lightly to level. Bake for about 1¼ hours, or until a metal skewer inserted in the centre comes out clean. Cool in the tin for 10 minutes, then turn the cake out on to a wire rack and leave to cool completely.

> **Cook's Tips**
> • *Madeira cake is ideal for using as a celebration cake as it keeps better than a sponge cake and so will last for longer while you decorate it. It also has a firm texture that will be easy to ice with butter icing and sugarpaste.*
> • *Level the domed top before icing the cake by putting a deep cake board inside the cake tin (pan) that the cake was baked in and placing the cake on top. Cut the part of the cake that extends above the top of the tin using a sharp knife.*

Chocolate Shortcrust Pastry (1)

Suitable for sweet flans and tarts, this quantity will line a 23cm/9in flan tin.

Makes one 23cm/9in flan

115g/4oz plain (semisweet) chocolate, broken into squares

225g/8oz/2 cups plain (all-purpose) flour
115g/4oz/½ cup unsalted (sweet) butter
15–30ml/1–2 tbsp cold water

1 Melt the chocolate in a heatproof bowl over hot water. Remove from the heat and allow to cool, but not set.

2 Place the flour in a mixing bowl. Rub in the butter until the mixture resembles fine breadcrumbs.

3 Make a well in the centre of the rubbed-in mixture. Add the cooled chocolate and mix in together with just enough cold water to mix to a firm dough. Knead lightly, then wrap in clear film (plastic wrap) and chill before rolling out. Once you have chilled the flan tin (pan), chill again before baking.

Chocolate Shortcrust Pastry (2)

This is an alternative sweet chocolate pastry, this time made with cocoa.

Makes one 23cm/9in flan

175g/6oz/1½ cups plain (all-purpose) flour

30ml/2 tbsp unsweetened cocoa powder
30ml/2 tbsp icing (confectioners') sugar
115g/4oz/½ cup butter
15–30ml/1–2 tbsp cold water

1 Sift the flour, cocoa powder and icing sugar into a bowl.

2 Place the butter in a pan with the water and heat gently until just melted. Cool.

3 Stir into the flour to make a smooth dough. Chill until firm, then roll out and use as required.

Madeira Cake Energy 453kcal/1894kJ; Protein 6.1g; Carbohydrate 51.4g, of which sugars 30g; Fat 26.3g, of which saturates 15.5g; Cholesterol 155mg; Calcium 74mg; Fibre 0.9g; Sodium 208mg.
Pastry (1) Energy 2209kcal/9238kJ; Protein 27.6g; Carbohydrate 248.5g, of which sugars 76.1g; Fat 129.7g, of which saturates 79.7g; Cholesterol 252mg; Calcium 374mg; Fibre 9.8g; Sodium 711mg.
Pastry (2) Energy 1664kcal/6950kJ; Protein 22.8g; Carbohydrate 171.5g, of which sugars 34.7g; Fat 103.3g, of which saturates 64.1g; Cholesterol 245mg; Calcium 321mg; Fibre 9.1g; Sodium 989mg.

Chocolate Fudge Frosting

A darkly delicious creamy chocolate frosting, this sumptuous topping can transform a simple sponge cake into one worthy of a very special occasion.

Makes 350g/12oz/1½ cups
50g/2oz plain (semisweet)
   chocolate

225g/8oz/2 cups
   icing (confectioners')
   sugar, sifted
50g/2oz/¼ cup butter
45ml/3 tbsp milk or
   single (light) cream
5ml/1 tsp vanilla extract

1 Break or chop the chocolate into small pieces. Put the chocolate, icing sugar, butter, milk or cream and vanilla extract in a heavy pan.

2 Stir over a very low heat until both the chocolate and the butter have melted. Remove the mixture from the heat and stir until it is evenly blended.

3 Beat the icing frequently as it cools until it thickens sufficiently to use for spreading or piping.

4 Use the icing immediately and work as quickly as possible once it has reached the right consistency. If you let it cool too much it will become too thick to work with.

Cook's Tips
• Spread fudge frosting smoothly over the cake or swirl it. Or be even more elaborate with a little piping – it really is very versatile.
• This recipe makes enough to fill and coat the top and sides of a 20cm/8in or 23cm/9in round sponge cake.
• This icing should be used immediately.
• Use a good quality chocolate so that you achieve a pronounced flavour for this frosting.
• Because the frosting contains cream, it is best to keep the finished cake in the refrigerator until ready to serve.

Glossy Chocolate Fudge Icing

A rich glossy chocolate icing using eggs, which sets like chocolate fudge, this is versatile enough to smoothly coat, swirl or pipe, depending on the temperature of the icing when it is used.

50g/2oz/¼ cup unsalted
   (sweet) butter
1 egg, beaten
175g/6oz/1½ cups icing
   (confectioners') sugar, sifted

Makes 450g/1lb/2 cups
115g/4oz plain (semisweet)
   chocolate, in squares

1 Place the chocolate and butter in a heatproof bowl over a pan of hot water.

2 Stir the mixture occasionally with a wooden spoon until both the chocolate and butter are melted. Add the egg and beat well until thoroughly combined.

3 Remove the bowl from the pan and stir in the icing sugar, then beat until smooth and glossy.

4 Pour immediately over the cake for a smooth finish, or leave to cool for a thicker spreading or piping consistency.

Cook's Tips
• Melt chocolate slowly, as overheating will spoil both the flavour and the texture. Avoid overheating – dark (bittersweet) chocolate should not be heated above 49°C/120°F; milk and white chocolate should not be heated above 43°C/110°F.
• Never allow water or steam to come into melting chocolate, as this may cause it to stiffen. If the chocolate comes into contact with steam, and forms a solid mass, add a small amount of pure vegetable oil and mix in. If this does not work, you will have to start again. Don't discard spoiled chocolate – it will probably melt when added to another ingredient such as milk, butter or cream.

Frosting Energy 1534kcal/6468kJ; Protein 5.5g; Carbohydrate 269.3g, of which sugars 268.8g; Fat 55.9g, of which saturates 34.9g; Cholesterol 112mg; Calcium 199mg; Fibre 1.3g; Sodium 339mg.
Icing Energy 1722kcal/7235kJ; Protein 13.2g; Carbohydrate 256.2g, of which sugars 255.2g; Fat 78.8g, of which saturates 46.9g; Cholesterol 304mg; Calcium 168mg; Fibre 2.9g; Sodium 390mg.

Satin Chocolate Icing

A luxuriously rich and fudgy chocolate topping for cakes, which gives them a shiny satin finish.

150ml/¼ pint/⅔ cup double (heavy) cream
2.5ml/½ tsp instant coffee powder

Makes 225g/8oz/1 cup
175g/6oz plain (semisweet) or dark (bittersweet) chocolate, chopped into small pieces

1 Put the chocolate, cream and coffee in a small heavy pan.

2 Place the cake to be iced on a wire rack over a baking sheet or tray.

3 Place the pan over a very low heat and stir the mixture with a wooden spoon until all the pieces of plain or dark chocolate have melted and the mixture is smooth and evenly blended.

4 Remove from the heat and immediately pour the icing over the cake. Allow the icing to run down the sides slowly to coat the cake completely. Spread the icing with a metal spatula as necessary, working quickly before the icing has time to thicken.

5 Cover the cake, being careful to avoid any contact with the icing, and leave until completely hardened before adding any further decoration.

> **Cook's Tips**
> • *Take care to avoid touching the icing once it has fully hardened. The attractive all-over satin finish can be easily spoilt by fingers or utensils.*
> • *Cakes covered with this icing need little by way of any extra decoration. However, a minimal decoration can look very attractive on top of a satin-finished cake. Try cherries half-dipped in white chocolate, or a few leaves or curls of chocolate.*

Glossy Chocolate Icing

A rich, smooth glossy icing, this can be made with plain or milk chocolate.

Makes 350g/12oz/1½ cups
175g/6oz plain (semisweet) chocolate
150ml/¼ pint/⅔ cup single (light) cream

1 Break up the chocolate into small pieces and place it in a pan with the cream.

2 Heat gently, stirring occasionally, until the chocolate has melted and the mixture is smooth.

3 Allow the icing to cool until it is thick enough to coat the back of a wooden spoon. Use it at this stage for a smooth glossy icing, or allow it to thicken to obtain an icing which can be swirled or patterned with a cake decorating scraper.

Chocolate Butterscotch Frosting

Soft light brown sugar, treacle and chocolate make a rich and tempting frosting.

Makes 675g/1½lb/3 cups
75g/3oz/6 tbsp unsalted (sweet) butter
45ml/3 tbsp milk
25g/1oz/2 tbsp soft light brown sugar

15ml/1 tbsp black treacle (molasses)
350g/12oz/3 cups icing (confectioners') sugar, sifted
15ml/1 tbsp unsweetened cocoa powder

1 Place the butter, milk, sugar and treacle in a bowl over a pan of simmering water. Stir until the butter melts and the sugar dissolves completely.

2 Remove from the heat and stir in the icing sugar and cocoa powder until well combined. Beat until smooth. Pour over the cake, or cool for a thicker consistency.

Satin Energy 1637kcal/6801kJ; Protein 11.2g; Carbohydrate 113.7g, of which sugars 112.1g; Fat 129.6g, of which saturates 79.5g; Cholesterol 216mg; Calcium 131mg; Fibre 4.4g; Sodium 44mg.
Glossy Energy 1182kcal/4937kJ; Protein 13.7g; Carbohydrate 114.4g, of which sugars 112.8g; Fat 77.7g, of which saturates 47.6g; Cholesterol 93mg; Calcium 191mg; Fibre 4.4g; Sodium 54mg.
Butterscotch Energy 2095kcal/8850kJ; Protein 4g; Carbohydrate 404.5g, of which sugars 404.5g; Fat 62.4g, of which saturates 39.5g; Cholesterol 163mg; Calcium 349mg; Fibre 0g; Sodium 523mg.

White Chocolate Frosting

This rich white chocolate icing is thick enough for you to create delightful sculpted patterns on your finished cakes. The frosting should hold its shape, making it possible to create rugged shapes resembling drifts of freshly fallen snow.

Enough to cover a 20cm/8in round cake
175g/6oz white chocolate, chopped into small pieces
75g/3oz/6 tbsp unsalted (sweet) butter
115g/4oz/1 cup icing (confectioners') sugar
90ml/6 tbsp double (heavy) cream

1 Melt the chopped white chocolate with the butter in a double boiler or a heatproof bowl over a pan of barely simmering water.

2 Stir the chocolate constantly until it has completely melted and the mixture is smooth and glossy.

3 Remove the bowl from the heat and beat in the icing sugar, a little at a time, using a wire whisk to ensure the sugar is well combined with the chocolate mixture.

4 Whip the cream in a separate bowl until it just holds its shape, then beat it into the chocolate mixture. Stir until the cream and chocolate are thoroughly blended.

5 Allow the mixture to cool, stirring occasionally, until it begins to hold its shape. Use immediately.

Cook's Tips
• *White chocolate frosting is a rich frosting suitable for a dark chocolate sponge without a filling. Use a metal spatula to form peaks for an attractive finish.*
• *This is the ideal covering for festive cakes and other treats during the Christmas period. Give the frosting a rugged finish with a metal spatula or fork so that it resembles a blanket of snow over your cake.*

Butter Icing

This icing has a creamy, rich flavour and silky smoothness. It can easily be flavoured with chocolate, coffee, lemon, orange or lime.

Makes 350g/12oz/1½ cups
75g/3oz/6 tbsp soft margarine or butter, softened
225g/8oz/2 cups icing (confectioners') sugar, sifted
5ml/1 tsp vanilla extract
10–15ml/2–3 tsp milk

For a chocolate flavouring
Blend 15ml/1 tbsp unsweetened cocoa powder with 15ml/1 tbsp hot water. Cool before beating into the icing.

For a coffee flavouring
Blend 10ml/2 tsp coffee powder with 15ml/1 tbsp boiling water. Omit the milk. Cool before beating the mixture into the icing.

For a lemon, orange or lime flavouring
Substitute the vanilla extract and milk with lemon, orange or lime juice and 10ml/2 tsp of finely grated citrus rind. Omit the rind if using the icing for piping. Lightly tint the icing with food colouring, if you like.

1 Put the margarine or butter, icing sugar, vanilla extract and 5ml/1 tsp of the milk in a bowl.

2 Beat with a wooden spoon or an electric mixer, adding sufficient extra milk to give a light, smooth and fluffy consistency. For flavoured butter icing, follow the instructions above for the flavour of your choice.

Cook's Tips
• *The icing will keep for up to three days in an airtight container stored in a refrigerator.*
• *Butter icing can be coloured with paste colours. Add a little at a time using a cocktail stick (toothpick) until you reach the desired shade.*
• *You can apply butter icing with a knife and make a smooth finish, or you can pipe the icing on to your cake using a plain or fluted nozzle, or use a serrated scraper for a ridged finish.*

Crème au Beurre

The rich, smooth texture of this icing makes it ideal for spreading, filling or piping on to cakes and gateaux.

Makes 350g/12oz/1½ cups
60ml/4 tbsp water
75g/3oz/scant ½ cup caster (superfine) sugar
2 egg yolks
150g/5oz/10 tbsp unsalted (sweet) butter, softened

For a chocolate flavouring
Add 50g/2oz plain (semisweet) chocolate, melted.

For a coffee flavouring
Add 10ml/2 tsp instant coffee granules, dissolved in 5ml/1 tsp boiling water, cooled.

For a citrus flavouring
Replace water with orange, lemon or lime juice and 10ml/2 tsp grated rind.

1 Put the water in a pan and bring to the boil, then stir in the sugar. Heat gently, stirring, until the sugar has dissolved.

2 Boil rapidly until the mixture becomes syrupy, or reaches the 'thread' stage (107°C/225°F on a sugar thermometer). To test, place a little syrup on the back of a dry teaspoon. Press a second teaspoon on to the syrup and gently pull apart. The syrup should form a fine thread. If not, return to the heat, boil rapidly and re-test a minute later.

3 Whisk the egg yolks together in a bowl. Continue to whisk while slowly adding the sugar syrup in a thin stream. Whisk until thick, pale and cool. Beat the butter until light and fluffy. Add the egg mixture gradually, beating well after each addition, until thick and fluffy.

4 For chocolate or coffee crème au beurre, fold in the flavouring at the end.

> **Cook's Tip**
> It is important that the syrup reaches the correct stage and does not cook any further, as it will become too firm and you will not be able to whisk it into the egg yolks smoothly.

Meringue Frosting

This light frosting needs to be used immediately.

Makes 450g/1lb/2 cups
2 egg whites
115g/4oz/1 cup icing (confectioners') sugar, sifted

150g/5oz/⅔ cup unsalted (sweet) butter, softened

For a chocolate flavouring
Add 50g/2oz plain (semisweet) chocolate, melted.

1 Whisk the egg whites in a clean, heatproof bowl, add the icing sugar and gently whisk to mix well. Place the bowl over a pan of simmering water and whisk until thick and white. Remove the bowl from the pan and continue to whisk until cool, when the meringue stands up in soft peaks.

2 Beat the butter in a separate bowl until light and fluffy. Add the meringue gradually, beating well after each addition, until thick and fluffy. Fold in the chosen flavouring, using a metal spatula.

Chocolate Buttercream

This filling is perfect for rich cakes such as chocolate logs.

Enough to fill a 20cm/8in round layer cake
75g/3oz/6 tbsp unsalted (sweet) butter or margarine, softened

175g/6oz/1 cup icing (confectioners') sugar
15ml/1 tbsp cocoa powder
2.5ml/½ tsp vanilla extract

Place all the ingredients in a large bowl. Beat well to a smooth, spreadable consistency.

> **Variation**
> To make plain buttercream, blend 75g/3oz butter, 225g/8oz/ 1½ cups icing (confectioners') sugar, 5ml/1 tsp vanilla extract and 10–15ml/2–3 tbsp milk.

Crème Energy 1534kcal/6354kJ; Protein 7.1g; Carbohydrate 79.3g, of which sugars 79.3g; Fat 134.3g, of which saturates 81.3g; Cholesterol 723mg; Calcium 114mg; Fibre 0g; Sodium 932mg.
Meringue Energy 1592kcal/6620kJ; Protein 7.2g; Carbohydrate 121.1g, of which sugars 121.1g; Fat 123.3g, of which saturates 78.1g; Cholesterol 320mg; Calcium 91mg; Fibre 0g; Sodium 1038mg.
Buttercream Energy 1294kcal/5431kJ; Protein 4.1g; Carbohydrate 185g, of which sugars 183.3g; Fat 64.9g, of which saturates 41g; Cholesterol 160mg; Calcium 126mg; Fibre 1.8g; Sodium 608mg.

Royal Icing

This white icing gives a professional finish. This recipe makes enough icing to cover the top and sides of an 18cm/7in cake.

about 675g/1½lb/6 cups icing (confectioners') sugar, sifted
7.5ml/1½ tsp glycerine
a few drops of lemon juice
food colouring (optional)

Makes 675g/1½lb/3 cups
3 egg whites

1 Put the egg whites in a bowl and stir lightly with a fork to break them up.

2 Add the sifted icing sugar gradually, beating well with a wooden spoon after each addition.

3 Add enough icing sugar to make a smooth, shiny icing that has the consistency of very stiff meringue.

4 Beat in the glycerine, lemon juice and food colouring, if using.

5 Leave for 1 hour before using, covered with damp clear film (plastic wrap), then stir to burst any air bubbles.

Cook's Tips
• The icing will keep for up to three days in a refrigerator, stored in a plastic container with a tight-fitting lid.
• This recipe is for an 'icing' consistency suitable for flat-icing a marzipanned rich fruit cake. When the spoon is lifted, the icing should form a sharp point, with a slight curve at the end, known as 'soft peak'. For piping, the icing needs to be slightly stiffer. It should form a fine sharp peak when the spoon is lifted.
• Royal icing is not appropriate for a sponge cake, as its stiff consistency would easily drag on the surface.
• Never use royal icing direct on to the cake's surface; a layer of marzipan will make a smooth surface for icing and stop cake crumbs mixing with the icing.

Apricot Glaze

Used as a sweet adhesive to stick marzipan to cake surfaces, apricot glaze is a simple combination of warm apricot jam and water. It is a good idea to make a large quantity, especially when making celebration cakes.

Makes 450g/1lb/2 cups
450g/1lb/2 cups apricot jam
45ml/3 tbsp water

1 Place the jam and water in a pan. Heat gently, stirring occasionally, until the jam has melted.

2 Boil the jam rapidly for 1 minute, then rub through a sieve (strainer), pressing the fruit against the sides of the sieve with the back of a wooden spoon. Discard the skins left in the sieve.

3 Use the warmed glaze to brush cakes before applying marzipan, or use for glazing fruits on gateaux and cakes.

Pastillage

This paste sets very hard and is used for making firm decorative structures from icing sugar.

Makes 350g/12oz/1½ cups
300g/11oz icing (confectioners') sugar
1 egg white
10ml/2 tsp gum tragacanth

1 In a large bowl, sift most of the icing sugar over the egg white, a little at a time, stirring until the mixture sticks together. Add the gum tragacanth and transfer the mixture to a work surface which has been dusted with icing sugar.

2 Knead the mixture well until the ingredients are thoroughly combined and the paste has a smooth texture.

3 Knead in the remaining icing sugar and mix until stiff.

Royal Energy 2694kcal/11494kJ; Protein 12g; Carbohydrate 705.4g, of which sugars 705.4g; Fat 0g, of which saturates 0g; Cholesterol 0mg; Calcium 363mg; Fibre 0g; Sodium 223mg.
Apricot Glaze Energy 1175kcal/5022kJ; Protein 1.8g; Carbohydrate 311.9g, of which sugars 311.9g; Fat 0g, of which saturates 0g; Cholesterol 0mg; Calcium 45mg; Fibre 0g; Sodium 207mg.
Pastillage Energy 1453kcal/6190kJ; Protein 8g; Carbohydrate 365.8g, of which sugars 365.8g; Fat 5.6g, of which saturates 1.6g; Cholesterol 190mg; Calcium 214mg; Fibre 0g; Sodium 91mg.

Chocolate Fondant

A highly versatile cake covering, chocolate fondant is a soft, creamy confection made with chocolate, liquid glucose, egg whites and icing sugar. It is very malleable and is rolled before laying on cakes, giving them an attractive, smooth finish with rounded edges.

Enough to cover and decorate a 23cm/9in round cake
350g/12oz plain (semisweet) chocolate, chopped into small pieces
60ml/4 tbsp liquid glucose
2 egg whites
900g/2lb/7 cups icing (confectioners') sugar

1 Put the chocolate and glucose in a heatproof bowl or in a double boiler.

2 Place the bowl over a pan of barely simmering water and leave to melt, stirring the mixture occasionally.

3 When it is smooth, remove the bowl from the heat and leave the mixture to cool slightly.

4 In a clean, grease-free bowl, whisk the egg whites with a hand-held electric mixer or wire whisk until soft peaks form.

5 Stir the egg whites into the chocolate mixture with about 45ml/3 tbsp of the icing sugar.

6 Continue to beat the icing, gradually adding enough of the remaining icing sugar to make a stiff paste.

7 Wrap the fondant in clear film (plastic wrap) if you are not using it immediately.

Cook's Tip
Fondant is the classic covering used on wedding cakes and other elaborately decorated cakes. It is ideal for giving them a smooth, professional finish.

Sugarpaste Icing

This type of icing is wonderfully pliable and can be coloured, moulded and shaped in many imaginative ways.

Makes 350g/12oz/1½ cups
1 egg white
15ml/1 tbsp liquid glucose, warmed
350g/12oz/3 cups icing (confectioners') sugar, sifted

1 Put the egg white and glucose in a mixing bowl. Stir them together to break up the egg white.

2 Add the icing sugar and mix together with a metal spatula, using a chopping action, until well blended and the icing begins to bind together.

3 Knead the mixture with your fingers until it forms a ball.

4 Knead the sugarpaste on a work surface that has been lightly dusted with icing sugar for several minutes until it is smooth, soft and pliable.

5 If the icing is too soft, knead in some more sifted sugar until it reaches the right consistency.

Cook's Tips
• *Sugarpaste icing is sometimes known as rolled fondant and is available ready made in sugarcraft stores. It is easy to make yourself, but if you are using a large quantity and are in a hurry you could purchase it ready made. It is available in a variety of colours.*
• *If you want to make the sugarpaste in advance, wrap it up tightly in a plastic bag. The icing will keep for about three weeks.*
• *The paste is easy to colour with paste colours; add a little at a time using the tip of a knife.*
• *Roll out sugarpaste on a surface lightly sprinkled with icing (confectioners') sugar or a little white vegetable fat (shortening) to avoid the paste sticking.*

Sugarpaste Icing Energy 1435kcal/6123kJ; Protein 4.7g; Carbohydrate 377.6g, of which sugars 377.6g; Fat 0g, of which saturates 0g; Cholesterol 0mg; Calcium 190mg; Fibre 0g; Sodium 122mg.
Fondant Energy 5545kcal/23519kJ; Protein 27.8g; Carbohydrate 1213.6g, of which sugars 1183.7g; Fat 98g, of which saturates 58.8g; Cholesterol 21mg; Calcium 601mg; Fibre 8.8g; Sodium 287mg.

Chocolate Ganache

This is a justifiably classic chocolate icing or filling, deliciously creamy and therefore ideal for mousse cakes and chocolate logs. It has been in use since about 1850, with France and Switzerland arguing ever since over who was responsible for creating it.

Enough to cover a 23cm/9in round cake
225g/8oz plain (semisweet) chocolate, chopped into small pieces
250ml/8fl oz/1 cup double (heavy) cream

1 Melt the chocolate with the cream in a pan over a low heat.

2 Pour into a bowl, leave to cool, then whisk until the mixture begins to hold its shape.

Chocolate Glacé Icing

This glacé recipe is an instant icing solution for quickly finishing the tops of all sizes of cake.

10ml/2 tsp unsweetened cocoa powder
30–45ml/2–3 tbsp hot water
food colouring (optional)

Makes 350g/12oz/1½ cups
225g/8oz/2 cups icing (confectioners') sugar

1 Sift the icing sugar and cocoa powder into a bowl. Using a wooden spoon, gradually stir in enough of the hot water to obtain the consistency of thick cream.

2 Beat until white and smooth, and the icing thickly coats the back of the spoon.

3 Tint with a few drops of food colouring, if you wish. Use immediately to cover the top of the cake.

Petal Paste

This paste is perfect for making small cake decorations, such as petals and leaves. It is exceptionally strong and can be moulded into very fine flowers or cut into individual sugar pieces which dry very quickly. Liquid glucose and gum tragacanth are available from pharmacies or cake-icing specialists. Petal paste can also be bought in a powdered form, ready to mix. This is very convenient for small quantities but can be rather expensive if you need to use large amounts.

Makes 500g/1¼lb/2½ cups
10ml/2 tsp powdered gelatine
25ml/1½ tbsp cold water
10ml/2 tsp liquid glucose
10ml/2 tsp white vegetable fat (shortening)
450g/1lb/4 cups icing (confectioners') sugar, sifted
5ml/1 tsp gum tragacanth
1 egg white

1 Place the gelatine, water, liquid glucose and white fat in a heatproof bowl set over a pan of hot water until melted, stirring occasionally.

2 Remove the bowl from the heat.

3 Sift the icing sugar and gum tragacanth into a large bowl. Make a well in the centre and add the egg white and the gelatine mixture.

4 Thoroughly combine the ingredients to form a soft malleable white paste.

5 Knead the paste on a surface dusted with icing sugar until smooth, white and free from cracks.

6 Place in a plastic bag or wrap in clear film (plastic wrap), sealing well to exclude all the air.

7 Leave the paste for about two hours. When ready to use, knead the paste again and use small pieces at a time, leaving the remaining petal paste well sealed.

Ganache Energy 2388kcal/9911kJ; Protein 15.3g; Carbohydrate 147.1g, of which sugars 145.1g; Fat 197.3g, of which saturates 121.3g; Cholesterol 356mg; Calcium 197mg; Fibre 5.6g; Sodium 69mg.
Glacé Icing Energy 887kcal/3782kJ; Protein 1.1g; Carbohydrate 235.1g, of which sugars 235.1g; Fat 0g, of which saturates 0g; Cholesterol 0mg; Calcium 119mg; Fibre 0g; Sodium 14mg.
Petal Paste Energy 1888kcal/8044kJ; Protein 5.2g; Carbohydrate 478.3g, of which sugars 478.3g; Fat 8.2g, of which saturates 3.6g; Cholesterol 2mg; Calcium 242mg; Fibre 0g; Sodium 195mg.

Honey Icing

A simple and tasty topping
for decorated cakes.

Makes 275g/10oz/1¼ cups
75g/3oz/6 tbsp butter, softened

175g/6oz/1½ cups icing
(confectioners') sugar
15ml/1 tbsp clear honey
15ml/1 tbsp lemon juice

Put the softened butter into a bowl and gradually sift over the
icing sugar, beating well after each addition. Beat in the honey
and lemon juice. Spread over the cake immediately.

Chocolate Fondue

This smooth, not-too-sweet
fondue is made using equal
quantities of chocolate and
cream, so you can easily
increase the quantities to
feed more people.

Serves 4
150ml/¼ pint/⅔ cup double
(heavy) cream
15ml/1 tbsp orange or coffee liqueur
150g/5oz dark (bittersweet)
chocolate

1 Pour the cream into the ceramic cooking pot and switch the
slow cooker to high. Stir in the orange or coffee liqueur, then
cover with the lid and heat for about 30 minutes.

2 Finely chop the chocolate and sprinkle over the hot cream
mixture. Stir with a wooden spoon until melted and well
blended, then switch the slow cooker to low.

3 Keep the chocolate fondue warm for up to 30 minutes,
or serve immediately. For a thicker fondue, turn off the slow
cooker and leave to cool for 10 minutes.

> **Cook's Tip**
> This recipe can also be used as a guide for a fudge fondue.
> Simply omit the liqueur and add 65g/2½oz chopped caramel
> chocolate bars in place of the dark (bittersweet) chocolate.

Sugar-frosted Flowers

When frosting real flowers,
make sure you choose edible
varieties, such as pansies,
primroses, violets, roses,
freesias, apple blossom,
wild bergamot, borage,
carnations, honeysuckle,
jasmine and marigolds.

**Makes 10–15 flowers,
depending on their size**
1 egg white
caster (superfine) sugar
10–15 edible flowers

1 Lightly beat an egg white in a small bowl and sprinkle some
caster sugar on a plate.

2 Wash the flowers, then dry on kitchen paper. Evenly brush
both sides of the petals with the egg white. Hold the flower by
its stem over a plate lined with kitchen paper, sprinkle it evenly
with the sugar, then shake off any excess. Place on a wire rack
covered with kitchen paper and leave to dry in a warm place.

White Chocolate and Orange Sauce

A delectably rich and tangy
sauce that is perfect for
pouring over ice cream.
Or enjoy it with hot
waffles or fresh crêpes.

Serves 6
150ml/¼ pint/⅔ cup double
(heavy) cream

50g/2oz/¼ cup butter
45ml/3 tbsp caster
(superfine) sugar
175g/6oz white chocolate,
chopped into small pieces
30ml/2 tbsp orange-flavoured
liqueur
finely grated rind of 1 orange

1 Pour the cream into a heavy pan. Dice the butter into cubes
and add it to the pan, along with the sugar. Heat gently, stirring
the mixture occasionally, until the butter has melted.

2 Add the chocolate to the cream. Stir over a very low heat
until it is melted and thoroughly combined. Stir in the orange
rind, then add the liqueur a little at a time. Leave to cool.

Sugar-frosted Flowers Energy 15kcal/63kJ; Protein 0.3g; Carbohydrate 3.5g, of which sugars 3.5g; Fat 0g, of which saturates 0g; Cholesterol 0mg; Calcium 8mg; Fibre 0.1g; Sodium 9mg.
Orange Sauce Energy 380kcal/1577kJ; Protein 2.8g; Carbohydrate 26.1g, of which sugars 26.1g; Fat 29.3g, of which saturates 18.1g; Cholesterol 52mg; Calcium 96mg; Fibre 0g; Sodium 89mg.
Honey Icing Energy 1291kcal/5420kJ; Protein 1.4g; Carbohydrate 194.8g, of which sugars 194.8g; Fat 61.6g, of which saturates 39.1g; Cholesterol 160mg; Calcium 107mg; Fibre 0g; Sodium 467mg.
Chocolate Fondue Energy 387kcal/1608kJ; Protein 2.5g; Carbohydrate 25.7g, of which sugars 25.4g; Fat 30.7g, of which saturates 18.8g; Cholesterol 54mg; Calcium 31mg; Fibre 1g; Sodium 11mg.

Quick Chocolate Sauce

A quick and easy sauce, perfect for when you need a chocolate treat in a flash.

Makes 225ml/8fl oz/1 cup
150ml/¼ pint/⅔ cup double (heavy) cream

15ml/1 tbsp caster (superfine) sugar
150g/5oz plain (semisweet) chocolate, chopped into pieces
30ml/2 tbsp dark rum or whisky (optional)

1 Bring the cream and sugar to the boil. Remove from the heat, add the chocolate and stir until melted. Stir in the rum or whisky.

2 Pour the chocolate sauce into a jar. When cool, cover and store for up to 10 days. Reheat by standing the jar in a pan of simmering water, or remove the lid and microwave on high for 2 minutes. Stir before serving.

Glossy Chocolate Sauce

This sauce will add a stunning satin sheen to your desserts. It is also ideal as a chocolate fondue – serve with fresh fruits and dessert biscuits as dippers.

Serves 6
115g/4oz/generous ½ cup caster (superfine) sugar

60ml/4 tbsp water
175g/6oz plain (semisweet) chocolate, chopped into small pieces
25g/1oz/2 tbsp unsalted (sweet) butter
30ml/2 tbsp brandy or orange juice

1 Place the sugar and water in a pan and heat gently, stirring occasionally until all the sugar has dissolved.

2 Stir in the chocolate until melted, then add the butter in the same way. Do not allow the sauce to boil.

3 Stir in the brandy or orange juice and serve warm.

Chocolate Sauce for Ice Cream

Rich, dark and irresistible. Pour the warm or cold sauce over vanilla or milk chocolate ice cream or serve with an ice cream sundae made with your favourite flavours.

Makes about 400ml/14fl oz/1⅔ cups
25g/1oz/2 tbsp butter

25g/1oz/2 tbsp caster (superfine) sugar
30ml/2 tbsp golden (light corn) syrup
200g/7oz luxury plain (semisweet) cooking chocolate
150ml/¼ pint/⅔ cup semi-skimmed (low-fat) milk
45ml/3 tbsp double (heavy) cream

1 Mix the butter, caster sugar and syrup in a pan. Break the chocolate into pieces and add it to the mixture. Heat very gently, stirring occasionally, until the chocolate has melted.

2 Gradually stir in the milk and cream and bring just to the boil, stirring constantly until smooth. Serve hot or cool, refrigerate and reheat when required. Smooth and glossy, this creamy toffee sauce is extremely rich. It is delicious with vanilla, coffee or yogurt ice creams. Once made, it can be stored in the refrigerator for up to 4 days.

French Chocolate Sauce

For an extra-indulgent flavour, try adding alcohol to this rich chocolate sauce.

Makes 150ml/¼ pint/⅔ cup
75g/3oz plain (semisweet) chocolate, chopped

90ml/6 tbsp double (heavy) or whipping cream
15–30ml/1–2 tbsp brandy or liqueur

In a small pan, bring the cream to the boil, then remove from the heat. Add the chocolate all at once and stir gently until melted and smooth. Stir in the brandy or liqueur, pour into a sauceboat and keep warm until ready to serve.

Quick Sauce Energy 1568kcal/6519kJ; Protein 10g; Carbohydrate 113.5g, of which sugars 112.1g; Fat 122.6g, of which saturates 75.3g; Cholesterol 215mg; Calcium 131mg; Fibre 3.8g; Sodium 43mg.
Glossy Sauce Energy 273kcal/1144kJ; Protein 1.6g; Carbohydrate 38.6g, of which sugars 38.3g; Fat 12.3g, of which saturates 7.5g; Cholesterol 12mg; Calcium 21mg; Fibre 0.7g; Sodium 33mg.
Ice Cream Energy 1686kcal/7051kJ; Protein 16.2g; Carbohydrate 184.8g, of which sugars 183g; Fat 103.3g, of which saturates 63.3g; Cholesterol 136mg; Calcium 291mg; Fibre 5g; Sodium 320mg.
French Sauce Energy 862kcal/3578kJ; Protein 5.2g; Carbohydrate 49.2g, of which sugars 48.5g; Fat 69.3g, of which saturates 42.7g; Cholesterol 128mg; Calcium 69mg; Fibre 1.9g; Sodium 24mg.

Chocolate Fudge Sauce

A thick, utterly delicious sauce with a kick of brandy. Once you have tried it, you will be pouring it over anything you can.

50g/2oz/¼ cup butter
50g/2oz/¼ cup vanilla sugar
175g/6oz plain (semisweet) chocolate, chopped into small pieces
30ml/2 tbsp brandy

Serves 6
150ml/¼ pint/⅔ cup double (heavy) cream

1 Heat the cream, butter and sugar together in a heatproof bowl or a double boiler which has been set over a pan of barely simmering water.

2 Stir the mixture until it is smooth, then take off the heat.

3 Add the chocolate pieces to the cream mixture and return the bowl to the pan.

4 Stir the mixture over simmering water until all the chocolate has melted and the ingredients are thoroughly combined.

5 Stir in the brandy a little at a time, mixing well after each addition, until well combined.

6 Serve the sauce hot or cold depending on accompaniments.

Cook's Tips
There are so many uses for this delicious sauce that you may find yourself making it on a very frequent basis.
Ice cream: *Many people swear that this sauce is at its best when served hot over some creamy vanilla ice cream.*
Profiteroles: *Make a batch of cream-filled profiteroles. Pile them into a stack and pour over the sauce while still warm. It will set as it cools, binding the profiteroles — if you can wait that long.*
Hot chocolate cake: *Warm fudge sauce poured over a slab of delicious chocolate cake is pure heaven.*

Dark Chocolate Sauce

This rich, decadent sauce is for serious chocolate lovers – creamy, dark, and with a hint of vanilla. It can be used warm, and you can pour it over almost any dessert you can think of.

25g/1oz/2 tbsp unsalted (sweet) butter, diced
60–90ml/4–6 tbsp single (light) cream
2.5ml/½ tsp vanilla extract

Makes about 350ml/ 12fl oz/1½ cups
45ml/3 tbsp sugar
120ml/4fl oz/½ cup water
175g/6oz dark (bittersweet) chocolate, chopped into pieces

1 Combine the sugar and water in a heavy pan.

2 Bring to the boil over a medium heat, stirring constantly until all the sugar has dissolved.

3 Add the chocolate and butter to the syrup. Stir with a wooden spoon until the mixture is well combined.

4 Remove the pan from the heat and continue to stir until the mixture is smooth.

5 Add in the single cream and vanilla extract. Stir occasionally until ready to use.

6 If you are not using the sauce immediately, cover it and store in a cool place.

Cook's Tip
This sauce is easy enough to quickly whip up whenever you wish to add a delicious dark chocolate element to a dessert. Serve it warm, over vanilla ice cream, profiteroles, poached pears, hot waffles or crêpes.

Dark Sauce Energy 1194kcal/4983kJ; Protein 10.9g; Carbohydrate 112.6g, of which sugars 111g; Fat 81g, of which saturates 49.7g; Cholesterol 97mg; Calcium 116mg; Fibre 4.4g; Sodium 179mg.
Fudge Sauce Energy 379kcal/1575kJ; Protein 2g; Carbohydrate 27.7g, of which sugars 27.4g; Fat 28.5g, of which saturates 17.6g; Cholesterol 54mg; Calcium 28mg; Fibre 0.7g; Sodium 58mg.

Melting Chocolate over Water

Ensure that the hot water doesn't touch the bottom of the pan or bowl, or the chocolate may stiffen.

1 Chop or cut the chocolate into small pieces. Put the chocolate in the top of a double boiler or in a heatproof bowl over a pan of barely simmering water.

2 Heat gently until the chocolate is melted and smooth, stirring occasionally. Remove from the heat and stir.

Melting Chocolate over Direct Heat

When a recipe recommends melting chocolate with a liquid such as milk, cream or even butter, this can be done over direct heat in a pan.

Choose a heavy pan. Add the chocolate and liquid and gently heat, stirring frequently, until the chocolate is melted and the mixture is smooth. Remove from heat immediately.

Melting Chocolate in the Microwave

These times are for a 650–700W oven and are approximate, as microwave ovens vary.

1 Place 115g/4oz chopped or broken dark (bittersweet) or plain (semisweet) chocolate in a microwave-safe bowl and microwave on medium for about 2 minutes. The same quantity of milk or white chocolate should be melted on low for about 2 minutes.

2 Check the chocolate frequently during the cooking time. The chocolate will not change shape, but will start to look shiny. It must then be removed from the microwave and stirred until completely melted and smooth.

Tempering Chocolate

To temper light or dark chocolate successfully, you will need a marble slab or a similar cool, smooth surface, such as an upturned baking sheet.

1 Break up the chocolate into small pieces and place it in a heatproof bowl over a pan of hot water. Heat gently until melted.

2 Remove from the heat. Spoon about three-quarters of the melted chocolate on to a marble slab or other cool, smooth, non-porous work surface. With a plastic scraper or metal spatula, spread the chocolate thinly, then scoop it up before spreading it again. Repeat the sequence, keeping the chocolate constantly on the move, for about 5 minutes.

3 Using a chocolate thermometer, check the temperature of the chocolate as you work it. As soon as the temperature registers 28°C/82°F, tip the chocolate back into the bowl and stir into the remaining chocolate. With the addition of the hot chocolate, the temperature should now be 32°C/90°F, making the chocolate ready for use. To test, drop a little of the chocolate from a spoon on to the marble; it should set very quickly.

Cook's Tip

Tempering is the process of gently heating and cooling chocolate to stabilize the emulsification of cocoa solids and butterfat. This technique is generally used by professionals handling couverture chocolate. It allows the chocolate to shrink quickly (to allow easy release from a mould, for example with Easter eggs) or to be kept at room temperature for several weeks or months without losing its crispness and shiny surface. All solid chocolate is tempered in production, but once melted loses its 'temper' and must be tempered again unless it is to be used immediately. Untempered chocolate tends to 'bloom' or becomes dull and streaky or takes on a cloudy appearance. This can be avoided if the melted chocolate is put in the refrigerator immediately: chilling the chocolate solidifies the cocoa butter and prevents it from rising to the surface and 'blooming'.

Making a Piping Bag

A non-stick paper cone is ideal for piping small amounts of messy liquids, such as chocolate. It is easy to make one yourself using baking parchment. As well as being small and easy to handle, an added advantage is that it is disposable, unlike a conventional piping (pastry) bag, which will need cleaning.

1 Fold a square of baking parchment in half to form a triangle. With the triangle point facing you, fold the left corner down to the centre.

2 Fold the right corner down and wrap it around the folded left corner to form a cone. Fold the ends into the cone.

3 Spoon the melted chocolate into the cone and fold the top edges over. When ready to pipe, snip off the end of the point neatly to make a tiny hole, about 3mm/⅛in in diameter.

4 Another method is to use a small heavy-duty freezer or plastic bag. Place a piping nozzle in one corner of the bag, so that it is in the correct position for piping.

5 Fill as above, squeezing the filling into one corner and twisting the top to seal. Snip off the corner of the bag, if necessary, so that the tip of the nozzle emerges, and squeeze gently to pipe the design.

Cook's Tip

Pipe chocolate directly on to a cake, or on to baking parchment to make run-outs, small outlined shapes or irregular designs. After melting the chocolate, allow it to cool slightly so it just coats the back of a spoon. If it still flows freely it will be too runny to hold its shape when piped. When it is the right consistency, you then need to work quickly because the chocolate will set quickly. Use a paper piping (pastry) bag and keep the pressure very tight, as the chocolate will flow readily without encouragement.

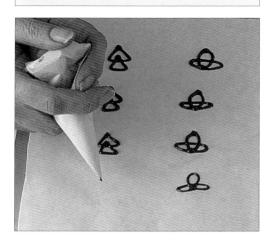

Piping on to Cakes

Chocolate can be piped directly on to a cake, as long as you work quickly. This chocolate design looks effective on top of a cake iced with coffee glacé icing.

1 Melt 50g/2oz each of white and plain (semisweet) dark chocolate in separate bowls, and allow to cool slightly. Place the chocolates in separate paper piping (pastry) bags. Cut a small piece off the pointed end of each bag in a straight line.

2 Hold each piping bag in turn above the surface of the cake and pipe the chocolates all over, as shown in the picture. Alternatively, pipe a freehand design in one continuous curvy line, first with one bag of chocolate, then the other.

Drizzling Chocolate

You can have great fun making random, irregular chocolate shapes or, if you have a steady hand, you could create some really special designs that will look great on special occasion cakes or cookies. Why not try your hand at flowers or butterflies.

1 Melt some chocolate and pour it into a paper cone or small piping (pastry) bag fitted with a very small plain nozzle. Drizzle the chocolate on to a baking sheet lined with baking parchment to make small, self-contained lattice shapes, such as circles or squares. Allow to set for 30 minutes, then peel off the paper.

2 Chocolate can be used in many designs, such as flowers or butterflies. Use baking parchment as tracing paper and pipe the chocolate over the chosen design or decorative shape.

3 For butterflies, pipe chocolate on to individually cut squares and leave until just beginning to set. Use a long, thin box (such as an egg carton) and place the butterfly shape in the box or between the cups so it is bent in the centre, creating the butterfly shape. Chill until needed.

Feathering or Marbling Chocolate

These two related techniques provide some of the easiest ways of decorating the top of a cake or dessert.

Melt two contrasting colours of chocolate and spread one over the cake to be decorated. Spoon the contrasting chocolate into a piping (pastry) bag and pipe lines or swirls over the chocolate base. Draw a skewer or cocktail stick (toothpick) through the swirls to create a feathered or marbled effect.

Making Chocolate Run-outs

Try piping the outline of a shape in one chocolate colour and fill in the middle with a contrasting colour.

1 Tape a piece of baking parchment to a baking sheet or flat board. Draw around a shaped biscuit (cookie) cutter on to the paper several times. Secure a piece of parchment over the top.

2 With a paper piping (pastry) bag, pipe over the outline of your design in a continuous thread. Cut the end off another bag, making the hole slightly wider than before, and pipe the chocolate to fill in the outline so it looks slightly rounded. Leave the shapes to set in a cool place, then carefully lift them off.

Piping Chocolate Curls

Make lots of these curly shapes and store them in a cool place ready for using later as cake decorations.

Melt 115g/4oz chocolate. Cover a rolling pin with baking parchment and attach it with tape. Fill a paper piping (pastry) bag with the chocolate and cut a small piece off the end. Pipe lines of chocolate backwards and forwards over the parchment. Leave the curls to set, then carefully peel off the baking parchment. Use a metal spatula to lift the curls on to the cake.

Making Mini Chocolate Curls

Delicate chocolate curls make an ideal decoration for many desserts and cakes, whether these are made from plain, dark or white chocolate. These mini curls can be made very quickly using a swivel-bladed vegetable peeler, and can be stored for several weeks in an airtight container in a cool, dry place.

1 Bring a thick piece or bar of chocolate to room temperature. (Chocolate that is too cold will 'grate', or if too warm will slice.)

2 With a swivel-bladed peeler held over a plate or baking sheet, pull the blade firmly along the edge of the chocolate and allow curls to fall on to the plate or baking sheet in a single layer.

Making Chunky Chocolate Curls

If you want to make chunkier curls, it is best to use chocolate that has been melted with pure white vegetable fat, which keeps it from hardening completely. The finished decorations are suitable for all kinds of cakes and desserts, and look even more striking if you use contrasting colours of white and dark chocolate.

1 Melt 175g/6oz plain (semisweet) or dark (bittersweet) chocolate with 30ml/2 tbsp pure white vegetable fat (shortening), stirring until smooth.

2 Pour into a small rectangular or square tin (pan) lined with foil or baking parchment to produce a block about 2.5cm/1in thick. Chill until set.

3 Allow the block to come to room temperature, remove it from the tin, then hold it with a piece of folded foil or paper towel (to stop it melting) and use a swivel-bladed peeler to produce short chunky curls. The block can also be grated.

Making Chocolate Scrolls

Use chocolate as prepared for Chunky Chocolate Curls to produce these long or cup-shaped scrolls.

1 Pour the chocolate evenly on to a marble slab or the back of a baking sheet. Using a metal spatula, spread to about 3mm/⅛in thick and allow to set for about 30 minutes, until just firm.

2 To make long scrolls, use the blade of a long, sharp knife on the surface of the chocolate, and, with both hands, push away from your body at a 25–45 degree angle to scrape off a thin layer of chocolate. Twist the handle of the knife about a quarter of a circle to make a slightly wider scroll. Use a teaspoon to make cup-shaped curls.

Grating Chocolate

Chocolate can be grated by hand or in a food processor. Make sure you grate it at the correct temperature.

1 Chill the chocolate and hold it with a piece of folded foil or paper towel to prevent the heat of your hand melting it. Hold a hand- or box-grater over a plate and grate with an even pressure.

2 A food processor fitted with the metal blade can also be used, but be sure the chocolate is soft enough to be pierced with a sharp knife. Cut the chocolate into small pieces and, with the machine running, drop the chocolate pieces through the feeder tube until very fine shavings are produced.

> **Cook's Tips**
> • If using a metal grater for grating chocolate, chill it in the freezer before use and the chocolate will be less likely to melt.
> • Experiment with different utensils when making chocolate curls. Metal spatulas, paint scrapers, tablespoons and even wide, straight pastry scrapers can be used.

Making Chocolate Cut-outs

It is fun to make geometric shapes such as circles, squares and diamonds out of chocolate by cutting them out free-hand with a sharp knife. More complex shapes can be made using a biscuit (cookie) cutter.

1 Cover a baking sheet with a sheet of baking parchment and tape down at each corner.

2 Melt 115g/4oz dark (bittersweet), milk or white chocolate. While still warm, pour the chocolate evenly on to the prepared baking parchment.

3 Spread the chocolate evenly with a metal spatula. Allow to stand until the surface is firm enough to cut, but not so hard that it will break. It should no longer feel sticky when touched lightly with your finger.

4 Press a shaped biscuit (cookie) cutter firmly through the chocolate and carefully lift it off the paper with a metal spatula. Try not to touch the surface of the chocolate while you do this, otherwise you will leave marks on it and spoil its appearance.

5 The finished shapes can be left plain or you can pipe over them with a contrasting colour of chocolate for an attractive decorative effect.

6 Abstract shapes can be cut with a knife free-hand. They look particularly effective pressed on to the sides of a cake iced with plain or chocolate buttercream.

> **Cook's Tip**
> If you do not feel confident about cutting chocolate cut-outs free-hand, use biscuit (cookie) or aspic cutters. Cut-outs look particularly good decorating the sides of cakes or gateaux. Space them at regular intervals or allow them to overlap. Be creative, and see where your imagination takes you.

Making Chocolate Leaves

You can use any fresh, non-toxic leaf with distinct veins to make these decorations. Rose, bay or lemon leaves work well. If small leaves are required – for decorating petits fours, for instance – use mint or lemon balm leaves.

1 Thoroughly wash and dry some fresh leaves.

2 Melt plain (semisweet) or white chocolate and use a pastry brush or spoon to coat the veined side of each leaf completely.

3 Place the coated leaves chocolate-side up on a baking sheet lined with baking parchment to set.

4 Starting at the stem end, gently peel away each leaf in turn. Store the chocolate leaves in a cool place until needed.

Making Chocolate Cups

Large or small cupcake papers or sweet cases can be used to make chocolate cups to fill with ice cream, mousse or liqueur. Use double liners inside each other for extra support.

1 Melt some chocolate. Using a paintbrush or pastry brush, completely coat the bottom and sides of the paper cases.

2 Allow the chocolate to set, then repeat once or twice to build up the layers. Allow to set for several hours or overnight.

3 Carefully peel off the paper case, set the chocolate cups on a baking sheet and fill as desired.

> **Cook's Tip**
> These cups are ideal as a container for sweets, or fill with nuts and fruit for petits fours. Use bigger cases for larger-sized treats.

Making Chocolate Baskets

These impressive baskets make pretty, edible containers for mousse or ice cream.

Makes 6
*175g/6oz plain (semisweet)
milk or white chocolate
25g/1oz/2 tbsp butter*

1 Cut out six 15cm/6in rounds from baking parchment.

2 Melt the chocolate with the butter in a heatproof bowl over barely simmering water. Stir until smooth.

3 Spoon one-sixth of the chocolate over each round, using a teaspoon to spread it to within 2cm/¾in of the edge.

4 Carefully lift each covered paper round and drape it over an upturned cup or ramekin, curving the edges to create a frilled effect on the chocolate.

5 Leave until completely set, then carefully lift off the chocolate shape and peel away the paper.

6 Add your chosen filling to the basket, taking care not to break the chocolate.

> **Variation**
> *For a different effect, brush the chocolate over the parchment, leaving the edges jagged. Build up the layers by leaving each prior layer to set before painting with more chocolate.*

> **Cook's Tips**
> • *These chocolate baskets not only look impressive but they are also ideal for holding many kinds of delicious desserts, such as mousse, ice cream and tiramisu.*
> • *For a simple filling, whip cream with a little orange-flavoured liqueur, pipe the mixture in swirls in the chocolate cups and top with mandarin segments, half-dipped in chocolate.*

Coating Cookies with Chocolate

Before coating cookies in melted chocolate, make sure that the chocolate is just starting to cool; chocolate that is hot or even very warm will soak into the cookies and spoil the finished texture.

1 Place the cookies on a wire rack with a sheet of baking parchment underneath. Spoon cooled melted chocolate over each cookie, then tap the rack to help it run down the sides and to level the top. Leave to set on the rack, then cover with a second coat, if you like. Scrape the chocolate off the baking parchment, return to the bowl and re-melt to coat more cookies.

2 To decorate coated cookies, drizzle or pipe with a contrasting colour of chocolate. For a smooth surface, do this before the first layer of chocolate has set; for a raised surface, wait until the first layer of chocolate has hardened.

Dipping Cookies in Chocolate

Round or shaped cookies are often half-coated in chocolate, and finger cookies sometimes have one or both ends dipped in chocolate. This method is simpler than completely covering cookies in chocolate. If you're planning to sandwich cookies together, they are best dipped in chocolate before filling as the warmth of the chocolate may melt the filling if dipped afterwards.

1 Melt the chocolate in a narrow deep bowl. Holding the cookie by the part that you don't want to coat, dip it briefly in the melted chocolate, then allow any excess to drip back into the bowl.

2 Place the cookie on a sheet of baking parchment and leave to set. When the chocolate is firm, carefully peel off the paper. If you want to sprinkle chopped nuts or other decorations on the top, do this before the chocolate sets.

Coating Florentines with Chocolate

The flat undersides of florentines are traditionally coated with chocolate, decorated with wavy lines.

Holding the florentine between finger and thumb, spread the flat base with chocolate. With the prongs of a fork, create wavy lines in the chocolate. Place the florentine on a wire rack, and leave to set.

Piping Chocolate on to Cookies

Use a small paper piping (pastry) bag with the end snipped off to pipe thin lines of chocolate. Once you have mastered the art of decorating your cookies, vary the combinations. Try drizzling milk or dark (bittersweet) chocolate over different cookies.

Place cookies on a sheet of baking parchment and pipe over thin lines of chocolate. Try wavy lines or criss-cross patterns.

Stencilling Chocolate Designs

You can buy stencils made for cake or cookie decorating, or make your own by drawing a small design on thin cardboard and cutting it out, or use paper doilies. Make sure there is a contrast between the colour of the cookie and the dusting ingredient; icing (confectioners') sugar works well on chocolate cookies, while cocoa powder is better on pale cookies.

Place the stencil over the cookie. Dust with icing sugar or cocoa powder through a fine sieve (strainer), then carefully remove the cardboard. To create a dramatic light and dark effect on cookies, lightly dust a whole cookie with icing sugar, then cover half of it with a piece of cardboard or a sheet of paper and carefully dust the other half with cocoa powder.

Index

Alexander the Great 234
Alhambra Royale 233
almonds
  almond brownies 156
  almond-scented chocolate cherry
    wedges 164
  chocolate almond meringue pie 68
  chocolate almond mousse cake 41
  chocolate almond torrone 208
  chocolate and almond cake 31
  chocolate gooey cake 31
  chocolate, date and almond filo coil 67
  chocolate-topped coffee gateau 46
amaretti 77, 180
amaretto marquise 78
amaretto mousse with chocolate
  sauce 87
American chocolate cheesecake 141
American chocolate fudge brownies 155
Arago 232
army tank cake 58
autumn passionettes 147

baked Alaska, chocolate 67
bananas
  banana chocolate brownies 157
  banana cookies 174
  Boston banoffee pie 137
  chocolate, banana and toffee pie 138
  chocolate banana cake 12
  chocolate chip and banana pudding 66
  chocolate chip banana pancakes 69
  chocolate cinnamon cake with banana
    sauce 60
  chocolate fudge and banana
    sundae 104
  chunky chocolate and banana
    muffins 145
  double chocolate banoffee pie 137
  honey and banana smoothie with
    hot chocolate sauce 230
Barbara 232
battenburg 17
Belgian chocolate mousse 83
best-ever chocolate sandwich 12
bitter chocolate fondue with rosemary
  and vanilla poached pears 74
bitter chocolate mousse 84
bitter marmalade chocolate loaf 20
black and white chocolate mousse 85
black bottom pie 135
Black Forest and Kirsch ice cream 113
Black Forest gateau 33
Black Forest sundae 105
black rum and chocolate pie 134
blackberries
  rich chocolate tart with blackberry
    sauce 132
  white chocolate brûlées with
    blackberry coulis 118
blancmange 91
Blue Lady 233
blueberry chocolate muffins 147
bourbon balls 223
box of chocolates cake 56
brandy
  Brandy Alexander 234
  chocolate and brandied fig torte 98
  chocolate and brandy parfait 93
  chocolate brandy snap gateau 39
  chocolate teardrops with cherry
    brandy sauce 119
  French chocolate cake with brandy 30
  layered chocolate, chestnut and brandy
    bombes 107
brioche bake 61
brioches au chocolat 152
brioches with hot chocolate fudge sauce 152
brownies 98, 116, 155–62
bûche de Noël 44
butter icing 240
buttercream 241

butterscotch
  butterscotch and white chocolate
    brownies 159
  chocolate butterscotch bars 173

candied peel crumble cookies 175
cappuccino choc cones 120
cappuccino chocolate panettone 23
cappuccino chocolate torte 96
Captain Kidd 235
caramel
  chocolate box with caramel mousse 53
  chocolate caramel nuggets 186
  chocolate caramel torte 42
  marbled caramel chocolate slice 167
Caribbean chocolate ring with rum
  syrup 39
champurrada 227
cheese
  American chocolate cheesecake 141
  baked ravioli with chocolate and
    ricotta filling 71
  chilled chocolate zucotto sponge 79
  chocolate and lemon fromage frais 90
  chocolate cheesecake brownies 162
  chocolate cheesecake tart 141
  chocolate mandarin trifle 91
  fruity chocolate ricotta creams 79
  Italian chocolate ricotta pie 136
  luxury white chocolate cheesecake 142
  marbled chocolate cheesecake 142
  meringue gateau with chocolate
    mascarpone 95
  raspberry and white chocolate
    cheesecake 143
  walnut and ricotta cake with
    chocolate curls 14
cherries
  almond-scented chocolate cherry
    wedges 164
  Black Forest and Kirsch ice cream 113
  Black Forest gateau 33
  Black Forest sundae 105
  chocolate and cherry colettes 214
  chocolate and cherry polenta cake 13
  chocolate and fresh cherry gateau 36
  chocolate ice cream with hot cherry
    sauce 117
chestnuts
  chocolate and chestnut pots 81
  chocolate and chestnut Yule log 45
  layered chocolate, chestnut and
    brandy bombes 107
  meringues with chestnut cream 219
  two-chocolate chestnut roulade 44
chewy chocolate cookies 176
choca mocha sherbet 124
chocolate almond meringue pie 68
chocolate almond mousse cake 41
chocolate alphabetinis 199
chocolate amaretti 180
chocolate amaretti peaches 77
chocolate amaretto marquise 78
chocolate and almond cake 31
chocolate and brandied fig torte 98
chocolate and brandy parfait 93
chocolate and cherry colettes 214
chocolate and cherry polenta cake 13
chocolate and chestnut pots 81
chocolate and chestnut Yule log 45
chocolate and coconut slices 166
chocolate and coffee bombe with
  Marsala 117

chocolate and coffee mousse 87
chocolate and coffee roulade 43
chocolate and fresh cherry gateau 36
chocolate and hazelnut brittle
  ice cream 110
chocolate and lemon fromage frais 90
chocolate and mandarin truffle slice 92
chocolate and orange angel cake 11
chocolate and orange mousse 86
chocolate and orange Scotch
  pancakes 70
chocolate and orange soufflé 62
chocolate and pine nut tart 129
chocolate and prune cake 14
chocolate and prune cookies 191
chocolate and toffee bars 171
chocolate and vanilla ice cream 102
chocolate apple tree 55
chocolate apricot linzer tart 131
chocolate apricots 212
chocolate, banana and toffee pie 138
chocolate banana cake 12
chocolate birds' nests 216
chocolate blancmange 91
chocolate blueberry muffins 147
chocolate bombes with hot sauce 106
chocolate box cookies 200
chocolate box with caramel mousse 53
chocolate brandy snap gateau 39
chocolate bread 21
chocolate brownies 155
chocolate brownies, very low-fat 160
chocolate buttercream 241
chocolate butterscotch bars 173
chocolate butterscotch frosting 239
chocolate cake with coffee icing 13
chocolate cappuccino cake 26
chocolate caramel nuggets 186
chocolate caramel torte 42
chocolate cheesecake brownies 162
chocolate cheesecake tart 141
chocolate chiffon pie 140
chocolate chip and banana pudding 66
chocolate chip and hazelnut cookies 175
chocolate chip banana pancakes 69
chocolate chip brownies 156
chocolate chip marzipan loaf 21
chocolate chip muffins 145
chocolate chip walnut loaf 20
chocolate Christmas cakes 54
chocolate Christmas cups 209
chocolate Christmas log with cranberry
  sauce 45
chocolate cinnamon cake with banana
  sauce 60
chocolate cinnamon doughnuts 148
chocolate citrus candies 210
chocolate coconut roulade 43
chocolate coin treasure chest 58
chocolate cookie ice cream 103
chocolate cookies 174
chocolate cookies on sticks 204
chocolate crackle-tops 179
chocolate cream roll 18
chocolate crêpes with plums and port 70
chocolate crispy cookies 192
chocolate, date and almond filo coil 67
chocolate, date and walnut pudding 65
chocolate date cake 24
chocolate-dipped hazelnut crescents 186
chocolate dominoes 163
chocolate double mint ice cream 109
chocolate eclairs 149
chocolate fairy cakes 144
chocolate flake cookies 205
chocolate flake ice cream 102
chocolate florentines 188
chocolate fondant 243
chocolate fondant hearts 215
chocolate fondue 74, 245
chocolate frosted layer cake 9
chocolate fruit birthday cake 47
chocolate fruit fondue 72
chocolate fudge and banana sundae 104
chocolate fudge frosting 238
chocolate fudge gateau 38

chocolate fudge sauce 247
chocolate fudge triangles 207
chocolate ganache 244
chocolate gateau terrine 33
chocolate ginger crunch cake 24
chocolate glacé icing 244
chocolate gooey cake 31
chocolate Hallowe'en pumpkin cake 53
chocolate ice cream in florentine
  baskets 115
chocolate ice cream with hot cherry
  sauce 117
chocolate ice cream with lime sabayon
  123
chocolate-iced anniversary cake with
  exotic fruits 47
chocolate kisses 180
chocolate layer cake 11
chocolate lemon tart 130
chocolate lemon tartlets 124
chocolate loaf with coffee sauce 94
chocolate macaroons 184
chocolate mandarin trifle 91
chocolate, maple and walnut swirls 190
chocolate millefeuille slice 121
chocolate mint ice cream pie 121
chocolate mint-filled cupcakes 144
chocolate mousse gateau 40
chocolate orange battenburg cake 17
chocolate orange tondue 76
chocolate orange marquise 61
chocolate pavlova with passion fruit
  cream 95
chocolate, pear and pecan pie 140
chocolate pecan nut torte 28
chocolate pecan pie 68
chocolate porcupine cake 55
chocolate potato cake 38
chocolate pretzels 187
chocolate profiteroles with white
  chocolate sauce 151
chocolate pudding with rum custard 66
chocolate puffs 150
chocolate puppies in love 54
chocolate raspberry macaroon bars 171
chocolate redcurrant torte 50
chocolate ripple ice cream 111
chocolate risotto 77
chocolate rum roulade 19
chocolate, rum and raisin roulade 122
chocolate sailing boat 57
chocolate salami 167
chocolate sauce for ice cream 246
chocolate shortcrust pastry 237
chocolate sorbet 123
chocolate sorbet with red fruits 124
chocolate soufflé crêpes 69
chocolate teardrops with cherry brandy
  sauce 119
chocolate thumbprint cookies 181
chocolate tiramisu tart 131
chocolate treacle snaps 182
chocolate truffle tart 130
chocolate vanilla cooler 228
chocolate vanilla timbales 81
chocolate walnut delights 185
chocolate wands 199
chocolate whirls 195
choux pastries with two custards 154
Christmas cakes 54
Christmas cups 209
Christmas log 45
chunky choc and nut brownies 156
chunky chocolate bars 172
chunky chocolate coffee bean and Kahlúa
  ice cream 112
chunky chocolate drops 177
chunky chocolate ice cream 110
chunky double chocolate cookies 184
cinnamon
  chocolate cinnamon cake with banana
    sauce 60
  chocolate cinnamon doughnuts 148
  chocolate cinnamon tuiles 198
  chocolate-dipped cinnamon and
    orange tuiles 198

coconuts
chocolate and coconut slices 166
chocolate coconut roulade 43
coffee
cappuccino choc cones 120
cappuccino chocolate panettone 23
cappuccino chocolate swirls 179
cappuccino chocolate torte 96
chilled chocolate and espresso
mousse in chocolate cups 88
chocolate and coffee bombe with
Marsala 117
chocolate and coffee mint thins 214
chocolate and coffee mousse 87
chocolate and coffee roulade 43
chocolate cake with coffee icing 13
chocolate cappuccino cake 26
chocolate loaf with coffee sauce 94
chocolate-topped coffee gateau 46
chunky chocolate coffee bean and
Kahlúa ice cream 112
chunky white chocolate and coffee
brownies 161
coffee and chocolate flip 233
coffee chocolate mousse cake 41
coffee-chocolate soda 235
coffee chocolate truffles 222
coffee cognac cooler 30
coffee ice cream with choc beans 118
coffee profiteroles with white
chocolate sauce 151
coffee, vanilla and chocolate stripe 89
coffee with mocha ice cream 125
crunchy-topped coffee meringue pie 136
dark chocolate and coffee mousse
cake 96
grasshopper coffee 230
hot mocha rum soufflés 62
iced coffee cups with chocolate
dusting 114
iced coffee mousse in a chocolate
case 88
luxury mocha mousse 89
mocha Brazil layer torte 27
mocha chocolate panettone 23
mocha chocolate Victoria sponge 9
mocha cookies 174
mocha cooler 228
mocha hazelnut battenburg 17
mocha, prune and Armagnac terrine 101
mocha sponge cake 26
mocha truffles with café noir 224
mocha velvet cream pots 82
mocha Viennese swirls 185
petits pots de cappuccino 82
rich chocolate and coffee pudding 64
vanilla and chocolate caffè latte 231
vanilla poached pears with choc-
dusted cappuccino sauce 75
walnut coffee gateau with chocolate
frosting 28
white chocolate cappuccino gateau 27
white chocolate, frosted raspberry
and coffee terrine 100
cream
black bottom pie 135
chocolate cookie ice cream 103
chocolate cream puffs 150
chocolate cream roll 18
creamy fudge 206
double chocolate snowball 78
fruits of the forest with white
chocolate creams 90

heavenly mud 83
iced paradise chocolate cake 99
iced praline chocolate torte 99
mango and chocolate crème brûlée 92
white chocolate and mango cream
tart 132
crème au beurre 241
crème brûlée 92
crumbled chocolate brownie ice
cream 116
cupcakes 144
custard 66, 154
custard layer cake with chocolate
icing 15

dark chocolate and coffee mousse cake 96
dark chocolate and hazelnut tart 128
dark chocolate fingers 194
dark chocolate ice cream 108
dark chocolate orange mousse 86
dark chocolate ravioli 71
dark chocolate sauce 247
death by chocolate 34, 229
decorated chocolate lebkuchen 201
devil's food cake with orange frosting 10
dolly cookies with chocolate centres 203
double chocolate banoffee pie 137
double chocolate chip muffins 146
double chocolate cookies 184
double chocolate-dipped fruit 211
double chocolate slices 169
double chocolate snowball 78
double heart engagement cake 49
double white chocolate ice cream 109

Easter egg nest cake 52

fairy cakes 144
florentines 155, 188, 189, 253
florentine bites 217
fondue 72, 74, 76, 245
French chocolate cake 30
French chocolate cake with brandy 30
French chocolate soufflé 63
French-style coupe glacée with chocolate
ice cream 105
frosted chocolate fudge cake 25
frosting 238, 239, 240, 241
fruit
autumn passionettes 147
chilled chocolate zucotto sponge 79
chocolate fruit and nut cookies 193
chocolate fruit fondue 72
chocolate meringues with mixed fruit
compote 219
chocolate sorbet with red fruits 124
chocolate-topped candied fruit pie 139
double chocolate-dipped fruit 211
dried fruit cookies 174
fruit-and-nut white chocolate
clusters 216
fruit fondant chocolates 215
fruit kebabs with chocolate and
marshmallow fondue 72
fruit tartlets with chocolate pastry 127
fruits of the forest with white
chocolate creams 90
fruity chocolate cookie-cakes 149
fruity chocolate ricotta creams 79
steamed chocolate and fruit pudding
with chocolate syrup 64
white chocolate castles with fresh
summer berries 122
fudge
chocolate fudge and banana
sundae 104
chocolate fudge frosting 238
chocolate fudge sauce 247
chocolate fudge triangles 207
creamy fudge 206
easy chocolate hazelnut fudge 206
frosted chocolate fudge cake 25
fudge-frosted starry roll 52
fudge-glazed chocolate brownies 158
fudge-nut chocolate bars 170
glossy chocolate fudge icing 238
pears in chocolate fudge blankets 73

rich chocolate pistachio fudge 207
two-tone fudge 206
ganache 244
giant birthday cookie 203
giant triple chocolate cookies 178
ginger
chocolate ginger crunch cake 24
Cognac and ginger creams 213
double gingerbread cookies 197
ginger florentines 189
gingerbread family 196
gingerbread teddies 197
gingered semi-freddo in dark chocolate
cases 111
gingered truffles 223
iced chocolate ginger cookies 196
Tia Maria and ginger gateau 32
glossy chocolate fudge icing 238
glossy chocolate icing 239
glossy chocolate sauce 246
gluten-free chocolate chip cookies 174
gluten-free chocolate gooey cake 31
gluten-free rocky road wedges 165
grasshopper coffee 230
grasshopper milkshake 230
Greek chocolate mousse tartlets 126

Hammer Horror 234
hazelnuts
chocolate and hazelnut brittle ice
cream 110
chocolate chip and hazelnut cookies 175
chocolate-dipped hazelnut
crescents 186
dark chocolate and hazelnut tart 128
easy chocolate hazelnut fudge 206
hazelnut and chocolate cake 10
mocha hazelnut battenburg 17
pear and hazelnut meringue torte 94
heavenly mud 83
Hollywood Nuts 233
honey and banana smoothie with hot
chocolate sauce 230
honey icing 245
hot chocolate cake 60
hot chocolate zabaglione 76
hot mocha rum soufflés 62

iced chocolate nut gateau 120
iced coffee cups with chocolate dusting 114
iced coffee mousse in a chocolate case 88
iced paradise chocolate cake 99
iced pear terrine with Calvados and
chocolate sauce 101
iced praline chocolate torte 99
Irish chocolate velvet 229
Italian chocolate ricotta pie 136

jazzy chocolate gateau 50
jelly bean chocolate-topped cones 205

Kahlúa
chunky chocolate coffee bean and
Kahlúa ice cream 112
kumquats with rich chocolate mousse 85

ladies' kisses 178
late night cookies 183
layered chocolate, chestnut and brandy
bombes 107
lebkuchen 201
lemon
chocolate and lemon fromage frais 90

chocolate lemon tart 130
chocolate lemon tartlets 124
lime sabayon with chocolate ice
cream 123
liqueur-spiked dark chocolate orange
mousse 86
luxurious chocolate cake 29

macaroons 171, 184
mini chocolate macaroons 183
Madeira cake 237
magic chocolate mud cake 65
malt whisky truffles 222
mandarin trifle 91
mango
mango and chocolate crème
brûlée 92
white chocolate and mango cream
tart 132
maple and pecan nut brownies 157
maple, chocolate and walnut swirls 190
marbled caramel chocolate slice 167
marbled chocolate and peanut cake 16
marbled chocolate brownies 159
marbled chocolate cheesecake 142
marbled chocolate ring cake 16
marbled chocolate Swiss roll 19
marmalade chocolate loaf 20
marquises 61, 78
marshmallow
fruit kebabs with chocolate and
marshmallow fondue 72
nutty marshmallow and chocolate
squares 160
meringue
chocolate almond meringue pie 68
chocolate meringues with mixed fruit
compote 219
chocolate pavlova with passion fruit
cream 95
meringue frosting 241
meringue gateau with chocolate
mascarpone 95
meringues with chestnut cream 219
mini praline pavlovas 218
mint chocolate meringues 218
pear and hazelnut meringue
torte 94
Mexican hot chocolate 227
midnight chocolate chip cookies 190
mini chocolate marylands 182
mint
chocolate and coffee mint thins 214
chocolate mint ice cream pie 121
chocolate mint truffle filo parcels 225
iced mint and chocolate cooler 228
mint chocolate meringues 218
mint-filled cupcakes 144
minty choc madness ice cream 114
Mississippi mud cake ring 15
Mississippi mud cake with filling 35
Mississippi mud pie 139
Mississippi pie 138
Mistress 233
mocha Brazil layer torte 27
mocha chocolate panettone 23
mocha chocolate Victoria sponge 9
mocha cookies 174
mocha cooler 228
mocha hazelnut battenburg 17
mocha ice cream 125
mocha mousse 89
mocha, prune and Armagnac terrine
101
mocha rum soufflés 62
mocha sherbet 124
mocha sponge cake 26
mocha tart 129
mocha truffles with café noir 224
mocha velvet cream pots 82
mocha Viennese swirls 185
mousse
Belgian chocolate mousse 83
bitter chocolate mousse 84
black and white chocolate mousse 85
chilled chocolate and espresso
mousse in chocolate cups 88

chocolate almond mousse cake 41
chocolate and coffee mousse 87
chocolate and orange mousse 86
chocolate box with caramel
   mousse 53
chocolate mousse strawberry layer
   cake 46
coffee chocolate mousse cake 41
dark chocolate and coffee mousse
   cake 96
Greek chocolate mousse tartlets 126
iced coffee mousse in a chocolate
   case 88
liqueur-spiked dark chocolate orange
   mousse 86
luxury mocha mousse 89
raspberry chocolate mousse
   gateau 97
rich chocolate mousse gateau 97
rich chocolate mousse with glazed
   kumquats 85
white amaretto mousse with
   chocolate sauce 87
white chocolate mousse with dark
   sauce 84
mud from Gerritje 83
multi-layer chocolate cake 35

New York egg cream 231
nuts
   almonds 31, 41, 46, 67, 68, 164, 208
   chestnuts 44, 45, 81, 107
   chocolate and pine nut tart 129
   chocolate coated nut brittle 209
   chocolate fruit and nut cookies 193
   chocolate macaroons 184
   chocolate nut clusters 208
   chocolate nut slice 168
   chocolate nut tart 133
   chunky choc and nut brownies 156
   chunky chocolate drops 177
   coconuts 43, 168
   fruit-and-nut white chocolate
      clusters 216
   hazelnuts 10, 17, 94, 110, 128, 175,
      186, 206
   iced chocolate nut gateau 120
   marbled chocolate and peanut
      cake 16
   mocha Brazil layer torte 27
   nut bar chocolate cookies 191
   nut cookies 174
   nut wafers with chocolate drizzle 195
   nutty chocolate chip cookies 177
   nutty chocolate squares 158
   nutty marshmallow and chocolate
      squares 160
   pecans 28, 68, 140, 157
   pistachios 113, 165, 207
   rich chocolate nut cake 37
   walnuts 14, 20, 28, 37, 65, 146, 172,
      174, 190
   white chocolate macadamia slices 166

oat chocolate chip cookies 176
oat, date and chocolate brownies 161
oat florentines 188
one-stage chocolate sponge 8
orange
   bitter marmalade chocolate loaf 20
   chocolate and mandarin truffle
      slice 92
   chocolate and orange angel cake 11
   chocolate and orange mousse 86
   chocolate and orange Scotch
      pancakes 70
   chocolate and orange soufflé 62
   chocolate mandarin trifle 91
   chocolate orange battenburg cake 17
   chocolate orange marquise 61
   chocolate orange sponge drops 148
   chocolate-dipped cinnamon and
      orange tuiles 198
   devil's food cake with orange
      frosting 10
   liqueur-spiked dark chocolate orange
      mousse 86

pain au chocolat 153
pancakes
   chocolate and orange Scotch
      pancakes 70
   chocolate chip banana pancakes 69
   chocolate crêpes with plums and
      port 70
   chocolate soufflé crêpes 69
pane al cioccolato 22
panettone 23
passion fruit
   chocolate pavlova with passion fruit
      cream 95
pastillage 242
pastry 237
pavlovas 95, 218
peaches
   chocolate amaretti peaches 77
   peachy chocolate bake 76
pears
   bitter chocolate fondue with
      rosemary and vanilla poached
      pears 74
   chocolate pear tart 133
   chocolate, pear and pecan pie 140
   iced pear terrine with Calvados and
      chocolate sauce 101
   pear and hazelnut meringue torte 94
   pear tartlets with chocolate sauce 75
   pears in chocolate fudge blankets 73
   poached pears with chocolate 74
   puffy chocolate pears 154
   vanilla poached pears with choc-
      dusted cappuccino sauce 75
pecans
   chocolate, pear and pecan pie 140
   chocolate pecan nut torte 28
   chocolate pecan pie 68
   maple and pecan nut brownies 157
peppermint chocolate sticks 213
petal paste 244
petits pots de cappuccino 82
Piranha 234
pirate's hat with chocolate coin
   treasure 59
pistachios
   bitter chocolate and pistachio
      wedges 165
   pistachio ice cream in choc cones 113
   rich chocolate pistachio fudge 207
polenta cake 13
Pompeii 232
port
   chocolate crêpes with plums and
      port 70
potatoes
   chocolate potato cake 38
prunes
   chocolate and prune cake 14
   chocolate and prune cookies 191
   mocha, prune and Armagnac
      terrine 101
   prune beignets in chocolate sauce 73
   stuffed chocolate prunes 212

quick-mix sponge cake 236

rainbow ice cream with chocolate
   candies 107
raisins
   baked chocolate and raisin
      cheesecake 143
   chocolate, rum and raisin roulade 122
   raisin chocolate brownies 156
raspberries
   chocolate raspberry macaroon
      bars 171
   raspberry and white chocolate
      cheesecake 143
   raspberry chocolate mousse gateau 97
   white chocolate, frosted raspberry
      and coffee terrine 100
   white chocolate raspberry ripple 103
redcurrants
   chocolate redcurrant torte 50
rice pudding with chocolate sauce 80
rich chocolate and coffee pudding 64

rich chocolate brioche bake 61
rich chocolate brownies 156
rich chocolate cake 40
rich chocolate cookie slice 168
rich chocolate leaf cake 25
rich chocolate mousse gateau 97
rich chocolate mousse with glazed
   kumquats 85
rich chocolate nut cake 37
rich chocolate pie 135
rich chocolate tart with blackberry
   sauce 132
rich tea-time chocolate cake 32
rocky road chocolate bars 173
rocky road ice cream 106
rocky road wedges 165
rose petal truffles 224
roulades
   chocolate and coffee roulade 43
   chocolate coconut roulade 43
   chocolate rum roulade 19
   classic chocolate roulade 42
   two-chocolate chestnut roulade 44
royal icing 242
rum
   black rum and chocolate pie 134
   Caribbean chocolate ring with rum
      syrup 39
   chocolate pudding with rum
      custard 66
   chocolate rum roulade 19
   chocolate, rum and raisin roulade 122
   hot mocha rum soufflés 62

sachertorte 36
satin chocolate icing 239
sauces 246, 247
Savoy Hotel 235
Scotch pancakes 70
shape and bake chocolate cookies 192
Sicilian brioches with hot chocolate
   fudge sauce 152
simnel cookies with chocolate eggs 200
simple buttercream 241
simple chocolate cake 8
snowball 78
soufflés 62, 63, 69
spicy hearts and stars 202
spider's web cake with chocolate icing 58
sponge cake, quick-mix 236
sponge, one-stage chocolate 8
sponge roll 236
steamed chocolate and fruit pudding with
   chocolate syrup 64
strawberries
   berry chocolate savarin 34
   chocolate mousse strawberry layer
      cake 46
   strawberries in a chocolate basket
      57
   strawberry chocolate Valentine
      cake 48
sugar-frosted flowers 245
sugarpaste icing 243
sundaes 104, 105
Swedish rose chocolates 211
sweet hearts 201
Swiss roll 19

three chocolate bread 22
Tia Maria and ginger gateau 32
Tia Maria and walnut gateau 37
Tia Maria truffle tarts 128

tiramisu
   chocolate tiramisu tart 131
   iced tiramisu 112
   tiramisu biscuits 187
   tiramisu in chocolate cups 80
   tiramisu tart 131
toffee
   chocolate and toffee bars 171
   chocolate, banana and toffee
      pie 138
torte Varazdin 29
tree cookies 202
triple chocolate sandwiches 194
triple chocolate terrine 100
truffle filo tarts 127
truffles
   chocolate cherry brandy truffles 220
   chocolate truffle medley 221
   classic Belgian chocolate truffles 221
   coffee chocolate truffles 222
   gingered truffles 223
   malt whisky truffles 222
   mixed chocolate truffles 220
   mocha truffles with café noir 224
   rose petal truffles 224
   truffle Christmas puddings 225
Turkish delight sorbet with white
   chocolate drizzle 125
twice-baked mocha soufflé 63

Valentine's box of chocolates cake 49
velvety mocha tart 129

walnuts
   chocolate chip and walnut
      cookies 174
   chocolate chip walnut loaf 20
   chocolate, date and walnut
      pudding 65
   chocolate walnut bars 172
   chocolate walnut delights 185
   chocolate walnut muffins 166
   sticky chocolate, maple and walnut
      swirls 190
   Tia Maria and walnut gateau 37
   walnut and ricotta cake with
      chocolate curls 14
   walnut coffee gateau with chocolate
      frosting 28
wedding cake 51
white chocolate
   black and white chocolate mousse 85
   chunky white chocolate and coffee
      brownies 161
   luxury white chocolate cheesecake 142
   raspberry and white chocolate
      cheesecake 143
   stripy white chocolate canes 204
   white amaretto mousse with
      chocolate sauce 87
   white chocolate and brownie ice
      cream 116
   white chocolate and brownie torte 98
   white chocolate and mango cream
      tart 132
   white chocolate and orange
      sauce 245
   white chocolate brownies 162
   white chocolate brûlées with
      blackberry coulis 118
   white chocolate cappuccino gateau 27
   white chocolate castles with fresh
      summer berries 122
   white chocolate celebration cake 48
   white chocolate, frosted raspberry
      and coffee terrine 100
   white chocolate frosting 240
   white chocolate macadamia slices 166
   white chocolate mousse with dark
      sauce 84
   white chocolate parfait 93
   white chocolate raspberry ripple 103
   white chocolate slices 164
   white chocolate snowballs 217
Whiteout 232

zabaglione 76